The Supreme Court in American Society

Equal Justice Under Law

Series Editor

Kermit L. Hall
North Carolina State University

Series Contents

The Least Dangerous Branch

Separation of Powers and Court-Packing

Edited with introductions by

Kermit L. Hall

North Carolina State University

Routledge
Taylor & Francis Group
NEW YORK AND LONDON

First published 2000 by Garland Publishing, Inc.

This edition published 2013 by Routledge
605 Third Avenue, New York, NY 10017
4 Park Square, Milton Park, Abingdon, Oxon OX14 4RN

Routledge is an imprint of the Taylor & Francis Group, an informa business

Library of Congress Cataloging-in-Publication Data

The least dangerous branch : separation of powers and court-packing / edited with introductions by Kermit L. Hall
p. cm. — (The Supreme Court in American society ; 5)
Includes bibliographical references.
ISBN 0-8153-3428-1 (alk. paper)
1. Judicial power—United States—History. 2. Separation of powers—United States—History. 3. Judges—Selection and appointment—United States—History. 4. United States. Supreme Court—History. I. Hall, Kermit. II. Series.

KF5130 .L43 2000
342.73'262—dc21 00-062250

ISBN 13: 978-0-8153-3428-6 (hbk)

Contents

Series Introduction

The inscription carved above the entrance to the Supreme Court of the United States is elegant in its brevity and powerful in its directness: "Equal Justice Under Law." No other words have been more regularly connected to the work of the nation's most important judicial tribunal. Because the Court is the highest tribunal for all cases and controversies arising under the Constitution, laws, and treaties of the United States, it functions as the preeminent guardian and interpreter of the nation's basic law. There was nothing, of course, in the early history of the Court that guaranteed that it would do just that. The justices in their first decade of operation disposed of only a handful of cases. During the subsequent two centuries, however, the Court's influence mushroomed as it became not only the authoritative interpreter of the Constitution but the most important institution in defining separation of powers, federalism, and the rule of law, concepts at the heart of the American constitutional order.

Chief Justice Charles Evans Hughes once declared that the Court is "distinctly American in concept and function." Few other courts in the world have the same scope of power to interpret their national constitutions; none has done so for anything approaching the more than two centuries the Court has been hearing and deciding cases. During its history, moreover, the story of the Court has been more than the sum of either the cases it has decided or the justices that have decided them. Its story has been that of the country as a whole, in war and peace, in prosperity and depression, in harmony and discord. As Alexis de Tocqueville observed in *Democracy in America*, "I am unaware that any nation on the globe has hitherto organized a judicial power in the same manner as the Americans. . . . A more imposing judicial power was never constituted by any people." That power, as Tocqueville well understood, has given the justices a unique role in American life, one that combines elements of law and politics. "Scarcely any political question," Tocqueville wrote, "arises in the United States that is not revolved, sooner or later, into a judicial question." Through the decisions of the Supreme Court, law has become an extension of political discourse and, to that end, the rule of law itself has been embellished. We appropriately think of the high court as a legal institution, but it is, in truth, a hybrid in which matters of economics, cultural values, social change, and political interests converge to produce what we call our constitutional law. The Court, as a legal entity, speaks through the law but its decisions are shaped by and at the same time shape the social order of which it is part. All of which is to say that, in the end, the high court is a human institution, a place where justices make decisions by applying precedent, logic, empathy, and a respect for the Constitution as informed by the principle of "Equal Justice Under Law." That the Court has at times, such as the struggle over slavery in the 1850s, not fully grasped all of the implications of those words does not, in the end, diminish the importance of the Court. Instead, it reminds us that no other institution in American life takes as its goal such a lofty aspiration. Given the assumptions of our constitutional system, that there is something like justice and freedom for all, the Court's operation is unthinkable without having the concept of the rule of law embedded in it.

As these volumes attest, interest in the Court as a legal, political, and cultural entity has been prodigious. No other court in the American federal system has drawn anything approaching the scholarly attention showered on the so-called "Marble Palace" in Washington, D.C. As the volumes in this series make clear, that scholarship has divided into several categories. Biographers, for example, have plumbed the depths of the judicial mind and personality; students of small group behavior have attempted to explain the dynamics of how the justices make decisions; and scholars of the selection process have tried to understand whether the way in which a justice reaches the Court has anything to do with what he or she does once on the Court. Historians have lavished particular attention on the Court, using its history as a mirror of the tensions that have beset American society at any one time, while simultaneously viewing the Court as a great stabilizing force in American life. Scholars from other disciplines, such as political science and law, have viewed the Court as an engine of constitutional law, the principal agent through which constitutional change has been mediated in the American system, and the authoritative voice on what is constitutional and, thereby, both legally and politically acceptable. Hence, these volumes also address basic issues in the American constitutional system, such as separation of powers, federalism, individual expression, civil rights and liberties, the protection of property rights, and the development of the concept of equality. The last of these, as many of the readings show, has frequently posed the most difficult challenge for the Court, since concepts of liberty and equality, while seemingly reinforcing, have often, as in the debate over gender relations, turned out to be contradictory, even puzzling at times.

These volumes also remind us that substantial differences continue to exist, as they have since the beginning of the nation, about how to interpret the original constitutional debates in the summer of 1787 in Philadelphia and the subsequent discussions surrounding the adoption of the Bill of Rights, the Civil War amendments, and Progressive-era constitutional reforms. Since its inception, the question has always been whether the Court , in view of the changing understandings among Americans about equality and liberty, has an obligation to ensure that its decisions resonate with yesterday, today, tomorrow, or all three.

Volume Introduction

Few concepts in American constitutionalism are more important and less understood than the doctrine of separation of powers. It is, in the end, more a name than a description of reality. None of the three branches of the federal government are clearly separated from one another. The Supreme Court, on first impression, seems the most infirm of the three. It has, as Alexander Hamilton observed in the *Federalist Papers*, neither the power of the sword nor the purse. Yet, remarkably, it is the most separated and the least checked of the branches of government. When, for example, the justices in *Hammer* v. *Dagenhart* (1918) held unconstitutional congressional restraints on child labor, only five of them needed to agree to do so; at the same time, the legislative requirement to pass such a measure in the first place rested on the majority approval of the Congress. The justices, moreover, are not directly accountable to the public, as is much more the case with both the President and the Congress. While the impeachment power would seem an important weapon to use against the nine members of the Court, it has proven in practice to be a weak instrument. Only one justice, Samuel Chase, in 1805, has been impeached, and he avoided conviction by a narrow margin. Even the specter of constitutional amendment in opposition to the justices' exercise of judicial review has proven relatively harmless. Supreme Court decisions have been overridden by an amendment in only four instances — the Eleventh, Fourteenth, Sixteenth, and Twenty-sixth Amendments. Moreover, numerous amendments aimed at relieving the Court of its jurisdiction over certain highly controversial matters, such as abortion, school prayer, and busing to achieve racial integration, have foundered in Congress.

The following essays, however, reveal that the Court does not live in a political vacuum and that it has been responsive to electoral and congressional imperatives. Presidents have often sought to reshape the Court through the selection process, imposing something like a prospective check on the Court's decision-making. Still, as several of these essays argue, the peculiar American institution of judicial review has given the Supreme Court enormous supervisory power over the other branches of government and, as such, the critical role in defining the meaning of separation of powers constitutionally. In some ways, therefore, the doctrine of separation of powers has come to mean what the Supreme Court says it means.

West Virginia Law Review

Vol 71 | February, 1969 | Number 2

The Supreme Court and the Political Question: Affirmation or Abdication?*

RALPH J. BEAN, JR.**

Scarcely any political question arises in the United States that is not resolved, sooner or later, into a judicial question.—De Tocqueville, Democracy in America.

Although more than 100 years have elapsed since the young Frenchman Alexis De Tocqueville made this observation, its accuracy has not been disproved by a century of American democracy at work. Indeed, the truth of his remark may have prompted Justice Frankfurter to express "disquietude that the line is often very thin between cases in which the Court felt compelled to abstain from adjudication because of their 'political' nature, and the cases that so frequently arise in applying the concepts of 'liberty' and 'equality'."[1]

Today that line has been worn even thinner. Recent Supreme Court decisions seem actually to have erased the line for all practical purposes by placing certain aspects of the political question in a position of subservience to concepts of individual liberty and equality. The significance of these decisions lies not only in new substantive norms which have been created but also in the crippling blow that has been dealt to what is perhaps the most ancient and "potentially the widest and most radical avenue of escape from adjudicaion" in the federal courts.[2]

In terms of age the political question claims an ancestry which began prior to the birth of the American institution of judicial review.

* This article represents a condensed version of a paper presented in partial fulfillment of the requirements for "The Supreme Court and Judicial Review" Seminar at the Law School, Harvard University, April 10, 1967.

** A.B., 1963, J.D., 1966, W. Va. University; LL.M., 1967, Harvard University; Member, W. Va., Va., and D.C. Bars.

[1] Frankfurter, *John Marshall and the Judicial Function*, 69 HARV. L. REV. 217, 227-28 (1955).

[2] The quoted portion is taken from Bickel, *Foreword: The Passive Virtues*, 75 HARV. L. REV. 40, 45 (1961).

In *Hayburn's Case*[3] the Court took under advisement an attempt to mandamus a federal circuit court to accept pension applications of disabled war veterans, war orphans and widows and to recommend eligible applicants to the Secretary of War as provided by an act of Congress.[4] Although the case was never decided by the Supreme Court because Congress subsequently amended the statute, letters and memoranda of the circuit court judges reported in a note to the report of *Hayburn's Case* question the constitutionality of the statute. The justices emphasized that the division of the federal government into three independent and distinct branches forbade encroachment by one branch upon the duties of another. It was felt that the act assigned duties to the circuit courts which they could not constitutionally perform because the duties were not judicial tasks; subsequent review by another branch of government was thought to be inconsistent with the very nature of judicial power.[5]

Although *Hayburn's Case* was not technically a political question case, refusal by the federal courts to perform a function thought to be committed by the Constitution to another department of government is strongly reminiscent of the political question. Furthermore, the concern expressed for preservation of separation of powers has been the traditional explanation for the political question.

Ten years after the decision in *Hayburn's Case* the political question doctrine received express recognition in *Marbury v. Madison*[6] when Chief Justice Marshall stated that the federal courts will not adjudicate political questions even though such questions involve actual controversies. Thus, by the time the institution of judicial review was established, the doctrine that an issue is nonjusticiable because its determination is committed to one of the so-called political departments of government—the executive or legislative—was given content.[7]

---

[3] 2 U.S. (2 Dall.) 409 (1792).

[4] Act of March 23, 1792, ch. 11, § 1, 1 Stat. 243. The act suspended prior acts of Congress which barred certain claims for pensions and made additional provision for pensions for certain disabled veterans. Application was to be made to the federal circuit courts which were to determine the degree of disability and to certify the information to the Secretary of War who was at liberty to disregard a name placed on the pension list by a court.

[5] The justices of the circuit court for the district of New York agreed to administer the act in the capacity of commissioners while the justices for the districts of North Carolina and Pennsylvania refused to proceed in any capacity.

[6] 5 U.S. (1 Cranch) 137, 164-66 (1803).

[7] The roots of the political question reach deep into English law. Development of the doctrine probably began with the Duke of York's Claim to the Crown (1460) (reported in 1 Wambaugh, Cases on Constitutional

Establishment of the political question doctrine as a part of American constitutional law, however, is only the beginning of the story. The generality of a doctrine forbidding justiciability because it is the prerogative of another branch of government to make the determination has proved to be readily adaptable to a great variety of circumstances. Moreover, the political question has tended to lend itself to a general policy of judicial self-restraint.

As a consequence of its general applicability and the negative results that flow from its use, the political question has been applied broadly to a variety of seemingly unrelated subject matter. These have ranged from the exclusion and deportation of aliens to the legal status of Indian tribes and to the apportionment of governments. Thus, it is not surprising that the amorphism of the doctrine has provoked a barrage of critical commentary. As one writer has charged, "[t]he term 'political question' is . . . one of the least satisfactory terms known to law. The origin, scope and purpose of the concept elude all attempts at precise statement."[8]

It is in this setting that recent decisions of an activist court have eliminated the doctrine as an obstacle in some areas while reducing its significance in others. *Bond v. Floyd*[9] is perhaps the most current decision having negative implications for the political question doctrine. Julian Bond, a Negro, was duly elected as representative to the Georgia House of Representatives from the 136th House district. A civil rights organization of which Bond was a member

---

Law 1 (1915)) in which the judges refused to consider the Duke's suit to have himself declared the rightful heir to the throne.

Perhaps the most significant English case having bearing on the political question was *Nabob of the Carnatic v. East India Co.*, 1 Ves. Jr. 370 (1791), 2 Ves. Jr. 56 (1793). Suit was brought against the East India Company for having breached a contract with the Nabob. The court reasoned that the East India Company was acting as a delegate of the sovereign power of England in making contracts with potentates and for this reason the matter could not be decided by a court of law. More than any other decision the *Nabob of the Carnatic* is said to have established the political question doctrine as part of English law. *See* Finkelstein, *Judicial Self-Limitation*, 37 HARV. L. REV. 338 (1924).

The influence of the English decisions must have been felt in the development of the American counterpart to the doctrine, as the *Nabob* is cited in Luther v. Borden, 4 U.S. (7 How.) 1 (1849) which is one of the earliest of the leading American cases applying the doctrine of judicial non-interference with political questions. The *Borden* decision was the first of a long line of cases from which emerged the rule that the constitutional guarantee of a republican form of government is not enforceable in the courts. A subsequent portion of this paper is devoted to these cases.

[8] FRANK, POLITICAL QUESTIONS, IN SUPREME COURT AND SUPREME LAW 80 (Cahn ed. 1954).

[9] 385 U.S. 116 (1966).

and officer issued a statement criticizing United States Government policy in Vietnam and United States draft laws; Bond publicly endorsed the statement.

Before the Georgia House convened, House members challenged Bond's right to be seated. A special committee appointed to hear the matter concluded that Bond did not support the Constitution of the United States or of the state of Georgia, that he adhered to the enemies of the state of Georgia and gave comfort to the enemies of the United States, that his statements violated the Selective Service laws of the United States, and that his statements would bring discredit and disrespect to the Georgia House. When the House adopted the committee report and voted not to allow Bond to take the oath of office or to be seated as a House member, Bond brought an action in the appropriate federal district court for injunctive relief and a declaratory judgment that the House action was not authorized by the Georgia constitution and violated his rights under the first amendment to the Federal Constitution. Two members of the three-judge federal district court concluded the action of the Georgia House was proper, and Bond appealed directly to the United States Supreme Court.

Reversing the three-judge court, a unanimous Supreme Court rejected the state's argument that there should be no judicial review of a state legislature's power to judge whether or not a prospective member may conscientiously take the oath required by the state and Federal Constitutions and concluded that the controversy was justiciable. Addressing itself to the merits of the controversy, the Court held that disqualification on account of statements Bond had made violated the free speech provisions of the first amendment which are made applicable to the states by the fourteenth amendment.[10]

The *Bond* case is significant because it represents the first time in American constitutional history that a federal court has interferred with a state legislature's decision regarding membership in the legislature. Such questions were heretofore considered non-justiciable because of separation of powers conceptualism; *i.e.*, decisions of a legislature pertaining to its membership have tradi-

---

[10] The Court stated that "[l]egislators have an obligation to take positions on controversial political questions so that their constituents can be fully informed by them, and be better able to assess their qualifications for office; also so they may be represented in governmental debates by the person they have elected to represent them." *Id.* at 136.

tionally been considered nonjusticiable political questions.[11] Thus, the *Bond* case is unique; yet it is not surprising because the groundwork had already been laid for it by the Court, notably in the landmark decision of *Baker v. Carr.*[12]

Baker held justiciable a suit under the equal protection clause of the fourteenth amendment to compel reapportionment of a state legislature in which representation was not based on numerical equality in voting power. In deciding *Baker* the Court was confronted with a respectable line of adverse precedent which was anchored to the political question doctrine.

As a result of the Court's treatment, the future of the political question doctrine will probably be confined primarily to conflicts between the federal judiciary and coordinate branches of the federal government. Partly for this reason the recent refusal of the House of Representatives to seat Representative Adam Clayton Powell is likely to be treated as a political question in the event the case is decided by the Supreme Court.[13] According to the Court, the relationship between state governments and the federal judiciary cannot raise a political question unless judicially discoverable standards are found to be lacking, and, as the *Bond* and *Baker* cases illustrate, the Court has little difficulty discovering standards where concepts of individual liberty and equality are involved.

Given the tendency of the present Court to limit the application of the political question doctrine, it seems appropriate to consider what distinguishes nonjusticiable political issues from justiciable issues. Is the political question doctrine required by the Constitution or is it a mere technique of avoidance by which the Court screens cases which it deems appropriate for decision by other departments of government? Or is there a more subtle quality to the doctrine

---

[11] 13 U.C.L.A. L. REV. 1317 (1966). In 1920 five New York socialists were suspended from the New York Legislature because of their opposition to United States participation in World War I. When the Bond story became news, a writer for the *New York Times* interviewed Louis Waldman (one of the five) and inquired why no redress had been sought in the courts. He received this reply: "We regarded the concept of separation of powers . . . as far more important than our own case . . . . If judges can decide who can sit in the legislature, they can decide who shouldn't sit. This would be a much greater offense to democratic government than anything a stupid majority might do in an individual case." N. Y. Times, Jan. 12, 1966, at 18, col. 1 (city ed.).

[12] 369 U.S. 186 (1962).

[13] The *Powell* case is discussed in greater detail in a subsequent portion of this paper beginning at page 132.

which is somehow related to the role which courts should play in a democracy?

EXPLANATION AND PURPOSE OF THE DOCTRINE

The Classical Explanation

As previously mentioned, the political question has traditionally been explained in terms of judicial respect for the principle of separation of powers.[14] For Professor Wechsler this means that, "all the doctrine can defensibly imply is that the courts are called upon to judge whether the Constitution has committed to another agency of government the autonomous determination of the issue raised, a finding that itself requires an interpretation."[15] According to Wechsler, a judicial decision not to adjudicate the merits of a particular controversy conforms with *Marbury v. Madison* in that it amounts to a constitutional adjudication that the matter in question is vested in the uncontrolled discretion of another department of government.

Wechsler does concede the Court's discretion to grant or to deny review of judgments of lower courts whenever the jurisdictional statute permits certiorari but fails to provide for an appeal. Even so, he is quick to note that the Court has defined standards for the exercise of its discretion[16] and argues for "their faithful application."[17] Beyond this, Wechsler would favor greater elimination of the Court's discretion through revision of the applicable jurisdictional statutes. Thus, he finds comfort in the following dicta in *Cohens v. Virginia*:

> It is most true that this court will not take jurisdiction if it should not; but it is equally true, that it must take jurisdiction if it should. The judiciary cannot, as the legislature may, avoid a measure because it approaches the confines of the Constitution. We cannot pass it by because it is doubtful, with whatever doubts, with whatever difficulty, a case may be attended. We must decide if it be brought before us. We have no more right

---

[14] *See, e.g.*, Weston, *Political Questions*, 38 HARV. L. REV. 296 (1925). Weston describes a political question as "one which is by law for the determination of the executive or legislative departments, or possibly of the people themselves. . . . [T]he line between judicial and political questions . . . is the line drawn by the constitutional delegation, and none other." *Id.* at 331.

[15] Wechsler, *Toward Neutral Principles of Constitutional Law*, 73 HARV. L. REV. 1, 7 (1959).

[16] U.S. SUP. CT. R. 19.

[17] Wechsler, *supra* note 15, at 11.

> to decline the exercise of jurisdiction which is given, than to usurp that which is not given. The one or the other would be treason to the Constitution.[18]

As examples of proper judicial abstention resulting from acts of constitutional interpretation, Wechsler mentions the Senate's constitutional power to try impeachment cases, the power of each House of the Congress to seat or to expel members[19] and the guarantee of a republican form of government. An additional example is the constitutional power of Congress to make or alter state regulations of the "[m]anner of holding Elections for Senators and Representatives"[20] which operates to exclude courts from considering constitutional objections to state gerrymanders.[21]

Wechsler's explanation of the political question doctrine is wedded to an elaboration of the so-called classical theory of judicial review which denies judicial discretion to withhold judgment upon a matter properly before the Court.[22] In articulating the classical theory,

[18] 19 U.S. (6 Wheat.) 264, 404 (1821).

[19] Wechsler, *supra* note 15, at 8. One writer has suggested quite properly that these examples are unique because the functions to be performed pursuant to the grants of power are essentially adjudicative. Scharpf, *Judicial Review and the Political Question: A Functional Analysis*, 75 YALE L.J. 517, 539 (1966). The recent expulsion of Representative Adam Clayton Powell by the House of Representatives may test Wechsler's assertion that actions of either house of Congress in seating or expelling members are political questions. The relevant constitutional language is as follows: "Each House shall be the Judge of the Elections, Returns and Qualifications of its own Members. . . . Each House may determine the Rules of its Proceedings, punish its members for disorderly Behaviour, and, with the Concurrance of two thirds, expel a Member." U.S. CONST. art. 1, sec. 5. The *Powell* case is dealt with in more detail in the concluding portion of this paper.

[20] U.S. CONST. art. I, § 4.

[21] Wechsler, *supra* note 15, at 8. Whatever validity there once may have been in this proposition, it is today in serious need of qualification. Gomillion v. Lightfoot, 364 U.S. 339 (1960) invalidated state racial gerrymandering used to deprive Negroes of the right to vote in a municipal election. More recently, the Court decided the merits of a claim alleging that voting districts created by the New York legislature were motivated by racial considerations. Wright v. Rockfeller, 376 U.S. 52 (1964). Although the relief prayed for by the plaintiffs was denied, the result did not rest on the political question doctrine but upon the insufficiency of evidence to prove the allegations.

[22] The classical theory draws heavily upon the following language in *Marbury v. Madison:*

> It is, emphatically, the province and duty of the judicial departments to say what the law is. Those who apply the rule to particular cases, must of necessity expound and interpret that rule. If two laws conflict with each other, the courts must decide on the operation of each. So, if a law be in opposition to the constitution; if both the law and the constitution apply to a particular case, so that the court must either decide that case, conformable to the law, disregarding the constitution; or conformable to the constitution, disregarding the law; the court must determine which of these conflicting rules governs the case: this is of the very essence of judicial duty. Marbury v. Madison, 5 U.S. (1 Cranch) 137 (1803).

Wechsler was responding in part to Judge Hand's assertion that the Court is free to adjudicate a constitutional objection or to decline to do so when a case is properly before the Court, according to "how importunately the occasion demands an answer."[23] In fact, Judge Hand viewed the political question as an illustration of the kind of discretion he thought was involved in judicial review[24] and alluded to the doctrine as a "stench in the nostrils of strict constructionists."[25]

The Political Question and the "Passive Virtues"

Concurring with Judge Hand's disagreement with Wechsler is Professor Bickel who declares that it is a play on words to say that the broad discretion which the Court has exercised may be explained solely in terms of constitutional interpretation.[26] Bickel's emphasis, however, differs from Hand's. For Professor Bickel, judicial review is justified by the value to society with results from the Court's capacity to define and pronounce principles of the community.[27]

The thrust of the Bickel analysis is upon "passive virtues"—techniques employed by the Court to avoid the exercise of judicial review, whenever, in the Court's prudential judgment, a principled decision on the merits is not possible. Among these techniques the political question occupies the seat of honor. Stated in Bickel's words: "[t]he culmination of any progression of devices for withholding the ultimate constitutional judgment of the Supreme Court—and in a sense their sum—is the doctrine of political questions."[28]

According to Bickel, the political question doctrine "resists being domesticated" in the fashion suggested by Professor Wechsler:

> There is something different about it, in kind, not in degree, from the general 'interpretative process'; something greatly more flexible, something of prudence, not construction and not principle. And it is something which cannot exist within the four corners of *Marbury v. Madison*.[29]

---

[23] L. HAND, THE BILL OF RIGHTS 15 (1958).

[24] *Id.* at 15-18.

[25] *Id.* at 15.

[26] Bickel, *Foreword: The Passive Virtues*, 75 HARV. L. REV. 40, 46 (1961).

[27] A. BICKEL, THE LEAST DANGEROUS BRANCH 23-28 (1962). For a criticism of Professor Bickel's thesis, see Gunther, *The Subtle Vices of the "Passive Virtues"—A Comment on Principle and Expediency in Judicial Review*, 64 COLUM. L. REV. 1 (1964).

[28] A. BICKEL, *supra* note 27, at 463.

[29] Bickel, *supra* note 26, at 46.

Bickel does not deny that the political question may sometimes be adequately explained as an act of constitutional interpretation. His point of departure, however, is Wechsler's insistence that constitutional interpretation is "all the doctrine can defensibly imply."[30]

A "Functional" Analysis

While in general agreement with the Bickel thesis that the passive virtues are legitimate "because they make possible performance of the Court's grand function as proclaimer and protector of goals,"[31] Professor Scharpf has expressed the opinion that the political question cannot be justified in the same manner.[32] This is so because the political question is uniquely distinguishable from other techniques of avoidance such as standing and ripeness.

In contrast to other "passive virtues," when the Court refuses to decide an issue because it is political and leaves it for determination by another department of government, its purpose is not to postpone decision until the time is ripe for a truly principled decision on

---

[30] Other critics of the constitutional quality of the political question include Maurice Finkelstein, who has recorded the following description of the doctrine:

> It [the political question] applies to all those matters of which the court, at a given time, will be of the opinion that it is impolitic or inexpedient to take jurisdiction. Sometimes this idea of inexpediency will result from the fear of the vastness of the consequences that a decision on the merits might entail. Sometimes it will result from a feeling that the Court is incompetent to deal with the particular type of question involved. Sometimes it will be induced by the feeling that the matter is 'too high' for the courts. But always there will be a weighing of considerations in the scale of political wisdom. Finkelstein, *supra* note 7, at 344.

Mention should also be made of Mr. Field's laudable attempt to review the political question cases; his conclusion was that "the true basis of a political question is the lack of legal principles for the courts to apply in their consideration of cases involving certain types of subject matter. . . ." Field, *The Doctrine of Political Questions in the Federal Courts*, 8 MINN. L. REV. 485, 513 (1924). The Field analysis has been labeled a "cognitive" theory of the political question. Scharpf, *supra* note 19, at 555.

It has been said that a great variety of considerations, acting alone or in various combinations, contribute to the conclusion that a question is political. H. M. HART & H. WECHSLER, THE FEDERAL COURTS AND THE FEDERAL SYSTEM 192 (1953). Among these considerations the following are salient:

> the inability of courts to secure facts necessary for decision; the need for discretion in decision and the courts' inability to develop or apply controlling principles of law; the superiority of political checks as guides to decisions; the existence of special dangers, as for example in foreign relations of having the government speak with more than one voice; the inability of courts to deal with the possible consequences of decision, such as would follow, for example, a holding that an entire state government was unconstitutional; the push of express constitutional provisions; etc., etc.

[31] A. BICKLE, *supra* note 27, at 71.

[32] Scharpf, *supra* note 19, at 534-35.

the merits (as Bickel suggests). On the contrary, the Court relinquishes all responsibility to decide the issue, unless, of course, the Court later overrules or distinguishes a political question.[33] In short the contention is that the political question doctrine cannot be explained satisfactorily in terms of a procedural or jurisdictional technique of avoidance.[34]

Instead, Professor Scharpf would explain the political question "in functional terms, as the Court's acknowledgment of the limitations of the American judicial process."[35] He enumerates several functional factors and considerations which, in various combinations, are likely to convince the Court that decision of a particular issue would transgress "the limits of its own responsibility."[36] The first factor or consideration which may cause the Court to invoke the political question doctrine is difficulty in gaining access to information.[37] This factor may be manifest in cases dealing with foreign affairs in which decision depends upon evaluation of a foreign fact-situation, especially if relevant information is in the special competence of the executive department.

A second factor or consideration which may be germane in determining whether an issue is a nonjusticiable political question is the need for uniformity of decision.[38] This factor has been operative in cases in which the Court has respected determinations by the political departments establishing the duration of war. As a third factor, Professor Scharpf lists deference by the Court to the wider responsibility of the political departments.[39] This has been a salient factor in many of the cases in which the Court has found the issue to be political for the reason that judicial interference would be embarrasing to another branch of government.

---

[33] The political question should also be distinguished from other rules of self-restraint which the Court has, from time to time, imposed upon itself. See for example the self-imposed rules enumerated by Brandeis, J., concurring in Ashwander v. T.V.A., 297 U.S. 288 (1936). These rules have a procedural quality, the thrust of which is to postpone decision of the constitutional question that is raised.

[34] Scharpf, *supra* note 19, at 535-38.

[35] *Id.* at 566. Professor Scharpf defines the term "functional" to refer to the "interrelationship between the nature of the task which the Court is performing and the means which it can employ for the performance of this task. If its ordinary means prove inadequate for a particular task, the Court may react either by enlarging its arsenal of means or by limiting the tasks which it will perform." *Id.* at 523, n.21.

[36] *Id.* at 567.

[37] *Id.*

[38] *Id.* at 573.

[39] *Id.* at 578.

On the other hand, the political question has not invariably provided the technique by which the Court has seemingly deferred to the wider responsibility of the political departments. Thus, in *Korematsu v. United States*[40] a majority of the Court upheld the exclusion of American citizens of Japanese extraction from designated areas of the West Coast as a valid exercise of the war power, even as applied to a citizen of Japanese extraction whose loyalty to the United States was unquestioned. The Court rejected the contention that it was sanctioning an obvious racial discrimination in violation of the fifth amendment as well as the deprivation of other constitutional rights.[41]

A final consideration is characterized by Scharpf as the normative limitations of the political question. That is, except for the cases in which the Court has applied the political question doctrine to allow exclusion and deportation of aliens in spite of appealing due process claims, the Court has refused to apply the doctrine to the guarantees of the Bill of Rights.[42] So also has the doctrine been held inapplicable when the Court was presented with "conflicting claims of competence among the departments of the federal government, or between the federal government and the states."[43]

In regard to the Wechsler-Bickel dichotomy, Scharpf suggests that the political question has provided a "touchstone for the validity of competing theories of judicial review."[44] Concluding that the doctrine cannot satisfactorily be explained in terms of a

---

[40] 323 U.S. 214 (1944).

[41] Three justices filed separate dissenting opinions. Justice Murphy said the exclusion not only amounted to racial discrimination depriving persons of Japanese ancestry of equal protection of the laws as guaranteed by the fifth amendment but that "[i]t further deprives these individuals of their constitutional rights to live and work where they will, to establish a home where they choose and to move about freely. In excommunicating them without benefit of hearings, this order also deprives them of all their constitutional rights to procedural due process." *Id.* at 235.

[42] Scharpf, *supra* note 19, at 583-84. An additional qualification of this generalization is suggested in Justice Jackson's dissenting opinion in Korematsu v. United States, 323 U.S. 214, 242 (1944). While agreeing with his fellow dissenters that the military order directing the exclusion exceeded permissible constitutional limits, Justice Jackson concluded that the civil courts should refuse to enforce such an order. He counseled against sustaining the order under the due process clause, for to do so "is a far more subtle blow to liberty than the promulgation of the order itself," and said that to lead the people to rely on the Court for review was "wholly delusive." By intimating that restraint should be imposed upon the military through the political processes and not through the judicial process, Justice Jackson was favoring what amounted to the political question doctrine; *i.e.*, by refusing to adjudicate, the Court could avoid legitimating an order repugnant to the Constitution.

[43] *Id.* at 585.

[44] Scharpf, *supra* note 19, at 517.

consistent interpretation of constitutional grants of power or as a discretionary retreat to avoid an unprincipled decision, he advances a "functional" explanation—acknowledgment by the Court of the limitations of the judicial process. In support of this he adumbrates functional factors or considerations which have made the acknowledgment necessary in a number of cases.

Conceding that the factors which Scharpf lists have been prominent in a number of cases, one wonders whether or not he has been successful in divorcing the explanation from theories of judicial review in the American system. If the bulk of the political question cases represents no more than an acknowledgment by the Court of the limitations of the judicial system, perhaps Scharpf has done little more than state a theory of judicial self-limitation.

As the debate over the meaning of the political question illustrates, the doctrine contains an evanescent quality which evades precise articulation. Evaluation of the doctrine is further complicated by the staggering number of cases in which it has been involved. For this reason exhaustive treatment of the cases, though desirable, is beyond the scope of this article. Short of this, however, an effort will be made to examine significant areas of the doctrine with emphasis on current decisions.[45]

SCOPE OF THE DOCTRINE

Promulgation and Adoption of Constitutional Amendments

Coleman v. Miller[46] is noteworthy for its holding that the validity of a state legislature's ratification of a proposed amendment to the Federal Constitution is a political question to be left to the determination of the Congress in exercising its control over the promulgation of the adoption of amendments. Factually, the case revolved around the child labor amendment which Congress had proposed in 1924. The following year the Kansas Legislature adopted a

[45] Limitations of time and space have made it necessary to eliminate discussion of categories of the political question relating to the duration of war, the legal status of Indian tribes, foreign affairs and the deportation of aliens. For commentary on these subjects see, Note, *Judicial Determination of the End of War*, 47 COLUM. L. REV. 255 (1947); Hudson, *The Duration of War Between the United States and Germany*, 39 HARV. L. REV. 1020 (1926); POST, THE SUPREME COURT AND THE POLITICAL QUESTION 112-17 (1936); Dickinson, *Law of Nations as National Law: "Political Questions,"* 104 U. PA. L. REV. 451 (1956); Bullit, *Deportation as a Denial of Substantive Due Process*, 28 WASH. L. REV. 205 (1953); Note, *Resident Aliens and Due Process: Anatomy of a Deportation*, 8 VILL. L. REV. 566 (1963).

[46] 307 U.S. 433 (1939).

resolution rejecting the proposed amendment, and a certified copy of the resolution was sent to the United States Secretary of State. Twelve years later—in 1937—the Kansas Legislature passed a resolution ratifying the proposed amendment by a narrow margin. There was a tie vote in the state senate which was broken when the presiding officer cast an affirmative vote.

Thereafter, members of both houses of the state Legislature brought a mandamus proceeding in the state supreme court to compel legislative officials to declare that the bill had not passed and to restrain them from authenticating it. A majority of the United States Supreme Court affirmed dismissal of the writ by the highest court in Kansas. Although the Court was divided to the point of indecision with rspect to the question whether or not the power of the Lieutenent Governor, as presiding officer of the state Senate, to break a tie vote should be considered a political question, another aspect of the political question was decisive. The Court said the efficacy of the ratification was committed to Congress as part of its authority in exercising its control over the promulgation of the adoption of amendments.[47]

It was argued that Congress, having set no time limit within which the proposed amendment could be ratified, had in effect said that ratification must take place within a reasonable time to be determined by the Supreme Court. The Court, however, was unpersuaded and expressed concern that relevant criteria for making a judicial determination were absent.[48] As the Court stated it:[49]

> In short, the question of a reasonable time in many cases would involve . . . an appraisal of a great variety of relevant conditions, political, social and economic, which can hardly be said to be within the appropriate range of evidence receivable in a court of justice and as to which it would be an extravagant extension of judicial authority to assert judicial notice as the basis of deciding a controversy. . . . On the other hand, these conditions are appropriate for the consideration of the political departments of Government. The questions they involve are essentially political and not justiciable.

[47] *Id.* at 450.

[48] The Court said that in determining whether a question is political and not justiciable, "the appropriateness under our system of government of attributing finality to the action of the political departments and also the lack of satisfactory criteria for a judicial determination are dominant considerations." *Id.* at 454-55.

[49] *Id.* at 453-54.

Notwithstanding the theme of judicial abstention in the majority opinion, Mr. Justice Black in a concurring opinion criticized the Court for not expressly disapproving the conclusion in an earlier decision (*Dillion v. Gloss*)[50] that the Constitution impliedly required ratification of a proposed amendment within a reasonable amount of time. The Court distinguished the *Dillion* case as deciding only that Congress *might* fix a reasonable time for ratification, but Justice Black argued that it should be overruled. Characterizing the entire amendment process as political, he said the process was subject to no judicial review because article V of the Constitution grants power over the amending of the Constitution to Congress alone.[51]

To regard the reasonable time question as having complete immunity from judicial review seems the preferable position. In the first place, the problem invites application of Professor Jaffe's observation that for many problems "[w]e may believe that the job is better done without rules, or that even though there are applicable rules, these rules should be only among the numerous relevant considerations."[52] Although little difficulty would be involved in devising rules defining a reasonable time, this problem is one for which we do not want rules. As the Court pointed out, a determination of the vitality of a proposed amendment requires evaluation of a broad range of conditions in society. These give rise to sharply contested issues of social policy (such as the child labor law) which cut deeply into society and which are not always susceptible to reasoned elaboration. Such issues are more appropriately resolved by the legislature whose members are directly responsible to the electorate.

Secondly, there is a certain tension between the institution of judicial review and the democratic principle of majority rule. To the extent that judicial review is counter-majoritarian it is essentially undemocratic.[53] Thus, it is one thing to attempt to justify

[50] 256 U.S. 368 (1921) (congressional resolution proposing the eighteenth amendment which contained a specification declaring the proposed amendment inoperative unless ratified within seven years held to be a reasonable amount of time).

[51] Coleman v. Miller, 307 U.S. 433, 459 (1939) (Black, J. concurring).

[52] Jaffe, *Standing to Secure Judicial Review: Public Actions,* 74 HARV. L. REV. 1265, 1303 (1961). Professor Bickel adopts the Jaffe formula in developing his thesis. See A. BICKEL, *supra* note 27, at 183-198.

[53] For a discussion of whether or not judicial review is compatible with democracy, see McCleskey, *Judicial Review in a Democracy: A Dissenting Opinion,* 3 HOUSTON L. REV. 354 (1966). The writer concludes that "tradi-

judicial annulment of legislation as an expression of community principle—the "sober second thought," as Bickel has put it—yet it is entirely another thing to allow the Court to hold a reasonable time has expired and thereby frustrate the very process by which the community may wish to reverse what the Court has done.

On the other hand, to regard the *entire* amendment process as being subject to *no* review is to ignore important functions which the Court might legitimately perform. Redress for irregularities or fraud in obvious disregard of explicit constitutional requirements could be sought in court. For example, assuming there are no questions concerning the efficacy of a state's ratification such as were involved in *Coleman v. Miller,* if Congress should declare an amendment adopted which plainly had not been approved by three-fourths of the states as required by the Constitution, the Court's doors should not be closed. Although the likelihood of such a patent violation of the Constitution is improbable, the possibility of judicial relief should not be foreclosed.[54] The Court could declare the amendment void or refuse to enforce it because approval of the requisite number of states had not been secured. As the Court's order would be framed in the negative, compliance would not present a significant problem.

When, however, one passes from the more outrageous violations of article V, nice questions are presented. A potential problem is illustrated by current attempts to secure applications of two-thirds of the state legislatures requesting Congress to call a convention for the purpose of proposing amendments in regard to the apportionment of state governments. Segments of the community, unhappy

tion, and sentiment, and some really spendid rhetoric, have blinded us to 'the essential reality that judicial review is a deviant institution in the American democracy.' " *Id.* at 366.

[54] A more likely situation would be a judicial contest of congressional certification that three-fourths of the states had approved a proposed amendment. Assuming the approval is authenticated by the proper officers, what evidence, if any, would be admissible to impeach their authentication? Two early cases dealing with legislation cut in different directions. Field v. Clark, 143 U.S. 649 (1892) held that it is incompetent to show from committee reports or the journals of either house of Congress that a bill, which was signed by the presiding officers of each house and the President, was not the one actually passed by the Congress. *But cf.* Gardner v. Barney, 73 U.S. (6 Wall) 499 (1868) in which the Court held it was proper to resort to extrinsic evidence show that the date affixed to a bill signed by the President was defective. "[W]henever a question arises in a court of law of the existence of a statute, or of the time when a statute took effect, or of the precise terms of a statute, the judges who are called upon to decide it, have a right to resort to *any* source of information which in its nature is capable of conveying to the judicial mind a clear and satisfactory answer to such questions. . . ." *Id.* at 511 (dictum) (emphasis supplied).

with the Court's conception of one-man, one-vote, have set into motion the cumbersome amending process. If two-thirds of the states should apply to Congress to call such a convention, would the Court review a congressional refusal or failure to comply?

If the Court decides the merits, it must interpret the explicit language of article V which uses the word "shall" in connection with the duty of Congress to call such a convention. However, as the Court's interpretation of the rendition clause of article IV, section 2 exemplifies, mandatory language is not always construed to create an enforceable duty.[55] Thus, the Court might well hold that the congressional duty to call a convention is not used in the mandatory or compulsory sense but is only declaratory of a moral duty created by the Constitution. Such a construction would avoid a head-on confrontation with Congress and compliance problems growing out of the affirmative action which a contrary construction might necessitate.

On the other hand, the Court could accomplish the same result by applying the political question and thus refusing to decide the merits. Besides avoiding hostile confrontation with the legislative branch, use of the political question would help preserve the prestige and public confidence on which the Court's ultimate authority rests. By refusing to legitimate or sanction congressional non-compliance with a constitutional directive, the Court will emerge from the fray unscarred and final solution of the question will be left to the political processes.

The Politics of the People: The Apportionment Cases

> *The Court's authority—possessed of neither the purse nor the sword—ultimately rests on sustained public confidence in its moral sanction. Such feeling must be nourished by the Court's complete detachment, in fact and in appearance, from political entanglements and by abstention from injecting itself into the clash of political forces in political settlements.—Frankfurter, J., dissenting in Baker v. Carr, 369 U.S. 186, 267 (1962).*

Considering the wide range of issues to which the political question has been applied, it is not surprising that it should have raised its head in suits to compel reapportionment where state legislative and congressional representation was based on considerations other than numerical equality at the ballot box. As the justiciability of malapportionment claims has important social, political and economic consequences, this has proved to be one of the most active and most controversial categories of the political question. Thus,

[55] Kentucky v. Dennison, 65 U.S. (24 How.) 66 (1860).

it may be more than a matter of mere coincidence that the earliest apportionment suits were commenced at the threshold of an era in American history which subjected American institutions to a serious re-evaluation.

After the 1930 census, approximately two-thirds of the states were affected by congressional reapportionment. States with increasing and with decreasing populations were affected, and many state legislatures were reapportioned.[56] Voters instituted suit challenging the new districts, and several of the cases ultimately reached the Supreme Court.

In one of these cases the two houses of the Minnesota Legislature had passed a congressional districting bill and had sent it to the Governor who had returned it without approval. The Minnesota constitution provided that a bill should become law upon approval by the Governor or in the absence of his approval by two-thirds vote of each House. Even though the necessary two-thirds approval had not been obtained, the bill was deposited with the state Secretary of State to become effective as law.

Alleging (1) that the bill had not been repassed by the Legislature and (2) that the proposed congressional districts were not compact and did not contain an equal number of inhabitants as required by the congressional Reapportionment Act of 1929, the plaintiff sought to enjoin all proceedings pursuant to the bill. The Supreme Court held for the plaintiff on the ground that there is nothing in article 1, section 4 of the Constitution to allow a state legislature to enact law except in accordance with the method set forth in its own constitution.[57]

The Court was confronted with what in effect had been the plaintiff's second contention in *Wood v. Broom*.[58] The 1911 congressional Reapportionment Act specified that each district should have, among other things, as nearly as practicable the same number of inhabitants, and a federal district court declared a Mississippi statute invalid for failure to comply with this requirement. Reversing, the Supreme Court held that the provision of the 1911 act relied upon by the district court had expired and was not included in the

---

[56] Dixon, *Legislative Apportionment and the Federal Constitution*, 27 LAW & CONTEMP. PROB. 329 (1962).

[57] Smiley v. Holm, 285 U.S. 355 (1932). *Accord*, Carrol v. Becker, 285 U.S. 380 (1932); Koenig v. Flynn, 285 U.S. 375 (1932).

[58] 285 U.S. 1 (1932).

1929 congressional Reapportionment Act.[59] Four justices, however, thought the only ground for dismissing the bill was want of equity.

Precedent against the justiciability of apportionment claims continued to mount and reached its high water mark with the decision of *Colegrove v. Green.*[60] A divided Court dismissed a complaint under the federal Declaratory Judgment Act for a decree declaring Illinois' statutes apportioning the state into congressional districts invalid on the theory that the districts lacked compactness of territory and approximate equality of population. The prevailing opinion was written by Justice Frankfurter who thought *Wood v. Broom* was controlling.[61] Moreover, he hinted that lack of jurisdiction was the basis for the decision because the Constitution grants to Congress the exclusive authority to regulate congressional elections.

The actual ground of the decision, however, proceeded on the assumption that the judiciary is incompetent to entertain claims based on unequal voting power. Thus:

> We are of the opinion that the appellants ask of this Court what is beyond its competence to grant. [Such a demand on judicial power] must be resolved by considerations on the basis of which this Court, from time to time, has refused to intervene in controversies. It has refused to do so because due regard for the effective working of our Government revealed this issue to be of a peculiarly political nature and therefore not meet for judicial determination.
>
> . . . .
>
> Courts ought not to enter this political thicket.[62]

At the heart of *Colegrove* was Justice Frankfurter's conviction that excessive reliance on courts weakens the responsibility of the electorate in a democracy. One thought, more than any other, permeates the opinion: "It is hostile to a democratic system to involve the judiciary in the politics of the people."[63]

In an opinion by Justice Black, three dissenters took a different view of the role of courts in a democracy. The dissenters emphasized that the plaintiffs lived in congressional election districts with popu-

[59] *Accord,* Mahan v. Hume, 287 U.S. 575 (1932).

[60] 328 U.S. 549 (1946).

[61] Three justices dissented, and one justice was of the opinion that the bill should be dismissed for want of equity.

[62] Colegrove v. Green, 328 U.S. 549, 552-56 (1946).

[63] *Id.* at 553. For an article challenging both the legatlity and practicality of *Colegrove,* see Lewis, *Legislative Apportionment and the Federal Courts,* 71 HARV. L. REV. 1057 (1958).

lations three to four times as great as other such districts; and that state legislators were chosen on the basis of state election districts apportioned in a manner similar to the congressional election districts, which had not been reapportioned for approximately forty years. The interdependence between state and congressional apportionment made it in the self-interest of state legislators to perpetuate the inequalities in voting power. Given this situation, the dissenters felt it was the duty of the Court to declare the existing Illinois apportionment act "a wholly indefensible discrimination against appellants and all other voters in heavily populated districts" in violation of the equal protection clause of the fourteenth amendment.[64]

Following the *Colegrove* decision, the Court continued to remain aloof from the political thicket and dismissed a number of apportionment claims in short *per curiam* decisions.[65] While reflecting the *Colegrove* philosophy to a degree, an additional concept appeared to justify non-intervention:

> To assume that political power is a function exclusively of numbers is to disregard the practicalities of government. . . . It would be strange indeed, and doctrinaire, for this Court, applying such broad constitutional concepts as due process and equal protection of the laws, to deny to a State the power to assure a proper diffusion of political initiative as between its thinly populated counties and those having concentrated masses. . . . The Constitution—a practical instrument of government—makes no such demands on the States.[66]

On the other hand, the same Court which declared nonjusticiable malapportionment claims based on the equal protection clause of the fourteenth amendment had considerably less difficulty striking down racially motivated legislation which created a disparity in voting power. Thus, Justice Frankfurter who wrote the opinion in *Colegrove v. Green* spoke for the Court in *Gomillion v. Lightfoot*.[67]

---

[64] Colegrove v. Green, 328 U.S. 549, 569 (1946) (Black, J., dissenting).

[65] Matthews v. Handley, 361 U.S. 127 (1959); Hartsfield v. Sloan, 357 U.S. 916 (1958); Radford v. Gray, 352 U.S. 991 (1957); Kidd v. McCanless, 352 U.S. 920 (1956); Anderson v. Jordan, 343 U.S. 912 (1952); Cox v. Peters, 342 U.S. 936 (1952); Remmey v. Smith, 342 U.S. 916 (1952); Tedesco v. Board of Supervisors of Elections, 339 U.S. 940 (1950); South v. Peters, 339 U.S. 276 (1950); MacDougall v. Green, 335 U.S. 281 (1948); Colegrove v. Barret, 330 U.S. 804 (1946); Cook v. Fortson (Turner v. Duckworth), 329 U.S. 675 (1946). Only a few of these decisions were by a unanimous Court.

[66] MacDougall v. Green, 335 U.S. 281, 283-84 (1948).

[67] 364 U.S. 339 (1960).

The plaintiffs in *Gomillion* were Negro citizens who sought an injunction in a federal district court in Alabama to restrain the enforcement of a state statute which altered the boundaries of the city of Tuskegee. According to the allegations in the bill, the act eliminated practically all of the city's 400 Negro voters without eliminating any white voters,[68] and the plaintiffs argued that the effect of the statute was to disenfranchise them solely for racial reasons. More specifically, the alleged effect of the act was "to deprive the Negro petitioners discriminatorily of the benefits of residence in Tuskegee, including, *inter alia,* the right to vote in municipal elections."[69] Reversing the district court's dismissal of the bill, the Court said that if the allegations were proved, the effect of the act would be to deprive Negroes of the right to vote on account of race in violation of the fifteenth amendment.

Attempting to distinguish *Colegrove v. Green,* Mr. Justice Frankfurter pointed out that *Colegrove* involved a complaint based on discriminatory apportionment of congressional districts in the form of legislative inaction over a period of years resulting in a dilution of the strength of the plaintiff's votes. In contrast, the complaint in *Gomillion* centered around affirmative legislation which was racially inspired. As Justice Frankfurter expressed it:

> In no case involving unequal weight in voting distribution that has come before the Court did the decision sanction a differentiation on racial lines whereby approval was given to unequivocal withdrawal of the vote solely from colored citizens. Apart from all else, these considerations lift this controversy out of the so-called "political" arena and into the conventional sphere of constitutional litigation.[70]

Although *Gomillion* did involve a kind of apportionment problem in that the contested legislation in effect deprived the plaintiffs of the right to vote in municipal elections, the distinction drawn by Justice Frankfurter seems correct. In the first place, there was ample precedent in support of the result in *Gomillion,*[71] while there

[68] It was alleged that the act altered the shape of the city from a square to an irregular twenty-eight sided figure.

[69] Gomillion v. Lightfoot, 364 U.S. 339, 341 (1960).

[70] Gomillion v. Lightfoot, 364 U.S. 339, 346-47 (1960).

[71] Guinn v. United States, 238 U.S. 347 (1915) and Myers v. Anderson, 238 U.S. 368 (1915) held so-called Grandfather clauses—statutes fixing the qualifications of voters based on the right of the voter or his ancestor to vote at a date prior to the adoption of the fifteenth amendment—void because in violation of the fifteenth amendment. In Nixon v. Herndon, 273 U.S. 536 (1927) the Court held unconstitutional under the equal protection

was no precedent permitting justiciability where the sole claim was numerical inequality in voting strength. Secondly, the force of history presented an appealing argument for finding justiciability in *Gomillion* while denying it in *Colegrove*: perhaps the principal purpose behind the fifteenth amendment was enfranchisement and legal equality for the Negro. Thirdly, judicial abstention in *Colegrove* could co-exist with judicial interference in *Gomillion* because "apportionment is necessarily a very high percentage of politics with a very small admixture of definable principle. In race relations the proportions are reversed."[72] For this reason the political question was not even mentioned in the school segregation cases.[73]

In this state of the art, the apportionment issue appeared to have been placed beyond the competence of the federal judiciary. There were few warnings in the Court's opinions that *Baker v. Carr*[74] was on the horizon. It should be noted, however, that a majority of the Court had never been able to agree upon the reasons for holding apportionment suits nonjusticiable. In addition, only four of the judges who sat on the Court at the time *Colegrove v. Green* was decided remained when *Baker* was argued, and two of them—Justices Black and Douglas—had dissented in *Colegrove*. Just prior to Baker these two justices had reiterated their positions by way of a memorandum dissent in which they were joined by Chief Justice Warren and Justice Brennan.[75]

Actually there was nothing new or innovating in the claim set forth in the complaint in *Baker*. The Tennessee Constitution provided for representation in proportion to the number of qualified

clause of the fourteenth amendment a Texas statute making Negroes ineligible to participate in a primary election of a political party. Speaking for the Court Mr. Justice Holmes said, "[t]he objection that the subject matter of the suit is political is little more than a play upon words." *Id.* at 540.

A majority of the Court in Smith v. Allwright, 321 U.S. 649 (1944) found that exclusion of Negroes from voting in a Democratic primary election to select nominees for a general election constituted state action in contravention of the fifteenth amendment, even though membership in the party was limited to white persons by resolution of a state convention. More recently, eight of nine members of the Court thought the fifteenth amendment was violated because Negroes were not allowed to vote in primary elections of a Texas county political organization which placed the names of its nominees on the regular Democratic primary ballot. Terry v. Adams, 345 U.S. 461 (1953).

72 A. BICKEL, *supra* note 27, at 193.

73 *Id.*

74 369 U.S. 196 (1962).

75 Hartsford v. Sloan, 357 U.S. 916 (1958). (involving an attack on the Georgia county unit system). *See* Neal, *Baker v. Carr: Politics in Search of Law*, 1962 SUP. CT. REV. 252.

voters in the state. Suit was instituted in a federal district court in which the plaintiffs alleged that the state legislature had failed to apportion since 1901 and that the Supreme Court of Tennessee had declined jurisdiction in a similar case. For these reasons plaintiffs claimed denial of the equal protection of the laws guaranteed by the fourteenth amendment.

Agreeing that the claim presented a justiciable controversy, six members of the Court amassed four separate opinions. Justices Frankfurter and Harlan dissented. Although Mr. Justice Stewart in his concurring opinion stressed that the Court decided only the questions of jurisdiction, justiciability and standing, subsequent decisions have made it unequivocally clear that the political question is no longer an impediment to justiciability in apportionment litigation.[76]

---

[76] After *Baker*, the Court, in a series of decisions, overturned the line of cases dating from *Smiley v. Holm* and *Wood v. Broom* in 1932. Thus, in Gray v. Sanders, 372 U.S. 368 (1963), the Court struck down use of Georgia's county unit system in primary elections for state-wide officers. According to Mr. Justice Douglas, "[t]he conception of political equality from the Declaration of Independence, to Lincoln's Gettysburg Address, to the Fifteenth, Seventeenth, and Nineteenth Amendments can mean only one thing—one person, one vote." *Id.* at 381. In like manner the Court invalidated a Georgia statute creating congressional districts because the statute abridged the guarantee of article I, section 2 of the federal constitution, providing that congressmen shall be chosen "by the People of the several States."

By 1964 the Court had come full circle, Reynolds v. Sims, 377 U.S. 533 (1964) held the existing and two proposed apportionment plans allowing substantial variances between population and representation for the Alabama Legislature unconstitutional. The dominant theme of the opinion was, of course, equal protection: "We hold, that as a basic constitutional standard, the Equal Protection Clause requires that the seats in *both* houses of a bicameral state legislature must be apportioned on a population basis." *Id.* at 568 (emphasis supplied). As for the political question: "We are cautioned about the dangers of entering into political thickets and mathematical quagmires. Our answer is this: a denial of constitutionally protected rights demands judicial protection; our oath and our office require no less of us." *Id.* at 566.

On the same day *Reynolds v. Sims* was decided—June 15, 1964—the Court held the legislatures of five other states had been unconstitutionally apportioned. Lucas v. Forty-Fourth General Assembly, 377 U.S. 713 (Colorado); YMCA, Inc. v. Lomenzo, 377 U.S. 633 (New York); Maryland Committee for Fair Representation v. Tawes, 377 U.S. 656 (Maryland); Davis v. Mann, 377 U.S. 678 (Virginia); Roman v. Sincock, 377 U.S. 695 (Delaware). Shortly after these cases were decided, the Court found apportionments in nine additional states unconstitutional; they are reported beginning at 378 U.S. 553.

But cf., Fortson v. Morris 385 U.S. 231 (1966), where the Court by a five-four decision upheld a provision of the Georgia Constitution allowing members of the Georgia General Assembly to elect the governor in the event no candidate receives a majority of the popular votes cast in a general election. The Court refused to enjoin the Georgia Legislature from proceeding to elect a Governor even though the Legislature was malapportioned.

In holding that the challenge to an apportionment presents no nonjusticiable political question, Mr. Justice Brennan, who wrote the majority opinion, found it necessary to review the contours of the political question doctrine. He sidestepped the *Colegrove v. Green* line of precedent upon which the district court had relied in dismissing the suit by saying "[t]he cited cases do not hold to the contrary."[77] He said that a review of the cases revealed that in the political question cases, "it is the relationship between the judiciary and the coordinate branches of the Federal Government, and not the federal judiciary's relationship to the States, which gives rise to the 'political question.' "[78] Furthermore, he listed a number of variables which distinguish a political question and which, at the same time, identify it as essentially a function of separation of powers. As Mr. Justice Brennan expressed it:

> Prominent on the surface of any case held to involve a political question is found a textually demonstrable constitutional commitment of the issue to a coordinate political department; or a lack of judicially discoverable and manageable standards for resolving it; or the impossibility of deciding without an initial policy determination of a kind clearly for nonjudicial discretion; or the impossibility of a court's undertaking independent resolution without expressing lack of the respect due coordinate branches of government; or an unusual need for unquestioning adherence to a political decision already made; or the potentiality of embarrassment from multifarious pronouncements by various departments on one question.
>
> Unless one of these formulations is inextricable from the case at bar, there should be no dismissal for nonjusticiability on the ground of a political question's presence.[79]

As Professor McCloskey has pointed out,[80] with the exception of the formulation described as "a lack of judicially discoverable and manageable standards," Brennan's primary emphasis is upon the

[77] Baker v. Carr, 369 U.S. 186, 209 (1962). Brennan read *Smiley v. Holm* and the other 1932 cases as having "settled the issue in favor of justicability of questions of congressional redistricting," Such a reading seems questionable as the only questions decided in these cases were the applicability of the governor's veto power to a state redistricting and the expiration of the voter numerical equality requirement in the 1911 congressional Reapportionment Act.

[78] *Id.* at 210.

[79] Baker v. Carr, 369 U.S. 186, 209 (1962).

[80] McCloskey, *Foreword: The Reapportionment Case,* 76 HARV. L. REV. 54, 61 (1962).

intra-federal relationship. Not only are the variables which he lists concerned in the main with separation of powers at the federal level, but the precedents he considers in fields such as foreign affairs, duration of war and validity of enactments bear the same message. Although Brennan does not expressly foreclose application of the political question for want of judicially discoverable standards when the federal judiciary's relationship to the states is involved, it seems implicitly clear that this will seldom be an insuperable barrier. Thus, in *Baker* such a contention was disposed of in one sentence, and no breath was wasted on elaboration:

> Judicial standards under the Equal Protection Clause are well developed and familiar, and it has been open to the courts since the enactment of the Fourteenth Amendment to determine, if on the particular facts they must, that a discrimination reflects *no* policy, but simply arbitrary and capricious action.[81]

More recently the Court in the Julian Bond case had little difficulty discovering free speech standards by which actions of the Georgia Legislature were invalidated.

Mr. Justice Brennan's treatment of the political question has been praised for several reasons. First, some crystalization of such an amorphous concept is desirable, and there is a strong implication that his list of specific elements which make an issue into a political question is exclusive. Even if the list is not exclusive, it has confined the doctrine to more manageable proportions.[82] Secondly, as a by-product of enumerating the elements of the political question, Mr. Justice Brennan has assembled the political question cases with an orderliness of doctrine that previous majority opinions lacked.[83] At the same time, however, he seems to have rejected blanket application of the doctrine to any one broad area and to have emphasized the need for case by case development.[84]

On the other hand, this undertaking has not escaped criticism. Thus, he has been accused of engaging in "a type of logomachical legerdemain without squarely facing the more fundamental problem; namely, the distinction between *law* and *politics*."[85] Another com-

---

[81] Baker v. Carr, 369 U.S. 186, 226 (1962).

[82] *See* Emerson, *Malapportionment and Judicial Power*, 72 YALE L.J. 64 (1962).

[83] McKay, *Political Thickets and Crazy Quilts: Reapportionment and Equal Protection*, 61 MICH. L. REV. 645 (1963).

[84] Emerson, *supra* note 82.

[85] Tollett, *Political Questions and the Law*, 42 U. DET. L.J. 439, 441 (1965).

mentator has advanced a similar observation, although in more practical language: "The Court seems to have decided justiciability in such a generalized context as to amount to judicial adventuring on the high seas of politics with no assurance of a safe return to shore."[86] Perhaps the most stinging criticism, however, was voiced by Mr. Justice Frankfurter who was of the opinion that the Court's decision not only reversed a "uniform course of decision established by a dozen cases" but amounted to a "massive repudiation of the experience of our whole past."[87]

Part of the past experience Justice Frankfurter thought the Court had repudiated was the *Colegrove* doctrine. While admitting there had been no unanimity of agreement on the reasoning behind *Colegrove,* he said that the political question in the *Colegrove—Baker* type of case embodied a confluence of the following considerations: (1) a concern with avoiding involvement of the judiciary in matters traditionally left to legislative policy; (2) difficulty of devising judicial standards to determine the precise role of numerical equality in the allocation of political power; (3) difficulty of finding appropriate kinds of relief. Each of these considerations converged to make the *Colegrove—Baker* kind of controversy nonjusticiable. "To classify the various instances as 'political questions' is rather a form stating this conclusion than a revealing of analysis."[88]

Emanating from his dissenting opinion was the Frankfurter philosophy of complete judicial detachment from the politics of the people. To embroil the Court in the apportionment controversy would be "hostile to a democratic system"[89] because apportionment lies at the heart of the political process.

> Apportionment . . . [involves] considerations of geography, demography, electoral convenience, economic and social cohesions or divergencies among particular local groups, communications, the practical effects of political institutions like the lobby and the city machine, ancient traditions and ties of settled usage, respect for proven incumbents of long experience and senior status, mathematical mechanics, censuses compiling relevant data, and a host of others.[90]

---

[86] Dixon, *supra* note 56, at 355.

[87] Baker v. Carr, 369 U.S. 186, 266-67 (1962) (Frankfurter, J., dissenting).

[88] *Id.* at 280-81.

[89] Colegrove v. Green, 328 U.S. 549, 553 (1946).

[90] Baker v. Carr, 369 U.S. 186, 323 (1962) (Frankfurter, J., dissenting). As Professor Bickel has put it, "apportionment is a very high percentage of politics with a small admixture of definable principles." A. BICKEL, *supra* note 27, at 193.

Factors such as these make apportionment extraordinarily complex—so complex that equal protection provides no clear guide for judicial examination.

The Court simply had no answer for this argument, and it is suggested that the Frankfurter position is the preferable one. In the first place, precedent dating from *Colegrove v. Green* called for rejection of apportionment suits. Moreover, there was no compelling historical justification for making representation proportional to population; and what justification there was had not been initiated at the behest of the judiciary.[91] Secondly, conceding that the flexible language of equal protection lends itself to a formula of equality in numbers, there are still other relevant considerations—to return to Professor Jaffe's formula. Even though equal representation of qualified voters may be an ideal of American democracy, our political institutions have invariably found it necessary to compromise the ideal to conform with the practicalities of political life.

Different groups, regions and interests clamor for recognition. Strength of political parties depends to a degree upon which group of voters wields the most power at the polls. In short, the apportionment question is too "high," and "too nakedly power-oriented, and perhaps too explosive for judicial control."[92] By using the political question the Court can refrain from blessing or legitimating "the expedient arrangements made by political institutions."[93] Correction of these arrangements should be initiated at the grass roots level—by the people who exert ultimate control in a democracy.

The Guarantee of a Republican Form of Government

For more than a century article IV, section 4 of the Constitution, guaranteeing to each state a republican form of government, has consistently been held not to be enforceable through the courts. The grandfather of this long line of cases is *Luther v. Borden*,[94] which grew out of Dorr's rebellion of 1841. As the 1633 Charter of Rhode Island contained no provision for amendment and allowed only limited suffrage, dissatisfied citizens elected representatives to attend a constitutional convention, which, in turn, drew up a pro-

[91] Representation proportional to population was not a prevalent practice in colonial times, at the time the Constitution was adopted, or at the time the fourteenth amendment became part of the Constitution; nor was it employed by a large number of states at the time *Baker v. Carr* was argued. Baker v. Carr, 369 U.S. 186 (1962) (Frankfurter, J., dissenting).
[92] McCloskey, *supra* note 80, at 62.
[93] A BICKEL, *supra* note 27, at 194.
[94] 48 U.S. (7 How.) 1 (1849).

posal for a new state government. The new government was adopted by a majority vote of the adult male population, and its Governor-elect Dorr tried unsuccessfully to uphold its authority by force. Thereafter, issue was joined in a trespass action on the question whether or not officials of the charter government had acted pursuant to martial law to suppress an insurrection against the state government. Thus, the ultimate issue was which of the two competing governments was legitimate and lawful. Describing the question as political, the Supreme Court refused to decide the matter.

The Court pointed out that the guarantee clause guaranteed to each state not only a republican form of government but protection against domestic violence upon application of the legislature or the executive (when the legislature cannot be convened). In accordance with the latter guarantee, the Congress had enacted a statute in 1795 empowering the President to curb insurrection within a state upon request by the proper state governmental authority. Thus, the President would necessarily have to determine which government was legitimate before he could exercise his statutory power. As events would have it, the militia was not summoned in the *Luther* case, although the President did in fact recognize the Governor of the charter government. The Court bowed to the President's decision and declared that the political departments had the sole power to determine which of the two competing state governments was legitimate.[95]

Although the actual holding of the *Luther* case was rather narrow, the decision has been the cornerstone in the development of a line of decisions establishing the principle that the federal courts will not enforce guarantee clause claims. Particularly important has been the following dictum:

> Under [the guarantee clause] it rests with Congress to decide what government is the established one in a State. . . . Congress must necessarily decide what government is established in the State before it can be determined whether it is republican or not. And when the senators and representatives of a State are admitted into the councils of the Union, the authority of the government under which they are appointed, as well as its republican character, is recognized by the proper constitutional authority. And its decision is binding on every other department

[95] *See* Bonfield, *The Guarantee Clause of Article IV, Section 4: A Study in Constitutional Desuetude,* 46 MINN. L. REV. 513 (1962).

of the government, and could not be questioned in a judicial tribunal.[96]

This dictum has been taken for granted in a number of decisions,[97] notably *Pacific States Tel. & Tel. Co. v. Oregon.*[98] After the Oregon Constitution was amended in 1902 to provide for the initiative and referendum, the initiative was used in 1906 to enact a law taxing certain classes of corporations. In a proceeding brought by the state to enforce the tax, the taxpayer's two principal contentions were that the initiative and referendum violated the guarantee of a republican form of government and that the tax measure was forbidden by the equal protection clause of the fourteenth amendment. The Court reasoned that the taxpayer's sole objection to the tax was based on its guarantee clause claim and therefore the matter was nonjusticiable on the authority of *Luther v. Borden.*

One could read the *Pacific States* decision rather narrowly to mean only that the republicanism of a mode of statutory enactment cannot be asserted as a defense to resist enforcement of the statute created under it.[99] Such an interpretation, however, has been rejected as subsequent decisions demonstrate, and the *Pacific States* decision has bulked large in a number of instances where efforts have been made to enforce the guarantee clause. More specifically, the Court has declared all issues raised under the guarantee clause to be political primarily on the authority of *Pacific States;* [100] enforcement of the guarantee is said to be for the Congress and not for the Courts.

In contrast with the central role played by the equal protection clause of the fourteenth amendment in decisions of the present Court such as the school segregation decisions and the reapportionment decisions, the Court in *Pacific States* regarded the taxpayer's

---

[96] Luther v. Borden, 48 U.S. (7 How.) 1, 42 (1849).

[97] During the Reconstruction era the Court refused to enjoin the operation of statutes dividing former confederate states into military districts. As such matters affected the structure of a state's government, they were political and not justiciable. See *e.g.*, Georgia v. Stanton, 73 U.S. (6 Wall.) 50 (1867); Mississippi v. Johnson, 71 U.S. (4 Wall.) 475 (1866).

[98] 223 U. S. 118 (1912).

[99] Bonfield, *supra* note 95.

[100] *See, e.g.*, Highland Farms Dairy, Inc. v. Agnew, 300 U.S. 608, 612 (1937) (attack on a statute establishing a state commission to regulate the licensing, sales, prices and market areas of milk producers held nonjusticiable); Ohio *ex rel.* Bryant v. Akron Metropolitan Park Dist., 281 U.S. 74, 79-80 (1930) (challenge to a constitutional provision requiring the concurrence of all but one of the justices on the state supreme court to invalidate a statute held nonjusticiable); other cases in which attacks based on guarantee clause have been declared nonjusticiable are collected in Bonfield, *supra* note 95.

equal protection claim as mere surplusage. In like manner the Court in *Taylor & Marshall v. Beckham (No. 1)*[101] avoided an alleged due process violation on rather technical grounds. The Kentucky Board of Election Commissioners declared two candidates—Taylor and Marshall—in a general election to have been elected Governor and Lieutenant Governor respectively. After they had been inducted into office, Goebel and Beckham, the opposing candidates, contested the election in the state's General Assembly, which the state constitution gave them the right to do, and the General Assembly awarded the election to them.

Shortly after the oath of office was administered, Goebel died and Beckham succeeded him as Governor. Beckham thereafter successfully sought a judgment of ouster against Taylor and Marshall in the state courts. On appeal to the United States Supreme Court, it was alleged that because the General Assembly had acted without evidence the judgment of ouster deprived Taylor and Marshall of due process of law and deprived the people of Kentucky of a government republican in form. The Court rejected the due process claim on the ground that an office in a state government was not property within the meaning of the fourteenth amendment; as for the latter claim, the Court felt that *Luther v. Borden* was controlling.[102]

It is quite probable that the outcome in the *Taylor* case would be different if it were decided by the present Court. In the first place, the Court in *Taylor* seems to have applied *Luther* almost indiscriminately without regard to what *Luther* did or said. Actually, the *Luther* Court abstained from deciding which of two competing governments was legitimate, and its dicta declared that Congress determines whether or not a state has a republican form of government by admitting Senators and Representatives to " the councils of the Union." If Congress determines a state's republicanism by seating its elected Representatives, it is difficult to see how *Luther* applies to the validity of a gubernatorial election. Neither the holding nor dicta in *Luther* embraces the manner in which a state governor is chosen.

Secondly, separation of powers between the federal judiciary and the states is no longer a formidable barrier to justiciability. Writing for the Court in *Baker v. Carr,* Justice Brennan was at pains to emphasize that it is the federal judiciary's relationship to co-

[101] 178 U.S. 548 (1900).
[102] Three justices dissented.

ordinate branches of the federal government that creates a political question. Since *Baker*, the Court's review of the Georgia Legislature's action in refusing to seat a newly elected member supplies further evidence that the federal judiciary's relationship to the states will not give rise to a political question.

In his dissenting opinion in *Baker v. Carr*, Justice Frankfurter analyzed many of the guarantee clause cases, although the *Taylor* case was not among them. He concluded that the combination of three discernible principles was responsible for the proposition that guarantee clause claims are nonjusticiable, namely: (1) refusal to decide when standards meet for judgment were lacking; (2) non-interference with state governmental matters in the absence of a clear mandate (such as the fifteenth amendment's mandate in *Gomillion v. Lightfoot*); (3) abstention from broad issues of political organization. Justice Frankfurter thought each of these elements was present in the *Baker* case and argued that the claim in *Baker* was, in effect, "a Guarantee Clause claim masquerading under a different label. . . . [W]here judicial competence is wanting, it cannot be created by invoking one clause of the Constitution rather than another.[103]

Justice Brennan's majority opinion, on the other hand, purported to leave the guarantee cluase cases undisturbed. Differing with Justice Frankfurter, he stated that, "it is the involvement in Guaranty Clause claims of the elements thought to define 'political questions,' and no other feature, which could render them nonjusticiable. Specifically, . . . such claims are not held nonjusticiable because they touch matters of state governmental organization."[104] Notwithstanding statements such as these, the substance of the complaint in *Baker*—that representation based on geographical units without regard to numerical equality violates the equal protection clause of the fourteenth amendment—is practically indistinguishable from a charge that the Tennessee government is not republican in form.[105]

[103] Baker v. Carr. 369 U.S. 186, 297 (1962) (Frankfurter, J., dissenting).

[104] *Id.* at 229. It has been observed that "[t]he Brennan-Frankfurter dichotomy was a salient illustration of Llewellyn's notion of 'leeways'—that is, . . . that the choice of applicable precedents to govern current cases, is one of the principal leeways of the law." Rosenblum, *Justiciability and Justice: Elements of Restraint and Indifference*, 15 CATH. U.L. REV. 141, 146 (1966); K. LLEWELLYN, JURISPRUDENCE: REALISM IN THEORY AND PRACTICE 120 (1962).

[105] According to one commentator, "the net conclusion of . . . [Brennan's] opinion seems to be that the issue presented in *Baker v. Carr* is justiciable when presented under the equal protection clause, but nonjusticiable when raised under the guarantee." Bonfield, *Baker v. Carr: New Light on the Constitutional Guarantee of Republican Government*, 50 CALIF. L. REV. 245 (1962).

That is, it is difficult to see how the Court could decide the equal protection issue without considering the republican form issue as a preliminary question for the reason that what violates equal protection depends upon the frame of government being used. As Justice Frankfurter put it, "since 'equal protection of the laws' can only mean an equality of persons standing in the same relation to whatever governmental action is challenged, the determination whether treatment is equal presupposes a determination concerning the nature of the relationship."[106]

Thus, in deciding *Baker* and subsequent apportionment decisions, the Court has in a sense defined a government republican in form. The Court has carried over to the ballot box the aspiration of American democracy that every person counts one. Having done this, the next step may well be specific judicial enforcement of guarantee clause claims. Witness, a recent statement by Justice Fortas:[107]

> They [the voting rights cases and apportionment cases] represent . . . an acknowledgment that the republican form of government guaranteed by the Constitution, read in light of the General Welfare Clause, the guarantees of equal protection of the law and the privileges and immunities of citizens of the United States, requires something more than an adherence to form.

It is reasonable to say, however, that judicial enforcement of the guarantee of a republican form of government would be an undesirable extension of judicial power. Such an extension would be undesirable not because of the impossibility of finding judicial standards, for in deciding equal protection claims in the apportionment cases the Court has, in effect, crossed this hurdle. Instead, nonjusticiability of republican guarantee claims should be dictated by other relevant considerations. As indicated above, there is an interrelation between a state's scheme of representation and its frame of government. Hence, much of the criticism which was aimed at the Court's holding malapportionment claims justiciable is applicable here.

The form of a state's government involves potentially explosive and power-packed issues which cut deep into the heart of American political institutions. For the Court to regulate the structure of a state's government would be "hostile to a democratic system"; judicial regulation would deprive the people of an important func-

[106] Baker v. Carr, 369 U.S. 186, 301 (1962) (Frankfurter, J., dissenting).
[107] Fortson v. Morris, 385 U.S. 231, 249 (1966), (Fortas, J., dissenting).

tion in a democracy. A related consideration, moreover, concerns the division of sovereignty between nation and states in our federal system. As power to determine the structure of government is one of the essential attributes of sovereignty, due regard for the role of state government in an effective, viable federal system compels judicial non-intervention.

CONCLUSION

Prior to *Baker v. Carr* perhaps the most important generalization one could make about the political question was that there was no readily ascertainable test for determining whether or not a matter was justiciable. It was, in a sense, a conclusion that followed from the weighing of various policy considerations concerning the appropriateness of judicial review.[108] Although an attempted enumeration of these considerations would be incomplete, three underlying ideas have been dominant in the application of the political question;[109] each idea has had its own independent impact while at the same time converging and overlapping with one or both of the other two.

First, is the idea that the Court should not interfere with matters which because of their nature or because of express constitutional language are committed to or are clearly the prerogative of one of the political departments of government. In point is *Coleman v. Miller.*[110] Chief Justice Hughes' opinion, which was accepted by only two other members of the Court, asserted that the nature of the question before the Court—whether ratification of a proposed constitutional amendment was valid—committed it to the determination of Congress. Because appraisal of a great variety of relevant conditions, political, social and economic, was involved, the question was essentially political and better suited for Congress. Justice Black, on the other hand, in a concurring opinion which was joined by three other justices, said that Article V of the Constitution granted "power over the amending of the Constitution to Congress alone."[111] So exclusive was this power that the amending process was " 'political' in its entirely, from submission until an amendment becomes part of the Constitution. . . ."[112]

[108] See Taylor, *Legal Action to Enjoin Legislative Malapportionment: The Political Question Doctrine*, 34 So. CALIF. L. REV. 179 (1961).

[109] These ideas are discussed in McCloskey, *supra* note 80, at 61.

[110] 307 U.S. 433 (1939).

[111] *Id.* at 459 (Black, J., concurring).

[112] *Id.* at 458 (Black, J., concurring).

The cases dealing with foreign relations—the area where the political question has traditionally been given emphasis—also express this idea in various ways. Thus, in the cases involving recognition of governments, jurisdiction over territory, boundary determinations and abrogation and violations of treaties, the Court emphasized that judicial inquiry was withheld because the conduct of foreign relations is committed by the Constitution to the political departments of government. In addition, the very nature of many of the foreign affairs issues has been a significant factor. For example, the Court has recognized the need for uniform decisions in the conduct of international relations:[113]

> If this were not the rule, cases might often arise in which, on the most important questions of foreign jurisdiction, there would be an irreconcilable difference between the executive and judicial departments. By one of the departments a foreign island or country might be considered at peace with the United States; whilst the other would consider it in a state of war. No well regulated government has ever sanctioned a principle so unwise, and so destructive of national character.

The need to speak with one voice only is sometimes said to be necessary in order to avoid the danger of embarrassment abroad. Certainly this was a factor in *Chicago & So. Air Lines, Inc. v. Waterman,*[114] in which the Court refused to review the validity of a Civil Aeronautics Board decision on the ground that judicial intervention might prove embarrasing to the President in executing foreign policy. The *Waterman* case, moreover, illustrates yet another consideration which sometimes contributes to the Court's conclusion that a matter is beyond the realm of judicial competence because committed to another branch of government, namely: the inability of the Court to acquire information necessary for decision. As Justice Jackson expressed it:[115]

> The President, both as Commander-in-Chief and as the Nation's organ for foreign affairs, has available intelligence services whose reports are not and ought not to be published to the world. It would be intolerable that courts without the relevant information, should review and perhaps nullify actions of the Executive taken on information properly held secret.

[113] Williams v. Suffolk Ins. Co., 38 U.S. (13 Pet.) 415, 420 (1839).
[114] 333 U.S. 103 (1948).
[115] *Id.* at 111.

Of course this factor has not been without significance in domestic disputes.[116]

A second idea which has run through the political question has been the Court's inability to develop or to apply principles of law. To put it another way, "standards meet for judicial judgment" have sometimes been said to be lacking;[117] some situations have been thought to be judicially unmanageable. This idea has been prevalent in the apportionment cases in which the Court has felt incompetent or ill equipped to render decision because apportionment involves the weighing of such factors as geography, economics and the urban-rural conflict. Thus, complaints with legislative districting could not be addressed to the courts. Instead, "[a]ppeal must be to an informed, civically militant electorate. In a democratic society . . . relief must come through an aroused popular conscience that sears the conscience of the people's representatives."[118] Inequities in representation should not be corrected by the judiciary because such a practice deprives the people of an important function in a democracy.

Related to the idea of lack of judicial standards is a third idea of judicial non-intervention where the organization of a government forms the basis of the complaint. This idea has frequently been reflected in the guarantee clause cases. Thus, in the *Pacific States* case the Court said that the taxpayer's attack was "not on the tax as a tax, but on the State as a State. It is addressed to the framework and political character of the government by which the statute levying the tax was passed."[119] In cases such as this one, the Court has refused to administer relief because of the fear, whether real or supposed, of the consequences that might follow from a holding that a state government is not republican in form. That is, the Court has been afraid that such a decision would invalidate all state laws and create a state of general lawlessness.[120]

The sum of these two concepts—non-intervention when "standards meet for judicial judgment" are lacking and when the organiza-

---

[116] *See e.g.*, Coleman v. Miller, 307 U.S. 433, 453-54 (1939) where the Court said: "[T]he question of a reasonable time in many cases would involve . . . an appraisal of . . . conditions . . . which can hardly be said to be within the appropriate range of evidence receivable in a court of justice and as to which it would be an extravagant extension of judicial authority to assert judicial notice as the basis of deciding a controversy. . . ."

[117] Baker v. Carr, 369 U.S. 186, 289 (1962), (Frankfurter, J., dissenting).

[118] *Id.* at 270.

[119] Pacific States Tel. & Tel. Co. v. Oregon, 223 U.S. 118, 150-51 (1912).

[120] *Id.* at 141-42; Luther v. Borden 48 U.S. (7 How.) 1, 38-39 (1849).

tion or framework of a government is in question—"amounts to respect, either prudential of normative in origin, for the arrangements the political process has worked out for shaping the political process."[121] *Baker v. Carr* and subsequent decisions, however, have made it clear that it is the relationship between the federal judiciary and the coordinate branches of the federal government and not the judiciary's confrontation with the states which gives rise to the political question, with the possible exception of situations in which there is an absence of judicially discoverable standards. The standards problem, however, was dismissed in *Baker* by the simple statement that "[j]udicial standards under the Equal Protection Clause are well developed and familiar. . . ."[122] Having thus settled the issue of justiciability, the Court wasted little time in reading the democratic ideal of one person, one vote into the elastic language of equal protection, while at the same time paying lip service to the guarantee clause cases. Yet, by insuring numerical equality in voting, the Court has in one sense determined what frame of government is proper because equality under the equal protection clause cannot be defined without reference to the frame of government being employed.

The short of it is that respect for federalism and the principle of separation of powers as between the federal judiciary and the states have been subordinated to concepts of individual liberty and equality for which the Court claims to have no difficulty discovering standards. Thus in the Julian Bond case the Court did not hesitate to review the action of the Georgia Legislature in determining the qualifications of a prospective member and to hold the Georgia Legislature's action an unconstitutional interference with free speech.[123]

On the other hand, there is less likelihood that the Court would review the action of either house of Congress in disciplining or refusing to seat a member. At least this would seem a fair implication to be drawn from the stress placed on the intrafederal character of the political question by Justice Brennan in *Baker v. Carr*. Apparently, the Court will invoke the political question where the doctrine otherwise would not be used in order to avoid confrontation with Congress. In addition, the push of express constitutional language favors the political question. Article I, section 5 of the Con-

[121] McCloskey, *supra* note 80, at 62.
[122] Baker v. Carr, 369 U.S. 186, 226 (1962).
[123] Bond v. Floyd, 385 U.S. 116 (1966).

stitution is quite clear in saying that "[e]ach House shall be the Judge of the . . . Qualifications of its own Members . . . and may . . . punish its Members for disorderly Behaviour, and, with the Concurrence of two thirds, expel a Member."

Recent House activities disciplining Representative Adam Clayton Powell, Jr. for alleged misconduct invite attention. The House denied Powell his seat pending an investigation by a special Select Committee. In its concluding report, the Committee recommended, among other things, that Powell be seated and publicly censured by the Speaker of the House and that he be fined to repay government funds he was alleged to have misused. The House, however, rejected the Committee's report and denied Powell his seat by a two-thirds vote, although the Speaker in calling the vote said that only a majority was necessary.

Powell has sought relief in the federal courts, and the case has now reached the Supreme Court.[124] One of Powell's grievances is the Speaker's failure to call for a two-thirds vote. He also alleges that he was denied his seat for racial reasons. Undoubtedly, the racial claim will tempt the Court to decide the case on the merits, as it can be argued that a holding of nonjusticiability will be viewed as tacit judicial approval of racial discrimination by the House of Representatives in regard to the qualifications of one of its members. A further factor in Powell's favor is the fact that the Court in the *Bond* case seemed to approve the Hamilton-Madison view that the qualifications of legislators as defined and fixed by the Constitution cannot be altered.[125]

Having said all these things, still it is likely that the Supreme Court will apply the political question and refuse to decide Powell's case. Although Powell is seeking a seat that was denied to him after a regular congressional election, in terms of years of service he was one of the senior members of the House. Article I, section 5 of the Constitution clearly states that the House by two-thirds vote may expel a member for "disorderly [b]ehaviour," and no restrictions are placed on the expulsion power. Apparently, a

[124] The federal district court and the circuit court of appeals have refused to decide the merits of Powell's case. Powell v. McCormack, 266 F. Supp. 354 (D.D.C. 1968), *aff'd*, 395 F.2d 577 (D.C. Cir. 1968), *cert. granted*, 37 U.S.L.W. 3184 (U.S. Nov. 18, 1968). Although the Congress has recently seated Powell, he is prosecuting his appeal in the Supreme Court. The case is not altogether moot because payment of the fine has not been forgiven and Powell's seniority has not been reinstated.

[125] Bond v. Floyd, 385 U.S. 116, 135 (1966).

member may be expelled for any reason. If judicial abstention seems inconsistent with the *Bond* case, the explanation for the difference is that separation of powers remains an operative factor where the Court confronts one of its peers—the Congress or the President.

Results such as the one projected in the *Powell* case, however, will not be common, for decisions such as *Baker* and *Bond* have a clear message: the significance of the political question as a curb on justiciability has been reduced substantially, and its prestige has been dealt a severe blow; no longer will it occupy the seat of honor among the techniques of avoidance.

In a broader context the demise of the political question has paralleled the activist tendencies of the present Court in its zealous protection of individual rights. Of course those who would cast the political question aside in order to protect individual rights see a strong constitutional duty to adjudicate. Only a small percentage of the political question cases, however, can be explained solely in terms of the Court's duty to say what the law is in accordance with the admonition in *Marbury v. Madison.* As Professor Bickel has suggested, the political question "resists being domesticated" in such a fashion, for there has been "something greatly more flexible" about it;[126] the doctrine is indicative of the discretion that has accompanied the exercise of judicial review.

Whether or not these ingredients of flexibility and discretion have been coupled with an equal dosage of prudence depends in the final analysis upon one's philosophy of judicial review. To explain the doctrine "in functional terms, as the Court's acknowledgment of the limitations of the American judicial process"[127] really does no more because the limits of the process depend in large measure upon one's conception of the judiciary's role in our constitutional scheme.

Viewed in this context, the political question has been a useful tool for allowing the Court to dispose of issues, such as apportionment of governments, for example, which are inappropriate for judicial decision. Prior to *Baker* the Court had steadfastly rejected apportionment suits; furthermore, there was a dearth of historical justification for making representation proportional to population. Yet, in the face of its own precedent and despite the absence of

---

[126] Bickel, *supra* note 26, at 46.
[127] Scharpf, *supra* note 19, at 567.

compelling historical justification, the Court has been able to find the political ideal of representation according to numerical equality written into the vague contours of equal protection to the extent that it is legally enforceable. Accordingly, one is inescapably confronted with Justice Frankfurter's charge that what the Court has done "is to choose among competing bases of representation—ultimately, really among competing theories of political philosophy . . . ."[128]

Reform in matters such as these should come from the political branches—from the people striving "however blindly and inarticulately, toward their own conception of the Good Life."[129] If brave new worlds are to be ushered in, the responsibility for their creation does not lie with the judiciary. In placing responsibility for such issues where it properly belongs and in limiting the judiciary to the decision of cases and controversies, the political question has performed a valuable function. The doctrine affirms Alexander Hamilton's observation that the judiciary from the nature of its functions should be "the least dangerous [branch] to the political rights of the Constitution."[130]

---

[128] Baker v. Carr, 369 U.S. 186, 300 (1962) (Frankfurter, J., dissenting).
[129] L. Hand, The Spirit of Liberty 105-06 (3d ed. Dillard 1960).
[130] A. Hamilton, The Federalist (1961 ed.).

Constitution, Congress, and Court: On the Theory, Law, and Politics of Appellate Jurisdiction of the United States Supreme Court

By LELAND E. BECK

Table of Contents

Constitution, Congress, and Court: On the Theory, Law, and Politics of Appellate Jurisdiction of the United States Supreme Court

By LELAND E. BECK*

Introduction

Since the founding of the Republic, relations between the United States Congress and the Supreme Court often have exhibited the institutional tension and occasional conflict embodied in the constitutional and political doctrines of separation of powers and the system of checks and balances. Any understanding of the constitutional relationship between Congress and the Court must begin with the premise that this tension is essential to the functioning of the government; that it is not only accepted, but expected. The variety of tensions and conflicts are exemplified in the confirmation and attempted impeachment of justices; the judiciary's procedure, remedies, and jurisdiction; and the legitimacy, scope, and application of the doctrine of judicial review.[1] This article will undertake the exposition of one constitutional question of current tension and potential conflict between Congress and the Court: whether the exceptions and regulations clause authorizes Congress to preclude the Supreme Court from adjudicating particular constitutional claims by excepting those cases from the Court's appellate jurisdiction.[2]

Establishing the contours of the Court's appellate jurisdiction is as obtuse a process as establishing the original jurisdiction is acute: The appellate jurisdiction is conceptualized in the Constitution, while the

* Member of the District of Columbia Bar. Legislative Attorney-Advisor, American Law Division, Congressional Research Service, Library of Congress. B.A., 1973, M.A., 1975, Kent State University; J.D., 1977, The American University; LL.M., 1981, Harvard University. The author would like to thank Professor Archibald Cox and Mr. Johnny H. Killian for their critical commentaries on drafts of this article. The views presented in this article are those of the author and do not represent the views of the Congressional Research Service or any other organization of the United States Government.

1. Examples of each of these types of tension are included in the conceptual level discussion at notes 30-57 and accompanying text *infra*.

2. The elements of this question are discussed at notes 6, 21-25 and accompanying text *infra*.

original jurisdiction is enumerated. The relevant portions of the jurisdiction clauses of article III provide:

> The judicial Power of the United States, shall be vested in one supreme Court, and in such inferior Courts as the Congress may from time to time ordain and establish . . . .
>
> The judicial Power shall extend to all Cases, in Law and Equity, arising under this Constitution, the Laws of the United States, and Treaties made, or which shall be made, under their Authority; . . .
>
> In all Cases affecting Ambassadors, other public Ministers and Consuls, and those in which a State shall be Party, the Supreme Court shall have original Jurisdiction. In all other Cases before mentioned, the supreme Court shall have appellate Jurisdiction, both as to Law and Fact, with such Exceptions, and under such Regulations as the Congress shall make.[3]

Had the Framers unequivocally provided for the Court's appellate jurisdiction, or had they unequivocally provided the Congress with plenary power to determine affirmatively the Court's appellate jurisdiction, there would be little room for political concern. Instead, the Court's appellate jurisdiction was only facially outlined, with at least facial authority in Congress to except from that jurisdiction.

Jurisdiction over cases arising under the Constitution is the predicate for the development of the misnomered doctrine of "constitutional causes of action" under the Fourth Amendment,[4] the Fifth Amendment's due process clause,[5] and the Eighth Amendment's cruel and unusual punishment clause, among others.[6] Substantial scholarly commentary exists over the scope of constitutional causes of action, but consideration of congressional limitation of that concept has been limited.[7] Thus far, commentary on constitutional causes of action has not reached the idea of excepting particular causes of action from the Court's appellate jurisdiction as a means of regulating the causes of action.

Debate on the jurisdictional predicate to the judicial enforcement of constitutional rights, however, has drawn the attention of Congress

3. U.S. CONST. art. III, §§ 1-2.

4. *See, e.g.*, Bivens v. Six Unknown Named Agents, 403 U.S. 388 (1971).

5. *See, e.g.*, Davis v. Passman, 442 U.S. 228 (1979).

6. *See, e.g.*, Carlson v. Green, 446 U.S. 14 (1980). Interest here is limited to causes and cases arising directly under the Constitution, not correlative statutes, *e.g.*, 42 U.S.C. § 1983 (1976); 28 U.S.C. §§ 1331, 1343 (1976, as amended 1980).

7. Literature concerning *Bivens*-type actions, for example, has consistently focused on the scope of the remedy, not the jurisdictional predicate for the case. Presumably, jurisdiction lies only under 28 U.S.C. § 1331 (1976, as amended 1980) in cases involving state or federal officer defendants, and under § 1346 in suits against the United States.

in the form of excepting from the Court's jurisdiction certain species of cases. Since 1956, over one hundred proposals to restrict the Court's jurisdiction can be found in the *Congressional Record*, although many are mere reintroductions or variations of previous bills. Only three have received serious consideration by either the House or the Senate. The first proposal responded to a series of Court decisions curbing some of the excesses of McCarthyism.[8] The second proposal responded to the reapportionment decisions.[9] The third proposal focuses on the contemporary debate concerning prayer in the public schools and the efficacy of *Engel v. Vitale*[10] and *Abington School District v. Schempp*.[11]

Like its predecessors, the school prayer proposal[12] is a response to

8. *See, e.g.*, Watkins v. United States, 354 U.S. 178 (1957); Service v. Dulles, 354 U.S. 363 (1957); Schware v. Board of Bar Examiners, 353 U.S. 232 (1957); Konigsberg v. State Bar of California, 353 U.S. 252 (1957); Cole v. Young, 351 U.S. 536 (1956); Pennsylvania v. Nelson, 350 U.S. 497 (1956); Slochower v. Board of Higher Educ., 350 U.S. 551 (1956). *See also* S. 2646, 85th Cong., 1st Sess. (1957); *Limitation of Appellate Jurisdiction of the United States Supreme Court: Hearings before the Subcomm. to Investigate the Administration of the Internal Security Act and other Internal Security Laws of the Senate Comm. on the Judiciary*, 85th Cong., 1st & 2d Sess. (1957, 1958) [hereinafter cited as *1958 Senate Hearings*]; S. REP. No. 1586, 85th Cong., 2d Sess. (1958). *Cf.* H.R. 10775, 85th Cong., 2d Sess. (1958). S. 2646 would have removed Supreme Court jurisdiction over cases involving contempts of Congress, federal employee security separations, state "subversive activities" programs, teacher employment and "subversive activities" control, and state bar admissions. Certain of these exceptions would be only statutory, while others, because of the nature of the claim, could only be characterized as constitutional. The Senate passed a modified version of the bill, but the proposal died on a point involving its germaneness to new language in a conference committee report. *See generally* W. MURPHY, CONGRESS AND THE COURT: A CASE STUDY IN THE AMERICAN POLITICAL PROCESS (1962); C. PRITCHETT, CONGRESS VERSUS THE SUPREME COURT, 1957-1960 (1961).

9. *See, e.g.*, Reynolds v. Sims, 377 U.S. 533 (1964); Baker v. Carr, 369 U.S. 186 (1962). *See also* H.R. 11926, 88th Cong., 2d Sess. (1964); H.R. Res. 893, 88th Cong., 2d Sess., 110 CONG. REC. 20213-301, 21236 (1964). H.R. 11926 was introduced by Congressman Tuck in 1964 to remove all cases involving the apportionment or reapportionment of state legislatures from both the Supreme Court's and the inferior federal courts' jurisdiction. After an acrimonious debate, the bill was passed. This bill is not as well-known as the "stay" bill which was introduced, modified, and passed by the Senate. Both bills died in the Senate when a move to invoke cloture on the Conference Report failed by a substantial margin. *See generally* McKay, *Court, Congress and Reapportionment*, 63 MICH. L. REV. 255 (1964).

10. 370 U.S. 421 (1962).

11. 374 U.S. 203 (1963).

12. On April 5, 1979, Senator Helms proposed an amendment to the Department of Education organic bill that would remove school prayer issues from the Court's jurisdiction. This amendment was subsequently attached to a bill that would have provided broader discretion for the Court to handle its docket. Both were passed in the Senate, but the Supreme Court jurisdiction bill languished in the House Judiciary Committee and died at adjournment. *See* S. 450, 96th Cong., 1st Sess., 125 CONG. REC. 3057-58 (1979). *See also Prayer in Public Schools and Buildings: Hearings Before the Subcomm. on Courts, Civil Liberties and the Administration of Justice, House Comm. on the Judiciary*, 96th Cong., 2d Sess. (1980). At the beginning of the 97th Congress, Senator Helms and Congressman Crane

a perceived erroneous interpretation of the Constitution by the Court. Unlike its predecessors, however, which responded to unentrenched and limited Court interpretations, this proposal is a reaction against the long-term development of constitutional standards under the establishment clause.[13] Even as the school prayer proposal was being delayed by the House Judiciary Committee near the end of the Ninety-sixth Congress,[14] the Court summarily decided *Stone v. Graham*,[15] which declared the display of the Ten Commandments in all Kentucky public classrooms unconstitutional, even though it contained a statement of secular purpose and even though it was financed by private contributions to the state treasury in accordance with state law.[16] During the Ninety-seventh Congress, debate on limiting the judiciary's jurisdiction and remedial powers in abortion, busing, and school prayer cases flourished.[17] The contemporary debate is also distinguishable because it is

reintroduced the proposal. S. 481, 97th Cong., 1st Sess. (1981); H.R. 865, 97th Cong., 1st Sess. (1981).

13. *See, e.g.*, Stone v. Graham, 449 U.S. 39 (1980); New York v. Cathedral Academy, 434 U.S. 125 (1977); Wolman v. Walter, 433 U.S. 229 (1977); Roemer v. Maryland Pub. Works Bd., 426 U.S. 736 (1976); Meek v. Pittenger, 421 U.S. 349 (1975); Wheeler v. Barrera, 417 U.S. 402 (1974); Sloan v. Lemon, 413 U.S. 825 (1973); Committee for Pub. Educ. & Religious Liberty v. Nyquist, 413 U.S. 756 (1973); Hunt v. McNair, 413 U.S. 734 (1973); Levitt v. Committee for Pub. Educ. & Religious Liberty, 413 U.S. 472 (1973); Lemon v. Kurtzman, 411 U.S. 192 (1973) (*Lemon II*); Lemon v. Kurtzman, 403 U.S. 602 (1971) (*Lemon I*); Tilton v. Richardson, 403 U.S. 672 (1971); Walz v. Tax Comm'n, 397 U.S. 664 (1970); Board of Educ. v. Allen, 392 U.S. 236 (1968). This is not the first attempt to nullify, alter, or obviate past decisions in this area. *See School Prayers: Hearings Before the House Comm. on the Judiciary*, 88th Cong., 2d Sess. (1964) (constitutional amendments); *School Prayer: Hearings Before the Subcomm. on Constitutional Amendments of the Senate Comm. on the Judiciary*, 89th Cong., 2d Sess. (1966) (constitutional amendments). An attempt to catalogue the introductions and reintroduction of constitutional amendments and simple legislation in this area has, in light of limited space, not been undertaken.

14. *See* note 11 *supra*.

15. 449 U.S. 39 (1980).

16. *Id.* at 42-43.

17. *See Constitutional Restraints upon the Judiciary, Hearings Before the Subcomm. on the Constitution of the Comm. on the Judiciary*, 97th Cong., 1st Sess. (1981); *The Fourteenth Amendment and School Busing, Hearings Before the Subcomm. on the Constitution of the Comm. on the Judiciary*, 97th Cong., 1st Sess. (1981) (S. 528, S. 1005, S. 1147, S. 1760, *infra* note 19); *The Human Life Bill, Hearings Before the Subcomm. on Separation of Powers of the Comm. on the Judiciary*, 97th Cong., 1st Sess. (1981) (S. 158, *infra* note 19); *School Desegregation, Hearings Before the Subcomm. on Civil and Constitutional Rights of the Comm. on the Judiciary*, 97th Cong., 1st Sess. (1981). During the first half of the second session of the 97th Congress, the Senate passed a provision to limit the remedial power of the federal courts in school desegregation cases by prohibiting orders that would require busing pupils more than 10 miles round trip or more than 30 minutes per day beyond the nearest school that offered the classes in which the pupil was matriculating, as part of the Department of Justice Appropriations Authorization Act, Fiscal Year 1982. S. 951, 97th Cong., 2d Sess. § 2 (1982) (as passed the Senate). The need to reconcile this bill with a House-approved version was obviated by the passage of a continuing resolution funding the Department of Justice for the

part of a broader congressional debate. The school prayer proposal has been the prototype for bills[18] to limit jurisdiction and relief in abortion and school desegregation cases as well.[19] Test cases will inexorably follow passage of any school prayer, abortion, or busing proposal, given the emotion committed to their debate. Thus, Congress and the Court may have begun in earnest to travel the road from constitutional tension to constitutional conflict.

This political history has elicited responsive, if fragmented, scholarly literature on the scope of the exceptions and regulations clause.[20]

remainder of the fiscal year. H.R.J. Res. 409, 97th Cong., 2d Sess., Act of Mar. 31, 1982, Pub. L. No. 97-161.

18. The language of these school prayer bills, S. 481, 97th Cong., 1st Sess. (1981), H.R. 865, 97th Cong., 1st Sess. (1981), provides an excellent legislative prototype. In order to cover other areas of cases arising under the Constitution, only the direct object need be changed. S. 481 and H.R. 865 both provide, in pertinent part:

"§ 1259. Appellate Jurisdiction; limitations

"(a) Notwithstanding the provisions of section 1253, 1254, and 1257 of this chapter the Supreme Court shall not have jurisdiction to review, by appeal, writ of certiorari, or otherwise any case arising out of any State statute, ordinance, rule, regulation, or any part thereof, or arising out of any act interpreting, applying or enforcing a State statute, ordinance, rule, or regulation, which relates to voluntary prayers in public schools and public buildings. . . ."

"§ 1363. Limitations on jurisdiction

"Notwithstanding any other provision of law, the district courts shall not have jurisdiction of any case or question which the Supreme Court does not have jurisdiction to review under section 1259 of this title." This is precisely what has been done with H.R. 869, 97th Cong., 1st Sess. (1981), a bill to limit the Supreme Court's and inferior courts' jurisdiction over the assignment of children to public schools. *See* note 19 *infra*.

19. *See, e.g.*, in the 97th Congress, 1st & 2d Sess. (1981): H.R. 72, 326, 408, 865, 989, 1335, 2347, 4756, S. 481, 1742 (Supreme Court and inferior courts, jurisdiction, prayer); H.R. 311, § 106 (Supreme Court, jurisdiction, prayer and qualification of teachers); H.R. 867 (Supreme and inferior courts, jurisdiction, abortion); S. 583 (Supreme Court and inferior courts, remedies, abortion); H.R. 73, 900, 3225, S. 158, 1741 (inferior courts, remedies, abortion); H.R. 869 (Supreme Court and inferior courts, jurisdiction, school desegregation); H.R. 340, 761, 1079, 1180, 2047, 3332, 5200, S. 528 (Supreme Court and inferior courts, remedies, school desegregation); S. 1647, 1743, 1760 (inferior courts, remedies, school desegregation). Additional bills exist on such diverse topics as equal protection (sex discrimination) in draft registration and *habeas corpus*. The classification of bills here does not necessarily coincide with the perceptions of their authors. For example, the language of S. 158, § 2, is couched in terms of "jurisdiction to issue any restraining order, temporary or permanent injunction, or declaratory judgment," which is remedial in character, not jurisdictional. *See* notes 21-23 *infra*.

20. Berger, *Congressional Contraction of Federal Jurisdiction*, 5 WIS. L. REV. 801 (1980); Brant, *Appellate Jurisdiction: Congressional Abuse of the Exceptions Clause*, 53 OR. L. REV. 3 (1973); Forkosch, *The Exceptions and Regulations Clause of Article III & A Person's Constitutional Rights: Can the Latter be Limited by Congressional Power under the Former?*, 72 W. VA. L. REV. 238 (1970); Hart, *The Power of Congress to Limit the Jurisdiction of Federal Courts: An Exercise in Dialectic*, 66 HARV. L. REV. 1362 (1953); Lenoir, *Congressional Control Over the Appellate Jurisdiction of the Supreme Court*, 5 U. KAN. L. REV. 16 (1956); Levy, *Congressional Power over the Appellate Jurisdiction of the Supreme Court: A Reappraisal*, 22

In contrast, illuminating the scope of this article requires the statement of several *caveats*. First, this article is concerned only with the appellate jurisdiction of the Supreme Court. Thus, contemporary bills on inferior federal court consideration of, for example, abortion issues, while germane to a discussion of the political context, will not be considered. The appropriate authority for the disposition of these questions is the power of Congress to ordain and establish inferior federal courts under article III, section 1, and article I, section 8, clause 9 (the inferior courts clause), not a power over the Supreme Court under the exceptions and regulations clause.[21] Second, this article addresses only questions of subject matter jurisdiction. Thus, issues of remedy, such as the busing remedy and the *Bivens*[22] damage remedy, are germane only to contextual discussion.[23] Third, the scope of this article is lim-

N.Y.U. INTRA. L. REV. 178 (1967); Merry, *Scope of the Supreme Court's Appellate Jurisdiction: Historical Basis*, 47 MINN. L. REV. 53 (1962); Ratner, *Congressional Power Over the Appellate Jurisdiction of the Supreme Court*, 109 U. PA. L. REV. 157 (1960); Sager, *Foreword: Constitutional Limitations on Congress' Authority to Regulate the Jurisdiction of the Federal Courts*, 95 HARV. L. REV. 17 (1981); Tribe, *Jurisdictional Gerrymandering: Zoning Disfavored Rights Out of the Federal Courts*, 16 HARV. C.R.-C.L. L. REV. 129 (1981); Van Alstyne, *A Critical Guide to* Ex parte McCardle, 15 ARIZ. L. REV. 229 (1973); Wechsler, *The Courts and the Constitution*, 65 COLUM. L. REV. 1001 (1965); Note, *Limitations on the Appellate Jurisdiction of the Supreme Court*, 20 U. PITT. L. REV. 99 (1958); Comment, *Removal of Supreme Court Appellate Jurisdiction: A Weapon Against Obscenity?*, 1969 DUKE L.J. 291 [hereinafter cited as Comment, *Obscenity*]; Comment, *Congressional Power Over Appellate Jurisdiction of the Supreme Court: A Reappraisal*, 22 N.Y.U. INTRA. L. REV. 178 (1967).

See generally Symposium on Limiting Federal Court Jurisdiction, 65 JUDICATURE 177 (1981). *See also* Fite & Rubenstein, *Curbing the Supreme Court—State Experiences and Federal Proposals*, 35 MICH. L. REV. 762 (1937); Martig, *Congress and the Appellate Jurisdiction of the Supreme Court*, 34 MICH. L. REV. 650 (1936); Nagel, *Court-Curbing Proposals in American History*, 18 VAND. L. REV. 925 (1965); Richter, *A Legislative Curb on the Judiciary*, 21 J. POL. ECON. 281 (1913); Stumpf, *Congressional Response to Supreme Court Rulings: The Interrelation of Law and Politics*, 14 J. PUB. L. 377 (1965). *Cf.* Eisenberg, *Congressional Authority to Restrict Lower Federal Court Jurisdiction*, 83 YALE L.J. 498 (1974); Estreicher, *Congressional Power and Constitutional Rights: Reflections on Proposed 'Human Life' Legislation*, 68 VA. L. REV. 333 (1982); Redish & Woods, *Congressional Power to Control the Jurisdiction of the Lower Federal Courts: A Critical Review and a New Synthesis*, 124 U. PA. L. REV. 45 (1975).

21. The inferior courts clause of article III, § 1, along with the restrictions imposed by the Bill of Rights and the Fourteenth Amendment, is a distinct authority, separable from the exceptions and regulations clause of article III, § 2, clause 2, which concerns the appellate jurisdiction of the Supreme Court. On numerous occasions, however, the question of the Supreme Court's jurisdiction has been discussed in terms of practice consequent to the powers of the inferior courts clause. For clarity of analysis, this article is restricted to the authority establishing the Supreme Court under article III and seeks to avoid the folly of confusing the Supreme Court with the inferior courts.

22. Bivens v. Six Unknown Named Agents, 403 U.S. 388 (1971).

23. Jurisdiction is a separable issue from either procedure or remedy. It must be noted, however, that the use of jurisdiction, procedure, and remedy as means of controlling activities of the federal courts (historically in the context of inferior federal courts) has often

ited to "exceptions" from jurisdiction. It must be remembered that the exceptions and regulations clause has two distinct, yet interrelated, parts and may be considered as two clauses. By the term "exception," it is generally understood[24] that a *part* is removed or excluded from the *whole*, removing the entirety of that part of the whole. In the context of constitutional claims, an exception must preclude the Court from entertaining the claim. A regulation, on the other hand, does not take away or preclude—it merely sets order or method to the process of doing a thing.[25] Fourth, this article considers only the question of excepting those cases in which constitutional, not merely statutory, rights are claimed.

Although the language of the exceptions and regulations clause does not provide any "plain meaning," several initial interpretations of the clause are summarized here and detailed later.[26] By linguistic modification, the reading implicit in the congressional proposals is that "the supreme Court shall have appellate jurisdiction . . . with such Exceptions . . . as the Congress shall make." This reading relates the "exceptions" component directly to the appellate jurisdiction of the Court. An alternative reading relates the "exceptions" component directly to the law and fact clause. This reading might be extended to exclusivity, *i.e.*, exceptions *solely* related to the law and fact clause, leaving the jurisdiction of the Court beyond congressional action.[27] These two readings appear to represent polar extremes—either complete or non-

blurred the distinctions between them, and, indeed, the distinctions themselves have changed over time. For example, the provision of the Norris-LaGuardia Act, Act of Mar. 23, 1932, ch. 229, 47 Stat. 70, which restricts the district courts from issuing injunctions in labor disputes, was initially referred to as a jurisdictional limitation but is now referred to as a remedial restriction. This distinction may not be important in light of the restriction of this article to the Supreme Court, since there have been no attempts to restrict remedies available to the Court or to limit its remedial power jurisdictionally. The analytic framework proposed is one composed of six discrete questions: (1) Supreme Court jurisdiction; (2) Supreme Court procedure; (3) Supreme Court remedies; (4) inferior court jurisdiction; (5) inferior court procedure; and (6) inferior court remedies. Within this framework, this article is concerned only with question (1).

24. Modern common-sense definitions, as well as technical definitions, comport with those of the Framers. *See* Ratner, *supra* note 20, at 168-71. There seems to be no need to delve into the definitional development of these terms again.

25. To be oversimplistic, exceptions may be best illustrated in jurisdictional terms, while regulations are exemplified by procedure and remedies. This illustration, however, does not recognize that there clearly are procedural and remedial exceptions and jurisdictional regulations; further, the illustration tends to confuse the sources of congressional power over the Supreme and inferior courts with the effects of congressional concern with the latter. The discussion of the history of congressional consideration of the federal courts will illustrate this complexity of ideas.

26. *See* text accompanying notes 212-27, *infra*.

27. *See* Merry, *supra* note 20.

existent congressional authority over the Supreme Court's appellate jurisdiction. Such extremes of interpretation, however, illustrate only that diagrammatical analysis is inconclusive. A variety of middle grounds may be derived, principally from the interplay with other clauses of the Constitution and the Bill of Rights. For example, the exceptions and regulations clause, together with the inferior courts clause, may be interpreted to authorize Congress to place appellate jurisdiction in inferior federal courts.[28] These clauses also may be, and indeed have been, interpreted to authorize Congress to make the Court's original jurisdiction concurrent with such inferior federal courts, just as the inferior courts clause has been interpreted to allow the original jurisdiction of the inferior federal courts to be concurrent with the jurisdiction of state courts.[29] In light of the possible multiple readings of the exceptions and regulations clause, particularly when read in conjunction with the inferior courts clause, the only thing that is clear about the "plain meaning" of the exceptions and regulations clause is that there is nothing plain at all.

Accordingly, this article is confined to the narrow question of the validity of the interpretation of the exceptions and regulations clause that would authorize Congress to except particular constitutional claims from the Supreme Court's appellate jurisdiction. Although there are a multitude of questions concerning the regulatory powers of Congress, the powers over the processes and remedies available to the Court, and the entire existence of inferior courts, this article undertakes to explore a limited but important and volatile issue. It focuses on that issue from several angles. First, the article stresses the conceptual framework of the issue by examining the tensions within theories of constitutional jurisdiction, judicial review, the doctrine of separation of powers, and the system of checks and balances. Second, the article develops a historical perspective from the Federal Convention of 1787, the state ratifying conventions, and the initial amendments to the Con-

28. Judiciary Act of 1789, ch. 20, § 13, 1 Stat. 73, 80; 28 U.S.C. §§ 41-48 (1976). *Contra* 3 J. STORY, COMMENTARIES ON THE CONSTITUTION OF THE UNITED STATES 546-626 (1831).

29. Ames v. Kansas *ex rel.* Johnson, 111 U.S. 449 (1884); Börs v. Preston, 111 U.S. 252 (1884); Judiciary Act of 1789, ch. 20, § 9, 1 Stat. 73, 78; 28 U.S.C. § 1351 (Supp. 1980). The converse theory has also been proposed that Congress had authority to make cases within the appellate jurisdiction original in the Supreme Court. *See generally Hearings Before the Subcomm. on Separation of Powers of the Senate Comm. on the Judiciary*, 90th Cong., 2d Sess. 169-70 (1969) (testimony of Mr. Van Alstyne) [hereinafter cited as *1969 Hearings*]; Van Alstyne, *A Critical Guide to* Marbury v. Madison, 1969 DUKE L.J. 1, 30-33; Comment, *Obscenity, supra* note 20, at 294-95. General federal question jurisdiction naturally devolved to the state courts of general jurisdiction by congressional omission in the organization of the inferior federal courts.

stitution. Third, this strain is continued with a review of the implementation of the Constitution by the Congress and the Court through the formative period, the Great Insurrection, and the more contemporary substantive regulation of the federal courts. Finally, the article applies the precedents and principles discerned to the current question of the constitutionality of excepting from the Court's appellate jurisdiction particular classes of cases arising under the Constitution.

I. Conceptual Framework

Underlying the political and constitutional discussion of the instant question are conceptual differences of opinion and theory. In considering the detail of legislative and judicial interpretation under the exceptions and regulations clause, the conceptual framework will be a constant reference. Four concepts will be useful: constitutional jurisdiction, the legitimacy of judicial review, the doctrine of separation of powers, and the system of checks and balances.

The theory of constitutional jurisdiction simply suggests that the source of the Supreme Court's appellate jurisdiction is the Constitution itself. If the vesting of judicial power affirmatively grants jurisdiction without action by the Congress and the President, or if it contemplates only mandatory action by the political branches of government, a more restrictive view of the exceptions and regulations clause of article III is warranted than if jurisdiction is dependent on an affirmative discretionary action. If the Supreme Court's appellate jurisdiction is not self-executing, *i.e.*, its source is statutory authority, some congressional and executive action is necessary and a liberal view of the exceptions and regulations clause would be warranted. Accepting that premise, the next logical question is whether, and to what extent, that action is mandatory, and thus merely ministerial.

The Constitution commences each article with an organic clause stipulating authority and the mandatory nature of that authority, with certain modifications based on the branch organized.[30] From the beginning of the Federal Convention of 1787, the term "jurisdiction" was used with regard to the judiciary in the senses of both organization and

30. *Compare* art. I, § 1, cl. 1 *and* art. II, § 1, cl. 1 *with* art. III, § 1, cl. 1. The phrases in articles I and II that "all legislative Powers herein granted shall be vested in a Congress of the United States" and "The executive Power shall be vested in a President of the United States of America," compare favorably with the article III notion that "[T]he judicial Power of the United States, shall be vested in one supreme Court," as an affirmative organic grant. By contrast, the organizational structure and detail of articles I and II are conspicuously absent from article III. Those omissions have been consistently considered a delegation to Congress of the power to reorganize the judiciary.

authority.[31] The displacement of the term "jurisdiction" by the broader word "power" in the organic and authority clauses[32] came in marked stages during the Convention.[33] In the major debate on the authority of the judiciary, Doctor Johnson proposed the "arising under this Constitution" clause, with Madison agreeing on the assumption that the clause was limited to judicial cases and with the understanding that the clause was self-executing.[34] The state ratifying conventions debated the jurisdiction of the Court in strident terms, a fact which gives further support to the notion that the jurisdictional language was complete.[35] Contemporaneous external sources, such as the *Federalist Papers*, also appear to have been operating under the assumption that the Constitution itself was a grant of effective jurisdiction.[36]

Be that as it may, the practice of Congress and the Court under the Constitution has been markedly different. The First Congress, in the

31. 1 THE RECORDS OF THE FEDERAL CONVENTION OF 1787 20 (J. Madison May 29, 1787) (M. Farrand ed. 1937) [hereinafter cited as RECORDS and accompanied by a parenthetical indicating the source, action, and date]. *See* 3 RECORDS 593-94 (App. C: Note on the "Virginia Plan.") In dealing with the *Records*, it should be kept in mind that a compilation was not published until 1911. History has suffered greatly from its absence until that late date. As Farrand has noted, 1 RECORDS xi-xxv, Madison's widely utilized notes are replete with amendments made over 40 years after the fact. *See* note 121 *infra*.

32. The term "judicial power" is a broader term than "jurisdiction." It encompasses not only the authority to hear and determine cases, but a certain power over its processes deriving from the inherent power of a court, especially in a coordinate branch.

33. The first deviation from the use of "jurisdiction" appears in the report of the Committee on Detail as a means of providing symmetry to the organic clauses utilizing the term "power." *Compare* 2 RECORDS, *supra* note 31, at 177, 185 *with id.* at 186 (Madison, *Report of the Comm. on Detail*) (August 6th). In this posture, the draft organized the judiciary under "power" and enumerated and divided the "jurisdiction" of the Supreme Court. Nonetheless, the term "jurisdiction" appears in both the authority subsection and the original and appellate jurisdiction subsections. *Id.* Note also that the judicial authority did not include cases "arising under" the Constitution. In the major debate on the judiciary, the style of the authority clause beginning in § 6 of article III was changed from "jurisdiction" to "the judicial Power." 2 RECORDS, *supra* note 31, at 430, 431 (Madison), 425 (Journal) (Aug. 27th). This change arguably broadened the scope of § 2 in the areas of procedure and remedies, but it appears doubtful that this alteration was intended to be more than a stylistic change.

34. 2 RECORDS, *supra* note 31 at 430, 431 (Madison), 425 (Journal) (Aug. 27th), *quoted in full in* text accompanying note 73 *infra*. The other alteration, adding cases in which the United States was a party, further indicates that the Convention understood that the Constitution alone was the source of authority to hear and determine cases. *Id. See* text accompanying note 72 *infra*.

35. The conceptualization of the Court's jurisdiction as embodied in the Constitution did not arise directly, but was the product of a clear debate on subordinate questions which presumed that fact. *See* notes 70-85 and accompanying text *infra*.

36. THE FEDERALIST No. 80, at 499-500 (A. Hamilton) (B. Wright ed. 1961). For a compilation of essays questioning the efficacy of the Constitution, see THE COMPLETE ANTI-FEDERALISTS (H. Storing ed. 1981).

Judiciary Act of 1789,[37] vested legislative jurisdiction to hear appeals[38] from the highest state courts and the inferior federal courts in many of, but by no means all, the cases and controversies contemplated in the Constitution.[39] The Court never has been squarely faced with the choice of taking jurisdiction that is provided under the Constitution but not by statutes, although Chief Justice Ellsworth,[40] Chief Justice Marshall,[41] and Justice Story[42] each had occasion to support the concept in dicta. Even as Justice Story penned his *Commentaries*,[43] debate on this issue was in decline and has only recently been resurrected.[44]

The historical question of constitutional jurisdiction poses a fundamental problem, however, given the lack of a concept of desuetude in American law. If the jurisdiction of the Court flows directly from the Constitution and remains extant though unexercised, the scope of the exceptions and regulations clause may be interpreted more narrowly in light of the Court's mere statutory, as contrasted with constitutional, past exercise of power. On the other hand, if the question of

37. Judiciary Act of 1789, ch. 20, §§ 13-14, 25, 1 Stat. 73.

38. "Appeal" is used here in the generic, nontechnical sense.

39. For example, legislative jurisdiction to hear criminal appeals from inferior federal courts was not vested until 1891, and then only by the confluence of judicial interpretation and subsequent legislation. Act of Feb. 6, 1889, ch. 113, § 6, 25 Stat. 655 (providing Supreme Court appeal in all cases of conviction of crime, the punishment of which is death, tried before any court of the United States); *In re* Classen, 140 U.S. 200 (1891) (writ of error issued by the Court where the conviction for the crime occurred before the act of March 3, 1891, but sentencing was imposed thereafter); Act of Mar. 3, 1891, ch. 517, § 5, 26 Stat. 826 (providing for direct appeal to the Supreme Court in specific cases regarding jurisdiction or constitutionality). The gap between the constitutional jurisdiction theory and legislative vesting has occurred only in the instance of cases arising under statutes and, indeed, was not fully closed until 1980, 28 U.S.C. § 1331 (Supp. 1980), although some residual difference may remain.

40. Chief Justice Ellsworth indicated that the Court's jurisdiction flowed directly from the Constitution, even though this dictum appears contrary to his authorship of the Judiciary Act of 1789. Wiscart v. Dauchy, 3 U.S. (3 Dall.) 321, 327 (1796) (discussed at notes 140-44 *infra*).

41. Chief Justice Marshall took a self-execution stand with regard to the original jurisdiction of the Court in Marbury v. Madison, 5 U.S. (1 Cranch) 137 (1803), but took the contrary stand in Durousseau v. United States, 10 U.S. (6 Cranch) 307, 313-17 (1810), suggesting that while the Constitution grants appellate jurisdiction, an exception from that jurisdiction could be inferred from a lack of statutory jurisdiction affirmatively granted—a position consistent with the Judiciary Act of 1789. *See* text accompanying notes 146-50 *infra*.

42. Justice Story took a more radical stance on the question than did Chief Justices Marshall or Ellsworth. He asserted not only that the Court's jurisdiction flowed directly and completely from the Constitution, but that if Congress created inferior federal courts, those courts as well would automatically be vested with the full panoply of constitutional jurisdiction. Martin v. Hunter's Lessee, 14 U.S. (1 Wheat.) 304, 374 (1816).

43. J. STORY, COMMENTARIES ON THE CONSTITUTION OF THE UNITED STATES (1833).

44. *See, e.g.*, Sager, *supra* note 20, at 23-25.

constitutional jurisdiction has died for lack of exercise, so too may have the power of Congress to except constitutional questions from the Court's jurisdiction. In short, constitutional jurisdiction cannot be divorced from the question of the power of Congress under the exceptions and regulations clause.

The second conceptual point focuses on judicial review. Unlike constitutional jurisdiction, the concept of judicial review has been exercised by the Court on numerous occasions—sparingly at first, but more frequently in recent years.[45] During the formative and middle periods of constitutional history, the legitimacy of the concept was widely debated.[46] The search for evidence of the Framers' intent and understanding of the concept has proven to be a frustrating endeavor. The concept was not stated explicitly in the Convention of 1787 or in the state ratifying debates, but was implicit in the rejection of the Council of Revision.[47] In response to early declarations of unconstitutionality,

45. At last count, the Court had invalidated 105 acts of Congress, 908 state statutes, and 101 municipal ordinances as contrary to the Constitution. J. KILLIAN, CONSTITUTION OF THE UNITED STATES OF AMERICA—ANALYSIS AND INTERPRETATION S272, S275, S291, S293 (1972 & Supp. 1978). The first direct exercise of judicial review to void an act of Congress was Marbury v. Madison, 5 U.S. (1 Cranch) 137 (1803); the second was Dred Scott v. Sandford, 60 U.S. (19 How.) 393 (1857) (voiding the "Missouri Compromise"). *See* Pollock v. Farmers' Loan & Trust Co., 157 U.S. 429, *further opinion*, 158 U.S. 601 (1895) (overruled by the 16th Amendment in 1913 (income taxation)); Oregon v. Mitchell, 400 U.S. 112 (1970) (reversed, in part, by the 26th Amendment in 1972 (age of suffrage)). *Compare* Hammer v. Dagenhart, 247 U.S. 251 (1918), *with* J. KILLIAN, *infra*, at 52. Once only circumspectly applied, the doctrine now has an active role in the Court's decisions.

46. The classic works on the subject are C. BEARD, THE SUPREME COURT AND THE CONSTITUTION (A. Westin ed. 1962), and Thayer, *The Origin and Scope of the American Doctrine of Constitutional Law*, 7 HARV. L. REV. 129 (1893). *See also* A. BICKEL, THE LEAST DANGEROUS BRANCH: THE SUPREME COURT AT THE BAR OF POLITICS (1962); E. CORWIN, COURT OVER CONSTITUTION (1938); W. CROSSKEY, POLITICS AND THE CONSTITUTION IN THE HISTORY OF THE UNITED STATES (1953). Alan Westin has compiled an extensive bibliography on the subject through 1962 in the reissue of Beard's volume. C. BEARD, *supra*, at 133-49.

47. Numerous ideas were circulated during the Convention regarding the formation of a "Council of Revision," to be composed of the President and "a convenient number of the Judiciary," for the purpose of deciding whether congressional enactments should become law. 1 RECORDS, *supra* note 31, at 97-98 (Madison), 109 (Pierce) (June 4th); 2 RECORDS, *supra* note 31, at 71-72 (Journal), 73-80 (Madison) (July 21st). The Council of Revision developed into the President's veto power under article I, § 7, clause 2. Madison records Luther Martin's objection to judicial participation in the veto in this way: "And as to the Constitutionality of laws, that point will come before the Judges in their proper official character. In this character they have a negative on the laws. Join them with the Executive in the Revision and they will have a double negative." 2 RECORDS, *supra* note 31, at 76 (Madison) (July 21st). Madison also notes, "Mr. Gerry doubts whether the Judiciary ought to form a part of [a Council of Revision], as they will have a sufficient check against encroachments on their own department by their exposition of the laws, which involved a power of deciding on their Constitutionality." 1 RECORDS, *supra* note 31, at 97 (Madison)

Congress was petitioned to limit the Court's authority to review federal and state enactments, but no formal action was ever taken to that end.[48] It is not the province of this article to debate the broad contours of the concept, but merely to note the more limited scope of contemporary debate. Although contemporary debate over the Court's jurisdiction is, as before, a response to the Court's exercise of judicial review, the thrust of the debate is currently directed toward overturning, obviating, or circumventing the rules laid down in particular decisions.

The importance of reintroducing the idea of judicial review here is that, while there may not be a concept of desuetude in American law, there is clearly a concept of legitimation in American politics. While the debate on judicial review will surely continue, the concept has been all but fully legitimized in the structure of American government. The proposals to limit the Court's appellate jurisdiction run counter to this strain of legitimation.

The third and fourth conceptual points are interrelated. Separation of powers and the system of checks and balances must be considered respectively as methods of animating the structure of government and of insuring the existence of liberty. While the ideas of separation of powers and checks and balances can be traced to Plato and Aristotle, the Framers were specifically influenced by Montesquieu's *L'Esprit des Lois*.[49] The doctrine of separation of powers does not demand that the functions of each branch be completely separate from the others, but rather that certain fundamental functions cannot be usurped from one branch by another.[50] The concept of separation of powers has been fleshed out by the Court in notable instances of the President exercising

(June 4th). Pierce recorded, "Mr. King was of opinion that the Judicial ought not to join in the negative of a Law, because the Judges will have the expounding of those laws when they come before them; and they will no doubt stop the operation of such as shall appear repugnant to the constitution." *Id.* at 109 (Pierce) (June 4th).

48. The most famous attacks were probably the Kentucky and Virginia Resolutions of 1798, passed after stay laws were struck down and as Virginia's response to the Court accepting jurisdiction over Cohens v. Virginia, 19 U.S. (6 Wheat.) 264 (1821). *See* 1 THE OLIVER WENDELL HOLMES DEVISE, HISTORY OF THE SUPREME COURT OF THE UNITED STATES 1-24 (1971) [hereinafter cited as 1 HOLMES DEVISE]; J. GOEBEL, 1 C. WARREN, THE SUPREME COURT IN UNITED STATES HISTORY 651-52 (1922).

49. C. MONTESQUIEU, L' ESPRIT DES LOIS (1748).

50. As Madison posed the doctrine, "It is agreed on all sides, that the powers properly belonging to one of the departments ought not to be directly and completely administered by either of the other departments. It is equally evident, that none of them ought to possess, directly or indirectly, an overruling influence over the others, in the administration of their respective powers. It will not be denied, that power is of an encroaching nature, and that it ought to be effectually restrained from passing the limits assigned to it. After discriminating, therefore, in theory, the several classes of power, as they may in their nature be legislative, executive, or judiciary, the next and most difficult task is to provide some practical security

a legislative function or the Congress exercising an executive function.[51] The most notable case for the instant purpose involved a usurpation of both executive and judicial power by the Congress.[52] Proper functioning of the doctrine of separation of powers, however, relies on the interdependence of the various departments of government as expressed through the operation of the system of checks and balances.

The most common examples of the system of checks and balances can be found in the division of the war powers and the spending powers—in short, the sword and the purse. In terms of its impact on the Court, the system of checks and balances has had a very finite history. Only on two occasions has the House attempted to impeach a sitting justice; neither attempt was successful.[53] The Senate has, however, rejected nominees to the Court on numerous occasions, including the rejection of John Rutledge as Chief Justice after a recess appointment and after he had sat on two terms of the Court.[54] The rejection of a nominee reflects more fully the tripartite nature of the federal government because rejection affects the capacity of a president to contribute philosophy to the Court rather than creating direct conflict between Congress and the Court. Similarly, Congress has altered the number of justices in order to grant or to deny a president vacancies on the Court.[55] Finally, Congress has had an impact on the Court by altering the duties of the justices[56] and the terms of the Court.[57]

for each, against the invasion of the others. What this security ought to be, is the great problem to be solved." THE FEDERALIST, *supra* note 36, No. 48, at 343 (J. Madison).

51. *E.g.*, Buckley v. Valeo, 424 U.S. 1 (1976); United States v. Nixon, 418 U.S. 683 (1974); Youngstown Sheet & Tube Co. v. Sawyer, 343 U.S. 579 (1952); Myers v. United States, 272 U.S. 52 (1926).

52. United States v. Klein, 80 U.S. (13 Wall.) 128 (1872), discussed at notes 181-89 and accompanying text *infra*. *See generally* A. VANDERBILT, THE DOCTRINE OF SEPARATION OF POWERS AND ITS PRESENT-DAY SIGNIFICANCE 98-114 (1953).

53. 14 ANNALS OF CONG. 726-63 (House), 81-676 (Senate) (1804) (attempted impeachment of Chase, J.); HOUSE COMM. ON THE JUDICIARY, 91ST CONG., 2D SESS., FINAL REPORT BY THE SPECIAL SUBCOMM. ON H. RES. 920 (1970) (proposed impeachment of Douglas, J.).

54. *See* J. HARRIS, THE ADVICE AND CONSENT OF THE SENATE 42-43, 385 (1953); 1 C. WARREN, THE SUPREME COURT IN UNITED STATES HISTORY 127-39 (1922); 1 THE HOLMES DEVISE, *supra* note 48, at 748 n.120.

55. Act of Sept. 24, 1789, ch. 20, § 1, 1 Stat. 73 (six); Act of Feb. 13, 1801, ch. 4, § 3, 2 Stat. 89 (five; never implemented); Act of Mar. 2, 1802, ch. 8, § 1, 2 Stat. 132 (repealing Act of Feb. 13, 1801); Act of Feb. 24, 1807, ch. 16, § 5, 2 Stat. 420-21 (seven); Act of Mar. 3, 1837, ch. 34, § 1, 5 Stat. 176 (nine); Act of Mar. 3, 1863, ch. 50, 12 Stat. 794 (ten); Act of July 23, 1866, ch. 210, § 1, 14 Stat. 209 (seven); Act of Apr. 10, 1869, ch. 22, § 1, 16 Stat. 44 (nine).

56. The circuit-riding duties are the best remembered changes. *See generally* F. FRANKFURTER & J. LANDIS, THE BUSINESS OF THE SUPREME COURT 4-55 (1928).

57. Act of Feb. 13, 1801, ch. 4, § 1, 2 Stat. 89; Act of Mar. 2, 1802, ch. 8, 2 Stat. 132.

The contemporary proposals to limit the Court's jurisdiction have clearly been conceived as a check on the Court. The perception of proponents of the contemporary debate is that the exceptions and regulations clause, besides extending to the question of jurisdiction—particularly jurisdiction over cases arising under the Constitution—is a proper method for the Congress to check what Congress perceives as improvident exercises of judicial review. Whether or not the Framers considered this proposition as flowing from their handiwork is of utmost importance.

II. The Constitutional History of the Exceptions and Regulations Clause

The Federal Convention of 1787, the state ratifying conventions, and the contemporaneous amendments to the Constitution must all be reviewed in order to understand the purpose and intent of the exceptions and regulations clause. Little of the material presented in this part could be considered as new, but this basic material is essential in order to draw useful conclusions.

A. The Federal Convention of 1787

The exceptions and regulations clause is first recognizable in the report of the Committee on Detail, but much previous discussion during the Convention animated the clause. The original Virginia Resolutions submitted by Edmund Randolph on May 29th included several notable points: (1) more than one supreme tribunal might be established; (2) inferior courts were to be chosen by the Congress; and (3) the jurisdiction of both of these courts was enumerated, including "questions which may involve the national peace and harmony."[58] During the first debate, several of the specific jurisdictional clauses were stricken, and the resolution was reduced to general principle.[59] The task of detailing the jurisdiction of the judiciary was to be delegated to the Committee on Detail.[60]

58. 1 RECORDS, *supra* note 31, at 21-22 (Madison: Randolph's resolutions) (Journal) (May 29th). Particular attention should be paid to the manner in which Farrand has assembled the *Records*, including changes that Madison made in his notes late in life and discrepancies between recorders. Bearing that in mind, Farrand's *Records* remain the best, and in many instances the only, source of information on the Constitution's development.

59. *Id.* at 211 (Journal), 220 (Madison) (June 12th), 232 (Madison), 231 (Journal), 233 (Yates) (June 13th). Farrand notes that Madison's entry of June 13th appears to be an instance of Madison revising the Journal 40 years later.

60. *Id.* at 238 (Yates) (June 13th).

On June 15th, William Paterson presented alternative resolutions, called collectively the New Jersey Plan, which were based in part on previously accepted versions of Randolph's resolutions; however the general tenor was toward a federal league of sovereign states and a revision of the Articles of Confederation. Paterson's resolution dealing with the judiciary proposed that there be one supreme tribunal and that it have a specified, limited jurisdiction, both original and appellate.[61] Paterson's proposal was rejected, but parts of it would later reappear. On this scanty basis, in marked contrast to the detailed resolutions and debates on the legislature and executive, the Committee on Detail was erected.[62]

1. The Committee on Detail

Only a few documents survive to illuminate the construction of article III within the Committee on Detail; only three appear useful. The first document, in outline form, provides:

> 7. The jurisdiction of the supreme tribunal shall extend
> 1. to all cases, arising under laws passed by the general Legislature . . . and,
> 3. to *such* other cases, as the national legislature may assign, as involving the national peace and harmony, . . .

The outline then enumerates many of the jurisdictions of article III:

> But this supreme jurisdiction shall be appellate only, except in Cases of Impeachmt. & those instances, in which the legislature shall make it original, and the legislature shall organize it . . . .
>
> 8. The whole or a part of the jurisdiction aforesaid according to the discretion of the legislature may be assigned to the inferior tribunals, as original tribunals.[63]

In exercising its delegated authority, the Committee on Detail reverted to many of the enumerations previously discussed in the Convention. The delegation of the division of jurisdiction between the Supreme and inferior courts is "new" in this document. At this point, the choice of making appellate jurisdiction original and delegating trial jurisdiction to the inferior courts is the only recognizable concern of the Committee.

61. *Id.* at 244 (Madison, Paterson's resolutions) (June 15th).

62. 2 *id.* at 97 (Journal), 106 (Madison) (July 24th). The Committee on Detail was composed of Edmund Randolph of Virginia, John Rutledge of South Carolina, James Wilson of Pennsylvania, Oliver Ellsworth of Connecticut, and Nathanial Gorham of Massachusetts. All of these men were involved with the later ratification and implementation of the Constitution.

63. *Id.* at 146-47 (Committee on Detail, IV); 4 *id.* at 47-49 (Corrections).

The second document may be no more than an extract of the Paterson resolutions, but to such an extract Wilson appears to have appended a new idea: "[a]n appeal for the Correction of all Errors both in Law and Fact."[64] The third document, apparently late in the Committee's work, presents a more complete picture:

> The Jurisdiction of the Supreme [National] Court shall extend to all Cases arising under Laws passed by the Legislature of the United States; . . . In Cases of Impeachment, Cases affecting Ambassadors other public Ministers & Consuls, and those in which a State shall be a Party, this Jurisdiction shall be original. In all the other Cases beforementioned, it shall be appellate, with such Exceptions and under such Regulations as the Legislature shall make. The Legislature may assign any part of the Jurisdiction above mentd.,—except the Trial of the Executive—, in the Manner and under the Limitations which it shall think proper to such inferior Courts as it shall constitute from Time to Time.[65]

The next-to-last sentence appears to be a new version of the predecessor language giving Congress authority to make the appellate jurisdiction original. The last sentence clearly indicates that Congress may assign jurisdiction to the inferior federal courts. If the meaning of the provisions overlapped, the question remains why two separable delegations were made. Thus the first appearance of the clause allows only a narrow interpretation. The law and fact clause is also conspicuously absent. The division of appellate jurisdiction between the Supreme and inferior federal tribunals would appear to be a consistent interpretation to this point in development. It was also during the initial constructions of a constitution and deliberations of the Committee on Detail that the authority to constitute inferior courts was enumerated in the legislative article for the first time.[66]

The report of the Committee on Detail was the basis for future discussion. The relevant provision of the Committee's report was in the following terms:

> Sect. 3. The Jurisdiction of the Supreme Court shall extend to all cases arising under laws passed by the Legislature of the United States; to all cases affecting Ambassadors, other Public Ministers and Consuls; to the trial of impeachments of Officers of the United States; to all cases of Admiralty and maritime jurisdiction; to controversies between two or more States, (except such as shall regard Territory or Jurisdiction) between a State and Citizens of another State, between Citizens of different States, and

64. 2 RECORDS, *supra* note 31, at 157 & n.15 (Committee on Detail, VII).
65. *Id.* at 172-73 (Committee on Detail, IX).
66. *Id.* at 136 (Committee on Detail, III), 144 (IV), 168 (IX).

> between a State or the Citizens thereof and foreign States, citizens or subjects. In cases of impeachment, cases affecting Ambassadors, other Public Ministers and Consuls, and those in which a State shall be party, this jurisdiction shall be original. In all the other cases before mentioned, it shall be appellate, with such exceptions and under such regulations as the Legislature shall make. The Legislature may assign any part of the jurisdiction above mentioned (except the trial of the President of the United States) in the manner, and under the limitations which it shall think proper, to such Inferior Courts, as it shall constitute from time to time.[67]

The Convention took up the provisions of the report of the Committee on Detail *seriatim*. On August 17th, during debate on the powers of the legislative branch, the Convention agreed to the establishment of inferior courts.[68] An additional charge was given to the Committee on Detail on August 20th: To consider whether "The Jurisdiction of the supreme Court shall be extended to all controversies between the U. S., and an individual State, or the U. S. and the Citizens of an individual State."[69]

2. *The Debate on the Judiciary*

The records of the main debate on the jurisdiction of the federal courts, held on August 27th, pose a singular problem: Many of the amendments are noted only in the technical linguistic sense, without notation of discussion and debate. The first amendment added the law and equity clause over the objection that the powers of common law courts and chancery courts, as known at that time, should not be consolidated into a single court system.[70] After considerable debate on what eventually became the good behavior and diminution clauses, the Convention reached the formal questions of jurisdiction.[71] The proposition that the United States should be able to sue in its own courts was accepted when the Convention specifically added to the jurisdictional

---

67. *Id.* at 186 (presumably Madison's copy) (Aug. 6th). While the report is substantially the same as document IX from the Committee, it is necessary to set it out in full in order to follow the various changes.

68. *Id.* at 315 (Madison) (Aug. 17th).

69. *Id.* at 342 (Madison), 335 (Journal) (Aug. 20th).

70. *Id.* at 428 (Madison), 422 (Journal) (Aug. 27th). The objection reflected the contemporary state of judicial systems while the accepted motion established the idea of perhaps the first unified court system.

71. *Id.* at 428-30 (Madison), 423 (Journal) (Aug. 27th). In addition, the question of jurisdiction over impeachment of national officers was raised but postponed. *Id.* at 430 (Madison), 423 (Journal) (Aug. 27th). Eventually, the trial of impeachments would be shifted to the Senate, with the Chief Justice presiding in cases of impeachment of the President. U.S. CONST. art. I, § 3.

enumeration of controversies to which the United States was a party.[72]

The next amendment considered by the Convention has created the most substantial debate about the scope of the federal courts' authority and is a premise to this article. As Madison reports the debate:

> Docr. Johnson moved to insert the words "this Constitution and the" before the word "laws."
>
> Mr. Madison doubted whether it was not going too far to extend the jurisdiction of the Court generally to cases arising Under the Constitution, & whether it ought not to be limited to cases of a Judiciary Nature. The right of expounding the Constitution in cases not of this nature ought not to be given to that Department.
>
> The motion of Docr. Johnson was agreed to nem: con: it being generally supposed that the jurisdiction given was constructively limited to cases of a Judiciary nature.[73]

At this point in the Convention, the exceptions and regulations clause had been postulated by the Committee on Detail as applicable only to statutes and past treaties. The entire jurisdictional section would soon be brought up without discussion of the applicability of the clause.

After agreeing as to a conforming amendment on future treaties, Secretary Jackson's Journal of the Convention (Journal) and Madison's notes record events differently. Only the Journal records a reduplication of the jurisdiction of the federal courts to hear cases in which the United States was a party, but both the Journal and Madison's notes agree that the Convention again postponed the impeachments clause.[74] The Journal entries continue:

> It was moved and seconded to agree to the following amendment.
>
> "In all the other cases beforementioned original jurisdiction shall be in the Courts of the several States but with appeal both as to Law and fact to the courts of the United States, with such exceptions and under such regulations, as the Legislatures shall make."
>
> The last motion being withdrawn,
>
> It was moved and seconded to amend the clause to read:

72. 2 RECORDS, *supra* note 31, at 430 (Madison), 423 (Journal) (Aug. 27th).

73. *Id.* It is also important to note that in this brief exchange, the Convention sets the stage for the classic debates on the doctrines known under the rubric of standing, ripeness, mootness, political questions, and advisory opinions. *See generally* J. KILLIAN, *supra* note 45, at 633-69. This mere fragment of debate also fertilizes the contemporary question of the Court's power to independently enforce its own remedies. In this light, further study of the remedial aspect of the "constitutional causes of action" can be found in the constitutional history, although the Supreme Court has not consciously done so. *See* Carlson v. Green, 446 U.S. 14 (1980); Davis v. Passman, 442 U.S. 228 (1979); Bivens v. Six Unknown Named Agents, 403 U.S. 338 (1971).

74. 2 RECORDS, *supra* note 31, at 423 (Journal), 431 (Madison) (Aug. 27th).

"In cases of impeachment, cases affecting Ambassadors, other public Ministers and Consuls, and those in which a State shall be Party, this jurisdiction shall be original. In all the other cases before mentioned it shall be appellate both as to law and fact with such exceptions and under such regulations as the Legislature shall make"

which passed in the affirmative

It was moved and seconded to add the following clause to the last amendment.

"But in cases in which the United States shall be a Party the jurisdiction shall be original or appellate as the Legislature may direct"

(To strike out the words "original or" Ayes—6; noes—2)

which passed in the negative.[75]

This attempt to amend the report to utilize definitively the state courts as trial courts was broader than the language being amended. It would have delegated even cases arising under the Constitution to state courts for trial, with an appeal to the federal court if Congress did not except those cases from the federal jurisdiction. The amendment that the Convention did adopt contained a narrower division of when the Supreme Court shall have original or appellate jurisdiction, and it provided for a delegation to Congress, which, in context, would be limited to establishing that division.

Professor Farrand has inserted a notation from the voting record that a motion to strike the words "or original" from the last motion was successful, but concedes that he so placed the motion "merely because it is the only place that it seems to fit in the proceedings."[76] The Journal then records that the last quoted motion was defeated.[77] That last motion would have made explicit the delegation of authority to decide when cases in which the United States was a party would be within the original or appellate jurisdiction.

Madison's notes record that at some point during this debate (in all likelihood during the consideration of the second motion, the only motion affecting the product thus far), the Convention was confronted with the "law-fact" and "common-civil" distinctions. Madison's notes provide the only illumination of the debate and genesis of the question:

Mr. Govr. Morris wished to know what was meant by the words "In all cases before mentioned it (jurisdiction) shall be appellate with such exceptions &c," whether it extended to matters

75. *Id.* at 424-25 (Journal) (Aug. 27th).

76. *Id.* at 424 & n.3 (Farrand's organization). This organizational problem will recur in the *Records*, but is specifically mentioned here because there is no corroboration from Madison's notes in this case, contrasted with such corroboration in other cases of interest.

77. *Id.* at 424-25 (Journal) (Aug. 27th).

> of fact as well as law—and to cases of Common as well as Civil law.
>
> Mr. Wilson. The Committee he believed meant facts as well as law & Common as well as Civil law. The jurisdiction of the federal Court of Appeals [under the Articles of Confederation] had he said been so construed.
>
> Mr. Dickinson moved to add after the word "appellate" the words "both as to law & fact[''] which was agreed to nem: con:[78]

It appears implicit from the discussion that neither Morris, Wilson, nor Dickinson saw a connection between the exceptions and regulations clause and the "cases arising under this Constitution" language that had previously been added. In the questions posed by Morris, the concerns were explicit; Wilson responded directly to them. The motion by Dickinson appears to be an attempt to make the choice vested in Congress over questions of law and fact explicit, yet assumes Wilson's answer that "law" includes both common and statutory law. Dickinson's amendment does not appear in Secretary Jackson's Journal; the defeated amendment that would have expressly authorized legislative determination of whether cases in which the United States was a party would be original or appellate does not appear in Madison's notes. The defeat of a motion, of course, does not carry the weight of the passage of a motion in determining intent. The discussion of power to except cases from the Court's jurisdiction focused on the distinctions between law (civil and common) and fact; it did not relate to the question on which both the Journal and Madison agree—that the Convention had included cases arising under the Constitution within the ambit of the Court's jurisdiction.

Madison's notes and Secretary Jackson's Journal are in agreement that the next motion was to delete "The jurisdiction of the Supreme Court" and insert in lieu thereof "The Judicial Power."[79] In yet another inconsistency, however, the Journal records the approval of a motion deleting the phrase "this jurisdiction shall be original" and inserting the familiar "the supreme Court shall have original jurisdiction," yet no trace of the motion appears in Madison's notes.[80]

In one of the more telling negative actions, the Convention defeated a motion that would have disposed entirely of the exceptions and regulations clause and replaced it with the affirmative: "In all the

78. *Id*. at 431 (Madison) (Aug. 27th).

79. *Compare id.* at 425 (Journal) *with id.* at 431 (Madison) (Aug. 27th). This illustrates the vexing problem of a lack of convention on such details as capitalization, much in the same vein as the lack of convention on punctuation, which has been illustrated continuously.

80. *Id*. at 425 (Journal) (Aug. 27th).

other cases before mentioned the Judicial power shall be exercised in such manner as the legislature shall direct."[81] Had the motion been accepted, the authority of Congress to regulate the method of the federal courts (both Supreme and inferior) would have been clear, and the question of excepting from jurisdiction would have been foreclosed. The defeat of the proposed amendment, however, ought not to be construed to foreclose exceptions from jurisdiction, even though it appears consistent with the previous discussions of the law (civil and common) and fact. An even more specific interpretation of this rejection flows from the next, unanimous action of the Convention—striking from the end of the section: "The Legislature may assign any part of the jurisdiction above mentioned (except the trial of the President of the United States) in the manner, and under the limitations which it shall think proper, to such Inferior Courts, as it shall constitute from time to time."[82] The Convention's rejection of a specific delegation of power to divide jurisdiction between the Supreme and inferior courts, of course, cannot be cited as conclusive evidence that the Convention did not wish the Congress to have that power; the rejection may have been because the Convention felt it was mere surplusage. Nevertheless, the discussion until then had been focused on jurisdiction over statutory and common law, and this particular language was so all-inclusive that it undoubtedly would have specifically given Congress power to divide jurisdiction over cases arising under the Constitution. Thus, the rejection of such language and its effect, though not conclusive of the point, cannot be ignored. It is evidence that the Convention did not wish to extend congressional authority over the jurisdiction of the Supreme Court to cases arising under the Constitution.

The Convention continued to amend article III for the remainder of August 27th. The Journal records the conforming addition of a law and equity clause preceding the "arising under" language, but Madison fails to record the motion.[83] The Journal and Madison's notes agree that the last substantive motion of the day was the addition of cases of "citizens of the same state claiming lands under grants of different States."[84]

One final amendment was made to the jurisdiction section on August 28th. In order to "prevent uncertainty" as to whether the Supreme

81. *Id.* at 425 (Journal), 431 (Madison) (Aug. 27th). Madison appears to have copied this entry from the published Journal before publishing his notes.

82. *Id.* The language is from 2 RECORDS, *supra* note 31, at 186-87 (presumably Madison's copy of the report of the Committee on Detail) (Aug. 6th).

83. *Id.* at 425 (Journal) (Aug. 27th).

84. *Id.* at 425 (Journal), 431 (Madison) (Aug. 27th).

Court alone or the whole judicial power that might be created would have appellate jurisdiction, the subject pronoun and verb of the clause were struck and "The supreme Court shall have appellate jurisdiction" was substituted.[85] This change, in itself, can be construed as merely conforming the style of the sentence to that of the preceding sentence detailing the original jurisdiction of the Court. If Madison's attribution of purpose is to be taken seriously, however, the change was a specific delineation of the Court's jurisdiction.

The question of jurisdiction of the Supreme Court arose only one more time before the draft constitution, as amended, was committed to the Committee on Style, and that motion—to include land claims between the states and the United States under the treaty of peace with Great Britain—was defeated.[86] Professor Farrand's compilation of the amended report provides the following text:

> Sect. 3. The Judicial Power shall extend to all cases both in law and equity arising under this Constitution and the laws of the United States, and treaties made or which shall be made under their authority; to all cases affecting Ambassadors, other Public Ministers and Consuls; to all cases of Admiralty and Maritime Jurisdiction; to Controversies to which the United States shall be a party, to controversies between two or more States (except such as shall regard Territory and Jurisdiction) between a State and citizens of another State, between citizens of different States, between citizens of the same State claiming lands under grants of different States, and between a State or the citizens thereof and foreign States, citizens or subjects. In cases affecting Ambassadors, other Public Ministers and Consuls, and those in which a State shall be party, the Supreme Court shall have original jurisdiction. In all other cases beforementioned the Supreme Court shall have appellate jurisdiction both as to law and fact with such exceptions and under such regulations as the Legislature shall make.[87]

The report of the Committee on Style, while not differing markedly in terms from its charge, made improvements on the enumeration of jurisdiction. As to the original jurisdiction clause, the stylization was nominal, and as to the appellate jurisdiction clause, the stylization may have been detrimental:

> In cases affecting ambassadors, other public ministers and consuls, and those in which a state shall be a party, the supreme court shall have original jurisdiction. In all the other cases before mentioned, the supreme court shall have appellate jurisdiction,

85. *Id.* at 434 (Journal), 437 (Madison) (Aug. 28th).
86. *Id.* at 434 (Journal), 465 (Madison) (Aug. 30th).
87. *Id.* at 565, 576 (Farrand's Compilation).

> both as to law and fact, with such exceptions, and under such regulations as the Congress shall make.[88]

The division of jurisdiction was complete with the exception of a return to the archaisms of capitalization and certain punctuation styles. It is important to reiterate that the problems of "plain meaning" are the product of the Committee on Style, not an intentional substantive set of amendments.[89]

One final attempt was made to include a provision for the right to a jury in civil cases, but the motion was defeated, according to Madison's notes, after it was suggested that the nature of a jury trial varied among the states.[90] In this form, the Constitution was approved and forwarded to the Continental Congress, and then to the states for ratification or rejection.

B. The State Ratifying Conventions

The ratifying conventions in the thirteen states provided a forum for the discussion of the Constitution and for the final decision as to whether the proposed document would become the frame of national government. Although in some respects the ratifying conventions provide the major explanations of the terms and meaning of the Constitution, this is not the case for the exceptions and regulations clause. Convention debate on the clause, to the extent that it exists, is of a very limited scope.

The explanation by Wilson, quite probably the author of the clause, to the Pennsylvania Convention warrants substantial quotation:

> In two cases the Supreme Court has original jurisdiction—that affecting ambassadors, and when a state shall be a party. It is true it has appellate jurisdiction in more, but it will have it under such restrictions as the Congress shall ordain. I believe that any gentleman, possessed of experience or knowledge on this subject, will agree that it was impossible to go further with any safety or propriety, and that it was best left in the manner in which it now stands.
>
> "*In all the other cases before mentioned, the Supreme Court shall have appellate jurisdiction, both as to law and fact.*" The jurisdiction as to fact may be thought improper; but those possessed of information on this head see that it is necessary. We find it essentially necessary from the ample experience we have had in the courts of admiralty with regard to captures. Those gentlemen who, during the late war, had their vessels retaken,

88. *Id.* at 601 (Committee on Style, Madison's copy).
89. *See* notes 27-28 and accompanying text *supra*.
90. 2 RECORDS, *supra* note 31, at 628 (Madison) (Sept. 15th).

> know well what a poor chance they should have had when those vessels were taken in their states and tried by juries, and in what a situation they would have been if the Court of Appeals [under the Articles of Confederation] had not been possessed of authority to reconsider and set aside the verdicts of those juries. Attempts were made by some of the states to destroy this power; but it has been confirmed in every instance.
>
> There are other cases in which it will be necessary; and will not Congress better regulate them, as they rise from time to time, then could have been done by the Convention? Besides, if the regulations shall be attended with inconvenience, the Congress can alter them as soon as discovered. But any thing done in Convention must remain unalterable but by the power of the citizens of the United States at large.
>
> I think these reasons will show that the powers given to the Supreme Court are not only safe, but constitute a wise and valuable part of the system.[91]

This is the extent of Wilson's remarks on the subject, and these remarks appear only in the context of the arduous debate over the need for protection of the right to a civil jury trial and appellate review of jury-found facts. General Charles Pinckney addressed the problem in similar terms before the South Carolina Ratifying Convention.[92] These two references comprise the entire recorded discussion of the exceptions and regulations clause before the state ratifying conventions of those states participating in the ratification of the Constitution (as contrasted with states affirming the Constitution after ratification was, by its terms, complete).[93]

91. 2 J. ELLIOT, THE DEBATES IN THE SEVERAL STATE CONVENTIONS ON THE ADOPTION OF THE FEDERAL CONSTITUTION 493-94 (1836) (Pa., Wilson (C), Dec. 7, 1787) [hereinafter cited as DEBATES and accompanied by a parenthetical indicating the debate cited, the speaker, whether the speaker was a member of the Federal Convention of 1787 (indicated by (C)), and the date of the remarks]. Over the formation of the Republic, a number of individuals played multiple roles, and it is important to stress the continuity or fragmentation of their opinions.

92. 4 DEBATES, *supra* note 91, at 306-08 (S.C., C. Pinckney (C), Jan. 18, 1788).

93. There is at least a theoretical methodological concern for this strict classification of the various State Conventions. On June 21, 1788, New Hampshire became the ninth state to ratify the Constitution. 34 JOURNALS OF THE CONTINENTAL CONGRESS 281 (1937 (July 2, 1788)) [hereinafter cited as JS. CONT. CONG.]; 2 DOCUMENTARY HISTORY OF THE CONSTITUTION, 141-44 (1902) [hereinafter cited as DOC. HIST.]. By the terms of article VI of the Constitution, the ratification of New Hampshire was sufficient to make the Constitution operative as among the states that had ratified it: Delaware, Pennsylvania, New Jersey, Georgia, Connecticut, Massachusetts, Maryland, South Carolina, and New Hampshire. Presumably a consistent, intrinsic, constitutive history ends here. The remainder of state convention debates would normally be treated as extrinsic aids to interpretation, similar to after-enactment commentary. However, a number of problems were evident even at that time. For one, New York was the seat of the Continental Congress, and the State of New York had not yet ratified the Constitution. Virginia was also seen as politically necessary to

The argument of need for a guarantee of a right to a jury trial in civil cases was raised numerous times during the other state conventions. Almost invariably, the response to this argument was that the variation of trial practice before the state courts—and within the state court systems of law, chancery, and admiralty—would not lend to the development of a uniform rule for the inferior federal courts and that therefore the Congress should be free to determine and redetermine the manner of civil trials.[94] Nonetheless, the proposal found its way into the pleadings of at least four states for amendments to the Constitution.[95]

The Virginia and North Carolina State Conventions are the most extensively reported, and these debates illuminate a variety of concerns about the federal judiciary. As already noted, the primary concern of the state debates in this area was the guarantee of a civil trial by jury and the appellate review of jury-found facts, but there are also references within those debates to perceived problems regarding the accessibility of a centralized court, the oppressive appeals of small or frivolous claims,[96] and, on one occasion, the detail of jurisdiction over a state as a party defendant.[97]

the efficacy of the new government. Virginia convened its convention on June 2, 1788, and ratified the Constitution on June 25, 1788, 3 DEBATES, *supra* note 91, at 1, 653. Thus, Virginia's Convention straddles the date of actual ratification of the Constitution for the relevant states, but there is no indication on the record that the Virginians were aware of that fact. *But cf. id.* at 617-18 (Madison (C), June 24, 1788) (reference to failure if only eight states ratify). The North Carolina Convention commenced on July 21, 1788, and neither ratified nor rejected the Constitution prior to adjournment on Aug. 2, 1788. 4 DEBATES, *supra* note 91, at 34, 251. That convention was aware before it adjourned that the question before it was that of joining the union rather than that of ratifying the Constitution. *Id.* at 208 (N.C., Spaight (C), Aug. 2, 1788). Eventually, North Carolina joined the union after the government had been formed and had become operational. Thus, while methodologic problems are posed by including the Virginia and North Carolina debates as intrinsic aids to interpretation, the historical circumstances appear to outweigh the difficulties of methodologic inconsistency, and those debates are therefore included.

94. 2 DEBATES, *supra* note 91, at 488 (Pa., Wilson (C), Dec. 7, 1787); 3 DEBATES, *supra* note 91, at 518-20 (Va., Pendleton, June 19, 1788), 524 (Mason (C)), 534 (Madison (C)), 540-42 (Henry) (June 20, 1788); 4 DEBATES, *supra* note 91, at 141-42 (N.C., Johnston, July 28, 1788), 146 (Iredell), 157 (Davie) (July 29, 1788), 166 (Iredell), 306-08 (S.C., Pinckney (C, Jan. 18, 1788).

95. Massachusetts' 8th Resolution, 2 DOC. HIST., *supra* note 93, at 95; New Hampshire's 7th and 8th Resolutions, *id.* at 143; New York's 14th Resolution, *id.* at 193; Virginia's 11th Resolution and 14th Proposed Amendment, 3 DEBATES, *supra* note 91, at 653, 660-61.

96. Many of the more detailed arguments were during the North Carolina debates which led to a decision to neither ratify nor reject. *See, e.g.*, 4 DEBATES, *supra* note 91, at 143 (N.C., M'Dowall), 144 (Spaight (C)), 144-45 (Iredell), 147-48 (Iredell), 151 (Bloodworth), 154-55 (Spencer), 164 (Maclaine), 165-66 (Iredell), 170-71 (Iredell) (July 28, 1788).

97. In one of the more interesting colloquies, Patrick Henry claimed that a state was subject to being hailed before the Supreme Court as a defendant; John Marshall opposed

Patrick Henry, though not a member of the Federal Convention, argued in a flourish of oratory to the Virginia Convention that: (1) Civil trial by jury was abolished by neglect in drafting the Constitution; (2) Congress could not alter the jurisdiction of the Supreme Court under the pretense of authority of the exceptions and regulations clause (arguing partially in the vein of the concept of constitutional jurisdiction);[98] (3) such a law, being contrary to the Constitution, would be a nullity and that judges would so declare in conformity with the concept of judicial review;[99] and (4) under the enumeration of original jurisdiction, a state could be hailed before the Court as a defendant.[100] Marshall, also not a member of the Federal Convention, rose later to rejoin Henry on the issue of interpretation of the exceptions and regulations clause and argued that the clause answered his first point:

> What is the meaning of the term *exception*? Does it not mean an alteration and diminution? Congress is empowered to make exceptions to the appellate jurisdiction, as to law and fact, of the Supreme Court. These exceptions certainly go as far as the legislature may think proper for the interest and liberty of the people. Who can understand this word, *exception*, to extend to one case as well as the other?[101]

Marshall's response to Henry is clearly founded on the expressed attitude of Henry that the clause had no effect, but Marshall's interpretation does not sweep far in the opposite direction. Marshall's particular concern is to rebut Henry's statement on jury trials and appeals as to fact. Marshall engaged in Henry's technique of hyperbole in reinforcing the concept of judicial review and in stating that Congress had plenary authority over the Court's jurisdiction. This becomes clearer when Marshall continues by drawing analogy to the Virginia practice in civil jury trials and appeals of facts.[102] Others entered limited remarks on the use of the exceptions and regulations clause for the security of civil jury trials and jury-determined facts where Congress deemed appropriate, further supporting the limited nature of Mar-

this notion, saying that a state could only be a party plaintiff before the Supreme Court. 3 DEBATES, *supra* note 91, at 545 (Va., Henry), 555 (Va., Marshall) (June 20, 1788). *See* Chisholm v. Georgia, 2 U.S. (2 Dall.) 419 (1793); U.S. CONST. amend. XI (1796). This would appear to be a case of Henry winning the battle and Marshall winning the war by changing the rules.

98. *Compare* 3 DEBATES, *supra* note 91, at 540-41 (Va., Henry June 20, 1788) *with* J. STORY, COMMENTARIES ON THE CONSTITUTION OF THE UNITED STATES, *supra* note 28, *and* notes 21-32 and accompanying text *supra*.

99. *See* notes 40-45 and accompanying text *supra*.

100. 3 DEBATES, *supra* note 91, at 540-42, 546 (Va., Henry, June 20, 1788).

101. *Id*. at 560 (Va., Marshall, June 20, 1788).

102. *Id*. at 561.

shall's comment.[103] Whatever the state of Marshall's and Henry's knowledge of the proceedings of the Federal Convention, the positions staked out at the Virginia Convention appear more rhetorical than substantive.

The North Carolina Convention considered the question of the exceptions and regulations clause in the context of the administrative concerns for a centralized court and the attendant problems of small or frivolous claims, exacerbated by the concern for the right to a jury trial in civil cases and the finality of jury-found facts.[104] Although these debates were probably the best recorded of the state conventions, no light is shed on the jurisdictional question.

The New York Convention convened and adjourned without mentioning or interpreting the exceptions and regulations clause; however, the *Federalist Papers*, addressed to those delegates through a public, yet anonymous, medium, approached the subject several times.[105] Although Hamilton had left the federal Convention before the judicial article was discussed, his discussion of jurisdiction in essay No. 80 sounds in the Constitution alone as the source of authority and is followed by a cursory review of the clause:

> From this review of the particular powers of the federal judiciary, as marked out in the Constitution, it appears that they are all conformable to the principles which ought to have governed the structure of that department, and which were necessary to the perfection of the system. If some partial inconvenience should appear to be connected with the incorporation of any of them into the plan, it ought to be recollected that the national legislature will have ample authority to make such *exceptions*, and to prescribe such regulations as will be calculated to obviate or remove these inconveniences. The possibility of particular mischiefs can never be viewed, by a well-informed mind, as a solid objection to a general principle, which is calculated to avoid general mischiefs and to obtain general advantages.[106]

This broad approach is limited in essay No. 81 by a discussion of the particular flaw that Hamilton perceived Congress might remedy: the division of jurisdiction among the Supreme and inferior courts, should the latter be established, and the question of the "abolition" of trial by

103. *Id.* at 546-50 (Va., Pendleton, June 20, 1788), 572-73 (Randolph (C) June 21, 1788).

104. *See* note 96 *supra*.

105. The New York Convention convened on June 17, 1788, and adjourned *sine die* on July 26, 1788. 2 DEBATES, *supra* note 91, at 205-414. The *Federalist*, *supra* note 36, appeared in New York newspapers between October 17, 1787 and April 4, 1788, over the famous pseudonym. Essays No. 78-85, the essays relevant here, did not appear until a publication of a second volume of collected essays on May 28, 1788.

106. THE FEDERALIST, *supra* note 36, No. 80, at 505-06 (A. Hamilton).

jury in civil cases.[107] Language is often politically turned in the *Federalist* rather than legally refined, and here the broad language is limited by its contextual discussion, and particularly by the conclusion that Hamilton reaches:

> The amount of the observations hitherto made . . . is this: that it has been carefully restricted to those causes which are manifestly proper for the cognizance of the national judicature; that in the partition of this authority a very small portion of original jurisdiction has been reserved to the Supreme Court, and the rest consigned to the subordinate tribunals; that the Supreme Court will possess an appellate jurisdiction, both as to law and fact, in all cases referred to them, both subject to any *exceptions* and *regulations* which may be thought advisable; that this appellate jurisdiction does, in no case, *abolish* the trial by jury; and that an ordinary degree of prudence and integrity in the national councils will insure us solid advantages from the establishment of the proposed judiciary, without exposing us to any of the inconveniences which have been predicted from that source.[108]

Hamilton's view would appear to be narrowly confined to the authority to hear and determine, and particularly redetermine, facts found by a jury, as well as the authority in certain cases to hear and determine facts initially in the Supreme Court as a trial court. There is no indication that Hamilton, in a series of essays designed to indicate how narrow the respective powers of the proposed government should be in order to better secure acceptance, needed to brush a broad picture of legislative power over the judicial power, especially since the legislative was considered the more controversial of the two powers to be granted. Additionally, the responsiveness of the essays to specific complaints about the proposed Constitution reinforces the notion that the exceptions and regulations clause was understood as a particularly narrow authority. As in the ratifying debates, discussion of the exceptions and regulations clause was tuned to narrow, yet major, concerns, several of which were reconsidered and altered soon after the consummation of the Constitution.

C. Reconsiderations: The Seventh and Eleventh Amendments

Concern over the right to jury trials in civil cases and the finality of jury-found facts surfaced repeatedly during the state ratifying conventions and during the ratifiers' pleas to the Continental Congress and the First Congress for alteration of the Constitution. It is thus not surprising that the First Congress took up the question of a right to jury

107. *Id*. No. 81, at 512 (A. Hamilton).
108. *Id*. at 513-14.

trial in civil cases almost immediately, delaying consideration of the overall organization of the judiciary.[109]

The ascension of the right to a jury trial in civil cases from statutory to constitutional[110] status made three important changes. First, obviously, a major objection to the Constitution was laid to rest. Second, Congress relinquished a substantial amount of control over the federal courts, a concession that, over time, has all but disappeared with the displacement of common with statutory law. Third, control of jury trials, at least at common law, and the review of jury findings were vested in the courts as interpreted at that time and were thereafter frozen. Congress retained authority over statutory, admiralty, and equitable proceedings, while common law questions were relegated to common law. The Court has defined the right to a jury trial as "limited to rights and remedies peculiarly legal in their nature, and such as it was proper to assert in courts of law, and by the appropriate modes and proceedings of courts of law."[111]

The effect of the Seventh Amendment on the scope of the exceptions and regulations clause was finite. The concern for the right to a jury trial in civil cases and the finality accorded jury-found facts in the Federal Convention and the state ratifying conventions suggests that the exceptions and regulations clause applied directly to the law and fact clause. It has been suggested that the right to a jury trial was the primary, if not conclusive, purpose for the exceptions and regulations clause, and further that the Seventh Amendment obviated the exceptions and regulations clause completely.[112] Congressional concern for the mode of amendment of the Constitution may have resulted in the

109. 1 ANNALS OF CONG. 443 (Madison, (C), Va.) (introducing resolutions for amendment to Constitution, June 8, 1789). *See* note 96 *supra*. Adoption of the final version of the 7th Amendment by Congress made consideration of several provisions of the bill under consideration to reorganize the judiciary unnecessary.

110. U.S. CONST. amend. VII: "In suits at common law, where the value in controversy shall exceed twenty dollars, the right of trial by jury shall be preserved, and no fact tried by a jury, shall be otherwise reexamined in any Court of the United States, than according to the rules of common law."

111. Shields v. Thomas, 59 U.S. (18 How.) 253, 262 (1856). The right to a jury trial exists in civil cases as it existed "under the English common law when the Amendment was adopted." Baltimore & Carolina Line v. Redman, 295 U.S. 654, 657 (1935); Parsons v. Bedford, 28 U.S. (3 Pet.) 433, 446-47 (1830). Two recent cases illustrate the breadth of the right—a landlord/tenant case and a discrimination in rental housing case brought under federal law: Pernell v. Southall Realty, 416 U.S. 363 (1974); Curtis v. Loether, 415 U.S. 189 (1974). Congressional power to vest the fact-finding function under statute in an administrative body does not violate the 7th Amendment. Atlas Roofing Co. v. OSHRC, 430 U.S. 442 (1977).

112. *E.g.*, Merry, *supra* note 20.

language of the law and fact clause not being altered and the Seventh Amendment being appended,[113] but this does not stand as a barrier to the interpretation; the substance must be considered separately from the means used to alter the effect of the Constitution, even if the means makes the interpretation more difficult. To suggest that Congress intended to repeal the exceptions and regulations clause interpretation of the law and fact clause ignores the variety of other concerns evident in the debates of the Federal Convention and the state ratifying conventions, as well as contemporaneous congressional action to regulate the processes and remedies of the judiciary. The Seventh Amendment no doubt altered congressional power under the exceptions and regulations clause insofar as jury trials and appellate review of facts in common law cases were concerned, but an interpretation of the amendment that emasculates the clause entirely is not tenable.

The Seventh Amendment did not reach jurisdiction as closely as did the Eleventh Amendment.[114] The exchange between Henry and Marshall during the Virginia Convention was shortly replayed by the Court in *Chisholm v. Georgia*,[115] and within a decade by Congress and the states.[116] The Eleventh Amendment may be viewed as a complex defensive pleading because of the restriction it places on the manner in which the Court may construe and effectuate its power. Such a construction of the Amendment is in stark contrast to the possible alternative available to Congress, namely, the elimination of the constitutional jurisdiction of the Court to hear and determine cases in which a state is a party defendant. Still more important was the congressional approval of the amendment as a determination that it could not except such cases from the jurisdiction of the Court by simple legislative means. Had Congress been satisfied that a repeal of a legislative grant or an affirmative jurisdictional exception of cases in which a state was a party defendant would have been sufficient to overrule *Chisholm*, the more onerous process of constitutional amendment would not have

113. A preliminary decision was made by Congress that the Constitution should be amended by supplementation rather than deletion or modification of existing language. 1 ANNALS OF CONG. 743 (Aug. 13, 1789). This decision has remained in effect throughout the history of the Republic and has contributed to numerous constitutional debates besides the current focus of this article.

114. U.S. CONST. amend XI: "The Judicial power of the United States shall not be construed to extend to any suit in law or equity, commenced or prosecuted against one of the United States by Citizens of another State, or by Citizens or Subjects of any Foreign State." The 11th Amendment was ratified in 1795, but for reasons unknown, ratification was not announced until 1798. *See* note 45 *supra*.

115. 2 U.S. (2 Dall.) 419 (1793).

116. 4 ANNALS OF CONG. 30-31 (Jan. 14, 1794), 476-78 (Mar. 4, 1794) (proposed).

been necessary. Congressional desire to put the question, once and presumably for all time, beyond its own unratified power, much in the vein of the Seventh Amendment, nominally militates against this interpretation.[117]

The problem of interpretation has not been answered by the Court or by Congress, although each for its part has recognized that the interpretive aspect is important. The interpretation of when a state is a real party in interest has led to numerous decisions by the Court, but once it has been ascertained that a state is the real party in interest, each case has been dismissed for want of jurisdiction.[118] The Court has also held that the Eleventh Amendment is limited by other amendments.[119] Congress' use of the rigorous course of constitutional amendment, rather than statutory exception, suggests that Congress did not believe it had the power to make such an exception to the Court's jurisdiction by statutory means. This inference is suggested by congressional actions on several other occasions as well.[120]

D. Lessons from the Constitutional History

The draft Constitution and its development provide one of the classic problems of interpretation—the record as it is known today is incomplete, inconsistent, and ambiguous. What seems clear from both the language and the development of the Constitution is Congress' broad authority over the inferior federal courts' jurisdiction. Less clear, but still stated with conviction, is the authority of Congress to decide what the scope of jurisdiction of inferior federal courts and the Supreme Court will be with regard to particular statutory provisions, and though not discussed in the development of the Constitution, this would also apply to treaties, given the structure of treaties within the law and their method of amendment by statute. Also supportable in the history of the Convention is the notion that Congress may divide

117. The problem of ascribing legislative intent to congressional silence is perhaps insoluble. The most telling example of this problem lies in the propounding of the 14th Amendment. *See generally* R. BERGER, GOVERNMENT BY JUDICIARY (1969).

118. The Court will "look behind and through the nominal parties on the record, to ascertain who were the real parties to the suit." *In re* Ayers, 123 U.S. 443, 490 (1887). *See generally* J. KILLIAN, *supra* note 45, at 1277, 1279 (collected cases).

119. Fitzpatrick v. Bitzer, 427 U.S. 445, 456 (1976) ("[T]he Eleventh Amendment, and the principle of state sovereignty which it embodies, . . . are necessarily limited by the enforcement provisions of § 5 of the Fourteenth Amendment"). The limitation of one clause by another must be intentional, however. *See* Craig v. Boren, 429 U.S. 190 (1976) (equal protection under 14th Amendment limits authority of states to control alcoholic beverages under the 21st Amendment).

120. *See* note 45 *supra*.

the jurisdiction of the Supreme Court in terms of whether it will be original in cases where it would otherwise be appellate, but that suggestion has not been accepted. The lack of discussion in the Convention of 1787 on whether or not Congress should have the power to except cases arising under the Constitution from the Supreme Court's appellate jurisdiction, particularly in light of the Convention having established the jurisdiction over such cases and having entertained multiple considerations of statutory or common law and fact, suggests, albeit inconclusively, that the exceptions and regulations clause was not intended to reach so far.

The state ratifying conventions reinforce the notion that detailed problems of the right to a jury trial and appellate review of jury facts, as well as a variety of administrative concerns about a centralized court and procedure, animated the discussions of the exceptions and regulations clause. When jurisdiction was formally considered in the ratifying conventions, it was viewed as flowing directly from the Constitution. The only limitations that the ratifiers perceived to be within the ambit of Congress dealt with statutory and common law or fact distinctions. It does not appear that jurisdiction over cases arising under the Constitution was ever questioned in ratifying or acceptance debates, nor does the concept of judicial review appear to be other than embraced.

Finally, the first relevant modifications to the Constitution dealt with preserving the right to jury trials in civil cases—the primary concern over the judicial article during ratification—and with limiting jurisdiction over cases to which a state was a party, a particular construction of the judicial power. The Seventh Amendment limited congressional power to determine the right to jury trials in common law cases by removing that power to the judiciary in accord with the common law. This alteration impedes only one interpretation of the exceptions and regulations clause, and then only at common law. It does not dispose of all exceptions and regulations clause questions. The Eleventh Amendment restricted the construction of the judicial power to exclude cases in which a state was defendant to an out-of-state private party. This alteration was of very limited effect despite the wealth of case law it has spawned. The key to interpreting the exceptions and regulations clause, however, is posed in the implicit question of why Congress would proceed along the more difficult route of amendment if a statutory exception would have sufficed.

In sum, the constitutional history does not support a purpose or intent on the part of the Framers or ratifiers that the exceptions and regulations clause reaches questions of jurisdiction to hear cases arising under the Constitution. The first Congresses, in amending the Constitution, also do not evidence such an intent. To the contrary, the constitutional history shows a more limited scope of congressional authority under the exceptions and regulations clause.

III. Congress, the Court, and Implementation of the Constitution

The history of the Constitution can be divided for purposes of this article into three substantial divisions: the Formative Era, running roughly from 1789 through the publication of the *Journal*, *Debates*, and Madison's notes to about 1850;[121] the Great Insurrection and its aftermath, running from about 1850 through about 1880; and the era of developing substantive regulation of the federal courts, from appoximately 1880 to the present. The development during those periods of statutory jurisdiction and decisional statements, both *ex cathedra* and dicta, present a wide range of policy and constitutional views.

A. The Formative Era

Congressional consideration of proposed amendments to the Constitution and legislation to organize the judiciary overlapped in both time and substance. The right to a civil trial by jury and the mandate against appellate review of facts are additions to the Constitution that must be understood within the framework of contemporaneous congressional actions to organize and regulate the judiciary. During the

121. It should be remembered that the proceedings of the Convention were, with few minor exceptions, held in unviolated secrecy. The Journal was committed to the President for such disposition as the Continental Congress might deem appropriate. George Washington transferred the Journal to the Department of State in 1796, and it was published in 1819 for the first time. Yates' notes were published in a politically edited form in 1808 as an attack on Madison and were formally published shortly after the appearance of the Journal. Madison's voluminous and detailed, although often postured, notes were not published until 1840, after his death. Many other writings, including the drafts of the Committee on Detail, were not assembled until Farrand published the first edition of the *Records* in 1911, or until publication of the second edition in 1937. Farrand, *Introduction* to 1 RECORDS, *supra* note 31, at xi-xxv. These documents were preceded by both Luther Martin's Letter, 1 DEBATES, *supra* note 91, at 344, and THE FEDERALIST, *supra* note 36. Elliot's *Debates* of the ratifying conventions were compiled and first published in 1830, with a second edition issued in 1836. The point of such publication and disclosure history—aside from its use in documenting the personal histories of the Framers, ratifiers, members of congress, and justices during the formative period—was that only political debate and personal recollections were available to each writer in considering the purpose and intent of the Convention. Thus, understanding the role that each individual played in the formative era is of great value in evaluating what that individual has said in interpreting the Constitution during that period.

First Congress, the Senate appointed a committee to draft a bill to organize the judiciary. The bill was reported on June 12, 1789, and debate commenced on June 22nd.[122] After debate and alteration, the bill passed the Senate and was referred to the House on July 17th.[123]

Madison had proposed resolutions in the House to amend the Constitution in June, and debate was commenced on August 14th.[124] Several amendment proposals overlapped provisions of the Senate-passed judiciary bill; consideration of the latter was therefore postponed.[125] The House agreed to amendment resolutions on August 22nd and referred them to the Senate.[126] House consideration of the judiciary bill was again postponed while the Senate altered the amendment resolutions.[127] Only after the Senate passed the resolutions did the House take up the judiciary bill.[128] The Judiciary Act of 1789 was signed on September 24th, one week after the Bill of Rights was referred to the states.[129]

Details of several sections of the Judiciary Act of 1789 would have provided a useful record of legislative purpose and intent, but such records, common to the processes under which Congress today operates, were embryonic at best in 1789.[130] Warren's review of the Judiciary Act of 1789 appears to be the only attempted reconstruction of the process, and his conclusions generally reach only the subject of the

122. 1 ANNALS OF CONG. 18 (Committee appointed, Apr. 7, 1789), 47 (bill reported, Lee, (C), June 12, 1789). (There are two different editions of *Annals of Congress*. The edition used here bears the running head "History of Congress." The other edition bears the running head "Debates in Congress." Page citations to "History" do not correspond with material in "Debates.") The Committee originally included four members of the Federal Convention and their respective state ratifying conventions: Ellsworth of Connecticut, Paterson of New Jersey, Bassett of Delaware, and Few of Georgia.

123. *Id.* at 48 (debate commenced, June 22, 1789), 50 (recommitted, July 13, 1789), 51 (passed, July 17, 1789).

124. *Id.* at 439-40 (Va., Madison (C), June 8, 1789), 745 (debate begun, Aug. 14, 1789).

125. *Id.* at 685-90 (July 20-21, 1789); Warren, *New Light on the History of the Federal Judiciary Act of 1789*, 37 HARV. L. REV. 49, 111 (1923).

126. 1 ANNALS OF CONG. 808 (Aug. 24, 1789). *See generally* Warren, *supra* note 125.

127. 1 ANNALS OF CONG. 812-14 (Aug. 24, 1789). *See generally* Warren, *supra* note 125.

128. 1 ANNALS OF CONG. 826 (Aug. 29, 1789). *See generally* Warren, *supra* note 125.

129. Act of Sept. 24, 1789, ch. 20, 1 Stat. 73.

130. For example, there was substantial debate during the early years of the Republic as to whether the federal courts' jurisdiction extended to common law crimes. This was settled in the negative in United States v. Hudson, 7 U.S. (11 Cranch) 32 (1807). Nevertheless, there was argument to the contrary even after the decision. *See* F. SERGEANT, A DISSERTATION OF THE NATURE AND EXTENT OF THE JURISDICTION OF THE COURTS OF THE UNITED STATES (1824). Warren suggested that the Court may have been unaware of contrary legislative intent to the effect that the courts were expected to exercise such jurisdiction. Warren, *supra* note 125, at 51.

newly established inferior courts' jurisdiction.[131] The alteration of jurisdiction during this process has only been noted in the form of documentary changes (similar to the documentation of the Committee on Detail), but none of the changes with respect to the Court's appellate jurisdiction appear to be significant.[132]

Section 25 of the Act provides for statutory appellate jurisdiction of the Court over judgments of state courts of last resort:

> [W]here is drawn in question the validity of a treaty or statute of, or an authority exercised under the United States, and the decision is against their validity; or where is drawn in question the validity of a statute of, or an authority exercised under any State, on the ground of their being repugnant to the constitution, treaties or laws of the United States, and the decision is in favour of such their validity, . . . or where is drawn in question the construction of any clause of the constitution, or of a treaty, or statute of, or commission held under the United States, and the decision is against the title, right, privilege or exemption specially set up or claimed by either party, under such clause of the said Constitution, treaty, statute or commission, may be re-examined and reversed or affirmed in the Supreme Court of the United States upon a writ of error.[133]

It does not appear on the face of the statute that all constitutional questions are included, but the Act provides for inclusion of all cases in which the supremacy of federal law has been denied in the state court of last resort or when a right claimed under a federal authority has been denied, thereby including all cases in which federal constitutionality might be raised and not effected.[134] Where a federal or state stat-

131. "The broad pro-Constitution men took the position that Congress had no power to withhold from the Federal Courts which it should establish any of the judicial power granted by the Constitution. On this point, they were forced to yield; for the Congress withheld from the Federal Courts much of the jurisdiction which it might have bestowed under the Constitution. On the other hand, the narrow pro-Constitution men were anxious to give to the Federal Courts as little jurisdiction as possible and to leave to the State Courts, in the first instance, jurisdiction over most of the Federal questions, subject to Federal revision through the appellate power of the United States Supreme Court. On this point, this faction also was forced to yield. The result was a compromise." Warren, *supra* note 125, at 67-68.

132. *See generally id.*

133. Act of Sept. 24, 1789, ch. 20, § 25, 1 Stat. 73, 85. The provision goes on to detail the process of review by the Supreme Court, including a requirement, in the form of a limitation, that the error assigned appear in the record below.

134. Congress appears to have been concerned with the denial of the validity of a congressional enactment, the validity of a state enactment against a claim of supremacy or constitutionality, and the denial of a personal claim or right granted under the Constitution, laws, or treaties of the United States. This suggests that Congress has seen fit to exclude from the Court's jurisdiction, cases where supremacy and uniformity are not abridged. The continuing concern of Congress—often manifested in the defeat of proposals to alter this ostensibly self-executing constitutional balance—appears to lie in Congress' belief that it

ute was attacked as repugnant to the Constitution and a state court of last resort held the statute unconstitutional, the Court would not have jurisdiction under the first or second clause to hear a claim that a federal or state statute had been improperly declared invalid. This incompleteness was not corrected until 1914,[135] but these same questions might have been brought before the Court under the third clause on the theory that the validation of a statute under the Constitution is a *claimable* denial of an equivalent constitutional right to be free of the statute. If a state were to set up a defense to such an attack on the basis of a constitutional right under the third provision (the decision being against that right), review in the Supreme Court is quite possible, but this view apparently has never been tested.[136] No parallel problem existed in cases in which the United States was the defendant because the state courts could not compel the superior authority of the United States to appear. Thus, insofar as review of judgments of state courts of last resort are concerned, the statute appears to provide review for the full panoply of constitutional questions. This suggests that all cases arising under the Constitution *could* have been brought to the Supreme Court *if properly pleaded or defended*.

The provisions for inferior federal court jurisdiction were more complex and posed substantial statutory exceptions, which consequently were also exceptions to the Supreme Court's appellate jurisdiction. The lack of Supreme Court jurisdiction to review circuit court decisions on statutory questions in criminal cases prior to 1891 is the most obvious example;[137] however, the writ of *habeas corpus* would lie to review all jurisdictional questions, including all questions of the con-

was fully implementing the provisions of article III. This suggestion comports with such concepts as the independent state grounds for state court decisions, which the Court will not review.

135. The alteration of the section was a direct result of Ives v. South Buffalo Ry. Co., 201 N.Y. 271 (1911), which was perceived to be nonappealable. "Federal right had been vindicated, not denied. Under the existing appellate jurisdiction there was no way of reviewing the *Ives* result by the Supreme Court. When, shortly after, the Supreme Court of Washington upheld the constitutionality of a similar statute, the demand for review by the Supreme Court was intensified by a wide-spread feeling that, in practice, constitutionality turned on geography." F. FRANKFURTER & J. LANDIS, *supra* note 56, at 195. The result was Act of Dec. 23, 1914, ch. 2, 38 Stat. 790.

136. *Ives*, 201 N.Y. 271 (1911), posed a particularly good opportunity to make this form of argument. The State of New York not only has an interest in the constitutionality of its laws, but has a constitutional claim, which is not that the law violates the due process clause, but rather that the invalidation violates the right of the state to enact laws under its police power. Of course, this is mere speculation, for if the argument had been asserted, the results are unreported.

137. *See* note 38 *supra*.

stitutionality of the court's process.[138]

More notable was a possible gap in admiralty jurisdiction, which appears to extend not only to statutory questions, but, because of the way the statute operated, to constitutional questions that might also arise. Jurisdiction in admiralty cases included an escalating jurisdictional amount, together with a choice of appeal or writ of error in certain cases from the district to the circuit courts, with the possibility of a loss of jurisdiction if counsel were to commit an error in judgment.[139] The fundamental difference between the writ of error and appeal illustrates the potential for a tactical error that could preclude taking an

138. The writ of *habeas corpus* is provided for by implication from the restriction on its suspension in article 1, § 9, clause 2 of the Constitution. Applying the English practice, § 14 of the Judiciary Act of 1789 provides that the writ may issue to contest the authority of confinement on a writ or other process, or the jurisdiction of the court to try a criminal offense, but not to review the judgment of conviction by a proper court. This reading is confirmed by *Ex parte* Bollman, 4 U.S. (8 Cranch) 75 (1807). An oft-cited dictum appears in Chief Justice Marshall's (Va., 1st Cong.) opinion: "As preliminary to any . . . [decision] of the merits of this motion, this court deems it proper to declare that it disclaims all jurisdiction not given by the constitution, or by the laws of the United States." *Id.* at 93. This dictum can be read as embracing the principle of constitutional jurisdiction, strictly statutory jurisdiction or neither of these. As the Court in *Ex parte Bollman* found that it had statutory jurisdiction, there was no need for it to determine whether jurisdiction existed otherwise. *See also* United States v. Palmer, 16 U.S. (3 Wheat.) 610 (1818) (via certified questions). In United States v. More, 7 U.S. (3 Cranch) 159 (1805), a conviction under indictment at common law was brought up by writ of error from the Circuit Court for the District of Columbia and was dismissed. On its face, the dismissal may have been the result of (1) the Court exercising its discretion due to the unsettled nature of the common law crimes, (2) the civil nature of the writ of error, making its pleading in a criminal case improper, or (3) the position of the circuit court as a possible article I court under the territory clause of § 8, clause 17. *See also* Palmore v. United States, 411 U.S. 389 (1973); American Ins. Co. v. Canter, 26 U.S. (1 Pet.) 511 (1828). *See generally* F. FRANKFURTER & J. LANDIS, *supra* note 56, at 109-20; Ratner, *supra* note 20, at 195-201.

139. Section 9 of the Judiciary Act of 1789 grants the district courts, exclusive of the state courts, admiralty and maritime jurisdiction over waters accessible from the ocean by ships of 10 tons loaded. Section 21 of the Act provides that an appeal will lie from final judgments of the district courts in admiralty and maritime cases where the amount in controversy exceeds $300. It is not clear whether a writ of error would lie in cases exceeding $50, but not exceeding $300, under the general civil actions provisions of § 22. Section 22 also provides the Supreme Court with jurisdiction to review by writ of error cases in which the circuit court had issued a writ of error and the amount controverted exceeded $2000. There does not appear to be a specific jurisdictional provision for the Supreme Court to hear admiralty cases other than by way of general civil cases. Thus, if the navigability jurisdictional requirement is met, (1) district court decisions in which the amount controverted does not exceed $50 are final, (2) decisions in which the amount controverted exceeds $50 but not $300 might have been reviewable by the circuit court by way of writ of error, and (3) decisions in which the controverted amount exceeds $300 may be taken to the circuit court by writ of error or appeal. If the appeal route is chosen, there is apparently no further review possible in the Supreme Court. There appears to be no distinction whether the question raised is one of treaty, of statute, or of constitutional magnitude.

admiralty case to the Supreme Court. That difference is described by Chief Justice Ellsworth in *Wiscart v. D'Auchey*:[140]

> An appeal is a process of civil law origin, and removes a cause entirely; subjecting the fact as well as the law, to a review and re-trial: but a writ of error is a process of common law origin, and it removes nothing for re-examination but the law. Does the Statute observe this obvious distinction? I think it does.[141]

The jurisdictional amount is a product of the recurrent problem of appellate review of facts. Even here, there is no express exception from the Court's appellate jurisdiction of cases arising under the Constitution, but only of cases in which particular sums have not been alleged or proven, or in which the tactical decisions of counsel have been erroneous.[142]

Wiscart, a diversity rather than an admiralty case, was the first of many cases in which the Court has discussed its appellate jurisdiction. *Wiscart* involved an equity suit to enforce a judgment against petitioner to compel transfer of title. After the equity decree, Wiscart appears to have transferred the real estate and other effects that could have been used to satisfy the judgment. D'Auchey acquired a judgment in the circuit court, and Wiscart petitioned the Supreme Court by writ of error, appending the decree and a statement of fact from the court below. The issue for decision was whether such a statement of fact was conclusive as to its contents, and, although its relevancy is unclear, whether such a statement is conclusive when the evidence is attached. Answering both points in the affirmative and providing for Judge Wilson's dissent on the latter point, Chief Justice Ellsworth stated:

> The constitution, distributing the judicial power of the *United States*, vests in the Supreme Court, an original as well as an appellate jurisdiction. The original jurisdiction, however, is confined to cases affecting ambassadors, other public ministers and consuls, and those in which a State shall be a party. In all other cases, only an appellate jurisdiction is given to the court; and even the appellate jurisdiction is, likewise, qualified; inasmuch as it is given "with such exceptions . . . as the Congress shall make." Here then, is the ground, and the only ground, on which we can sustain an appeal. If Congress has provided no rule to regulate our proceedings, we cannot exercise an appellate jurisdiction; and if the rule is provided, we cannot depart from it.

140. 3 U.S. (3 Dall.) 321, 327 (1796).

141. *Id.* at 327.

142. For example, failure to plead the jurisdictional amount in the inferior court was fatal to review by writ of *habeas corpus*. Barry v. Mercein, 46 U.S. (5 How.) 103 (1847). *Barry* is also noted for its dicta on jurisdiction of the Supreme Court.

> The question, therefore, on the constitutional point of an appellate jurisdiction, is simply, whether Congress has established any rule for regulating its exercise?[143]

Chief Justice Ellsworth went on to distinguish the civil law appeal from the common law writ of error, as well as admiralty from civil actions. He then returned to the regulation of appellate jurisdiction:

> It is observed, that a writ of error is a process more limited in its effects than an appeal: but whatever may be the operation, if an appellate jurisdiction can only be exercised by this court conformably to such regulations as are made by the Congress, and if Congress has prescribed a writ of error, and no other mode, by which it can be exercised, still, I say, we are bound to pursue that mode, and can neither make, nor adopt another. The law may, indeed, be improper and inconvenient; but it is of more importance, for a judicial determination, to ascertain what the law is, than to speculate upon what it ought to be.[144]

Chief Justice Ellsworth's experience with the Federal Convention of 1787, the Connecticut Ratifying Convention, and the First Congress, in which he apparently authored the Judiciary Act of 1789, led him to conclude that the exceptions and regulations clause clearly extends congressional control to the question of appellate review of facts, and perhaps generally to the regulation of the Court's procedure. In *Wiscart*, however, the question was not one of jurisdiction to hear and determine the case, or to hear and determine a constitutional claim; rather, the issue was the extent to which the record may be brought up to redetermine factual background. Insofar as *Wiscart* involved a question of congressional regulation of the Court's process, the Chief Justice's remarks might appear to be *ex cathedra*; however, as *Wiscart* did not involve the question of the Court's jurisdiction, the Chief Justice was issuing mere dicta about jurisdiction.

Another important Supreme Court case of the era concerning the original jurisdiction of the inferior federal courts contains useful statements about Supreme Court jurisdiction. *Durousseau v. United States*[145] arose on a question of the scope of the jurisdiction of the District Court for New Orleans. That court had been given the same jurisdiction as the District Court for Kentucky under Section 10 of the Judiciary Act of 1789, which also provided that the District Court for Kentucky had circuit court jurisdiction. The questions before the Court were whether the district court had jurisdiction and, if so, what methods of review were available for decisions of that court. Marshall

143. 3 U.S. (3 Dall.) at 327 (Ellsworth, C.J. (C, Conn., 1st Cong.)).
144. *Id.* at 328.
145. 10 U.S. (6 Cranch) 307 (1810).

accepted the notion of the constitutional jurisdiction of the Supreme Court, but then suggested that the affirmative statutory recitation of the Court's jurisdiction worked a negative implication of exception of all other jurisdiction, even though other jurisdiction was enumerated by the Constitution.[146] Later in the opinion, however, Chief Justice Marshall indicated that this would be an argument of convenience, and reached the opposite conclusion in attempting to determine the law controlling the jurisdiction of the lower federal courts, and in particular the jurisdiction of the court below:

> It would be difficult to conceive an intention in the legislature to discriminate between judgments rendered by the district court of Kentucky, while exercising the powers of a district court, and those rendered by the same court while exercising circuit powers, when it is demonstrated that the legislature makes no distinction

146. "It is contended that the words of the constitution vest an appellate jurisdiction in this court, which extends to every case not excepted by congress; and that if the court had been created without an express definition or limitation of its powers, a full and complete appellate jurisdiction would have vested in it, which must have been exercised in all cases whatever.

"The force of this argument is perceived and admitted. Had the judicial act created the supreme court, without defining or limiting its jurisdiction, it must have been considered as possessing all the jurisdiction which the constitution assigns to it. The legislature would have exercised the power it possessed of creating a supreme court as ordained by the constitution; and, in omitting to exercise the right of excepting from its constitutional powers, would have necessarily left those powers undiminished. The appellate powers of this court are not given by the judicial act. They are given by the constitution. But they are limited and regulated by the judicial act, and by such other acts as have been passed on the subject.

"When the first legislature of the Union proceeded to carry the third article of the constitution into effect, they must be understood as intending to execute the power they possessed of making exceptions to the appellate jurisdiction of the supreme court. They have not, indeed, made these exceptions in express terms. They have not declared that the appellate power of the court shall not extend to certain cases; but they have described affirmatively its jurisdiction, and this affirmative description has been understood to imply a negative on the exercise of such appellate power as is not comprehended within it.

"The spirit as well as the letter of a statute must be respected, and where the whole context of the law demonstrates a particular intent in the legislature to effect a certain object, some degree of implication may be called in to aid that intent.

"It is upon this principle that the court implies a legislative exception from its constitutional appellate power in the legislative affirmative description of those powers.

"Thus, a writ of error lies to the judgment of a circuit court, where the matter in controversy exceeds the value of 2,000 dollars. There is no express declaration that it will not lie where the matter in controversy shall be of less value. But the court considers this affirmative description as manifesting the intent of the legislature to except from its appellate jurisdiction all cases decided in the circuits where the matter in controversy is of less value, and implies negative words.

"This restriction, however, being implied by the court, and that implication being founded on the manifest intent of the legislature, can be made only where that manifest intent appears. It ought not to be made for the purpose of defeating the intent of the legislature." 10 U.S. (6 Cranch) at 313-15 (Marshall, C.J. (Va., 1st Cong.)).

> in the cases from their nature and character. Causes of which the district courts have exclusive original jurisdiction are carried into the circuit courts, and then become the objects of the appellate jurisdiction of this court. It would be strange if, in a case where the powers of the two courts are united in one court, from whose judgment an appeal lies, causes, of which the district courts have exclusive original jurisdiction, should be excepted from the operation of the appellate power. It would require plain words to establish this construction.[147]

Chief Justice Marshall went on to pose the question in an argumentative, if not rhetorical, form, but in doing so he undercut the value of his original statement and introduced the foundation of one of the more prominent contemporary theories on the power of Congress under the exceptions and regulations clause:

> [C]an it be conceived to have been the intention of the legislature to except, from the appellate jurisdiction of the supreme court, all the causes decided in the western country, except those decided in Kentucky? Can such an intention be thought possible? Ought it to be inferred from ambiguous phrases?
>
> The constitution here becomes all important. The constitution and the laws are to be construed together. It is to be recollected that the appellate powers of the supreme court are defined in the constitution, subject to such exceptions as congress may make. Congress has not expressly made any exceptions; but they are implied from the intent manifested by the affirmative description of its powers. It would be repugnant to every principle of sound construction, to imply an exception against the intent.
>
> This question does not rest on the same principles as if there had been an express exception to the jurisdiction of this court, and its power, in this case, was to be implied from the intent of the legislature. The exception is to be implied from the intent, and there is, consequently, a much more liberal operation to be given to the words, by which the courts of the western country have been created.
>
> It is believed to be the true intent of the legislature to place those courts precisely on the footing of the court of Kentucky, in every respect, and to subject their judgments, in the same manner, to the revision of the supreme court. Otherwise the court of Orleans would, in fact, be a supreme court. It would possess greater and less restricted powers than the court of Kentucky, which is, in terms, an inferior court.[148]

In order to understand Chief Justice Marshall's reasoning fully, it must be remembered that he was a member of the House of Representatives that passed the Judiciary Act of 1789, and therefore approached the

147. *Id.* at 315-16.
148. *Id.* at 317-18.

Act with noticeable prejudice. Since the Court ultimately accepted jurisdiction in the case, however, Chief Justice Marshall's remarks on exceptions from the Court's jurisdiction are somewhat beside the point.

Implication of an affirmative power has been accepted on a number of occasions to justify the exercise of that power, but implication of a negative power or restriction has neither been so widely accepted nor based on so little precedent.[149] Chief Justice Marshall cited neither congressional nor judicial precedent in *Durousseau*. In a conflict between express constitutional language and its negative implication, the latter may not be relied upon for the destruction of the former. Thus, Chief Justice Marshall's conclusion that an implied exception to jurisdiction is to be found from the affirmative statutory enumeration of jurisdiction does not necessarily follow from the affirmative jurisdiction that he accepts under the Constitution and from the specification of statutory jurisdiction. In any event, the question of exception from the Court's jurisdiction was no more before Chief Justice Marshall in *Durousseau* than it was before Chief Justice Ellsworth in *Wiscart*. The question in *Durousseau* rested on jurisdiction of an inferior (and perhaps territorial) court and the consequences flowing from the determi-

149. The most obvious example of implication of affirmative power lies in the necessary and proper clause. U.S. CONST. art. I, § 8, ¶ 18. The elasticity of the clause is illustrated in Chief Justice Marshall's classic formula: "Let the end be legitimate, let it be within the scope of the constitution, and all means which are appropriate, which are plainly adopted to that end, which are not prohibited, but consist with the letter and spirit of the constitution, are constitutional." McCulloch v. Maryland, 17 U.S. (4 Wheat.) 316, 421 (1819). The Constitution also provides substantial bases for inherent powers in each of the branches of the government, for example, the power of Congress to investigate, Eastland v. United States Servicemen's Fund, 421 U.S. 491, 503-07 (1975); executive privilege, United States v. Nixon, 418 U.S 683, 703-13 (1974); and the inherent power of the courts to admit and disbar attorneys, *Ex parte* Garland, 71 U.S. (4 Wall.) 333, 378-79 (1867). Negative power, or prohibition, is conversely more narrowly construed. For example, the power of national supremacy has received substantial elucidation over the years, but, as Justice Black observed, no single standard has controlled review under this power to negative: "There is not—and from the very nature of the problem there cannot be—any rigid formula or rule which can be used as a universal pattern to determine the meaning and purpose of every act of Congress. This Court, in considering the validity of state laws in the lights of treaties or federal laws touching the same subject, has made use of the following expressions: conflicting; contrary to; occupying the field; repugnance; difference; irreconcilability; inconsistency; violation; curtailment; and interference. . . . Our primary function is to determine whether, under the circumstances of this particular case, [a particular] law stands as an obstacle to the accomplishment and execution of the full purposes and objectives of Congress." Hines v. Davidowitz, 312 U.S. 52, 67 (1941). Whatever the verbiage, the ultimate test is simply stated: "The principle to be derived from our decisions is that federal regulation of a field of commerce should not be deemed preemptive of state regulatory power in the absence of persuasive reasons—either that the nature of the regulated subject matter permits no other conclusion, or that the Congress has unmistakably so ordained." Florida Lime & Avocado Growers, Inc. v. Paul, 373 U.S. 132, 142 (1963).

nation of the inferior jurisdiction.[150]

In neither case was the Court faced with an inexorable conflict between its constitutional or statutory jurisdiction to hear cases arising under the Constitution and an express exception from that jurisdiction by the Congress; yet two conclusions can be drawn from *Wiscart* and *Durousseau*. First, Congress had clearly *regulated* the process of the Court, both as a statutory matter and in amendment to the Constitution. Congress had also regulated the structure and functions of the inferior federal courts. Second, Congress did not create an *exception* to jurisdiction to hear cases arising under the Constitution. Language in *Wiscart* and *Durousseau* to the contrary is mere dicta. It is possible that statutory jurisdictional requirements may have deterred counsel from presenting the Court with an appeal or writ of error that, though arguably within the constitutional framework, clearly fell outside the statutory framework. It is also possible that counsel may have been deterred from presenting the Court with an implied exception from the Court's jurisdiction. Those possibilities, however, do not show that the Congress had the power to except such cases; rather, they merely confirm that counsel failed to raise the arguments.[151]

In summary, the actions of Congress must be noted for what Congress did *not* do during the formative period. On numerous occasions, the exercise of judicial review resulted in calls to repeal the Court's jurisdiction or to limit it in a prescribed manner, but none of these

150. The disposition of the case on the matter of inferior court jurisdiction, while it has obvious implications for the Court's jurisdiction, is quite independent from the latter question. True, an appellate court cannot be appellate without an inferior trial court, but at the same time, lack of jurisdiction in the inferior court goes only to the capacity to bring the suit below. Many of the decisions during the formative period that raise this question involve questions of inferior court jurisdiction, particuarly questions concerning common and statutory law. *See, e.g.*, Sheldon v. Sill, 8 U.S. (49 How.) 441 (1850) (diversity); Barry v. Mercein, 5 U.S. (46 How.) 103 (1847) (pleading jurisdictional amount in *habeas corpus*); Turner v. Bank of North America, 4 U.S (4 Dall.) 8 (1799) (remarks from oral argument noted in margin).

151. Another Supreme Court case, Cohens v. Virginia, 19 U.S. (6 Wheat.) 264 (1821), by answering the question of the source of the Court's jurisdiction could have also answered the underlying questions concerning the exceptions and regulations clause. The dispute in *Cohens* was whether a civil writ of error had been properly exercised to review Cohens' criminal conviction before a state court. While § 25 of the Judiciary Act of 1789 provided for the denial of any claim under the Constitution to be reviewed by writ of error (presumably the case in *Cohens*), Chief Justice Marshall found the writ to apply only in civil cases. Counsel for Virginia appears to have been instructed only to argue jurisdiction of the Court, but there seems to be no record of jurisdictional argument on this point. Even so, this might be argued to be a procedural jurisdiction rather than a substantive jurisdiction. *See* P. Bator, P. Mishkin, D. Shapiro and H. Wechsler, Hart & Wechsler's The Federal Courts and the Federal System 455-56 n.1 (1973).

measures was enacted. This most volatile period did not lead to the establishment of precedent for congressional exertion of power over the Court's jurisdiction to hear cases arising under the Constitution.[152] Thus, the law and politics of the formative era of American constitutional law do not provide answers to the central question of the power of Congress to make exceptions from the jurisdiction of the Court in general, and to make exceptions from jurisdiction to hear cases arising under the Constitution in particular. Despite numerous *dicta* of the Court and arguments propounded in Congress during that period, congressional authority, if it exists, was neither exercised nor challenged. In essence, whatever the basis and range of the Court's jurisdiction, Congress enacted no legislation to except affirmatively cases arising under the Constitution (or for that matter, any class of cases), and accordingly, the Court was never placed in the position of determining the validity of such an exception.

B. The Great Insurrection and Its Aftermath

As the late ante-bellum period drew to a close, the relative calm between Congress and the Court was shattered by the Court's exercise of judicial review in *Dred Scott v. Sandford*.[153] While there were initially calls for reprisal against the Court, little action was taken; however, but the course was charted toward the Great Insurrection.[154] A decade later, with the Civil War fresh within memory, the Court decided that the President could not suspend the civil courts and detain a civilian before a military tribunal outside the actual theater of war.[155] That decision, in turn, led to concern that the Court might overturn the

152. There were calls for the repeal of § 25 of the Judiciary Act of 1789 almost immediately after its enactment and again in 1831, but none succeeded; nor did Congress change the Court's statutory operation in any major way. Congress did, however, make an unsuccessful attempt to avoid federalist developments like *Marbury v. Madison*. F. FRANKFURTER & J. LANDIS, *supra* note 56, at 4-55; 1 C. WARREN, *supra* note 54, at 10-11; 2 *id*. at 12, 16, 123, 196-201. *See generally* 1 HOLMES DEVISE, *supra* note 48; 2 G. HASKINS & H. JOHNSON, THE OLIVER WENDELL HOLMES DEVISE, HISTORY OF THE SUPREME COURT OF THE UNITED STATES—FOUNDATIONS OF POWER: JOHN MARSHALL, 1801-1815 (1981) [hereinafter cited as 2 HOLMES DEVISE]. *See also* 3 C. WARREN, *supra* note 54, at 55, 57.

153. 60 U.S. (19 How.) 393 (1856) (declaring the prohibition of slavery in the Missouri territory unconstitutional; subsequently vitiated by § 1 of the 14th Amendment).

154. 5 C. SWISHER, HISTORY OF THE SUPREME COURT OF THE UNITED STATES—THE TANEY PERIOD, 1836-1864, 631-52 (1974) [hereinafter cited as 5 HOLMES DEVISE]; 2 C. WARREN, *supra* note 54.

155. *Ex parte* Milligan, 4 U.S. (71 Wall.) 2 (1866). *See* 6 HOLMES DEVISE, HISTORY OF THE SUPREME COURT OF THE UNITED STATES—RECONSTRUCTION AND REUNION, 1864-1888 (pt. 1), 182-252 (C. Fairman ed. 1971) [hereinafter cited as 6 HOLMES DEVISE (pt. 1)]; 3 C. WARREN, *supra* note 54, 140-76.

convictions of those who had conspired to kill President Lincoln. Since four of those individuals had been executed, such an action would have effectively branded the executions as murder.[156] Against the backdrop of this newly heightened political tension, the Court was faced with the petition of a violently anti-Reconstruction Vicksburg editor named McCardle.

1. Ex parte McCardle (I & II)

Congress set the stage for *Ex parte McCardle (I & II)*[157] in February, 1867, by expanding the *habeas corpus* jurisdiction of the inferior federal courts to better protect newly freed slaves and by providing a right of appeal to the Supreme Court.[158] In March, 1867, Congress also established military districts for the administration of ten states and authorized military trials to enforce Reconstruction.[159] McCardle was charged before such a military tribunal after publishing editorials opposing—indeed encouraging defiance of—the Reconstruction administration. Late in 1867, McCardle won his bonded release in circuit court from military custody under the *habeas corpus* provisions of the 1867 Act; McCardle then took advantage of the right under the Act to appeal to the Supreme Court.

Thus, McCardle was poised to challenge military Reconstruction by invoking the provisions of one of its sister acts. The government—through counsel Lyman Trumbull—moved to dismiss the appeal for want of jurisdiction, citing a number of technical grounds under the 1867 Act. The Court rejected these contentions and, on February 17, 1868 (*McCardle I*), specifically declared its jurisdiction to hear the appeal under the provisions of the Act.[160] Oral argument on the merits was commenced on March 2, 1868. Chief Justice Chase was called to the Senate chamber to preside over the impeachment trial of President Johnson on March 5th, while oral argument in *McCradle* was not concluded until March 9th.[161] Three days later, with *McCardle sub judice*,

156. 6 HOLMES DEVISE (pt. 1), *supra* note 155, at 237-39, 488-92; 3 C. WARREN, *supra* note 54, at 165-66. A petition for *habeas corpus* was filed in 1869, and oral argument appears to have been heard, but the case was mooted by President Johnson's pardon of March 1, 1869.

157. 73 U.S. (6 Wall.) 318 (1867) (*McCardle I*); 74 U.S. (7 Wall.) 506 (1868) (*McCardle II*).

158. Act of Feb. 5, 1867, ch. 28, 14 Stat. 385.

159. Act of Mar. 2, 1867, ch. 153, 14 Stat. 428.

160. 73 U.S. (6 Wall.) 318 (1867).

161. CONG. GLOBE, 40th Cong., 2d Sess. 1644 (1868) (letter from Chief Justice Chase on proceedings and oath of senators); *id.* at 1696 (Chief Justice Chase takes chair of Court of

the House and Senate—under the leadership of Senator Lyman Trumbull—adopted the Repealer Act, providing, in pertinent part,

> That so much of the act approved February [5, 1867] . . . as authorizes an appeal from the judgment of the circuit court to the Supreme Court of the United States, or the exercise of any such jurisdiction by said Supreme Court on appeals which have been or may hereafter be taken, be, and the same is, hereby repealed.[162]

President Johnson vetoed this Act, despite his own perilous condition before the Senate, in a ringing defense of the Court, on March 25th.[163] The veto was summarily overridden on March 27th.[164]

The Court met on March 30th at 11:00 a.m., but Chief Justice Chase was due in the Senate to preside at the opening argument of the trial of impeachment at 12:30 p.m. Justice Nelson presided after the Chief Justice's departure, and the suggestion he made to counsel in another case like McCardle's was prescient: It might be better to plead under section 14 of the Judiciary Act of 1789.[165] The Court did not opt to make *McCardle II* a race with Congress to a decision; rather, they suggested the need for argument on the effect of the Repealer Act.[166] The Court adjourned on April 6th, averting for the time any exacerbation of the situation, leaving McCardle to his bail and the Chief Justice to the trial of impeachment.[167]

This review of history may appear stark, but further detail only darkens the shadows of the politics of the time. Before turning to the decision in *McCardle II*, one ever-controlling fact must be reiterated: The law of the case from *McCardle I* was that the Court had jurisdiction under the Act of February 5, 1867, to hear an appeal of the cause.[168]

Impeachment). *See also* 6 HOLMES DEVISE (pt. 1), *supra* note 155, at 455, 459; 3 C. WARREN, *supra* note 54, at 165.

162. *See* text of Act of Mar. 27, 1868, ch. 34, § 2, 15 Stat. 44, *passed* CONG. GLOBE, 40th Cong., 2d Sess. 2062 (1868).

163. CONG. GLOBE, 40th Cong., 2d Sess. 2165 (1868).

164. Act of Mar. 27, 1868, ch. 34, 15 Stat. 44. The trial of impeachment of Andrew Johnson is set out in CONG. GLOBE, 40th Cong., 2d Sess. (Supp. 1868). 6 HOLMES DEVISE (pt. 1), *supra* note 155, at 458-60.

165. Section 14 of the Judiciary Act of 1789 provides for a writ of *habeas corpus* to be taken in challenging the legality of confinement or the jurisdiction of the tribunal ordering confinement. 6 HOLMES DEVISE (pt. 1), *supra* note 155, at 472-78.

166. 6 HOLMES DEVISE (pt. 1), *supra* note 155, at 472-78. There is some suggestion that the Court could not have decided the case within this short a time period had they attempted to do so, for the Court was continuing to sit six days each week.

167. *Id.*

168. 73 U.S. (6 Wall.) at 324. The decision that the Court had jurisdiction under the Act of 1867 is critical because of the historical inference that the further actions of Lyman Trum-

The Court decided *McCardle II* on April 12, 1869, over a year after the political intrigue generated by the Repealer Act and impeachment proceedings, making the decision almost anticlimactic. Chief Justice Chase began by accepting two principles previously discussed: (1) the origin of jurisdiction in the Constitution; and (2) Chief Justice Marshall's negative inference from the statutory enumeration.[169] From these premises, Chief Justice Chase stated and answered the question before the Court:

> The exception to appellate jurisdiction in the case before us, however, is not an inference from the affirmation of other appellate jurisdiction. It is made in terms. The provision of the Act of 1867, affirming the appellate jurisdiction of this court in cases of *habeas corpus* is expressly repealed. It is hardly possible to imagine a plainer instance of positive exception.
>
> We are not at liberty to inquire into the motives of the legislature. We can only examine into its power under the Constitution; and the power to make exceptions to the appellate jurisdiction of this court is given by express words.
>
> What, then, is the effect of the repealing act upon the case before us? We cannot doubt as to this. Without jurisdiction the court cannot proceed at all in any cause. Jurisdiction is power to declare the law, and when it ceases to exist, the only function remaining to the court is that of announcing the fact and dismissing the cause. And this is not less clear upon authority than upon principle.[170]

Chief Justice Chase dismissed several state authorities in the next paragraph as not on point, and went on to affirm the nonexistence of acts after their repeal except as to transactions previously concluded. The Chief Justice then returned to the effect of the Repealer Act on the Court's jurisdiction:

> It is quite clear, therefore, that this court cannot proceed to pronounce judgment in this case, for it has no longer jurisdiction of the appeal; and judicial duty is not less fitly performed by declining ungranted jurisdiction than in exercising firmly that which the Constitution and the laws confer.
>
> Counsel seem to have supposed, if effect be given to the repealing Act in question, that the whole appellate power of the court, in cases of habeas corpus, is denied. But this is in error. The Act of 1868 does not except from that jurisdiction any cases but appeals from Circuit Courts under the Act of 1867. It does

bull, as Senator, were specifically designed to derogate that decision by removing the jurisdictional act. Indeed, the Repealer Act reads more like a judicial order than legislation.

169. *See* notes 146-50 *supra*.

170. 74 U.S. (7 Wall.) at 513-14.

not affect the jurisdiction which was previously exercised.[171]

At this point, the Court reached its conclusion, with no dissent: "The appeal of the petitioner in this case must be dismissed for want of jurisdiction."[172]

Three critical questions must be answered about *McCardle II*: (1) whether or not the Court had jurisdiction as pleaded; (2) whether or not the Repealer Act was an exception from cases arising under the Constitution or a regulation of the procedure for review; and (3) whether or not an exception or regulation can be made applicable to a case *sub judice*.

The question before the Court in *McCardle II* was one of jurisdiction over the particular case. McCardle based his case on the Act of February 5, 1867, and prosecuted it throughout under the aegis of the Act. His plea to the Court appears to harbor no alternative source of jurisdiction, and the jurisdictional attack in *McCardle I* was based solely on that Act.[173] Thus, when the Court held that it had jurisdiction under the Act of February 5, 1867, it did more than affirm its power under that Act—it also limited its jurisdiction to that conferred by the Act. The intimation of "jurisdiction previously exercised" in *McCardle II* and Justice Nelson's advice to counsel in another case[174] suggest an alternative source of jurisdiction, namely, section 14 of the Judiciary Act of 1789, which provides that the writ of *habeas corpus* may be invoked to challenge the legality of confinement or the jurisdiction of the tribunal ordering confinement.[175] Within a year, the Court answered these intimations, in the less celebrated but equally important case of *Ex parte Yerger*,[176] by declaring that section 14 was unimpaired by the Repealer Act and remained an appropriate method of invoking

171. *Id.* at 515.

172. *Id.*

173. 73 U.S. (6 Wall.) at 324. The government's motion to dismiss set up the law of the case; the Court implemented that law with a narrow holding. *See* Brief to Resist Motion for Judgment (undated), *McCardle II*, 74 U.S. (7 Wall.) 506, at 511-12 (1868).

174. *See* note 165 and accompanying text *supra*.

175. Section 14 of the Judiciary Act of 1789 provides:

"*And be it further enacted*, that all the before-mentioned courts of the United States, shall have power to issue writs of *scire facias*, *habeas corpus*, and all other writs not specially provided for by statute, which may be necessary for the exercise of their respective jurisdictions, and agreeable to the principles and usages of law. And that either of the justices of the district courts, shall have power to grant writs of *habeas corpus* for the purpose of an inquiry into the cause of commitment.—*Provided*, that writs of *habeas corpus* shall in no case extend to prisoners in gaol, unless where they are in custody, under or by colour of the authority of the United States, or are committed for trial before some court of the same, or are necessary to be brought into court to testify." Judiciary Act of 1789, ch. 20, § 14, 1 Stat. 73.

176. 75 U.S. (8 Wall.) 85 (1868).

the Court's jurisdiction. *Yerger* stands for the narrow proposition that the repeal of the more convenient appeal did not impair the right to petition for the more complex and narrow writ of *habeas corpus*. In short, McCardle's reliance on the right of appeal, to the exclusion of the alternative plea for a writ of *habeas corpus*, was the fatal error in *McCardle I* that controlled the decision of *McCardle II*. Dismissal in *McCardle II* was for want of jurisdiction over a particular party who pleaded under a particular statute.[177] Therefore, the conclusion that the Court had no jurisdiction must be read narrowly and technically, as the Court appears to have read it subsequently. The Court lacked jurisdiction only over the appeal taken, not necessarily over any alternative petition that could have been filed.

177. In *A Critical Guide to* Ex parte McCardle, Professor Van Alstyne asks: "Given this consideration, should not the Court have proceeded to reach the merits [in *McCardle II*] acknowledging that the technical basis on which appeal had been perfected from the circuit court had been withdrawn by Congress, but declining to reject the case in view of the existing alternative basis for retaining jurisdiction as confirmed by section 14 of the Judiciary Act of 1789? In favor of this result it might be observed that the Supreme Court has generally not been overly technical in holding parties to the particular source of appellate jurisdiction they have invoked." Van Alstyne, *supra* note 20, at 247. He goes on to conclude that the appropriate criticism of the Court is that it "simply declined, under the circumstances, to proceed *sua sponte* on a different jurisdictional basis than that previously relied upon." *Id.* at 254.

The only rebuttal to Van Alstyne's remark that the Court has not been "overly technical" about jurisdiction, is that the Court was in fact quite technical. At the time of *McCardle II*, the perils of erroneous common law pleading were still firmly entrenched. Common law pleadings would not become comatose for another 70 years, and they are not completely lifeless even today. The distinctions between detinue, replevin, and assumpsit were hardly dead in contract law of 1969, nor were the distinctions between appeal and writ of error lost. *See* O. HOLMES, THE COMMON LAW (1881). Professor Van Alstyne cites contemporary authority (28 U.S.C. § 2103 (1976)), for the proposition that the Court may consider appeals improvidently taken as petitions for writs of certiorari. However, this authority was not added until the famous Judge's Bill of 1925. Judicial Code of 1911, § 237(c), *amended by* Act of Feb. 13, 1925, ch. 229, 43 Stat. 936, 937, 938. Even this did not entirely do away with the problem of prejudicial pleadings between the statutory appeal and the common law writs of certiorari or error. *See* F. FRANKFURTER & J. LANDIS, *supra* note 56, at 285 n.114. It was not until Erie R.R. Co. v. Tompkins, 304 U.S. 64 (1938), and the modern merger of law and equity in the Federal Rules of Civil Procedure, 308 U.S. 645-766 (effective Sept. 16, 1938), that the decline of common law pleading in the federal courts became irreversible. In some states today, the problem of prejudicial pleading still exists.

Thus, the criticism that Van Alstyne feels is appropriate does not meet its mark; the Court could not consistently have accepted jurisdiction other than as had been pleaded. The ascendency of the radical Reconstruction Congress and the trial of impeachment being held just steps away, while certainly no justification for shirking judicial duty, may have reinforced the Court's resolve not to depart from an established practice. Nor can the result be said to have been unjust to the petitioner. He was then on bail, and the dismissal did not prejudice his capacity to file the suggested *habeas corpus* petition, nor did it recommit him to the custody of military authority.

The answer to the second question has already been suggested. Even after the Repealer Act had become law, there remained alternative jurisdiction by way of petition for a writ of *habeas corpus*,[178] and Congress is presumed to have been fully aware of that legal fact. The language of the Repealer Act itself—"so much of the Act" under which the appeal was taken—was narrowly and precisely drawn by the government's counsel to fit the appeal of *McCardle*, an appeal "which ha[s] been or may hereafter be taken."[179] Thus, *McCardle II* cannot be fairly judged to be an *exception* to the Court's jurisdiction; rather, it must be regarded as a *regulation* of the Court's process.

Finally, the question of legislative timing of the change in the regulation of the Court's process must be considered. The Court's disposition of *McCardle II*, in which it respected a statutory change in the fabric of the law while an affected case was *sub judice*, emphatically stands for the proposition that there is nothing sacred about the intonation that the "case is submitted" at the close of oral argument. If nothing else, *McCardle II* settles the power of Congress to alter the premises of a case right up to the time the case is decided.

Thus, for all that *McCardle II* is thought to settle, it actually settles very little. Historically, to paraphrase Professor Hart's "Dialogue," *McCardle II* has been read for all that it *might* be worth rather than for the least that it *must* be worth.[180] Under the concept of *ratio decidendi*, the least that it must be worth is the narrow rule of the case discussed above.

2. *United States v. Klein*

In determining the scope of exceptions that Congress may make in the Court's appellate jurisdiction, *McCardle II* has limited value and is perhaps overshadowed by *United States v. Klein*.[181] *Klein* is the product of a long and complex legal travail over the effect of presidential pardons on the right to the return of property confiscated during the Great Insurrection.[182] In 1870, Congress responded to the travail by

178. *See* note 177 *supra*.

179. *See* text accompanying note 162 *supra*.

180. Hart, *supra* note 20, at 1364-65.

181. 80 U.S. (13 Wall.) 128 (1871). Greater background on the *Klein* case can be found in 6 HOLMES DEVISE (pt. 1), *supra* note 155, at 840-48.

182. In 1862, Congress had authorized confiscation of the property of all persons in rebellion. Act of July 17, 1862, ch. xx, § 5, 12 Stat. 589. The act also "authorized" the President to issue pardons (an unnecessary action in light of the plenary authority of article II, § 2, clause 1, of the Constitution). In *Ex parte* Garland, 71 U.S. (4 Wall.) 333, 380 (1867), the Court held that a presidential pardon had the effect of not only relieving the punishment for an offense, but obliterating the guilt as well, "so that in the eye of the law the offender is

enacting the "Drake proviso," which provided that (1) evidence of a pardon was not admissible in the Court of Claims to support any claim against the United States; (2) a recitation in a pardon that the claimant had taken part in the insurrection was to be treated as conclusive proof of disloyalty, and thus bar the return of confiscated property; (3) if already in evidence, a pardon was not to be considered by the Court of Claims or by the Supreme Court, except to prove disloyalty; and (4) the Court of Claims and the Supreme Court were to dismiss any pending claims based on such a pardon *for want of jurisdiction*.[183] The Reconstruction Congress apparently considered the decision in *McCardle II* to be a victory, for the Drake proviso had a far broader effect. On December 22, 1870, the Court of Claims held that Wilson, Klein's decedent, had been absolved of any offenses or disloyalties by the amnesty oath he had executed. The holding conformed with previous Supreme Court interpretations but was contrary to the express requirements of the Drake proviso.[184]

The Court was thus caught on the horns of a dilemma, with the pardoning power on one hand and what facially appears to be an exception on the other. While the opinion of the Court in *Klein* leaves much to be desired, its path is clear. After the incantation of the familiar dicta regarding congressional power over inferior court jurisdiction and the Supreme Court's appellate jurisdiction, Chief Justice Chase addressed his Scylla and Charybdis: "But the language of the proviso shows plainly that it does not intend to withhold appellate jurisdiction except as a means to an end. Its great and controlling purpose is to deny to pardons granted by the President the effect which this court had adjudged them to have."[185] Chief Justice Chase went on to outline the requirements of the Drake proviso, and continued:

> It seems to us that this is not an exercise of the acknowledged power of Congress to make exceptions and prescribe regulations to the appellate power.
>
> The court is required to ascertain the existence of certain facts and thereupon to declare that its jurisdiction on appeal has ceased, by dismissing the bill. What is this but to prescribe a rule for the decision of a cause in a particular way? In the case before

as innocent as if he had never committed the offence." Given that the President's pardons had all provided for the restoration of confiscated property, the Court, in United States v. Padelford, 76 U.S. (9 Wall.) 531 (1870), held that a claimant under such a pardon was entitled to his property. Congress intervened with the "Drake proviso," which was attached to an appropriation authorization statute.

183. Act of July 12, 1870, ch. 251, 16 Stat. 235.

184. 4 Ct. Cl. 559 (1870).

185. 80 U.S. (13 Wall.) at 145.

> us, the Court of Claims has rendered judgment for the claimant and an appeal has been taken to this court. We are directed to dismiss the appeal, if we find that the judgment must be affirmed, because of a pardon granted to the intestate of the claimants. Can we do so without allowing one party to the controversy to decide it in its own favor? Can we do so without allowing that the legislature may prescribe rules of decision to the Judicial Department of the government in cases pending before it?[186]

Chief Justice Chase was posing rhetorical questions in light of the conclusion reached by the Court. After distinguishing cases of congressional alteration of decisions where the power to alter the effect of the decision was otherwise within its province, the Court concluded, "We must think that Congress has inadvertently passed the limit which separates the legislative from the judicial power."[187] Were this the only question before the Court, the result would make it clear that Congress could not except cases arising under the Constitution in which the government was the party defendant and the statutory exception conclusively favored the government's litigative position. However, the Drake proviso also deprived the President's pardon of efficacy, so that another conclusion could be independently reached: "The rule prescribed is also liable to just exception as impairing the effect of a pardon, and thus infringing the constitutional power of the Executive."[188] Thus, *Klein* cannot be said to stand for the proposition that Congress cannot except cases from the jurisdiction of the Court because the basis for the exception was held substantively invalid. Moreover, the effect of the exception was to impose a particular rule of decision that was conclusive in the government's favor. Since the Court did not treat these issues as separable, even though they would appear to be separable, there is no clear *ratio decidendi* for *Klein*.

Just as *McCardle II* proved too little, *Klein* may have proved too much. What would otherwise have been a clear exception from the Court's jurisdiction was clouded by the manner of the exception's implementation—a biased rule of decision. *Klein*, however, is instructive of how cases arising under the Constitution will be viewed. These cases will inexorably pit a right or power under the Constitution against the power of Congress under the exceptions and regulations clause. In *Klein*, the right conferred by a presidential pardon was raised against the Reconstruction Congress' attempt to deny the Court's jurisdiction to effectuate that pardon. This clear conflict is clouded by the require-

186. *Id.* at 146.
187. *Id.* at 147.
188. *Id.*

ment that the Court find a state of facts and dismiss after finding that state of facts, a rule of decision that does violence to the doctrine of separation of powers. Thus, *Klein* does not stand for the proposition that there are limits on the power of Congress to make exceptions, but for the broader proposition that Congress may not violate the principles of separation of powers to accomplish a forbidden act by casting legislation in terms of the Court's jurisdiction.[189]

The attention of Congress and the Court slowly turned away from the constitutional fencing that left both weary and neither victorious. The question of the scope of congressional authority to make exceptions from the Supreme Court's appellate jurisdiction remained in flux.[190] In its haste to rein the Court, the Reconstruction Congress may politically have succeeded, but legally have failed. *McCardle II* stands for the proposition that Congress, by repealing a statute, may reach into the Court's conference to excise a case that is dependent on that statute. *Yerger* stands for the proposition that Congress must leave no residuum of jurisdictions if it is ever to make an exception that will be free of a litigable alternative. *Klein* stands for the proposition that the Congress may not direct decisional results in the effectuation of its powers over the jurisdiction of the Court. Where the limits imposed by statute dispose of the merits of the case, *Klein* clearly indicates that the statute cannot stand. Even these holdings, however, were subject to further elucidation in the following century. The debate since that time has been relatively tame, and the acts of Congress that set *McCardle*, *Yerger*, and *Klein* in motion precipitated the last truly critical bouts of constitutional sparring.

C. The Developing Substantive Regulation of the Federal Courts

For the last century, the Court has undergone a series of philosophical and personal clashes, but the fundamental power of the Court itself has not again been raised. Prior to the outset of the contemporary debates, two formidable periods of conflict took place: (1) the clash between substantive due process and the progressive movement early in the twentieth century; and (2) Franklin Roosevelt's Court-packing plan. Otherwise, little effort has been made to curb the Supreme Court or to alter its power substantially. The Court, for its part, has continued to comment only in the vein of dicta.

189. *Id.*

190. Further dicta deferential to Congress can be found in The Francis Wright, 105 U.S. 381 (1881); Daniels v. Railroad Co., 3 U.S (70 Wall.) 250 (1865).

The progressive era of the early twentieth century led to a variety of social legislation, much of which, to the disgruntlement of its proponents, was struck down by state courts of last resort. During this period, the Supreme Court was perceived as unable to review these decisions because its statutory jurisdiction did not extend to cases in which a state court of last resort had declared a state statute unconstitutional.[191] The predicament was sharply focused when the New York Court of Appeals struck down a workmen's compensation law and the Supreme Court of Oregon upheld a similar law.[192] The end result of this conflict—over which the Supreme Court held statutory jurisdiction to review only the Oregon decision of constitutionality—was the expansion of statutory jurisdiction.[193] During this period, the recall of both judicial decisions and judges was advocated, but no action was taken.[194] With the exception of the expansion of statutory jurisdiction, the question of the Court's jurisdiction was not raised.

The more formidable attack on the Court came from Franklin D. Roosevelt and his attempt to "pack" the Court.[195] The idea of altering the size of the Court was not novel; indeed, such an idea had a history of political use.[196] Even today the Court-packing plan is not fully understood, but the substantial question of why jurisdictional exceptions, if available, were not employed instead must be asked.[197] Whatever the intentions of the architects of the Court-packing plan, the idea of excepting from the Court's jurisdiction was not raised as a congressional alternative.

Congress has passed numerous enactments restricting the jurisdiction, procedure, and available remedies of inferior federal courts over the years.[198] Alteration of the statutory mandates of Supreme Court

191. F. FRANKFURTER & J. LANDIS, *supra* note 56, at 193-96.

192. *Compare* Ives v. South Buffalo Ry. Co., 201 N.Y. 271, 294 (1911), *with* State v. Clausen, 65 Wash. 156, 195-96 (1911).

193. Act of Dec. 23, 1914, ch. 2, 38 Stat. 790.

194. *See* F. FRANKFURTER & J. LANDIS, *supra* note 56, at 169-70. Other examples of conflict are: Pollock v. Farmers' Loan & Trust Co., 157 U.S. 429, *further opinion*, 158 U.S. 429 (1895), overruled by the 16th Amendment; Hammer v. Dagenhart, 247 U.S. 251 (1918); and the still-pending proposed amendment on Child Labor. *See* J. KILLIAN, *supra* note 45, at 51-52.

195. *See* Leuchtenburg, *The Origins of Franklin D. Roosevelt's "Court-Packing Plan,"* 1966 SUP. CT. REV. 347 (P. Kurland ed. 1966).

196. *See* note 55 *supra*.

197. *Compare* Leuchtenburg, *supra* note 195, *with* R. BERGER, CONGRESS V. THE SUPREME COURT 291-92 (1969).

198. *E.g.*, Oestereich v. Selective Serv. Sys. Bd., 393 U.S. 233 (1968); South Carolina v. Katzenbach, 383 U.S. 301 (1966); Yakus v. United States 321 U.S. 414 (1944); Lockerty v. Phillips, 319 U.S. 182 (1943); Lauf v. E.G. Shinner Co., 303 U.S. 323 (1938); Military Selec-

writ jurisdiction has consisted of minor changes in wording and the addition of omnibus remedial authority.[199] Changes in Supreme Court statutory jurisdiction have only been expansive.

Congress also began investing varying amounts of adjudicatory power in "article I courts" and administrative bodies during the development of the regulatory model of government.[200] Corresponding restrictions on the scope of judicial review by article III courts also became commonplace, but a new approach to the theory arose in the dicta of the Court. The Court began to pose a new question, not one of deference to Congress, but, as Chief Justice Hughes noted, "rather a question of the appropriate maintenance of the Federal judicial power."[201] In *Crowell v. Benson* the Court intimated that the adjudication of "constitutional facts"—those facts that form the predicate of a constitutional claim—must be reviewable by an article III court.[202] This approach has not been fully tested or explicated in the context of congressional attempts to limit the power of the federal courts, but should the Court hold that an article III court review of constitutional facts is mandated, proposals that eliminate all federal court jurisdiction over a constitutional cause of action (thus delegating final adjudication

tive Serv. Act of 1967, Pub. L. No. 90-40, 81 Stat. 100; Voting Rights Act of 1965, Pub. L. No. 89-110, 79 Stat. 437; Emergency Price Control Act of 1942, ch. 26, 56 Stat. 23; Norris-LaGuardia Act, ch. 229, 47 Stat. 70 (1932).

199. The writs issued—error, certiorari, and habeas corpus—historically controlled the scope of review within the law-fact distinction, a distinction developed at common law and occasionally changed by congressional enactment. None of these enactments removed a writ in such a way as to preclude constitutional as opposed to statutory consideration.

200. We must distinguish here between administrative boards, article I courts, state courts, and district and territorial courts. Delegation of adjudicatory power to administrative bodies began in earnest with the Interstate Commerce Act in 1887. Such bodies—for example, the late Board of Tax Appeals (administrative), now the United States Tax Court (an article I court)—have long had adjudicatory powers subject to judicial review by an article III court. State courts, on the other hand, ordinarily share concurrent jurisdiction with inferior federal courts, and their decisions are subject to review by the Supreme Court. The District of Columbia and territorial courts have territorial jurisdiction that is reviewable, but which depends on the power of Congress to affirmatively legislate under special authorities of article IV, § 3, clause 2, and article I, § 3, clause 16, respectively. *See generally* Key v. Doyle, 434 U.S. 59 (1977); Palmore v. United States, 411 U.S. 389 (1973); Durousseau v. United States, 10 U.S. (6 Cranch) at 312-15.

201. Crowell v. Benson, 285 U.S. 22, 56 (1932).

202. *Id.* This approach has been further expanded in the article I courts area. In United States v. Raddatz, 447 U.S. 667 (1980), the Court upheld the use of an adjunct magistrate's fact-finding, but only if that magistrate is subject to sufficient control by an article III court. In Northern Pipeline Constr. Co. v. Marathon Pipe Line Co., 50 U.S.L.W. (U.S. June 28, 1982) (Nos. 81-150 & 81-546), the Court struck down the use of an article I judge to determine (and enter judgment on which execution could be made) state law claims pendent to a bankruptcy matter when one of the parties objected. *Marathon* is reminiscent of the badly divided decision in Glidden Co. v. Zdanok, 370 U.S. 530 (1962).

of such claims to state courts) would be constitutionally dubious on this score alone. This has not yet been the case. This approach appears to leave open the possibility that an inferior federal court might be designated to review administrative action without the possibility of review by the Supreme Court.[203]

Perhaps beginning with *Klein*, and particularly corresponding with the development of modern bureaucratic government, the Court has developed a more holistic approach to constitutional decisionmaking. More conservative dicta began to appear with regard to the exceptions and regulations clause. The elder Justice Harlan's comment in *United States v. Bitty*[204] illustrates this point while discussing congressional power over jurisdiction: "[W]hat such exceptions and regulations should be it is for Congress, in its wisdom, to establish, having of course due regard to all the provisions of the Constitution."[205] Similarly, Justice Black eventually concluded that since the Constitution, in its original form, is replete with grants of authority that may complement, converge, diverge, conflict, and even contradict, "these granted powers are always subject to the limitation that they may not be exercised in a way that violates other specific provisions of the Constitution."[206]

Dicta with respect to the Court's jurisdiction were not limited in the development of a more holistic approach. The constitutional origin of jurisdiction, while it declined as a subject of dicta, saw occasional resurgence.[207] Statements regarding the dependence of the Court on congressionally determined jurisdiction were guided by Justice Frankfurter's oft-cited dissent in *National Mutual Insurance Co. v. Tidewater Transfer Co.*:[208] "Congress need not give this Court any appellate power; it may withdraw appellate jurisdiction once conferred and it may do so even while a case is *sub judice*."[209] Justice Frankfurter appears to have stated the modern efficacy of a broad view of *McCardle II*, as apparently did the younger Justice Harlan.[210] By 1962, however, Justice Douglas, in a dissent joined by Justice Black, eschewed the *McCardle II* holding, whether broad or narrow, observing, "There is a serious question whether the *McCardle* case could command a majority

203. *But see* notes 230-35 and accompanying text *infra*.
204. 208 U.S. 393 (1908).
205. *Id.* at 399-400.
206. Williams v. Rhodes, 393 U.S. 23, 29 (1968).
207. *See, e.g.*, Plaquemines Tropical Fruit Co. v. Henderson, 170 U.S. 511 (1898).
208. 337 U.S. 582 (1949).
209. *Id.* at 655 (Frankfurter, J., dissenting).
210. Bruner v. United States, 343 U.S. 112, 117 n.8 (1952).

view today."[211] Yet again, the composition of the Court has changed, and its present view of *McCardle II* and of the power of Congress over its appellate jurisdiction is unclear.[212]

In conclusion, history illuminates no hard and fast rule, no distinct contours of power, nor does it reveal a void. Like many powers and rights under the Constitution, at this late day there remains only resort to the structure and function of the Constitution to determine the proper sphere of congressional action. Many of the cases here cited are grounded on the regulation or establishment of inferior federal courts, whatever the consequential effects these changes may have on the manner in which a cause may reach the Supreme Court. Those cases dealing directly with the Court's appellate jurisdiction have concerned congressional action that is regulatory in nature.

Neither constitutional history nor the manner in which the Constitution has been implemented by the Congress and the Court provides a basis for reaching a conclusive decision on whether Congress may except classes of cases arising under the Constitution from the appellate jurisdiction of the Supreme Court. Both the Congress and the Court have suggested that the Court is wholly dependent on Congress for its appellate jurisdiction, but Congress has never attempted to limit constitutional claims in this way. The Court, in its proper role of adjudicating only that which is properly brought before it, has not been asked the question. In short, whether founded on regulation of constitutional causes of action through exception of the jurisdictional predicate or as a response to controversial or unpopular Court decisions, the proposition of excepting cases arising under the Constitution from the Court's appellate jurisdiction is unprecedented.

IV. Legislating and Adjudicating Exceptions of Cases Arising Under the Constitution

The central question of legislating and adjudicating exceptions of cases arising under the Constitution must be answered on the basis of (1) the constitutional purpose and intent of the exceptions and regulations clause as revealed by the Federal Convention of 1787 and the

211. Glidden Co. v. Zdanok, 370 U.S. 530, 605 n.11 (1962) (Douglas, J., dissenting). *Compare* Justice Harlan's majority reliance on *McCardle* for what it did not do. *Id.* at 567-68. Justice Harlan cites *McCardle* with approval even though noting that Congress' "authority is not, of course, unlimited." *Id.* at 568. The regulations aspect may cover much more, however, and may perhaps extend to the regulation of the entire judicial power, but that question is beyond the scope of this article.

212. *See, e.g.*, United States v. Sioux Nation, 448 U.S. 371, 425, 427-34 (1980) (Rehnquist, J., dissenting).

state ratifying conventions (discussed in part II), and (2) the historical interpretations given the clause by Congress and the Court (discussed in part III). In this part, first, the affirmative theories of interpretation of the clause are reiterated. Second, assuming a legislative exception of a class of cases arising under the original Constitution, an eclectic view of the original Constitution will help to determine whether the Court is likely to strike down the exception as unconstitutional. Finally, assuming a legislative exception of a class of cases arising under a provision of the Bill of Rights or a right derived from another provision, a synergetic view of the Constitution is utilized to make a parallel determination.

A. Affirmative Interpretations of the Exceptions and Regulations Clause

Four relevant categories of affirmative interpretation and application of the exceptions and regulations clause appear to be supported by the foregoing discussion: (1) exceptions and regulations based on the law-fact distinction; (2) regulation of judicial process, such as procedure and remedies; (3) regulation of the division of jurisdiction between the Supreme Court, inferior federal courts, and the state court systems; and (4) regulation, and possibly exceptions, of statutory claims. History does *not* provide affirmative support for an interpretation of the power to except from jurisdiction to hear cases arising under the Constitution or constitutional claims.

The law-fact distinction animated much of the discussion of the exceptions and regulations clause during the construction, ratification, and implementation of the Constitution. The intention of the Framers was clearly to delegate the determination of the availability of civil jury trials and the finality of jury-found facts to the Congress, but this reliance on future determination was insufficient for the ratifiers. Thus, the First Congress, supported by the state legislatures' ratifications, constitutionalized the finality of jury-found facts on appeal and the common law right to a jury trial in controversies involving more than twenty dollars.[213] Limiting the exceptions and regulations clause to delegating the law-fact controversy to Congress has the appeal of simplicity, but simplicity merely obfuscates underlying concerns.[214]

213. U.S. CONST. amend. VII, discussed at notes 109-12 and accompanying text *supra*.

214. *See, e.g.*, R. BERGER, *supra* note 197, at 286-87; Merry, *supra* note 20, at 68-69. Although the Federal Convention may have been satisfied with Wilson's explanation of the exceptions and regulations clause, *supra* note 78, the issue arose in several contexts, including the variations discussed in both the federal convention and the state ratifying conventions.

Procedure and remedies were another major focus of the Convention of 1787 and the state ratifying conventions and were a considered part of the exceptions and regulations clause insurance against any "inconveniences" that might arise.[215] While many enactments of Congress confirmed the common law, equity, and admiralty practice of the times, there were specific procedures provided by Congress that were indigenous to the new system of government.[216] While not germane to this discussion, the circuit-riding duties of the justices to the statutory enactment of civil, criminal, and appellate rules of procedure until the 1930's, and beyond, exhibit this interpretation. Legislation to regulate remedies under statutes of the Supreme and inferior courts also is clearly constitutional.[217] Any constitutional limitations on this regulatory, and possibly excepting, power are the subject of a separate debate of great magnitude.[218]

The divisions of jurisdiction between federal and state courts,[219] and between the Supreme and inferior federal courts,[220] pose substantial possibilities for interpretation of the exceptions and regulations clause. First, unless precluded by Congress, the state courts naturally have, and commonly exercise, general jurisdiction to hear and determine federal questions of law between private parties and that State, or even another state, but not between private parties and the federal government.[221] As to the choice of federal court, Congress has specifically provided concurrent jurisdiction in the district courts of cases involving ambassadors, and, contrary to *Marbury v. Madison*,[222] the Court may well have exercised original jurisdiction in issuing original writs of *habeas corpus* when it lacked jurisdiction to review the lower federal court's denial of that writ.[223] Whatever the potential for this line of

215. *See generally* notes 122-90 and accompanying text *supra*.

216. Perhaps the first of these indigenous procedures was the removal of cases in which the defendant was an officer of the United States from state to federal court. Judiciary Act of 1789, ch. 20, § 12, 1 Stat. 72, 79 (codified at 28 U.S.C. § 1441 (1976)).

217. *See, e.g.*, Norris-LaGuardia Act, ch. 229, 47 Stat. 70 (1932).

218. *See* notes 15 & 21 *supra*.

219. *See* notes 74 & 75 and accompanying text, *supra*. In essence, however, this question was resolved by the compromise to delegate inferior courts.

220. *See* note 20 *supra*.

221. Testa v. Katt, 330 U.S. 386 (1947). The limitations on jurisdiction of the state courts of one state over another are obvious. *But see* Nevada v. Hall, 440 U.S. 410 (1979). The limitation of a state court jurisdiction in cases to which the United States is a party is clear and, where avoided by suits against an officer, such cases are removable. 28 U.S.C. § 1441 (1976).

222. 5 U.S. (1 Cranch) 137 (1803). *See 1969 Hearings*, *supra* note 29; Van Alstyne, *supra* note 29.

223. *See* note 29 *supra*.

argument, it adds nothing to the question of precluding Supreme Court jurisdiction.

The final affirmative interpretation applies the exceptions and regulations clause to all civil (*i.e.*, statutory) rights, an interpretation far narrower than the reading implicit in current bills that "the Supreme Court shall have appellate jurisdiction . . . with such exceptions . . . as the Congress shall make." The broader interpretation appears to have been adopted in the *Federalist Papers*.[224] Further, it is widely argued that this interpretation animates the holding in *McCardle II*.[225] Indeed, given the lack of checks other than confirmation and impeachment (which have historically proved fruitless), the interpretation would appear to have substantial structural and political support. True, Congress has exempted whole classes of statutory cases from review, and criminal cases generally until 1892,[226] yet none of those exceptions appears to have been raised or argued to the point of a constitutional claim. Rather, as in *McCardle I* and *II*, the exceptions have been merely statutory.

Thus, the affirmative interpretations historically appear to reach many of the possible combinations of exception and regulation of the Supreme and inferior courts with respect to jurisdiction, procedure, and remedies arising under constitutional, statutory, or common law claims. The one subject *not* reached is that of exceptions to the Supreme Court's jurisdiction over constitutional claims.[227] We must turn, then, from history to more eclectic and synergetic legal considerations.

B. An Eclectic View of the Original Constitution and the Limits of the Constitutional Exceptions Theory

It is axiomatic to say that the Constitution must be read so as to be internally consistent, at least within the framework of the original unamended Constitution. Should any of the current proposals to except constitutional claims from the Court's jurisdiction become acts of Con-

224. THE FEDERALIST, *supra* note 36, at 505. *But see id.* at 513-14.

225. Van Alstyne, *supra* note 20. *Contra* notes 157-80 *supra*.

226. See, *e.g.*, the lack of general jurisdiction to review federal criminal cases, discussed at note 38 *supra*. Congress has also regulated the degree of discretion in the Court's determination of the right to review. *Compare* 28 U.S.C. § 1257 (1) (1976) *with id.* at § 1257 (2) (certiorari and appeals jurisdiction in the Supreme Court over judgments of state courts).

227. It has been suggested that in order to analyze fully any distinct constitutional problem, the specific categorization of what is done is imperative. *See* notes 6 (constitutional/statutory), 21 (Supreme/inferior), 23 (jurisdiction/procedure/remedy) & 25 (exception/regulation) and accompanying text *supra*. Many of these theoretical constructions can be disposed of *en bloc*, such as the inferior court possibilities.

gress, such an act must initially be read as consistent with the Constitution, original and as amended, because of the presumption of constitutionality of Acts of Congress.[228] Thus, in reviewing the constitutionality of these presumably constitutional Acts, the appropriate method may be more akin to an attack on the legislation *per se*. Finding no affirmative support or impregnable defense in history, we turn to the adjudicative process.[229]

The first perceivable limitation on the exception of constitutional cases from the Court's jurisdiction theory of the exceptions and regulations clause is the structural and functional argument of the "essential functions" of the Supreme Court.[230] The structural aspect of the "essential functions" argument lies in the concept of "one supreme Court" as the body to insure the functional aspect, the uniformity and the supremacy of federal law—particularly the Constitution.

It should be recalled that the delegates to the Convention of 1787 generally agreed early in the proceedings to the idea that there should be a Supreme Court.[231] Under the Constitution, little time elapsed until Supreme Court dicta on the role of the Court began to appear. *Durousseau*, clearly a case on lower (even article I, territorial) court jurisdiction of the District Court for Louisiana, presented Chief Justice Marshall with an occasion for comment on the structure and function of the Court under the Constitution, but Marshall's argument that to

228. A presumption of the constitutionality of a congressional enactment may effectively range from a mere catchword for the burden of going forward, to a nearly irrebuttable presumption, where persuasion may be futile (*e.g.*, in an area in which the legislative ambit is substantively within the political arena). *See* C. BLACK, THE PEOPLE AND THE COURT 215-20 (1960).

229. It should be kept in mind that the Court will initially postpone jurisdiction over the merits in order to determine its jurisdiction where a question of jurisdiction *per se* such as this is apparent. This practice is necessary for the elucidation of the jurisdiction of the Court in any sense where the Court determines that it does not have jurisdiction. In essence, this jurisdiction is "jurisdiction to determine jurisdiction."

According to contemporary Supreme Court practice, in cases brought by way of appeal, the appropriate order would be to postpone the question of jurisdiction to the hearing on the merits. SUP. CT. R. 16 (as amended Nov. 18, 1980). In the case of a petition for a statutory or common law writ of certiorari, the Court would necessarily grant certiorari and dismiss the writ as improvidently granted if the Court later determined a want of jurisdiction. SUP. CT. R. 17. In the case of jurisdiction of certified questions, the Court may simply dismiss the matter. SUP. CT. R. 25.2.

230. The origin of the caption for this theory may be traced to Ableman v. Booth, 62 U.S. (21 How.) 506 (1858). *See* note 238 and accompanying text *infra*.

231. In the Virginia Resolutions presented by Randolph, the question of whether there should be one or more such courts was left undecided. 1 RECORDS, *supra* note 31, at 21-22 (Madison) (May 29th). The alternate resolutions proposed by Paterson on behalf of the New Jersey delegation settled on a "supreme Tribunal." 1 RECORDS, *supra* note 31, at 244 (Madison) (June 15th).

allow no appeal from the district court would arrogate that court to a "supreme" court is mere dicta.[232] The fundamental problem with a structural approach,[233] of course, remains that there are numerous historical instances in which inferior federal courts have been the final arbiters of at least statutory questions.[234] In review of state court decisions, however, the Supreme Court has always enjoyed statutory jurisdiction to review any judgment that upheld a state action against a challenge of repugnancy to the Constitution or federal law.[235] In the limited sphere of the constitutional questions, therefore, the structural approach has historical legitimacy.

The rationale for a structurally supreme tribunal was voiced in the Convention of 1787 as being the need for uniformity of both interpretation and judgment as to federal law.[236] Chief Justice Marshall carried the theme forward in *Cohens v. Virginia*:

> [T]he necessity of uniformity, as well as correctness [of decision] in expounding the constitution and laws of the United States, would itself suggest the propriety of vesting in some single tribunal the power of deciding, in the last resort, all cases in which they are involved . . . .
>
> [The Framers] declare, that in such cases, the Supreme Court shall exercise appellate jurisdiction. Nothing seems to be given which would justify the withdrawal of a judgment rendered in a State Court, on the constitution, laws, or treaties of the United States, from this appellate jurisdiction.[237]

Thus, Chief Justice Marshall embraced both the structural and functional aspects of the "essential functions" approach. It was Chief Justice Taney in *Abelman v. Booth*, however, who joined these two aspects with the requirements of the supremacy clause:

232. *See* note 148 and accompanying text *supra*.

233. A structural approach has been used in the context of a proposed National Court of Appeals. *See, e.g*, Goldberg, *One Supreme Court*, THE NEW REPUBLIC 14 (Feb. 10, 1973); Gressman, *The Constitution v. The Freund Report*, 41 GEO. WASH. L. REV. 951, 960-70 (1973).

234. *See* notes 38 (general federal question jurisdiction in inferior courts) & 39 (general jurisdiction to review criminal cases in Supreme Court) *supra*.

235. At a minimum, all substantial claims of unconstitutionality in a state action could be reviewed by the Supreme Court. Judiciary Act of 1789, ch. 20, § 25, 1 Stat. 73, 85 (current version at 28 U.S.C. § 1257 (1976)).

236. Even the staunch states' rights advocate, John Rutledge, is reported by Madison as suggesting: "[T]he State Tribunals might and ought to be left in all cases to decide in the first instance the right of appeal to the supreme national tribunal being sufficient to secure the national rights & uniformity of Judgmts . . . ." 1 RECORDS, *supra* note 31, at 124 (Madison) (June 31st).

237. 19 U.S. (6 Wheat.) 264, 416-17 (1822).

> But the supremacy thus conferred on this Government could not peacefully be maintained, unless it was clothed with judicial power, equally paramount in authority to carry it into execution; for if left to the courts of justice of the several States, conflicting decisions would unavoidably take place . . . [a]nd the Constitution and laws and treaties of the United States, and the powers granted to the Federal Government, would soon receive different interpretations in different States, and the Government of the United States would soon become one thing in one State and another thing in another. It was essential, therefore, to its very existence as a Government, that . . . a tribunal should be established in which all cases which might arise under the Constitution and laws and treaties of the United States, whether in a State court or a court of the United States, should be finally and conclusively decided . . . . And it is manifest that this ultimate appellate power in a tribunal created by the Constitution itself was deemed essential to secure the independence and supremacy of the General Government in the sphere of action assigned to it; to make the Constitution and laws of the United States uniform, and the same in every State . . . .[238]

The use of the supremacy clause as the binding force is a complementary interpretation to that of the finality of judicial review, but is clearly antithetical to allowing use of the exceptions and regulations clause to relegate certain constitutional decisions to finality in state courts.[239]

238. 62 U.S. (21 How.) at 517-18 (1858). Uniformity is specifically mentioned as a requirement in the constitutional grants of power to Congress over naturalization and bankruptcy law. U.S. CONST. art. I, § 8, cl. 4. The "imperative demand [for] a single uniform rule" as contrasted with "that diversity, which alone can meet the local necessities" has enlivened much of the judicial interpretation of the commerce clause, U.S. CONST. art. I, § 8, cl. 3, in instances in which Congress has not acted. Cooley v. Board of Wardens, 53 U.S. (12 How.) 299, 319 (1851). Instances in which the Court has required uniform minimum standards of affirmative conduct are also clear. Minnesota v. Clover Leaf Creamery Co., 449 U.S. 456 (1981) (application of equal protection standards by state court); Oregon v. Hass, 420 U.S. 714 (1975) (confessions during detention; state court may impose a higher standard of conduct or more stringent limitation of use than required as a matter of state law, but not as a matter of constitutional interpretation); Harris v. New York, 401 U.S. 222 (1971); Miranda v. Arizona, 384 U.S. 436 (1966). The Court's decision to grant certiorari is also stimulated by a concern for the uniformity of federal law. SUP. CT. R. 17.1(a) (effective June 30, 1980, as amended). Thus, the root of uniformity in American constitutional jurisprudence is far deeper than the suggestion in the above text would indicate.

239. The supremacy clause, U.S. CONST. art. VI, § 1, has been the source of the doctrinal development of "preemption" of state authority by federal authority. The exact contours are not ascertainable. Hines v. Davidowitz, 312 U.S. 52, 67 (1941) (Black, J., for the Court). As we have noted, finality is now beyond peradventure, with perhaps one exception—the commerce clause. Finality of judgments of the Supreme Court as to the constitutionality of a state regulation of interstate commerce are constantly subject to alteration by Congress. For example, the affirmance of the constitutionality of a Montana coal severance tax, Commonwealth Edison Co. v. Montana, 453 U.S. 609 (1981), may be preempted by congressional prohibition of such a tax under the commerce clause. Also, the invalidation of an

It was on this foundation that Professor Hart built his test for the limits of "Exceptions." In response to the rhetorical question of whether Congress might provide a minimum federal jurisdiction over patent cases, Professor Hart responded:

> The measure is simply that the exceptions must not be such as will destroy the essential role of the Supreme Court in the constitutional plan. *McCardle*, you will remember, meets that test. The circuit courts of the United States were still open in habeas corpus, and the Supreme Court itself could still entertain petitions for the writ which were filed with it in the first instance.[240]

The addition of review authority over federal questions in general and over criminal cases was only statutory. Hart states that the original *habeas corpus* could be brought and that this common law writ could be used to challenge only the jurisdiction of the court or the authority of the jailer, either of which would encompass the constitutionality of procedure or confinement. In light of this circumvention of statutory gaps by the Court, Professor Ratner states his conclusions about the first bill to propose exceptions of constitutional claims:

> Despite some impediments in early statutes, the Supreme Court from its inception has performed the essential constitutional functions of maintaining the uniformity and supremacy of federal law. These functions provide a standard for testing the validity of legislation limiting the Court's appellate jurisdiction. Even though the legislation may narrowly restrict the procedures for obtaining Supreme Court review, constitutional limitations are not transgressed so long as the Court remains available ultimately to resolve conflicts between state and federal law and conflicting interpretations of federal law by lower courts. But legislation that precludes Supreme Court review in every case involving a particular subject is an unconstitutional encroachment on the Court's essential functions. Thus, [the Jenner proposal] was clearly invalid. Its enactment would have allowed the courts of each state to determine for themselves the constitutionality of state statutes and regulations on the specified subjects and would have permanently foreclosed Supreme Court resolution of inconsistent state and federal decisions concerning the application of the federal constitution and laws to such matters. The exceptions and regulations clause does not give Congress power thus to ne-

Iowa safety regulation prohibition of double trailers as excessively burdening interstate commerce, Kassel v. Consolidated Freightways, 450 U.S. 662 (1981), is subject to preemption by congressional authorization of such regulations. Nonetheless, the judgment of the Court remains final in its sphere. Congress, like the Court, cannot directly reach and alter state law.

240. Hart, *supra* note 20, at 1365.

gate the essential functions of the Supreme Court.[241]

Professor Ratner's argument of the essential functions relies heavily on the structural and functional aspects of the Court's existence. The historic lack of complete review of lower federal court decisions and the Court's jurisdictional dependence on the substantive decision of state courts substantially restrict the efficacy of this claim. The mere *capacity* to provide uniformity and maintain supremacy, however, may be all that is required under the theory.[242] Professor Ratner's ultimate conclusion would appear to rest on the existence of a separate right to animate the structural and functional aspects of the essential functions theory, although he does not explain this factor. Professor Wechsler, on the other hand, simply does not accept this limited view of the exceptions and regulations clause, the supremacy clause, and the "essential functions" that devolved upon the Court:

> Federal courts, including the Supreme Court, do not pass on constitutional questions because there is a special function vested in them to enforce the Constitution or police the other agencies of government. They do so rather for the reason that they must decide a litigated issue that is otherwise within their jurisdiction and in doing so must give effect to the supreme law of the land. . . .
>
> The difficulty with legislative [preclusion] of jurisdiction is not one of constitutional dimension . . . . Congress could not, for example, employ federal courts as organs of enforcement and preclude them from attending to the Constitution in arriving at decision of the cause.[243]

Professor Wechsler suggests that a limitation is imposed on any attempt to use the federal courts to enforce a given statute without reference to the Constitution. He cites cases or remedial limitations,[244] but his enforcement approach is functionally limited to the federal courts because Congress cannot providently dictate these limitations to the state court systems.[245] Professor Wechsler's claim would also appear to have no validity as applied to self-executing constitutional rights in need

241. Ratner, *supra* note 20, at 201-02.

242. If that is the case, the historic capacity of the Court to hear all constitutional attacks that have failed, together with the concurrent jurisdiction of the state courts until the federal courts had general federal question jurisdiction and the Supreme Court gained plenary (albeit discretionary) review powers, would fill that need.

243. Wechsler, *supra* note 20, at 1006.

244. *Id*. at 1006 n.10 (citing Lockerty v. Phillips, 319 U.S. 182 (1943); Yakus v. United States, 321 U.S. 414 (1944)).

245. The Court does not have supervisory power over the state court systems. The Congress may gain limited power over state court systems through the use of conditional monetary grants to the states; however, because of federalism and the limited degree of retained sovereignty, Congress cannot mandate state court jurisdiction or procedure.

only of enforcement. At any rate, the question is begged as to the substance of the statute itself, as was the case of infringing on the judicial decisionmaking process in *Klein*.[246]

As Professor Sager notes, review of decisions of the state court systems is where the primary value of the essential functions theory lies.[247] In addition to the lack of systemic congressional or judicial supervision of the state courts, the sheer potential for conflicting interpretations of the Constitution among fifty-four courts of last resort is great. Further, the implication that constitutional facts must be reviewable by at least *some* federal court[248] poses a substantial limitation on removing Supreme Court review. Here, however, history has been entirely consistent: the Court has always had statutory jurisdiction to review decisions of state courts that have denied claims arising under the Constitution.[249]

Thus, the essential functions theory is diametrically opposed to excepting from the jurisdiction of the Court constitutional questions arising from, at the least, state court judgments. Should such a bill progress so far, the essential functions theory provides a formidable model and deserves attention in the policymaking functions of the Congress and veto decisions of the executive. Standing alone, however, it lacks vitality as a means of adjudicating the constitutionality, both procedurally and substantively, of a particular legislative preclusion of an article III case or controversy of constitutional dimension.[250] From here, attention must turn to the second aspect of *Klein* for aid in constitutional adjudication. Just as it was the substantive effect and interpre-

246. *See* notes 181-89 and accompanying text *supra*.

247. Sager, *supra* note 20, at 42-57.

248. Crowell v. Benson, 285 U.S. 22, 56-57 (1932). *See* Northern Pipeline Constr. Co. v. Marathon Pipe Line Co., 50 U.S.L.W. 4892 (U.S. June 28, 1982) (Nos. 81-150 & 81-546).

249. Judiciary Act of 1789, § 25, 1 Stat. 73.

250. Adding the operative condition of the doctrine of separation of powers does not add appreciably to the substantiality of the argument, for, in effect, the "essential functions" theory *is* a separation of powers argument. Separation of powers has been the formulation for several invalidations either of legislative or executive action as intrusive on authority vested in the other. *See* note 99 *supra*. One example of this doctrine over the judiciary's authority was the declination to exercise power to initially determine war veterans' claims on the theory that review would lie in the executive branch, making the judges' actions nonjudicial. Hayburn's Case, 2 U.S. (2 Dall.) 408 (1792). The only other example of the use of a separation of powers rationale by the judiciary to protect "essential functions" was *United States v. Klein*, *see* text accompanying notes 181-90, in which it was claimed that a statute intruded on the decisionmaking function of the court of claims and the Supreme Court. It will be remembered, however, that the *Klein* decision was intermeshed with a separate claim, *i.e.*, that the Court must give effect to the presidential pardon granted to Klein's decedent.

tation of a presidential pardon that breathed life into Klein's claim,[251] all constitutional adjudicatory analysis of exceptions must accordingly include, as a factor, consideration of whether or not a specific constitutional right is being affected by operation of the challenged exception.

C. A Synergetic View of the Amended Constitution and Jurisdictional Exceptions to Constitutional Claims

In considering the scope of the original (unamended) Constitution, we have already noted that the various clauses must be read as internally consistent. The Bill of Rights and the subsequent amendments to the Constitution serve different purposes and have different effects. The Bill of Rights, as has been noted in the limited context of the Seventh and Eleventh Amendments,[252] was corrective by design. The guarantee of enumerated individual rights was intentionally a limitation on the government, and those enumerated rights have since been supplemented on several occasions.[253] Professor Wechsler has stated:

> There is, to be sure, a school of thought that argues that "exceptions" has a narrow meaning, not including cases that have constitutional dimension; or that the supremacy clause or the due process clause of the fifth amendment would be violated by an alteration of the jurisdiction motivated by hostility to the decisions of the Court. I see no basis for this view and think it antithetical to the plan of the Constitution for the courts.[254]

From the point of view that the original Constitution appears to include sufficient room for the proposition that Congress may limit the Court's jurisdiction over "constitutional" cases, via the supremacy clause or otherwise, this may be true. The reference to the Fifth Amendment's due process clause must be considered, however, to be a reference to a *per se* theory that the clause is violated by an exception of constitutional cases. On the contrary, as a matter of application to inferior courts, Judge Augustus Hand noted:

> We think . . . that the exercise by Congress of its control over jurisdiction is subject to compliance with at least the requirements of the Fifth Amendment. That is to say, while Congress has the undoubted power to give, withhold, and restrict the jurisdiction of courts other than the Supreme Court, it must not so

251. Only when the existence and effect of the pardon was established could the issue of the statute's constitutionality arise.

252. *See* notes 109-18 and accompanying text *supra*.

253. The specific guarantees of the 13th, 14th, 15th, 19th, 24th, and 26th Amendments are in marked contrast to the government organization and powers of the 16th, 17th, 20th, and 25th Amendments.

254. Wechsler, *supra* note 20, at 1005.

> exercise that power as to deprive any person of life, liberty, or property without due process of law or to take private property without just compensation.[255]

This dictum by a lower federal court runs counter to Professor Wechsler's commentary that there is no *per se* violation of the due process clause, but the real issue is whether the *application* of the exception deprives a person of due process. In this functional mode, an exception must also be tested against the particular enumerated rights of the Bill of Rights and subsequent explicit guarantees. The powers of government are in all ways restricted by explicit rights guaranteed in the Constitution.[256]

A major debate over passage of the Bill of Rights focused, as today, on the effect of enumerating rights. Madison's oft-quoted remarks on the subject provide a useful starting point.

> It has been objected also against a bill of rights, that, by enumerating particular exceptions to the grant of power, it would disparage those rights which were not placed in that enumeration; and it might follow, by implication, that those rights which were not singled out, were intended to be assigned into the hands of the General Government, and were consequently insecure. This is one of the most plausible arguments I have ever heard urged against the admission of a bill of rights into this system; but, I conceive, that it may be guarded against. I have attempted it, as gentlemen may see by turning to the last clause of the fourth resolution [eventually the Ninth Amendment].
>
> It has been said, that it is unnecessary to load the constitution with this provision, because it was not found effectual in the constitution of the particular States. It is true, there are a few particular States in which some of the most valuable articles have not, at one time or another, been violated; but it does not follow but they may have, in a certain degree, a salutary effect against the abuse of power. If they are incorporated into the constitution, independent tribunals of justice will consider themselves in a peculiar manner the guardians of those rights; they will be an impenetrable bulwark against every assumption of power in the

255. Battaglia v. General Motors Corp., 169 F.2d 254, 257 (2d Cir.), *cert. denied*, 335 U.S. 887 (1948). *Battaglia* challenged the jurisdictional limitations of the Portal-to-Portal Act on the basis of a 5th Amendment due process challenge. As the court found no due process right, there was no need to determine whether the court had jurisdiction to adjudicate that right.

256. The multitude of cases that underline this common statement need not be catalogued here. The most conspicuous of cases suffices to illustrate that unless a particular governmental powers amendment was intended to alter or limit a specific right guaranteed by a previous amendment, the previous amendment will effectively limit a later governmental power. *See* Craig v. Boren, 429 U.S. 190 (1976) (state power to regulate intoxicating liquors under 21st Amendment limited by equal protection clause of the 14th Amendment).

> legislative or executive; they will be naturally led to resist every encroachment upon rights expressly stipulated for in the constitution by the declaration of rights.[257]

For organizational purposes, though not adoption, the conservative political notion might be introduced that the degree to which rights are guaranteed in the Bill of Rights and subsequent amendments is dependent upon whether the action in their regard is expressly prohibited, implicit from the requirement of governmental protection, or assumed from the structure and function of the government and the clauses of the Constitution.

If any limitation on the power of Congress to enact exceptions of constitutional claims from the Court's appellate jurisdiction must be activated by invoking the rights themselves, the device of limiting rights by removing jurisdiction to adjudicate them must also be subjected to review under those rights. Any limitation on the power of Congress in this regard must flow directly from the incapacity of Congress to effect the rights in question. Thus, it is necessary to examine the several rights involved in contemporary exceptions legislation.

Assuming that the affected right is one expressly, directly guaranteed in the Bill of Rights or another substantive guarantee, the question becomes whether that particular right limits the exceptions and regulations clause. Assuming instead, however, that the right affected is not textually established and defined, one must look to the contextual framework of the right and, if all else fails, the substantive values of the Constitution and how these values are interpreted. It is along this shifting spectrum of lessening certainty that the analysis will proceed.[258]

The dual rights to the free exercise of religion and to be free from the governmental establishment of religion might be the premier examples from the contemporary debate of rights textually found in the Constitution that may restrict the right of Congress to except "constitutional cases" from the Court's jurisdiction. In the first instance, the preamble of the First Amendment prohibits congressional action in the area of religious liberty: "Congress shall make no law respecting an establishment of religion, or prohibiting the free exercise thereof

257. 1 ANNALS OF CONG. 456-57 (Madison, (C), Va.) June 8, 1789).

258. The spectrum itself is disputable. We might begin with the least controversial and most acceptable form of constitutional interpretation, that of textual review, go so far as the enumeration of substantive values that an individual may embrace, and posit all such positions as legitimately a part of the judicial power. The last of these are clearly minority views. *See, e.g.*, Parker, *The Past of Constitutional Theory—and Its Future*, 42 OHIO ST. L.J. 223 (1981); Tribe, *supra* note 20; Tribe, *The Puzzling Persistence of Process-Based Constitutional Theories*, 89 YALE L.J. 1063 (1980).

. . . ." This provision does not directly guarantee the right; rather, it assumes the right and prohibits interference. The extant standards for the interpretation of the right are to be found in the cases of the very type that Congress seeks to limit—*Engel v. Vitale*[259] and *Abington Township School District v. Schempp*.[260] In *Engel*, the Court dealt with a specific regulation and practice of the New York state schools of reciting the "Regents' Prayer" each day:

> We think that by using its public school system to encourage recitation of the Regents' prayer, the State of New York had adopted a practice wholly inconsistent with the Establishment Clause. There can, of course, be no doubt that New York's program of daily classroom invocation of God's blessings as prescribed in the Regents' prayer is a religious activity. . . . [W]e think that the constitutional prohibition against laws respecting an establishment of religion must at least mean that in this country it is no part of the business of government to compose official prayers for any group of the American people to recite as a part of a religious program carried on by government.[261]

H.R. 865 and S. 481, in the Ninety-seventh Congress, definitionally exclude this type of written prayer from their ambit.[262] Furthermore, the limitation of the statute to "voluntary" prayer is an attempted "savings" clause; however, there is substantial doubt as to whether the "voluntariness" device would work. The statute could be held invalid on the ground that public school regulation of student conduct inherently vitiates voluntariness.[263] Even so, as the Court noted directly in *Engel*:

> Neither the fact that the prayer may be denominationally neutral nor the fact that its observance on the part of the students is voluntary can serve to free it from the limitations of the Establishment Clause, as it might from the Free Exercise Clause . . . . The Establishment Clause . . . does not depend upon any showing of direct governmental compulsion and is violated by the enactment of laws which establish an official religion whether those laws operate directly to coerce nonobserving individuals or

259. 370 U.S. 421 (1962).

260. 374 U.S. 203 (1963).

261. 370 U.S. at 424-25.

262. *See* note 12 *supra*.

263. It is possible to avoid the entire question of constitutionality by reaching a conclusion that school children can exercise no constitutional voluntarism in complying with even the faintest suggestion by a teacher that they may pray if they so choose and that, in effect, any suggestion at all may be deemed coercive. This is merely a use of the common tactic of avoiding constitutional decisions wherever possible. Begging additional litigation by beginning down this road, however, without concluding the trip to a firm rule, is itself reason to reach the constitutional issue. Thus, if the choice is one of reaching the constitutional issue or creating a rule with unknown long-term effects, the former is preferable.

not.[264]

The direct relation of the state law to the limitation of power under the First Amendment obviates any need for coercive action on the part of the state.

Shortly after *Engel*, a requirement that verses of the Holy Bible be read at the beginning of each school day was challenged in *Schempp*. The Court rejected the secular purposes proffered by the state and stipulated future standards:

> [W]hat are the purpose and primary effect of the enactment? If either is the advancement or inhibition of religion then the enactment exceeds the scope of legislative power as circumscribed by the Constitution. That is to say that to withstand the strictures of the Establishment Clause there must be a secular legislative purpose and a primary effect that neither advances nor inhibits religion.[265]

In addition, the Court has added a third test—that the statute in question not foster "an excessive government entanglement with religion."[266]

"Secular purpose," "principal or primary effect," and "non-excessive entanglement" are the three separate tests under which the school prayer proposals, such as H.R. 865[267] and S. 481[268] in the Ninety-seventh Congress, could be declared unconstitutional. Considering the ongoing litigation of government-religion separation, the impatience of the Court with that litigation, and the rhetoric supporting such proposals, survival of the school prayer bill from a constitutional attack appears doubtful. In the first instance, such bills do not appear to meet the substantive requirements of the *Engel* and *Schempp* cases which they seek to limit.[269] Also, the device of "voluntariness" may be seen as ineffectual, since prayer is suggested by the authority figure of teachers.[270]

Of similar contextual clarity is the issue of "busing." If the current proposals were recast in a form more amenable to treatment as jurisdictional—for example, to except appellate jurisdiction over cases relating

264. 370 U.S. at 430.

265. 374 U.S. at 222.

266. *E.g.*, *Lemon I*, 403 U.S. 602, 612-13 (1971). *See generally* note 13 *supra*.

267. 97th Cong., 1st Sess. (1981).

268. *Id.*

269. This is to suggest that the current school prayer bill is unconstitutional because it is an "encouragement" of religion in violation of *Engel*; its primary and principal effect is to remove the Supreme Court from adjudicating complaints about religious exercises, thereby suggesting to local authorities license to engage in establishment of religion in schools.

270. *See* note 263 *supra*.

to pupil composition of schools based on race—the proposal would be within the analytical framework of this article. The prohibition of racial discrimination is contextually founded in the Fourteenth Amendment's equal protection clause. It seems clear that a direct proposal to limit desegregation would be suspect.[271]

The removal of the Supreme Court's capacity to review school desegregation cases is not distinguishable from other methods implicating student assignment that were formally nondiscriminatory criteria but that were discriminatory in application—such as direct pupil placement laws;[272] freedom of choice plans,[273] zoning, or a combination of the two;[274] minority transfer plans;[275] and school closings.[276] State interference with the process of desegregation has been struck down,[277] and it seems doubtful that the Court would welcome a congressionally mandated end to its overseeing of the process. Assuming only a case that might necessarily be brought in federal court where past discriminatory practice could be proved, the action of Congress in removing jurisdiction would become the predicate action continuing that discrimination. Accordingly, the jurisdictional exception would fail for the same reason that all the other facially neutral actions failed: discriminatory impact.[278] Furthermore, such a proposal would encourage public educational discrimination far more significantly than did the California constitutional prohibition of statutes providing for equal treatment in housing opportunities that was struck down in *Reitman v. Mulkey*;[279] the Akron charter provision—requiring housing opportunity legislation to traverse a more rigorous gauntlet than normal ordinances—that was

271. Columbus Bd. of Educ. v. Penick, 443 U.S. 449 (1979); Dayton Bd. of Educ. v. Brinkman, 443 U.S. 526 (1979); North Carolina State Bd. of Educ. v. Swann, 402 U.S. 43 (1971); Brown v. Board of Educ., 347 U.S. 483 (1954), 349 U.S. 294 (1955).

272. *E.g.*, Hall v. St. Helena Parish School Bd., 417 F.2d 801 (5th Cir.), *cert. denied*, 396 U.S. 904 (1969); Henry v. Clarksdale Mun. Separate School Dist., 409 F.2d 682 (5th Cir.), *cert. denied*, 396 U.S. 940 (1969).

273. *E.g.*, Green v. County School Bd., 391 U.S. 430 (1968); Raney v. Board of Educ., 391 U.S. 443 (1968).

274. *E.g.*, Northcross v. Board of Educ., 333 F.2d 661 (6th Cir. 1964).

275. *E.g.*, Goss v. Board of Educ., 373 U.S. 683 (1963).

276. *E.g.*, Griffin v. County School Bd., 377 U.S. 218 (1964). *See also* Hall v. St. Helena Parish School Bd., 197 F. Supp. 649 (E.D. La. 1961), *aff'd*, 368 U.S. 515 (1962); Bush v. Orleans Parish School Bd., 187 F. Supp. 42, 188 F. Supp. 916 (E.D. La. 1960), *aff'd*, 365 U.S. 569 (1961).

277. McDaniel v. Barresi, 402 U.S. 39 (1971); North Carolina State Bd. of Educ. v. Swann, 402 U.S. 43 (1971).

278. Only H.R. 869, 97th Cong., 1st Sess. (1981), would appear to fail on this point. Most busing bills are limitations on remedies, although these may fail as an interference under *Barresi*, 402 U.S. 39 (1971), and *Swann*, 402 U.S. 43 (1971).

279. 387 U.S. 369 (1967).

struck down in *Hunter v. Erickson*;[280] or the state of Washington's assumption of direct control (here, by referendum) over whether to use busing in a school district's desegregation plan that was struck down in *Washington v. Seattle School District No. 1*.[281] Jurisdictional modification that encourages racial discrimination would appear no less suspect than legislation that would have the same effect more directly. This is not to say that Congress could not repeal the entirety of the civil rights laws currently in the United States Code, assuming its intent was not to encourage discrimination, but only to say that Congress cannot affirmatively enact legislation having a discriminatory effect. Nor does section 5 of the Fourteenth Amendment provide shelter from such an analysis under the congressional authority specifically provided—authority to legislate implementation of the requirements of equal protection under the Fourteenth Amendment—even though this type of proposal appears to be antithetical to equal protection.

At the other end of the spectrum, where perhaps the least textual and contextual support for the substantive rights involved may be found, lies the question of abortion.[282] *Roe v. Wade*[283] and *Doe v. Bolton*[284] establish the right of a woman to choose to have an abortion during the first trimester of pregnancy and base that right on the Fourteenth Amendment. Whatever one's view regarding the legitimacy of that right, it must be admitted that there is no textual or contextual support for the conclusion reached. Rather, the right to an abortion is a substantive right created by the Court and is based on the values of the Constitution as interpreted by the Court at the time of the decision.[285] The lack of textual or contextual support for the right of a woman to choose to have an abortion is the underlying basis for much of the political debate over the efficacy of the right, whether couched in terms of granting the state and Congress the power to regulate abortion by a constitutional amendment[286] or of prohibiting the Supreme Court

280. 393 U.S. 385 (1969).

281. 50 U.S.L.W. 4998 (U.S. June 30, 1982) (No. 81-9). A more direct approach was taken and struck down in Lee v. Nyquist, 318 F. Supp. 710 (W.D.N.Y.), *aff'd*, 402 U.S. 935 (1971). The Court has distinguished these evasive tactics from the mere repeal, without more, of statutory requirements greater than the minimum imposed by the 14th Amendment. Crawford v. Board of Educ., 50 U.S.L.W. 5016 (U.S. June 30, 1982) (No. 81-38).

282. The decisional history concerning abortion indicates substantial vacillation over the "morality" of the act. Morality, however, ought to play no part in the process of constitutional decisionmaking. Here the problem is one of the lack, until recently, of any contextual reference, consideration, or concern for abortion.

283. 410 U.S. 113 (1973).

284. 410 U.S. 179 (1973).

285. *See* Tribe, *supra* note 20.

286. *E.g.*, S.J. Res. 16, 97th Cong., 2d Sess. (1982).

from reviewing state or inferior federal court decisions on abortion.[287]

Substantial differences will arise over the order and relative merit of the spectrum of constitutional interpretation of rights, and these are but some preliminary thoughts on the manner of addressing the interface of an exception of cases based on a constitutional right with the legitimacy of that right *in se*. Contextually supported rights are more likely to receive protection against exceptions from Supreme Court appellate review than rights newly created by the Court. Nonetheless, the question of excepting constitutional claims from the Supreme Court's appellate jurisdiction will arise in this substantive manner.

Conclusion: The Adjudicatory Framework

The adjudicatory path for reaching an outcome in a case of exception of classes of constitutional rights, at least, is clear. Assuming that a particular bill becomes law and that the law provides for an exclusion of jurisdiction from the lower federal courts, a case and controversy must arise in a state court system. The adjudication of the right by the state courts need not affirm or deny the federal right, for, as a general matter, the Supreme Court has jurisdiction to hear the case by varying methods.[288] The immediate question facing the Court is whether it has jurisdiction to hear and determine the matter presented. There are only two alternative consequences of accepting jurisdiction to determine jurisdiction; either (a) the limitation of jurisdiction is constitutional and the Court has no jurisdiction to proceed further, or (b) the limitation on jurisdiction is unconstitutional and the Court must proceed to the merits of the claim.

The claim must be of a constitutional dimension in order to raise the current question, and obviously it must be the claim sought to be excepted from the Court's jurisdiction. The question of the jurisdiction of the Court, however, is not immediately tied to the claim itself. First, the Court must consider the authority under which Congress has enacted the exception. The plaintiff bears the burden of going forward and persuading the Court to look beyond the presumption that the enactment is constitutional. As has been discussed, the text and direct context of the Constitution do not provide support for the notion that Congress has authority to make constitutional exceptions, nor does his-

287. *E.g.*, H.R. 867, S. 583, 92d Cong., 1st Sess. (1981). This should not be read to suggest that the right to an abortion is any less constitutional than other rights, merely that there is less textual support, and, thus, greater vulnerability to attack.

288. *Compare* 28 U.S.C. § 1257(1) *with id.* at § 1257 (2) (1976). *See* notes 192-93 and accompanying text *supra*.

tory support that notion, nor is such a notion precluded. In essence, the question before the Court will be novel. The party claiming the right will advocate that the essential functions of the Court are implicated and that only the Supreme Court is capable of providing for uniform interpretation of the Constitution in compliance with the supremacy clause and the doctrine of separation of powers. This argument will be pitted against the plethora of the Court's own dicta of deference to the Congress over the scope of jurisdiction. An outcome on this issue alone is unlikely.

Next, the party claiming the right must show that the exception itself does violence to the right claimed. Here it is inescapable that the Court will extend the line of jurisprudence under the Constitution in order to resolve the argued collision of right and congressional power. Indeed, the right claimed and the power asserted by Congress must in fact collide in order for the party claiming the right to argue the cause. Further, the legitimacy of the right asserted will be again tested. Textually and contextually based rights provide a clear path to adjudicatory choice within the bounds of the clauses of the Constitution itself. Rights that the Court has interpolated from the Constitution and contemporary values will face a far sterner challenge.

Thus, the question returns remarkably to the bifurcated analysis and decision of *Klein*. The case would be clearer if, as in *Klein*, the outcome were proscribed by the statute. Nonetheless, the litigatory requirement that the right animate and collide with the asserted power provides sufficient clarity of the outcome-determinativeness of the exceptions of constitutional claims from the Court's jurisdiction. If the Court ultimately finds that the claim is of the constitutional nature jurisdictionally proscribed by the statute, the only alternative short of declaring the statute unconstitutional would be dismissal. Thus, *Klein*, not *McCardle*, is the appropriate standard for consideration, and constitutional development should hinge on this precedent.

The impact of legislating and adjudicating exceptions of constitutional claims from the Supreme Court's appellate jurisdiction is highly speculative. Exceptions from jurisdiction in which the constitutional claim is founded on express textual prohibitions of governmental action, such as the First Amendment's prohibition of congressional enactments respecting an establishment of religion, are unconstitutional, whether such a claim is based on the infringement on the Court's essential functions in violation of the doctrine of separation of powers, or directly as a violation of the First Amendment. Exceptions from jurisdiction in which the constitutional claim is founded on contextual rights, such as the prohibition of racial discrimination in the Fourteenth Amendment, are more problematic, but past decisions indicate that the discrimination that would be established by such an exception would be struck down.[289] Exceptions from jurisdiction based on nontextual rights, such as abortion, pose much more substantial problems—first, in establishing a nexus between the right to an abortion and the Court's jurisdiction; second, in pressing the effects of the limitation on the Court's essential functions. The question of whether the constitutional fabric of government would withstand such a direct conflict between the powers of Congress and the Court warrants the most serious avoidance.

289. Read together, Washington v. Seattle School District No. 1, 50 U.S.L.W. 4998 (U.S. June 30, 1982) (No. 81-9), Crawford v. Board of Education, 50 U.S.L.W. 5016 (U.S. June 30, 1982) (No. 81-38), and Northern Pipe Line Constr. Co. v. Marathon Pipeline Co., 50 U.S.L.W. 4892 (U.S. June 28, 1982) (Nos. 81-150 & 81-546), indicate that the Court is fully cognizant of the potential for further evasion of desegregation by either the states or Congress.

CAN A PRESIDENT PACK—OR DRAFT—THE SUPREME COURT? FDR AND THE COURT IN THE GREAT DEPRESSION AND WORLD WAR II

*Michael Comiskey**

I. INTRODUCTION

For many years, students of the Supreme Court have concerned themselves with the possibility that Presidents can "pack" the Court.[1] Behind that concern is an often unstated fear that if Presidents can pack the Court, they can dictate the Court's decisions on vital matters concerning the proper constitutional distribution of powers or the constitutional rights of citizens.[2] It is "entirely understandable"[3] that Presidents try to appoint Justices who share their views. Yet our society cherishes the impersonality of the law. It is therefore appropriate to question whether one individual has the ability to acquire excessive influence over "the supreme Law of the Land"[4] by capturing the most powerful constitutional court in the world.[5]

This Article examines the efforts of one President, Franklin Roosevelt, to pack the Court. The choice of Roosevelt may surprise some readers, since his titanic struggle with the Court over the New Deal, the spectacular failure of his infamous "Court-packing" bill,[6] and his ultimate success at staffing the Court with New Dealers are

---

* Assistant Professor of Political Science, Penn State Fayette Campus, Uniontown, Pa. A version of this work was originally presented at the 1993 annual meeting of the Midwest Political Science Association and subsequently at the annual meeting of the American Political Science Association.

1 For two fairly recent (and different) perspectives, see Henry Abraham, *Can Presidents Really Pack the Supreme Court?*, *in* AN ESSENTIAL SAFEGUARD: ESSAYS ON THE UNITED STATES SUPREME COURT AND ITS JUSTICES 37 (D. Grier Stephenson, Jr. ed., 1991); William H. Rehnquist, *Presidential Appointments to the Supreme Court*, 2 CONST. COMMENTARY 319 (1985).

2 For an expression of fears that Reagan appointees would limit individual rights, see *Justice Rehnquist's Assurances*, N.Y. TIMES, Oct. 23, 1984, at A32.

3 HENRY ABRAHAM, THE JUDICIAL PROCESS: AN INTRODUCTORY ANALYSIS OF THE COURTS OF THE UNITED STATES, ENGLAND, AND FRANCE 73 (6th ed. 1993).

4 U.S. CONST. art. VI.

5 For a sophisticated statement of this concern, see Bruce A. Ackerman, *Transformative Appointments*, 101 HARV. L. REV. 1164 (1988).

6 *See* GERALD GUNTHER, CONSTITUTIONAL LAW: CASES AND MATERIALS 168-70 (9th ed. 1975) (describing a bill that proposed adding six members to the Court for a total of 15 Justices).

well known. But Roosevelt had other goals he hoped to achieve through the Court, and few scholars have systematically examined his success or failure in achieving those ends.[7]

In addition to securing judicial approval for the New Deal, Roosevelt had two specific goals he hoped to effect through his judicial appointments. First, he sought to fortify the Court's role as the ultimate protector of individual (noneconomic) liberties.[8] And in the last six years of his tenure, he also sought, as previous Presidents did with great success, a Court supportive of wartime executive authority.[9]

This Article compares and contrasts Roosevelt's complete success at winning the Court's blessing for the New Deal with his success or lack thereof at attaining his goal of securing a Court compliant with his wartime actions. The study has three objectives: first, to assess, insofar as we can learn from one notable case, the ability of Presidents to pack the Court; next, to shed light on the factors governing their ability to do so; and finally, to examine the Court's ability to restrain executive actions in wartime, an area where the Court has often displayed great deference to Presidents.[10]

The term "pack" is often defined as: "to influence the composition of (as a political agency) so as to bring about a desired result."[11] If we use this definition of Court packing, "Every president who has made nominations to the Supreme Court has been guilty of Court-packing in some measure" because they all *try* to "influence the composition of [the Court] *so as to* bring about a desired result."[12] To test whether Presidents can pack the Court in some meaningful sense, we must redefine "pack" as: "to influence the composition of [the Court] *and thereby bring about* a desired result."

For several reasons, Roosevelt was better positioned to pack the Supreme Court than any President since George Washington. First, Roosevelt appointed[13] a total of nine Justices,[14] more than any Pres-

---

7 Partial exceptions to this generalization are HENRY ABRAHAM, JUSTICES AND PRESIDENTS: A POLITICAL HISTORY OF APPOINTMENTS TO THE SUPREME COURT 208-50 (3d ed. 1992), and ROBERT SCIGLIANO, THE SUPREME COURT AND THE PRESIDENCY 23-60, 125-60 (1971).

8 SCIGLIANO, *supra* note 7, at 137.

9 ABRAHAM, *supra* note 7, at 212; SCIGLIANO, *supra* note 7, at 137.

10 For a description of the Court's historical performance on this issue, see *infra* notes 43-84 and accompanying text.

11 WEBSTER'S NINTH NEW COLLEGIATE DICTIONARY 845 (1983).

12 Abraham, *supra* note 1, at 44.

13 Of course, Presidents only nominate, not "appoint," Justices. But I will follow what seems to be the convention by speaking of Presidents "appointing" Justices.

14 They were: Hugo Black (1937), Stanley Reed (1938), Felix Frankfurter (1939), William O. Douglas (1939), Frank Murphy (1940), James Byrnes (1941), Harlan Stone (elevated to Chief

ident since Washington. He ultimately "filled" seven seats. (Two pre-Roosevelt Justices remained on the Court at the time of Roosevelt's death: Owen Roberts, a Hoover appointee, and Harlan Stone, appointed initially by Coolidge.[15]) Second, Roosevelt took great care in selecting his Justices.[16] Third, unlike some Presidents, he knew *exactly* what qualities he was seeking. In order to achieve the three policy goals described above, Roosevelt specifically sought Justices who possessed: an unwavering belief in the constitutionality of economic regulatory and social welfare legislation; an adherence to a generally libertarian and egalitarian constitutional philosophy; and a willingness to support broad executive authority to lead the nation in war.[17]

A final factor in Roosevelt's favor was a friendly Senate ready to confirm his nominees.[18] He never had to compromise significantly on the above criteria in selecting Justices.

The next two sections examine how and whether he succeeded in packing the Court, thereby achieving his goals of winning judicial approval for both the New Deal and his exertions of wartime executive authority. As the New Deal cases are by far the better known, the treatment of them is somewhat abridged and the wartime cases more elaborately described. Following the discussion of these cases is a section summarizing and comparing the findings on the two issue areas and a concluding section assessing their implications.

II. The New Deal in Court

After Roosevelt's supreme legislative successes in 1933 and 1934, the Court provoked his wrath when it: "waged what was, in effect, a constitutional war against the economic programs that FDR's administration . . . and some state governments had enacted to cope with the Great Depression. As a result of these decisions, lower federal judges issued 1600 injunctions against enforcement of federal

Justice in 1941), Robert Jackson (1941), and Wiley Rutledge (1943). *See* Ted Morgan, FDR: A Biography 480 (1985).

15 One Roosevelt appointee, James Byrnes, served only one year before resigning and being replaced by another Roosevelt appointee, Wiley Rutledge. These two appointments thus filled only one seat. And Roosevelt's elevation of Harlan Stone to Chief Justice merely shifted him from one seat to another. *See, e.g.*, Abraham, *supra* note 7, at 212, 232.

16 *Id.* at 212.

17 *Id.*

18 *See, e.g.*, *id.* at 222, 226.

statutes."[19] After his landslide reelection in 1936, Roosevelt responded with his infamous "court-packing" plan of February 1937.[20]

By July 1937, when the plan died a humiliating death in the Senate, two events had rendered it superfluous. First, the Supreme Court, in particular Chief Justice Hughes and Justice Roberts, executed its famous "switch in time that saved nine." In the three terms from 1933-34 to 1935-36, the Court struck down or limited New Deal measures in eleven of thirteen cases.[21] From December 1936 to May 1937, the Court upheld New Deal-style social and economic measures in each of the eighteen cases it decided.[22] As Pritchett de-

---

19 WALTER F. MURPHY ET AL., AMERICAN CONSTITUTIONAL INTERPRETATION 230 (1986).

20 JAMES M. BURNS, ROOSEVELT: THE LION AND THE FOX 293 (1956) (detailing the events of 1937).

21 *See* Lewis Wood, *New Deal Victor in Court Tests*, N.Y. TIMES, May 30, 1937, § 4, at 7. The 11 cases invalidating or limiting New Deal measures are: Ashton v. Cameron County Water Improvement Dist., 298 U.S. 513 (1936) (invalidating an amendment to the Bankruptcy Act that extended that act's provisions to municipal subdivisions of a state); Carter v. Carter Coal Co., 298 U.S. 238 (1936) (invalidating portions of the Bituminous Coal Conservation Act of 1935); Jones v. SEC, 298 U.S. 1 (1936) (limiting the power of the SEC to compel production of records); Rickert Rice Mills, Inc. v. Fontenot, 297 U.S. 110 (1936) (returning impounded Agricultural Adjustment Act processing taxes to agricultural processors); United States v. Butler, 297 U.S. 1 (1936) (invalidating parts of the Agricultural Adjustment Act as an attempt by Congress to regulate state agricultural production); Hopkins Fed. Sav. & Loan Ass'n v. Cleary, 296 U.S. 315 (1935) (invalidating as an unconstitutional encroachment on states' reserved powers a provision of the Federal Home Owners' Loan Act that allowed state building and loan associations to convert into federal savings and loan institutions over state protest); Louisville Joint Stock Land Bank v. Radford, 295 U.S. 555 (1935) (invalidating a section of the Bankruptcy Act that allowed farmers who had defaulted on their mortgages to retain possession of their farms for five years under leasing arrangements with options to repurchase); Humphrey's Ex'r v. United States, 295 U.S. 602 (1935) (construing the Federal Trade Commission Act to deny the President the power to remove the Federal Trade Commissioner from office at will); Schecter Poultry Corp. v. United States, 295 U.S. 495 (1935) (deeming unconstitutional significant portions of the National Industrial Recovery Act as invalid delegations of legislative power to the President and to industry and trade associations); Railroad Retirement Bd. v. Alton R.R., 295 U.S. 330 (1935) (declaring the original Railroad Retirement Act unconstitutional); Panama Refining Co. v. Ryan, 293 U.S. 388 (1935) (invalidating as an executive branch abrogation of legislative power a section of the National Industrial Recovery Act that prohibited shipment in interstate commerce of certain quantities of petroleum).

The two cases decided during this period upholding New Deal legislation were: Ashwander v. Tennessee Valley Auth., 297 U.S. 288 (1936) (upholding the sale by the Alabama Power Company to the Federal Tennessee Valley Authority ("TVA") of transmission lines and certain real property and the subsequent sale by the TVA to the Power Company of excess hydroelectric power produced at the TVA's Wilson Dam); Norman v. Baltimore & Ohio R.R., 294 U.S. 240 (1936) (upholding the establishment of a new currency system and the abrogation of the gold clause).

22 For a concise account and tally of New Deal wins and losses, see Wood, *supra* note 21, at 7. The 18 cases are: Helvering v. Davis, 301 U.S. 619 (1937) (upholding Social Security Act pension payments as a valid exercise of Congress's power to remedy the social "ill" of unemployment—even that caused by old age); Charles C. Steward Mach. Co. v. Davis, 301 U.S. 548 (1937) (upholding certain taxes on employers under the Social Security Act and

scribed this transformation: "In the 1936[-37] term, when the Court's conversion to the New Deal was accomplished, Hughes and to a lesser extent Roberts became practically full-fledged adherents of the Court's left wing, thus giving it control of the situation."[23]

Why did Hughes and Roberts alter course so abruptly? As Abraham reports, "[F]ew students of the Court view their move as anything but a recognition of, and inevitable bowing to, the handwriting on the wall."[24] Since both had changed their minds by December 1936, two months before Roosevelt announced his court-packing plan,[25] scholars agree that Roosevelt's overwhelming electoral triumph, not the court-packing bill, induced their change of heart.[26]

The second development that rendered superfluous Roosevelt's defeat on the plan was the May 1937 retirement of Justice Willis Van

---

credits toward those taxes for payments made to state unemployment insurance funds); Carmichael v. Southern Coal & Coke Co., 301 U.S. 495 (1937) (upholding Alabama's statutory complement to the Social Security Act); Anniston Mfg. Co. v. Davis, 301 U.S. 337 (1937) (upholding a statutory provision curtailing refunds of processing taxes collected under the Agricultural Adjustment Act); West Coast Hotel v. Parrish, 300 U.S. 379 (1937) (upholding Washington State's minimum wage law for women); Cincinnati Soap Co. v. United States, 301 U.S. 308 (1937) (upholding an excise tax imposed on the first domestic processor of coconut oil); Washington, Va. & Md. Coach Co. v. NLRB, 301 U.S. 142 (1937) (unanimously upholding the National Labor Relations Act as applied to an operator of an interstate coach company); Associated Press v. NLRB, 301 U.S. 103 (1937) (upholding the National Labor Relations Act); NLRB v. Jones & Laughlin Steel Corp., 301 U.S. 1 (1937); Virginian Ry. v. System Fed. No. 40, 300 U.S. 515 (1937) (upholding provision of the Railway Labor Act requiring interstate rail lines to engage in collective bargaining with their employees); Sonzinsky v. United States, 300 U.S. 506 (1937) (upholding Congress's imposition of an annual license tax on firearms dealers under the National Firearms Act); Wright v. Vinton Branch of Mountain Trust Bank, 300 U.S. 440 (1937) (upholding Congress's imposition of an annual license tax on firearms dealers under the National Firearms Act); Holyoke Water Power Co. v. American Writing Paper Co., 300 U.S. 324 (1937) (reforming a contract term calling for payment in gold to conform with the Gold Reserve Act of 1934); United States v. Hudson, 299 U.S. 498 (1937) (upholding the 35-day retroactive period on a congressionally-imposed tax on profits from the transfer of interests in silver bullion); Kentucky Whip & Collar Co. v. Illinois Cent. R.R., 299 U.S. 334 (1937) (upholding a valid use of the congressional power to regulate interstate commerce a restriction on importation of prison-made goods into states barring their sale); United States v. Curtiss-Wright Export Corp., 299 U.S. 304 (1936) (upholding as not an unconstitutional delegation of legislative power a joint resolution of Congress that authorized the President to declare an embargo on the sale of arms to promote peace); Landis v. North Am. Co., 299 U.S. 248 (1936) (removing barriers to the enforcement of the Public Utility Holding Company Act of 1935); AT&T v. United States, 299 U.S. 232 (1936) (upholding accounting system prescribed by the FCC for telephone companies).

23 C. HERMAN PRITCHETT, THE ROOSEVELT COURT: A STUDY IN JUDICIAL POLITICS AND VALUES 1937-1947, at 249 (Quadrangle Paperback 1969) (1948).

24 ABRAHAM, *supra* note 7, at 211. *But see* Felix Frankfurter, *Mr. Justice Roberts*, 104 U. PA. L. REV. 311, 314-15 (1955).

25 BURNS, *supra* note 20, at 303-04.

26 *See, e.g.*, BURNS, *supra* note 20, at 303-04; MORGAN, *supra* note 14, at 473-74; MURPHY ET AL., *supra* note 19, at 945-46.

Devanter, one of the Court's four staunch opponents of the New Deal.[27] Although the precise timing of his retirement had been coordinated with opponents of the court-packing plan, Van Devanter, at age seventy-eight the longest serving Justice, had wished to retire for some time.[28] Van Devanter may also have reasoned that the battle within the Court was lost after Hughes's and Roberts's "switch" had left four Justices in the minority, with no prospect of picking up support over the next four years.

As it happened, Van Devanter's retirement was the first in a quick series of vacancies. Roosevelt placed a majority of five Justices on the Court by January 1940.[29] The Roosevelt Justices proved so tolerant of federal economic legislation as to allow Congress, in *Wickard v. Filburn*,[30] to restrict the amount of wheat a farmer could grow for his own use. In *United States v. Appalachian Electric Power Co.*[31] they granted federal sovereignty over the Virginias' New River despite the fact that the stretch of river in question was not used in commerce and was unnavigable by any but the smallest boat.

Thus, the Court was converted by overwhelming political realities and subsequently packed. One might expect the political imperatives of world war to produce much the same effect.

III. The Supreme Court in World War II

A. *The Historical Background*

After 1939, Roosevelt focused on another criterion for would-be Justices: a willingness to give the President a free hand to marshal the country's resources and wage war.[32] His success on this score must be judged in the context of a long tradition of judicial deference to the President in foreign and military affairs. Historically, the Court has hesitated to involve itself in disputes over the President's

---

27 Known as the "Four Horsemen," these Justices were Sutherland, VanDevanter, Butler, and McReynolds. *See* Stephen B. Presser & Jamil S. Zainaldin, Law and Jurisprudence in American History 749 (2d ed. 1989).

28 Burns, *supra* note 20, at 306; *see* Morgan, *supra* note 14, at 469, 474-75.

29 Morgan, *supra* note 14, at 480.

30 317 U.S. 111 (1942).

31 311 U.S. 377 (1940). This decision prompted Wendell Willkie to remark that: "Now the toilet water in the men's room is navigable." Morgan, *supra* note 14, at 480.

32 Abraham, *supra* note 7, at 212; *see also supra* text accompanying note 17 (listing all three criteria).

foreign and military powers, relying instead on Congress and the people to restrain presidential abuse of these powers.[33]

During the Civil War, the Supreme Court did nothing to check President Lincoln's clearly unconstitutional exertions for the Union cause.[34] His many extraordinary acts were subsequently ratified by Congress or the Court,[35] or simply became faits accompli, until the Court decided *Ex parte Milligan*[36] in 1866. However, the Court subsequently avoided applying *Milligan* to invalidate military trials in the postwar South.[37]

In World War I, "Congress simply recognized a state of war when passing broad legislation delegating vast discretionary powers to the president."[38] The Court upheld this legislation in such cases as the *Selective Draft Law Cases*,[39] the *War Prohibition Cases*,[40] the *Emergency Rent Cases*,[41] and the notorious *Espionage Act Cases*.[42]

Similarly, in 1936 and 1937 the Supreme Court permitted expanded presidential discretion in foreign affairs. In 1936, a presidential arms embargo issued pursuant to a congressional delegation of power was upheld by the Court, including most of the Justices still hostile to broad executive discretion in domestic affairs.[43] In 1937,

---

33 *See generally* 1 DAVID M. O'BRIEN, CONSTITUTIONAL LAW AND POLITICS: STRUGGLES FOR POWER AND GOVERNMENTAL ACCOUNTABILITY 190-248 (1991); CLINTON ROSSITER & RICHARD P. LONGAKER, THE SUPREME COURT AND THE COMMANDER IN CHIEF (expanded ed. 1976) (1951).

34 *See* ABRAHAM, *supra* note 7, at 116-17. Chief Justice Taney, while riding circuit, invalidated Lincoln's suspension of the writ of habeas corpus in *Ex parte* Merryman, 17 F. Cas. 144 (C.C.D. Md. 1861) (No. 9,487), but Lincoln dismissed the ruling. EDWARD S. CORWIN, THE PRESIDENT: OFFICE AND POWERS 1787-1957, at 144-47 (N.Y. Univ. Press 1957) (1940).

35 *See, e.g.*, The Prize Cases, 67 U.S. (2 Black) 635 (1863) (upholding as constitutional the Union blockade of Southern ports).

36 71 U.S. (4 Wall.) 2 (1866) (invalidating the President's authorization of a military judicial commission when civil courts were operational).

37 *Ex parte* McCardle, 74 U.S. (7 Wall.) 506 (1868) (dismissing for lack of jurisdiction a challenge to a military court's validity).

38 O'BRIEN, *supra* note 33, at 217.

39 Arver v. United States, 245 U.S. 366 (1918) (holding Selective Service Act was constitutional); *see also* ROSSITER & LONGAKER, *supra* note 33, at 99-100 & n.69 (discussing cases following the holding of one of the *Selective Draft Law Cases*).

40 Hamilton v. Kentucky Distilleries & Warehouse Co., 251 U.S. 146 (1919) (upholding the War-Time Prohibition Act); Jacob Ruppert, Inc. v. Caffey, 251 U.S. 264 (1920) (upholding the National Prohibition Act).

41 Marcus Brown Holding Co. v. Feldman, 256 U.S. 170 (1921); Block v. Hirsh, 256 U.S. 135 (1921) (both upholding laws extending terms of rental property during the wartime emergency); *see* ROSSITER & LONGAKER, *supra* note 33, at 98 n.63.

42 Abrams v. United States, 250 U.S. 616 (1919); Schenck v. United States, 249 U.S. 47 (1919) (both upholding the Espionage Act of 1917).

43 United States v. Curtiss-Wright Export Corp., 299 U.S. 304 (1936) (the vote was seven to one with Justice McReynolds dissenting and Justice Stone abstaining).

the Court unanimously upheld the constitutionality of executive agreements with foreign governments.[44]

B. *The World War II Cases*

Against this background one must examine the Supreme Court's handling of three types of cases resulting from World War II: the *Wartime Price Regulation Cases*, the *Wartime Civil Liberties Cases*, and the *Selective Service Cases*.[45]

In the 1941 through 1946 Terms, the Court decided at least nineteen cases involving the wartime Office of Price Administration ("OPA").[46] The Justices were more divided in OPA cases than in cases involving the seven other regulatory agencies that most frequently came before the Court in those years, all of which were pre-

[44] United States v. Belmont, 301 U.S. 324 (1937) (holding that the President has the power to make certain compacts with foreign nations without congressional approval).

[45] In reviewing these cases, one must acknowledge that the Court's rulings are an incomplete measure of its attitude toward the Roosevelt administration's wartime actions, for we do not know in how many cases the Court denied certiorari or what the results would have been in those cases.

[46] PRITCHETT, *supra* note 23, at 190 tbl. xix; *see* Fleming v. Mohawk Wrecking & Lumber Co., 331 U.S. 111 (1947) (holding that OPA Administrator has authority under Emergency Price Control Act ("EPCA") to delegate authority to issue subpoenas); Parker v. Fleming, 329 U.S. 531 (1947) (holding that tenants subject to orders issued pursuant to EPCA were entitled to judicial review); United States v. Bruno, 329 U.S. 207 (1946) (upholding conviction for violating waste paper ceiling prices set pursuant to EPCA); Bihn v. United States, 328 U.S. 633 (1946) (reversing conviction for conspiracy to violate gasoline rationing regulations due to confusing jury instructions); Davis v. United States, 328 U.S. 582 (1946) (upholding conviction for violating gasoline rationing regulations); Porter v. Warner Holding Co., 328 U.S. 395 (1946) (holding that district court has power to order restitution of rents charged over ceiling price of EPCA); Utah Junk Co. v. Porter, 328 U.S. 39 (1946) (reinstating protest to price schedule despite subsequent supersession of regulations); M. Kraus & Bros. v. United States, 327 U.S. 614 (1946) (remanding for new trial with clearer jury instructions regarding EPCA regulations); Hulbert v. Twin Falls County, 327 U.S. 103 (1946) (subjecting county tractor sale to EPCA); Bowles v. Seminole Rock & Sand Co., 325 U.S. 410 (1945) (holding that OPA construction of EPCA regulation must be given weight); Case v. Bowles, 327 U.S. 92 (1946) (holding that EPCA applies to timber sales from school lands despite statutory language directing sale only at market value); Weiler v. United States, 323 U.S. 606 (1945) (reversing perjury conviction for perjury arising out of OPA enforcement action); ICC v. Jersey City, 322 U.S. 503 (1944) (reinstating ICC's denial of OPA's request for a price modification); L.P. Steuart & Bro. v. Bowles, 322 U.S. 398 (1944) (upholding presidential power delegated to OPA, to issue retailer suspension orders); Bowles v. Willingham, 321 U.S. 503 (1944) (upholding EPCA rent control provisions); Vinson v. Washington Gas Light Co., 321 U.S. 489 (1944) (holding that OPA is not authorized by EPCA to regulate public utilities); Yakus v. United States, 321 U.S. 414 (1944) (holding that EPCA was not an unconstitutional delegation of legislative power); Hecht Co. v. Bowles, 321 U.S. 321 (1944) (holding that court retains discretion whether to grant OPA an injunction for violation of EPCA); Davie's Warehouse Co. v. Bowles, 321 U.S. 144 (1944) (holding that a public warehouse is included in the public utilities exemption to EPCA).

war agencies.[47] The Court divided in seventy-four percent of OPA cases, versus an average of sixty-one percent for cases involving the other seven agencies.[48] The OPA prevailed in sixty-three percent, or about five in eight, of its cases,[49] a less than remarkable level of support from a Court friendly to economic regulation, supportive of broad interpretations of administrative authority, and operating under wartime exigencies.[50] Moreover, the OPA's sixty-three percent success rate fell below the average success rate of seventy-three percent for the other agencies.[51] In short, the Court was somewhat less unified in OPA cases than in other regulatory cases, and somewhat less accommodating of the OPA than of the other major regulatory agencies whose work likely had a less direct connection to the war effort.

In the 1941 through 1946 Terms, the Supreme Court heard thirteen cases involving persons accused or convicted of wartime offenses such as treason, disloyalty, espionage, and sabotage. The government won six[52] of these cases and lost seven.[53] In eight cases involving persons accused of pro-German acts or sympathies, the Court ruled against the government five times.[54] Excluding the case of the German saboteurs, the government lost five of the seven cases involving Americans only, displaying what Pritchett called an "urge to lean over backwards" to avoid "applying wartime penalties."[55] An example is the case of *Cramer v. United States*,[56] in which the Court overturned the treason conviction of a naturalized American citizen of German birth who knowingly met with two of the saboteurs, drank with them, and agreed to keep their money for them. From these cases, Pritchett concluded that:

47 The seven were the National Labor Relations Board, Securities and Exchange Commission, Interstate Commerce Commission, Federal Trade Commission, Federal Communications Commission, the Federal Power Commission, and the Wage and Hour Division of the Department of Labor. PRITCHETT, *supra* note 23, at 189-90.

48 *Id*. at 190.

49 *Id*.

50 *Id*. at 167-89.

51 *Id*. at 190.

52 Haupt v. United States, 330 U.S. 631 (1947); Knauer v. United States, 328 U.S. 654 (1946); *In re* Yamashita, 327 U.S. 1 (1946); Korematsu v. United States, 323 U.S. 214 (1944); Hirabayashi v. United States, 320 U.S. 81 (1943); *In re* Quirin, 317 U.S. 1 (1942).

53 Duncan v. Kahanamoku, 327 U.S. 304 (1946); Keegan v. United States, 325 U.S. 478 (1945); Cramer v. United States, 325 U.S. 1 (1945); Baumgartner v. United States, 322 U.S. 665 (1944); Hartzel v. United States, 322 U.S. 680 (1944); *Ex parte* Endo, 323 U.S. 283 (1944); Viereck v. United States, 318 U.S. 236 (1943).

54 *Keegan*, 325 U.S. 478; *Cramer*, 325 U.S. 1; *Baumgartner*, 322 U.S. 665; *Hartzel*, 322 U.S. 680; *Viereck*, 318 U.S. 236.

55 PRITCHETT, *supra* note 23, at 118.

56 325 U.S. 1 (1945).

> The strong bias of the Roosevelt Court toward the maintenance of civil liberties was responsible to a large degree for the serious and on the whole successful effort made to prevent the development of intolerance and witch-hunts during World War II on the scale which had marred American participation in the preceding war. The Espionage Act of 1917, a convenient weapon of oppression in the first war, was strictly construed by the Court to prevent any such result the second time.[57]

The Court was not, however, so protective of civil liberties in cases emanating from the Pacific theater. The Court ruled *against* the government in a case[58] involving the imposition of martial law and the use of military courts to try civilians in wartime Hawaii, but it did not do so until 1946, a year after hostilities had ceased.

Three of the other four cases from the Pacific theater were the infamous *Japanese Exclusion Cases*.[59] The most important of these holdings was the *Korematsu* decision, which upheld the forced evacuation and relocation in prison camps of more than 100,000 Japanese and Japanese Americans against whom the government had no evidence of any crime.[60] At the Justices' conference on *Korematsu*, the initial vote was five to four in favor of the government, with one member of the majority, Wiley Rutledge, a Roosevelt appointee and staunch civil libertarian, deeply troubled by the decision.[61] Over subsequent weeks of maneuver, negotiation, and general upheaval within the Court, Rutledge remained in the majority while Chief Justice Stone and Justice Black persuaded Justice Douglas, initially a dissenter and another confirmed libertarian troubled by the case, to join the majority.[62] Had Douglas held firm and Rutledge switched his position, rather than vice-versa, the decision would have gone against the government.

In the end, the prevailing factor was the Justices' traditional deference to military judgments in wartime. But as Pritchett implied,[63] this deference prevailed over a powerful contrary value that

---

57 PRITCHETT, *supra* note 23, at 117.

58 *Duncan*, 327 U.S. at 304.

59 *Ex parte* Endo, 323 U.S. 283 (1944); Korematsu v. United States, 323 U.S. 214 (1944); Hirabayashi v. United States, 320 U.S. 81 (1943). In the fourth case, *In re* Yamashita, 327 U.S. 1 (1946), the Court refused to review the conviction of a Japanese general convicted of war crimes.

60 *Korematsu*, 323 U.S. at 215-24.

61 MURPHY ET AL., *supra* note 19, at 66.

62 *Id.* at 62-75 (describing the Court's internal politics and the anguish of some Justices in the *Korematsu* case).

63 PRITCHETT, *supra* note 23, at 117.

Roosevelt had endeavored to augment on the Court: the civil libertarianism of some of his appointees, most notably Justices Black, Douglas, Murphy, and Rutledge. The anguish of several Justices on both sides in *Korematsu*[64] resulted from an evident conflict between Roosevelt's second and third criteria for selecting Justices: civil libertarianism simply does not fit well with broad deference to executive authority even, and perhaps especially, in wartime. This libertarianism prevailed in most of the cases involving German sympathizers[65] but lost in *Korematsu*.

This conflict is most apparent in the records of the three Justices Roosevelt appointed after the start of war in Europe. These Justices were the presumed objects of his intention to appoint Justices supportive of his administration's wartime actions. Of the seven Roosevelt appointees,[66] the earlier four—Black, Reed, Douglas and Frankfurter—were the most supportive of the government's position in the *Wartime Civil Liberties Cases*. The three least supportive were those appointed after September 1939: Murphy, Jackson, and Rutledge supported the government in only one of twelve,[67] five of nine,[68] and three of eleven[69] of these cases, respectively. These Justices voted against the government by three to zero,[70] two to one,[71] or two to zero[72] in nine of the eleven *Wartime Civil Liberties Cases* in which two or more of them participated.

The *Selective Service Cases* are the third category of wartime cases. From 1941 to 1946, the Court heard nine *Selective Service Cases*, with the government winning five[73] and losing four.[74] The

64 MURPHY ET AL., *supra* note 19, at 62-75.

65 *See supra* note 54.

66 *See supra* notes 13-15 and accompanying text.

67 Hirabayashi v. United States, 320 U.S. 81 (1943).

68 Haupt v. United States, 330 U.S. 631 (1947); Keegan v. United States, 325 U.S. 478 (1945); Hartzel v. United States, 322 U.S. 680 (1944); *Hirabayashi*, 320 U.S. at 81; *In re* Quirin, 317 U.S. 1 (1942).

69 *Haupt*, 330 U.S. at 631; Korematsu v. United States, 323 U.S. 214 (1944); *Hirabayashi*, 320 U.S. at 81.

70 Cramer v. United States, 325 U.S. 1 (1945); *Ex parte* Endo, 323 U.S. 283 (1944); Baumgartner v. United States, 322 U.S. 665 (1944).

71 *Keegan*, 325 U.S. at 478; *Korematsu*, 323 U.S. at 214; *Hartzel*, 322 U.S. 680 (1944).

72 *In re* Yamashita, 327 U.S. 1 (1946); Duncan v. Kahanamoku, 327 U.S. 304 (1946); Knauer v. United States, 328 U.S. 654 (1946).

73 Eagles v. United States *ex rel.* Horowitz, 329 U.S. 317 (1946); Eagles v. United States *ex rel.* Samuels, 329 U.S. 304 (1946); Singer v. United States, 323 U.S. 338 (1945); Falbo v. United States, 320 U.S. 549 (1944); Bowles v. United States, 319 U.S. 33 (1943).

74 Gibson v. United States, 329 U.S. 338 (1946); Estep v. United States, 327 U.S. 114 (1946); Billings v. Truesdell, 321 U.S. 542 (1944); Bartchy v. United States, 319 U.S. 484 (1943).

government won three of the five cases decided during the war[75] and lost two of the four cases decided after hostilities ceased.[76]

The most important decision in a wartime draft case was *Falbo v. United States*,[77] in which the Court upheld the conviction of a man who failed to report for duty as ordered. The majority relied on the contention that the administrative selection process was not complete when Falbo received a "final" order to report for military service; only when a draftee reported for duty was the selection process complete.[78] Since Falbo had not reported for duty, he had failed to complete the administrative process and thus could not challenge his draft classification at his trial.[79] The Court relaxed the severity of this ruling after the war.[80]

The three Justices named after war began in Europe—Murphy, Jackson, and Rutledge—were not especially supportive of the administration's position in draft cases. Among the nine Justices sitting on the Court at war's end, Justice Murphy ranked last in support of the administration in draft cases, Justice Rutledge ranked next to last, and Justice Jackson was tied for fourth.[81] The three Justices together gave the administration a majority of their votes in four[82] of the nine *Selective Service Cases* and in only two[83] of the five *Selective Service Cases* decided during the war.

IV. Comparison of the New Deal and World War II Cases

Concerning the New Deal, Roosevelt unquestionably packed the Court. In the *Wickard*[84] and *Appalachian Electric Power Co.*[85] cases, his Justices endorsed an extremely expansive conception of

---

[75] *Singer*, 323 U.S. at 338 (government won); Falbo v. United States, 320 U.S. 549 (1944) (government won); *Bowles*, 319 U.S. at 33 (government won); *Billings*, 321 U.S. at 542 (government lost); *Bartchy*, 319 U.S. at 484 (government lost).

[76] *Gibson*, 329 U.S. at 338 (government lost); Eagles v. United States *ex rel.* Horowitz, 329 U.S. 317 (1946) (government won); Eagles v. United States *ex rel.* Samuels, 329 U.S. 304 (1946) (government won); *Estep*, 327 U.S. at 114 (government lost).

[77] 320 U.S. 549 (1944).

[78] *Id.* at 553.

[79] *Id.* at 554.

[80] *Gibson*, 329 U.S. at 350 (permitting challenge because only "purely formal steps" in administrative process not completed); *Estep*, 327 U.S. at 123 (permitting challenge because administrative process completed except for submission to induction).

[81] Since Reed and Frankfurter tied for third, Jackson actually *trailed* four others in his support for the draft.

[82] Eagles v. United States *ex rel.* Horowitz, 329 U.S. at 317; Eagles v. United States *ex rel.* Samuels, 329 U.S. at 304; *Falbo*, 320 U.S. 549; *Bowles*, 319 U.S. at 33.

[83] *Falbo*, 320 U.S. 549; *Bowles*, 319 U.S. at 33.

[84] Wickard v. Filburn, 317 U.S. 111 (1942); *see supra* note 30 and accompanying text.

[85] United States v. Appalachian Elec. Power Co., 311 U.S. 377 (1940); *see supra* note 31 and accompanying text.

the Interstate Commerce Clause and a correspondingly thorough denigration of property rights.

In the war-related cases, the Court erected no major obstacles to government action, though given wartime pressures and the Court's long history of deference to the President in the conduct of war, it would have been quite extraordinary if it had. In the wartime price regulation cases, however, the Court clearly did not give free reign to the Executive. The Court was actually somewhat less supportive of the administration than in other regulatory matters, a surprising result given the obvious connection between wartime price regulation and the war effort. In the *Wartime Civil Liberties Cases*, the civil libertarianism of several of the Roosevelt Justices clearly clashed with the administration's prosecutions of pro-German figures.[86] The result was that the Court was much less cooperative with these prosecutorial efforts than in World War I. This bias toward civil liberties also threatened to, but did not, interfere with the most important cases from the Pacific theater: the *Japanese Exclusion Cases*.[87] Still, the three Justices appointed after the war began had a conspicuously poor record of support for the government in *Wartime Civil Liberties Cases*. In the *Selective Service Cases*, the Court gave the administration what it required. But once again its cooperation was less than complete, and two of the three Justices appointed after the war began supported the administration the least often.

Thus, the evidence from the wartime cases suggests that, in comparison to the Court's obeisance to presidential authority during previous wars, the Roosevelt Court was substantially less cooperative with the Executive in World War II. Additionally, the behavior of Justices Murphy, Rutledge, and Jackson in the *Wartime Civil Liberties Cases* and *Selective Service Cases* suggests that Roosevelt largely failed in his post-1939 effort to recruit Justices highly cooperative with his wartime actions.

V. Can a President Pack—or Draft—the Court?

Based on this history, two questions are examined in conclusion. First, what does the (insufficiently studied) behavior of the Supreme Court in World War II reveal about the capabilities of the Court in wartime? And second, what does the comparison of the Roosevelt

86 *See supra* notes 52-58 and accompanying text.

87 *See supra* note 59 and accompanying text.

Court's handling of the New Deal and World War II cases reveal about a President's ability to pack the Court?

Regarding the Court's role in war, there is considerable evidence from wars both before and after World War II to justify the view that the Court has seldom intervened to block executive wartime actions.[88] The conspicuous prominence of the *Korematsu* decision greatly reinforces this perception.

By no means, however, did Roosevelt win an unconditional surrender from the Court in World War II. As the analysis above has shown,[89] the *Korematsu* decision might well have gone the other way and is not entirely representative of the Court's record in World War II. While the Court did nothing to derail the war effort (as unimaginable as such an attempt might be), neither did the Justices assume the supine posture of the Court in previous wars. In the price regulation cases, the Court demonstrated surprising independence in view of the wartime pressures it faced and its general attitude toward economic regulation and administrative authority.[90] In the *Wartime Civil Liberties Cases*, the Court did much to prevent a replay of the World War I prosecutions; in the *Selective Service Cases*, the Court was less than entirely cooperative with the administration. This record demonstrates that the Justices need not hibernate in wartime and that the Court is capable of speaking with an independent voice in the resolution of war-related issues even as war rages.

As for our second question, what does the Court's behavior in the Depression and the War imply about a president's ability to pack the Court? Any final assessment of Roosevelt as a Court-packer must await a thorough review of his success at achieving his other aspiration for the Court: sending the Court in a permanently more libertarian direction. It is possible on the basis of the present analysis, however, to hazard three observations, no matter how tentative they may necessarily be.

88 O'Brien, *supra* note 33, at 216-20; Rossiter & Longaker, *supra* note 33, at 65-77.

89 *See supra* notes 59-62 and accompanying text.

90 *See supra* note 46 and accompanying text.

A. *Roosevelt's Conversion of the Court on the New Deal Demonstrates That Court Packing is Possible, But Various Factors Unique to that Event Suggest That Such Successes Will be Infrequent, if Not Rare.*

On the New Deal, Roosevelt's triumph over the Court was complete. One might attempt to discount this achievement by noting that he served a now unattainable twelve years in the presidency and appointed more Justices than any President since Washington. These considerations are certainly relevant, but Roosevelt did not need more than two terms to convert the Court to the New Deal. Even had he faced the Twenty-Second Amendment's two-term limit, the New Deal would have had the overwhelming support of eight Justices at the end of his second term, with Justice McReynolds the lone remaining dissenter. Nor was Roosevelt's ability to fill five seats in his first two terms[91] highly unusual: the odds that a two-term President will fill five or more seats are approximately forty-three percent, just a little less than half.[92]

Against these considerations, however, one can point out the unique political context of the New Deal era. Seldom is one issue as dominant in American politics as the government's response to the Great Depression was in the 1930s, and rarely do political elites choose sides so clearly. As a result, Roosevelt avoided a difficulty that has bedeviled other Presidents' attempts to pack the Court: he had no difficulty in predicting how his appointees would vote on the central issue of the day, the New Deal. Almost all other Presidents, with the exception of George Washington, have been substantially less successful at forecasting their appointees' future votes.[93]

---

91 The five new Justices were Black (1937), Reed (1938), Frankfurter (1939), Douglas (1939), and Murphy (1940).

92 In the 125 years since the size of the Supreme Court was set at nine in 1869, Presidents have replaced Justices appointed by earlier Presidents a total of 68 times, for an average of about .54 per year. Since Supreme Court vacancies follow what statisticians call a Poisson distribution, we can calculate the probability that a President serving a given number of years will appoint any number of Justices. After eight years in office, a President's chances of filling five or more seats are 43%. *See* S. Sidney Ulmer, *Supreme Court Appointments as a Poisson Distribution*, 26 Am. J. Pol. Sci. 113 (1982). Note that some of the figures in Ulmer's Table 3 are incorrect. The figures that I give here have been recalculated from the formula for a Poisson distribution.

93 President Eisenhower, to take one admittedly extreme example, regarded his appointments of liberal Justices Earl Warren and William Brennan as his two biggest mistakes. For these and other examples of presidential misjudgments and Washington's contrastingly sagacious choices, see Abraham, *supra* note 1, and Abraham, *supra* note 7.

Just as American elites chose sides on the question of the government's response to industrial capitalism, so did the American public. An overwhelming majority took Roosevelt's side. FDR's landslide reelection in 1936 was the greatest popular vote victory in any presidential election up to that time.[94] As Bruce Ackerman has written:

> [A] decisive majority of Americans had voted for the New Deal with their eyes open to the practical and constitutional implications of their collective decision. If ever there was a time that the People could be said to have endorsed a sharp break with their constitutional past, it was when Roosevelt and the Senate self-consciously began to make transformative Supreme Court appointments.[95]

Rarely has a decisive majority of the nation made such a clear and conscious decision on a fundamental issue that had disturbed the body politic for sixty years.[96]

One additional consideration advises against viewing Roosevelt's packing of the Court with New Dealers as highly replicable. While the transformation of American politics wrought by the rise of the New Deal coalition does have parallels—though only a few—in previous eras, Presidents in those eras have not been consistently able to lead the Court as Roosevelt eventually did. John B. Gates concludes from his careful empirical analysis of 743 Supreme Court decisions during four periods of major political upheaval in the nineteenth and twentieth centuries that, "there is no consistent role"[97] played by the Court in such eras. It is therefore appropriate to view Roosevelt's New Deal triumph over the Court as, at the very least, highly unusual.

B. *Even a President Who is Particularly Well-Positioned to Pack the Court Will Succeed Only on a Limited Number of Issues.*

Roosevelt's attempted Court packing was much more successful on the New Deal than on wartime issues. One could, of course, point out that judicial approval for the New Deal was his first and earliest

---

[94] Roosevelt received 60.8% of the popular vote to Landon's 36.5%. Popular vote figures for the pre-1824 elections are sketchy because most members of the Electoral College were not chosen by popular vote prior to that year. HOWARD W. STANLEY & RICHARD G. NIEMI, VITAL STATISTICS ON AMERICAN POLITICS 102-06 (2d ed. 1990).

[95] Ackerman, *supra* note 5, at 1175.

[96] The only parallel that suggests itself is the abolition of slavery in 1865.

[97] JOHN B. GATES, THE SUPREME COURT AND PARTISAN REALIGNMENT: A MACRO—AND MICROLEVEL PERSPECTIVE 183 (1992).

goal and that his opportunities to appoint Justices compliant with his future wartime actions were relatively few in number.

Yet something more than the lack opportunities accounts for Roosevelt's relative lack of success at procuring a Court acquiescent to his wartime acts. In the *Wartime Freedoms* and *Selective Service Cases*, his last three Justices, all appointed after war had begun in Europe, were substantially less cooperative with the administration than the earlier appointees. Circumstantial evidence points strongly to a likely explanation: the clear conflict between the demand for libertarianism in peacetime and the support of broad executive powers on the home front in wartime. Two of his last three appointees, Justices Murphy and Rutledge, were also his two most libertarian Justices.[98] As a result of this conflict, Roosevelt received much less reflexive support from the Court than any previous wartime President.

C. *The President's Limited Ability to Control or Predict Future Issues Will Limit his Ability to Pack the Court.*[99]

The arrival of World War II demonstrates how a new issue beyond the President's control can add to the President's selection criteria a new item—support for broad executive authority—that conflicts with a pre-existing criterion—an expansive view of personal liberties. This example also implies that longevity in office is a mixed blessing for Presidents wishing to pack the Court: the longer they serve, the more appointments they make, but the more likely it is that their predominant concerns will change.

In sum, this assessment of Roosevelt as a Court-packer is limited by its admittedly partial survey of his judicial concerns, in particular by its omission of any assessment of his success at making the Court permanently more libertarian. The analysis does, however, lend preliminary support to three conclusions: (1) only under unusual circumstances will Presidents achieve complete success at packing the Court on the issue of principal interest to them; (2) even relatively successful Court-packers will achieve success only on a limited number of issues; and (3) Presidents' limited ability to know the prominent issues of the future will impede their ability to pack the Court.

---

98 PRITCHETT, *supra* note 23, at 131, 141, 162.

99 This is predicted by GATES, *supra* note 97, at 182-83, and Rehnquist, *supra* note 1, at 326.

Reneging on History? Playing the Court/Congress/President Civil Rights Game

William N. Eskridge, Jr.†

Brenda Patterson is a woman of color. She worked for McLean Credit Union as a file clerk and teller from 1972 until she was fired in 1982. Brenda Patterson sued McLean for racial discrimination based on its conduct towards her while she was an employee. She testified at trial that her employer and its supervisors gave her more demeaning work than similarly situated white employees, passed over her for promotions given less qualified white employees and did not even inform her of promotion opportunities, denied wage increases routinely given other employees, and subjected her to gratuitous racial slurs, such as the opinion that "blacks are known to work slower than whites by nature."[1]

Section 1981 of title 42 provides that all persons "shall have the same right . . . to make and enforce contracts . . . as is enjoyed by white citizens."[2] Brenda Patterson's claim asserted that the racial harassment she experienced while a McLean Credit Union employee violated her right "to make and enforce contracts," in this case, her employment contract. The district court refused to submit her claim to the jury on the ground that racial harassment relating to conditions of employment is not actionable under section 1981. On June 15, 1989, the United States Supreme Court, by a five-to-four vote, agreed with that interpretation. The Court in *Patterson v. McLean Credit Union*[3] reasoned, in part, that

---

† Professor of Law, Georgetown University Law Center. B.A. 1973, Davidson College; M.A. 1974, Harvard University; J.D. 1978, Yale University. I am grateful to Ron Cass, Dan Farber, Phil Frickey, and Dick Posner for their comments on an earlier draft of this Article, and to John Ferejohn, Edward Schwartz, and Barry Weingast for informal conversations about the game theory used in the Article. I presented a version of this Article at the Legislation Section of the 1991 annual meeting of the Association of American Law Schools and received useful comments from the other panelists and participants. Dean Judy Areen and Associate Dean Wendy Webster Williams of the Georgetown University Law Center provided intellectual encouragement and financial support for my work on this Article, for which I am grateful. I appreciate the research assistance provided by Matt Bernstein and Ken Smurzynski.

1. Patterson v. McLean Credit Union, 491 U.S. 164, 213 (1989) (Brennan, J., concurring in the judgment in part and dissenting in part).

2. 42 U.S.C. § 1981 (1988).

3. 491 U.S. 164 (1989). The facts of Brenda Patterson's case are taken from the trial transcript, summarized and quoted in *id.* at 212-15 (Brennan, J., concurring in part and dissenting in part).

interpreting section 1981 to cover claims of on-the-job racial harassment would interfere with the operation of Congress' more recent regulation of workplace discrimination in title VII of the Civil Rights Act of 1964.[4]

Ironically, however, the Court was giving title VII a narrow construction. On June 5 by a five-to-four vote, the Court in *Wards Cove Packing Co. v. Atonio*[5] held that in discriminatory impact cases under title VII, the employee must prove not only a disparate impact, but also that the employer has no reasonable business justification for its discriminatory practices.[6] On May 1, a Court divided on other issues indicated in *Price Waterhouse v. Hopkins*[7] that employment decisions motivated in part by prejudice do not violate title VII if the employer can show after the fact that the same decision would have been made irrespective of the intentional discrimination.[8]

Following the trend set by *Price Waterhouse* and *Wards Cove,* the Court held in *Martin v. Wilks*[9] that white employees who were not parties to the original litigation could nonetheless challenge court-approved consent decrees providing for affirmative action to remedy past violations of title VII and the fourteenth amendment. The *Martin* case was decided by a five-to-four vote on June 12. That same day, a five-to-three majority held, in *Lorance v. AT&T Technologies,*[10] that title VII's statute of limitations for challenging seniority plans begins to run when the plan is adopted, rather than when the plan is applied to an individual.[11] On June 22, a five-to-two vote of the Court in *Independent Federation of Flight Attendants v. Zipes*[12] held that title VII does not provide for the statutory award of counsel fees against intervening defendants unless the intervenors' action is frivolous.[13]

These six Supreme Court decisions of May and June 1989 triggered a national political debate. Each decision created practical difficulties for plaintiffs seeking relief for workplace discrimination under either title VII or section 1981. As a group, the decisions appeared an effort by five Justices[14] to narrow the protections provided by federal law for work-

4. *Id.* at 180-81.
5. 490 U.S. 642 (1989).
6. *Id.* at 659-60.
7. 490 U.S. 228 (1989).
8. *Id.* at 244-45, 258.
9. 490 U.S. 755 (1989).
10. 490 U.S. 900 (1989).
11. *Id.* at 911.
12. 491 U.S. 754 (1989).
13. *Id.* at 761.
14. These five Justices form the core majority in most of these cases: Chief Justice Rehnquist and Justices White, O'Connor, Scalia, and Kennedy. The exception is Price Waterhouse v. Hopkins, 490 U.S. 228 (1989), for which Justice Brennan wrote the plurality opinion, which was joined by Justices Marshall, Blackmun, and Stevens. Justices White and O'Connor concurred in the judgment; Chief Justice Rehnquist and Justices Scalia and Kennedy dissented.

place discrimination. Civil rights groups in Washington, D.C., immediately started to devise legislation to overrule as many of the decisions as possible. Legislation was introduced in February 1990 to overrule all six decisions, as well as three earlier Supreme Court decisions that also affected workplace discrimination lawsuits.[15] Congress passed the legislation, with amendments, in early October. The President vetoed the bill on the grounds that it did more than just overrule the unpopular decisions, and Congress was not able to override the veto. The debate continues. Similar legislation has been introduced in the 102nd Congress.[16]

The debate over the proposed Civil Rights Act of 1990 dramatizes the centrality of statutes and their interpretation to the nation's civil rights[17] agenda. The debate also raises issues about the nature of statutory interpretation and the role of Congress. What interests me about the 1990 debate is the rhetoric about the dynamics of Court/Congress interaction in the implementation of civil rights statutes. Consider this representative passage that appeared during the House discussion:

> One thing is true about our history, and that [is] there always has been an ever-continuing struggle, a struggle for freedom and justice and equality.
>
> . . . And by the 1960's we reached a consensus, a consensus that we would move in a direction that would allow the doors to be opened and allow remedies to be put in place and say that discrimination was wrong.
>
> For 25 years that process worked. Then in 1988 and 1989 a series of court decisions came about that changed that fundamental process and those definitions.[18]

Such rhetoric whiggishly oversimplifies the Court/Congress interaction over civil rights.

Certainly the proposed Civil Rights Act of 1990 was unprecedented in its sweeping reform of the civil rights agenda. The Act, however, did not emerge out of thin air as a simple retort to *Patterson* and the other decisions. Actually the Act was the culmination of a fifteen-year process during which the political preferences of the Court and Congress have diverged. As I argue in more detail in Part I, the "consensus" of the

15. The three cases were: Crawford Fitting Co. v. J.T. Gibbons, Inc., 482 U.S. 437 (1987) (limiting reimbursement by losing party of prevailing party's expert witness fees); Evans v. Jeff D., 475 U.S. 717 (1986) (Civil Rights Attorney's Fees Awards Act of 1976 does not prohibit waiver of attorney's fees in exchange for settlement of case on the merits); Library of Congress v. Shaw, 478 U.S. 310 (1985) (title VII's allowance of reasonable attorney's fees to prevailing party does not provide for recovery of interest from government).

16. *See* H.R. 1, 102d Cong., 1st Sess., 137 CONG. REC. H53 (daily ed. Jan. 3, 1991).

17. I am using the term "civil rights" in this Article to refer to measures attacking discrimination. I do not limit the discussion to racial discrimination, and several of the issues tracked in this Article relate to discrimination against women, the aged, and the handicapped. (I do not address legislation and decisions dealing with other civil rights, such as freedom of speech and association, criminal procedure rights, and various privacy protections.)

18. 136 CONG. REC. H6765 (daily ed. Aug. 3, 1990) (statement of Rep. Gray, D-Pa.).

1960s was largely driven by the Court and the President. The consensus was the coincidence of leftward movement on civil rights by a *Brown*-inspired Warren Court, by a Presidency that came to pursue the *Brown* revolution aggressively, and by a Congress slowly overcoming the long-standing Southern obstruction of civil rights legislation. This consensus began to break down in the 1970s. The Court and the Presidency moved to the right while Congress and the relevant committees moved to the left. Between 1976 and 1988, this divergence of opinion manifested itself in a series of legislative overrides of Supreme Court decisions. At times, the acrimony between the branches was just as intense as that in the 1990 debate.

The rhetoric quoted above also wrongly assumes a mechanical role for the Court. The Congressman seems shocked that the Court "changed that fundamental process" by which civil rights laws had been enforced since the 1960s. Much of Congress' criticism of the 1989 decisions accused the Court of ignoring the original legislative intent in title VII. In my view, this criticism is off the mark. Statutory interpretation is an inherently dynamic process: the text evolves as it is interpreted. The Court's interpretation of our civil rights laws has been particularly dynamic.[19] Thus, Congress' objection should not be that the Court has changed the statute, but that the Court has changed it in ways the current legislative majorities do not like.

To be sure, traditional theory emphasizes a mechanical approach to statutory interpretation under which the Court is nothing more than the "honest agent" of Congress.[20] However, the Constitution itself considers the Court a co-equal branch of the national government. Indeed, at least some of the original constitutional debates considered the Court a political branch, whose statutory as well as constitutional interpretations would serve as checks on the other branches.[21] Part II of this Article adopts that original constitutional perspective and develops a model of the Court as a political actor in statutory interpretation. The model is based upon a game played by the Court, Congress, and the President in statutory implementation. Part II uses the game model as a way of understanding the historical evolution of the Court/Congress/President interaction for civil rights statutes from 1962 to 1990.

The model suggests that the Court's influence on policymaking was

19. This is the argument in Eskridge, *Dynamic Statutory Interpretation*, 135 U. PA. L. REV. 1479 (1987), and subsequent articles.

20. This theory, too, has been vigorously criticized. For a variety of perspectives on the honest agent metaphor and its inability to constrain judicial discretion, see Eskridge, *Spinning Legislative Supremacy*, 78 GEO. L.J. 319 (1989); Farber, *Statutory Interpretation and Legislative Supremacy*, 78 GEO. L.J. 281 (1989); Posner, *Legal Formalism, Legal Realism, and the Interpretation of Statutes and the Constitution*, 37 CASE W. RES. L. REV. 179 (1986).

21. *See, e.g.*, THE FEDERALIST No. 78 (A. Hamilton).

most significant at two points: at the period's beginning (1962-72), when the Court was to the left of Congress and relevant committees, and at the period's end (1981-90), when both the Court and the President were significantly to the right of Congress and its committees. The model's success in explaining the Court/Congress/President interaction reaffirms the original constitutional understanding that the Court *and* the President *and* the Congress (not Congress alone) would determine statutory policy. The model also predicts that, given the likelihood that the Court will remain to the right of Congress, the most important variable for civil rights policy in the 1990s will be the President's agenda.

Part III explores some normative and doctrinal implications of these game theoretic dynamics. In particular, Part III explores the model's suggestion that the Court is a political actor implementing its own preferences about civil rights policy. This suggestion involves a rethinking of what we mean by "judicial activism." The model suggests that the Court tends to slight the preferences of enacting Congresses in favor of the current Congress, which is a form of activism. I argue, further, that the Rehnquist Court has been more activist than the Burger and Warren Courts, for so far the Rehnquist Court, unlike the Burger and Warren Courts, has also tended to slight current congressional preferences. This activism has made Congress more willing to overrule the Court's interpretations of civil rights statutes. An important question for the 1990s is whether the Court will curtail its activism. If it does not, Congress might reduce the Court's role in civil rights cases by imposing new procedural requirements on the Court and by shifting interpretive power from the Court to alternative fora.

I
A Conventional Political History of the Court/Congress/President Interaction on Civil Rights Issues, 1962-90

Traditional interest group and institutional theories identify three dynamic elements of the Court/Congress/President interaction in civil rights statutes in the last thirty years. First is the changing nature of the Democratic majority in Congress, from a majority whose leadership and membership were sharply divided on civil rights issues, to a solidly liberal majority on such issues. The second element is the development of a strong, institutionalized civil rights lobby aligned with the members of the relevant committees. The third is a shift of the Court's and the President's preferences on civil rights issues, from the left of Congress to the right of Congress.

In the 1960s, the Court and the Presidency pushed civil rights statutes in a liberal direction. Congress generally went along with the judicial and presidential initiatives, and there was surprisingly little open conflict between the Court and Congress. This changed in the mid-1970s, however, as Congress moved to the left and the Court, less sharply, to the right. Congress started to override some of the Court's statutory civil rights decisions in the 1970s. Through the 1980s, when the President was aligned with the Court, the Court has shifted dramatically to the right, and there has been a fair amount of conflict between Congress on one side, and the Court and President on the other.

A. Court/Congress/President Cooperation: 1962-72

In the 1950s, the federal government became cautiously interested in creating a progressive national civil rights policy.[22] Sporadically progressive on civil rights issues, the Eisenhower administration created the Civil Rights Division of the Department of Justice; deployed armed forces to enforce desegregation decrees in Little Rock, Arkansas; appointed progressive, *Brown*-enforcing federal judges in the South; and pressed for national civil rights legislation in 1957 and 1961. The legislation that emerged in those two years was watered down in the legislative process because Southern Democratic opposition was strategically placed (especially in the Senate) and because the administration and the Democratic congressional leadership lacked the intense resolve needed to pass legislation.

The Warren Court contributed little to the evolution of statutory policy during this period. It was preoccupied with the frustrating school desegregation battle, where it had only vague nineteenth-century statutes and unhelpful precedents to interpret. Moreover, the Justices could not agree on how activist the Court should be on civil rights.[23]

All three branches, but most notably the Presidency and the Supreme Court, shifted to the left in the 1960s. By 1963, the Kennedy administration had made enactment of a comprehensive civil rights statute a top priority. President Johnson pressed for major civil rights legislation in every year of his administration.[24] As for the legislative branch,

22. For a brief history of civil rights policy in this period, see H. GRAHAM, THE CIVIL RIGHTS ERA: ORIGINS AND DEVELOPMENT OF NATIONAL POLICY, 1960-1972, at 16-24 (1990). For additional material on earlier developments during the Truman administration, see TO SECURE THESE RIGHTS: THE REPORT OF THE PRESIDENT'S COMMITTEE ON CIVIL RIGHTS (1947).

23. Chief Justice Warren (1953-69) and Justices Black (1937-71), Douglas (1939-75), and Brennan (1956-90) were activist on civil rights issues in this period. Justices Frankfurter (1939-62), Clark (1949-67), Harlan (1955-70), Whittaker (1957-62), and Stewart (1958-81) were less so. *See generally* B. SCHWARTZ, SUPER CHIEF: EARL WARREN AND HIS SUPREME COURT—A JUDICIAL BIOGRAPHY 175-96, 204-17, 252 (1983) (Court polarized during 1956-58 between Frankfurter wing and a Black-Brennan-Douglas-Warren wing, sarcastically dubbed "B.B.D. and W." by Frankfurter); 4 ENCYCLOPEDIA OF THE AMERICAN CONSTITUTION 2023-31 (L. Levy, K. Karst & D. Mahoney eds. 1986) (discussing the Warren Court).

24. Specifically, President Johnson carried forth President Kennedy's civil rights bill in 1963,

the Democratic Party remained sharply split on civil rights issues throughout the 1960s, though its congressional leadership was more liberal than it had been in the 1950s.[25] While the median Democrat in Congress moved somewhat to the left on civil rights issues during this period,[26] opponents of civil rights legislation controlled some of the critical committees.[27] On the Court, sentiments shifted dramatically to the left after 1962, mainly due to changes in personnel.[28] The retirement of

signing the landmark Civil Rights Act in 1964; in addition, he introduced and procured enactment of the Voting Rights Act in 1965, introduced and pushed unsuccessfully for a second omnibus civil rights statute in 1966 and 1967 (but was able to procure enactment of the Fair Housing Act in 1968—originally title IV of the 1966 and 1967 comprehensive bills), and introduced and procured enactment of the Age Discrimination Act of 1967. *See generally* H. GRAHAM, *supra* note 22, at 125-300.

25. Majority Leader Mike Mansfield (D-Mont.), 1961-73, was more liberal on civil rights matters than Majority Leader Lyndon Johnson (D-Tex.), 1955-61. *See generally* Davidson, *Senate Leaders: Janitors for an Untidy Chamber?*, in CONGRESS RECONSIDERED 225, 228-32 (L. Dodd & B. Oppenheimer eds. 1985) (contrasting Johnson's and Mansfield's leadership styles); Stewart, *Two Strategies of Leadership: Johnson and Mansfield*, in CONGRESSIONAL BEHAVIOR 61 (N. Polsby ed. 1971) (describing the strikingly different approaches that the two had to the job of Senate Democratic majority leaders). Speaker of the House McCormack (D-Mass.), 1962-71, was more liberal on civil rights matters than Speaker Sam Rayburn (D-Tex.), 1940-47, 1949-53, 1955-61. *See* Peabody, *Party Leadership Change in the United States House of Representatives*, in NEW PERSPECTIVES ON THE HOUSE OF REPRESENTATIVES 359, 388-89 (R. Peabody & N. Polsby eds. 1969). The Speaker in the 1960s also began to exercise greater power over the Rules Committee. *See, e.g.*, N. MACNEIL, FORGE OF DEMOCRACY 412-47 (1963) (detailing the packing of the House Rules Committee in 1961).

26. Taking into account voting on civil liberties issues generally, which would include first amendment and not just civil rights/antidiscrimination protection, the Democratic record is more stable. *See* Sinclair, *Agenda, Policy, and Alignment Change From Coolidge to Reagan*, in CONGRESS RECONSIDERED, *supra* note 25, at 291, 301-04 (discussing Democratic and Republican voting records on civil liberties from 1953 to 1968). For a discussion of the importance of the median legislators, see *infra* note 197.

27. Representative Howard W. Smith (D-Va.) chaired the House Rules Committee until 1967, succeeded by William Colmer (D-Miss.). Although the Southern Democrats did not hold a majority on the Rules Committee, they were able to use the power of the chair and other senior members to slow down or kill civil rights legislation throughout the 1950s and 1960s. *See* N. POLSBY, CONGRESS AND THE PRESIDENCY 149-52 (3d ed. 1976) (describing Smith's use of the powerful Rules Committee to thwart civil rights legislation, and the Democratic caucus' attempt to make the Rules Committee better reflect the will of the majority). Representative Emanuel Celler (D-N.Y.) chaired the House Judiciary Committee until 1973. Celler was strongly on the left in civil rights matters, as was a solid majority of that committee throughout the 1960s. *See* C. WHALEN & B. WHALEN, THE LONGEST DEBATE: A LEGISLATIVE HISTORY OF THE 1964 CIVIL RIGHTS ACT 29-67 (1985) (Celler and the Judiciary Committee deliberations on the 1964 Act).

Senator James Eastland (D-Miss.) chaired the Senate Judiciary Committee from the 1950s until 1979, and through most of the 1960s about half of the committee (Southern Democrats Eastland, McClellan, Ervin, and Smathers, plus conservative Republicans Dirksen, Hruska, and Thurmond) was center-to-right on civil rights matters. Senator Lister Hill (D-Ala.) chaired the Committee on Labor and Public Welfare until 1969, but the composition of the committee was strongly to his left. To see the membership of the House and Senate committees during this period, see the *Congressional Quarterly Almanac* for each of the relevant years.

28. The key event was the retirement in 1962 of Justice Frankfurter, the leader of the Court's cautious wing, and his replacement with Justice Arthur Goldberg (1962-65). Together with the Warren Court's core of four civil rights activists (Justices Warren, Douglas, Black, and Brennan),

Chief Justice Warren and resignation of Justice Fortas resulted in a rightward shift in 1969. Nevertheless, the Court in 1971 was still substantially to the left of its position before 1962.

The national shift to the left was reflected in the significant, Presidency-led enactment of the Civil Rights Act of 1964 and the Voting Rights Act of 1965,[29] and the Court's lopsided votes upholding the constitutionality of both statutes.[30] At the same time, the Supreme Court began interpreting Reconstruction era civil rights statutes dynamically to expand civil rights protections without waiting for legislative updating. In *Louisiana v. United States,*[31] a unanimous Court interpreted the Enforcement Act of 1870[32] in a consciously dynamic way to invalidate a literacy test based upon its potential as well as its actual effect upon the fundamental right to vote.[33] Civil rights leaders and the Johnson administration used *Louisiana* to prod Congress to expand statutory protection by enacting the Voting Rights Act.[34]

In *United States v. Guest,*[35] the Court liberally interpreted another post-Civil War statute to criminalize some private conspiracies to deprive civil rights activists of their fourteenth amendment rights.[36] The Court

---

Justice Goldberg gave the activist wing a working majority on most civil liberties issues. *See* B. SCHWARTZ, *supra* note 23, at 445-50; 2 ENCYCLOPEDIA OF THE AMERICAN CONSTITUTION, *supra* note 23, at 848-49. The working majority continued when Justice Goldberg retired and was replaced with Justice Abe Fortas (1965-69), and the Court moved further to the left when Justice Thurgood Marshall replaced Justice Clark in 1967. *See* 3 *id.* at 1209-11. Justice Black moved discernibly to the right in the later 1960s, but after the appointment of Justice Marshall, Black's vote was not necessary for the progressive working majority. *See* B. SCHWARTZ, *supra* note 23, at 629-79.

29. For accounts of the Civil Rights Act of 1964, see H. GRAHAM, *supra* note 22, at 74-152; C. WHALEN & B. WHALEN, *supra* note 27. For accounts of the Voting Rights Act of 1965, see H. GRAHAM, *supra* note 22, at 162-76; S. LAWSON, BLACK BALLOTS: VOTING RIGHTS IN THE SOUTH, 1944-1969, at 307-22 (1976). *See generally* A. THERNSTROM, WHOSE VOTES COUNT? (1987).

30. *See* South Carolina v. Katzenbach, 383 U.S. 301 (1966) (9-0 vote); Katzenbach v. McClung, 379 U.S. 294 (1964) (9-0 vote); Heart of Atlanta Motel, Inc. v. United States, 379 U.S. 241 (1964) (9-0 vote).

31. 380 U.S. 145 (1965).

32. Act of May 31, 1870, ch. 114, 16 Stat. 140 (current version at 42 U.S.C. § 1971(a) (1988)).

33. This is not a test but a trap, sufficient to stop even the most brilliant man on his way to the voting booth. The cherished right of people in a country like ours to vote cannot be obliterated by the use of laws like this, which leave the voting fate of a citizen to the passing whim or impulse of an individual registrar.

Louisiana, 380 U.S. at 153; *cf.* Lassiter v. Northampton Election Bd., 360 U.S. 45, 51 (1959) (upholding a state literacy test against similar statutory and constitutional challenge, but suggesting that Congress could constitutionally prohibit the practice through affirmative legislation).

34. *See Voting Rights: Hearings on H.R. 6400 Before Subcomm. No. 5 of the House Comm. on the Judiciary,* 89th Cong., 1st Sess. 13-18 (1965) (statement of Nicholas Katzenbach, Attorney General of the United States) (asserting the constitutionality of the bill, and citing *Louisiana* in support), 469-98 (discussing and inserting into the record *Louisiana*).

35. 383 U.S. 745 (1966).

36. *Id.* at 754-56, 759 n.17; *see also* United States v. Price, 383 U.S. 787 (1966) (extending criminal liability for deprivation of civil rights to private parties in conspiracy with state officials).

was closely divided on the statute's exact reach,[37] but a majority called upon Congress to expand the statute to reach a greater number of private conspiracies.[38] Title V of President Johnson's omnibus 1966 civil rights bill followed the Court's suggestion precisely.[39] The House passed the bill in 1966, but an incipient end-of-session Senate filibuster killed it. The same bill was resubmitted in 1967.[40] The House passed the title V portion in 1967, and in 1968 the House bill became the mechanism by which most of the 1966 administration proposals, including the protection of civil rights workers, were enacted into law.[41]

Although title VIII, which established rights to nondiscrimination in housing, was the centerpiece of the Civil Rights Act of 1968, the Court dynamically interpreted a much earlier statute to afford victims of such discrimination significantly greater protection. Within weeks of title VIII's enactment, the Supreme Court in *Jones v. Alfred H. Mayer Co.*[42] interpreted the Civil Rights Act of 1866 to provide parallel remedies. Section 1982 of title 42, the current codification of part of the 1866 Act, protects against racial discrimination in the sale, lease, or other conveyance of real or personal property. After making a detailed historical interpretation of section 1982 in its original form as part of the 1866 Act,[43] the Court held that the statute applied to more than state action: It held the statute comprehended purely private discrimination as well.[44]

Following the lead of lower courts, the Supreme Court similarly

37. *Guest,* 383 U.S. at 782 n.6 (Brennan, J., joined by the Chief Justice and Justice Douglas, concurring in part and dissenting in part).

38. *See id.* at 782-83, 786; *id.* at 762 (Clark, J., concurring) ("[T]here now can be no doubt that the specific language of [the Fourteenth Amendment] empowers the Congress to enact laws punishing all conspiracies—with or without state action—that interfere with Fourteenth Amendment rights.").

39. *See* H.R. 14765, 89th Cong., 2d Sess. (1966); *see also Civil Rights, 1966: Hearings Before Subcomm. No. 5 of the House Comm. on the Judiciary,* 89th Cong., 2d Sess. 1073 (1966) [hereinafter *Civil Rights, 1966 Hearings*] (title V is "a responsible answer to the *Guest* case"); *id.* at 1129-69 (*Guest* opinions inserted into the hearings record), 1097-128 (also inserting language from the opinions in United States v. Price, 383 U.S. 787 (1966)). Title V was written not only to codify and expand upon *Guest,* but also to modify the interpretation of section 241 in United States v. Screws, 325 U.S. 91 (1945). *See Civil Rights, 1966 Hearings, supra,* at 1074.

40. *See* H.R. 5700, 90th Cong., 1st Sess. (1967); S. 1026, 90th Cong., 1st Sess. (1967). Soon after its introduction, the omnibus bill was broken up into separate bills, each focusing on one of the titles of the original bill. S. 1362 embodied title V, but it was never reported from committee. H.R. 2516 embodied title V and was passed by the House in 1967, with amendments and after the House had passed an anti-riot bill.

41. *See* Act of Apr. 11, 1968, Pub. L. No. 90-284, 82 Stat. 73.

42. 392 U.S. 409 (1968).

43. *See id.* at 422-36. The dissenting opinion's arguments for a contrary interpretation found much scholarly support. *See, e.g.,* C. FAIRMAN, RECONSTRUCTION AND REUNION, 1864-1888, at 1258 (1971); Casper, Jones v. Mayer: *Clio, Bemused and Confused Muse,* 1968 SUP. CT. REV. 89.

44. *Jones,* 392 U.S. at 437. One Justice found that current conditions alone required the Court's expansive interpretation. *See id.* at 444-49 (Douglas, J., concurring) (describing continuing "badges of slavery").

reinterpreted section 1981 (the 1866 protection against racial discrimination in the making of contracts) to apply to purely private conduct.[45] The Supreme Court's dynamic interpretation of sections 1982 and 1981 effectively gave more liberal remedies for racial discrimination in housing and workplace discrimination than those afforded by title VIII and title VII, respectively.

Jones v. Mayer is one of the Warren Court's last statutory interpretation decisions. *Jones* was the only Supreme Court civil rights decision of this period to come close to a congressional override. Referring to the Civil Rights Act of 1866 by name, Senator Hruska introduced an amendment during debate on the Equal Employment Opportunity Act of 1972[46] to make title VII and the Equal Pay Act the exclusive remedies for workplace discrimination.[47] The Hruska amendment would have overruled *Jones v. Mayer* insofar as it interpreted that part of the 1866 Act which is codified in section 1981. The amendment was rejected by a tie vote in the Senate,[48] but a similar amendment was adopted on the House floor.[49] In conference, the House backed off from its earlier position, and the final version of the 1972 Act had no exclusive remedy provision.[50]

The progressive position of the late Warren Court and early Burger Court carried over into a dynamic and liberal interpretation of the 1960s civil rights statutes. The key development in this period was the Court's policy shift from equality in opportunity (the focus of legislation in the 1960s) to equality of result (the practical focus of the legislation as implemented by the executive and the judiciary).[51] In short, the Court deemphasized the original goal of creating a colorblind society where only individual qualifications matter, and emphasized the new goal of creating a society where group results matter and reference to race is appropriate in decisionmaking (in order to advance the substantive goal). In one case, *Allen v. State Board of Elections*,[52] the Court by a seven-to-two vote interpreted the Voting Rights Act very liberally (and contrary to some important legislative history)[53] to invalidate even minor electoral changes

45. *See* Runyon v. McCrary, 427 U.S. 160 (1976) (private schools); Johnson v. Railway Express Agency, 421 U.S. 454 (1975) (private employers); Tillman v. Wheaton-Haven Recreation Ass'n, 410 U.S. 431 (1973) (community swimming pool).

46. Pub. L. No. 92-261, 86 Stat. 103.

47. 118 CONG. REC. 3172-73 (1972).

48. *Id.* at 3373; *see also id.* at 3965 (lopsided vote on reconsideration).

49. *See* 117 CONG. REC. 31,973, 32,111 (1971) (House discussion of Erlenborn amendment and its adoption).

50. *See* H.R. CONF. REP. NO. 899, 92d Cong., 2d Sess. 17 (1972).

51. *See generally* H. GRAHAM, *supra* note 22, at 233-54 (early administrative shift to equal results); *id.* at 366-92 (judicial shift); A. THERNSTROM, *supra* note 29 (similar shift for voting rights).

52. 393 U.S. 544 (1969).

53. *Compare id.* at 564-69 (majority opinion's discussion of the legislative history) *with id.* at

that potentially diluted the votes of blacks.[54] In another case, a unanimous Court in *Griggs v. Duke Power Co.*[55] interpreted title VII to prohibit employment practices that unintentionally have a disparate impact upon minorities.

Both decisions were dynamic interpretations of recently enacted statutes, developed by the Court in cooperation with the executive's vigorous implementation. They were also probably much more progressive than the view of a median Member of Congress. Yet when Congress extended the Voting Rights Act in 1970,[56] it made no effort to overrule *Allen.* Moreover, the House committee report used the Supreme Court's precedents to explain the statute's importance and operation.[57] When Congress amended title VII in 1972, both the House and Senate committee reports explicitly endorsed the *Griggs* decision and its equality-of-result implications.[58]

B. Court/Congress Confrontations: 1972-86

Escalating conflict between the Court and Congress over the nation's civil rights agenda marked the second decade of the modern statutory civil rights era. The most important development during this era was the gradual rightward drift of the Presidency and the Supreme Court, relative to Congress. The Nixon and Carter administrations progressively interpreted and vigorously enforced existing civil rights laws, albeit not as strongly as the Johnson administration.[59] The Reagan administration, however, took a sharp turn to the right on most key

588-91 (Harlan, J., concurring in part and dissenting in part) (criticizing majority opinion's discussion of legislative history).

54. Section 5 of the Act requires "preclearance" by the Attorney General of any changes in the electoral systems of designated states whose prior systems had discriminated against black voters. *Allen* found that the following changes, among others, were covered by section 5: (1) a change from district to at-large voting for county officials; (2) a system change making a county official position only appointive rather than elective *or* appointive; and (3) rules making it harder for an independent candidate to get on the ballot. *Id.* at 550-51, 572.

55. 401 U.S. 424 (1971) (proscribing employee tests not related to job performance).

56. Pub. L. No. 91-285, 84 Stat. 314 (1970).

57. H.R. REP. NO. 397, 91st Cong., 2d Sess. 2, 4-8, *reprinted in* 1970 U.S. CODE CONG. & ADMIN. NEWS 3277, 3278, 3280-84.

58. *See* H.R. REP. NO. 238, 92d Cong., 1st Sess. 21-22 (1971), *reprinted in* 1972 U.S. CODE CONG & ADMIN. NEWS 2137, 2156-67; S. REP. NO. 415, 92d Cong., 1st Sess. 14 (1971).

59. The Nixon and Carter administrations look alike, even though President Carter personally was more committed to civil rights than was President Nixon. The key boosters of the progressive agenda in both administrations were the Assistant Attorneys General for Civil Rights—Stanley Pottinger (Nixon) and Drew Days (Carter). In both administrations, my impression is that the Attorneys General—Mitchell, Kleindienst, Saxbe, and Levi (Nixon-Ford), and Bell and Civiletti (Carter)—were not as committed as the Assistants were. *See generally* H. GRAHAM, *supra* note 22, at 301-420 (information on the Nixon period); Days, *Fullilove,* 96 YALE L.J. 453 (1987) (information on the Carter period).

aspects of civil rights statutory interpretation.[60]

The Supreme Court's shift to the right was more gradual. It began in 1972, when Justices Rehnquist and Powell first started to cast votes.[61] Subsequent appointments in 1975, 1981, and 1986 moved the Court further to the right.[62] Although there was internal migration to the left by individual Justices during this same period,[63] by 1986 the Rehnquist Court stood significantly to the right of the early Burger Court.

In contrast, congressional preferences were moving to the left after 1973.[64] By the 1970s, a reliable civil rights coalition emerged, consisting of a rainbow of unions, black groups, women's groups, and other public interest groups. The House Democratic leadership and the relevant committees agreed with the coalition's civil rights agenda.[65] The story in the Senate was more complicated, because from 1981 to 1987 it was controlled by Republicans. Although the Republican leadership in the Senate was not hostile to the civil rights coalition outright, it was never as strongly nor consistently allied with the coalition as was the Democratic leadership. The relevant Senate committees continued to

60. I believe this generalization applies particularly to President Reagan, Attorney General Edwin Meese, and Assistant Attorney General William Bradford Reynolds. *Cf.* Days, *The Courts' Response to the Reagan Civil Rights Agenda,* 42 VAND. L. REV. 1003 (1989) (noting judicial resistance to Reagan's anti-affirmative action agenda); Days, *Turning Back the Clock: The Reagan Administration and Civil Rights,* 19 HARV. C.R.-C.L. L. REV. 309 (1984) ("[T]he Reagan Administration has inadequately enforced and otherwise undermined, if not violated outright, settled law in the field of civil rights.").

61. These two Justices were appointed to succeed Justices Harlan and Black, respectively, in 1971, but did not begin to vote in cases until 1972. One study has suggested that their pre-Court preferences were very conservative and that their Court votes simply reflected that conservatism. *See* Segal & Cover, *Ideological Values and the Votes of U.S. Supreme Court Justices,* 83 AM. POL. SCI. REV. 557, 560 table 1 (1989).

62. *Id.* at 559-60. The events were Justice Stevens' succession to Justice Douglas' seat (1975), Justice O'Connor's succession to Justice Stewart's seat (1981), Chief Justice Rehnquist's succession to Chief Justice Burger's seat (1986), and Justice Scalia's succession to Justice Rehnquist's seat (1986).

63. The most dramatic movement was by Justice Blackmun, who moved from being a "Minnesota Twin" of Chief Justice Burger, to become an ally of Justices Brennan and Marshall (the remnants of the 1960s Warren Court). Also gravitating to the left were Justices Stevens and Powell. On the other hand, Justice White gravitated to the right during the 1980s, as did Chief Justice Burger (who is, however, harder to pin down because of his strategic voting).

64. *See* Sinclair, *supra* note 26, at 306-11 (big jump in "civil liberties" support scores from 1969-72 to 1973-76, 1977-80, and 1981-82).

65. Liberal Peter Rodino (D-N.J.) chaired the Judiciary Committee from 1973 to 1989, and with him was a solid liberal majority through those years. Liberal Carl Perkins (D-Ky.) chaired the Education and Labor Committee until 1985, when he was succeeded by the even more liberal Augustus Hawkins (D-Cal.); both chairs have enjoyed solid liberal majorities (including Republican votes) during these years. See the lists of Committee members and their ADA scores in M. BARONE, G. UJIFUSA & D. MATTHEWS, THE ALMANAC OF AMERICAN POLITICS [hereinafter THE ALMANAC OF AMERICAN POLITICS] published for 1974, 1976, 1978, 1980, 1982, 1984, 1986, and 1988. The Rules Committee, long controlled by Southern Democrats, fell under the control of the liberal Democratic leadership after 1973. *See* R. DAVIDSON & W. OLESZEK, CONGRESS AND ITS MEMBERS 273-74 (1983).

have at least slim majorities in support of the coalition[66] but did not have supportive committee chairs.[67]

As the Court moved to the right of Congress, the cooperative relationship between the Court and Congress began to erode. While there were no legislative overrides of the Court's civil rights statutory interpretations between 1962 and 1972, there were significant overrides between 1972 and 1986. Several Congressmen publicly accused the Court, not only of creating bad policy, but also of affirmatively misinterpreting legislative intent.

1. Civil Rights Attorney's Fees Statutes

In the first of these legislative overrides, Congress reacted to the Court's own invitation. In *Alyeska Pipeline Service Co. v. Wilderness Society*,[68] a five-to-two Court held that attorney's fees were generally not recoverable by "private attorneys general" enforcing important public rights, unless the relevant federal statute contained explicit provisions for fee-shifting.[69] The Court's decision had what critics in Congress termed a "devastating impact" on civil rights litigation.[70] Within a year, Congress enacted the Civil Rights Attorney's Fees Awards Act,[71] which provided for fee-shifting in favor of civil rights plaintiffs. The Voting Rights Act Extension in 1975 included similar fee-shifting provisions in response to *Alyeska*.[72] The Equal Access to Justice Act of 1980, which permitted counsel fee awards against the federal government in some cases, was also in part a congressional response to *Alyeska*.[73]

66. Although the Judiciary Committee was chaired by conservative Senator Thurmond (R-S.C.) during this period, liberals had a theoretical working majority, consisting of the eight Democrats and two moderate Republicans (Senators Mathias (R-Md.) and Specter (R-Pa.)). Although the Labor and Human Resources Committee was chaired by conservative Senator Hatch (R-Ut.) during this period, liberals here too had a working majority, consisting of the seven Democrats and two moderate Republicans (Senators Stafford (R-Vt.) and Weicker (R-Ct.)). For the members of these committees and their ADA scores, see THE ALMANAC OF AMERICAN POLITICS 1982, 1984, and 1986, *supra* note 65.

67. Senator Hatch chaired the Labor and Human Resources Committee, and Senator Thurmond chaired the Judiciary Committee. Both were much more conservative than the median Republican Senator, and are hardly on the same chart as the median Democratic Senator. *See* sources cited *supra* note 66.

68. 421 U.S. 240 (1975).

69. *Id.* at 247-71.

70. *See* H.R. REP. NO. 1558, 94th Cong., 2d Sess. 3 (1976); S. REP. NO. 1011, 94th Cong., 2d Sess. 4 (1976) [hereinafter *Fees Act Senate Report*] (*Alyeska* "created anomalous gaps in our civil rights laws"). Note that *Alyeska* itself did not involve civil rights litigation (as I am using the term, *see supra* note 17), but I include it because the congressional overrides of it focused on civil rights litigation.

71. Pub. L. No. 94-559, 90 Stat. 2641 (1976) (codified at 42 U.S.C. § 1988 (1988)).

72. Pub. L. No. 94-73, § 402, 89 Stat. 400, 404 (1975); *see* S. REP. NO. 295, 94th Cong., 1st Sess. 40-43 [hereinafter *Voting Rights Senate Report*], *reprinted in* 1975 U.S. CODE CONG. & ADMIN. NEWS 774.

73. Pub. L. No. 96-481, § 203, 94 Stat. 2325 (codified as amended at 5 U.S.C. § 504 (1988)).

The legislative debates indicate that a majority of Congress approved of the prior lower court fee-shifting practice and did not agree with *Alyeska.* "This bill creates no startling new remedy—it only meets the technical requirements that the Supreme Court has laid down if the Federal courts are to continue the practice of awarding attorneys' fees which had been going on for years prior to the Court's May [1975] decision."[74] Thus, *Alyeska* may be seen as stimulating Congress to enact into law what it already approved of, and expected, in practice.

2. Age Discrimination Act Amendments of 1978

The next congressional override was more confrontational. It involved the Court's interpretation of the Age Discrimination in Employment Act of 1967 (ADEA). The ADEA's stated purpose was to promote the employment of older persons and to "prohibit arbitrary age discrimination in employment."[75] An issue arising under the ADEA was whether section 4(f)(2)'s exception for any "bona fide employee benefit plan . . . which is not a subterfuge to evade" the statute[76] justified the continuation of age-based mandatory retirement plans already in force when the ADEA was enacted. The Department of Labor's regulations implementing the Act narrowly construed the exception to protect only those plans that offered "equal benefit or equal cost" to older workers.[77] The circuits had split on the issue of whether the exclusion validated some mandatory retirement plans. To resolve the split, the Senate committee, in a report dated October 12, 1977, specifically approved the Fourth Circuit's decision in *McMann v. United Airlines*[78] as the correct interpretation of the provision.[79]

Only two months later, the Supreme Court reversed the Fourth Circuit's *McMann* decision by a five-to-two majority. The Court interpreted the ADEA in line with the cases the Senate committee had criticized and rejected in favor of the Fourth Circuit's interpretation.[80] The dissenting opinion argued that the original expectations of Congress in

74. *Fees Act Senate Report, supra* note 70, at 4; *see also id.* at 1 ("The purpose of this amendment is to remedy anomalous gaps in our civil rights laws created by the United States Supreme Court's recent decision in [*Alyeska*] . . . ."); *Voting Rights Senate Report, supra* note 72, at 42 ("The *Alyeska* decision created an unexpected and anomalous gap in our civil rights laws whereby awards of fees are barred in the most fundamental civil rights cases.").

75. Age Discrimination in Employment Act of 1967, Pub. L. No. 90-202, § 2(b), 81 Stat. 602 (codified at 29 U.S.C. § 621(b) (1988)).

76. *Id.* § 4(f)(2), 81 Stat. 602, 603 (codified at 29 U.S.C. § 623(f)(2) (1988)).

77. *See* 29 C.F.R. §§ 860.110, 860.120 (1976); *see also* Public Employees Retirement Sys. v. Betts, 109 S. Ct. 2854, 2862 (1989) (interpreting these sections).

78. 542 F.2d 217 (4th Cir. 1976) (ruling that ADEA proscribed mandatory retirement of employees at age 60 solely because of employee's membership in a retirement plan).

79. S. REP. No. 493, 95th Cong., 1st Sess. 10 (1977), *reprinted in* 1978 U.S. CODE CONG. & ADMIN. NEWS 504, 513.

80. United Airlines v. McMann, 434 U.S. 192, 197-98 (1977).

1967 had been to invalidate plans like United's.[81] The majority responded that the statutory exception for bona fide plans was unambiguous.[82]

Predictably, Congress immediately overrode the Court's construction with the Age Discrimination in Employment Act Amendments of 1978.[83] Senator Javits (R-N.Y.), who had authored section 4(f)(2), explained that the Labor Department in its regulations, and not the Supreme Court, had correctly interpreted the section.[84] The conference committee reiterated the ADEA's "original purposes" and the original legislative expectation that plans such as United's would be invalidated: "In [*McMann*] the Supreme Court held to the contrary . . . . The conferees specifically disagree with the Supreme Court's holding and reasoning in that case."[85] This decisive overriding marked the beginning of the present Court/Congress conflict over the interpretation of civil rights laws.

3. *The Pregnancy Discrimination Act of 1978*

By a six-to-three vote, the Supreme Court in *General Electric Co. v. Gilbert*[86] held that an employer's exclusion of pregnancy-related disabilities from its employee disability plan does not violate title VII's proscription against discrimination " 'because of [the] individual's . . . sex.' "[87] Had the Court looked to the exclusion's disparate impact as it had in *Griggs*,[88] it might have reached a different conclusion, since excluding pregnancy-related conditions has an obvious gender-based effect.[89] The Court, however, interpreted title VII in light of its decision in *Geduldig v. Aiello*,[90] where it held that pregnancy-based state regulation does not violate the equal protection clause of the Constitution.[91] *Gilbert* reasoned

---

81. *Id.* at 211-18 (Marshall, J., dissenting).

82. *Id.* at 199, 203. Ironically, the Court still responded (somewhat lamely) to the dissent's legislative history arguments. *See id.* at 199-202.

83. Pub. L. No. 95-256, § 2, 92 Stat. 189 (codified in scattered sections of 29 U.S.C. (1988)).

84. S. REP. No. 493, 95th Cong., 1st Sess. 31 (1977).

85. H.R. CONF. REP. No. 950, 95th Cong., 2d Sess. 8, *reprinted in* 1978 U.S. CODE CONG. & ADMIN. NEWS 528, 529.

86. 429 U.S. 125 (1976).

87. *Id.* at 133 (quoting 42 U.S.C. § 2000e-(a)(1) (1988)).

88. Griggs v. Duke Power Co., 401 U.S. 424 (1971).

89. There is a *Griggs*-based counterargument: Surveys suggested that firms spent more money on women's health plans even without pregnancy benefits, and the addition of pregnancy benefits increased the already existing disparity even more in favor of female workers. *See Legislation to Prohibit Sex Discrimination on the Basis of Pregnancy: Hearing on H.R. 5055 and H.R. 6075 Before the Subcomm. on Employment Opportunities of the House Comm. on Education and Labor*, 95th Cong., 1st Sess. 84, 85-86 (1971) [hereinafter *PDA House Hearings*] (statement of G. Brockwel Heylin, labor relations attorney, Chamber of Commerce of the United States) (describing surveys).

90. 417 U.S. 484 (1974).

91. *Gilbert*, 429 U.S. at 134 (citing *Geduldig*, 417 U.S. at 494).

that classifications based upon pregnancy divide the world into two groups: pregnant women versus men and nonpregnant women. Consequently, the rule did not exclude anyone from benefits solely on the basis of gender, and only "remove[d] one physical condition—pregnancy—from the list of compensable disabilities."[92] Although the majority acknowledged that the exclusion was gender-related, it noted that the plaintiffs had failed to demonstrate that this exclusion was a pretext for sex-based discrimination.[93] The Court's decision in *Gilbert* raised questions about the future viability of *Griggs*.[94]

The political response to *Gilbert* was swift and furious. The decision came down in December 1976, and within a week, women's organizations, progressive unions, civil rights groups, and several general public interest groups formed an umbrella lobbying group, the Campaign to End Discrimination Against Pregnant Workers.[95] Early in 1977, legislation was introduced in both chambers to overrule *Gilbert* by defining discrimination on the basis of gender to include pregnancy-based distinctions.[96] Hearings were held in both chambers in April 1977.[97] Although business and insurance groups vigorously opposed the new legislation, it was even more vigorously supported by the administration, labor unions and the AFL-CIO, various women's groups, and assorted civil rights and public interest groups. The relevant committees enthusiastically reported the bills (though the House committee bowed to pressure from the National Conference of Catholic Bishops to add a proviso that employers would not have to pay for abortion-related expenses[98]).

The resulting Pregnancy Discrimination Act (PDA) is notable in part because the key legislative players rushed to declare, with unusual fervor, that the Court had misinterpreted title VII. The committee

92. *Id.*

93. *Id.* at 134-36.

94. *Compare id.* at 146 (Blackmun, J., concurring in part) (raising the issue of *Griggs* but refusing to join in any suggestion that it is not still good law) *with id.* (Stewart, J., concurring) (saying viability of *Griggs* is not an issue and stating that in any event the Court's opinion does not retreat from *Griggs*).

95. *See PDA House Hearings, supra* note 89, at 30-42, 47.

96. H.R. 5055, 95th Cong., 1st Sess. (1977) (introduced by Rep. Hawkins (D-Cal.) with 81 sponsors) (superseded by H.R. 6075, 95th Cong., 1st Sess. (1977) (introduced by Rep. Hawkins with 119 sponsors by 1978, when the bill was reported)); S. 995, 95th Cong., 1st Sess. (1977).

97. *See PDA House Hearings, supra* note 89 (hearings held April 6, 1977, and June 29, 1977); *Discrimination on the Basis of Pregnancy, 1977: Hearings on S. 995 Before the Subcomm. on Labor of the Senate Comm. on Human Resources,* 95th Cong., 1st Sess. (1977) [hereinafter *PDA Senate Hearings*] (hearings held on April 26, 27, and 29, 1977).

98. *See* H.R. REP. NO. 948, 95th Cong., 2d Sess. (Mar. 13, 1978) [hereinafter *PDA House Report*], *reprinted in* 1978 U.S. CODE CONG. & ADMIN. NEWS 4749. The Senate bill did not have this proviso, *see* S. REP. NO. 331, 95th Cong., 1st Sess. (1977) [hereinafter *PDA Senate Report*], and the House conference committee subsequently watered down the House version. *See* H.R. CONF. REP. NO. 1786, 95th Cong., 2d Sess. (1978), *reprinted in* 1978 U.S. CODE CONG. & ADMIN. NEWS 4765.

reports asserted that "the dissenting Justices [in *Gilbert*] correctly interpreted the Act."[99] The statements of the PDA's sponsors were even stronger: "By concluding that pregnancy discrimination is not sex discrimination within the meaning of title VII, the Supreme Court disregarded the intent of Congress in enacting title VII. That intent was to protect all individuals from unjust employment discrimination, including pregnant women."[100]

4. *The Voting Rights Act of 1982*

The next major confrontation between the Court and Congress followed the Court's decision in *City of Mobile v. Bolden.*[101] The lower courts had invalidated, as a violation of the fifteenth amendment, the at-large method of electing city commissioners in Mobile, Alabama. The Supreme Court reversed. The Court's plurality opinion[102] admonished the lower courts for not considering the statutory issue first—whether the at-large system violated section 2 of the Voting Rights Act—but then held that section 2 merely "restated" fifteenth amendment requirements.[103] The plurality opinion then found that the fifteenth amendment required that challengers to a voting mechanism prove a discriminatory intent in order to prevail. A fifth Justice articulated a different, and arguably more restrictive, fifteenth amendment standard.[104] The dissenting Justices argued that the plurality's fifteenth amendment test represented a significant departure from the precedents established by the Warren Court and early Burger Court.[105]

Because there was no majority opinion, *Bolden* provoked as much

99. *PDA House Report, supra* note 98, at 2; *see also id.* ("It is the Committee's view that [the EEOC] guidelines rightly implemented the Title VII prohibition of sex discrimination in the 1964 Act."); *PDA Senate Report, supra* note 98, at 2-3 (same, almost verbatim).

100. *PDA Senate Hearings, supra* note 97, at 1 (opening statement of Sen. Williams (D-N.J.), committee chairman). Williams was also a key supporter of the 1964 Civil Rights Act. *See also id.* at 6-20 (statement of Sen. Bayh (D-Ind.)); *id.* at 20-23 (statement of Sen. Mathias (R-Md.)); *PDA House Hearings, supra* note 89, at 1 (opening statement of Rep. Hawkins (D-Cal.), committee chairman). Senator Bayh, then-Representative Mathias, and Representative Hawkins were all supporters of the 1964 Civil Rights Act.

101. 446 U.S. 55 (1980).

102. The plurality was authored by Justice Stewart, *id.* at 58, one of the most conservative of the Warren Court Justices. *See* Segal & Cover, *supra* note 61, at 561-62 (indicating Justice Stewart's relative conservatism as compared to Justices Warren, Brennan, Fortas, Goldberg, Marshall, and White). The opinion was joined by three of the four Nixon Justices, namely Burger, Powell, and Rehnquist. Justice Blackmun, the other Nixon appointee, concurred in the result. *Bolden,* 446 U.S. at 80-83. Justice Stevens, appointed by Ford, concurred in the judgment. *Id.* at 83-94. The three other Warren Court holdovers—Justices Brennan, Marshall, and White—dissented. *Id.* at 94-141.

103. *Id.* at 61.

104. *See id.* at 83-94 (Stevens, J., concurring in the judgment).

105. *See id.* at 94 (White, J., dissenting); *id.* at 108-12 (Marshall, J., dissenting) (relying on White v. Regester, 412 U.S. 755 (1973), Burns v. Richardson, 384 U.S. 73 (1966), and Fortson v. Dorsey, 379 U.S. 433 (1965)).

confusion as outrage. Decided in April 1980, *Bolden* came at the worst possible time for a legislative override. It was decided at the end of Congress' second session and in a critical presidential election year. As a consequence, Congress did not have adequate time to override *Bolden*, and so postponed serious consideration until 1981.

That year, Republicans took control of the Presidency and the Senate. Nevertheless, serious efforts were mounted early in the next Congress to override *Bolden*'s interpretation of the Voting Rights Act.[106] Hearings during the summer of 1981 yielded virtually unchallenged testimony from law professors, litigation groups, and groups in the civil rights coalition that *Bolden* was a radical departure from the Court's statutory, as well as constitutional, precedents and that *Bolden* had fashioned an approach to voting rights that was both confusing and counterproductive.[107] With little open opposition, Congress overrode *Bolden* in the Voting Rights Act Amendments of 1982.[108]

Just as had occurred twice in 1978, the 1982 legislative override was accompanied by a congressional claim that it was defending the statutory status quo. Key legislators stated that the Court, not the Congress, had shifted policy direction; Congress was merely correcting the Court's erroneous interpretation. The Republican-controlled Senate Judiciary Committee put it most carefully:

> While the Committee finds that Congress did not seek to include an intent test in the original provision of section 2, a plurality of four justices in [*Bolden*] thought that it did. The Court is the ultimate interpreter of laws once enacted. But in any event, there is no question that Congress may now decide that an intent requirement is inappropriate for section 2, and amend [the] statute to make that point clearly.[109]

5. *Rehabilitation Act Amendments of 1986*

In 1986, Congress enacted three different statutes to override three Supreme Court decisions, all involving the rights of handicapped Americans. The first of these overridings was fairly routine. In *United*

106. *See* H.R. 3112, 96th Cong., 1st Sess. 70 (1981) (introduced by Rep. Rodino (D-N.J.) on April 7); H.R. 3198, 96th Cong., 1st Sess. 72 (1981) (introduced by Rep. Hyde (R-Ill.) on April 9); S. 995, 96th Cong., 1st Sess. (1981) (introduced by Sens. Mathias (R-Md.) and Kennedy (D-Mass.)).

107. *See Extension of the Voting Rights Act: Hearings Before the Subcomm. on Civil and Constitutional Rights of the House Comm. on the Judiciary*, 97th Cong., 1st Sess. *passim* (1981).

108. Pub. L. No. 97-205, § 3, 96 Stat. 131, 134 (codified at 42 U.S.C. § 1973 (1988)).

109. S. REP. NO. 417, 97th Cong., 2d Sess. 17 n.49, *reprinted in* 1982 U.S. CODE CONG. & ADMIN. NEWS 177, 194 n.49; *see also id.* at 26, *reprinted in* 1982 U.S. CODE CONG. & ADMIN. NEWS 177, 203 ("A fair reading of *Bolden* reveals that the plurality opinion was a marked departure from earlier Supreme Court and lower court vote dilution cases."); *id.* at 27, *reprinted in* 1982 U.S. CODE CONG. & ADMIN. NEWS 177, 205 ("The 'results' standard is meant to restore the pre-*Mobile* legal standard . . . .").

States Department of Transportation v. Paralyzed Veterans of America,[110] the Court had interpreted section 504 of the Rehabilitation Act of 1973 to be inapplicable to air carriers.[111] Within the year, Congress responded with the Air Carrier Access Act of 1986,[112] which authorized the Department of Transportation to develop regulations protecting handicapped people against discrimination. Unlike the PDA, the ADEA Amendments, or the Voting Rights Act Amendments, this statute reflected congressional disagreement with the Court's outcome, not its role in the case.[113]

The same cannot be said of Congress' response to *Atascadero State Hospital v. Scanlon.*[114] By a five-to-four vote, the Court held that the Rehabilitation Act had not abrogated the states' eleventh amendment immunity. The Court's holding was based upon its increasingly aggressive stance toward protecting state sovereign immunity.[115] The decision greatly surprised Congress, which believed that it had specifically abrogated the sovereign immunity defense in the Act. Section 504 prohibited discrimination against the handicapped in "any program or activity receiving Federal financial assistance."[116] Obviously, this included many state programs. Moreover, Congress had conducted its debates under the assumption that the states could be sued.[117] Within a month of the Court's decision, a bill was introduced to override it.[118] The override provisions were incorporated into the omnibus Rehabilitation Act Amendments of 1986.[119]

The override of *Atascadero* was not a difficult decision for Congress. It considered the Court's interpretation simply wrong. "The Supreme Court's decision misinterpreted congressional intent," stated the committee report. "Such a gap in Section 504 coverage was never intended. It would be inequitable for Section 504 to mandate state compliance with

---

110. 477 U.S. 597 (1986).

111. *Id.* at 599 (quoting 29 U.S.C. § 794 (1982)).

112. Pub. L. No. 99-435, 100 Stat. 1080.

113. *See* S. REP. NO. 99-400, 99th Cong., 2d Sess. 2 (1986) ("In recognition of the unique difficulties now faced by handicapped air travelers, [the bill] would mitigate the effect of *DOT v. PVA* by amending section 404 of the Federal Aviation Act of 1958 to prohibit specifically discrimination against otherwise qualified handicapped individuals."), *reprinted in* 1986 U.S. CODE CONG. & ADMIN. NEWS 2328, 2330.

114. 473 U.S. 234 (1985).

115. *See id.* at 242 ("Our reluctance to infer that a State's immunity from suit in the federal courts has been negated stems from recognition of the vital role of the doctrine of sovereign immunity in our federal system.") (quoting Pennhurst State School & Hosp. v. Halderman (*Pennhurst II*), 465 U.S. 89, 99 (1984)).

116. *Id.* at 245 (quoting 29 U.S.C. § 794 (1988)).

117. *See id.* at 248 (Brennan, J., dissenting).

118. S. 1579, 99th Cong., 2d Sess. (1986) (introduced on August 1 by Sen. Cranston (D-Cal.), with five cosponsors, including two liberal Republicans—Sen. Stafford (R-Vt.) and Sen. Weicker (R-Conn.)).

119. Pub. L. No. 99-506, § 1003, 100 Stat. 1845 (codified at 42 U.S.C. § 2000d-7 (1988)).

its provisions and yet deny litigants the right to enforce their rights in Federal courts when State or State agency actions are at issue."[120] This reasoning was precisely that of the *Atascadero* dissenters, whose views the committee report endorsed.

6. *The Handicapped Children's Protection Act of 1986*

The third statutory override of 1986 also involved the rights of the handicapped. In *Smith v. Robinson,*[121] the Court held that the Education of All Handicapped Children Act of 1975 (EHA)[122] was handicapped children's exclusive source of remedies.[123] As a consequence, handicapped children could not sue under section 504 of the Rehabilitation Act, which offered the advantage of counsel fee awards to prevailing plaintiffs.[124] Bills to overrule *Smith v. Robinson* were introduced within months of the decision and enjoyed substantial bipartisan support. Although bills passed both the House and Senate in 1985, the measure languished in conference for almost a year. The source of the delay was a provision in the Senate bill imposing limits on fee awards to publicly funded legal aid lawyers.[125] In July 1986, after that issue was resolved, both chambers approved by voice vote the Handicapped Children's Protection Act (HCPA).[126] Congressional rhetoric about being disappointed with the Court was not so keen for this bill as it had been in earlier overrides. Nevertheless, the committee report suggested that once again Congress agreed with the dissenting opinion.[127]

In overriding *Robinson,* however, Congress adopted a more tangible way of registering its disapproval. Enacted at the end of 1986, the HCPA provided that it would apply to all EHA actions pending on July 4, 1984 (the day before the Court's decision), as well as to all actions initiated after July 3, 1984.[128] This provision was not only a slap at the Court, but also triggered open presidential opposition and risked a veto. Nonetheless, the President ultimately signed the bill, over his constitu-

120. S. REP. NO. 99-388, 99th Cong., 2d Sess. 27-28 (1986).

121. 468 U.S. 992 (1984).

122. 84 Stat. 175 (codified as amended at 20 U.S.C. § 1400 *et seq.* (1988)).

123. *Robinson*, 468 U.S. at 1009, 1021.

124. *See id.* at 1021.

125. *See* 1985 CONG. Q. ALMANAC 297; 1986 CONG. Q. ALMANAC 271-72.

126. Pub. L. No. 99-372, 100 Stat. 796 (1986) (codified at 20 U.S.C. § 1415 (1988)).

127. *See* S. REP. NO. 99-112, 99th Cong., 2d Sess. 2 [hereinafter *HCPA Senate Report*] ("The situation which has resulted from the *Smith v. Robinson* decision was summarized by Justices Brennan, Marshall, and Stevens in their dissenting opinion: 'Congress will now have to take the time to revisit the matter.' " (quoting *Robinson,* 468 U.S. at 1031)), *reprinted in* 1986 U.S. CODE CONG. & ADMIN. NEWS 1798, 1799.

128. Handicapped Children's Protection Act, § 5, 100 Stat. 798 (1986) (codified at 20 U.S.C. § 1415 (1988)); *see HCPA Senate Report, supra* note 127, at 3, *reprinted in* 1986 U.S. CODE CONG. & ADMIN. NEWS 1800.

tional objections.[129]

C. Court/Congress/President Conflict: 1985-90

Even though no general preference shifts occurred in the late 1980s, the Court/Congress conflict heated up, intensified by more presidential involvement. The Court continued its rightward drift, with personnel changes in 1987 and 1990.[130] Congress moved to the left on civil rights matters after the 1986 election.[131] The Presidency showed the most significant movement by implementing a virtually unprecedented confrontational strategy *against* civil rights legislation. Presidents Kennedy and Johnson had battled Congress *for* civil rights legislation; Presidents Nixon, Ford, and Carter had cooperated with Congress-driven initiatives in the 1970s. And, although the early Reagan administration had publicly expressed reluctance about the Voting Rights Amendments of 1982, it did not take a strong public position against the Rehabilitation Act Amendments of 1986 or the Air Carrier Access Act of 1986. The later Reagan administration and the Bush administration reversed this trend, actively opposing important congressional overrides of civil rights precedents, using the veto threat aggressively, and actually vetoing civil rights legislation for the first time since Reconstruction.

1. The Civil Rights Restoration Act of 1988

The most important override since the PDA involved Congress' response to the Supreme Court's decision in *Grove City College v. Bell.*[132] Title IX of the Education Amendments of 1972 prohibits sex discrimination in any "education program or activity receiving Federal financial

129. Statement on Signing S. 415 Into Law, 1986 PUB. PAPERS 1056 (Ronald Reagan, Aug. 5, 1986) ("The retroactive application of the act to cases that are no longer pending permits the Congress to displace the judicial function by interfering with a final judgment.").

130. The Court shifted to the right when Justice Kennedy succeeded Justice Powell in 1987, and Justice Souter succeeded Justice Brennan in 1990. Note that Segal & Cover, *supra* note 61, at 560-62, list Justice Powell as more conservative than Justice Kennedy on civil liberties issues (including due process, freedom of expression, criminal justice as well as civil rights issues). In my opinion, on such issues as affirmative action, Justice Powell is more liberal. For example, Justice Powell joined the Court in Johnson v. Transportation Agency, 480 U.S. 616 (1987), whereas Justice Kennedy has joined opinions, such as *Wards Cove*, that are hostile to affirmative action.

131. The Democrats picked up eight Senate seats and control of the Senate. That re-established a liberal civil rights leadership in the Senate (Senators Mitchell and Cranston), and strengthened liberal control over the key committees. Senator Biden's (D-Del.) Judiciary Committee has had a liberal majority of nine to five on most issues (the eight Democrats plus Senator Specter (R-Pa.)). Senator Kennedy's Labor and Human Services Committee has had a liberal majority of eleven to five on most issues (nine Democrats and Senators Stafford (R-Vt.) and Weicker (R-Conn.) in 1987-89; nine Democrats and Senators Durenberger (R-Minn.) and Jeffords (R-Vt.) in 1989-91). See THE ALMANAC OF AMERICAN POLITICS 1988, *supra* note 65, for lists of Senators, committee memberships, and ADA scores for committee members.

132. 465 U.S. 555 (1984).

assistance."[133] Grove City College accepted no direct federal assistance, but its students received federal financial aid. A begrudging, albeit unanimous, Supreme Court[134] held that even indirect financial assistance brought the college within the coverage of title IX, but by a six-to-two vote it held that only Grove City's financial aid department (and *not* other departments) fell within the statute's "program or activity" language.[135] The dissenting Justices argued that this interpretation of "program or activity" was inconsistent with the assumptions Congress made when it passed the amendments in 1972.[136]

The dissenters' view was widely held in Congress. Within a month and a half of the decision, bills to override *Grove City* had been introduced in Congress, with dozens of members eager to cosponsor.[137] If rhetoric is any gauge, the level of congressional outrage was at its highest since *Gilbert.*[138] One member exclaimed:

> It is sort of shocking that the Supreme Court of the United States has to get this kind of a lesson in 1984. This is not unsettled law. As a matter of fact, they are going against their own decisions. It leaves me slightly amazed that on a matter of this rather elementary nature in civil rights law that we're forced to come back to the ramparts one more time.[139]

Many of the key legislative players involved in creating title IX were still in Congress. They readily came forward to denounce the Court's conclusions about the original legislative intent.[140]

On May 23, less than three months after the *Grove City* decision,

133. Pub. L. No. 92-318, 86 Stat. 373 (codified as amended at 20 U.S.C. § 1681(a) (1988)).

134. Justice Powell (a Nixon appointee) wrote a separate opinion, in which Chief Justice Burger (a Nixon appointee) and Justice O'Connor (a Reagan appointee) joined, to express the view that "the case is an unedifying example of overzealousness on the part of the Federal Government." *Grove City,* 465 U.S. at 576.

135. Justice Stevens refused to join the Court's holding on this point but did not express a view on the merits. *Id.* at 579-81 (Stevens, J., concurring in part and dissenting in part). The only dissenters were Justices Brennan and Marshall, the remnants of the Warren Court's liberal majority. *Id.* at 581-604 (Brennan, J., concurring in part and dissenting in part).

136. *Id.* at 581-604 (Brennan, J., concurring in part and dissenting in part).

137. H.R. 5490, 98th Cong., 2d Sess. (1984) (introduced on April 12 by Rep. Simon, together with 71 cosponsors, which increased to 129 cosponsors when hearings began in May 1984); S. 2568, 98th Cong., 2d Sess. (1984) (introduced on April 12 by Sen. Kennedy).

138. *See supra* text accompanying notes 86-100.

139. *Civil Rights Act of 1984: Joint Hearings Before the House Comm. on Education and Labor and the Subcomm. on Civil and Constitutional Rights of the House Comm. on the Judiciary,* 98th Cong., 2d Sess. 36 (1984) (statement of Rep. Conyers (D-Mich.), who was an original supporter of title IX); *see also id.* at 13 (statement of Rep. Simon) ("In *Grove City* the Supreme Court ignored the congressional intent and rejected a long history of broad executive branch enforcement of Title IX of the 1972 Education Amendments. We must correct this result."); *id.* (statement of Rep. Sensenbrenner (R-Wis.)) (Court's decision "does not enunciate the intent of Congress when title IX was passed almost 10 years ago").

140. *See id.* at 40-53 (statement of Sen. Bayh, whom the *Grove City* Court had acknowledged as the key player for title IX (*Grove City,* 465 U.S. at 567)); *id.* at 55-56 (statement of Sen. Javits (R-N.Y.), the key player on the Republican side).

relevant House committees reported a broad override bill. The day before, the President had publicly indicated a willingness to veto the bill.[141] During extensive hearings, the administration was virtually the only force opposing the override.[142] The House passed the bill on June 26 by an overwhelming margin (375 to 32).[143] Because the Senate bill had been bottled up in its committee by Senator Hatch (R-Utah), the House bill became the mechanism by which the Senate considered overriding *Grove City.* Pressured by the administration and Hatch, the Republican leadership refused to bring up the bill for consideration unless a compromise were worked out, and compromise negotiations occupied the remainder of the summer. At the end of September, the bill's supporters (there were by then 63 sponsors) forced the Senate to consider it. But Senator Hatch and the bill's other opponents vexed the bill with so many killer amendment proposals that the bill's supporters ultimately agreed to table it.[144]

The next Congress immediately took up the *Grove City* issue. Again, Senator Hatch's committee buried the Senate bill, while the relevant House committees reported a strong *Grove City* bill.[145] The bill, however, never came up for a vote in the House. It ran into difficulties when the U.S. Catholic Conference expressed strong opposition, claiming that the bill would have the practical effect of forcing Catholic hospitals to perform abortions and schools to fund student abortions. One House committee accepted the Catholic Conference's position. But the bill's supporters were unwilling to compromise the right to abortion, and negotiations continued through the summer and fall without result.

When Congress next reconvened, Democrats controlled both the House and Senate. The Senate acted first, with 56 Senators sponsoring its *Grove City* bill.[146] The Senate bill received expedited hearings in a committee no longer chaired by Senator Hatch. The Senate committee

141. 1984 CONG. Q. ALMANAC 240.

142. H.R. REP. NO. 829, 98th Cong., 2d Sess. pts. 1 & 2 (1984).

143. 130 CONG. REC. 18,761, 18,817 (1984).

144. This was procedurally complicated. On September 20, sponsoring Senators Kennedy and Packwood (R-Ore.) announced that talks with the Administration had broken down. On September 27, Senator Byrd (D-W.Va.) introduced the bill as an amendment to the fiscal 1985 continuing appropriations resolution, H.R.J. Res. 648, 98th Cong., 2d Sess. (1984). The presiding officer sustained the Republican majority leadership's objection that the amendment was out-of-order, but the full Senate overruled the officer (51 to 48). 130 CONG. REC. 27,452, 27,487 (1984).

A blur of further amendments followed, including a Hatch amendment to restrict federal judges' authority to order school busing, but the Senate invoked cloture on September 29. 130 CONG. REC. 27,826 (1984). Despite cloture, the Senate was now—at the end of the session in a presidential election year—faced with voting on a number of controversial amendments, and on whether some of them (such as the busing amendment) were in order. Because of these circumstances, the Republican sponsors agreed to kill the bill for that Congress.

145. *See* H.R. REP. NO. 963, 99th Cong., 1st Sess., pts. 1 & 2 (1985).

146. S. 557, 100th Cong., 1st Sess., 133 CONG. REC. S2249-56 (daily ed. Feb. 19, 1987).

reported the bill on June 5, 1987.[147] The Senate committee report argued that Congress had originally intended for title IX and related statutes to have institution-wide coverage. It maintained that executive implementation and interpretation of those statutes was premised upon that understanding, as were judicial interpretations prior to *Grove City*. "The purpose of the Civil Rights Restoration Act of 1987 is to reaffirm pre-*Grove City College* judicial and executive branch interpretations and enforcement practices which provided for broad coverage of the anti-discrimination provisions of these civil rights statutes."[148] The report stated that *Grove City* misconstrued congressional intent and created absurd results.

Despite the committee report's strong wording, a Senate preoccupied with the Bork confirmation hearings did not get to the bill in 1987. In January 1988, the Senate passed the bill[149] after accepting an amendment that restricted some protections for women seeking abortions; the House followed in March.[150] President Reagan vetoed the bill on March 16, arguing that it would unnecessarily expand the federal government's power at the expense of religious and other private freedoms. Within a week, both chambers of Congress overrode the veto by lopsided margins.[151]

2. *Older Workers Benefit Protection Act of 1990*

When the Court's *McMann* decision was being debated in Congress in 1978, the committee report and Senator Javits disapproved of the Court's reasoning as well as result. However, the actual statute that overruled *McMann* only added a proviso to protect against involuntary retirement. As a consequence, employee plans that were not a "subterfuge" to evade the statute were still exempt. Debate over this exemption returned to the Court in *Public Employees Retirement System of Ohio v. Betts*.[152] The case involved a denial of disability benefits because of age—a situation which on its face seemed to violate the Act. Relying in part on the *McMann* understanding of subterfuge, the Court by a seven-to-two vote upheld the discriminatory disability plan.[153] This immedi-

147. S. REP. NO. 64, 100th Cong., 1st Sess. (1987) (vote to report was 12-4), *reprinted in* 1988 U.S. CODE CONG. & ADMIN. NEWS 3. This report contains an excellent summary of the history of the Senate's attempts to override *Grove City* from 1984 to 1987.

148. *Id.* at 2, *reprinted in* 1988 U.S. CODE CONG. & ADMIN. NEWS 4.

149. 134 CONG. REC. S266 (daily ed. Jan. 28, 1988).

150. 134 CONG. REC. H597-98 (daily ed. Mar. 2, 1988).

151. 134 CONG. REC. S2765 (daily ed. Mar. 22, 1988) (vote of 73-24); 134 CONG. REC. H1071-72 (daily ed. Mar. 22, 1988) (vote of 292-133).

152. 109 S. Ct. 2854 (1989).

153. *See id.* at 2861 ("As Congress did not amend the relevant statutory language, we see no reason to depart from our holding in *McMann* that the term 'subterfuge' is to be given its ordinary meaning . . . .").

ately reinvigorated the *McMann* understanding of "subterfuge," which had been attacked as a misinterpretation of legislative intent by the very legislators responsible for the ADEA's passage in 1978. The Court held that under the statute's "plain meaning," the plan at issue was not a subterfuge and, hence, was exempt from the statutory prohibition.[154] The Court rejected, as inconsistent with the statute's plain meaning, the Department of Labor's "equal benefit or equal cost" regulations that had been endorsed by the key players in 1978.[155]

Betts shocked most people who followed post-1978 ADEA developments, because it was widely assumed that the congressional override of *McMann* had cemented the equal benefit or equal cost rule into the statute. Within two months of the *Betts* decision, bills were introduced in both the House and Senate to override *Betts.*[156] These bills stated on their face: "The Congress finds that, as a result of the decision of the Supreme Court in [*Betts*], legislative action is necessary to restore the original congressional intent in passing and amending the [ADEA]."[157] The bill's sponsors barely concealed their distrust of the Court: "In *Betts,* the Supreme Court once again showed its disdain for civil rights by reaching the completely unexpected conclusion that employers are free to engage in age-based discrimination against their employees in the area of employee benefits."[158]

The report of the Senate Committee on Labor and Human Resources also sharply criticized the Supreme Court's "erroneous" interpretation not once, but twice:

> The Committee regrets that the Supreme Court in *Betts* chose not to credit the language of the 1978 Conference Report, language that appeared in the Congressional Record and was overwhelmingly approved by both Houses of Congress. The Committee hopes that in the future, the Supreme Court will take more seriously such expressions of legislative intent, particularly when they are subject to the same review and ratification as the language of the statute.[159]

The report also defended a retroactive overruling of *Betts.*[160]

---

154. *See id.* at 2863-64.

155. *See id.* at 2862 ("The requirement that employers show a cost-based justification for age-related reductions in benefits appears nowhere in the statute itself.").

156. H.R. 3200, 101st Cong., 1st Sess. (1989); S. 1511, 101st Cong., 2d Sess. (1990).

157. H.R. 3200, 101st Cong., 1st Sess. § 2 (1989); S. 1511, 101st Cong., 2d Sess. § 101 (1990).

158. 135 CONG. REC. S9949 (daily ed. Aug. 3, 1989) (statement of Sen. Pryor (D-Ark.), sponsor of S. 1511); *see also id.* at S9949-50 (statement of Sen. Metzenbaum (D-Ohio)) (commenting that in a "stunning" decision, Supreme Court "reverses 20 years of the settled law," and castigating "the tortured logic and cruel result of the Supreme Court decision"); *id.* at S9950 (statement of Sen. Jeffords (R-Vt.)) ("I am personally convinced that the Congress which enacted the ADEA had no intention of broadly exempting from coverage so integral a portion of the employment relationship as employee benefits.").

159. S. REP. NO. 263, 101st Cong., 2d Sess. 29 (1990).

160. *See id.* at 30-31.

The committee bill's strong expression of disapproval met resistance in the Senate. Through the summer, Senators from both parties negotiated a broadly acceptable compromise bill. The compromise adjusted the bill's substantive provisions and largely removed its retroactivity provisions but retained the textual provision overruling *Betts* by name.[161] The Senate and the House passed the override bill by overwhelming margins in late September and early October [162]

3. The Proposed Civil Rights Act of 1990

The Court decided *Patterson, Wards Cove, Martin v. Wilks, Hopkins, Zipes,* and *Lorance* at the end of the 1988 Term, about the same time as *Betts.*[163] All six decisions had implications for title VII. During the summer of 1989, civil rights groups in Washington drafted legislation to overrule all the decisions. They coordinated their efforts with the Senate Democrats, especially Senators Kennedy (D-Mass.) and Metzenbaum (D-Ohio). Because of the number of decisions to be overruled and the complexity of the political and constitutional issues, negotiations over the terms of the draft continued through the autumn and winter. Finally, on February 7, 1990, Senator Kennedy and thirty-three cosponsors introduced a bill to overrule these six decisions, as well as three earlier Supreme Court cases having similar implications for title VII.[164] The same bill was introduced in the House by Representative Hawkins (D-Cal.) and many cosponsors.[165]

The bill's language and content indicated Congress' wholehearted rejection of the Court's decisions. The bill announced that "in a series of recent decisions addressing employment discrimination claims under Federal law, the Supreme Court cut back dramatically on the scope and effectiveness of civil rights protections."[166] It added that the bill was designed "to respond to the Supreme Court's recent decisions by restoring the civil rights protections that were dramatically limited by those decisions."[167] The substantive sections of the bill then amended title VII or section 1981 to override one or more of the offending Supreme Court

161. *See* S. 1511, 101st Cong., 2d Sess. § 101, 136 CONG. REC. S13,611 (daily ed. Sept. 24, 1990).

162. *See* 136 CONG. REC. S13,611 (daily ed. Sept. 24, 1990) (Senate vote 94-1); 136 CONG. REC. H8738 (daily ed. Oct. 3, 1990) (House vote 406-17).

163. *See supra* notes 3-13 and accompanying text.

164. S. 2104, 101st Cong., 2d Sess., 136 CONG. REC. S1018-21 (daily ed. Feb. 7, 1990). The other three cases were: Crawford Fitting Co. v. J.T. Gibbons, Inc., 482 U.S. 437 (1987), Evans v. Jeff D., 475 U.S. 717 (1986), and Library of Congress v. Shaw, 478 U.S. 310 (1985).

165. H.R. 4000, 101st Cong., 2d Sess., 136 CONG. REC. H364 (daily ed. Feb. 7, 1990).

166. S. 2104, 101st Cong., 2d Sess. § 2(a)(1), 136 CONG. REC. S1019 (daily ed. Feb. 7, 1990).

167. S. 2104, 101st Cong., 2d Sess. § 2(a)(1), (b)(1), 136 CONG. REC. S1019 (daily ed. Feb. 7, 1990).

cases.[168] With complex transition rules, the bill overruled most of the nine Supreme Court cases retroactively.[169] The sponsors of the bill roundly indicted the Supreme Court's performance in the 1988 Term. "I believe the Supreme Court's recent rulings represent an effort to renege on history," said Senator Jeffords (R-Vt.).[170]

At hearings on the bills in the House and Senate during February and March, the administration agreed that *Patterson* and *Lorance* should be overruled, but strongly opposed overruling *Wards Cove* and *Martin v. Wilks*.[171] The administration's position, eloquently articulated by Senator Hatch, was that the provision overriding *Wards Cove* would all but compel employers to adopt quotas by making title VII liability hinge on bad numbers.[172] Hatch later, during the floor debates, further argued that the provision overriding *Martin v. Wilks* was unfair to white males penalized by old consent decrees and, in fact, raised due process problems.[173] The administration and the business community were also concerned about the bill's creation of new compensatory and punitive damages remedies for violations of title VII. Attorney General Thornburgh explored these and other concerns in detail in a letter to Senator Kennedy, indicating that he would urge the President to veto the bill in anything like its current form.[174]

In negotiations that spring, Senate Democrats, moderate Senate

---

168. Section 4 overruled *Wards Cove* and set standards for proof of unlawful employment practices in disparate impact cases. Section 5 overruled *Hopkins* by stipulating that a discriminatory practice need not be the sole motivating factor to make out a violation of the statute. Section 6 replaced *Martin v. Wilks* with guidelines for assuring finality of consent decrees. Section 7 amended existing provisions of title VII to overrule *Lorance*. Section 9 included a series of technical procedural amendments to title VII to overrule *Zipes*, *Crawford*, and *Jeff D*. Section 10 provided for interest against the United States, overruling *Shaw*. Section 12 amended section 1981 to overrule *Patterson*.

169. Section 15(a) provided that most of the substantive provisions would be retroactively applicable, beginning on the dates the Court had handed down the relevant decisions.

170. 136 CONG. REC. S1022 (daily ed. Feb. 7, 1990); *see also id.* at S1018 (statement of Sen. Kennedy) ("In the past year . . . the Supreme Court has issued a series of rulings that mark an abrupt and unfortunate departure from its historic vigilance in protecting civil rights. The fabric of justice has been torn.").

171. *Civil Rights Act of 1990: Hearing on S. 2104 Before the Senate Comm. on Labor and Human Resources*, 101st Cong., 2d Sess. 111 (1990) [hereinafter *1990 Senate Civil Rights Hearings*]; *Civil Rights Act of 1990: Joint Hearings on H.R. 4000 Before the House Comm. on Education and Labor and the Subcomm. on Civil and Constitutional Rights of the House Comm. on the Judiciary*, 101st Cong., 2d Sess. 358-62 (1990). The administration's override bill was introduced on February 22 by Senator Hatch in S. 2166, 101st Cong., 2d Sess. (1990). *See* 136 CONG. REC S1522 (daily ed. Feb. 22, 1990).

172. *1990 Senate Civil Rights Hearings*, *supra* note 171, at 5 (stating that the bill "so dramatically change[s] title VII that the only way to aviod being sued is to hire solely by numbers, to use quotas for hiring and promotion").

173. 136 CONG. REC. S9830-31 (daily ed. July 17, 1990).

174. Letter from Attorney General Richard Thornburgh to Senator Edward Kennedy (Apr. 3, 1990).

Republicans, and the White House sought to resolve these problems. The *Wards Cove/Griggs* issue of how to express the proof required to establish and defend against disparate impact cases posed the biggest hurdle. Hoping to reach a compromise with the administration, the Senate twice postponed consideration of the bill. With the same purpose, the Democratic and Republican supporters offered several amended bills.[175] On July 12, it appeared that the Democrats and the administration had reached agreement on the key provision (a definition of "business necessity").[176] However, the deal immediately unraveled, possibly because of cold feet in the administration.[177] The negotiations continued.

The Senate voted for cloture of debate on July 17,[178] over the bitter objections of the Republican leadership and despite bipartisan irritation over the lengthy impasse with the administration. After the cloture vote, the White House urged continuation of the negotiations.[179] Negotiations continued, and yet another Kennedy-Jeffords substitute was offered up. The negotiations lasted into the final day of the Senate's consideration of the bill,[180] when, at the eleventh hour, they collapsed over the quota issue. ("Quotas shmotas," grumbled Senator Kennedy.)[181] The Senate passed the second Kennedy-Jeffords substitute by a vote of 65 to 34.[182] The House passed a similar bill on August 3, by a vote of 272 to 154.[183]

As is often the case, negotiations over the bill's content continued almost without interruption after passage by both chambers and during the conference committee process. One conference report was submitted to Congress on September 26.[184] The House voted to recommit so that the conferees could add further language to appease the President.[185] A

175. The Kennedy-Danforth amended version of S. 2104 that emerged from committee was to be superseded by a Kennedy-Jeffords substitute. *See* 136 CONG. REC. S9325-27 (daily ed. July 10, 1990). A Kassebaum-Gorton compromise proposal also appeared, *see* 136 CONG. REC. S9756 (daily ed. July 16, 1990), but was then withdrawn.

176. *See* 136 CONG. REC. S9824-25 (daily ed. July 17, 1990) (statement of Sen. Danforth describing the oral agreement and its mysterious unraveling); *id.* at S9829-30 (statement of Sen. Kennedy describing the apparent deal and the apparent impasse that nonetheless developed).

177. *See* Holmes, *Accord Is Sought on Rights Measure to Avert a Veto,* N.Y. Times, July 20, 1990, at A1, col. 6.

178. 136 CONG. REC. S9823 (daily ed. July 17, 1990) (vote of 62-38, including 8 Republicans voting for cloture).

179. *Id.* at S9836 (statement of Sen. Danforth).

180. 136 CONG. REC. S9918-19, S9934 (daily ed. July 18, 1990).

181. *Id.* at S9947.

182. *Id.* at S9966.

183. 136 CONG. REC. H6769 (daily ed. Aug. 3, 1990). The key moves during the House deliberation were the party-line vote to adopt a modified closed rule restricting amendments on the bill, *see* 136 CONG. REC. H6336 (daily ed. Aug. 2, 1990), and the defeat of a Republican substitute by a party-line 238-188 vote, *see* 136 CONG. REC. H6768 (daily ed. Aug. 3, 1990).

184. H.R. CONF. REP. NO. 755, 101st Cong., 2d Sess., *reprinted in* 136 CONG. REC. H8045-50 (daily ed. Sept. 26, 1990).

185. 136 CONG. REC. H9405-06 (daily ed. Oct. 11, 1990) (recommittal motion vote of 375-45).

second conference report was submitted on October 12.[186] The final conference bill made a number of changes in the *Wards Cove* provision in an attempt to gain White House support. These changes included a more liberal definition of the business necessity defense in disparate impact cases, statutory language discouraging employers from adopting quotas, confirmation that bad numbers alone do not violate title VII, and a requirement that plaintiffs prove which employer practices cause the disparate impact.[187]

By October, the White House position seemed more conservative than it had been in July, and the President seemed ready to veto the bill despite all concessions.[188] Nonetheless, both chambers adopted the conference bill by lopsided, but not veto-proof, margins.[189] On October 20, the President sent Congress his own civil rights bill, which would have overruled or modified most of the cases that Congress sought to overrule (but in different ways, of course). It was ignored by Congress. Two days later the President vetoed Congress' bill,[190] and the Senate failed by one vote to override the veto.[191]

II
POSITIVE GAME THEORY ANALYSIS OF CONGRESSIONAL RESPONSES TO THE SUPREME COURT'S INTERPRETATION OF CIVIL RIGHTS STATUTES

The story told in Part I demonstrates in a general but fairly concrete way that civil rights statutory policy is dynamic and interactive. Civil rights policy is interactive because it involves the cooperation, and often the conflict, among the Congress (which enacts the statutes), the President (who has veto power and influences the statute's implementation), and the Court (which presides over the statute's interpretation). Civil rights policy is also dynamic. For one thing, the actual mix of stat-

186. H.R. CONF. REP. NO. 856, 101st Cong., 2d Sess., *reprinted in* 136 CONG. REC. H9552-59 (daily ed. Oct. 12, 1990).

187. 136 CONG. REC. S15,327 (daily ed. Oct 16, 1990) (statement of Sen. Kennedy). These changes were made in response to negotiations among Senator Hatch, Senator Specter, and former Secretary of Transportation William Coleman. *Id.* at S15,328 (statement of Sen. Hatch).

188. *See id.* at S15341-42 (statement of Sen. Jeffords); Letter from Attorney General Richard Thornburgh to Senator Robert Dole (Oct. 12, 1990), *reprinted in* 136 CONG. REC. S15,328-29 (daily ed. Oct. 16, 1990). Apparently, Senator Hatch would have been willing to support the conference bill if the White House had acquiesced. *See* 136 CONG. REC. S15,328 (daily ed. Oct. 16, 1990) (statement of Sen. Hatch); *id.* at S15,332 (statement of Sen. Specter).

189. *Id.* at S15,407 (Senate vote, 62-34); 136 CONG. REC. H9994-95 (daily ed. Oct. 17, 1990) (House vote, 273-154).

190. 136 CONG. REC. S16,562-63 (daily ed. Oct. 24, 1990) (reprinting the veto message).

191. At 11:50 p.m. on October 24, 1990, the Senate voted by 66 to 34 to override the veto. Fifty-five Democrats and eleven Republicans voted to override. 136 CONG. REC. S16,589 (daily ed. Oct. 24, 1990).

utes changes constantly as Congress enacts new statutes. In addition, the interpretation and implementation by the President and the Court strongly affect the evolution of each statute and the way the statutes knit together over time. Therefore, the dramatic changes in the attitudes of the President and of the Court (and, to a lesser extent, of Congress) toward these statutes have significantly affected the statutory policy.

Part I makes traditional political theory assumptions (such as the importance of interest groups and committees), but is otherwise atheoretic. Part II borrows from positive political theory a model of Congress/agency interaction and uses it to construct a theoretical framework for thinking about the Congress/Court/President interaction over time. This model does not perfectly explain the data, and I then suggest a modified model that does. As modified, this political theory framework suggests some interesting twists on the history outlined in Part I and some directions for future interaction. It indicates that the Court/Congress conflict will continue into the 1990s (though it is not clear at what level of intensity). Perhaps surprisingly, it suggests that the main variable in the Court/Congress balance will be the political preferences of the Presidency.

A. A Game Theoretic Analysis of Supreme Court Policymaking in Civil Rights Statutes

For some time now, positive political theory has been developing game theoretical models of the legislative process. Much of the theory has focused on legislator incentives and, specifically, the operation of a legislature in which members are primarily motivated by a desire to be reelected.[192] Recently, positive political theory has explored issues arising from the legislature's interaction with agencies and the President.[193] Scholars, most notably John Ferejohn, have been developing a model of Congress/agency interaction to explain Congress' ability to influence agency decisionmaking over time, even when it does not enact statutes

192. *See* B. CAIN, J. FEREJOHN & M. FIORINA, THE PERSONAL VOTE: CONSTITUENCY SERVICE AND ELECTORAL INDEPENDENCE (1987); M. FIORINA, CONGRESS: KEYSTONE OF THE WASHINGTON ESTABLISHMENT (1977); D. MAYHEW, CONGRESS: THE ELECTORAL CONNECTION (1974). For a more public-regarding view of legislator motivations, see R. FENNO, CONGRESSMEN IN COMMITTEES (1973); K. KREHBIEL, INFORMATION AND LEGISLATIVE ORGANIZATION (1991); A. MAASS, CONGRESS AND THE COMMON GOOD (1983).

193. *See* Ferejohn & Shipan, *Congressional Influence on Administrative Agencies: A Case Study of Telecommunications Policy*, in CONGRESS RECONSIDERED 393 (L. Dodd & B. Oppenheimer 4th ed. 1989); Mathews, *Veto Threats: Rhetoric in a Bargaining Game*, 104 Q.J. ECON. 347 (1989); Moe, *An Assessment of the Positive Theory of Congressional Dominance*, 12 LEGIS. STUD. Q. 475 (1987); Weingast & Moran, *Bureaucratic Discretion or Congressional Control? Regulatory Policymaking by the Federal Trade Commission*, 91 J. POL. ECON. 756 (1983).

that overrule the agency directly.[194] Their model, the *positive political theory model,* might be applied to understand legislative control of judicial statutory interpretation as well.[195]

The *Court/Congress/President game,* which follows from this model, is relatively straightforward. It is played out on a one-dimensional linear field that starts with the optimal political preferences of the major players, charting those preferences from left/liberal to right/conservative (here, the preferences concern civil rights legislation). I start with the assumptions of the positive political theorists who developed the outlines of my Court/Congress/President game: The political players are the Supreme Court (C), which interprets existing civil rights statutes; the legislative gatekeepers (G), which substantially control Congress' agenda and which I consider to be the committees with jurisdiction over civil rights bills plus the majority party leadership;[196] the Congress, which has the power to overrule the Court and is treated here as a single chamber whose preferences are represented by those of its median member (hence the notation M);[197] and the President (P), who has the power to veto legislation.

The game is played in the following sequence. The Court makes the first move when it interprets a civil rights statute. Once the Court has

194. *See* Ferejohn & Shipan, *Congressional Influence on Bureaucracy,* J.L. ECON. & ORGANIZATION (1990).

195. The most notable paper is B. Marks, A Model of Judicial Influence on Congressional Policymaking: *Grove City College v. Bell* (May 1989) (Ph.D. dissertation, Washington University) (on file with author). *See also* J. Ferejohn & B. Weingast, Limitation of Statutes: A Strategic Theory of Interpretation (prepared for delivery at the Conference on Constitutional Law and Economics, Stanford Law School (Oct. 25-26, 1990)) (on file with author).

196. This is a departure from traditional positive political theory, which assumes a single gatekeeping committee. In both the House and Senate, there are two committees with potential jurisdiction over antidiscrimination legislation—the judiciary committee and the labor committee. The existence of the two committees in each chamber itself makes the assignment power (by the House Speaker and the Senate Majority Leader) significant, but in both chambers the leadership exercises other powers as well. The House Rules Committee, since 1973 an arm of the leadership, can do much to dictate the terms of the debate by seeking closed or modified closed rules. (This is another departure from Ferejohn and Shipan, who assume that the House can always overrule a closed rule suggestion.) The Senate Majority Leader has weaker power in this regard but often affects the agenda by orchestrating or frustrating unanimous consent agreements, by deciding which bills to call up and in which order, and by securing desired rulings on points of procedure. For example, Majority Leader Baker's delaying tactics in the summer of 1984 were instrumental in killing the *Grove City* bill that year.

197. Using the preferences of the median legislator to indicate the legislative outcome is itself a "strong" assumption based on other assumptions such as a one-dimensional political spectrum and the inability of legislative processes to aggregate intensity of preference. Nonetheless, the median voter rule is a powerful and well-established theoretical construct in the collective choice literature. Basically, it suggests that on a single left-right spectrum where only one outcome is possible and no vote trading is permitted, the favored position of the median voter will prevail. *See* A. DOWNS, AN ECONOMIC THEORY OF DEMOCRACY 114-41 (1957); Bowen, *The Interpretation of Voting in the Allocation of Economic Resources,* in READINGS IN WELFARE ECONOMICS 115-32 (K. Arrow & T. Scitovsky eds. 1969); Hotelling, *Stability in Competition,* 39 ECON. J. 41-57 (1929).

interpreted the statute, the gatekeepers then decide whether they want to seek a legislative override; if they do, Congress must decide what policy to adopt, and it is not constrained by the gatekeepers' choice. If Congress passes a statute, the President must decide whether to veto it. Should the President veto it, Congress must decide whether to override the President's veto. This sequence of decisionmaking is mapped out in the diagram below:

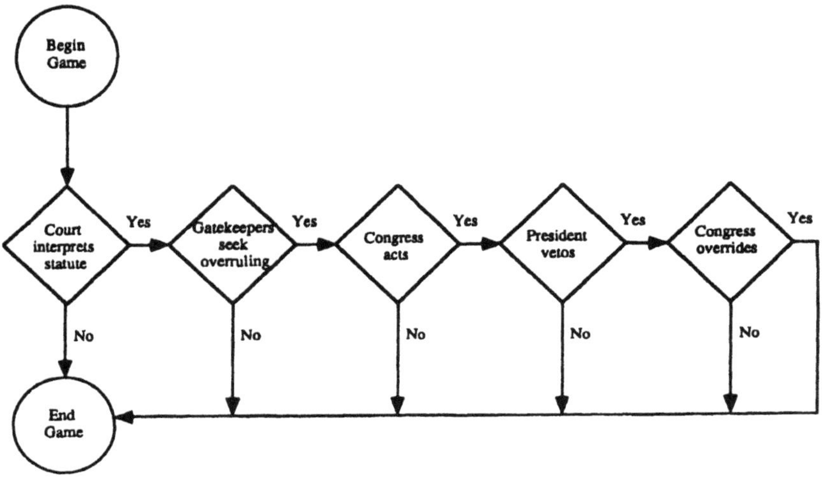

The Court/Congress/President game assumes that each player operates with complete information about other players' preferences, and, therefore, perfectly anticipates the future course of play. Moreover, each player in making its moves will not want to make a decision that will be overturned by another player with the authority to do so. In other words, in deciding whether to act, each player will do nothing if it realizes that its decision will be overturned by the next player.

The game's sequential nature, the players' possession of perfect information, and their reluctance to be overruled make two other preference points important. One is a player's "indifference point," the point on the spectrum that the player likes just as much as another point in the opposite direction (the player is indifferent as to the two points). For example, in our civil rights game, the gatekeepers' preferences (G) are usually to the left of those of the median member (M). The gatekeepers' indifference point (G(M)) is the point to the left of their preferred point that they like just as much as they like M, but in the other direction.[198]

198. Or stated more formally: If the gatekeepers' preferences were to the left of the median legislator's, and the intensity of the gatekeepers' preferences were single-peaked, then there would be

Indifference points are important to the gatekeepers, because they will not seek an overruling of a Supreme Court decision if it is between the legislative median and the gatekeepers' indifference point (G(M) < C < M). Knowing they will be overruled by Congress if they introduce a bill setting their preferences (G loses to M), the gatekeepers will simply not introduce override legislation.

According to the assumptions of the game's designers, the President only becomes involved when the gatekeepers seek an override *and* Congress responds with override legislation. When a President is faced with a decision of whether to veto the legislation, another salient point arises in our game, namely, the veto median (V). The veto median is the point that divides both legislative chambers so that a third of the members have ideal points to the right of V and two-thirds have ideal points to the left, or vice versa. V is obviously a strategic point of reference for a President who does not wish to have his veto overridden. Also, since V will lie to one side of the preferences of the median legislator, it has the

a point to the left of G that the gatekeepers like just as much as they like the position of the median legislator. This is their indifference point and is represented as G(M). This is demonstrated graphically below.

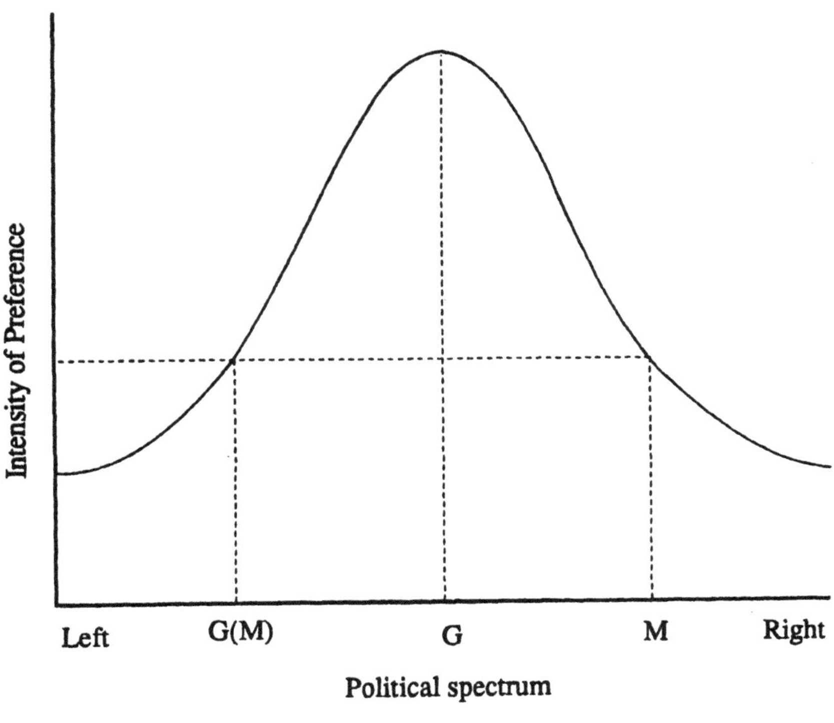

potential of increasing the range within which a Court decision could be protected from overruling legislation.

Despite its "strong" assumptions, the positive game provides a robust explanation for the behavior of the Court, Congress, and the President in three periods roughly tracking those described in Part I. The explanation, however, is not perfect. In this Part II(A), I identify data that the positive game does not explain. Later, I introduce a variation on the model that corrects those flaws.

1. Court/Congress/President Cooperation: 1962-72

Recall that in the first period we identified, 1962-70, the preferences of the Court and the President apparently were to the left of Congress' preferences, and the preferences of the gatekeepers in Congress were somewhat to the left of Congress' preferences.[199] Figure 1 maps these relationships linearly.[200] Using these relationships as our starting point, consider how the Court/Congress/President game plays out.

Figure 1
Civil Rights Preferences, 1962-71

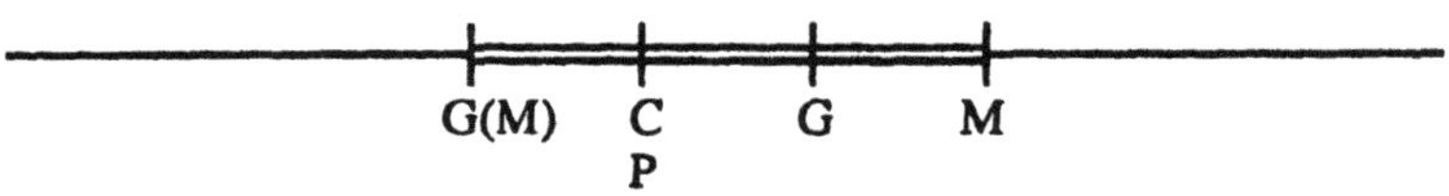

For purposes of this Figure, recall the abbreviations we are using:

C = Majority of Supreme Court
G = Gatekeepers (relevant committees & majority leadership)
M = Median Member of Congress
P = President
G(M) = Gatekeepers' Indifference Point
V = Veto Median

Given this array of preferences, one expects a short and simple game, in which the Court merely reads its preferences into civil rights statutes. This is our expectation, because the Court makes the first move

199. The House and Senate leadership—Speaker McCormack (D-Mass.) and Majority Leader Mansfield (D-Mont.) through most of this period—was decidedly in line with the preferences of Presidents Kennedy and Johnson and to the left of President Nixon's. The House Judiciary Committee (chaired by Representative Celler (D-N.Y.)) and Education and Labor Committee (chaired by Representative Perkins (D-Ky.)) were more liberal than the House median on both the Democratic and Republican sides. The same was not true of the Senate Judiciary Committee (chaired by Senator Eastland (D-Miss.)), which was to the right of the Senate median. The Senate Labor and Public Welfare Committee (although chaired by Senator Hill (D-Ala.) until 1969) was to the left of the Senate median. *See supra* notes 27 & 25.

200. With some alterations as to terminology, the figures in this Part are adapted from Ferejohn & Shipan, *supra* note 194.

and wants to interpret the statute as closely as possible to its own preferences (C) without being overruled by Congress. Figure 1 suggests that the Court can impose its own preferences in this manner, because the gatekeepers have no incentive to introduce override legislation. The gatekeepers have no incentive because if they did introduce override legislation to implement their preferences (G), Congress would simply implement its own preferences (M). Since the gatekeepers prefer the Court's result to Congress' ($G(M) < C < M$), they will not introduce override legislation.[201]

As explained above, Figure 1 describes the players' preferences during this period. Consider how the game changes (slightly) if the Court's position falls to the left of the gatekeepers' indifference point (that is, $C < G(M)$). In that event, the Court would not want to implement its desired policy (C), because that would stimulate the gatekeepers to propose a statute overruling its decision (since the gatekeepers prefer the congressional median to the Court's decision). Any time the Court implements a policy to the left of G(M), then Congress will simply respond by enacting the overruling statute (at $x = M$). In such a situation, the Court's best strategy would be to compromise its own preferences and choose the gatekeepers' indifference point as its decision ($x = G(M)$). In short, so long as the Court's decision falls on or to the right of G(M) (that is, $G(M) < C$)—the point the gatekeepers like just as much or more than M—the gatekeepers will not propose legislation. Without a proposal by the gatekeepers, Congress will have nothing to act upon. With no act from Congress, the President does not play in the game.

Hence, under Figure 1 and simple variations, the Court can make any decision (x) in the interval $\{G(M), M\}$ and not be overruled by Congress. In general, the Court will choose as its decision either its preferred point or the gatekeepers' indifference point, whichever is further to the right ($x = \max\{C, G(M)\}$). Note that I have drawn Figure 1 so that the Court's preferred point (C) is to the right of G(M). Thus, on issues for which this is the correct configuration, the Court will simply adopt its preferred point (C) as its final decision. I think this preferred point is where the Court actually was for most civil rights issues in the period 1962 to 1972—to the left of Congress generally, and usually to the left of the gatekeepers as well, but not so far to the left that it provoked legislative overruling.

The game in Figure 1 predicts that the Court would be able to interpret civil rights statutes more liberally than Congress or even its gate-

201. For the simple game in Figure 1, we do not assign a major role to the President. But note that the President would not always be able to protect the Court through a veto in the situation described in Figure 1.

keepers would have wanted during this period, without risking a legislative overruling so long as the Court's decision was not to the left of the gatekeepers' indifference point (G(M)). This game suggests a Court with a great deal of policy influence—a Court able to steer civil rights policy significantly to the left of what Congress desired.[202] The game just described does in fact capture much of what occurred during the period of 1962 to 1972: The Court's decisions interpreting civil rights statutes were in some cases to the left of decisions that Congress itself would have made, yet Congress overruled none of them, in part because the gatekeepers refused to initiate overruling proposals.

The best example of the positive game in action involves *Jones v. Mayer*. *Jones* reinterpreted section 1982 to create a substantially more liberal remedy for race discrimination in housing than Congress had been willing to create, just weeks before, in title VIII.[203] The Court's decision probably represented a more liberal remedy than that favored by the median Member of Congress. Nevertheless, there was no effort to overrule *Jones v. Mayer*. Indeed, there probably were no such proposals because the House gatekeepers—the Democratic Leadership and the Judiciary Committee—preferred the Court's decision to the compromise solution reached by Congress in title VIII.[204]

Following the *Jones* decision, lower federal courts began to apply its reasoning to section 1981 cases involving claims of employment discrimination.[205] Had it been asked to decide if section 1981 applied in these instances, Congress probably would have balked, since section 1981 procedures and remedies (including punitive damages) were quite liberal.

202. If we included the President in this game (as I do below for the last period, 1981-90), the Court's ability to move civil rights policy to the left would be even more pronounced. During most of the period 1962-72, the President was aligned with the Court and could be expected to veto any effort by Congress to overrule the Court. In such cases, the relevant preference becomes *either* the gatekeepers' indifference point (G(M)) *or* the veto median (V), whichever is further to the left. This would allow the Court to implement its own policy in some cases where $C < G(M)$.

203. Title VIII covered discrimination in transactions involving residential realty alone, while section 1982 as interpreted in *Jones v. Mayer* covered business and personal property as well. Title VIII was administratively enforced through a gradual phased-in process, but *Jones v. Mayer* immediately activated a private right of action. Title VIII contained a number of exemptions in order to procure Republican support (for example, religious institutions, small boardinghouses), none of which pertained to newly interpreted section 1982.

204. The year after *Jones v. Mayer*, the House Judiciary Committee was chaired by the very liberal Emanuel Celler, who prided himself above all on his sponsorship of the Civil Rights Act of 1964. The Committee consisted of 15 liberal Democrats, 5 southern Democrats, and 15 Republicans, of whom 5 were liberal eastern Republicans and another 4 were midwestern moderate conservatives who strongly supported civil rights legislation. *See* 1969 CONG. Q. ALMANAC 66 (listing Committee membership). Celler, the chair of the Committee, would have stalled any bill to overrule *Jones v. Mayer*. Moreover, even if the bill could have gotten to a Committee vote, it would have only received between eleven and fifteen of the thirty-five votes on the Committee.

205. *See* C. ABERNATHY, CIVIL RIGHTS: CASES AND MATERIALS 265-76 (1980) (collecting cases).

Indeed, they were much more liberal than those Congress had adopted (as a compromise to end the Senate filibuster) in title VII. When it came time to reexamine title VII, the congressional gatekeepers refused to propose that the parallel section 1981 cause of action be curtailed or eliminated by title VII. However, amendments to overrule the section 1981 cases were made in both chambers. A majority of Senators present favored the Senate amendment, but it failed on a tie vote because of maneuvering by the Senate leadership.[206] The House amendment was rejected in committee but adopted by a narrow vote on the House floor.[207] The House conferees—members of the gatekeeping committee that had rejected the proposal—predictably abandoned it in conference.[208]

Following *Jones v. Mayer*, the gatekeepers in Congress were able to use their institutional position to protect judicial decisions expanding *Jones*—a result they preferred to the congressional overrides that would have otherwise occurred. This example illustrates the various opportunities gatekeepers have to head off overruling proposals. The Court/Congress/President game explains this behavior fairly well. It also explains the gatekeepers' eagerness to write committee reports endorsing the Court's results in cases like *Allen* and *Griggs*, which the gatekeepers (more liberal than the median member in this initial period) preferred over results that Congress would have provided.

What the Court/Congress/President game does not explain as well is Congress' willingness to codify decisions like *United States v. Guest*[209] and *Louisiana v. United States*.[210] These liberal decisions represented highly dynamic interpretations of the 1870 Act. Not only did Congress fail to overrule the decisions, but it also ultimately went along with the suggestion made by both the Court and the gatekeepers that new and more expansive statutes be enacted to protect civil rights workers and voting rights. The positive political theory model would suggest that in these circumstances, Congress must have agreed with those decisions ($C = M$, not $C < M$). Although this scenario can neither be proved nor

206. The recorded vote was 33-33, which meant the defeat of the amendment. But there was a 34th Senator on the floor, Senator Gambrell (D-Ga.), who announced that he favored the amendment but was a "live pair" with an absent Senator opposed to the amendment. *See* 118 CONG. REC. 3372-73 (1972). This was very unusual: a Senator will rarely be in a live pair when doing so would affect the outcome. Apparently the Democratic leadership had made some special deal with Senator Gambrell.

207. 117 CONG. REC. 32,111 (1971).

208. Of the 20 Representatives named to the conference by the House leadership, *see* 118 CONG. REC. 5187 (1972), 11 (all but one of the Democrats) had voted against the amendment, *see* 117 CONG. REC. 32111 (1971).

209. 383 U.S. 745 (1966).

210. 380 U.S. 145 (1965).

disproved, I am doubtful that it represents the entire story. I present another explanation in Part II(B).

2. Court/Congress Conflict: 1972-81

Between 1971 and 1975, a dramatic change in institutional alignments occurred as the Court shifted to the right of Congress. For many issues, the shift yielded the configuration described in Figure 2.

Figure 2
Civil Rights Preferences, 1972-81

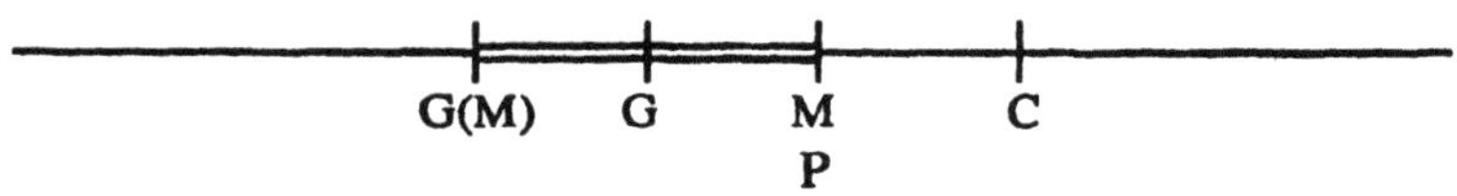

That is, the Court's preferences (C) were often to the right of the preferences of Congress (M), while the gatekeepers' preferences (G) remained slightly to the left of those of the median member. The President's preferences (P) moved closer to the congressional median during this period but were often to the left of that median.[211]

The dynamics of the institutional interactions are simpler in this second period. Under this new configuration (Figure 2), if the Court implements its own preferences (C) through interpretation of the civil rights statutes, it will be overridden, because the gatekeepers will have an incentive to introduce overruling legislation (they prefer any $x < C$, and the ultimate result $M < C$), and Congress will vote for its preferred outcome over that of the Court (it prefers M to C). As a result, the Court has a strong incentive to compromise its preferences and reach results that are at or to the left of the congressional median (M). Interestingly, because the Court's preferences are on the other side of the congressional median from the gatekeepers' preferences, the Court has lost much of its discretion to reach a result at variance with the median congressional preference (M) and, as a consequence, the Court runs a much greater risk of being overruled.

This Court/Congress/President game captures nicely much of what went on in the 1970s. A good example is the Supreme Court's decision in *Runyon v. McCrary.*[212] *Runyon* affirmed the application of *Jones v. Mayer*'s interpretation of section 1982 (discrimination in property transactions) to section 1981 (contract transactions). The Court's willingness

211. The Presidents during the 1970s held preferences not far from those of the median member. Because the Office of Civil Rights remained strongly to the left of M during this period, the administrations were on the whole at M or to the left of M and were, therefore, of no consequence in the game. The story changes substantially in the 1980s, as Part II(A)(3) will reveal.

212. 427 U.S. 160 (1976).

to extend the *Jones* reasoning here, by a seven-to-two vote, was explicitly premised upon the Court's belief that Congress, in 1971-72, had approved of the application of *Jones v. Mayer* to section 1981 cases.[213] Moreover, two of the seven majority Justices wrote concurring opinions suggesting that they thought *Jones v. Mayer* was in fact wrongly decided but that stare decisis, reinforced by current legislative policy, impelled them to go along with a liberal interpretation of section 1981.[214] A third Justice in the majority probably would have voted with the dissenters if the Court had split four-to-four.[215] *Runyon* is the rare case in which the Court all but announces that it is voting against its preferences in order to accommodate the preferences of the current Congress.

A number of other Burger Court decisions in the late 1970s relied on the Court's perception of legislative preferences to reach results that appeared more liberal than the Court's own preferences.[216] Indeed, the Court/Congress/President game provides an interesting explanation for *United Steelworkers v. Weber*,[217] which interpreted title VII to allow voluntary affirmative action. Justice Stewart, who voted with the *Weber* majority, had voted the year before against the constitutionality of voluntary state affirmative action.[218] Another majority Justice explained his vote in *Weber* as a response to societal developments that had overtaken the original congressional expectations.[219] Both these Justices may have been sensitive to the pressures for affirmative action created by *Griggs v.*

213. *Id.* at 174-75 & n.11. I argue that the Court was mistaken, in Eskridge, *Interpreting Legislative Inaction*, 87 MICH. L. REV. 67 (1988).

214. *See Runyon*, 427 U.S. at 186-89 (Powell, J., concurring); *id.* at 189-92 (Stevens, J., concurring).

215. The third Justice was Chief Justice Burger, who held preferences to the right of Justice Stevens, and who was notorious for voting against his preferences so that he could assign the majority opinion.

216. For the most prominent examples, see Cannon v. University of Chicago, 441 U.S. 677, 685-87, 694-708 (1979) (Court split 5-1-3, with the bare majority opinion resting on the apparent congressional assumption that title IX included a private cause of action); Monell v. Department of Social Servs., 436 U.S. 658, 691-701 (1978) (7-2 split Court relies upon recent legislative assumptions in overruling line of section 1983 cases); United States v. Board of Comm'rs, 435 U.S. 110, 131-34 (1978) (5-1-3 split Court endorses liberal interpretation of Voting Rights Act, based in part on congressional understandings when Act was renewed in 1975); *id.* at 138-39 (Blackmun, J., concurring) (more strongly stated reliance on subsequent legislative understandings); Franks v. Bowman Transp. Co., 424 U.S. 747 (1976) (5-1-2 split Court allowing affirmative remedies in title VII cases and relying in part on discussions underlying 1972 amendments). On the other hand, this sort of argument failed in International Brotherhood of Teamsters v. United States, 431 U.S. 324 (1977).

217. 443 U.S. 193 (1979).

218. Justice Stewart, the necessary fifth vote in *Weber* (the Court split 5-2), was part of the five-Justice majority invalidating the affirmative action plan in Regents of the University of California v. Bakke, 438 U.S. 265 (1978). Justices Stevens and Powell, who did not participate in *Weber*, were also part of the *Bakke* majority.

219. *Weber*, 443 U.S. at 209-16 (Blackmun, J., concurring).

Duke Power Co.[220] and to the gatekeeping committees' approval of *Griggs* in 1972. For these reasons, a Court critical of affirmative action in constitutional cases ended up interpreting title VII to allow a broad range of private affirmative action programs.[221] The conclusion from this *Weber* example suggests a broader observation: The Burger Court generally produced results in constitutional civil rights cases (where there was little chance of its being overridden) that were discernibly more conservative than the results it reached in analogous cases of statutory interpretation.[222]

If the positive political theory model's predictions were correct—namely, that the more conservative Court in the 1970s was often willing to subordinate its preferences to avoid being overruled—then *Gilbert, McMann, City of Mobile v. Bolden,* and *Atascadero*[223] were anomalies, because these decisions by a bitterly divided Court were overridden by an outraged Congress. The positive political theory model would view the overrides as instances where the game did not achieve perfect equilibrium, perhaps because of a failure of one or more assumptions. For the Court to avoid an override under the conditions of Figure 2, it must be able to predict accurately the views of the median Member of Congress. There is little room for error (unlike under the conditions of Figure 1). In *Gilbert, McMann,* and *Bolden,* the Court may have misjudged the location of M—placing it further to the right than the actual M—and suffered the consequences, namely, legislative overrides. This is a plausible explanation,[224] albeit one marred by the Court's substantial mis-

220. 401 U.S. 424 (1972).

221. Johnson v. Transportation Agency, 480 U.S. 616 (1987), confirmed this broad approval. The *Johnson* majority, formed when the Court was even more conservative, explicitly relied on current congressional preferences to expand on *Weber*. *Id.* at 629 n.7; *see also id.* at 642-47 (Stevens, J., concurring).

222. Contrast the Burger Court's broad tolerance of voluntary affirmative action in statutory interpretation cases like *Weber* and *Johnson* with its more critical attitude in constitutional cases like *Bakke*, Firefighters Local Union No. 1784 v. Stotts, 467 U.S. 561 (1984), and Wygant v. Jackson Board of Education, 476 U.S. 267 (1986). Contrast the Burger Court's willingness to look at effects upon racial groups to find actionable "discrimination" in statutory cases like Albemarle Paper Co. v. Moody, 422 U.S. 405 (1975), and *Griggs*, with its focus on only intentional conduct to find "discrimination" in constitutional cases like Arlington Heights v. Metropolitan Housing Corp., 429 U.S. 252 (1977), and Washington v. Davis, 426 U.S. 229 (1976).

223. *See supra* text accompanying notes 75-120.

224. The Court's subsequent willingness to follow the liberal dictates of the overrides and not just their bare text supports this explanation somewhat. *See* Thornburg v. Gingles, 478 U.S. 30 (1986) (divided Court applies Voting Rights Amendments of 1982 very liberally); Newport News Shipbuilding & Dry Dock Co. v. EEOC, 462 U.S. 669 (1983) (7-2 divided Court holds that Pregnancy Discrimination Act not only overruled holding of *Gilbert*, but also discredited its whole approach to gender discrimination). Congressional overrides of the Court's pregnancy discrimination and minority vote dilution opinions taught the Court much about the median member's preferences (M). As a consequence, the Court was able to stay out of trouble in later cases.

perceptions in each case.[225] In Part II(B), I present an alternative explanation.

3. *Court/Congress/President Confrontation: 1981-90*

In the final period, the President becomes a major player in the game. In the 1980s, the Court moved somewhat further to the right of Congress (especially after 1986, when the Court moved sharply to the right and Congress to the left). The decade's biggest shift, however, was the significant movement to the right by the Presidency. Figure 3 maps out the new preference configuration.

Figure 3
Civil Rights Preferences, 1981-90

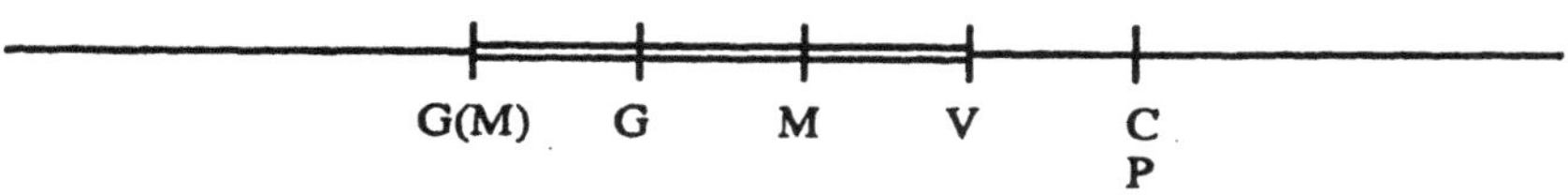

Recall that V is the veto median, or the point that divides the legislative chamber such that a third of the members have ideal points to the right of V and two-thirds have ideal points to the left. Figure 3 places the Court (C) and the Presidency (P) to the right of this veto point ($C > V$; $P > V$) for the main cases from this period discussed in Part I. However, I believe that the Court was to the left of the veto median ($C < V$) for many civil rights issues during this period. The administration's position, though, remains further to the right ($V < P$) for some of these issues.

Under this version of the Court/Congress/President game, the Court will not want to implement its own preferences when they are to the right of the veto median ($C > V$), because that decision would stimulate the gatekeepers to introduce overruling legislation set at V. Such legislation would not only be approved by Congress but also would survive an expected veto. Hence, the Court would want to shoot for a decision close to or to the left of the veto median (V). Although the gatekeepers would dislike that result, they would not introduce overruling legislation because they would realize that it would be vetoed and that they could not get Congress to override the veto. For this reason, they would live with V.

The game depicted in Figure 3 gives the conservative Court much more discretion than it had in Figure 2, because the addition of a presidential veto protects the Court's decisions against overrides. Hence, we

225. In *McMann*, for example, the Court was aware of the Senate committee report endorsing the Fourth Circuit's decision the Court was reversing. While the Court's vote in *McMann* was probably taken before the committee report was promulgated, Justices have been known to change their votes during the deliberative process.

would expect the Court's interpretation of civil rights statutes to have shifted markedly to the right in the 1980s—even more to the right than we might otherwise have expected simply from the rightward personnel changes. This scenario is basically what we find. The Court's composition changed only once between 1975 and 1986 (conservative Justice O'Connor replacing moderately conservative Justice Stewart). However, the Court's interpretations of civil rights statutes shifted dramatically to the right after 1981, when the Presidency emerged as a potential protection for the Court's conservative preferences.[226] The few liberal interpretations of civil rights statutes that occurred in this period tended to emphasize recent legislative signals,[227] suggesting that perhaps a few Justices were being careful to avoid results too far to the right, lest they fall athwart the veto median (V).

To see how this dynamic operates, consider the Court's position on the issue of tax exemptions for private institutions that segregate on the basis of race. Here, the positive political theory model offers a particularly good explanation for the Court's curious approach. Responding to lower court challenges, the Internal Revenue Service in 1970-71 amended its regulations to disallow income tax exemptions to racially discriminatory private schools.[228] Although the Code and its legislative history did not strongly support the Service's position, Congress in the 1970s turned back all efforts to reverse the new rules. It did, however, hamper the agency's efforts to devote substantial resources to the regulation's

226. *See, e.g.*, Marek v. Chesney, 473 U.S. 1 (1985) (6-3 split Court narrowly construes § 1988); Smith v. Robinson, 468 U.S. 992 (1984) (6-3 split Court narrowly construes Education of All Handicapped Children Act of 1975 and Rehabilitation Act); Grove City College v. Bell, 465 U.S. 555 (1984) (6-3 split Court narrowly construes title IX); Arizona Governing Comm. for Tax Deferred Annuity & Deferred Compensation Plans v. Norris, 463 U.S. 1073 (1983) (4-1-4 split Court extends liberal PDA interpretation to insurance companies but does so only prospectively); City of Lockhart v. United States, 460 U.S. 125 (1983) (5-3 split Court narrowly construes Voting Rights Act); General Bldg. Contractors Ass'n v. Pennsylvania, 458 U.S. 375 (1982) (6-1-2 split Court narrowly interprets section 1981); American Tobacco Co. v. Patterson, 456 U.S. 63 (1982) (5-4 split Court broadly construes exception to title VII); City of Memphis v. Green, 451 U.S. 100 (1981) (6-3 split Court narrowly interprets section 1982). *But see* Connecticut v. Teal, 457 U.S. 440 (1982) (Connecticut state agency's promotion of a greater overall percentage of black employees than of white employees did not preclude black employee plaintiffs from establishing a prima facie case of disparate impact under title VII); County of Washington v. Gunther, 452 U.S. 161 (1981) (Bennett amendment to title VII does not restrict title VII prohibition of sex-based wage discrimination to equal pay for equal work claims).

227. *See, e.g.*, Johnson v. Transportation Agency, 480 U.S. 616, 629 n.7 (1987) (5-1-3 split Court relies on subsequent congressional approval of *Weber* to reaffirm its view of title VII); School Bd. v. Arline, 480 U.S. 273, 277-80 (1987) (7-2 split Court relies on congressional review of HEW regulations to interpret Rehabilitation Act); North Haven Bd. of Educ. v. Bell, 456 U.S. 512, 530-35 (1982) (6-3 split Court relying on legislative review and deliberation over proposed HEW regulations).

228. The IRS policy was approved in Green v. Connally, 330 F. Supp. 1150 (S.D. Miss.), *aff'd mem.*, 404 U.S. 997 (1971), and formalized in Rev. Rul. 71-447, 1971-2 C.B. 230.

enforcement.[229] The Supreme Court's treatment of this issue tracks the well-publicized congressional treatment. In *Bob Jones University v. United States*,[230] a virtually unanimous Court upheld the agency regulation, relying heavily on Congress' supportive stance in the 1970s.[231] But a year later, in *Allen v. Wright*, a divided Court refused to allow citizens to enforce the agency regulations directly.[232]

Despite this success, the positive political theory model does not explain two important anomalies from this last period: the surprising amount and intensity of conflict between the Court/President and Congress; and the failure of each to avoid being reversed. The Court's interpretations were reversed five times after 1985 (with another nine vulnerable in the current Congress). The President's veto was overridden once. And Congress' action was thwarted once by a successful veto. The positive political theory model might attribute these reversals to insufficient information as to the location of the veto median (V). That explanation, however, is problematic. Why should the Court and President make such big mistakes in this period and not in earlier ones? Why should Congress have made the same mistake in 1990? This phenomenon is the biggest anomaly facing the positive political theory model as applied here, and it requires us to supplement the model.

B. Supplementing the Positive Political Theory Model: Informational Features of the Court/Congress/President Game

The game I have been using to model the Court/Congress/President interaction over the interpretation of civil rights statutes emphasizes the "distributive" features of the legislative process.[233] The positive political theory model assumes that Congress delegates duties to committees and outside agents (like courts) in ways that serve its members' reelection goals. Hence, the role of committees is to distribute rents to those members (and their constituents) who most intensely want them, and the role of agents is to carry out the members' current policies. Politics is seen as

229. For example, in 1978-79 the IRS issued regulations placing burdens on schools with low percentages of black students to "prove" nondiscrimination. Congress subsequently passed the Ashbrook Amendment, which barred the IRS from implementing those regulations. Other "back door" restrictions followed. *See IRS Tax Exemptions and Segregated Private Schools: Hearing Before the Subcomm. on Civil and Constitutional Rights of the House Comm. on the Judiciary*, 97th Cong., 2d Sess. 49-50 (1982).

230. 461 U.S. 574 (1983).

231. *Id.* at 599-602; *see also id.* at 607 (Powell, J., concurring).

232. 468 U.S. 737, 740 (1984). The 5-3 Court held that parents of black children did not have "standing" to sue for enforcement of the IRS regulation. *Id.* at 740. Read in conjunction with the *Bob Jones* ruling, *Wright* indicates that the Court shares congressional sentiment: The formal IRS rule stands, but enforcement will be lax.

233. *See* M. FIORINA, *supra* note 192; D. MAYHEW, *supra* note 192; K. SHEPSLE, THE GIANT JIGSAW PUZZLE (1978).

a zero-sum game, in which Congress and its members scheme to divide up the pie, with minimal friction and not much attention to what is "good" policy. Equilibrium means stable outcomes in which the various players operate under perfect information to satisfy their preferences (and those of important interest groups). Operating from these distributive assumptions, the model generates some intuitively appealing insights about civil rights overrides, but leaves several anomalies insufficiently explained, most notably the spate of legislative overrides and conflict in the past six years.

Several positive political theorists, most notably Professors Thomas Gilligan and Keith Krehbiel, have suggested that distributive features do not account for what goes on in the legislative process, and that informational features of the process deserve emphasis.[234] Under this view, legislators are policy outcome-oriented, as well as reelection-oriented, but are uncertain which policies produce desired outcomes. The legislature deals with uncertainty by delegating information-gathering and consensus-creating roles to committees and other agents. Under these assumptions, equilibrium is not rent-seeking stability: instead, it means a continuous exchange of information and views within committees and between the chamber and its committees until sufficient certainty finally allows the legislature to set policy.

These positive political theorists do not claim that informational assumptions explain all the data on the operation of Congress. They do claim, however, that distributive assumptions do not explain it either, and my case study bears this out. These theorists make an important advance by suggesting that in our game, the players' preferences are not entirely "exogenous," that is, determined prior to playing the game. To a substantial extent, they are "endogenous," formed in the process of playing the game and in response to the information and arguments adduced by the other players. This also suggests that there is no single Court/Congress/President game, but rather a series of games in which committees and agents have incentives to build up credibility by moving toward the legislative median (M). Reconsider our three periods of political interaction in light of the additional possibilities offered by considering the informational role of the players.

1. Court/Congress/President Cooperation: 1962-72

Informational assumptions provide a different way of thinking about

234. *See* K. Krehbiel, *supra* note 192; Gilligan & Krehbiel, *Organization of Informative Committees by a Rational Legislature*, 34 Am. J. Pol. Sci. 531 (1990); Gilligan & Krehbiel, *Collective Choice Without Procedural Commitment*, in Models of Strategic Choice in Politics 295 (P. Ordeshook ed. 1989); T. Gilligan, Performance of an Institutionalized Legislature (1989-90) (unpublished manuscript) (on file with author).

the initial period of cooperation among the Court, Congress, and the President on matters of civil rights policy (recall Figure 1). At the game's beginning, the views of Congress (M) and the gatekeepers (G) are incompletely formed, and open to change based upon more information. The Court's decision interpreting a civil rights statute (C) consequently becomes relevant information that might be considered, first, by the gatekeepers and, then, by the entire Congress. Three outcomes are possible, given the initial (and now only tentative) preference mapping for this period in Figure 1.

The first possible outcome I call the "information variation." Under this outcome, the relevant committees will examine the facts and reasoning of the Court's decision and agree with it. If the committee agrees with the decision, obviously it does not have to do anything. Moreover, sometimes the committee will even use the decision as a building block for new statutory initiatives. For example, the judiciary committees followed this course in using *Allen v. State Board of Elections* as a foundation for their thinking during the 1970 reenactment of the Voting Rights Act; the labor committees did the same when they considered *Griggs* similarly in the context of title VII's 1972 amendment. When the Court's opinion itself calls for legislative action to build upon its opinion, as in *Guest,* the committees will be particularly likely to press for codifying legislation.

The second possible outcome is the "distributive variation" discussed above: The gatekeeping committees will not agree with the Court's decision, but will not take action to overrule it because they do not prefer the decision Congress would probably adopt. Notwithstanding informational features of the political process, distributive features remain strong possibilities for the Court/Congress/President game.[235] Indeed, the distributive variation remains a robust positive political explanation of Congress' failure to overrule *Jones v. Mayer.*

The third possible outcome is a hybrid of the first two: The gatekeeping committees will be persuaded by the Court's decision and will shift their preferences (G) in the direction of the Court's (C); however, they will not initiate statutory proposals to codify or build upon the

235. Information theorists might argue, first, that this will occur in a narrow range of cases, because the preferences of committees (G) will not be far from those of the median Member (M). These theorists argue that committees are generally not composed of preference "outliers," and I think they are largely correct. However, even their own evidence suggests that the Labor and Judiciary committees in the 1980s were more liberal than the median Member.

Information theorists would argue, second, that the relevant committees are not gatekeepers, because they cannot prevent Congress from considering issues. There is much to this argument. In all the case examples I have discussed for this period, Congress had its chance to vote. But I consider the gatekeepers to be the committees plus the Democratic leadership, which together do substantially control the agenda of Congress and did play a critical role, for example, in turning back the floor challenges to the *Jones v. Mayer* interpretation in 1971-72.

Court's decision because they are unsure that Congress will agree (they are not sure M will shift toward C). This is a plausible explanation of the congressional response to *Griggs*: The very liberal labor committees in both chambers were persuaded by the *Griggs* opinion (and wrote committee reports to that effect) but never sought to codify it in title VII, since they were not certain that Congress would be similarly persuaded.

2. *Court/Congress Conflict: 1972-81*

Informational assumptions also provide a different way of looking at our second period, in which the Court's rightward shift yielded a number of overrides. The Court as an institution was trying to do more than just accommodate its preferences to those of Congress. Sometimes the Court was trying to change congressional preferences through persuasive opinions. Under this more complex set of assumptions, there are again three types of outcomes that might flow from the tentative preference mappings in Figure 2.

Under one possible outcome—the information variation—the Court will stick to its preferences and try to persuade the gatekeepers and Congress of its views. This is a very hard task, since it is especially important to persuade the gatekeepers, whose preferences (G) are more distant from the Court's (C) than Congress' (M) are. This scenario appears to be the one that the Court tried to follow in *Gilbert, Bolden,* and *Atascadero.* All three opinions were based upon the Court's conservative constitutional jurisprudence—fourteenth amendment gender discrimination, fifteenth amendment voting rights, and eleventh amendment state sovereign immunity, respectively—and might be interpreted as extensions of that jurisprudence. In these opinions, therefore, the Court was informing Congress of an important body of constitutional law and suggesting that the statutory law should run along parallel lines. Even though Congress declined to follow the Court's lead in each case, it did so only after considering the gatekeepers' thorough factfinding and reports, which discredited the Court's analysis.

Under the second possibility—the distributive variation—the Court will adjust its preferences in deference to those of the legislature and will successfully avoid an override. I think this is precisely what the Court did explicitly in *Runyon* and implicitly in *Weber* and a number of other civil rights decisions of the 1970s.[236] The distributive variation would explain cases like *Gilbert* by suggesting that the Court was simply mistaken about the congressional median. This conclusion strikes me as also plausible.

A third possible outcome, something of a hybrid, is that the Court

236. *See* cases cited *supra* note 216.

will signal Congress that its policy preferences might be different from its institutional preferences, thereby inviting a legislative override. This, I believe, is what the Court was doing in *Alyeska Pipeline.* The Court understood that, as a matter of policy, fee shifting made sense in public law litigation. The Court, however, did not feel comfortable adopting this fee shifting, in light of two factors: the relative clarity of the statutes limiting a court's authority to award counsel fees to the prevailing party and Congress' repeated willingness—in the 1960s and early 1970s—to adopt specific fee-shifting statutes tailored to specific statutory schemes when it wanted them. The Court's opinion provided Congress with useful information, and openly invited an override, to do what the Court felt incapable of doing.

3. Court/Congress/President Conflict: 1981-90

Informational assumptions also provide a useful perspective for thinking about our third period, in which a strong rightward shift in the Presidency not only supported the expected rightward shift in the Supreme Court opinions, but also ultimately contributed to four years of unprecedented conflict between the Court/President, on one side, and Congress, on the other. Again, these assumptions expand the possible outcomes of this revised game, in which the President became a major player in trying to protect the Court from Congress—especially after 1986, when Congress moved to the left and the Court sharply to the right (recall Figure 3).

One possible outcome is an information variation. The Court will implement its preferences as the decision ($x = C$) but will write an opinion providing Congress with useful information, in hopes of persuading enough Members of Congress to shift the veto median (V) to the right. The Court may have taken this attitude in *Grove City* and *Betts,* both of which proved dramatically unpersuasive to large majorities in Congress. Interestingly, the Court was probably trying to do this in *Wards Cove, Martin v. Wilks,* and *Zipes,* three of the six 1989 decisions subject to the 1990 civil rights bill.

In each of these opinions, the Court articulated important policy concerns that might have moved the veto median. *Wards Cove* and *Martin* reflected the Court's concern that the dynamics of title VII actions gave employers perverse incentives to adopt racial quotas. As a result, the Court in *Wards Cove* made plaintiffs' burden of proof in disparate impact cases more demanding to ensure that employers were not pressured to shoot for completely "proportional representation" by minorities, as through quotas.[237] The Court in *Martin v. Wilks* relied on

237. *See Wards Cove,* 490 U.S. at 652 (criticizing lower court's *Griggs*-based approach on the

standard due process values to assure procedural avenues for future white employees to reopen consent decrees to make "reverse discrimination" claims.[238] This is also a plausible explanation for *Zipes*, where the Court was concerned about the rights of intervening defendants.[239] That the President's veto of the 1990 civil rights bill was not overridden might suggest that the Court was successful in moving the veto median on these issues, though I think the third variation, described below, offers an even better explanation.

Another possible outcome is suggested by the distributive variation set forth initially: Even though the Court's decision is to the right of the preferences of Congress, it will try to avoid an override, by moving its own preferences toward what the Court perceives to be the veto median. This move does indeed explain most of the cases and suggests that some of the congressional overrides may have been a result of the Court's miscalculation of the veto median. For example, *Patterson* was clearly a compromise decision, in which the five-Justice majority reaffirmed *Runyon v. McCrary* as "consistent with our society's deep commitment to the eradication of discrimination based on a person's race,"[240] but then interpreted *Runyon* rather narrowly, based in part on its clash with the original assumptions of title VII.[241] Such a decision at least *seemed* to signal an accommodating attitude toward current legislative preferences.[242] Much the same story can be told for *Smith v. Robinson*, *Paralyzed Veterans of America*, and *Price Waterhouse v. Hopkins*.[243] On the other hand, this game does not adequately explain *Grove City*, *Betts*, and probably some of the 1989 decisions currently being considered for override by Congress (such as *Lorance*), where the Court's miscalculations were quite substantial.

A third possible outcome, a hybrid of the informational and distrib-

---

grounds that it would impel "many employers . . . to adopt racial quotas," in violation of section 703(j)).

238. *See Martin v. Wilks*, 490 U.S. at 761, 762 n.2 (ironically relying on Hansberry v. Lee, 311 U.S. 32, 40 (1940), which allowed a collateral challenge to a decree segregating a Chicago neighborhood).

239. *See* Independent Fed'n of Flight Attendants v. Zipes, 491 U.S. 754, 761-66 (1989).

240. Patterson v. McClean Credit Union, 491 U.S. 164, 174 (1989).

241. *Id.* at 177-82.

242. Members of Congress took the unusual step of filing an amicus brief in *Patterson*. The brief argued only for reaffirming Runyon v. McCrary, 427 U.S. 160 (1976); it did not tackle the difficult issue of applying *Runyon* to *Patterson*'s facts. *See* Brief of 66 Members of the United States Senate and 118 Members of the United States House of Representatives as *Amici Curiae* in Support of Petitioner, *Patterson* (No. 87-107). In light of this brief, the *Patterson* opinion may be seen as responding to congressional concerns, or at least to the Court's understanding of those concerns.

243. After being overridden three times in 1986 in its interpretations of statutes affecting the handicapped, *see* Department of Transp. v. Paralyzed Veterans of Am., 477 U.S. 597 (1986); Atascadero State Hosp. v. Scanlon, 473 U.S. 234 (1985); Smith v. Robinson, 468 U.S. 992 (1984), the Court changed course the next year by broadly construing section 504 of the Rehabilitation Act in School Board v. Arline, 480 U.S. 273 (1987).

utive variations, is that the Court will write an opinion trying to shift the veto median to the right, and the gatekeepers will respond by mounting an effort to shift the veto median to the left. The gatekeepers appear to have done just this in 1988 with the Restoration Act. The Act not only overruled *Grove City*'s interpretation of title IX, but went beyond the position of the *Grove City* dissenters and expanded federal antidiscrimination rules to entire "systems."[244] Seeking to repeat their 1988 success, the gatekeepers tried to do the same thing in 1990. The Court's decisions in the six 1989 cases—*Wards Cove, Martin v. Wilks, Patterson, Hopkins, Lorance, Zipes*—were extremely vulnerable in Congress because its policy preferences were too far to the right and so bereft of persuasive power that even the President deserted the Court on *Patterson* and *Lorance.*

As a result, the gatekeepers could have drafted a bill overruling most of these decisions (probably all but *Ward's Cove*) at the veto median (V) and could have been successful. But from the gatekeepers' point of view, such a decision (x = V) would have been little better than the Court's decisions (x = C > V). Hence, the gatekeepers themselves sought to move the veto median (V) and the median member (M) to the left on some of the relevant issues (especially the *Wards Cove* issue) through extensive hearings detailing the unfortunate practical effects of the decisions on civil rights enforcement. The 1990 experience suggests that the gatekeepers did not move the veto median far enough to the left (the veto was not overridden). But it also suggests that a less ambitious bill introduced to the current Congress could pass, because most of the Court's decisions appear to be to the right of the veto median.

C. Positive Predictions for Court/Congress/President Interaction on Civil Rights Issues in the 1990s

Positive political analysis not only provides explanations about the past but can suggest the direction of future Court/Congress/President interaction regarding civil rights statutes. One prediction is that Congress in 1991 or 1992 ought to be able to enact legislation overruling most or all of the nine Supreme Court decisions subject to the vetoed 1990 bill. The main obstacle to an override is not the prospect of another presidential veto, but the possible failure of the gatekeepers to develop a bill tailored to the veto median (yielding a bill the President would ordi-

244. *See Civil Rights Restoration Act of 1985: Joint Hearings on H.R. 700 Before the House Comm. on Education and Labor and the Subcomm. on Civil and Constitutional Rights of the House Comm. on the Judiciary,* 99th Cong., 1st Sess. 12, 174, 404-05, 599 (1985) (statements of Rep. Sensenbrenner (R-Wis.)). Rep. Sensenbrenner believed *Grove City* was wrongly decided and supported both bills but felt that the 1985 bill did more than overrule *Grove City*. *See also id.* at 231-36 (similar testimony by Assistant Attorney General Reynolds).

narily not veto, whatever his own preferences). For example, a bill overruling *Patterson* and *Lorance* (which the administration supported in 1990) could pass without a veto. A bill also overruling *Hopkins, Zipes,* and the three minor pre-1989 cases[245] could probably pass with veto-proof margins. With larger Democratic majorities in Congress, the gatekeepers also ought to be able to pass a bill modifying *Wards Cove* and *Martin v. Wilks.*

The more interesting question is what the dynamics for Court/Congress/President interaction will be for future Supreme Court decisions interpreting civil rights statutes. The dynamics are, I think, fairly established for the 1990s: The Court's preferences will remain to the right of Congress' preferences which in turn will be to the right of the preferences of the majority leadership and one of the two gatekeeping committees (the labor committees).[246] The three variables that will be important for the dynamics under the Court/Congress/President civil rights game developed in this Part are the preferences of the Presidency, the strategy of the Court, and the strategy of the gatekeepers. Consider some of the variations.

One possible (and in my view likely) scenario is a reduction of open Court/Congress conflict (after the 1991/92 bill is passed), even though the Court's own preferences will probably drift to the right, at least in the early 1990s.[247] The key variable will be whether the Court decides to compromise its preferences as it did in most of the civil rights cases of the

245. *See* cases cited *supra* note 15.

246. I assume here that the Democrats will retain their majorities in Congress, which seems very probable for the House and probable for the Senate. If so, Congress will remain substantially to the left of the Court, whose left-leaning Justices are relatively older than the right-leaning Justices (and hence more likely to be replaced). Even if the Republicans take control of the Senate, Congress as a whole will remain to the left of the Court on most civil rights issues.

If the Democrats retain their control of Congress, the majority leadership will likely remain to the left of the chamber median, as is currently the case with Majority Leader Mitchell (D-Me., 1988 ADA score 95) and Speaker Foley (D-Wash., 1988 ADA score 85). If the Republicans take control of Congress, the majority leadership will shift to the right of the chamber median, as is currently the case with House Minority Leader Michel (R-Ill., 1988 ADA score 10) and Senate Minority Leader Dole (R-Kan., 1988 ADA score 15). *See* THE ALMANAC OF AMERICAN POLITICS 1990, *supra* note 52 (listing the members' ADA scores).

Whichever party controls Congress, the labor committees will probably remain significantly to the left of the chamber median; the judiciary committees will probably stay pretty much at the chamber median (as has historically been the case). *See* K. KREHBIEL, *supra* note 192, ch. 4 (discussing House committees). For example, the 1990 Senate Judiciary Committee's Democratic members had an average 1988 ADA score of 74; its Republican members, 15. The two scores of 74 and 15 mirrored the chamber medians of 72 and 19, respectively. However, the average scores on the 1990 Senate Labor and Human Resources Committee differed significantly from these chamber medians. Democratic members had average 1988 ADA scores of 88, and its Republican members, 26. These numbers are markedly higher than the chamber medians, as listed above. See THE ALMANAC OF AMERICAN POLITICS 1990, *supra* note 52, for these ADA scores.

247. Liberal Justice Brennan's replacement by Justice Souter, who is probably more conservative, accounts for this rightward shift. Other moderate-to-liberal Justices (Marshall,

1970s. In the short term (with a conservative President), the Court only has to aim at the veto median (V). This strategy will still permit the Court plenty of discretion to reach conservative results. In the longer term, depending on the future preferences of the Presidency, the Court may have to aim at the congressional median (M) in order to accommodate the political system and avoid overrides.

The Court has strong incentives to follow this course under the Court/Congress/President civil rights game outlined here. Under the distributive variation, the Court's incentive to accommodate its preferences is simply to avoid being overridden. Under the information variation, the Court might want to risk being overridden in order to persuade Congress that the Court's policy is better. In that event, the Court still has an incentive not to be overridden constantly. That is, if the Court wants to be seen as generating useful information for Congress, it will lose its credibility if Congress continually rejects its information as unreliable by overruling its decisions. In the past, this incentive has motivated the Court to become more moderate when its policy initiatives were rebuffed by Congress.[248] On the other hand, if the Court decides to "dig in" and continue to try to persuade Congress to accept its policies, the Court/Congress conflict will continue into the 1990s.

Whether or not the Court/Congress conflict continues, the actual direction of civil rights statutory policy will depend largely on the preferences of the Presidency in the 1990s. If the Presidency remains where it is (on the right), policy will end up somewhere around the congressional veto median ($x = V$). This would mean greater restrictions on statutorily permitted affirmative action, narrower interpretations of section 1981 and other general civil rights laws, and greater procedural burdens on civil rights plaintiffs. If the Presidency shifts to the left, either to or beyond the congressional median ($P < M$), then the Court loses a great deal of its discretion, and the ultimate policy decision shifts toward the congressional median (M).

Given the Court's current preferences ($C > M$ for the entire decade), the election of a President whose civil rights preferences are at or to the left of Congress' preferences would clearly affect civil rights policy in the game. At the very least, a more liberal President would remove the veto protection for the Court, and policy would move back toward the congressional median. More dramatically, the President's ability to persuade and lead opinion could move the congressional median (M) to the left (as the President did in the 1960s). Such a movement would have a substantial influence on policy, notwithstanding the Court's position.

Blackmun, Stevens) may well leave the Court in time for the Bush administration to appoint more conservative Justices.

248. For example, see the Court's positive response to the PDA, discussed *supra* note 224.

The consequences would include statutory allowance of voluntary affirmative action, broader interpretations of the civil rights statutes to reach new and unanticipated problems, and fewer procedural obstacles to civil rights enforcement.

III
NORMATIVE IMPLICATIONS OF THE GAME THEORY ANALYSIS OF THE COURT/CONGRESS/PRESIDENT INTERACTION

The normative implications of the positive political theory model are also of interest. The model strongly suggests that the Court is a political actor: The Court imposes its own preferences onto civil rights statutes, subject mainly to the constraints imposed by the preferences of the current President and Congress. This positive political suggestion contrasts dramatically with the traditional law professor's view of the Court as merely an agent implementing the intent of the original legislature.[249] Yet the traditional view fails to account for the last thirty years of the Court's interpretations of civil rights statutes. Virtually all the important judicial interpretations of civil rights statutes during this period either do not explore the original legislative intent or expectations in any meaningful way,[250] or else they rely on arguments about those expectations that

249. *See, e.g.*, The FEDERALIST No. 78 (A. Hamilton) ("[T]he judiciary, from the nature of its functions, will always be the least dangerous to the political rights of the Constitution . . . ."); Maltz, *Statutory Interpretation and Legislative Power: The Case for a Modified Intentionalist Approach*, 63 TUL. L. REV. 1, 13 (1988) (an intentionalist approach to statutory interpretation "embodies widely shared, deeply embedded beliefs about the appropriate scope of legislative power"); Landes & Posner, *The Independent Judiciary in an Interest-Group Perspective*, 18 J.L. & ECON. 875, 877-87 (1975) (interest-group theory posits that an independent judiciary will enforce existing statutes in accordance with the enacting legislature's intent); Merrill, *The Common Law Powers of Federal Courts*, 52 U. CHI. L. REV. 1, 19-24 (1985) (the principle of separation of powers limits the legitimacy of lawmaking by federal courts). *But see* M. SHAPIRO, LAW AND POLITICS IN THE SUPREME COURT (1964) (the Supreme Court is often the agent of interest groups not represented adequately by other institutions of government).

250. *See* Public Employees Retirement Sys. v. Betts, 109 S. Ct. 2854, 2860-64 (1989) (skirting the legislative history arguments and concluding they have no relevance given the "plain statutory language," *id.* at 2864); Independent Fed'n of Flight Attendants v. Zipes, 491 U.S. 754, 758-66 (1989) (interpreting title VII "in light of the competing equities that Congress normally takes into account," *id.* at 761, but ignoring legislative intent); Patterson v. McLean Credit Union, 491 U.S. 164, 175-85 (1989) (analysis focuses on plain meaning and precedent with only scant attention to legislative history); Lorance v. AT&T Technologies, 490 U.S. 900 (1989) (similar); Martin v. Wilks, 490 U.S. 755 (1989) (ignoring title VII altogether); Wards Cove Packing Co. v. Atonio, 490 U.S. 642 (1989) (ignoring legislative intent); Atascadero State Hosp. v. Scanlon, 473 U.S. 234, 237-47 (1985) (emphasizing federalism policy and ignoring legislative expectations); City of Mobile v. Bolden, 446 U.S. 55, 60-61 (1980) (using admittedly scant legislative history to suggest that plaintiffs' statutory claim only duplicated their fifteenth amendment claim); General Elec. Co. v. Gilbert, 429 U.S. 125, 133-40 (1976) (interpreting title VII in light of equal protection jurisprudence and ignoring legislative intent); Louisiana v. United States, 380 U.S. 145, 147-56 (1965) (no discussion of legislative intent).

range from questionable[251] to untenable.[252] Furthermore, many of the decisions explicitly rely upon political developments after the statute's enactment.[253]

I am hardly the first to suggest that the Court is a political actor, for the legal realists long ago demonstrated that the Court's decisions do not necessarily flow from principled rules and that the Court decides cases based in part upon its own preferences. A fair amount of recent legal scholarship has demonstrated that many of the Court's decisions represent no consistent effort to replicate the original intent of the enacting Congress.[254] And there is a rich tradition of positive political theory that successfully explains outcomes from models that treat the Court as a political actor not much different from agencies, the President, and Congress.[255]

My historical account through the lens of a positive political theory model is further evidence that the Court does not faithfully follow the

251. *Compare* Library of Congress v. Shaw, 478 U.S. 310, 319-20 (1986) (majority opinion) (title VII provision making the United States liable "the same as a private person" waives the government's immunity from attorney's fees, but not interest, because neither the statute, nor the legislative history specifically mention "interest") *with id.* at 325-26 (Brennan, J., dissenting) (preclusion of interest inconsistent with actual congressional expectations). *Compare* Smith v. Robinson, 468 U.S. 992, 1006-13 (1984) (majority opinion's use of legislative intent) *with id.* at 1026-31 (Brennan, J., dissenting) (persuasive rebuttal based on underlying congressional assumptions). *Compare* United Airlines v. McMann, 434 U.S. 192, 199-202 (1977) (majority opinion's interpretation of legislative history) *with id.* at 210-16 (Marshall, J. dissenting) (detailed rebuttal). *Compare* Jones v. Alfred H. Mayer Co., 392 U.S. 409, 422-37 (1968) (majority opinion's detailed examination of legislative history) *with id.* at 450-76 (Harlan, J., dissenting) (even more detailed rebuttal).

252. A striking example is Grove City College v. Bell, 465 U.S. 555 (1984). In *Grove City,* a unanimous Court relied on legislative history to conclude that student receipt of federal financial aid triggers title IX's application to the college. *Id.* at 565-70. A majority then summarily rejected compelling legislative history which indicated that title IX was intended to cover a whole college. *Compare id.* at 570-71 (majority opinion) *with id.* at 582-99 (Brennan, J., concurring in part and dissenting in part). *See also* B. Marks, *supra* note 195 (original legislative history); *id.* at 71-78 (subsequent legislative history). *Compare also* Griggs v. Duke Power Co., 401 U.S. 424, 434-36 (1971) (unanimous Court's use of legislative intent in title VII) *with* H. GRAHAM, *supra* note 22 (Court's use of legislative intent in *Griggs* is spurious).

253. *See Patterson,* 491 U.S. at 180-82 (interpreting section 1981 narrowly so as not "to circumvent the detailed remedial scheme constructed" in [the later] title VII); *Atascadero,* 473 U.S. at 237-47 (relying on post-EHA eleventh amendment jurisprudence to interpret statute); *Bolden,* 446 U.S. at 60-74 (relying on post-Voting Rights Act fifteenth amendment jurisprudence to interpret statute); *Gilbert,* 429 U.S. at 133-40 (relying on post-title VII fourteenth amendment sex discrimination jurisprudence to interpret title VII).

254. Eskridge & Frickey, *Statutory Interpretation as Practical Reasoning,* 42 STAN. L. REV. 321, 325-32 (1990); Farber, *supra* note 20; Frickey, *Congressional Intent, Practical Reasoning, and the Dynamic Nature of Federal Indian Law,* 78 CALIF. L. REV. 1137, 1142-203 (1990) (careful demonstration of how the Court has ignored or abused legislative history in interpreting federal Indian law); Zeppos, *Judicial Candor and Statutory Interpretation,* 78 GEO. L.J. 353 (1989).

255. *See* C. PRITCHETT, THE ROOSEVELT COURT (1948); D. RHODE & H. SPAETH, SUPREME COURT DECISION MAKING (1976); G. SCHUBERT, THE JUDICIAL MIND: THE ATTITUDES AND IDEOLOGIES OF SUPREME COURT JUSTICES, 1946-1963 (1965); Segal & Cover, *supra* note 61.

traditional approach to statutory interpretation. This positive account also makes an interesting affirmative point: The Court is often attentive to the current Congress' preferences when it interprets statutes; therefore, these interpretations can then be interpreted as political efforts by the Court to accommodate its views to those of Congress, or to persuade Congress to change its views.

If the Court is—consciously or unconsciously—engaging in this sort of game with Congress, there are interesting normative ramifications. I explore three of them here: first, a reevaluation of traditional doctrines relating to the Court's interpretation of statutes; second, a rethinking of the meaning of judicial activism; and third, a reevaluation of the Court's role in civil rights policy.

A. Rethinking Specific Doctrines

Most traditional doctrines of statutory interpretation are, at least rhetorically, grounded upon original intent theory. Consequently, the Court's political role in the evolution of the nation's civil rights policy suggests that some of these doctrines should be reconsidered, at least in the context of implementing civil rights statutes. I shall examine three such doctrines here—the retroactivity of judicial decisions, the rule against using subsequent legislative history, and various legislative inaction rules.

1. Retroactivity of Supreme Court Interpretations of Civil Rights Statutes

The traditional, but not iron-clad, rule has been that legislation only applies prospectively, whereas judicial interpretation of legislation applies retroactively.[256] Sometimes when the Supreme Court overrules prior decisions (especially constitutional decisions), it will give the new rule only prospective effect.[257] Sometimes Congress will give retroactive effect to statutory changes it makes in the law.[258] But when the Court is merely interpreting statutes and not explicitly overruling prior interpretations, it almost always gives its decisions retroactive effect. So, too, Congress has traditionally overridden the Court's interpretations by legislating only prospectively.

This dichotomy is based on the traditional view of the different roles of Court and Congress. Since the Court "declares" the preexisting law, its decisions apply not only to the case or controversy at hand, but also to all others pending. Since Congress "creates" new law through the polit-

256. *See* W. ESKRIDGE & P. FRICKEY, LEGISLATION: STATUTES AND THE CREATION OF PUBLIC POLICY 264-77 (1987) (exploring the traditional view and some critiques of it).
257. *See id.* at 264-70.
258. *Id.* at 274-77.

ical process, it would be unfair to apply its "new" rules to preexisting transactions. The legal realists' demonstration that courts create law in some of the same ways that legislatures do has discredited this traditional rationale.[259] Yet a study of our present practices reveals how strongly the old dichotomy lives on. For example, even the very liberal House Education and Labor Committee came close to removing the retroactivity provisions of the omnibus 1990 bill, based upon these traditional arguments.[260]

This historical study also suggests a strong reason for why the Court and Congress should abandon the dichotomy in many cases. On the one hand, Congress should feel little reluctance to override judicial misinterpretations retroactively. Congress did this in the 1986 HCPA and tried to do so in the 1990 Civil Rights Act. The imperative towards retroactivity is greater when good evidence exists that the Court's interpretation alters "settled" expectations, as it did in *Jones v. Mayer, Gilbert, McMann, Bolden, Grove City, Robinson, Atascadero, Betts, Martin v. Wilks, Wards Cove,* and several of the other 1989 decisions. Indeed, when the Court's interpretation changes a settled agency and lower court consensus and Congress overrides the Court's novel interpretation, Congress ought to *presume in favor of* some form of retroactivity. On the other hand, the Court should reconsider its policy of retroactive application for decisions that in reality represent shifts of law. In such cases, it makes sense for the Court to give its decisions "prospective-prospective" effect; that is, the Court's interpretation should apply a year or two years from the date of the decision, so that Congress can respond to the Court's new information.[261]

2. *Subsequent Legislative History*

The traditional (original intent) theory suggests that the Court should not consider subsequent legislative history when interpreting stat-

259. *See, e.g.*, Traynor, *Quo Vadis, Prospective Overruling: A Question of Judicial Responsibility*, 28 HASTINGS L.J. 533, 534-42 (1977).

260. Representative Moorehead's (R-Cal.) motion to strike the retroactivity provisions passed by an 18-17 vote. Suddenly, another Democrat on the committee popped up (probably dragged from some other meeting) to vote with the chair and kill the motion on an 18-18 tie. It is interesting that this was the only significant Republican motion to come anywhere close to adoption by the liberal committee. *See* Marked Transcript of the House Education and Labor Committee (available from the Committee only).

261. This is hardly a novel strategy. State courts sometimes do this in seeking to call legislative attention to a problem. *See, e.g.*, Spanel v. Mounds View School Dist. No. 621, 264 Minn. 279, 118 N.W.2d 795 (1962) (prospectively overruling the doctrine of sovereign immunity for Minnesota school districts with respect to torts committed *after* the adjournment of the following regular session of the Minnesota Legislature). The Supreme Court used the same strategy in Northern Pipeline Co. v. Marathon Pipe Line Co., 458 U.S. 50 (1982) (prospective overruling only of an unconstitutional provision of the Bankruptcy Act of 1978). See G. CALABRESI, A COMMON LAW FOR THE AGE OF STATUTES (1982), for an excellent analysis of this concept.

utes. Indeed, the Burger Court in 1980 invoked "the oft-repeated warning that 'the views of a subsequent Congress form a hazardous basis for inferring the intent of an earlier one.' "[262] The Court, also in 1980, said that although arguments based on subsequent legislative history "must be weighed with extreme care, they should not be rejected out of hand as a source that a court may consider in the search for legislative intent."[263] And in yet a third 1980 case, the Court said that, "while the views of a subsequent Congress cannot override the unmistakable intent of the enacting one, . . . such views are entitled to significant weight . . . and particularly so when the precise intent of the enacting Congress is obscure."[264]

Obviously, the Burger Court had no hard-and-fast rule concerning subsequent legislative history. The positive political theory model developed in this Article would predict that the Court would be more likely to emphasize subsequent legislative history when it is trying to accommodate its preferences to those of Congress. Moreover, there is some evidence that the Court does exactly that. In *North Haven Board of Education v. Bell,*[265] for example, the Court liberally interpreted title IX to include employment discrimination. We could plausibly conclude that this interpretation reflected the Court's deference to a strong majority view in Congress to that effect. In fact, the Court's opinion emphasized subsequent legislative history.[266] Quoting another title IX case in which the Court bent its preferences toward those of the congressional median, the Court in *North Haven* said: "Although postenactment developments cannot be accorded 'the weight of contemporary legislative history, we would be remiss if we ignored these authoritative expressions concerning the scope and purpose of Title IX . . . .' "[267] The Court then reluctantly interpreted title IX to grant a private right of action. Two years later, the Court in *Grove City* relied on subsequent legislative history to reject the college's argument that federal financial aid to its students did not bring the college into title IX's ambit,[268] but then essentially ignored similarly informative subsequent legislative history cutting against its holding that only the college's financial aid operations (and not the entire college) fell within title IX.[269]

262. Consumer Prods. Safety Comm'n v. GTE Sylvania, 447 U.S. 102, 117-18 (1980) (quoting United States v. Price, 361 U.S. 304, 313 (1960)).

263. Andrus v. Shell Oil Co., 446 U.S. 657, 666 n.8 (1980).

264. Seatrain Shipbuilding Corp. v. Shell Oil Co., 444 U.S. 572, 596 (1980) (citations omitted).

265. 456 U.S. 512 (1982).

266. *Id.* at 531-35 (HEW regulations considered by Congress and not overruled; indeed, proposals to change the regulations were defeated).

267. *Id.* at 535 (quoting Cannon v. University of Chicago, 441 U.S. 677, 687 n.7 (1979)).

268. Grove City College v. Bell, 465 U.S. 555, 568-70 & 568 n.19 (1984).

269. *Id.* at 572-75; *cf. id.* at 592-99 (Brennan, J., concurring in part and dissenting in part) (detailed examination of subsequent legislative history bearing on this issue).

The Rehnquist Court's move to the right and its unwillingness to bend its interpretations to current congressional preferences are mirrored in its much more consistent rhetoric against the use of subsequent legislative history. In *Betts,* for example, the Court marginalized Congress' 1978 overruling of *McMann* and stated: "We have observed on more than one occasion that the interpretation given by one Congress (or a committee or member thereof) to an earlier statute is of little assistance in discerning the meaning of that statute."[270] The Rehnquist Court consistently inveighs against the use of subsequent legislative history,[271] though it has not hesitated to use subsequent statutes to inform its interpretations.[272] Indeed, the Rehnquist Court's refusal to acknowledge recent legislative expressions of preference is probably loosely correlated to the Court's provocatively conservative interpretations of civil rights laws.

Generally, the analysis in this Article suggests a normative justification for the Burger Court's practice of softening its conservative preferences as it looked to subsequent legislative history. The use of subsequent history may seem inconsistent with original intent theories of statutory interpretation; however, the practice of the Warren, Burger, and Rehnquist Courts has borne little resemblance to an original intent approach in civil rights cases. To the extent that the Court is a political actor in civil rights cases and is making public policy, it ought to consider current legislative views both to inform its own policy choices and to avoid an unnecessary legislative overruling. The analysis also suggests a normative problem with the Rehnquist Court's refusal to credit subsequent legislative history: that refusal has deprived the Court of useful political information and has contributed to confrontations with Congress.

Some current Justices may believe that it is healthy for the Court to prod Congress, rather than for the Court to update civil rights statutes (which they believe their conservative decisions do not). If that is the

270. Public Employees Retirement Sys. v. Betts, 109 S. Ct. 2854, 2861 (1989).

271. *See, e.g.,* United States v. Monsanto, 491 U.S. 600, 609-10 (1989) (disregarding postenactment statements of several legislators); Mackey v. Lanier Collections Agency & Serv., 486 U.S. 825, 839-40 (1988) (subsequent legislative history, absent an amendment to the original language of the statute, should not direct resolution of a case); Gwaltney of Smithfield v. Chesapeake Bay Found., 484 U.S. 49, 63 n.4 (1987) ("The conclusions of the 99th Congress, however, are hardly probative of the intent of the 92d Congress.").

272. *E.g.,* Jett v. Dallas Indep. School Dist., 491 U.S. 701, 711-31 (1989) (interpreting the Civil Rights Act of 1866 in light of the Civil Rights Act of 1871); Patterson v. McLean Credit Union, 491 U.S. 164, 181 (1989) ("We should be reluctant . . . to read an earlier statute broadly where the result is to circumvent the detailed remedial scheme constructed in a later statute."); United States v. Fausto, 484 U.S. 439, 453 (1988) ("[R]econciling many laws enacted over time, and getting them to 'make sense' in combination, necessarily assumes that the implications of a statute may be altered by the implications of a later statute.").

Justices' belief, the analysis in this Article carries with it a normative doctrinal suggestion: The Justices should at least consult subsequent legislative history and other recent materials before deciding whether to give their conservative decisions prospective-prospective effect. In sum, if the Court wants Congress to take responsibility for updating civil rights statutes, it should provide a clear signal to that effect by making its own decisions prospective (especially when they change previously settled understandings).

3. *Legislative Inaction*

The Court in general, and even the Rehnquist Court, has relied on one type of subsequent legislative history: "legislative inaction," namely, the failure of Congress to overrule Supreme Court decisions, lower court consensus, and/or agency regulations.[273] The analysis in this Article suggests that the Court's reliance on legislative inaction is most productive when it sheds light on current legislative preferences (as to either the congressional median or the veto median). To the extent this suggestion is correct, the Court ought to be more critical than it has been in the past.

The most questionable of the legislative inaction doctrines is the acquiescence rule, in which the Court follows a precedent or agency rule on the basis that Congress never overruled it. For example, in *Johnson v. Transportation Agency,*[274] the Court reaffirmed *Weber* based upon Congress' failure to overrule it and the mistaken belief that there had been no attempt to do so.[275] In reality, the failure of Congress to act against Supreme Court precedents says very little about the preferences of the congressional median. For the gatekeepers may favor the decision and, as a consequence, may not introduce or may at least block overruling legislation. The gatekeepers, however, may have preferences different from those of the chamber median; therefore, the failure to act may be attributed to gatekeeper preference rather than the preference of Congress as a whole. This may have been the case with *Weber.*[276]

273. *See* Eskridge, *supra* note 213 (analyzing the Court's recent treatment of legislative inaction); Grabow, *Congressional Silence and the Search for Legislative Intent: A Venture Into "Speculative Unrealities,"* 64 B.U.L. Rev. 737 (1985) (critically noting the Court's increased reliance on congressional silence or inaction as an aid to statutory construction).

274. 480 U.S. 616 (1987).

275. *Id.* at 629 n.7. The Court was wrong in thinking that no bill had even been introduced to overrule *Weber,* since that was the purpose of S.J. Res. 41, 97th Cong., 1st Sess. (1981), and was the basis for Senate hearings. *See Affirmative Action and Equal Protection: Hearings on S.J. Res. 41 Before the Subcomm. on the Constitution of the Senate Comm. on the Judiciary,* 97th Cong., 1st Sess. (1981).

276. There was no effort made to overrule *Weber* in 1979-80, for obvious reasons. Any bill to overrule *Weber* in the House would have gone to an immediate graveyard in either the Judiciary or Education and Labor Committee, both of which were probably to the left of the House on this issue. In the Senate, the chairs of the Judiciary and Labor Committees (Senators Kennedy and Williams, respectively) would have killed any such bill in 1979-80. The situation changed in the Senate when

The reenactment rule is somewhat less questionable. Under this rule, the Court finds support for following a precedent or agency decision because Congress had reenacted the statute without overruling the decision. This rule is less questionable because the gatekeepers are not able to prevent Congress itself from considering amendments to the new statute (as they often can when there is no action altogether under the acquiescence rule). Thus, Congress' failure to overrule *Griggs* in 1972 has some significance, not just because the gatekeeping committees endorsed it in their reports,[277] but also because each chamber had an opportunity to bring the matter up. In fact, the Senate did defeat an amendment seeking to bar race-conscious relief in title VII that went well beyond *Griggs.*[278] On the other hand, the reenactment rule should not apply if there is no sound reason to believe that Congress was aware of the Court's decision.

Legislative inaction is most persuasive, and appears most reliable, in the context of a rejected proposal. Under the rejected proposal rule, the Court will infer legislative intent from the defeat of a proposal to overrule a precedent or agency decision. So long as the rejection occurs on the floor of a chamber or in conference committee, it often will be reliable evidence of subsequent legislative preferences. Nevertheless, rejected proposals should always be approached critically. For example, the Court in *Runyon v. McCrary* relied heavily on the Senate's rejection of a proposal which would have overruled cases applying *Jones v. Mayer* to employment discrimination.[279] The Court, however, did not examine congressional actions in sufficient detail. It failed to note three crucial aspects: first, that the proposal was not opposed on the ground that anyone agreed with *Jones v. Mayer*; second, that the proposal was rejected on a tie vote; and third, that a majority of the Senators present actually favored the proposal, which was scuttled by a gatekeepers' gambit.[280] While the Senate's action does provide some evidence of median legisla-

---

the Republicans took control in 1981. Senator Hatch introduced S.J. Res. 41 and held hearings on it in the Judiciary Subcommittee, which he chaired. *See supra* note 275. But the committee was dominated by a pro-civil-rights coalition even during Republican control, *see supra* note 66, and S.J. Res. 41 went nowhere.

277. *See supra* notes 57-58 and accompanying text; *see also* 118 CONG. REC. 7166 (1972) (conference report operated under assumption that "the present case law as developed by the courts would continue to govern the applicability and construction of title VII").

278. Senator Ervin proposed an amendment to title VII to prohibit government agencies from requiring employers to adopt goals for the hiring of minorities. *See* 118 CONG. REC. 1663-64 (1972). Senator Javits led the opposition, which defended all sorts of remedial practices that addressed *Griggs*-like bad numbers. *Id.* at 1664-76. The Ervin amendment was defeated by a two-to-one vote. *Id.* at 1676. *See generally* H. GRAHAM, *supra* note 22, at 439-43 (describing the debate between Ervin and Javits).

279. Runyon v. McCrary, 427 U.S. 160, 174 n.11 (1976) (relying on the legislative history of the rejected proposal to legislatively overrule *Jones v. Mayer*).

280. This story, and more, is told in Eskridge, *supra* note 213, at 100-03.

tor preferences in the early 1970s, the *Runyon* Court overstated its significance.

B. Rethinking Judicial Activism

The Supreme Court's conduct has confounded traditional legal thinking about judicial activism.[281] Judicial activism has always been associated with the Warren Court, for it struck down many statutes to protect individual rights and interpreted statutes (especially civil rights statutes) dynamically and liberally. The Burger Court, however, taught us that a moderate-to-conservative Court too could be activist—it also struck down numerous statutes and interpreted others just as dynamically as the Warren Court did (albeit in different ways). The Rehnquist Court is now teaching us that a conservative Court can be activist also in a different way. The Rehnquist Court is (thus far) not keen on invalidating legislation on constitutional grounds, but it is more aggressively activist in the context of statutory interpretation than was either the Warren or Burger Court.

This Article's positive analysis suggests a new way of thinking about judicial activism. Consider the following normative framework: The Court is activist in interpreting civil rights statutes when it emphasizes dynamic considerations beyond the statutory text and original intent, because in so doing the Court is going beyond the expectations of the enacting Congress. This dynamic interpretation can be politically productive activism if the Court's interpretation provides useful information about the statute to Congress or contributes to the statute's goals. The Court is even more activist if its interpretation emphasizes its own preferences over those of both the enacting and current Congress. This self-interested interpretivism tends to be unproductive activism if the Court's preferences prove to be useless information or prove to thwart the statute's operation. The Court/Congress/President civil rights game developed in this Article suggests some interesting hypotheses for the various periods discussed.

1. The Warren Court: 1962-72

In civil rights decisions, the Warren Court was quite activist, but perhaps not so activist as lawyers often suppose. Its interpretations of nineteenth-century civil rights statutes certainly breathed new life into them. In most cases, the Court was interpreting very generalized statutes with little relevant legislative history. In addition, its dynamic interpretation reflecting current values strikes me as mild activism.[282] The

281. I am using "judicial activism" in its traditional sense, to mean the Court's substituting its own preferences for those of elected representatives.

282. I am specifically thinking of Louisiana v. United States, 380 U.S. 145 (1965) (interpreting

Court's liberal interpretations of title VII (*Griggs*) and of the Voting Rights Act (*Allen*) went beyond the original legislative expectations, but it is not clear that they went *against* those expectations. I would characterize the decisions as only moderately activist.

What is most striking about the Warren Court's dynamic interpretation of civil rights statutes is how politically productive it was. None of the decisions was overruled by Congress. Moreover, *Guest* and *Louisiana*, though dynamic interpretations, were codified and elaborated by Congress in statutes. *Allen* and *Griggs* were embraced as building-block interpretations by the legislature when it considered the voting rights extension in 1970 and title VII's amendment in 1972. In each case, the Court reached results that were perceived as just, gave reasons that made sense, and helped stimulate legislative responses to advance the statutory goals.

Although the Warren Court was probably to the left of Congress on most civil rights issues, its opinions proved persuasive and helped the Presidency move Congress to the left. To the extent that the Court and Congress worked so productively together (with critical leadership from the Presidency), the Warren Court's activism can be defended as not acutely countermajoritarian. It can also be characterized as politically astute. The Warren Court was in this way a very successful political actor in the Court/Congress/President civil rights game. This success is surely related to the substantial political experience of members of the Warren Court.[283]

2. *The Burger Court: 1972-86*

The Burger Court strikes me as more activist than the Warren Court in construing civil rights statutes. So far as I can tell, the Burger Court was no more faithful to original legislative intent than the Warren Court had been. *Runyon, Weber,* and *Bob Jones* were at least as dynamic on the liberal side as any of the Warren Court's decisions; *Gilbert, McMann, Bolden, Grove City, Robinson,* and *Atascadero* were equally

42 U.S.C. § 1971) and United States v. Guest, 383 U.S. 745 (1966) (interpreting 18 U.S.C. § 241 as a valid remedy for conspiracies to deprive individuals of their fourteenth amendment rights). The most controversial decision, *Jones v. Mayer,* strikes me as inconsistent with original legislative intent. My conclusion, however, is not so firm in light of recent historiography supporting the Court's interpretation. *See* Sullivan, *Historical Reconstruction, Reconstruction History, and the Proper Scope of Section 1981,* 98 YALE L.J. 541, 546 n.36 (1989) (surveying the historiography).

283. The Justices on the 1960s Warren Court were unusually experienced in the political arena. The "Super Chief" himself had been Governor of California for ten years and also the GOP's vice-presidential candidate in 1948. Others with substantial political experience were Justices Black (Senator from Alabama), Douglas (SEC Chair), Clark (Attorney General), Stewart (Mayor of Cincinnati), White (Deputy Attorney General), Goldberg (AFL-CIO Counsel, Secretary of Labor), and Fortas (presidential advisor). Justice Brennan, of course, proved the most politically savvy of all, although he never held elected or national political office.

dynamic on the conservative side. None of these decisions is easily defensible as an exercise in discerning the original legislative intent, and, for the last six, the testimony of Members of Congress involved in the original legislation provides additional evidence that in any event the Court was not seriously trying to implement the original legislative intent. Indeed, *Gilbert, Bolden,* and *Atascadero* were apparent efforts by the Court to transplant its conservative constitutional jurisprudence into statutory cases.[284] Unlike the Warren Court, whose statutory decisions tended to go "beyond" original legislative expectations, the Burger Court's civil rights decisions often went "against" original legislative expectations: They undermined the efficiency of the statutory schemes they interpreted. Acting against the original intent is arguably more activist than going beyond original intent, because it actually substitutes the Court's preferences for those of the legislature.[285]

The Burger Court's activism was often politically unproductive, for two reasons: its opinions failed to reflect current legislative preferences any better than historical ones; and the opinions contained unpersuasive reasoning. The Court's view of pregnancy discrimination in *Gilbert*—that it is not gender discrimination because it divides the world into one group consisting of pregnant women and another group consisting of men and women who are not pregnant—is bizarre. Not even employer groups bothered to defend it in the hearings on overruling *Gilbert.* In *Bolden,* the Court's failure even to come up with a position five Justices could accept, and the harsh approach of the plurality, created confusion and bewilderment in the voting rights area, one where the Court had traditionally been a productive leader. The Court's expansive view of state immunity in *Atascadero* can be defended as an effort to force Congress to deliberate more carefully before it abrogates state immunity. But the legislative overruling of *Atascadero* was so swift and perfunctory (there were no hearings) as to raise questions about whether it had a point at all.

Even though other Burger Court decisions were more productive,[286] the Burger Court did suffer several overrulings at the hands of an outraged Congress. Its statutory opinions were both more activist and less

284. *See* Atascadero State Hosp. v. Scanlon, 473 U.S. 234, 237-47 (1985) (eleventh amendment jurisprudence critical to Court's new clear statement rule against interpreting statutes to allow lawsuits against the states); City of Mobile v. Bolden, 446 U.S. 55, 60-74 (1980) (interpreting Voting Rights Act section 2 in accord with Burger Court fifteenth amendment precedents); General Elec. Co. v. Gilbert, 429 U.S. 125, 133-40 (1976) (interpreting title VII *in pari materia* with fourteenth amendment).

285. *See* Farber, *supra* note 20.

286. *See, e.g.,* Bob Jones Univ. v. United States, 461 U.S. 574 (1983); United Steelworkers v. Weber, 443 U.S. 193 (1979); Monell v. Department of Social Servs., 436 U.S. 658 (1978); Runyon v. McCrary, 427 U.S. 160 (1976); Cannon v. University of Chicago, 441 U.S. 677 (1975); Alyeska Pipeline Serv. Co. v. Wilderness Soc'y, 421 U.S. 240 (1975).

politically acceptable than those of the Warren Court. Under the normative scheme of the positive game, the Burger Court was a much less successful player than the Warren Court had been. One reason for the Burger Court's relatively poor performance is historical misfortune: The Warren Court may have been more liberal than Congress in the 1960s, but the *direction* of Congress' movement was toward the Court, and not away from it.[287] The Burger Court, in contrast, moved rightward as Congress was moving leftward, and so the dynamics of political discourse seemed to work against the Court after 1975. Also it appears that the Burger Court as a group was not quite as politically perceptive as the Warren Court had been.[288]

3. *The Rehnquist Court: 1986-Present*

Although it is too early to make definite assessments of the Rehnquist Court's performance in civil rights cases, its decisions to date indicate that it is more activist than the Burger Court and significantly more activist than the Warren Court. Consider the controversial cases from the 1988 Term. None of the opinions even attempted to justify its results based upon original legislative expectations.[289] The outcry in Congress reinforces the arguments made by dissenting opinions that the Court followed an interpretive methodology "which is so manipulative as virtually to invite the charge of result-orientation."[290]

It remains to be seen how productive the Rehnquist Court's activism will be. *Betts* has already been legislatively overruled. There seems to be overwhelming bipartisan support for overruling *Patterson* and *Lorance*, and substantial bipartisan support for overruling or modifying

287. The Warren Court was of course lucky to have Presidents sympathetic to its civil rights agenda, and even luckier to have sympathetic gatekeepers in 1962-72—the Democratic leadership in both chambers, the House Judiciary Committee, and the Senate Education and Labor Committee.

288. To be sure, the Burger Court Justices were no strangers to the world of Washington politics. Warren Court holdover Justices Stewart, White, Brennan, and Marshall had sophisticated political instincts, and Chief Justice Burger had been an Assistant Attorney General. But his political abilities (building coalitions, leading the Conference, avoiding doomed political battles with Congress) are widely considered inferior to those of Chief Justice Warren. And among the other Justices appointed between 1969 and 1983, only Justice Powell had impressive political experience and instincts.

289. Martin v. Wilks, 490 U.S. 755 (1989), never acknowledged that it was implicitly construing title VII's remedial scheme. Wards Cove Packing Co. v. Atonio, 490 U.S. 642 (1989), engaged only in perfunctory analysis of the statutory text, as did Public Employees Retirement System v. Betts, 109 S. Ct. 2854 (1989). Patterson v. McLean Credit Union, 491 U.S. 164 (1989), not only ignored legislative intent, but also selectively relied on subsequent legislative developments. The *Patterson* Court interpreted section 1981 narrowly, in part because a broad reading might "circumvent" the detailed statutory scheme adopted in title VII. *Id.* at 181. Given the legislative belief after Runyon v. McCrary, 427 U.S. 160 (1976), that section 1981 would be an additional remedy in race discrimination cases, the Court's reliance on title VII seems arbitrary.

290. *Betts*, 109 S. Ct. at 2870 (Marshall, J., dissenting).

Hopkins and *Zipes.*[291] In addition, there is a good chance that Congress will modify *Wards Cove* and *Martin v. Wilks,* albeit not without considering the Court's values.

Obviously, the Rehnquist Court was (in 1989 anyway) not a very successful player of the Court/Congress/President civil rights game. Like prior Courts, it did not interpret civil rights statutes by trying to discern original legislative intent; but, unlike the Warren and Burger Courts, it often missed the tenor of current legislative majorities. I find it quite puzzling that the Rehnquist Court might be less successful than the Burger Court. Although the Rehnquist Court is on the whole a sheltered group with unimpressive political experience, it is not vastly different from the Burger Court in its personnel. And the Rehnquist Court is historically lucky (for the time being) to enjoy the support of a President significantly to the right of Congress. My hypothesis in response to this puzzle is that the Rehnquist Court may currently be rethinking whether it wants to play this game, which was played (adroitly) by the Warren Court and (in a mediocre way) by the Burger Court. Consider the next Section.

C. The New Textualism and the Future Role of the Court in National Civil Rights Policy

The Rehnquist Court surely does not see itself as unusually activist and politically unpredictive. Some of the Justices on the Court (foremost among them Justice Scalia) have responded to these criticisms essentially by denying the legitimacy of the Court/Congress/President civil rights game that the Court has played for decades. According to the "new textualists" like Justice Scalia, the Court's role is not to implement the preferences of either the enacting or the current legislature, but to apply the "plain meaning" of the statutory text as passed by both chambers of Congress and presented to the President.[292] The new textualism posits that truly "neutral" statutory interpretation does not consider the "subjective" preferences of Congress, only the "objective" meaning of a stat-

291. *See 1990 Senate Civil Rights Hearings, supra* note 171, at 5-6 (statement of Sen. Hatch), 71-72 (statement of Prof. Fried), 111 (statement of Deputy Attorney General Ayer).

292. *See Statutory Interpretation and the Uses of Legislative History: Hearing Before the Subcomm. on Courts, Intellectual Property, and the Administration of Justice of the House Comm. on the Judiciary,* 101st Cong., 2d Sess. (1990) (hearings on new textualism); Eskridge, *The New Textualism,* 37 UCLA L. REV. 621 (1990) (discussing, inter alia, how the new textualism of Justice Scalia posits a radically different role for the Court); Ross, *Reaganist Realism Comes to Detroit,* 1989 U. ILL. L. REV. 399 (demonstrating how textualism and deference to administrative expertise currently favor the policies of a Republican administration over the policies of a Democratic Congress); Zeppos, *Legislative History and the Interpretation of Statutes: Toward a Fact-Finding Model of Statutory Interpretation,* 76 VA. L. REV. 1295 (1990) (criticizing the new textualism as insufficiently deferential to legislative preferences and proposing that such preferences be analyzed as judicially noticed "facts").

ute's words. If the plain meaning of the words runs counter to current legislative preferences, textualism's adherents reason, Congress can always amend the statute. New textualists believe it is better (and indeed constitutionally required) for Congress to do the amending than for the Court to do so through "interpretation."

The new textualism is an ideologically significant development. By excluding evidence of actual legislative expectations (past or present), the new textualism signals that the Court may no longer be willing to play the positive game, and that it is willing to tolerate tension between itself and Congress. Elsewhere, I have criticized the new textualism for failing to provide a persuasive justification for its rethinking of the Court's role.[293] I only want to suggest three points here. First, as it has actually operated in civil rights cases, the textual analysis engaged in by the right wing of the Rehnquist Court has not established its claims to objectivity. Second, textualism is an inappropriate way for the Court to fulfill its inherently subordinate role in statutory policymaking. And third, if the Court's embrace of the new textualism continues to move its decisions further from current legislative preferences, Congress might consider removing or diminishing the Court's role in civil rights statutory interpretation.

1. The New Textualism's Questionable Claim to Objectivity

A problem with textualism is that words do not interpret themselves, and the general and norm-filled language often favored by statutory drafters offers a variety of interpretive choices. How the statutory interpreter makes those choices depends heavily on her own perspective and often on her own preferences. The new textualists' claim that they can divine universal, objective meaning from such language is therefore suspect. Their performance in recent civil rights cases bears out this insight.

Recall *Patterson,* where the five-Justice majority held that the racial harassment Brenda Patterson endured at the hands of her employer did not violate section 1981's right "to make and enforce contracts" irrespective of race. The Court's only rationale was that protecting Brenda Patterson's right to "make" a contract "extends only to the formation of a contract, but not to problems that may arise later from the conditions of continuing employment,"[294] and that protecting Patterson's right to "enforce" the contract only "prohibits discrimination that infects the legal process in ways that prevent one from enforcing contract rights."[295] The Court cited no precedent or other authority to support its narrow

293. *See* Eskridge, *supra* note 292, at 669-78.

294. Patterson v. McLean Credit Union, 491 U.S. 164, 176 (1989).

295. *Id.* at 177.

interpretation of section 1981. Certainly, ordinary usage of the words "make" and "enforce" does not compel such a narrow reading. To say, as the Court did, that a broad statutory protection of a person's right "to make and enforce contracts" only applies to the original formation and to the legal process of contract enforcement is like saying that a sandwich consists only of two pieces of bread (and not the meat in the middle). To say that Brenda Patterson has "the same right . . . to make . . . contracts . . . as is enjoyed by white citizens" surely implies a right to nondiscriminatory terms throughout the duration of the employment contract, as a matter of plain meaning. To say that she has "the same right . . . to enforce . . . contracts . . . as is enjoyed by white citizens" explicitly protects her right to "give effect to" (the dictionary meaning of "enforce") a nondiscriminatory contract. This is all Brenda Patterson was claiming. Her interpretation of the plain meaning of section 1981 strikes me as more objective than that of the Court. Indeed, her reading is precisely the one that congressional critics of *Jones v. Mayer* felt was the plain meaning of the statute (and the reason they wanted it changed).[296]

Moreover, there is no persuasive reason to protect against racial discrimination in the acts of entering into a contract and suing upon a contract, without including the acts of performing the contract. Recall the facts of *Runyon,* which *Patterson* purported to reaffirm. In *Runyon,* the Court held that private segregated schools could not refuse to admit ("to make a contract" with) the parents of black children, under the plain meaning of section 1981. By implication, *Runyon* surely interprets section 1981 to prevent a school from admitting black children and then expelling them because of their race. It is virtually certain that the Court would have found that such expulsion would impair the children's ability to "enforce"—give effect to—their contracts. Yet *Patterson* disallows this interpretation. Hence, *Patterson* is internally incoherent: It explicitly reaffirms *Runyon* while simultaneously repudiating by implication a necessary part of *Runyon*'s holding.

In *Patterson,* the new textualists do not even present plausible textual arguments for their position. The case exemplifies their most naked activism, namely, their willingness to read a statute narrowly (contrary to its apparent textual meaning and precedent) based upon nothing more than their own policy preferences. *Patterson,* of course, may not represent the new textualist ideology at its best. Usually, the new textualists have more plausible semantic arguments about the meaning of specific

296. In the debates on the 1972 amendments to title VII, Senator Hruska complained that unless his amendment were adopted to make title VII the exclusive remedy for job discrimination, "a black female employee [claiming] a denial of either a promotion or a pay raise . . . because of her color" could bypass title VII by filing "a complaint in Federal court under the provisions of the Civil Rights Act of 1866." 118 CONG. REC. 3368-69 (1972). Brenda Patterson was a "black female employee [claiming] a denial of . . . a promotion . . . because of her color."

words, phrases, or sentences.[297] Even when well articulated, however, their semantic arguments are more suggestive than conclusive and do not exclude other "textual" readings. Because the *Patterson* Court did not even bother to clothe its decision in plausible textualist arguments, its (anti-civil-rights) result orientation is manifest. Thus far in civil rights cases, I find little (or in *Patterson,* nothing) objective about the new textualists' results or reasoning. That the new textualists' semantic arguments so often seem to favor defendants in civil rights cases further undermines the theory's claim to objectivity and neutrality.[298]

2. *False Modesty of the New Textualism*

Our system of government still assumes that the Court is a subordinate player in statutory policymaking, and at least some of the new textualists continue to argue that the Court is the "honest agent" of Congress.[299] If this is so, the new textualism is not a very helpful approach to statutory interpretation.[300] An honest agent does not consider himself bound by the narrowest, most literal meaning of the principal's commands, but instead seeks to carry out her commands in the context of the principal's original expectations, original goals, and even current expectations and goals—all as they relate to the situation at hand. An agent is neither competent nor faithful if he interprets the principal's command without really trying to move the enterprise forward. Thus, if the principal instructs the agent to make and enforce contracts for her (the *Patterson* situation), doesn't the agent know that he should monitor performance of the contracts? It is a pretty lame agent who sees monkey business going on in the operation of the contract and shrugs, "Well, that's too bad for the principal, but my orders were just to 'make and enforce' contracts, and I think they are pretty narrow commands."

In the context of this Article's game-theoretic analysis, the new textualists would respond that the best course for the agent is to consult the

297. For narrowly literalist analysis by the new textualists in civil rights cases, see Public Employees Retirement Sys. v. Betts, 109 S. Ct. 2854, 2861-64 (1989) (Kennedy, J., for the Court) (interpreting term "subterfuge" according to "ordinary meaning" rather than considering legislative and statutory context); Independent Fed'n of Flight Attendants v. Zipes, 491 U.S. 754, 758-61 (1989) (Scalia, J., for the Court) (rewriting title VII fee-shifting provision without reference to legislative intent); Price Waterhouse v. Hopkins, 490 U.S. 228, 279 (1989) (Kennedy, J., dissenting) (interpretation of "because of"); Johnson v. Transportation Agency, 480 U.S. 616, 669-77 (1987) (Scalia, J., dissenting) (criticizing Court's approach to statutory interpretation).

298. *See* Ross, *supra* note 292 (arguing that the new textualists' methodology systematically favors conservative values).

299. Easterbrook, *The Supreme Court, 1983 Term—Foreword: The Court and the Economic System,* 98 HARV. L. REV. 4, 60 (1984).

300. *See* R. POSNER, THE FEDERAL COURTS: CRISIS AND REFORM 291-93 (1985) (criticizing stingy textualist interpretation as not very helpful to legislative process).

principal when there is ambiguity in the directive.[301] Stringent textual interpretations of civil rights statutes that trigger legislative overrides can be useful, according to this ideology, insofar as they encourage clarification from the most legitimate party, the principal. What this response ignores is that overrides are costly. When the agent fails to monitor the contract's operation, those contract losses are lost to the principal even if she is able to correct the agent's misinterpretation later. And the whole point of having a sophisticated agent is that he will "act for" the principal, without having to bother the principal constantly with the details of implementation.

Similarly, a Court that distorts the congressional civil rights policy and thereby triggers legislative overrides is usually behaving in a countermajoritarian way. It takes time for Congress to override the Court's errant interpretations, and during that time, victims of discrimination are denied the remedies that Congress has established and, indeed, wants them to have. Sometimes, Congress will not override decisions it disagrees with, either because well-placed opposition (Senate filibuster, a hostile gatekeeping committee in either chamber, or a presidential veto) makes enactment unlikely or because the legislative agenda is already full. As the experiences in 1988 and 1990 have shown us, overriding the Court's statutory civil rights decisions is a mine field and usually requires substantial effort that would be better spent correcting new problems, not reiterating agreed-upon solutions to old ones. This is the most serious indictment of the Rehnquist Court's activism: by clogging the legislative agenda with issues settled yesterday, the Court is distracting Congress from understanding and addressing the tough civil rights issues of today and tomorrow.

3. *Shifting Responsibility for Civil Rights Interpretation Away From the Court*

The most important implication of our game-theoretic model is that if the Court is reluctant or obstructive in its implementation of congressional civil rights policy, Congress should consider establishing procedural rules to limit the Court's role. An important theme of positive political theory is that Congress can exercise control over its "agents" in how it structures "agency" procedures.[302] Because the Court is harder to discipline than executive departments or independent commissions,

301. The new textualists are not wont to find much ambiguity, however. *See* Scalia, *Judicial Deference to Administrative Interpretation of Law*, 1989 DUKE L.J. 511, 521 (indicating a propensity to find unambiguous statutory meaning).

302. Moe, *Control and Feedback in Economic Regulation: The Case of the NLRB*, 79 AM. POL. SCI. REV. 1094 (1985); Weingast & Moran, *Bureaucratic Discretion or Congressional Control: Regulatory Policymaking by the Federal Trade Commission*, 91 J. POL. ECON. 765 (1983).

this strategy might not work as well—and indeed it might clash with the checks and balances function of an independent judiciary—but several proposals bear consideration.

Probably the least useful is the rule, floated in the vetoed 1990 bill and in the proposed 1991 bill, directing the Court to interpret civil rights statutes "broadly" and to reflect legislative "intent."[303] Apart from the constitutional problems with such a rule,[304] it is hard for me to see how it would make much difference. Justice Kennedy, the author of *Patterson,* probably thought he *was* construing section 1981 broadly and consistently with the legislative intent (as he read it in the plain meaning of the statute's text). Should any of the cases mentioned in this Article be reconsidered under the broad construction rule, at least one—*Weber*—would probably be decided differently. *Weber,* after all, was a "narrow" interpretation of title VII's prohibition of discrimination, which is hard to square with original legislative "intent." (That would probably surprise the sponsors of the 1990 and 1991 bills!) In any event, this sort of interpretational "rule" would probably not make the Court a more cooperative player in the game outlined in this Article.

Rather than legislating such a general rule, Congress should consider more structural rules for civil rights cases. For example, Congress might be more specific about information it wants the Court to consider. An interpretation statute might require the Court to consider committee reports when construing civil rights statutes, to solicit amicus curiae briefs from designated public interest groups and the U.S. Civil Rights Commission, and to solicit information on the effect of the proposed interpretations on the ability of victims of discrimination to obtain effective redress. The difference between this sort of interpretation statute and the one contained in the 1990 and 1991 bills is that it not only gives a strong signal to the Court (as the current bills do), but also invites or requires the Court to become better informed about American civil rights policy. Information theory suggests (persuasively, to me) that confronting information itself can shift preferences in at least some cases.

Along precisely these lines is the suggestion that Congress shift responsibility for interpreting civil rights statutes from article III courts to one or more administrative agencies. There are several ways Congress can try to do this. The most logical approach would be to vest one or

303. As finally passed (and vetoed), the 1990 bill provided in section 1107(a): "All Federal laws protecting the civil rights of persons shall be interpreted *consistent with the intent* of such laws, and shall be *broadly construed* to effectuate the purpose of such laws to provide effective . . . remedies." 136 CONG. REC. H9554 (daily ed. Oct. 12, 1990) (emphasis added). This language has been carried over in H.R. 1, 102d Cong., 1st Sess. § 1107 (1991).

304. That is, it might be argued (though I am not persuaded) that such a rule represents a legislative usurpation of article III judicial functions. *See* R. DICKERSON, THE INTERPRETATION AND APPLICATION OF STATUTES 262 (1975).

more existing agencies (such as the EEOC) with formal rulemaking authority and legislate a very restrictive standard for judicial review. This approach has the advantage of building upon the Court's own precept of deferring to administrative interpretation of regulatory statutes.[305] The Court has tended to ignore that precept when agencies charged with enforcing civil rights laws try to help victims of discrimination (usually the Court relies upon the pretext that Congress did not give the agency "formal" rulemaking authority).[306] Giving agencies formal rulemaking authority would shift the responsibility for fleshing out and updating civil rights laws from an increasingly conservative Court to agencies that might better reflect and respond to congressional preferences.

This strategy, of course, will not guarantee that civil rights policy will be set at the congressional median (M). A conservative President can use his executive authority or his appointment and OMB review authority to press any agency to the right of the congressional median. The President can then use the veto threat to protect the agency from being overruled. Hence, policy might end up closer to the veto median (V) than to Congress' preferred point (M).

This scenario, however, is hardly inevitable. First, Congress can build a pro-civil-rights bias into the procedures the agency must follow to make policy and conduct adjudications. For instance, Congress might require the agency to consider the views of specified groups in the civil rights community. Or it might provide funding for reports on the impact of proposed rules on discrimination victims and on their access to justice. It might also allocate decisionmaking responsibility among long-term civil service personnel (such as administrative law judges) as well as political appointees. Second, Congress has more leverage over an agency than it has over the Court. Through oversight hearings, appropriations bills, and informal means of communication, Congress can influence agency policy to shift in the direction of congressional preferences.

Moreover, in a decade during which the Court's preferences concerning civil rights will surely lie significantly to the right of Congress' preferences, Congress may be better off with agency-driven policy even if the agency follows presidential, rather than congressional, direction. An agency that is controlled by a conservative Presidency and which sets

305. Chevron U.S.A. Inc. v. Natural Resources Defense Council, Inc., 467 U.S. 837 (1984) (deferring to EPA's construction of the Clean Air Act Amendments of 1977, when Congress had not directly addressed the question at issue); *see* Diver, *Statutory Interpretation in the Administrative State*, 133 U. PA. L. REV. 552 (1985) (arguing from a utilitarian perspective that courts "should presumptively defer to agency interpretations of statutes in situations where Congress has endowed the agency with significant policymaking responsibility").

306. *See* General Elec. Co. v. Gilbert, 429 U.S. 125 (1976) (refusing to defer to EEOC on pregnancy issue).

policy at the veto median (V) is preferable to a Court that sets policy to the right of the veto median (V). In other words, Congress prefers an interpreter that will play the Court/Congress/President civil rights game (an agency) to one that refuses to play it (the Court in 1989) or plays it badly (the Court in *Gilbert* or *Grove City*). Congress' agenda is simply too crowded to permit the repeated overruling of judicial interpretations of civil rights statutes. In addition, Congress can work more productively with an agency, which is well-informed about legislative preferences and the dynamics of civil rights, than with a Court that has demonstrated an inability or unwillingness to be cooperative. On the other hand, under a moderate or liberal Presidency, agency policymaking would quickly shift toward the congressional median (M), whereas a shift in the Court's preferences would probably take years and require appointments by a series of moderate or liberal Presidents as space on the Court becomes available.

Conclusion: Reneging on History?

Contrary to some statements made in the congressional debates in 1990, the Court's 1989 civil rights decisions have a certain continuity with what came before. The Court in *Patterson* and the other 1989 decisions was not faithfully seeking original legislative intent or neutrally applying the statutes' plain meaning. But, then, the Court has never acted that way in civil rights statutory interpretation. This sort of judicial activism in statutory interpretation is nothing new.

The Court that decided *Patterson* and the other 1989 decisions was producing results that did not reflect current legislative preferences. However, this was also true of the Warren Court (which thrived on such independence and never got overruled) and was often true of the Burger Court (which in almost every instance was promptly overruled). Therefore, again, ignoring current legislative preferences is nothing new. Finally, the Rehnquist Court approached *Patterson* and the other 1989 decisions from a perspective substantially more conservative than that of Congress. But that has been true of the Court since 1972, when Justices Rehnquist and Powell started voting.

Despite these points of continuity, there remains a deep sense of rupture, a dramatic unsettling of things in our political system, because of the 1989 civil rights decisions. The game-theory model of the Court/Congress/President dynamics in statutory interpretation is a formal (and of course incomplete) way of expressing this rupture. The big change in 1989 was the Court's seeming unwillingness, in a series of high-visibility cases, to play the game. In the short term, the Court's "attitude" has produced an intense political conflict involving all three branches of government. In the long term, I doubt the Court will sustain its uncooperative attitude, because the game is important to the Court as well.

The 1989 rupture ought to awaken the civil rights community to the fact that the Supreme Court is no longer the most appropriate mechanism for advancing progressive civil rights policies through statutory interpretation. This has been true for some time. The 1989 decisions dramatically confirmed exactly how far to the right the Court has drifted. The challenge for Congress and civil rights groups in the 1990s is to develop alternative approaches for implementation that do not depend upon the Court's cooperation. The Court has, as Republican Senator Jeffords charged, "reneged on history."[307] Like previous Courts, the Rehnquist Court has substituted its policy preferences for those of the enacting Congress. But it has also "reneged" on the historical tradition by which the Court has long attended to the preferences of Congress. This is a breach of political faith that underlies the sense of betrayal felt by Senator Jeffords and others. It remains to be seen whether that breach of faith will stimulate a larger rethinking of decisionmaking power to implement our nation's civil rights agenda.

307. 136 CONG. REC. S1022 (daily ed. Feb. 7, 1990).

CONSTRAINING "THE LEAST DANGEROUS BRANCH": THE TRADITION OF ATTACKS ON JUDICIAL POWER

WILFRED FEINBERG*

Chief Judge Feinberg delivered this address as the sixteenth James Madison Lecture at New York University School of Law on October 26, 1983. The Chief Judge focused on current legislative attempts to limit the jurisdiction of the federal courts. As background, he first recounted several of the many episodes in our history in which unpopular decisions by federal judges provoked attacks on the judicial branch. He then examined in detail the most comprehensive of the jurisdiction-stripping proposals recently before Congress, Senate Bill 3018. While noting that in the past nearly all efforts to curb the power of the federal bench have failed, he warned that today's politically motivated attacks may gain the decisive support of those groups which, historically, have defended the independence of the judicial branch but which, today, are alarmed about the courts' burgeoning workload. These groups' decision to support proposals such as S. 3018, the Chief Judge stressed, would be misguided and unfortunate.

I am pleased to have been invited to deliver the 1983 James Madison Lecture. Since the institution of this series in 1960, many distinguished members of the Supreme Court and of the federal courts of appeals have spoken about the Constitution and the Bill of Rights. I am honored to join this group.

My topic is appropriate, I think, for a lecture bearing the name of James Madison. I intend to discuss attempts, both current and past, by those who are upset by federal court decisions to make fundamental changes in the structure and jurisdiction of the federal judiciary. That structure, of course, owes much to James Madison. At the Constitutional Convention, many argued that the federal judiciary should consist only of a Supreme Court. Lower federal courts would not be necessary, they felt; the needs of the national government would be satisfied by the Supreme Court's exercise of appellate jurisdiction over state supreme court decisions. Madison and his allies disagreed, and the result was the compromise language that continues to fuel academic, and not so academic, debate about how much control Congress can exert over the jurisdiction of the federal courts.[1]

Article III, section 1 of the Constitution provides: "The judicial Power of the United States, shall be vested in one supreme Court, and

---

* Chief Judge, United States Court of Appeals for the Second Circuit. The assistance of Karen Goodyear Krueger and Richard L. Revesz in the preparation of this address is gratefully acknowledged.

[1] P. Bator, P. Mishkin, D. Shapiro & H. Wechsler, Hart and Wechsler's The Federal Courts and the Federal System 11-12 (2d ed. 1973).

in such inferior Courts as the Congress may from time to time ordain and establish." As the Chief Judge of one of those "inferior courts," I have more than a passing interest in the meaning and effect of that one not so simple declaratory sentence. The debate over whether the lower federal courts serve any function that could not be handled as well or better by state courts continues to this day. The Framers built further ambiguity into the Constitution by providing in article III, section 2 that the Supreme Court's appellate jurisdiction be subject to "such Exceptions, and . . . such Regulations as the Congress shall make."

There is controversy over the extent to which the language of section 1 authorizes Congress to exert substantial control over the lower federal courts by altering their jurisdiction. The exceptions clause of section 2 has given rise to similar dispute regarding Congress's power over the Supreme Court. These sections, particularly the first, are the backdrop to attempts by members of Congress and others in the body politic to change significantly and to limit the jurisdiction of the federal courts.[2]

As I will discuss in greater detail in a moment, it is not unusual for legislators to regard an independent federal judiciary as a political inconvenience or even as an outrage. And today, as always, the courts are making decisions that are unpopular with some segments of the political spectrum, and their representatives in Congress are seeking to undo those decisions, directly or indirectly. Some of the current proposals are benign in intent, but others are overtly hostile to an independent judiciary. As David R. Brink said when he was president of the American Bar Association, these measures "threaten the rights of all of us."[3] As a whole, the proposals are particularly dangerous because they come at a time when the federal courts are facing a critical overload that must be dealt with soon, or the system will collapse. This crisis can be used to justify attempts to alter and restrict the courts' jurisdiction.

---

[2] The literature on the constitutionality of court-stripping bills is extensive. Recent articles include Bator, Congressional Power Over the Jurisdiction of the Federal Courts, 27 Vill. L. Rev. 1030 (1982); Brilmayer & Underhill, Congressional Obligation to Provide a Forum for Constitutional Claims: Discriminatory Jurisdictional Rules and the Conflict of Laws, 69 Va. L. Rev. 819 (1983); Sager, The Supreme Court, 1980 Term—Foreword: Constitutional Limitations on Congress' Authority to Regulate the Jurisdiction of the Federal Courts, 95 Harv. L . Rev. 17 (1981). For a classic treatment of this issue, see Hart, The Power of Congress to Limit the Jurisdiction of Federal Courts: An Exercise in Dialectic, 66 Harv. L. Rev. 1362 (1953).

[3] Address by David R. Brink, The Separation of Powers: Whose Ox Is Being Gored?, National Press Club 13 (Apr. 28, 1982) (on file at New York University Law Review).

After a brief survey of the history of attacks on the federal courts, I will examine in detail a bill introduced in the last session of Congress.[4] My message is that such attacks are not new and that by and large they have not been successful. But given the current crisis in the workload of the federal courts and the resentment over their decisions on highly charged constitutional issues, all those who treasure the independence of the federal judiciary must be alert to attempts to override interpretations of the Constitution by drastic jurisdictional overhauls.[5] Of course, I shall not comment on the constitutionality of the proposals. That question might well come before the courts; until it does, I leave it to law professors and other commentators. And now for a little history, the better with which to understand the present.

I

Historical Background

1. Article III, section 1 of the Constitution, in the language I already have quoted, provides for the creation of federal courts. But another part of article III—section 2—defines the kinds of cases the Supreme Court and the "inferior courts" may hear. Section 2 states, among other things, that "the judicial Power shall extend . . . to Controversies . . . between a State and Citizens of another State." This provision gave rise to the first instance in which Congress attempted to overrule a judicial decision by restricting the federal courts' jurisdiction—in this case by successfully setting in motion the mechanism that led to a constitutional amendment.

Very early in our history, several suits were brought in federal court by individuals against states: Eleazer Oswald filed against New York in 1791,[6] and in 1792 William Grayson sued Virginia and Alex-

---

[4] S. 3018, 97th Cong., 2d Sess. (1982) (on file at New York University Law Review).

[5] Judge Leonard I. Garth, of the United States Court of Appeals for the Third Circuit, stated recently that congressional respect for federal court jurisdiction "may come to be regarded during the years of our lifetime as the most vital item on this Nation's agenda." Address by Judge Leonard I. Garth, Pruning the Least Dangerous Branch: Congressional Intrusions on the Federal Judicial Power, The Arthur T. Vanderbilt Lecture, Harvard Law School Association of New Jersey 29 (Feb. 10, 1982) (on file at New York University Law Review). For our titles, Judge Garth and I independently borrowed Alexander Bickel's phrase, see A. Bickel, The Least Dangerous Branch (1962), borrowed in turn from Alexander Hamilton, see The Federalist No. 78, at 483 (A. Hamilton) (H.C. Lodge ed. 1888) ("[T]he judiciary, from the nature of its functions, will always be the least dangerous to the political rights of the Constitution.").

[6] 1 J. Goebel, History of the Supreme Court of the United States: Antecedents and Beginnings to 1801, at 724 (1971).

ander Chisholm sued Georgia.[7] The defendant states refused to acknowledge effective service of process, and the attorneys for the State of Georgia even refused to argue in the Supreme Court on the question whether the federal courts had jurisdiction of the case.[8] The Supreme Court held that there was jurisdiction, and *Chisholm v. Georgia*[9] and the other two cases proceeded amidst angry protests and calls for a constitutional amendment from the legislatures of Georgia, Massachusetts, Virginia, and New York.[10] The temper of the time was revealed by an act of the Georgia House of Representatives, which provided that any federal marshal attempting to execute any process of the Supreme Court in a suit against the State of Georgia should be "deemed guilty of felony, and shall suffer death without the benefit of clergy, by being hanged."[11] On the day after the Supreme Court entered judgment for Chisholm in February 1793, the text of what became the eleventh amendment was introduced in the Senate.[12] When it was finally ratified in January 1798, suits by individual plaintiffs against states, which had continued in the interim, were no longer regarded as cognizable in the federal courts.[13]

2. A few years later, the federal courts became a focus of the battle between the Federalists and the Jeffersonians. The system of circuit courts established by the Judiciary Act of 1789 had developed a number of problems.[14] In particular, circuit riding by the Supreme Court Justices was intolerably difficult, dangerous, and time consuming, given travel conditions of the day.[15] Moreover, circuit riding placed the Justices in the unseemly position of passing judgment on appeals in cases they had decided below.[16] The Judiciary Act of 1801,

---

7 Id. at 724-25.

8 Id. at 725-28.

9 2 U.S. (2 Dall.) 419 (1793).

10 J. Goebel, supra note 6, at 734-36.

11 Warren, Legislative and Judicial Attacks on the Supreme Court of the United States—A History of the Twenty-Fifth Section of the Judiciary Act (pts. 1 & 2), 47 Am. L. Rev. 1, 161, 166 (1913).

12 J. Goebel, supra note 6, at 736.

13 Id. at 736-41. In February 1798, the Supreme Court decided that after the ratification of the eleventh amendment, the federal courts had no jurisdiction over cases in which a state was sued by citizens of another state or by the citizens or subjects of a foreign state. See Hollingsworth v. Virginia, 3 U.S. (3 Dall.) 378 (1798).

14 2 G. Haskins & H. Johnson, History of the Supreme Court of the United States: Foundations of Power: John Marshall, 1801-15, at 110-22 (1981).

15 Id. at 111-15.

16 Id. at 115-16.

enacted in the last days of the defeated Adams Administration, addressed these problems,[17] including the demands on the Justices' time caused by the "itinerant dispensation of justice."[18] The Judiciary Act eliminated circuit riding and created new circuit courts with sixteen new circuit judges and a full force of federal marshals, clerks, and United States Attorneys.[19]

The Jeffersonians, however, perceived the Judiciary Act as a last-ditch effort by a lame-duck President to control the country by appointing Federalist judges.[20] The Jeffersonians also were angered by what they considered the misuse of the judicial power by Federalist judges in following English common law precedents,[21] in enforcing the Sedition Act,[22] and in using grand jury charges to instruct the public in federalism.[23] Jefferson told his Attorney General that what was needed was a "removal of excrescences from the judiciary."[24] In 1802, the Jeffersonians repealed the Judiciary Act of 1801 and abolished the new judgeships,[25] legislatively recessed the Supreme Court for over one year,[26] and embarked on a program of impeaching Federalist judges with the ultimate aim, it seems, of bringing charges against the Chief Justice, John Marshall.[27]

For those of you who are puzzled that a dispute as intense as that between Jefferson and Marshall could stem merely from different views on the proper role of the judiciary, let me quote a little-known fact from Richard Morris's superb book, *Seven Who Shaped Our Destiny*.[28] Professor Morris explains that, as a youngster, Jefferson had courted Rebecca Burwell, then a sixteen-year-old orphan. Rebecca apparently was not responsive to Jefferson's overtures; while he was studying abroad, she married another man. Her daughter, in turn, married John Marshall. Richard Morris points out that "Jefferson's intense dislike for the jurist may well have, unconsciously, sprung

---

[17] Id. at 122-26.
[18] Id. at 117 (quoting Edmund Randolph).
[19] Id. at 108.
[20] Id. at 108-09, 138-39.
[21] Id. at 139.
[22] Id. at 140.
[23] Id. at 159-60.
[24] Id. at 153.
[25] Id. at 209.
[26] Id. at 184.
[27] Id. at 205-11.
[28] R. Morris, Seven Who Shaped Our Destiny: The Founding Fathers as Revolutionaries (1973).

from this relationship. After all, but for the vagaries of female passion, Marshall might have been [Jefferson's] own son-in-law!"[29]

It is interesting to note that the Jeffersonians regarded a program of impeachment as a proper means of popular control over judicial decisionmaking. James Monroe suggested that use of English common law precedent was a ground for impeachment;[30] Senator Giles added that impeachment was proper if a judge was "disagreeable in office" or "opposed to the administration & wrong headed."[31] To be sure, not all of the targets of impeachment were model judges. Judge Pickering of the District of New Hampshire, who was impeached and convicted, was mentally ill and alcoholic.[32] The impeachment of Justice Chase was triggered in part by his delivery of a charge to a grand jury in Baltimore criticizing the repeal of the Judiciary Act of 1801, universal suffrage in Maryland, and the Jeffersonian ideal of equal liberty and rights for all men.[33] Apparently, though, this kind of commentary was less shocking then than it would be now—judges were more outspoken politically, and politics was not yet considered incompatible with the judicial role.[34] After Justice Chase was narrowly acquitted, impeachment was abandoned as a common political method of attack, but at least one of the desired ends was achieved: grand jury charges became more cautious.[35]

3. In the meantime, the passage of the eleventh amendment had not ended the struggles between state governments and the national judiciary. Throughout the early nineteenth century, indeed, throughout the Civil War era, states and states' rightists railed against the power of the Supreme Court to review certain decisions of the state courts, and the power of the federal courts to declare state laws unconstitutional.[36] In some instances, states simply refused to comply with Supreme Court orders;[37] some state legislatures passed laws forbidding compliance.[38] In 1832, the South Carolina legislature passed a

---

[29] Id. at 126-27.

[30] G. Haskins & H. Johnson, supra note 14, at 205.

[31] Id. at 211.

[32] Id. at 211-12.

[33] Id. at 217-19.

[34] See id. at 217 n.60.

[35] Id. at 245.

[36] These powers had been established in Martin v. Hunter's Lessee, 14 U.S. (1 Wheat.) 304 (1816). See generally G. Haskins & H. Johnson, supra note 14, at 312-65.

[37] Warren, supra note 11, at 9-12, 22-23, 166-71, 174, 182-84.

[38] See, e.g., id. at 5, 166, 169; see text accompanying note 42 infra.

statute forbidding any appeals to the United States Supreme Court, but the state supreme court declared the law unconstitutional.[39]

Occasionally, violence threatened to break out, as in the so-called "Olmstead affair."[40] Two rival groups of claimants to the sloop *Active*, the first headed by a Connecticut sailor named Olmstead and the second connected with another armed sloop fitted out by the Commonwealth of Pennsylvania, made claims to the vessel in an action in the Pennsylvania Court of Admiralty in 1778. A jury awarded 25% of the net proceeds of the sale of the vessel to Olmstead and 75% of the proceeds to the Pennsylvania group.[41] In 1779, the Continental Congress's Standing Committee on Appeals, which had jurisdiction of appeals from state admiralty courts at the time, reversed the decision and gave the entire judgment to Olmstead. The Pennsylvania authorities, however, refused to execute the revised decree, arguing that pursuant to a Pennsylvania statute the jury's findings of fact were conclusive.[42] Eventually, the Pennsylvania Supreme Court so held.[43] In the meantime, Pennsylvania's share of the prize had been paid over to the Treasurer of that Commonwealth.[44] Olmstead's efforts to enforce the revised decree in his favor eventually led to a United States Supreme Court order that it be enforced.[45] The Pennsylvania legislature promptly enacted resolutions against the decision and called for the creation of an impartial tribunal to resolve federal-state disputes. The governor sent out the state militia to resist enforcement of the judgment, but a posse turned out to support the federal marshal. Eventually, the governor backed down and the legislature provided the losers with funds for satisfaction of the judgment. The state militia officers were convicted of treason and sentenced, but President Madison later pardoned them.[46]

In another typical but dramatic instance, Pennsylvania again came into conflict with the Supreme Court when the Court was asked to decide several questions regarding Pennsylvania's obligations to

---

[39] Warren, supra note 11, at 175.

[40] G. Haskins & H. Johnson, supra note 14, at 322-31.

[41] Id. at 322-23.

[42] Morris, The Forging of the Union Reconsidered: A Historical Refutation of State Sovereignty over Seabeds, 74 Colum. L. Rev. 1056, 1079-80 (1974).

[43] G. Haskins & H. Johnson, supra note 14, at 324 & n. 46.

[44] Id. at 323-24.

[45] United States v. Peters, 9 U.S. (5 Cranch) 115 (1809). The Court skirted the potential eleventh amendment problem by stating that the money in question "was in possession, not of the state of Pennsylvania, but of David Rittenhouse [the Treasurer of the Commonwealth] as an individual." Id. at 141; see G. Haskins & H. Johnson, supra note 14, at 326-27.

[46] G. Haskins & H. Johnson, supra note 14, at 327-31.

persons receiving land under a Pennsylvania statute enacted in 1792.[47] The Court treated the statute as a contractual obligation and determined that it could be enforced against the state.[48] The Pennsylvania legislature reacted by approving a resolution passed by the Kentucky legislature calling for a constitutional amendment depriving the federal courts of diversity jurisdiction and land-grant jurisdiction.[49] Another Pennsylvania resolution denied the authority of the federal courts to take jurisdiction over suits brought under the 1792 statute involving the interest and sovereignty of the state.[50] The governor of Pennsylvania, although an anti-Federalist, vetoed the resolution as an intrusion into the federal judicial process,[51] a principled act of statesmanship of the kind that would recur in the years that followed.

Congress did not remain aloof from these struggles. Many proposals to change the federal judiciary were introduced, although none was enacted. Section 25 of the Judiciary Act of 1789 provided for appeals from state court decisions to the United States Supreme Court. Attempts to repeal this section were frequent, as were proposals to require a supermajority of the members of the Court to hold state statutes unconstitutional.[52] It was also proposed that, in cases where a state was a party or where the constitution or laws of a state were questioned, appeal be had to the United States Senate rather than to the Supreme Court.[53]

Despite the strong sentiment in many states for curbing the federal courts, these and other measures for change failed to pass Congress. In some cases, this failure was a result of the efforts of influential lawmakers who opposed the measures. For instance, an 1830 bill to repeal section 25 was defeated largely because of the persuasive opposition of Representative James Buchanan, then Chairman of the House Judiciary Committee.[54] In other cases, changes in the Court itself forestalled more radical measures from the legislative branch. For example, a wave of proposals in the 1820's was deflected by the appointment to the Court of Smith Thompson, an advocate of states'

---

47 Huidekoper's Lessee v. Douglass, 7 U.S. (3 Cranch) 1 (1805); see G. Haskins & H. Johnson, supra note 14, at 317-21.

48 Huidekoper's Lessee, 7 U.S. at 70-71; G. Haskins & H. Johnson, supra note 14, at 320-21.

49 G. Haskins & H. Johnson, supra note 14, at 321.

50 Id.

51 Id. at 322.

52 Warren, supra note 11, at 22, 27-28, 30-34.

53 Id. at 26; see also id. at 168.

54 Id. at 164.

rights.[55] Congress's attack on the Court of the early 1830's was deterred by the Court's announcement that it would thenceforth not render judgment in constitutional law cases unless four Justices concurred in an opinion, even though one or more of the seven Justices (as the Court was then constituted) could not sit in a particular case.[56] All in all, then, despite the dissatisfaction with, and occasional outright defiance of, the federal courts in this period, those who sought to curb the federal judiciary achieved no permanent results.

4. The climactic struggle between the national government and the advocates of states' rights was, of course, the Civil War. We tend to think of the federal government as allied with antislavery forces against the southern states that asserted the right to maintain the institution of slavery. But before the war, many northerners feared that the federal government would force slavery on them.[57] Lincoln himself expressed this concern in his famous "House Divided" speech in the Senate in 1858.[58] The Supreme Court was a major cause of that fear, with its decision in *Dred Scott v. Sandford.*[59] The *Dred Scott* decision held that national citizenship could not extend to a freed slave[60] and went on to state that the Constitution prevented Congress from barring slavery from the territories.[61] Northern states attacked the decision. The Maine Supreme Judicial Court gave an advisory opinion to the legislature that blacks could vote in state and federal elections in Maine.[62] The Ohio Supreme Court held that any slave coming into Ohio with the consent of his master was permanently freed, even if he later returned to a slave state.[63] The New York Court of Appeals rendered a similar decision.[64] Other northern legislatures adopted antislavery and anti-*Dred Scott* resolutions and laws.[65] The issue was not destined to be resolved by legislation or by judicial

---

[55] Id. at 29.

[56] Mayor of New York v. Miln, 33 U.S. (8 Pet.) 118, 122 (1834) (Marshall, C.J.); see Warren, supra note 11, at 165.

[57] H. Hyman & W. Wiecek, Equal Justice Under Law: Constitutional Development 1835-1875, at 194-97, 201-02 (1982).

[58] Id. at 196-97.

[59] 60 U.S. (19 How.) 393 (1857); see H. Hyman & W. Wiecek, supra note 57, at 172-90.

[60] 60 U.S. at 404-05.

[61] Id. at 452.

[62] H. Hyman & W. Wiecek, supra note 57, at 191.

[63] Id. at 191-92.

[64] Id. at 192.

[65] Id. at 195-96.

decision, but by civil war. The Supreme Court as an institution survived that war, but *Dred Scott* did not; it was overruled by the fourteenth amendment.

5. In the midst of Reconstruction, William McCardle of Mississippi published a series of inflammatory editorials attacking military rule in the South. His editorials set in motion a series of events that were to ensure his future prominence in constitutional law casebooks. Arrested by order of General Ord, the Commander of the Fourth Military District, McCardle was held in military custody pending trial by a military commission.[66] On November 25, 1867, the United States Circuit Court for the District of Mississippi denied McCardle's application for habeas corpus.[67] McCardle then appealed to the Supreme Court, pursuant to the recently passed Habeas Corpus Act of 1867, which, for the first time, provided for direct appeal from a circuit court decision denying habeas relief.[68] It is ironic that this new act, which was intended to protect the wives and children of former slaves against obstinate former masters,[69] was invoked by an ex-Confederate who called the Reconstruction leaders "infamous, cowardly, and abandoned villains, who, instead of wearing shoulder straps and ruling millions of people, should have their heads shaved, their ears cropped, their foreheads branded, and their precious persons lodged in a penitentiary."[70]

The Republican majority in Congress moved quickly, concerned that, in response to McCardle's challenge to military trials for nonmilitary offenses, the Supreme Court might declare part of the Reconstruction Acts unconstitutional.[71] Two weeks after the oral argument in *Ex parte McCardle,* Congress repealed the portion of the Habeas Corpus Act of 1867 that permitted direct appeals from decisions of the circuit courts.[72] The Court then dismissed McCardle's suit in a terse opinion, ruling that as a result of the repeal it lacked jurisdiction to give the case further consideration.[73]

---

[66] 6 C. Fairman, History of the Supreme Court of the United States: Reconstruction and Reunion 1864-88, at 437 (1971).

[67] Id. at 438.

[68] Id. at 448-49.

[69] Id. at 448.

[70] See id. at 437-38.

[71] Id. at 449-51.

[72] Id. at 459, 467-69.

[73] 74 U.S. (7 Wall.) 506, 514-15 (1869).

Despite its anticlimactic ending, the *McCardle* case has spurred a long-lasting debate over the extent to which Congress can invoke the exceptions clause to restrict the appellate jurisdiction of the Supreme Court. For reasons already indicated, I will not give you my own reading of *Ex parte McCardle*. Instead, I will set out the competing positions, since they define the controversy that still exists today. Before doing that, a few observations are pertinent. First, before the passage of the Habeas Corpus Act of 1867, the Court reviewed habeas cases under its certiorari jurisdiction, pursuant to section 14 of the Judiciary Act of 1789.[74] Second, the Court acknowledged this power at the time it decided *Ex parte McCardle*. It stated in dictum that Congress's repealer act in 1868 did not remove any cases from the Supreme Court's appellate jurisdiction except appeals from circuit courts under the Act of 1867. The Court stated that the 1868 act did not "affect the jurisdiction which was previously exercised."[75] In addition, while *McCardle* was still under advisement, the Court suggested to a lawyer representing a group of prisoners charged with the murder of a black man that he invoke the jurisdictional provisions of the Judiciary Act of 1789.[76] And, in *Ex parte Yerger*, decided only a few months after *McCardle*, the Court explicitly rejected the government's contention that Congress's repeal of part of the Habeas Corpus Act of 1867 limited the appellate jurisdiction the Court had enjoyed over habeas cases prior to 1867.[77]

Based on these considerations, some commentators believe that *Ex parte McCardle* did not decide the question whether categories of constitutional law cases can be insulated from Supreme Court review by means of the exceptions clause. What *McCardle* decided, under this view, is that Congress can choose the mechanism by which the Supreme Court exercises its appellate jurisdiction over a given class of cases. Congress may eliminate certain avenues for review only when others remain open.[78]

---

[74] C. Fairman, supra note 66, at 440-44.

[75] 74 U.S. at 515.

[76] C. Fairman, supra note 66, at 471, 475-78.

[77] 75 U.S. (8 Wall.) 85, 105-06 (1869).

[78] See Van Alstyne, A Critical Guide to Ex Parte McCardle, 15 Ariz. L. Rev. 229, 249 & n.75 (1973) (discussing view of commentators that *McCardle* curtailed none of the Court's "essential" functions). For a discussion and criticism of the "essential functions" thesis, see Gunther, Congressional Power to Curtail Federal Court Jurisdiction: An Opinionated Guide to the Ongoing Debate, in The Courts: Separation of Powers 15, 21-22 (B. Goulet ed. 1984) (forthcoming).

Other commentators dispute this assessment. Instead of focusing on the facts surrounding the *McCardle* decision, they dwell on the Court's dictum linking the repeal of the Habeas Corpus Act with the exceptions clause. They argue that nothing in the opinion suggests that the power to "except" is limited to "inessential" exceptions, and thus urge us to read broadly the exceptions clause and congressional power over the Supreme Court's appellate jurisdiction.[79]

6. One year after *McCardle*, in *Hepburn v. Griswold*,[80] the Court declared that the Legal Tender Act of 1862, which made paper money legal tender for all debts, was unconstitutional as to debts contracted before the passage of the act. Had the Court's position remained law, there would have been a drastic gold shortage, and debtor classes would have suffered.[81] Only one year later, however, the Court upheld the constitutionality of the Legal Tender Acts in *Knox v. Lee*.[82] In the interim, President Grant had named William Strong and Joseph P. Bradley to the Court. Questions were raised at the time as to whether Grant chose these Justices with the knowledge that they would uphold the Legal Tender Acts. At least one historian has concluded from the available evidence that Grant did indeed "pack" the Supreme Court to obtain a politically desirable turnaround, an incident in which that historian saw obvious parallels to the Court-packing plans that were in the air as he wrote in 1935.[83]

7. A generation after *Hepburn*, in 1895, we come to *Pollock v. Farmers' Loan and Trust Co.*,[84] which was the third Supreme Court decision to be overruled by a constitutional amendment.[85] In *Pollock*, the Supreme Court held the income tax unconstitutional. The issue was a highly political one. In a separate opinion, Justice Field referred to "[t]he present assault upon capital" that, if unchecked, would bring about "the sure decadence of our present government."[86] One notes

---

[79] See Van Alstyne, supra note 78, at 257-60.

[80] 75 U.S. (8 Wall.) 603 (1870).

[81] See Knox v. Lee, 79 U.S. (12 Wall.) 457, 530 (1871).

[82] 79 U.S. (12 Wall.) 457 (1871).

[83] See Ratner, Was the Supreme Court Packed by President Grant?, 50 Pol. Sci. Q. 343 (1935).

[84] 157 U.S. 429 (1895).

[85] The sixteenth amendment was adopted in 1913. Since then, only one Supreme Court decision has been overruled by a constitutional amendment: the twenty-sixth amendment, which lowered the voting age to eighteen, overruled Oregon v. Mitchell, 400 U.S. 112 (1970).

[86] 157 U.S. at 607 (Field, J.).

with wistful longing for a bygone day that the actual tax imposed was two percent of ordinary income over $4,000, and two percent of corporate profits! The burden of paying this outrageous sum would have fallen on less than two percent of the population.[87] The sixteenth amendment, effective in 1913, reversed the result in *Pollock* by granting Congress the power to tax income "without apportionment among the several States, and without regard to any census or enumeration."

8. If we move ahead another four decades, we come to a classic political dispute with the federal courts at its center. The onset of the Depression and the election of Franklin D. Roosevelt in 1932 precipitated a dramatic clash between the Supreme Court and the other two branches of government. Even before the Supreme Court held much of the New Deal legislation unconstitutional, lower federal courts had intensified a trend toward enjoining enforcement of federal legislation. By late 1933, federal judges had granted some 1600 injunctions restraining the federal government from enforcing acts of Congress.[88] After the Supreme Court held the Agricultural Adjustment Act of 1933 unconstitutional, irate farmers hanged the six majority Justices in effigy.[89] Between 1934 and 1936, the Supreme Court invalidated more federal statutes than in any comparable period in the nation's history.[90] Between May 1935 and August 1937, over thirty different constitutional amendments aimed at changing the Court's membership or limiting its power to declare legislation unconstitutional were introduced in Congress.[91]

After his landslide victory in the 1936 election, Roosevelt considered several approaches to the problem, including a constitutional amendment and legislation curbing the Court's jurisdiction.[92] He ultimately proposed to Congress on February 5, 1937, that the President be empowered to appoint a new Justice for each Justice over seventy years old who failed to retire, with the proviso that the total membership of the Court not exceed fifteen. This measure would have assured Roosevelt the opportunity to appoint six new members of the Court.[93]

---

[87] Id. at 443-44 (argument for appellants).

[88] P. Murphy, The Constitution in Crisis Times 1918-1969, at 141 (1972).

[89] Id. at 146-48.

[90] Id. at 155 n.82.

[91] Elliott, Court-Curbing Proposals in Congress, 33 Notre Dame Law. 597, 605-06 (1958).

[92] P. Murphy, supra note 88, at 152.

[93] Id. at 152-53; Elliott, supra note 91, at 605.

Opposition to the proposal by the American Bar Association, Republicans, and dissident Democrats was fierce.[94]

In the midst of the fight, Justice Roberts joined the pro-New Deal faction on the Court, voting to uphold the Wagner Act and the State of Washington's minimum wage law.[95] This gave Roosevelt a five to four majority. Two months later, Justice Van Devanter announced his retirement, making possible a six to three division.[96] Even though the New Deal legislation now seemed relatively out of danger, Roosevelt continued to fight for the Court-packing bill. In the end, the bill was abandoned only after Senate majority leader Joe Robinson, who was shepherding the bill through the Senate, died of a heart attack.[97]

Within two and a half years after rejection of the measure, Roosevelt had made five appointments to the Court.[98] It is often said that Roosevelt lost the battle but won the war because the new Court greatly expanded the scope of permissible economic regulation. But a prominent historian of the New Deal, William Leuchtenburg, concludes that Roosevelt in fact lost the war, because, by pushing so hard for the Court plan, he destroyed the unity of the Democratic majority in Congress. Thus, Leuchtenburg notes, while the new Court "might be willing to uphold new laws . . . an angry and divided Congress would pass few of them for the justices to consider."[99]

9. Some twenty years later, the pendulum swung the other way with the federal courts again the center of contention. The Supreme Court's reaction to McCarthy-era legislation and to activities of congressional committees was mixed. Under Chief Justice Vinson, the Court upheld the legislative anti-Communist campaign.[100] After the appointment of Earl Warren in 1953, the Court's stance began to change. By the 1955 Term, the Court was using statutory interpretation to limit state antisedition legislation,[101] administrative inquiries,[102] and dismissals of government employees under the Internal

---

[94] P. Murphy, supra note 88, at 153; Elliott, supra note 91, at 605.

[95] W. Leuchtenburg, Franklin D. Roosevelt and the New Deal 1932-1940, at 236 (1963).

[96] Id. at 237.

[97] Id. at 237-38. See generally Leuchtenburg, The Origins of Franklin D. Roosevelt's "Court-Packing" Plan, 1966 Sup. Ct. Rev. 347.

[98] Id. at 238.

[99] Id. at 239.

[100] See P. Murphy, supra note 88, at 294-306.

[101] Pennsylvania v. Nelson, 350 U.S. 497 (1956).

[102] Communist Party v. Subversive Activities Control Bd., 351 U.S. 115 (1956).

Security Act of 1950.[103] The Court also ruled that the due process clause prevented the dismissal of a Brooklyn College professor solely on the ground that he had invoked the fifth amendment before a congressional committee.[104] In the next Term, the Court held that it was a violation of due process for state bar associations to deny admission to qualified applicants with a Communist background.[105] On so-called "Red Monday," June 17, 1957,[106] the Court announced decisions curbing prosecutions under the Smith Act[107] and dismissals of State Department employees under the McCarran rider,[108] and limiting congressional and state investigations of political activities.[109]

Congress responded with a flurry of bills designed to thwart these rulings.[110] Professor Shelden Elliott, then of this Law School, classified the various approaches as "selective scattergun" curbs on the Supreme Court's jurisdiction; "single-shot" curbs on the federal courts' jurisdiction; measures that would correct "mistaken" statutory interpretations; and bills to change the terms of office, qualifications, or selection processes for federal judges.[111] The most notable "scattergun" bill was introduced by Senator Jenner during the debates on the Civil Rights Act of 1957.[112] Professor Paul Murphy characterized it as "an omnibus anti-Court bill."[113] Professor Elliott summarized its provisions:

> [T]hey would deny the Supreme Court jurisdiction to review any case involving the validity of (1) the practices or jurisdiction of congressional committees, (2) the national government's enforcement of federal employee security regulations, (3) state control of intrastate subversive activities, (4) school board regulation of sub-

[103] Cole v. Young, 351 U.S. 536 (1956).

[104] Slochower v. Board of Higher Educ., 350 U.S. 551 (1956).

[105] Konigsberg v. State Bar, 353 U.S. 252 (1957); Schware v. Board of Bar Examiners, 353 U.S. 232 (1957).

[106] See P. Murphy, supra note 88, at 328.

[107] See Yates v. United States, 354 U.S. 298 (1957).

[108] Service v. Dulles, 354 U.S. 363 (1957).

[109] Sweezy v. New Hampshire, 354 U.S. 234 (1957); Watkins v. United States, 354 U.S. 178 (1957).

[110] See P. Murphy, supra note 88, at 330-33.

[111] Elliott, supra note 91, at 598, 600-02.

[112] Id. at 598 (discussing S. 2646, 85th Cong., 1st Sess. (1957)).

[113] P. Murphy, supra note 88, at 332.

versive activities of teachers, and (5) state action or regulation pertaining to admission to practice law in the state.[114]

The Senate Judiciary Committee generally reported the anti-Court bills favorably, but none was passed.[115]

10. At about the same time as the sedition and the red-hunt cases, the problem of pervasive racial discrimination came to a dramatic head in *Brown v. Board of Education*.[116] That watershed case and its implementation by the lower federal courts created a furor that inspired a number of bills designed to prevent school desegregation or busing.[117] A 1957 bill would have withdrawn federal court jurisdiction to hear suits challenging state laws on public schools.[118] Another bill would have withdrawn appellate jurisdiction from the Supreme Court in cases attacking a public school system "on grounds other than substantial inequality of physical facilities and other tangible factors."[119] A number of statutes and constitutional amendments were proposed to forbid courts to order busing.[120] None passed both Houses, although the House of Representatives passed a bill forbidding courts to order busing beyond the two schools closest to a student's home.[121]

A similar response was triggered by the legislative apportionment decisions.[122] After *Reynolds v. Sims*,[123] announcing the "one man, one vote" rule for state legislatures, Senator Dirksen proposed a constitutional amendment to override the decisions,[124] and a bill to withhold federal court jurisdiction over cases seeking reapportionment of state legislatures was introduced in the House.[125] Neither proposal received the necessary approval of Congress.[126]

---

[114] Elliott, supra note 91, at 598.

[115] P. Murphy, supra note 88, at 332-33.

[116] 347 U.S. 483 (1954).

[117] Eisenberg, Congressional Authority to Restrict Lower Federal Court Jurisdiction, 83 Yale L.J. 498, 498-99 (1974).

[118] Id. at 498 n.6 (discussing H.R. 1228, 85th Cong., 1st Sess. (1957)).

[119] Id. (discussing S. 3467, 85th Cong., 2d Sess. (1958)).

[120] Id. at 499 & n.13.

[121] Id. at 499 n.13 (discussing H.R. 13915, 92d Cong., 2d Sess. (1972)).

[122] See P. Murphy, supra note 88, at 386-91; Eisenberg, supra note 117, at 499 & n.10.

[123] 377 U.S. 533 (1964).

[124] P. Murphy, supra note 88, at 389.

[125] Eisenberg, supra note 117, at 499 & n.10 (discussing H.R. 11926, 88th Cong., 2d Sess. (1964)).

[126] See P. Murphy, supra note 88, at 389-91.

II

THE CURRENT ASSAULT

And so we come to the present day. This survey has, of course, been sketchy, but it is sufficient, I believe, to prompt a few observations.

First, it is clear that since its inception the federal judiciary has been at the center of turbulent controversy. Sometimes the outrage in the body politic has come from the right, sometimes from the left. But regardless of the source of the passion, over the course of our history particular decisions have upset segments of the citizenry enough to invite attempts to change the results by one means or another.

Second, the assaults on the federal courts have generally not been successful. In four instances, when the Supreme Court's interpretation of the Constitution was unpopular enough, decisions have been overruled by constitutional amendments—the eleventh, the fourteenth, the sixteenth, and the twenty-sixth. In other instances, the Court has changed an unpopular course because of new appointments or simply because of the pressure of public opposition; in the words of Mr. Dooley, the Court has displayed a capacity to follow the election returns.[127] These methods of change are built into our system, and that is as it should be: by and large, they do not damage the courts, but protect them by giving them a needed flexibility. For the most part, legislative attempts to nullify decisions of the federal courts indirectly by tinkering with their structure and jurisdiction for substantive, political ends have failed. It is true that, in the anti-court campaign of the early 1800's, the Jeffersonians stopped the Supreme Court dead in its tracks for over a year and were able to repeal the Judiciary Act of 1801, abolishing many new judgeships. But the plan to control the judiciary with politically motivated impeachments did not succeed in its ultimate aim.

No other similar legislative attack on the federal courts since then has met with true success. For example, the result in *Ex parte McCardle* turned out to be a limited victory, perhaps good for one performance only. In particular, Congress has in no other instance enacted any of the myriad bills to strip the federal courts of jurisdiction to hear certain classes of constitutional cases.[128] The attempts of states' right-

[127] M.F. McNamara, 2,000 Famous Legal Quotations 550 (1967).

[128] Committee on Federal Legislation, Jurisdiction-Stripping Proposals in Congress: The Threat to Judicial Constitutional Review, 36 Rec. A.B. City N.Y. 557, 559 (1981).

ists to curb federal review of state statutes and court decisions, the McCarthy-era Congress's efforts to prevent the courts from protecting individual liberties, and the battery of bills aimed at undercutting the school desegregation decisions have all failed. I am not sure why this is so. One can attribute the failure to the difficulty of changing fundamental institutions, to inertia, to a residual consensus regarding the courts, or, in some instances, to just plain chance. There is no doubt that, from time to time, acts of principled statesmanship by individual legislators or lawyers have helped to prevent the passage of ill-considered measures.

Third, despite this lack of success, the attacks have continued over most of our history. This is not surprising when one considers the depth of feeling stirred by the basic issues in the cases just discussed. Indeed, the surprise may be that such attempts have not occurred more often. The failures of the past rarely discourage outraged citizens of the present. It is true that we have come a long way since the turbulent days of the early 1800's. I doubt that any member of Congress would propose today, for example, that the Supreme Court be required to stay in recess for one year. But history has a way of repeating itself. When then-Congressman Gerald Ford led the attempt to impeach Justice Douglas in 1970, the Congressman stated that an impeachable offense is "whatever a majority of the House of Representatives considers [it] to be at a given moment in history."[129] This statement did not differ much from Senator Giles's definition in 1802 that impeachment was warranted if a judge was "opposed to the administration & wrong headed."[130]

Decisions in the last decade or two involving prayer in the schools, abortion, capital punishment, and school desegregation raise issues about which people feel strongly, even passionately. With this background in mind, perhaps you will not be too surprised to learn that in the last Congress there were more than thirty bills introduced that, according to former American Bar Association president Brink, "would deprive the federal courts of their historic and vital jurisdiction or power to grant remedies in what all agree are constitutional cases."[131] Almost all of these bills single out narrow categories of constitutional claims for jurisdictional oblivion. It is worthwhile, I

---

[129] 116 Cong. Rec. 11,913 (1970).

[130] See text accompanying note 31 supra.

[131] Address by David R. Brink, supra note 3, at 5.

believe, to examine more closely what may be the most comprehensive and in some ways the most sophisticated of these bills, the "Judicial Reform Act of 1982."[132] No action was taken last year on that bill, S. 3018, but Senator Joseph R. Biden, Jr., of Delaware, the ranking minority member of the Senate Judiciary Committee, expects it to be reintroduced in one form or another.[133]

S. 3018 proposes to limit the jurisdiction of the federal courts and to alter their decisions on important issues. One provision would repeal the general federal question jurisdiction of 28 U.S.C. § 1331,[134] thus depriving the federal courts of jurisdiction to hear cases arising under the Constitution, treaties, or federal law, unless Congress has specifically provided for jurisdiction in another provision of title 28 or in the substantive statute creating the alleged federal right.

The bill would also reverse several judicial rules designed to protect civil and statutory rights. It would render the incorporation doctrine, which applies many of the provisions of the Bill of Rights to the states, unenforceable in the federal courts by depriving the Supreme Court and the district courts of jurisdiction to hear cases claiming that a state or any state agency or subdivision has deprived a party of any right secured by the first eight amendments to the Constitution.[135] In addition, the exclusionary rule would be overturned, and in its place the courts would be given the power to punish violations of the fourth amendment connected with cases pending before them as contempt of court.[136] The bill would also provide that no cause of action may be implied from any federal statute; only those causes of action explicitly provided for by Congress would be cognizable.[137]

The bill would also curtail the courts' jurisdiction in several other areas. Federal habeas corpus relief for prisoners in custody under a state court judgment would be limited to cases involving a substantial constitutional claim, rather than *any* claim under the Constitution, laws, or treaties of the United States. Moreover, the federal courts could not entertain a habeas petition raising an issue that had been, could have been, or still could be raised and determined in a state

---

132 S. 3018, supra note 4.

133 Address by Senator Joseph R. Biden, The Radical Right and the Constitution: The Assault on Our Independent Federal Judiciary, Association of the Bar of the City of New York 2 (May 3, 1983) (on file at New York University Law Review).

134 S. 3018, supra note 4, § 161.

135 Id. §§ 111-112.

136 Id. §§ 121-123.

137 Id. § 171.

court proceeding subject to Supreme Court review by certiorari.[138] Thus, state prisoners would apparently face an almost inescapable Catch-22. The exhaustion doctrine would require resort to the state courts, but a determination on the merits there would bar a suit in the federal courts. In any event, I find it difficult to imagine that many petitioners could come up with substantial claims that would survive the emasculation of the incorporation doctrine. So it appears that habeas petitions from state prisoners would virtually disappear from the federal courts if this provision became law.

An analysis of the bill by the staff of the Senate Subcommittee on Separation of Powers, excerpts of which have been published—and I quote only from those—stated: " 'These provisions should provide both a practical solution to the habeas deluge and an opportunity to explore the jurisprudence which made that deluge inevitable. It would return to the states the power to establish rules of criminal law and thus restore the principle of federalism in this important area.' "[139]

The bill would also severely limit civil rights litigation in the federal courts. It would amend 42 U.S.C. § 1983 in four ways: (1) claims of deprivation of rights secured by federal statutes would be limited to those under statutes "providing for equal rights;" (2) courts would be unable to enjoin state court proceedings; (3) no action could be maintained against a local government, municipal corporation, or other local body; and, finally, (4) even those claims remaining within § 1983 could not be heard in the federal courts unless "[s]tate law provides no adequate remedy or the remedy is not as a practical matter available."[140] Those few hardy civil rights plaintiffs whose claims could still be brought in the federal courts would be further deterred by the repeal of the provision for award of attorneys' fees to successful plaintiffs.[141]

Another provision of Title I of the bill would require that injunctions against a state or a subdivision, agency, or officer of a state be entered by a three-judge district court.[142] Title I also provides for the

---

138 Id. § 131.

139 National Legal Center for the Public Interest, 2 Judicial/Legislative Watch Report No. 14, Nov. 5, 1982, at 3 (quoting memorandum of Staff of Senate Subcommittee on Separation of Powers).

140 S. 3018, supra note 4, §§ 141-142.

141 Id. § 151 (proposing to amend 42 U.S.C. § 1988).

142 Id. § 181. Former 28 U.S.C. §§ 2281-2282, repealed in 1976, imposed a similar requirement for injunctions against the enforcement of allegedly unconstitutional statutes, both state and federal.

elimination of two of the three categories of class actions: those under Federal Rule of Civil Procedure 23(b)(2), which is often used for civil rights suits seeking injunctive relief, and those under Federal Rule of Civil Procedure 23(b)(3), where the court, in its discretion, determines that a class action is the fairest and most efficient way to settle the controversy, and that common questions of law or fact predominate.[143] The Subcommittee staff's analysis makes clear what motivates this provision: " '[M]embers of a particular race or sex now easily constitute classes given the sociological bent of modern federal jurisprudence. Abstract rights provide the bases for classes which render modern federal litigation more like legislation than like traditional adjudication of rights among concerned litigants.' "[144]

Before I describe Title II, we should step back for a moment to examine the effect of Title I. Of course, there have been abuses in prisoner suits under section 1983 and in habeas corpus proceedings. Each of these topics, and the exclusionary rule, for example, could well be the subject of an entire speech. My focus is not, however, on specific provisions of the bill but on the effect of the bill as a whole. The message is clear enough: The federal courts are welcome to decide diversity cases under state law and routine federal law questions involving economic regulation or copyright infringement, but they had better not get the idea that one of their main functions is to guard the rights of individuals under the Constitution and laws of the United States. That function is left primarily to the states—and if the states choose to ignore the Bill of Rights, so be it.

The hostility toward the federal judiciary that permeates Title I of the bill is even more evident in Title II, called "Judgeships." Most revealing is Part A, "Oversight of Judiciary,"[145] which would repeal the recent statute providing for discipline of judges through the chief judges and judicial councils of the circuits,[146] and would set up a "Joint Committee on Judicial Conduct."[147] This committee would be composed of five senators and five representatives, appointed by the President pro tem of the Senate and the Speaker of the House,[148]

---

[143] S. 3018, supra note 4, § 191.

[144] National Legal Center for the Public Interest, supra note 139, at 5 (quoting memorandum of Staff of Senate Subcommittee on Separation of Powers).

[145] S. 3018, supra note 4, §§ 201-211.

[146] Id. § 210.

[147] Id. § 201.

[148] Id. § 201(b) (1), (2).

respectively. The committee would review the conduct of each federal judge—including Justices of the Supreme Court[149]—at least once every ten years,[150] and would recommend impeachment if the judge's conduct "fail[s] to meet the standard of good behavior."[151] Judicial "conduct" is defined to include a judge's decisions. "Good behavior" is said to have the same meaning as in the Constitution.[152] Conduct "failing to meet the standard of good behavior" is further defined, however, as including "usurpation of the authority of the Congress, the President or the States"[153] and the "exercise of will instead of judgment by substituting the pleasure of the judge for that of the legislature—either Congress or the ratifiers of the Constitution of the United States, as the case may be—rather than declaring the sense of the law."[154]

I think it is obvious that the bill as a whole is an attempt to overrule a judicial philosophy that is unpopular with the bill's proponents. The standard established in Title II seems dangerously vague. The very threat of review by these overseers would have a profound effect on federal judges—indeed, it would destroy their independence. It would lead to the precise dangers that Alexander Hamilton feared: that "representatives of the people" might attempt to act in ways incompatible with the provisions of the existing Constitution. According to Hamilton, to guard against "legislative invasions" of the Constitution requires an "uncommon portion of fortitude in the judges." Thus, he viewed the independence of the judiciary as an essential characteristic of our constitutional system of government.[155]

We have seen that in the two-hundred-year history of our Constitution there have been many attempts to subjugate the courts to the will of the political majority. These attempts have by and large been responses to particular decisions or trends of decision in the courts. But if this bill became law, it would end the need to proceed piecemeal. Congress would assume effective control of the judiciary. I wonder if the proponents have considered that the Supreme Court has often

---

149 Id. § 202(a).
150 Id. § 202(c).
151 Id. § 202(b).
152 Id.
153 Id. § 202(b) (4).
154 Id. § 202(b) (5).
155 The Federalist No. 78, supra note 5, at 488; see Kaufman, Chilling Judicial Independence, 88 Yale L.J. 681 (1979).

been attacked, as it was in the Roosevelt era, for defending conservative values against liberal legislation passed by Congress with the support of most voters. Similarly, in the 1970's, liberal dissatisfaction with Supreme Court decisions on standing led to introduction of a bill in Congress to remove the jurisdiction of the federal courts, under article III of the Constitution, to determine whether plaintiffs have standing to bring a suit in federal court.[156] Majority control of the courts is a two-edged sword.

You may wonder why, given the failure rate of similar anti-court proposals in the past, this speech is devoted to the current assault. There are several reasons. First, these attacks have failed in the past usually because opposing political forces have combined with those who value the independence of the judiciary for its own sake to blunt or thwart the attack. Senator Biden, in a passionate speech before the Association of the Bar of the City of New York last May, reported that the sponsors of the bill intend to present it to Congress piecemeal if, as is quite likely, it fails to pass in its present form.[157] Senator Biden expressed great concern that this second effort might succeed, since the issues involved "are difficult for the public at large to understand" and the method of attack is largely procedural. Thus, the measures are not likely to arouse widespread interest and opposition. Senator Biden called upon the organized bar to recognize this bill and others like it as a threat to the Constitution and to oppose them actively.[158]

The second principal reason for my concern is that the forces that resent federal decisions are today reinforced in their calls for change by the judges' complaints, including my own, about the excessive caseload in the federal courts. If there are aspects of S. 3018 with which you disagree, mere opposition to this bill and to others like it is not sufficient; you must put forth and support alternative proposals to strengthen the federal courts while relieving them of some of the current burden of work.

Those of us who work in the system are acutely aware that something must give soon. Filings on all three levels of the federal judiciary have increased spectacularly in the past twenty years. In the district courts, the number of civil cases filed has increased three-and-

---

[156] Address by Senator Joseph R. Biden, supra note 133, at 4.
[157] Id. at 3.
[158] Id. at 10-12.

a-third times.[159] The Supreme Court's docket has multiplied by a factor of two-and-a-half.[160] And the most staggering increases have been in the courts of appeals, where filings are almost six times what they were twenty years ago.[161] The addition of judgeships to the district and circuit courts has not kept pace with this increase in work, and of course the Supreme Court has not been enlarged at all.

S. 3018 would indubitably reduce the federal courts' workload considerably. But in the process it would substantially strip the courts of what I believe to be their special role in the federal system. While there may be room for constructive debate over some of the provisions of S. 3018, that debate should not be skewed by efficiency considerations because there are other, far more desirable, ways of reducing judicial workload. For example, the federal courts should not be deciding purely state law cases; if diversity jurisdiction were eliminated, 25% of the civil caseload of the district courts[162] and 17% of civil appeals in fiscal 1982[163] would have been removed, leaving the federal courts to do what we need them to do: enforce the Constitution's scheme of separation of powers; carry out the policies of the Constitution and of federal statutes; assure their supremacy in relation to the states; and guarantee federal constitutional rights against the encroachment of government, both federal and state. These functions are, of course, precisely what S. 3018 would in great part remove from the federal courts while leaving diversity jurisdiction intact.

While we ponder these questions, it might be instructive to recall a debate on overworked judges that took place over a century ago. Then, while Congress was deciding what to do about the appellate jurisdiction of the Supreme Court in habeas corpus cases, one senator argued that a statute that forces the Court to hear "long arguments upon a matter of trifling importance" when it is "two or three or four years behind in its business and the vast interests of the country are delayed" should be repealed. But when pressed, the senator admitted that he knew of no habeas appeal that had "overburdened" the Court

---

[159] Compare 1982 Annual Report of the Director of the Administrative Office of the United States Courts 4 (206,193 cases) [hereinafter 1982 Report] with 1962 Annual Report of the Director of the Administrative Office of the United States Courts 196 (61,836 cases) [hereinafter 1962 Report].

[160] Compare 1982 Report, supra note 159, at 189 (5,311 cases) with 1962 Report, supra note 159, at 176 (2,185 cases).

[161] Compare 1982 Report, supra note 159, at 190 (27,946 cases) with 1962 Report, supra note 159, at 180 (4,823 cases).

[162] See 1982 Report, supra note 159, at 4 (total civil cases: 206,193; diversity cases: 50,555).

[163] See 1982 Report, supra note 159, at 194-95 (total civil cases: 18,784; diversity cases: 3,217).

other than McCardle's.[164] Recalling this episode should make us wary when efficiency arguments are used to justify removing constitutional law questions from the federal courts.

Those of us who believe that James Madison was right—that the Supreme Court needs the help of a system of lower federal courts and that the country needs an independent federal judiciary—must be alert to the fact that even after almost 200 years, there are those who disagree. Now, when the federal judiciary faces a workload crisis of unprecedented proportions, the federal courts are particularly vulnerable to the attacks of those who do not like their decisions. As we seek to make the federal judicial system work better, let us remember the job we want it to do.

---

[164] C. Fairman, supra note 66, at 469.

HARVARD LAW REVIEW

Vol. XLII NOVEMBER, 1928 No. 1

THE SUPREME COURT UNDER THE JUDICIARY ACT OF 1925

SINCE May 13, 1925, the Supreme Court of the United States has been adjudicating under a new dispensation. To enable the Court to cope with the growth in its business and to conserve its energies for issues appropriate to the Supreme Bench, Congress by the Act of February 13, 1925,[1] acceded to the Court's desire for drastic limitations upon its jurisdiction. Speaking on behalf of the Court in 1924, Mr. Justice Van Devanter reported to Congress that "more than two-thirds of the cases which come to us under our obligatory jurisdiction — from State courts, circuit courts of appeals, district courts, and the Court of Claims — result in judgments of affirmance by our court, and also a goodly number are ultimately dismissed for want of prosecution. This, we think, illustrates that the present statutes are too liberal — that they permit cases to come to us as of right with no benefit to the litigants or the public. What we learn of the cases in examining them confirms and emphasizes this conclusion. Of course, in proportion as our attention is engaged with cases of that character, it is taken away from others which present grave questions and need careful consideration." [2]

The remedy proposed by the Supreme Court and adopted by Congress was a transference of numerous classes of cases from obligatory review by appeal or writ of error to discretionary review

[1] 43 Stat. 936, 28 U. S. C. §§ 344–50 (1926).

[2] Hearing before the Judiciary Committee, House of Representatives, on H. R. 8206, 68th Cong. 2d Sess., Dec. 18, 1924, at 13.

by *certiorari*. It will be recalled that the Act of 1925 entirely shut off access to the Supreme Court as a matter of right from the Court of Claims, the courts of the dependencies, and the Court of Appeals of the District of Columbia.[3] From the circuit courts of appeals review without leave was retained only in cases in which such a court finds a state statute in conflict with "the Constitution, treaties, or laws of the United States."[4] The Chief Justice enumerated not less than fourteen types of controversies in which a second right of appeal was thus eliminated.[5] Direct review by the Supreme Court was abolished as to decisions of the district courts, except as to five strictly confined categories of litigation: (1) suits under the Anti-trust and Interstate Commerce Acts; (2) suits to enjoin the enforcement of state statutes or administrative orders; (3) suits to enjoin orders of the Interstate Commerce Commission; (4) suits under the Stockyard and Packers Act of 1921; (5) writs of error by the United States in criminal cases. All other litigation arising in the district courts can now be reviewed only by the circuit courts of appeals. Finally, the litigation coming as of right to the Supreme Court from the state courts was restricted to two classes: (1) where the validity of a state statute was challenged under the Federal Constitution and its validity sustained; (2) where a federal statute or treaty was invoked and its validity denied. The 1925 Act has left the Supreme Court power to decide every case that could have come to it before that Act, but under the Act only controversies in which issues

[3] It remains doubtful whether any review as of right may be had over the decisions of the Court of Appeals of the District of Columbia. Section 240(b) of the Judicial Code as amended by the Act of February 13, 1925, provides for writs of error and appeals from circuit courts of appeals in cases where a state statute has been held repugnant to the Constitution, treaties, or laws of the United States. 43 STAT. 936, 28 U. S. C. 347(b) (1926). It may be that the Court of Appeals in a collateral proceeding might be called upon to determine the validity of a state statute. *Cf.* Wisconsin v. Pelican Ins. Co., 127 U. S. 265 (1888); Huntington v. Attrill, 146 U. S. 657 (1892). It is true that in the interpretation of other jurisdictional statutes the Supreme Court has held that the Court of Appeals is to be included within the general designation of circuit courts of appeals. Swift & Co. v. United States, 276 U. S. 311 (1928). But the express mention of the Court of Appeals in Sections 240(a) and 240(c) and its omission from Section 240(b), make doubtful such inclusion in the latter section.

[4] Section 240(b), JUDICIAL CODE, 28 U. S. C. 347(b) (1926).

[5] FRANKFURTER AND LANDIS, THE BUSINESS OF THE SUPREME COURT (1927) 261–62.

of a national or at least general concern are at stake can be carried to the Court as of right.[6] For all other cases, the Act requires leave of the Court through individual petitions of *certiorari*.

I

The Act has been in force for a little over three years, but its effective influence has been shorter. The new era really begins with the 1927 term. Many cases which originated prior to the Judiciary Act of 1925 were disposed of during the 1925 and 1926 terms. However, these terms reflected decisive changes. The last five terms cover the work of the Court under the old jurisdiction, the transition from the old to the new, and the operation of the new régime. A study of the 1923–1927 terms will thus afford a basis for a survey of tendencies under the present Act and lay the foundation for future comparisons.

A similar study of the work of British or continental courts would base its data upon official annual judicial statistics. Unfortunately, such a system of authoritative balance sheets of the business of the Supreme Court has not yet been established. Since 1922, Mr. Ernest Knaebel, the present Reporter of the Court, has prepared a very summary statement of the gross items in the Court's business for each term.[7] And since 1875 the annual reports of the Attorney General of the United States give a more detailed analysis of the year's business for the Supreme Court, and also for the lower federal courts. Neither set of figures purports to analyze the sources of the Court's business, the modes by which the cases reach the Court, the character of the litigation, its disposition, or the distribution of opinions and votes among the Justices. Until the European system of official judicial statistics finds its counterpart in the United States,[8] any analysis

[6] In the Revised Rules of the Supreme Court of the United States, adopted on June 5, 1928, a new practice was inaugurated by the adoption of Rule 12. 275 U. S. 595, 603 (1928). Within thirty days after docketing a case, counsel are required to file a detailed statement disclosing the basis for the Supreme Court's jurisdiction. Opposing counsel are then permitted to file a counter statement. These statements are then submitted to the Court without oral argument, unless at the special invitation of the Court. In this way the Court hopes to avoid the waste of oral arguments upon the merits, where no ground of jurisdiction is established.

[7] 262 U. S. 763 (1922).

[8] For the Supreme Court of New York in the First Judicial Department,

of the business of the Supreme Court must be based upon an independent investigation of the adjudged cases in the United States Reports.[9]

We are here concerned solely with the appellate jurisdiction of the Court. To be sure, issues of great moment and of considerable complexity arise under the Court's original jurisdiction. But in volume this head of litigation is relatively meager, and in any event beyond jurisdictional control by Congress.[10] The Court's appellate work may be broadly divided between the determination of cases that are before the Court for adjudication and the disposition of petitions seeking to bring the cases before the Court. Again, cases for adjudication may terminate without consideration by the Court, as, for instance, by consent of counsel. The great bulk of cases, however, requires consideration. These in turn fall into two modes of adjudication: decisions with opinions, and *per curiam* decisions, that is, without opinion.

Table I shows the volume of considered cases [11] for the period under scrutiny. It will be noticed that the variations in the totals of such cases between 1923 and 1927 are not very significant. The Act of 1925 was, on the whole, not intended to contract the volume of annual dispositions, but to guard against the inevitable increase and the resulting congestion. Indeed, the Act was an effort by the Court to cut the coat of jurisdiction according to the cloth of the time and energy of the nine Justices. While the total dispositions remain substantially unchanged, there is a noticeable readjustment in the proportions between cases disposed of by opinion and *per curiam* decisions. *Per curiams* are largely used in dismissals for want of jurisdiction.[12] On the other hand, some

detailed and comprehensive statistics have, since 1914, been published annually. In 1926 the Conference of Senior Circuit Judges appointed a committee to consider and report upon methods for securing and publishing appropriate statistics of the work of the federal courts. See REP. ATT'Y. GEN. (1926) 7. The death of Judge Hough, a leading member of the committee, has for a time apparently postponed the realization of this much needed reform.

[9] The figures in the following tables differ slightly from the attorney general's computations. The variations may be due to differences in classification.

[10] Marbury v. Madison, 1 Cranch 137 (U. S. 1803).

[11] The tabulation represents cases and not opinions. Several cases may be disposed of by one opinion.

[12] That dismissals for want of jurisdiction ordinarily present stereotyped situations governed by prior decisions of the Court, is illustrated by the constant

TABLE I

Disposition of Cases on Appellate Docket

Cases Disposed of by Full Opinion

	1923	*1924*	*1925*	*1926*	*1927*	*Total*
Affirmed	130	135	159	108	78	610
Reversed	83	93	78	95	112	461
Dismissed *	12	11	13	7	8	51
Certificate	5	10	9	7	6	37
Transferred	6	3	0	3	0	12
Miscellaneous †	4	3	4	3	10	24
Total	**240**	**255**	**263**	**223**	**214**	**1195**

Cases Disposed of Per Curiam ‡

	1923	*1924*	*1925*	*1926*	*1927*	*Total*
Affirmed	19	25	20	36	28	128
Reversed	8	3	3	11	10	35
Dismissed	45	59	55	74	73	306
Certificate	1	4	0	1	1	7
Transferred	2	7	3	3	0	15
Miscellaneous	2	0	0	0	1	3
Total	**77**	**98**	**81**	**125**	**113**	**494**

Total Dispositions With Consideration

	1923	*1924*	*1925*	*1926*	*1927*	*Total*
Affirmed	149	160	179	144	106	738
Reversed	91	96	81	106	122	496
Dismissed	57	70	68	81	81	357
Certificate	6	14	9	8	7	44
Transferred	8	10	3	6	0	27
Miscellaneous	6	3	4	3	11	27
Total	**317**	**353**	**344**	**348**	**327**	**1689**

* Including petitions for *certiorari* dismissed by full opinion.

† Including partial affirmances, decisions on petitions for *certiorari*, on motions, etc.

‡ Excluding petitions for *certiorari* disposed of *per curiam*.

important decisions are thus disposed of on the merits, by reference to authority.[13] It is significant that in several instances the controlling character of prior decisions on pending litigation has evoked the expression of dissents in *per curiams* — apparently an innovation, due to the use of *per curiams* on controverted issues.[14] If the Court's time were wholly given to the adjudication of cases and the preparation of opinions, the annual output of opinions would remain substantially the same. But if its labors also demand the prompt disposition of petitions for leave to come before the Court, there is a necessary deflection of the intellectual resources of the Court available for opinion writing. Therefore the desire and, indeed, the necessity to keep abreast of business will operate as a pressure to decide cases without opinions.[15] Thus we see the increase in opinions for the three terms beginning with 1923 and their decrease for the last two terms,[16] and the striking increase of nearly forty per cent in *per curiams* since the Act of 1925.

One other trend in the total dispositions during the last five terms is arresting. It will be noticed in Table I that since the Act of 1925 there has been a striking change in the proportion of reversals to affirmances. For years prior to the 1926 term, affirmances overwhelmingly exceeded reversals. The 1926 term discloses a decided rise in reversals, and at the last term of court there were 122 reversals as against 106 affirmances. This result was to be expected. In fact, the large percentage of affirmances was adduced by Mr. Justice Van Devanter as evidence of the un-

repetition of the same controlling authorities, such as Farrell v. O'Brien, 199 U. S. 89 (1905); Shulthis v. McDougal, 225 U. S. 561 (1912); Central Land Co. v. Laidley, 159 U. S. 103 (1895); Jett Bros. Distilling Co. v. City of Carrollton, 252 U. S. 1 (1920).

[13] See, *e.g.*, State Industrial Board of N. Y. v. Terry & Tench Co., 273 U. S. 639 (1926), commented upon in Note (1927) 40 HARV. L. REV. 485; Standard Oil Co. v. City of Lincoln, 275 U. S. 504 (1927), commented upon in Note (1928) 41 HARV. L. REV. 775.

[14] Murphy v. Sardell, 269 U. S. 530 (1925); Donham v. West-Nelson Mfg. Co., 273 U. S. 657 (1927).

[15] Of the significance of opinions in the development of English law, Edmund Burke said: "To give judgment privately is to put an end to reports; and to put an end to reports is to put an end to the law of England." Quoted in MAITLAND, ENGLISH LAW AND THE RENAISSANCE (1901) 78, n.50; 1 SELECT ESSAYS IN ANGLO-AMERICAN LEGAL HISTORY (1907) 193.

[16] Compare also the figures given in Table VII, *infra* pp. 16–17.

due liberality in the right of review prior to the Act of 1925. That legislation attempted, in part, to shut off types of litigation presumably unworthy of review by the Supreme Court. Since such litigation can now come to the Court only by permission, the probability is enhanced that cases on the docket present more doubtful issues than characterized the litigation prior to the present Judiciary Act.

A large proportion of these reversals, as disclosed by Table II, arises in cases coming from the circuit courts of appeals. Thus, for the 1923 term, in reviews of circuit courts of appeals decisions, there were 43 affirmances and 36 reversals compared with 29 affirmances and 72 reversals for the 1927 term. The Judiciary Act of 1925 made those courts the ultimate tribunals of review for the vast bulk of litigation arising in the federal courts. Further review by the Supreme Court was limited to cases of exceptional importance. Only in one class of cases, nominally negligible, was review as of right retained; the review in the remainder was subjected to specific leave of the Court. *Certiorari* is thus the normal method by which cases from the circuit courts of appeals reach the Supreme Court. Among the grounds for granting *certiorari,* as formulated by the Supreme Court in its Rules, is the probability of error in the decisions of the circuit courts of appeals in the light of the applicable local or general law.[17] Prior

---

[17] Revised Rules of the Supreme Court of the United States, Rule 38, § 5(b); 275 U. S. 595, 624 (1928). In cases where the issue does not concern the applicable local or general law but raises a problem of federal law, the scope of review upon *certiorari* to the circuit courts of appeals should be limited to federal questions. Where the case comes from a circuit court of appeals as a matter of right, the Supreme Court under the provisions of Section 240(b) of the Judicial Code is "restricted to an examination and decision of the Federal questions presented in the case." 43 STAT. 939 (1925), 28 U. S. C. § 347(b) (1926). It is difficult to justify a broader review where the same type of case comes from the same court by *certiorari.* The wise restriction imposed upon reviews by right should be extended to reviews by grace. In some instances the Supreme Court in granting *certiorari* has limited itself to the consideration of constitutional questions raised by the case. Olmstead v. United States, 48 Sup. Ct. 207 (U. S. 1928). Mr. Justice Stone, speaking for a minority, contended that the effect of the order was simply to limit the scope of argument, but did not restrain the Court from a consideration of any question presented by the record, inasmuch as the scope of review by *certiorari* was specifically stated by Section 240(a) of the Judicial Code to be the same as if the case "had been brought . . . by unrestricted writ of error or appeal." 48 Sup. Ct. 564, 576 (U. S. 1928).

TABLE II

COURTS FROM WHICH CASES CAME

	1923	*1924*	*1925*	*1926*	*1927*	*Total*
DISTRICT COURTS	**91**	**102**	**78**	**98**	**25**	**394**
Affirmed	47	60	48	47	16	218
Reversed	31	25	18	28	6	108
Dismissed	5	7	9	17	3	41
Transferred	8	10	3	6	0	27
CIRCUIT COURTS OF APPEALS	**103**	**82**	**83**	**83**	**119**	**70**
Affirmed	43	33	41	34	29	180
Reversed	36	31	25	38	72	202
Dismissed	15	6	7	4	5	37
Certificate	5	9	9	7	7	37
Miscellaneous	4	3	1	0	6	14
HIGHEST STATE COURTS	**94**	**119**	**100**	**124**	**160**	**597**
Affirmed	40	35	26	39	51	191
Reversed	18	28	26	27	33	132
Dismissed	36	56	48	58	73	271
Miscellaneous	0	0	0	0	3	3
COURT OF APPEALS, DISTRICT OF COLUMBIA	**10**	**15**	**28**	**12**	**4**	**69**
Affirmed	5	4	26	4	1	40
Reversed	3	6	1	5	2	17
Dismissed	0	5	1	2	0	8

TABLE II (*continued*)

	1923	*1924*	*1925*	*1926*	*1927*	*Total*
Certificate	1	0	0	1	0	2
Miscellaneous	1	0	0	0	1	2
COURT OF CLAIMS	**18**	**34**	**53**	**27**	**14**	**146**
Affirmed	13	27	37	21	6	104
Reversed	3	6	13	6	8	36
Dismissed	1	0	3	0	0	4
Miscellaneous	1	1	0	0	0	2
COURT OF CUSTOMS APPEALS	**0**	**1**	**0**	**1**	**2**	**4**
Affirmed	0	1	0	0	1	2
Reversed	0	0	0	1	1	2
Dismissed	0	0	0	0	0	0
PHILIPPINE SUPREME COURT	**1**	**0**	**2**	**3**	**3**	**9**
Affirmed	1	0	0	2	2	5
Reversed	0	0	2	1	0	3
Dismissed	0	0	0	0	0	0
Miscellaneous	0	0	0	0	1	1
Total	**317**	**353**	**344**	**348**	**327**	**1689**

to 1925, cases dependent on *certiorari* had to compete unduly with the extensive obligatory jurisdiction, the disposition of which operated as a practical restriction upon the Court's opportunities to exercise its discretionary corrective powers over the decisions of the circuit courts of appeals. Now that the Court has been relieved of the burden of litigation which heretofore came to it as of right, but ought never to have been there at all, it is freer to exercise its discretionary authority over the business of the circuit courts of appeals.

The expectation of reducing litigation from courts over which there ought not to be review as of right in the Supreme Court has been realized. The most marked decrease is in reviews of the district courts. The Court of Claims and the Court of Appeals of the District of Columbia also show a notable falling off. The decrease in litigation from these sources wrought by the Act of 1925 is far greater than the figures disclose. That Act not only secured a considerable decrease, but forestalled a considerable increase in Supreme Court litigation.

By the Act of 1925 the Supreme Court sought for itself a selective jurisdiction. The legislation which it obtained is a notable application of the principle of individualization in the exercise of appellate review. From this aspect the effect of the Act of 1925 is already decisive.

TABLE III

EXTENT OF DISCRETIONARY REVIEW

	1923	*1924*	*1925*	*1926*	*1927*	*Total*
Obligatory Jurisdiction	246	290	282	260	166	1244
Discretionary Jurisdiction	71	63	62	88	161	445
Total	**317**	**353**	**344**	**348**	**327**	**1689**
Obligatory Jurisdiction	80.8%	82.1%	81.5%	74.7%	50.8%	
Discretionary Jurisdiction	19.2%	17.9%	18.5%	25.3%	49.2%	

For the three terms preceding the Act, as shown in Table III, eighty per cent of the cases came to the Court as a matter of course, regardless of the Court's judgment as to the seriousness of the questions at issue. In less than twenty per cent did the

Court exercise discretion in assuming jurisdiction. The 1926 term already shows a drop in the obligatory jurisdiction to less than seventy-five per cent, and at the last term, the Court's business was almost evenly divided between its obligatory and discretionary jurisdiction. The analysis made in Table IV indicates that this enlargement of the use of *certiorari* is most operative in the Supreme Court's review of the labors of the circuit courts of appeals. Review as of right arises mainly in cases coming from the state courts, and these courts are likely to continue as the chief feeders of the Supreme Court's obligatory jurisdiction.

The future administration of the Court's business thus largely turns on *certioraris*. The number increased, as will be seen from Table V, from 389 in the 1923 term to 587 in the last term. Petitions for *certiorari* are disposed of without argument or opinions. But, as we have been authoritatively told, all the members of the Court make independent examination of these petitions, the underlying records, and supporting briefs preliminary to their disposition after deliberation by the full Court.[18] Petitions for *certiorari* will steadily increase. This means a growing absorption of the Court's time not in the adjudication of cases and the writing of opinions, but in determining whether cases should be adjudicated. How heavy the drain is likely to become is indicated by the action taken by the Court at the beginning of the present term. On October 1, the Chief Justice announced that since the close of the last term 244 petitions had been filed. Much time had already been devoted to them by members of the Court during the vacation, but in order that the accumulation might be disposed of "in the early days of this term," the Court set aside the entire first week of the term "for the consideration of the pending petitions for *certiorari*." [19] Here then are the seeds of competition between the task of deciding cases and the necessity of disposing of petitions for *certiorari*.

Undoubtedly, the 1925 Act has relieved the Court of some needless burdens for the more effective discharge of its great duties. No less true is it that the enlargement of the area of discretionary

---

[18] See Mr. Justice Van Devanter in Hearing before a Subcommittee of the Committee on the Judiciary, U. S. Senate, 68th Cong. 1st Sess., on S. 2060 and S. 2061, Feb. 2, 1924, at 29.

[19] N. Y. Times, Oct. 2, 1928, at 53.

TABLE IV

MODE OF ARRIVAL

	1923	*1924*	*1925*	*1926*	*1927*	*Total*
DISTRICT COURTS						
Appeal	75	64	56	74	19	288
Error	16	38	22	23	1	100
CIRCUIT COURTS OF APPEALS						
Appeal	27	20	31	13	2	93
Error	18	10	10	4	2	44
Certiorari	53	42	33	59	108	295
Certificate	5	10	9	8	11	43
HIGHEST STATE COURTS						
Appeal	0	0	0	0	2	2
Error	77	100	75	108	123	483
Certiorari	17	19	25	16	35	112
COURT OF APPEALS, DISTRICT OF COLUMBIA						
Appeal	5	8	26	7	0	46
Error	4	2	1	2	0	9
Certiorari	0	1	1	2	4	8
Certificate	1	4	0	1	1	7
COURT OF CLAIMS						
Appeal	18	33	52	20	5	128
Error	0	1	0	0	0	1
Certiorari	0	0	1	7	9	17
COURT OF CUSTOMS APPEALS						
Certiorari	0	1	0	1	2	4
PHILIPPINE SUPREME COURT						
Certiorari	1	0	2	3	3	9
Total	317	353	344	348	327	1689

TABLE V

Petitions for Certiorari *

	1923	*1924*	*1925*	*1926*	*1927*	*Total*
Granted	69	63	98	117	102	449
Denied	291	352	423	458	468	1992
Quashed	4	1	0	0	0	5
Denied for Failure to File in Time	3	4	0	1	1	9
Denied on Motion	14	4	7	6	6	37
Dismissed per Stipulation	3	2	3	2	1	11
Dismissed for Failure to Prosecute	0	4	0	0	0	4
Dismissed Pursuant to Rules of Court	4	4	0	0	5	13
Denied for Lack of Jurisdiction	1	0	1	0	0	2
Dismissed on Authorities Cited	0	0	1	0	0	1
Revocation of Prior Grant of Writ	0	0	2	1	4	7
Stricken from Files	0	0	0	1	0	1
Total	**389**	**434**	**535**	**586**	**587**	**2531**

TABLE VI

Appellate Business Finally Disposed Of

	1923	*1924*	*1925*	*1926*	*1927*	*Total*
Cases Disposed of with Consideration	317	353	344	348	327	1689
Cases Disposed of without Consideration	37	58	71	67	32	265
Petitions for Certiorari Denied and Dismissed	320	371	437	469	485	2082
Total	**674**	**782**	**852**	**884**	**844**	**4036**

* Exclusive of writs of error treated as petitions for *certiorari* under the provisions of the Act of Feb. 13, 1925, of petitions for *certiorari* disposed of by full opinion of the court, and of petitions for *certiorari* granted to enable reversal of a case without consideration. The disposition of these petitions has been excluded from this table in order to prevent duplication in the statistics relating to the disposition of cases.

jurisdiction opened the door to new difficulties. *Certioraris* have been granted sparingly enough — 102 out of 587 petitions is a fair index to the present law of probabilities governing this exercise of the Supreme Court's discretion. The greater the denials the less the load of adjudication. This is one way of relief. But the whole operation of the device of *certiorari* will be seriously affected if selection is determined not by the intrinsic importance of legal issues but by the arbitrary exactions of the size of the docket. Again, increase in petitions for *certioraris* may suggest other methods for their disposition than the present collective deliberation by the Court. It is inconceivable that the Court itself will ever accede to such a departure from the traditional habits of its judicial process. The Court, we may be confident, will not diminish the greatest source of its strength. But one thing is clear. If the present scope of the jurisdiction of the federal courts continues,[20] a steady increase in the present volume of litigation at Washington must be expected. Before long the dockets of the Supreme Court will again show signs of congestion, and the conditions under which the Court does business will once more call for relief.

Thus far the 1925 Act has enabled the Court to gain upon its arrears. Not for a hundred years has the Court reached for argument on the regular calendar cases docketed during the term. Last term it achieved this dispatch in its business.[21] When the Court rose last June only 190 cases were undisposed of as against 295 at the close of the preceding term.[22] This has recently led Mr. Justice Stone to express the hope that "by the end of another term the Court may be able to hear cases on their merits as soon after they are docketed as counsel are prepared to present

---

20 See Frankfurter, *Distribution of Judicial Power between United States and State Courts* (1928) 13 CORN. L. Q. 499.

21 The Supreme Court has demonstrated that the expedition of criminal appeals — so important an element in the efficacy of criminal justice — is largely within the control of courts. By its order of June 1, 1926, it advanced of its own motion the criminal cases on its docket and set them for hearing at the earliest opportunity. (1925) SUP. CT. J. 326. The automatic advancing of criminal cases upon the Court docket is now its established practice and they are promptly disposed of.

22 Stone, *Fifty Years' Work of the United States Supreme Court* (1928) 14 A. B. A. J. 428, 435.

them."[23] The vindication of this hope will depend on the volume of business that may in the future arise in the lower federal courts, upon the stream of *certioraris,* and the extent to which non-federal questions will remain open for review before the Supreme Court.[24]

A survey of the Court's work makes abundantly clear that opinions only in part tell the story of its labors. Nevertheless, the most enduring and interesting activity of the Court is expressed through its opinions. Having noted a diminution in the number of adjudicated cases since the Act of 1925, we are prepared to find a decrease in opinions. Their distribution among the members of the Court is happily not determined by a mechanical rule in their assignment, as is the case in some state courts. Here again considerations of individualization are operative. The complexity and bulk of the record, specialized equipment in certain fields of the law, and the burden of judicial administration are all factors which determine the nature and the volume of cases assigned to individual Justices and account for the differences set forth in Table VII in the number of opinions rendered by members of the Court.

The expression of dissents began with the first opinion of the Court,[25] and its practice may well be characterized as one of the settled traditions of the Court. Dissenting opinions have been among the most important influences in the development of our constitutional law.[26] Dissents prevent undue or premature generalizations of specific instances into rigid doctrine. The more constitutional adjudications turn upon judgment upon social and economic data, the more will they provoke differences of opinion among members of the Court. The last five terms reflect a rise in dissents and an increase in their expression. Dissents entail as

---

[23] *Ibid.*

[24] See *supra* note 12.

[25] Georgia v. Braislford, 2 Dall. 402 (U. S. 1792), 2 Dall. 415 (U. S. 1793).

[26] See HUGHES, THE SUPREME COURT OF THE UNITED STATES (1928) 67–70. "I am of the opinion," wrote Mr. Justice Story, in Briscoe v. Bank of Kentucky, 11 Pet. 257, 350 (U. S. 1837), "that upon Constitutional questions, the public have a right to know the opinion of every judge who dissents from the opinion of the court, and the reasons of his dissent." In Rhode Island v. Massachusetts, 12 Pet. 657, 752 (U. S. 1838), Chief Justice Taney wrote: "It has, I find, been the uniform practice in this Court, for the justices who differed from the Court on constitutional questions, to express their dissent."

TABLE VII

Distribution of Opinions

	1923	*1924*	*1925*	*1926*	*1927*	*Total*
	Opinions of the Court					
Taft	35	33	37	31	23	159
McKenna	17	4	0	0	0	21
Holmes	27	33	24	25	21*	130
Van Devanter	21	12	17	10	8	68
McReynolds	17	33	20	23	22*	115
Brandeis	25	31	27	23	24	130
Sutherland	25	27	17	20	9	98
Butler	25	24	26	21	22	118
Sanford	20	24	20	16	22	102
Stone	0	11	21	30	24	86
Total	**212**	**232**	**209**	**199**	**175**	**1027**
	Concurring Opinions					
Taft	1	0	0	0	0	1
McKenna	1	0	0	0	0	1
Holmes	0	0	0	0	0	0
Van Devanter	0	0	0	0	0	0
McReynolds	0	0	0	1	0	1
Brandeis	0	0	0	3	1	4
Sutherland	0	0	0	0	0	0
Butler	0	0	0	1	0	1
Sanford	0	0	0	0	0	0
Stone	0	0	0	2	1	3
Total	**2**	**0**	**0**	**7**	**2**	**11**
	Dissenting Opinions					
Taft	0	0	0	0	0	0
McKenna	1	0	0	0	0	1
Holmes	1	2	3	3	10	19
Van Devanter	1	0	0	0	0	1
McReynolds	3	7	5	3	3	21

* Including the opinion of four Justices in a divided court.

TABLE VII (*continued*)

	1923	*1924*	*1925*	*1926*	*1927*	*Total*
Brandeis	5	1	2	8	9	25
Sutherland	2	2	0	2	1	7
Butler	0	1	0	1	3	5
Sanford	0	0	0	1	0	1
Stone	0	0	1	3	5	9
Total	**13**	**13**	**11**	**21**	**31**	**89**

Total Opinions Delivered

	1923	*1924*	*1925*	*1926*	*1927*	*Total*
Taft	36	33	37	31	23	160
McKenna	19	4	0	0	0	23
Holmes	28	35	27	28	31	149
Van Devanter	22	12	17	10	8	69
McReynolds	20	40	25	27	25	137
Brandeis	30	32	29	34	34	159
Sutherland	27	29	17	22	10	105
Butler	25	25	26	23	25	124
Sanford	20	24	20	17	22	103
Stone	0	11	22	35	30	98
Total	**227**	**245**	**220**	**227**	**208**	**1127**

Dissenting Votes

	1923	*1924*	*1925*	*1926*	*1927*	*Total*
Taft	1	5	0	2	0	8
McKenna	4	1	0	0	0	5
Holmes	7	2	3	10 †	20	42
Van Devanter	2	2	1	2	0	7
McReynolds	13	12	11	11	10	57
Brandeis	13	6	9	14 †	17	59
Sutherland	2	8	4	8	7	29
Butler	3	3	1	9	5	21
Sanford	2	3	3	3	7	18
Stone	0	0	4	10 †	16	30
Total	**47**	**42**	**36**	**69**	**82**	**276**

† Including one "opinion dubitante."

much labor as majority opinions. They constitute a burden in addition to the average quota of opinions written by the individual Justice. A wise determination of the Court's jurisdiction ought to assure its members ample time for adequate expression of dissents, no less than for careful preparation of the Court's opinions.

2

The history of the Supreme Court since the Civil War shows a steady atrophy of ordinary private litigation and growing preoccupation by the Court with public law. In freeing the Court for litigation of national and public importance, the Act of 1925 furthered that tendency. When the Act of 1925 was passed, common law controversies constituted about five per cent of the Court's business,[27] and Table VIII indicates that the amount of common law litigation appears to be stabilizing at that ratio. Although the increased rôle played by *certiorari* has greatly enlarged the Court's power of preventing cases without a real public interest from reaching it, in several instances during the last term the Court assumed jurisdiction in cases where a public or general interest is hardly discernible. Special mention may be made of several cases under the Federal Employers' Liability Act presenting unique circumstances for decision rather than occasions for the formulation of general rules.[28]

Issues of public law, then, constitute the stuff of Supreme Court litigation. But the conflicts which they engender are due far less to differences over abstract principles than to disagreements in the application of recognized doctrine to the complex problems of modern industrial society. Differences of degree become more and more the vital differences. And a perception of these differences depends on familiarity with social and economic details and an understanding of their significance. What led the Supreme Court to sustain the Packers and Stockyards Act of 1921 was not any technical interpretation of the Commerce Clause but a vivid

[27] FRANKFURTER AND LANDIS, *op. cit. supra* note 5, at 306.

[28] *E.g.*, Atlantic Coast Line R. R. v. Southwell, 275 U. S. 64 (1927); Missouri Pac. R. R. v. Aeby, 275 U. S. 426 (1928); Gulf, M. & N. R. R. v. Wells, 275 U. S. 455 (1928); Toledo, St. Louis & Western R. R. v. Allen, 276 U. S. 165 (1928). See also Book Review (1928) 28 COL. L. REV. 516, n.4.

realization of the rôle played by the stockyards "as great national public utilities to promote the flow of commerce from the ranges and farms of the West to the consumers in the East." [29] And so again, Congress was justified in the novel provisions for the recapture of railroad earnings not by any abstruse legal dialectic but by due regard to the concrete consideration of railroad economics which the experience of the World War wrote into the Transportation Act of 1920.[30] Explicitly or implicitly, considerations of a like nature determine judgment upon legislation affecting economic enterprise through direct limitations upon the conduct of business or its indirect control through taxation. And this is true whether the controversies involve the determination of state powers under the Fourteenth Amendment or the eternal adjustments of authority under the Commerce Clause between the Federal Government and the states. In passing upon zoning laws, in sanctioning or disallowing "yellow dog contracts," in formulating the bases for rate fixing, the process of adjudication necessarily implies judgment upon the economic and social considerations from which such policies derive. The validity of the judgment made will therefore depend upon the adequacy and relevance of the extra-legal data upon which it ultimately rests.

A technique which will assure the effective presentation of these determining issues of fact becomes thus a matter of crucial importance in the administration of American public law. Since these adjudications turn so largely on the particularities of fact in individual cases, the specific circumstances should be established decisively by the record before the Court and not be shrouded in ambiguity or left to speculation. Otherwise, the Court will be driven to hypothetical judgments and moot decisions. Adherence to the traditional considerations against intruding into controversies regarding political power, whether as between the different departments of the Federal Government or as between the Federal Government and the states, becomes the more vital since the demarcation of power may depend upon minor variations of fact in individual cases. Unless adequate provision be made for the

---

[29] Stafford v. Wallace, 258 U. S. 495, 516 (1922).

[30] Dayton-Goose Creek Ry. v. United States, 263 U. S. 456 (1924).

TABLE VIII

SUBJECT MATTER OF OPINIONS

	1923	*1924*	*1925*	*1926*	*1927*	*Total*
Admiralty	6	11	8	7	12	44
Antitrust Laws	5	7	2	13	1	28
Bankruptcy	9	10	9	1	7	36
Bill of Rights (other than Due Process)	7	10	3	11	7	38
Commerce Clause						
1. Constitutionality of Federal Regulation	2	2	2	1	2	9
2. Constitutionality of State Regulation	3	7	2	10	6	28
3. Construction of Federal Regulation						
a. General	21	20	24	9	8	82
b. Federal Employers' Liability Act	3	5	5	0	11	24
Common Law Topics	9	8	11	8	11	47
Construction of Miscellaneous Statutes						
1. Federal	22	19	15	23	11	90
2. State	2	0	0	1	2	5
3. Territorial	1	4	0	3	0	8

TABLE VIII (*continued*)

	1923	*1924*	*1925*	*1926*	*1927*	*Total*
Due Process						
1. Regulation of Economic Enterprise	17	12	20	21	13	83
2. Relating to Procedure	1	5	3	4	4	17
3. Relating to Liberties of the Individual Citizen	4	2	0	7	1	14
Impairment of Contract	3	1	4	1	2	11
Indians	3	4	7	1	4	19
International Law	2	3	6	5	0	16
Jurisdiction, Practice and Procedure						
1. Supreme Court	12	10	9	8	8	47
2. Inferior Courts	23	23	20	19	18	103
Land Laws	6	8	3	3	3	23
Patents and Trademarks	10	1	4	4	4	23
Separation of Powers	1	1	0	2	2	6
Suits Against Government in Contract	6	24	17	10	2	59
Suits by States	6	3	8	2	2	21
Taxation						
1. Federal	9	19	19	13	20	80
2. State	18	13	8	12	13	64
3. Territorial	1	0	0	0	0	1
Total	**212**	**232**	**209**	**199**	**174**	**1026**

ascertainment of these controlling details, issues of gravest public concern may be determined in violation of the root principle of American constitutional theory, to wit, that the Supreme Court decides cases and does not announce abstract policy.

The dependence on fact in modern Supreme Court litigation was strikingly illustrated in two cases at the last term of the Court.[31] They involved perplexing problems of control over motor bus lines. Abstractly, the legal questions concerned limitations imposed by the Commerce Clause upon the state's power to regulate traffic and promote safety, but the decision turned on the particular traffic conditions and transportation facilities in the city of Hammond, Indiana. The record in these cases, however, failed to furnish the necessary light upon these decisive circumstances. In this state of the record, the Supreme Court found itself unable to decide the legal questions argued before it, and remanded the cases to the lower court for determination of the facts essential to their decision:

> "These questions have not, so far as appears, been considered by either of the lower courts. The facts essential to their determination have not been found by either court. And the evidence in the record is not of such a character that findings could now be made with confidence. The answer denied many of the material allegations of the bill. The evidence consists of the pleadings and affidavits. The pleadings are confusing. The affidavits are silent as to some facts of legal significance; lack definiteness as to some matters; and present serious conflicts on issues of facts that may be decisive. For aught that appears, the lower courts may have differed in their decisions solely because they differed as to conclusions of fact. Before any of the questions suggested, which are both novel and of far reaching importance, are passed upon by this Court, the facts essential to their decision should be definitely found by the lower courts upon adequate evidence." [32]

The *Hammond* cases indicate forcibly the burden cast upon the Court in searching the record for proof of facts underlying legal issues. The Supreme Court should be free from such tasks. Lower courts ought to be required to report findings of those facts which determine Supreme Court decisions. Such findings are

---

[31] Hammond v. Schappi Bus Line, Inc., 275 U. S. 164 (1927); Hammond v. Farina Bus Line & Co., 275 U. S. 173 (1927).

[32] Hammond v. Schappi Bus Line, Inc., 275 U. S. 164, 171 (1927).

demanded by the whole range of public law litigation — the review of rate regulation, the respective fields of control over interstate commerce, the various instances of state legislation challenged under the Fourteenth Amendment. It is not for the Supreme Court to disentangle confused testimony, nor for a Court charged with keeping our constitutional system in equilibrium to pass upon disputation over evidence. The credibility of witnesses, the reconciliation of conflicting testimony, the proof of economic data, and the reliability of experts are problems with which, as a rule, the Supreme Court ought not to be inflicted.[33] Carefully framed findings by the lower courts should serve as the foundation for review, leaving for the Supreme Court the ascertainment of principles governing authenticated facts, the accommodation between conflicting principles, and the adaptation of old principles to new situations. The mechanism for review of decisions of the Court of Claims and of common law actions tried without a jury should be generally adapted to cases coming from the federal courts, whether arising in equity or at law.[34]

The Supreme Court is equally dependent upon the thoroughness with which issues are sifted and explored before they reach the Court. In this process, the opinions below play an important rôle. They compel analysis and formulation of the issues in a controversy, sharpen responsibility in adjudication, and advise litigants and the appellate court of the factors that control decision. Only by such a process is the controversy adequately focussed for the consideration of the Supreme Court. Opinions by the lower courts are therefore indispensable for the adequate exercise by the Supreme Court of its *reviewing* function. Without them, as the Supreme Court has remarked on several occasions during the last two terms,[35] "the appellate court is denied an important aid in the consideration of the case; and the defeated party is often unable to determine whether the case presents a question worthy of consideration by the appellate court. Thus,

[33] FRANKFURTER AND LANDIS, *op. cit. supra* note 5, at 290.

[34] *Id.* at 291, notes 134–35.

[35] Cleveland, etc. Ry. v. United States, 275 U. S. 404, 414 (1928); Virginian Ry. v. United States, 272 U. S. 658, 674 (1926). *Cf.* Lawrence v. St. Louis-San Francisco Ry., 274 U. S. 588 (1927); Arkansas R. R. Comm. v. Chicago, R. I. & Pac. R. R., 274 U. S. 597 (1927); Hammond v. Schappi Bus Line Co., Inc., 275 U. S. 164 (1927); Hammond v. Farina Bus Line & Co., 275 U. S. 173 (1927).

both the litigants and this court are subjected to unnecessary labor." [36]

Furthermore, as the questions coming before the Court are "rooted in history and in the social and economic development of the nation," [37] the Court requires aid from counsel for a full presentation of the issues in the light of their political and social history.[38] The determination of the scope of the President's power of removal, in the famous *Myers* case, compelled an investigation into practices and opinions since the foundation of our government.[39] The constitutionality of legislation such as the New Jersey Employment Agency Act, considered at the last term of Court, cannot fairly be determined without regard to the voluminous data set forth in Mr. Justice Stone's dissenting opinion.[40] Their ascertainment, however, involves laborious research which counsel should supply. If the task of independent inquiry is left to the Court, only in relatively few cases will time permit its adequate pursuit. There is thus real danger that constitutional adjudications will be determined by abstractions or jejune generalizations on obsolete data. No longer does the Supreme Court possess a specialized bar of constitutional lawyers. But the character of its business requires a bar fully equipped to deal with the social and economic implications of the issues presented by modern Supreme Court litigation.

3

Judiciary acts have always required clarification through litigation, and the Act of 1925 has not proved an exception. The Supreme Court has been called upon to remove doubts and resolve ambiguities. In so doing it has determined the ambit of its jurisdiction, and thereby influenced the volume of its future litigation. In four cases [41] the Court construed the amendment to

[36] Cleveland, etc. Ry. v. United States, 275 U. S. 404, 414 (1928).

[37] Stone, *supra* note 22, at 435.

[38] FRANKFURTER AND LANDIS, *op. cit. supra* note 5, at 312–17.

[39] Myers v. United States, 272 U. S. 52 (1926).

[40] Ribnik v. McBride, 48 Sup. Ct. 545, 548–52 (U. S. 1928).

[41] *Ex parte* Buder, 271 U. S. 461 (1926); Moore v. Fidelity & Deposit Co., 272 U. S. 317 (1926); Smith v. Wilson, 273 U. S. 388 (1927); Board of Pub. Util. Comm'rs v. Middlesex Water Co., 275 U. S. 483 (1927).

Section 266 of the Judicial Code,[42] whereby the provision for a hearing before three judges in suits for an interlocutory injunction against the enforcement of state statutes or administrative orders was extended to apply " to the final hearing in such suit in the district court; and a direct appeal to the Supreme Court may be taken from a final decree granting or denying a permanent injunction in such suits." The Court had to decide " whether the phrase ' such suit ' was intended to refer only to a suit in which a preliminary injunction had in fact been sought or to a suit in which an application for such an interlocutory injunction might have been but in fact was not made." [43] In deciding that the Act did not " extend the application of the section with respect to the requirement of three judges or the right of direct appeal to any case in which an interlocutory injunction is not sought," the Court placed reliance on the fact that " the general purpose of the Act of February 13, 1925, was to relieve this Court by restricting the right to a review by it." [44]

These four decisions indicated that the Supreme Court would, when free to do so, deny obligatory jurisdiction. But in *King Manufacturing Co. v. City Council of Augusta* [45] it rejected an opportunity for realizing this purpose by a restrictive interpretation, which, as the minority forcibly contended, was supported by history and precedent. Prior to the Act of 1925, Section 237 of the Judicial Code allowed review on writ of error of judgments of state courts

> " where is drawn in question the validity of a statute of, or an authority exercised under any State, on the ground of their being repugnant to the Constitutions, treaties, or laws of the United States, and the decision is in favor of their validity. . . ." [46]

That Act struck from this section the words " or an authority exercised under any State." In the *King* case the challenge was to the validity of a city ordinance, and the question before the Court was whether such a case could come to the Court as a matter of right or only by grace through *certiorari*. More specifically, the Court had to determine whether a city ordinance was included in the phrase " statute of any State." In holding

[42] Now 28 U. S. C. § 380 (1926).

[43] Smith v. Wilson, 273 U. S. 388, 390 (1927).

[44] *Ibid.*

[45] 48 Sup. Ct. 489 (U. S. 1928).

[46] Act of Sept. 6, 1916, § 2, 39 STAT. 726.

that it was, the Court has opened the door to obligatory review in every case involving an attack upon an ordinance from the thousand municipalities throughout the country. The dissenting opinion of Mr. Justice Brandeis persuasively maintained that prior to the Act of 1925 the Court founded its jurisdiction in such cases on the fact that a municipal ordinance was " an authority exercised under any State," and not on the identification of such subordinate law making with a " statute of any State." The elimination of " an authority exercised under any State " in 1925 as a basis for obligatory jurisdiction transferred reviews affecting city ordinances to discretionary jurisdiction. And the dissenting opinion thus stated the reasons of policy that justified withdrawal of the right to review in such cases:

" When it is borne in mind that the severe limitations upon the right of review by this court imposed by the act of 1925 were made solely because the increase of the court's business compelled, the reasons why Congress should have taken away the right to a review by writ of error to the highest court of a state in cases involving the validity of ordinances, while leaving unaffected the right in cases involving the validity of statutes, becomes clear. There are only 48 states. In 1920 there were 924 municipalities in the United States of more than 8,000 inhabitants. The validity of ordinances of even smaller municipalities had come to this court for adjudication. The increasingly complex conditions of urban life have led, as this court noted in Village of Euclid v. Ambler Realty Co. 272 U. S. 365, 386, 387, 47 S. Ct. 114, 71 L. Ed. 303, to a corresponding increase in municipal police legislation. Recently, two classes of municipal ordinances, new in character — those relating to zoning and those relating to motor vehicles — had become the subject of many controversies. The constitutionality of these ordinances can rarely be determined simply by applying a general rule. The court must consider the effect of the ordinance as applied. As the validity of the particular ordinance depends ordinarily upon special facts, these must be examined whenever there is jurisdiction. Dahnke-Walker Milling Co. v. Bondurant, 257 U. S. 282, 42 S. Ct. 106, 66 L. Ed. 239. Though no burdensome factual inquiry is involved, the controversy may often be of trifling significance, as in the case at bar. Thus, persuasive reasons existed why Congress should have denied, in 1925, review by writ of error in cases which involved only the validity of a municipal ordinance." [47]

[47] King Mfg. Co. v. City Council of Augusta, 48 Sup. Ct. 489, 499 (U. S. 1928).

Three weeks later, in *Ex parte Collins*,[48] the Court had before it a cognate question of jurisdiction. It was called upon to decide whether a suit to enjoin the enforcement of a municipal ordinance is one to restrain "the enforcement . . . of any statute of a State" within the meaning of Section 266 of the Judicial Code. The Court unanimously held that the phrase applied only to the enforcement of a statute within the conventional meaning of the term, that is, an enactment of the state legislature.

The two decisions in combination create a further jurisdictional problem for the Court. Review in a case like *Ex parte Collins* cannot be taken directly from the district court to the Supreme Court inasmuch as it does not involve "a statute of a State." But after an adverse decision by a circuit court of appeals it may apparently be reviewed as a matter of right by the Supreme Court as a case "where is drawn in question the validity of a statute of any State . . . and the decision is against its validity."[49] For it is hardly conceivable that a municipal ordinance is a "statute of any State" within section 237(b) but not a "statute of any State" under section 240(b) of the same Act.[50]

A final change affecting the jurisdiction of the Supreme Court remains to be noticed. Professing to simplify the appellate procedure of the Supreme Court, Congress by Act of January 31, 1928,[51] abolished writs of error except in cases coming from the state courts. On April 26, 1928, this Act had to be amended.[52] The history of the original enactment and its amendment ought to serve as a warning on how not to legislate. Here was a reversal of methods of review which had prevailed since 1789. One would suppose that the reasons for such change would be clearly defined and the consequences of the change thoroughly explored. The fact is that the origin and the purposes of the Act of January 31, 1928, are shrouded in confusion and its implications appear hardly to have been canvassed.[53] Apparently the Act had its ori-

---

48 48 Sup. Ct. 585 (U. S. 1928).

49 Section 240(b), JUDICIAL CODE, 28 U. S. C. 347(b) (1926).

50 The language in Section 240(b), which was a Senate amendment to the Judges' Bill, was obviously taken from that employed in Section 237(b).

51 28 U. S. C. A. §§ 861(a), 861(b) (1928). See (1928) 41 HARV. L. REV. 673.

52 28 U. S. C. A. § 861(b) (1928).

53 The full history of the Act is set forth in (1928) 41 HARV. L. REV. 673.

gin with the American Bar Association. That body in 1921 proposed legislation with a view to eliminating the mishaps due to pursuing the wrong method of review in the Supreme Court.[54] The evil, however, had previously been remedied by allowing writs of error and appeals to serve interchangeably and to permit a writ of error to be treated as a petition for *certiorari*.[55] But the American Bar Association continued to urge legislation which, in substance, had been achieved. In passing the Act of January 31, 1928, Congress registered what it believed to be the desire of the American Bar Association on a technical matter and exercised practically no independent judgment.[56] It overlooked, too, its own legislation of 1922 and 1925. Not only was the new legislation redundant and empty; it was mischievous.[57] For no safeguards were provided in granting an appeal, no provision made against its abuse, and the usual conditions governing its allowance were neglected.[58] Plainly, the Supreme Court could have had nothing to do with the promotion of this legislation. But the Court promptly became aware of its difficulties and urged upon

[54] 46 A. B. A. REP. (1921) 387–88, 396. "In 1922 a bill passed the Senate similar to the one enacted, except that amendments were adopted omitting the proviso as to state courts, and inserting a provision for security as under the former practice with writs of error. 62 CONG. REC. 12, 298. The bill in one or the other of these forms was recommended each year thereafter by the American Bar Association. 47 A. B. A. REP. (1922) 356; 48 *ibid.* (1923) 332, 336; 49 *ibid.* (1924) 341; 50 *ibid.* (1925) 409–10; 51 *ibid.* (1926) 430; 52 *ibid.* (1927) 308." (1928) 41 HARV. L. REV. 673.

[55] Act of Sept. 6, 1916, 39 STAT. 726–27; Act of Feb. 13, 1925, 43 STAT. 936–37.

[56] The bill passed both Houses of Congress without debate. See (1928) 41 HARV. L. REV. 673.

[57] Referring to the effect of the Act of Jan. 31, 1928, Mr. Graham from the committee said: "It would appear, and an instance of it has already transpired, that this section would create such a loose method of practice with regard to cases in which the writ of error is abolished that there is great necessity for remedial legislation limiting the freedom with which appeals can be taken and restoring those safeguards which surrounded the granting of the writ of error and protected it from abuse." H. R. REP. No. 1071, 70th Cong. 1st Sess., Mar. 28, 1928.

[58] Section 2 of the Act provided "that the review of judgments of State courts of last resort shall be petitioned for and allowed in the same form as now provided by law for writs of error to such courts." It is significant of the slipshod method in which this Act and the amendatory Act were hurried through Congress that the report of the Judiciary Committee of the House of Representatives in recommending the passage of the amendatory Act, purports to quote Section 2 of the earlier Act, but its quotation omits any reference to this proviso. No reference to it can be found in the debates in either house. *Ibid.*

Congress their correction.[59] By the Act of April 26, 1928 the protective provisions governing review prior to the abolition of writs of error were restored.

The total effect of this legislation is that the writ of error has ceased to be one of the descriptions of review by the Supreme Court, and the term "appeal" is now applicable to what was heretofore either appeal or writ of error, but as a matter of substance the scope of review remains unaltered.[60] Though reviews will indiscriminately be called appeals, a differentiation must still be enforced by the Supreme Court between those cases which were traditionally reviewable by appeal and those traditionally reviewable by writ of error. In the former, facts were open for review, but not in the latter. That important distinction survives the simplification of nomenclature.

Felix Frankfurter.
James M. Landis.

HARVARD LAW SCHOOL.

---

59 "The chief justice and another member of the court" appeared before the Judiciary Committee of the House of Representatives and "approved of the amendment." *Ibid.*

60 Following the passage of these Acts, the Supreme Court on June 5, 1928, revised its rules of practice. It substituted the expression "appeal," "appellant," and "appellee" wherever the former rules used the terms "writ of error," "plaintiff in error," and "defendant in error." By Rule 46 it specifically stated that appeals in equity were not affected by the recent legislation but were governed by the statutes formerly in force. It confirmed the fact that the change effected by this legislation was simply a change in nomenclature, by requiring a petition, its accompaniment by an assignment of error, its allowance by the appropriate judge or justice, and the taking of adequate security, the traditional incidents in the allowance of a writ of error. 275 U. S. 595, 630 (1928).

WILLIAM E. LEUCHTENBURG

THE ORIGINS OF FRANKLIN D. ROOSEVELT'S "COURT-PACKING" PLAN

No event of twentieth-century American constitutional history is better remembered than Franklin D. Roosevelt's ill-fated "Court-packing" scheme of 1937; yet the origins of the plan remain obscure and often misstated. The proposal has been variously attributed to Felix Frankfurter, who abhorred it; to Benjamin Cohen and Thomas Corcoran, who favored a different remedy and had no hand in shaping this one; and to Samuel I. Rosenman, who played only a minor role after the decision had already been made.[1] Among those who have been said to have helped frame the plan were James M. Landis, who had heard only rumors of it before it was announced, and Robert H. Jackson, who first learned of the President's plan when he read about it in a Philadelphia newspaper.[2]

William E. Leuchtenburg is Professor of History, Columbia University.

[1] Mallon, *Purely Confidential*, Detroit News, Feb. 8, Apr. 2, May 21, 1937; MASON, BRANDEIS: A FREE MAN'S LIFE 625 (1946); MOLEY, AFTER SEVEN YEARS 357–59 (1939) (hereinafter MOLEY); Raymond Clapper MS Diary, Feb. 8, 1937, Clapper MSS, Library of Congress (hereinafter LC); 7 Frances Perkins, Columbia Oral History Collection 128 (hereinafter COHC); Washington Post, Feb. 13, 1937. Of Frankfurter, James M. Landis recalled that he "caught hell from him" for supporting the plan. Landis, COHC 49, 302. See, too, Clapper MS Diary, Sept. 28, 1938; Frank Buxton to William Allen White, June 2, 1937, White MSS, LC, Box 189.

[2] Mallon, *Purely Confidential*, Detroit News, Apr. 2, 1937; Landis, COHC 44–45; MICHELSON, THE GHOST TALKS 169–70 (1944); GERHART, AMERICA'S ADVOCATE: ROBERT H. JACKSON 105 (1958).

The project has been described either as an impulsive act born of the *hubris* created by FDR's landslide victory in 1936 or as a calculated plot hatched many months before in angry resentment at the *Schechter* verdict. Roosevelt himself never did anything to clear up the confusion. Three weeks after the President launched the proposal, Senator Hiram Johnson of California wrote a friend: "He has been beaten from pillar to post upon when he conceived the brilliant idea, and how he conceived it."[3]

I. Prologue

The constitutional crisis of 1937 had been brewing for a long time. Franklin Roosevelt began his political career at the time that his distant cousin Theodore was assaulting the sanctity of the courts and the air was loud with cries for the recall of judges and judicial decisions. In the 1920's there was mounting progressive animus toward the Taft Court manifested in such forms as the La Follette platform of 1924, which called for empowering Congress to override the Supreme Court. In the Hoover years, progressives had waged fierce contests against the confirmations of John J. Parker and Charles Evans Hughes. Increasingly, liberal critics of the Court believed that a majority of the Justices spoke for the interests of the rich and well-born.[4]

Even before Roosevelt took office, he had aroused speculation over whether his presidency would result in a confrontation with the Supreme Court. In a campaign speech in Baltimore on October 5, 1932, Roosevelt blurted out: "After March 4, 1929, the Republican party was in complete control of all branches of the government—the Legislature, with the Senate and Congress; and the executive departments; and I may add, for full measure, to make it complete, the United States Supreme Court as well."[5] This statement had been interpolated in the original text of the address, but the next day, Roosevelt told Senator James F. Byrnes: "What I said last night about the judiciary is true, and whatever is in a man's

---

[3] Johnson to John Francis Neylan, Feb. 26, 1937, Johnson MSS, Bancroft Library, University of California, Berkeley.

[4] St. Louis Star, June 23, 1930, clipping, Pierce Butler MSS, Minnesota Historical Society, St. Paul; 2 Pusey, Charles Evans Hughes 655–62 (1951).

[5] 1 Franklin D. Roosevelt, Public Papers and Addresses 837 (1938) (hereinafter Public Papers).

heart is apt to come to his tongue—I shall not make any explanations or apology for it!"[6] Republicans hopped on Roosevelt's statement as a warning that, if elected President, he might, in Herbert Hoover's words, "reduce the tribunal to an instrument of party policy."[7]

Roosevelt, who was right in thinking that the composition of the federal courts was heavily Republican,[8] found an even greater source of concern in the doctrines pronounced by the Court in such recent decisions as that in the *Oklahoma Ice* case.[9] The New Dealers recognized that much that they proposed to do would be invalidated by the Court if it followed the line of reasoning adopted by the Taft Court, but they hoped that the Court would recognize the depression to be an emergency justifying unprecedented government action. In his inaugural address on March 4, 1933, the new president stated: "Our Constitution is so simple and practical that it is possible always to meet extraordinary needs by changes in emphasis and arrangement without loss of essential form."[10]

Yet Roosevelt was wary of relying on the tolerance of the Court for New Deal experiments. The Administration deliberately postponed tests of the constitutionality of the legislation of the Hundred Days as long as possible; the Supreme Court did not have the opportunity to rule on a New Deal statute until 1935. Meanwhile, the New Dealers were heartened by two 1934 opinions which appeared to recognize that the emergency might be the occasion for governmental restrictions on property rights.[11] Especially encouraging was Justice Roberts' statement in the *Nebbia* case: "[T]his court from the early days affirmed that the power to promote the general welfare is inherent in government."[12]

---

[6] BYRNES, ALL IN ONE LIFETIME 65 (1958).

[7] N.Y. Times, Feb. 11, 1937.

[8] In the autumn of 1933, Roosevelt's Attorney General sent him a memorandum noting that of the 266 judges in the federal courts, only 28 per cent were Democrats. Homer Cummings to FDR, Nov. 8, 1933, Franklin D. Roosevelt Library, Hyde Park, N.Y. (henceforth cited as FDRL) OF 41, Box 114.

[9] New State Ice Co. v. Liebmann, 285 U.S. 262 (1932).

[10] 2 PUBLIC PAPERS 14–15.

[11] Home Building & Loan Ass'n v. Blaisdell, 290 U.S. 398 (1934); Nebbia v. New York, 291 U.S. 502 (1934).

[12] 291 U.S. at 524.

Such pronouncements served, for the moment, to dispel the conviction that a collision between Roosevelt and the Supreme Court was inevitable and that steps should be taken to reconstitute the Court, ideas that emerged remarkably early in the Roosevelt administration. Almost two years before the Court had invalidated the first New Deal law, an Illinois man wrote the President: "Sometimes I get thinking about the many millions who are unemployed, and I wonder if we really can get them back to work, and retain our social order. . . . If the Supreme Court's membership could be increased to twelve, without too much trouble, perhaps the Constitution would be found to be quite elastic."[13]

As early as January, 1934, the *Literary Digest* reported: "In the intimate Presidential circle the idea of reconstituting the Supreme Court has been considered. . . . In the conversation within the Roosevelt circle, a court of fifteen, instead of the present nine, has been mentioned."[14] The *Digest* added that the *Blaisdell* opinion, which appeared to indicate a liberal majority on the Court, had caused such talk among the New Dealers to subside. Yet conservatives remained uneasy. The following month, Henry Prather Fletcher, soon to be chosen Republican national chairman, wrote the columnist Mark Sullivan: "You seem to rely on the Courts for relief in the last analysis. Let us hope the Supreme Court will not bend before the storm—but even if it does not, it is the weakest of the three coordinate branches of the Government and an administration as fully in control as this one is can pack it as easily as an English Government can pack the House of Lords."[15]

II. Gold Clauses and Railroad Pensions

Early in 1935 the period of nervous calm was abruptly shattered. On January 7, 1935, in its first ruling on a New Deal law, the Court invalidated the "hot oil" provisions of the National Industrial Recovery Act.[16] The Republican New York *Herald-Tribune* commented:[17]

---

[13] John P. Byrne to FDR, Apr. 18, 1933, FDRL OF 41-A.

[14] *News and Comment from the National Capital,* 117 Literary Digest 10 (Jan. 20, 1934).

[15] Fletcher to Sullivan, Feb. 28, 1934, Fletcher MSS, LC, Box 16.

[16] Panama Refining Co. v. Ryan, 293 U.S. 388 (1935); Charles Fahy, COHC 148.

[17] *New Deal Meets Tests in Supreme Court,* 119 Literary Digest 5–6 (Jan. 19, 1935).

> In the skylarking days of 1933–34, the happy administrators of the New Deal brushed aside the Supreme Court as they brushed aside Congress and the Constitution.... The President paid perfunctory lip-service to the nation's charter of liberty. Behind the scene the whispers were loud enough to be beyond misunderstanding. Let the Supreme Court try to halt the march of the new order, according to F. D. R., an Act of Congress would be passed adding to its membership and packing it with enough Tugwellian jurists to overturn any conservative decision overnight.

Now, the *Tribune* exulted, the 8-to-1 decision had thrown "this revolutionary nonsense into the Potomac where it belongs."

In fact, the New Dealers took the "hot oil" decision in stride. Since the Court's objections had rested on procedural defects that could easily be corrected, the Administration was not greatly concerned by the judgment. Much more alarming were the series of tests of the constitutionality of gold legislation that were making their way relentlessly toward the Supreme Court. A ruling by the Court for the plaintiffs would deny Congress the right to regulate the currency at a time of national economic disaster and threatened financial chaos by increasing the country's debt by nearly $70 billion.[18] Washington officials, observed Arthur Krock, were more absorbed with the question of how the Court would decide than by any subject since the bank holiday of March, 1933. In contemplation of that opinion, cold shivers "chase up and down their spines when they waken in the night."[19]

At a cabinet meeting on January 11, 1935, Attorney General Homer Cummings reported on the gold clause cases, which he had just finished arguing. Secretary of the Interior Harold L. Ickes noted in his diary:[20]

> The Attorney General said that if the Court should decide against the Government in the gold certificate and Liberty Bond cases, the situation could be saved by Congress hurrying through a statute taking away from the citizens the right to sue the Government for the damages that they might claim by reason of having accepted payment in currency on bonds that, by their terms, were stated to be payable in gold....
>
> The Attorney General went so far as to say that if the Court

18 SCHLESINGER, THE POLITICS OF UPHEAVAL 255–56 (1960) (hereinafter SCHLESINGER).

19 N.Y. Times, Jan. 15, 1935.

20 1 SECRET DIARY OF HAROLD L. ICKES 273–74 (1953) (hereinafter ICKES).

> went against the Government, the number of justices should be increased at once so as to give a favorable majority. As a matter of fact, the President suggested this possibility to me during our interview on Thursday, and I told him that that is precisely what ought to be done. It wouldn't be the first time that the Supreme Court had been increased in size to meet a temporary emergency and it certainly would be justified in this case.

Many in the Administration had an almost apocalyptic sense of inevitable conflict. After the cabinet meeting on January 11, Ickes reported:[21]

> I told the President yesterday that only a few years ago I had predicted that sooner or later the Supreme Court would become a political issue as the result of its continued blocking of the popular will through declaring acts of Congress unconstitutional. During the discussion today the Vice President said that he had read a pamphlet which had been written about a hundred years ago in which the author advanced the theory that sooner or later, through the aggrandizement of power by the Supreme Court, a political crisis of major magnitude would be precipitated in this country.

Close observers anticipated that the President would not permit the Court to disrupt his attempts to achieve recovery, even if this led to a constitutional crisis. In his Kings Feature Syndicate column, Arthur Brisbane created a stir when he questioned whether there was any constitutional authority for the practice of judicial review. Brisbane wrote:[22]

> As a matter of constitutional law, as actually written by the constitutional convention, if the Supreme Court should say to the President of the United States "We find unconstitutional, and ask you to revoke, your law abolishing the gold clause," the President might reasonably reply, "I have your message and respectfully request that you show me what part of the Constitution authorizes you to nullify a law passed by the Congress of the United States and signed by the President."
>
> If he sent that message, the Supreme Court would be puzzled, for it could show nothing in the Constitution.

Roosevelt was, in fact, ready to act much as Brisbane suggested. A month earlier, in response to an inquiry from the President, Robert Jackson, general counsel of the Bureau of Internal Revenue,

---

21 *Id.* at 274.

22 Brisbane to FDR, Feb. 11, 1935, FDRL OF 41-A, Box 116.

had suggested that the government might withdraw its consent to be sued.[23] Accordingly, a message to Congress was drafted recommending the withdrawal of the right to sue the United States for more than the face value of government bonds and other obligations. In the event of an adverse decision, Roosevelt was ready with a proclamation of national emergency to regulate currency transactions; for ninety days, no payment on any contract would be permitted save at the rate of $35 for an ounce of gold, the rate fixed by the President on January 31, 1934, under authority of the Gold Reserve Act.[24]

If the Supreme Court ruled against the government, Roosevelt was prepared to deliver a defiant radio address in which he would declare that the decisions, if enforced, would result in "unconscionable" profit to investors, bankruptcy for almost every railroad and for many corporations, default by state and local governments, and wholesale mortgage foreclosures on farms and in cities. It would not only increase the national debt by a staggering sum but would catapult the nation "into an infinitely more serious economic plight than we have yet experienced."[25] He did not seek a quarrel with the Supreme Court, but he did think it appropriate to quote a sentence from Lincoln's First Inaugural Address: "At the same time, the candid citizen must confess that if the policy of the government, upon vital questions affecting the whole people, is to be irrevocably fixed by decisions of the Supreme Court, the instant they are made, in ordinary litigation between parties in personal actions, the people will have ceased to be their own rulers, having to that extent practically resigned their government into the hands of that eminent tribunal."

Neither the President nor Congress, Roosevelt planned to say, could "stand idly by and . . . permit the decision of the Supreme Court to be carried through to its logical, inescapable conclusion," because this would "imperil the economic and political security of this nation." He sought only to carry out the principle that "For value received the same value should be repaid," a doctrine "in accordance with the Golden Rule, with the precepts of the Scrip-

---

[23] Robert Jackson, COHC.

[24] 1 Blum, From the Morgenthau Diaries 126–27 (1959) (hereinafter Morgenthau).

[25] Draft of message, FDRL PSF Supreme Court.

tures, and the dictates of common sense." "In order to attain this reasonable end," the President intended to announce, "I shall immediately take such steps as may be necessary, by proclamation and by message to the Congress of the United States."

On February 18, as word reached the White House that the Court had assembled, Roosevelt took his place at the cabinet table to await word. Minutes later, the tension broke, as it became clear that in each of a series of cases, the government had won.[26] On the following day, the President sent a saucy note to Joseph P. Kennedy, chairman of the SEC:[27]

> With you I think Monday, February eighteenth, was an historic day. As a lawyer it seems to me that the Supreme Court has at last definitely put human values ahead of the "pound of flesh" called for by a contract.
>
> The Chairman of the Securities Exchange Commission turns out to be far more accurate than the Associated Press in that he reported the decisions accurately. How fortunate it is that his Exchanges will never know how close they came to being closed up by a stroke of the pen of one "J.P.K."
>
> Likewise, the Nation will never know what a great treat it missed in not hearing the marvelous radio address the "Pres" had prepared for delivery to the Nation Monday night if the cases had gone the other way.

Roosevelt could not have been pleased by the scolding he received from Chief Justice Hughes in the majority opinion, and he was aware that he had had a close call. "In spite of our rejoicing," he wrote, "I shudder at the closeness of five to four decisions in these important matters!"[28] Congressmen began to talk more seriously about the need to find some way to restrain the Court. Senator George Norris of Nebraska protested: "These five to four Supreme Court decisions on the constitutionality of congressional acts it seems to me are illogical and should not occur in a country like ours."[29] Yet, since the government had been upheld, most of the expressions of dissatisfaction came not from New Deal supporters but from the outraged conservatives, many of whom echoed

---

[26] Norman v. B. & O. R.R., 294 U.S. 240 (1935), and related cases; 1 MORGENTHAU 130.

[27] FDR to Kennedy, Feb. 19, 1935, 1 F.D.R.: HIS PERSONAL LETTERS 455 (1950) (hereinafter LETTERS).

[28] FDR to Angus MacLean, Feb. 21, 1935, FDRL OF 10-F.

[29] Norris to Layton Spicher, Mar. 29, 1935, Norris MSS, LC, Tray 27, Box 4.

Justice McReynolds' irate dissent: "Shame and humiliation are upon us now."[80]

Three months later, it was the liberals' turn to be discomforted by the Court. In another 5-to-4 decision, with Justice Roberts joining the majority, the Court invalidated the Railway Pension Act.[81] For the first time since Roosevelt took office, the Court had delivered an opinion that antagonized an important interest group who could demand restrictions on the Court's powers.[82] The president of one Railroad Brotherhood called the decision, which affected a million railroad workers, a "bitter disappointment."[83] From Wichita Falls, Texas, one man wrote Roosevelt: "I Had an idea they would turn Down that Railroad Pension. I told you the Rich Men always Run to the Supreme Court to Beat Our Laws. . . . The Supreme Court is a Public Nuisance."[84]

The implications of the rail pension decision were not limited to its effects on railroad workers. Many believed that if Justice Roberts disposed of other cases as he had this one, the pending social security legislation would also be invalidated. "Congratulations to rail carriers over pension decision yesterday," the general attorney for the Cudahy Packing Company wired a spokesman for the railroads: "That monumental decision so parallels our necessities in connection with Social Security legislation that we owe you a debt for fight now vindicating constitutional interpretation upon which all American business stands for future welfare all citizens."[85] The opinion, wrote *Business Week*, indicated that the

80 There is a copy of McReynolds' extemporaneous dissent, with corrections in his handwriting, in McReynolds MSS, Alderman Library, University of Virginia, Charlottesville, Va., Folder H-2. For conservative dismay, see L. E. Armstrong to Willis Van Devanter, Feb. 26, 1935, Van Devanter MSS, LC; James Beck to J. C. McReynolds, Apr. 13, 1934, Beck MSS, Princeton University Library, Carton 2; Alfred James McClure to Homer Cummings, Feb. 19, 1935, NA Dept. of Justice 105-42-11; letters in Charles Evans Hughes MSS, LC, Box 157.

81 Retirement Board v. Alton R. Co., 295 U.S. 330 (1935).

82 The Court had, of course, angered groups like bondholders by its decisions in the gold cases, but since these elements viewed the Court as a bulwark against social change, they were unlikely to support any movement to limit the Court's powers.

83 D. B. Robertson to FDR, Jan. 22, 1936, NA Dept. of Justice 235460.

84 P. J. Hasey to FDR, May 6, 1935, NA Dept. of Justice 235460.

85 Thomas Creigh to Paul Shoup, May 7, 1935, Shoup MSS, Stanford University Library, Stanford, California, Box 1.

Court "would smash any social security legislation that may be passed by Congress."[36]

Prodded by the rail pension decision, which raised the alarming likelihood that Justice Roberts had joined the conservatives to create a permanent 5-to-4 majority against the New Deal, Cummings began to explore possibilities of counter actions. Before the week was out, Cummings sent a memorandum to Assistant Attorney General Angus MacLean:[37]

> Has any study been made in this office of the question of the right of the Congress, by legislation, to limit the terms and conditions upon which the Supreme Court can pass on constitutional questions? I have seen several memoranda from time to time spelling out a theory by which this result could be achieved without a constitutional amendment. My recollection is that our files will somewhere disclose briefs on the theory that the Supreme Court has no right to pass on constitutional questions at all. Of course, quite a learned document could be prepared dealing with the historical aspects of this matter and the way in which it has developed.
>
> I think it would be well to have this pretty thoroughly covered, but in addition to this it would be well to cover the subject I first above mentioned; namely, the question of legislation which would not cut off the right of the Supreme Court to pass on constitutional questions, but which would limit it somewhere with a view to avoid 5 to 4 decisions.

III. Black Monday, 1935 Version

On "Black Monday," May 27, 1935, in three 9-to-0 decisions, the Court invalidated the National Industrial Recovery Act and the Frazier-Lemke Act and ruled, in the *Humphrey* case, that the President could not remove members of independent regulatory commissions save as Congress provided.[38] Roosevelt was incensed by the overturning of the NRA, the keystone of his industrial recovery program.[39] The Court's language in denouncing the dele-

[36] *5 to 4 Against,* Business Week 7–8 (May 11, 1935).

[37] Cummings to MacLean, May 11, 1935, NA Dept. of Justice 235773.

[38] Schechter Corp. v. United States, 295 U.S. 495 (1935); Louisville Bank v. Radford, 295 U.S. 555 (1935); Humphrey's Executor v. United States, 295 U.S. 602 (1935).

[39] It is often said that Roosevelt was relieved by the *Schechter* decision, because the NRA had become an intolerable burden. In fact, he believed strongly in the NRA approach, and persisted in later years in trying to revive it. On Roosevelt's

gation of powers and its narrow construction of the Commerce Clause appeared to place other New Deal laws in jeopardy and to bar the way to new legislation.[40] He was even more outraged by the *Humphrey* decision, which, in view of the history of the *Myers* opinion,[41] seemed a deliberate assault by the Court on his own prerogatives.[42] The unanimity of the Court in all three cases was bewildering. "Well, where was Ben Cardozo?" he asked. "And what about old Isaiah?"[43]

For four days, while the country speculated about what he would do, the President said nothing. On May 31, reporters were summoned to the White House. As they filed in, they saw on the President's desk a copy of the *Schechter* opinion and a sheaf of telegrams. Eleanor Roosevelt, seated next to her friend Mrs. Felix Frankfurter, busied herself knitting on a blue sock. For the next hour and a half, while reporters listened intently, Roosevelt, in an unusually somber mood, discoursed on the implications of the Court's opinion. Thumbing the copy of the *Schechter* decision as he spoke, the President argued that the Court's ruling had stripped the national government of its power to cope with critical national problems. "We are facing a very, very great national non-partisan issue," he said. "We have got to decide one way or the other . . . whether in some way we are going to . . . restore to the Federal Government the powers which exist in the national Governments of every other Nation in the world."[44] Of all the words the President spoke at the extraordinary conference, newspapermen singled out one sentence which headline writers emblazoned on late afternoon newspapers: "We have been relegated to the horse-and-buggy definition of interstate commerce."[45]

---

indignation at the *Schechter* opinion, see Raymond Clapper MS Diary, Feb. 24, 1937.

40 Roosevelt wrote: "It is the 'dictum' in the Schechter case opinion that is disturbing because . . . if the 'dictum' is followed in the future the Court would probably find only ten per cent of actual transactions to be directly in interstate commerce." FDR to Henry L. Stimson, June 10, 1935, 1 LETTERS 484.

41 Myers v. United States, 272 U.S. 52 (1926).

42 Landis, COHC 39–41; GERHART, *op. cit. supra* note 2, at 99.

43 GERHART, *op. cit. supra* note 2, at 99. "Isaiah" was a familiar term for Justice Brandeis.

44 4 PUBLIC PAPERS 200–22; Washington Post, June 1, 1935.

45 SCHLESINGER 284–87.

The President's "horse-and-buggy" conference created a furor. The next day, Raymond Clapper wrote in his Scripps-Howard column:[46]

> Within an hour after President Roosevelt held his press conference yesterday, you could almost feel the electric excitement about Washington.
>
> Gossip travels with lightning speed through the National Capital. . . . Long before the first newspapers reached the street corners . . . , the whole city knew that something of unusual importance had occurred.

Most commentators upbraided the President severely. The Washington *Post* typified much of the newspaper response with an editorial bluntly titled, "A President Leaves His Party." Henry Stimson wrote Roosevelt a long letter in which he protested that the "horse-and-buggy" observation "was a wrong statement, an unfair statement and, if it had not been so extreme as to be recognizable as hyperbole, a rather dangerous and inflammatory statement."[47] Senator Arthur Vandenberg, Michigan Republican, declared: "I don't think the President has any thought of emulating Mussolini, Hitler or Stalin, but his utterance as I have heard it is exactly what these men would say."[48]

Nor were all liberals pleased with Roosevelt's remarks. The Tennessee editor George Fort Milton wrote the President that his target should be not the Court but the Constitution. After all, Milton pointed out, men like Cardozo, Stone, Hughes, and the Brandeis of the *Oklahoma Ice* dissent had joined in the *Schechter* judgment; given our Constitution, they had had no other choice. Milton counseled:[49]

> Take the lead in a great program of constitutional reform. That is what we need to have done. Let the Constitution be amended so that the Congress will be given power to control indirect as well as direct effects of Interstate Commerce. Let the Constitution be amended to provide for an intelligent measure of delegation. I believe that you will get a very important and effective support from progressives all over the coun-

[46] Washington Post, June 1, 1935.

[47] Stimson to FDR, June 10, 1935, FDRL PPF 20.

[48] Washington Post, June 1, 1935; cf. Ralph Hayes to Newton Baker, June 8, 1935, Baker MSS, LC, Box 117.

[49] Milton to FDR, June 4, 1935, Milton MSS, LC, Box 18.

try on a program such as this. But I do not believe that there would be nearly so much support and strength for a program bottomed on a criticism of the Court itself.

Despite his lengthy press conference, Roosevelt never stated directly what he proposed to do. When reporters asked him in what manner the question might be resolved, he replied: "We haven't got to that yet." Nor did he suggest immediate action: "I don't mean this summer or winter or next fall, but over a period, perhaps of five or ten years."[50]

From both within and outside the Administration, Roosevelt was urged to act immediately. In the confusion after the horse-and-buggy conference, Raymond Moley, one of the original members of the Brain Trust, called Vice President John N. Garner and Senators Byrnes and Robert M. La Follette, Jr., together and found that they, like he, favored a constitutional amendment. Encouraged by the meeting, Moley wrote an editorial for *Today* advocating this course, and Byrnes spoke in support of the idea in Charleston, South Carolina. In Congress, the demand for action produced a freshet of new proposals. Some wanted to make constitutional grants of power to Congress more explicit; others, like Senator Norris, wished to require at least a 7-to-2 vote by the Supreme Court to invalidate legislation.[51]

In the nation there was growing anti-Court sentiment, which those who wished to act right away might tap. To the forces arrayed against the Court by the rail pension opinion, the *Schechter* decision had added both those groups which had benefited from the NRA and people who resented any setback to Roosevelt and the New Deal. A Memphis man advised the President to balk the Court by declaring martial law,[52] and a Kentucky attorney wrote: "I should think that you and Congress were as tired of the Supreme Court stunts as the people are."[53]

But Roosevelt decided against immediate action. For a moment, Moley recalls, the President showed a "flicker of enthusiasm," but

---

[50] 4 Public Papers 222.

[51] Moley 307; Schlesinger 288; H.R. No. 7997, Robert Ramsay MSS, University of West Virginia, Morgantown, W.Va.; Washington Post, May 29–June 1, 1935.

[52] Edward J. Brown to FDR, June 7, 1935, FDRL OF 41-A, Box 116.

[53] H. M. Stanley to FDR, July 2, 1935, FDRL OF 41-A, Box 116.

this soon dwindled.[54] Roosevelt sensed that the time was not yet ripe. The NRA had its supporters, but its detractors were more numerous; he could not go to the country with that kind of an appeal. The clamor raised by the horse-and-buggy conference indicated that the Court would have to antagonize a much larger portion of the nation before it would be politically safe to challenge it.[55] The difficulties in the way of winning approval for a constitutional amendment were inhibiting. Norris conceded: "It looks now as though it would be an absolute impossibility to pass it through the Senate or the House by the necessary two-thirds majority in order to submit it to the states."[56] Nor had the explorations in the Department of Justice proceeded far enough so that Roosevelt was ready with a specific proposal.

For the next year Roosevelt bided his time. He made no public reference to the Supreme Court even when additional adverse decisions appeared to require some sort of response. He left the impression that he was accepting the Court's verdicts without complaint and that, after having had his knuckles rapped for his horse-and-buggy remarks, he proposed neither to say nor to do anything further. In fact, as Tugwell has written, "If open battle was not at once joined, a kind of twilight war did begin."[57]

In June, 1935, the American ambassador to Italy, Breckinridge Long, returned for a brief visit to the United States; he found "one thing . . . uppermost on the minds of political America": the *Schechter* decision. At lunch alone with Long on the White House porch, Roosevelt spoke freely about the course he planned to pursue. He would move other cases up to the Supreme Court to give it an opportunity to modify its interpretation of the Commerce Clause. If the Court did not do so, then it might be necessary to

---

54 MOLEY 307.

55 TUGWELL, THE DEMOCRATIC ROOSEVELT 385 (1957).

56 George W. Norris to William A. Ahern, July 10, 1935, Norris MSS, Tray 27, Box 4.

57 TUGWELL, *op. cit. supra* note 55, at 385. For Roosevelt's continued concern, see FDR to Armstead Brown, July 6, 1935, FDRL PPF 2669. In a letter marked "Personal," he told the judge of the Supreme Court of Florida: "I am not worrying in any way about 1936, but I am, of course, concerned about future Supreme Court decisions. After all, we do not want to take away State's rights but, at the same time, there are a good many problems which, under modern conditions, can be solved only by Federal action."

propose an amendment. Long noted in his diary: "The amendments are not yet in specific or concrete form but might be broached under three headings: first, to define Inter-State Commerce with authority to Congress to legislate on the subject; second, to define certain phases of Inter-State Commerce; and third, taking a page from Lloyd George, to give authority to the Congress to pass over the veto of the Supreme Court legislation which the Court held unconstitutional."[58]

If and when the time came to act, the amendment route seemed the most promising path, although not everyone agreed about this. Some thought that the problem lay not in the Constitution but the Court; hence, they reasoned either that the composition of the Court must be altered or that the Court must, and perhaps could, be persuaded to change its views. The Felix Frankfurter cadre, which had always disliked the NRA anyway, opposed the amendment approach. From a different standpoint, Homer Cummings, angered by the *Schechter* decision, fumed: "I tell you, Mr. President, they mean to destroy us. . . . We will have to find a way to get rid of the present membership of the Supreme Court."[59] Yet the unanimity of the Court made it seem unlikely that the New Deal could win a majority, and it argued against solving the problem by appointing a few additional judges. After the *Schechter* opinion was handed down, Raymond Clapper wrote: "Talk of blackjacking the court by enlarging its membership collapsed when all nine justices joined in the decision. That subterfuge of packing the court, a weak and uncertain one at best, becomes ridiculous to think of now."[60]

Both Roosevelt and Cummings agreed that the Justice Department should continue to seek out solutions for the impasse. A week after the horse-and-buggy conference, Alexander Holtzoff, who was to be a central figure in the search for a plan, sent Cummings a memorandum responding to the suggestion that the Court might be stripped of most or all of its appellate jurisdiction. When Holtzoff explained that such a proposal would encounter too much

[58] Breckinridge Long MS Diary, LC, June 12, June 17, 1935. That same month, the President's son James Roosevelt, in a speech in Missouri, called for "an earlier determination of the constitutionality of the acts of the Legislature." Carlisle Bargeron, *Along the Potomac*, Washington Post, June 13, 1935, clipping in John Taber MSS, Cornell University Collection of Regional History, Ithaca, N.Y., Box 62.

[59] SCHLESINGER, 282, 288–89.

[60] Washington Post, May 29, 1935.

opposition and still would not eliminate all the problems confronting the Administration, Cummings was unsatisfied and told him to develop his point "a little more fully." On June 22 Holtzoff sent another five-page memorandum on the question, but the matter did not end there. On August 15, W. W. Gardner prepared a fourteen-page study for the Solicitor General in which he, too, looked into whether "the power of the Supreme Court to pass upon the constitutional validity of congressional legislation might be abolished or restricted by an Act of Congress." But he also found objections to the proposal, and the search for a satisfactory plan continued.[61]

The President displayed a lively interest in these inquiries. In July, for example, he sent Cummings a memorandum calling to his attention "two extremely interesting articles by Harold Laski" in the Manchester *Guardian*.[62] Roosevelt also corresponded with critics of the Court outside the government. In August, 1935, Charlton Ogburn, counsel for the American Federation of Labor, informed the President that he had submitted a proposed constitutional amendment to the executive council of the Federation for approval.[63] That same month, Roosevelt told Charles E. Wyzanski, Jr., solicitor of the Department of Labor: "Of course, if the Supreme Court should knock out the AAA, then the constitutional amendment would be the real issue. It probably will be anyway, and there will be less difficulty in phrasing it than many people think."[64]

Finding a satisfactory plan was only one part of Roosevelt's strategy; another part was building popular support for such a move. The horse-and-buggy conference had been one move toward that end. In August the President took another step when he met at the White House with George Creel. In collaboration with Creel, a veteran of reform wars, Roosevelt sometimes used the pages of *Collier's* to launch trial balloons. For an article entitled "Looking Ahead with Roosevelt," the President now dictated to Creel:[65]

---

61 Holtzoff, Memorandum for the Attorney General, June 6, 1935; Cummings, Memorandum for Mr. Holtzoff, June 13, 1935; Holtzoff, Memorandum for the Attorney General, June 22, 1935; W. W. Gardner, Memorandum for the Solicitor General, Aug. 15, 1935, NA Dept. of Justice 235773.

62 FDR to Cummings, July 5, 1935, FDRL OF 142.

63 Charlton Ogburn to FDR, Aug. 7, 20, 1935, FDRL OF 142.

64 3 SCHLESINGER 453. See, too, Rev. Francis Haas to FDR, Oct. 25, 1935, Haas MSS, Catholic University of America, Washington, D.C.

65 CREEL, REBEL AT LARGE 291–92 (1935).

> In the next few months, the Supreme Court will hand down fresh pronouncements with respect to New Deal laws, and it is possible the President will get another "licking." If so, much will depend on the language of the licking. In event that unconstitutionality is found, perhaps the decisions will point the way to statutory amendments. If, however, the Constitution is construed technically; if it is held that one hundred and fifty years have no bearing on the case, and that the present generation is powerless to meet social and economic problems that were not within the knowledge of the founding fathers, and therefore not made the subject of their specific consideration, then the President will have no other alternative than to go to the country with a Constitutional amendment that will lift the Dead Hand, giving the people of today the right to deal with today's vital issues.

He told Creel grimly: "Fire that as an opening gun."[66]

Contrary to Roosevelt's expectation, the trial balloon attracted almost no notice. Most of the nation in 1935 was still either indifferent to the Court question or outrightly opposed to tethering the Court. To the query: "As a general principle, would you favor limiting the power of the Supreme Court to declare acts of Congress unconstitutional?" the Gallup Poll in the autumn of 1935 received the following replies: yes, 31 per cent; no, 53 per cent; no opinion, 16 per cent. The most articulate anti-Court feeling came from those who felt they had been hurt by specific decisions. A Virginian objected: "The Supreme Court turned down my railroad pension." But many more thought the Justices wise, the system of checks and balances sacred, and Congress mercurial, even if their conception of these institutions was sometimes primitive. Asked his view of the Court, an Illinois man replied: "It's permanent. Congress is just the whims and fancies of the people." An Ohio reliefer said: "If they didn't know more than the other courts, they wouldn't be called the Supreme Court."[67]

Despite this discouraging response, the President pushed ahead quietly with his plans. At a long lunch at the White House on November 12, 1935, Ickes and Roosevelt fell to talking about the Court. The President remarked that he did not think that any Justices would retire and permit him to make new appointments. "Then," Ickes noted, "he said that while the matter could not be talked about now, he believed that the way to mend the situation was to adopt a constitutional amendment which would give

---

[66] *Id.* at 292.

[67] N.Y. Herald-Tribune, Nov. 3, 1935.

the Attorney General the right, if he has any doubt of the constitutionality of a legislative act, to apply to the Supreme Court for a ruling, that ruling to state specifically in which respects the act is unconstitutional. Then, if the next succeeding Congress, with this opinion of the Supreme Court before it, should re-enact that statute, it would, by that fact, be purged of its unconstitutionality and become the law of the land."[68]

During their conversation, the President made use of an analogy that was to crop up frequently in succeeding months in discussions of the judiciary crisis. Ickes wrote in his diary:[69]

> The President's mind went back to the difficulty in England, where the House of Lords repeatedly refused to adopt legislation sent up from the House of Commons. He recalled that when Lloyd George came into power some years ago under Edward VII, he went to the King and asked his consent to announce that if the Lords refused again to accept the bill for Irish autonomy, which had been pressed upon them several times since the days of Gladstone, he would create several hundred new peers, enough to outvote the existing House of Lords. With this threat confronting them, the bill passed the Lords.

Roosevelt's recollection was faulty—the episode actually concerned Asquith and the attempt to reform the House of Lords—but the British analogy was clearly important for him, because he recurred to it once more on December 27 at a cabinet meeting at which the Supreme Court question was again reviewed at length.[70] This time he referred not only to the Irish Home Rule Bill, but to Lloyd George's success in pushing through a social security act by the threat to create three hundred new peers.[71]

After the cabinet meeting, Ickes made a new entry in his diary:[72]

> Clearly, it is running in the President's mind that substantially all of the New Deal bills will be declared unconstitutional by the Supreme Court. This will mean that everything that this Administration has done of any moment will be nullified. The President pointed out that there were three ways of meeting such a situation: (1) by packing the Supreme Court, which

---

[68] 1 ICKES 467–68.

[69] *Ibid.*

[70] *Id.* at 494–95. The Asquith precedent was to be mentioned often during the Court fight. See, for example, Martin J. Lide to Kenneth McKellar, Feb. 16, 1937, McKellar MSS, Memphis Public Library, Memphis, Tenn., Box 229.

[71] 1 ICKES 495.

[72] *Ibid.*

> was a distasteful idea; (2) by trying to put through a number of amendments to the Constitution to meet the various situations; and (3) by a method that he asked us to consider very carefully.
>
> The third method is, in substance, this: an amendment to the Constitution conferring explicit power on the Supreme Court to declare acts of Congress unconstitutional, a power which is not given anywhere in the Constitution as it stands. The amendment would also give the Supreme Court original jurisdiction on constitutional questions affecting statutes. If the Supreme Court should declare an act of Congress to be unconstitutional, then—a congressional election having intervened—if Congress should repass the law so declared to be unconstitutional, the taint of unconstitutionality would be removed and the law would be a valid one. By this method there would be in effect a referendum to the country, although an indirect one. At the intervening congressional election the question of the constitutionality or unconstitutionality of the law would undoubtedly be an issue.

In essence, the President's strategy was to leave the power of decision to the Supreme Court. If the Court upheld New Deal legislation, the issue would fade away. But if all the legislation were thrown out, Roosevelt warned, there would be "marching farmers and marching miners and marching workingmen throughout the land." For almost half a year, while the Court was recessed, the conflict between the President and the Court had simmered on a low flame. But during those months, as Roosevelt was keenly aware, such significant questions as the AAA processing tax had been making their way through the lower courts; the Supreme Court could be expected to render decisions on such matters early in 1936. "If the Court does send the AAA flying like the NRA," the President had told Wyzanski, "there might even be a revolution."[73]

IV. The Court Nullifies the New Deal

On January 6, 1936, the Supreme Court handed down its long-awaited decision on the AAA processing tax.[74] Divided 6 to 3, the Court ruled the tax unconstitutional, thus overturning the second of the two most important New Deal recovery programs. In an opinion that earned him scorching comments from the law journals, Justice Roberts held the levy to be an illegitimate use of the

---

[73] 3 Schlesinger 453.

[74] United States v. Butler, 297 U.S. 1 (1936).

taxing power, "the expropriation of money from one group for the benefit of another."[75]

The *Butler* decision aroused acrimonious criticism of the Court. Coming on top of the 1935 opinions, the *Butler* verdict appeared to indicate a determination by the Court to wipe out all of the New Deal. "Is Poe's Raven who croaked 'Never More' their model?" asked one man. An Oklahoman penciled a letter to the Attorney General stating that he wanted to impeach every judge who had declared the AAA invalid, and another man wrote the President: "I'm in favor of doing away with the Constitution if it's going to interfere with the general welfare of the people." The head of a Chicago advertising agency asked: "Are you aware that the people at large are getting damned tired of the United States Supreme Court, and that, if left to a popular vote, it would be kicked out?"[76]

A nation of tinkerers, the country flooded Washington with home-made inventions to improve the government machinery. Many of the contrivances stressed either the age of the Justices or the device of packing the Court, or both. A South Carolina attorney wrote: "We are hoping and believing that you and the Congress of the United States will not allow six old men to destroy this Country." A Minnesota lawyer urged compulsory retirement at 65 or 70, "whichever would retire the majority of the present members of the Court." A Los Angeles man questioned the fitness of "that body of nine old hasbeens, half-deaf, half-blind, full-of-palsy men. . . . That they are behind the times is very plain—all you have to do is to look at Charles Hughes' whiskers."[77]

---

[75] *Id.* at 61.

[76] Maurice Daley to Homer Cummings, Jan. 13, 1936, NA Dept. of Justice 5-36-346; George Thomason to Cummings, NA Dept. of Justice 235773; John W. White to FDR, Jan. 7, 1936, NA Dept. of Justice 5-36-346; W. K. Cochrane to Stephen Early, Jan. 25, 1936, FDRL OF 41-A, Box 120. Governor George Earle of Pennsylvania denounced the Court as "a political body" with "six members committed to the politics of the Liberty League." Address of George H. Earle, Jan. 18, 1935, Earle MSS, Bryn Mawr, Pa., privately held, Speech and News File No. 73. Some of the indignation was aroused by the "windfall" millers anticipated as a consequence of the decision. Clifford Hope to Chester Stevens, Apr. 21, 1936, Hope MSS, Kansas State Historical Society, Topeka, Kans., Tax (Legis.) folder, Legislative Correspondence, 1935–36.

[77] Joe P. Lane to FDR, Jan. 7, 1936, FDRL OF 274, Box 3; S. C. Odenborg to FDR, Feb. 3, 1936, NA Dept. of Justice 235241; John B. Muller to FDR, Jan. 9, 1936, FDRL OF 1-K, Misc. 1936.

From different parts of the nation came calls for additional Justices "with younger minds." Some wanted four more Justices, like the Memphis businessman who pointed out: "Business does not accept an applicant with twelve gray hairs on his head." Others thought six new Justices would have to be added to "reverse this infamy." An Arizona attorney recommended: "In order to avoid the impending seizure of this government by the special interests it is incumbent on you to increase the membership of the Supreme Court to fifteen; and appoint the new membership from the Frankfurters, Olsons, and other men who place human rights above the rights of predatory wealth." From Richmond, Virginia, came a demand for a Court of "at least twenty or more members. Nine OLD MEN, whose total age amounts to about 650 years, should have additional help." A member of the Kansas House of Representatives had an even more radical suggestion: add sixteen new members, "the new members to be not over thirty-five years of age, and retired at forty. This would put men on the court that are in step with TO-DAY."[78]

A number of correspondents seemed to believe that Roosevelt was unaware of the Court's infamy or that he needed to be stiffened to oppose the Court. A Seattle woman wrote:[79]

> I have just this minute heard the decision of the U.S. Supreme Court on the A.A.A.
>
> Mr. Roosevelt, are you going to sit back and let these few men, controlled by the selfish elements of our country, control the destinies of intelligent, thinking and country-loving people, who really make this great country of ours?

A Kansan asserted: "One who is really a man will resist to the end being governed by men who lived one hundred and fifty years ago." A Miami attorney assured the President: "If you, as the Executive, and Congress will make the Supreme Court an issue in this country it will not fail. Jackson did not fail, Grant did not fail, and the Dred-Scott decision was treated with contempt."[80]

[78] W. J. Young to FDR, Jan. 7, 1936, NA Dept. of Justice 5-36-346; W. B. Mills to FDR, Jan. 13, 1936; Thomas Duncan to FDR, Jan. 7, 1936; Elmer Graham to FDR, Jan. 7, 1936, NA Dept. of Justice 235773; W. F. Betts to FDR, Jan. 6, 1936, FDRL OF 1-K Misc. 1936; W. H. (Bill) Reed to FDR, Jan. 21, 1936, NA Dept. of Justice 235868.

[79] Auzias de Turenne to FDR, Jan. 6, 1936, FDRL OF 1-K Misc. 1936.

[80] R. W. Sholders to FDR, Jan. 6, 1936, NA Dept. of Justice 5-36-246; Rudolph Isom to FDR, Jan. 13, 1936, FDRL OF 41-A, Box 120.

A Mississippi editor wired Roosevelt:[81]

> On behalf of farmers and workers urge that you set aside Supreme Court decision and destroy their assumed right to declare laws of Congress unconstitutional. . . . President Andrew Jackson, our greatest Democrat, defied Supreme Court on this very point. Hope you will do the same. Sincerely believe that future of Democratic government hinges on whether you will take the bull by the horns. Drastic action is imperative. America is depending on you. Perhaps civilization and its perpetuity is involved in your acts. God grant that you have the courage to do right.

Roosevelt's strategy of "watchful waiting" seemed to be paying off. The Court, which had antagonized groups like railway employees in 1935, had now angered farmers who would be denied more than two billion dollars in AAA benefit checks in the next year. Edward A. O'Neal, president of the American Farm Bureau Federation, warned: "Those who believe the American farmer will stand idly by and watch his program for economic justice fall without a fight are badly mistaken. The fight is on—and this time it will be with the gloves off."[82] O'Neal planned to meet with the A. F. of L.'s general counsel, Charlton Ogburn, to lay plans for a farmer-labor alliance to achieve common objectives.

Yet none of this agitation moved Roosevelt to act. Despite constant prodding, he refused even to comment on the *Butler* decision. He believed that the time had not yet come. An election year was not the propitious moment to give the opposition, which was bereft of issues, an opportunity to stand by the flag. Nor had the coalition against the Court yet reached full strength. If O'Neal denounced the *Butler* opinion, other farm leaders approved it, and a Gallup Poll, which appeared the day before the decision was rendered, showed a majority of the country opposed to the AAA.[83] Nor had opponents of the Court yet reached agreement on a proposal. Ogburn, for one, thought that nothing should be done at present save to make the amending process easier.[84]

Moreover, the Administration was not yet ready for a fight on the Court issue, because it had not yet come up with a satisfactory

---

81 H. B. Sanders to FDR, Jan. 7, 1936, NA Dept. of Justice 5-36-346.

82 Washington Post, Jan. 7, 1936.

83 Washington Post, Jan. 8, 1936.

84 Charlton Ogburn to FDR, Jan. 9, 1936, FDRL OF 274.

plan. Shortly after the *Butler* verdict was rendered, Assistant Attorney General John Dickinson wrote:[85]

> The way in which the high command has apparently decided to treat the AAA decision has been to smother its effect as much as possible. I am not at all sure that this is a wise strategy, but apparently the feeling is that there is a widespread readiness, throughout the country, to blaze up against the Supreme Court and that this state of mind must be wet-blanketed, for fear that otherwise it would drive the Administration into the position of either attacking the Court, or calling for an amendment, which they are not yet prepared to do.

While maintaining public silence, Roosevelt indicated privately that he was preparing for a showdown with the Court. At the cabinet meeting on January 24, 1936, Ickes recorded:[86]

> The President said that word is coming to him from widely separated parts of the country that people are beginning to show a great deal of interest in the constitutional questions that have been raised by recent Supreme Court decisions. . . . The President made the point, based upon some statement by Harold J. Laski, that the Supreme Court, in its decisions on New Deal legislation, was dictating what it believed should be the social philosophy of the nation, without reference to the law or the Constitution. . . . It is plain to see, from what the President said today and has said on other occasions, that he is not at all averse to the Supreme Court declaring one New Deal statute after another unconstitutional. I think he believes that the Court will find itself pretty far out on a limb before it is through with it and that a real issue will be joined on which we can go to the country.
>
> For my part, I hope so. Here is an issue that must be faced by the country sooner or later, unless we are prepared to submit to the arbitrary and final dictates of a group of men who are not elected by the people and who are not responsible to the people: in short, a judicial tyranny imposed by men appointed for life and who cannot be reached except by the slow and cumbersome process of impeachment.

That same day, Roosevelt prepared a memorandum for the files, with a copy to Moley, stating:[87]

> It has been well said by a prominent historian that fifty years from now the Supreme Court's AAA decision will, in all probability, be described somewhat as follows:

---

[85] Dickinson to George Fort Milton, Jan. 13, 1936, Milton MSS, Box 19.

[86] 1 Ickes 524.

[87] Memorandum, Jan. 24, 1936, FDRL OF 1-K.

(1) The decision virtually prohibits the President and Congress from the right, under modern conditions, to intervene reasonably in the regulation of nation-wide commerce and nation-wide agriculture.

(2) The Supreme Court arrived at this result by selecting from several possible techniques of constitutional interpretation a special technique. The objective of the Court's purpose was to make reasonableness in passing legislation a matter to be settled not by the views of the elected Senate and House of Representatives and not by the views of an elected President but rather by the private, social philosophy of a majority of nine appointed members of the Supreme Court itself.

Roosevelt continued to move ahead on the study of plans to curb the Court. A week after the *Butler* decision, he wrote Cummings: "What was the McArdle case . . .? I am told that the Congress withdrew some act from the jurisdiction of the Supreme Court."[88] The Attorney General replied: "The case of ex parte McCardle . . . to which you refer . . . is one of the classic cases to which we refer when considering the possibility of limiting the jurisdiction of Federal Courts. This whole matter has been the subject of considerable study in this Department, and, in view of recent developments, is apt to be increasingly important."

The exchange between the President and the Attorney General suggests the crucial development in the early weeks of 1936: loss of faith in the amendment solution and rising belief that the Court could be curbed by an act of Congress. Perhaps the most important influence on this change of plans was the division of the Court in the *Butler* case and Justice Harlan Stone's ringing dissent, less because the minority voted to sustain the processing tax than because of Stone's vigorous assault on judicial usurpation. Cummings wrote Stone:[89]

Your dissenting opinion is on a high plane—sound, constructive and human.

It may not be the law *now*—but it will be the law later, un-

[88] FDR to Cummings, Jan. 14, 1936; Cummings to FDR, Jan. 16, 1936, FDRL PSF Supreme Court.

[89] Cummings to Stone, Jan. 8, 1936, FDRL PSF Justice. Stone responded: "Thank you for your generous note. When one finds himself outvoted two to one he should be humble and perhaps skeptical of his own judgment. But I have a sincere faith that history and long time perspective will see the function of our court in a different light from that in which it is viewed at the moment." For Stone's views, see MASON, HARLAN FISKE STONE 417 (1956).

less governmental functions are to be permanently frozen in an unescapable mold.

You spoke at a great moment and in a great way. Congratulations.

The split in the Court confirmed those who had been arguing that the problem lay not in the Constitution but in the composition of this particular Court, and Justice Stone's dissent made it easier to argue that Congress must act to regain powers which the Court had usurped. The amendment route was not abandoned, but the search for a suitable amendment now concentrated for the first time on compelling the retirement of Justices at 70, thus altering the makeup of the Court. In addition, increasing attention was given to finding a way to meet the difficulty by statute.[90]

On January 29, 1936, after talking over the Court issue at lunch with Senator Norris, the President continued the same discussion with Ickes. He told Ickes that he had reached the conclusion that he could achieve Court reform without resort to an amendment; he had also confided this to Norris. Roosevelt favored an act of Congress which would strip the lower courts of the power to pass upon the constitutionality of statutes and would confer this power on the Supreme Court as a matter of original jurisdiction. The Supreme Court would be required to give an advisory opinion on the constitutionality of a bill before it was enacted. Congress could then alter the bill to conform with the advice of the Court or it could pass it once more in its original form, and it would then become the law of the land. Ickes noted:[91]

I made the obvious remark that the Supreme Court would declare unconstitutional such an act as the President had in mind and he said that of course it would. To meet that situation his plan would be somewhat as follows: Congress would pass a law, the Supreme Court would declare it unconstitutional, the President would then go to Congress and ask it to instruct him whether he was to follow the mandate of Congress or the mandate of the Court. If the Congress should declare

90 3 SCHLESINGER 493–94; FDR Memorandum to Homer Cummings, Feb. 24, 1936; FDR Memorandum for Chairman Hatton Sumners, FDRL OF 41, Box 114. During the 1936 campaign, one correspondent wrote the President: "Why not make a campaign on the opinions of Justice Stone? By taking the words of a member of the court itself there can be no justifiable charge of usurpation." Paul Webb to FDR, June 4, 1936, FDRL OF 41-A, Box 116.

91 1 ICKES 529–30.

that its own mandate was to be followed, the President would carry out the will of Congress through the offices of the United States Marshals and ignore the Court.

After their talk, Ickes reflected:[92]

There isn't any doubt at all that the President is really hoping that the Supreme Court will continue to make a clean sweep of all New Deal legislation, throwing out the TVA Act, the Securities Act, the Railroad Retirement Act, the Social Security Act, the Guffey Coal Act, and others. He thinks the country is beginning to sense this issue but that enough people have not yet been affected by adverse decisions so as to make a sufficient feeling on a Supreme Court issue.

I told the President that I hoped this would be the issue in the next campaign. I believe it will have to be fought out sooner or later, and I remarked to him that the President who faced this issue and drastically curbed the usurped power of the Supreme Court would go down through all the ages of history as one of the great Presidents.

Two days later, at a cabinet meeting, Cummings raised the question whether the government should appeal a lower court decision denying the federal government the right to condemn property for a low-cost housing project. Tom Corcoran and Ben Cohen were but two of the President's advisers who thought the government should drop the case, in part because they feared an adverse opinion from the Supreme Court that might wipe out the Public Works Administration. Ickes noted:[93]

The President was firmly of the opinion that we ought to go ahead with the case. He scouted the idea that anyone could draw an act which would pass the scrutiny of the Supreme Court in its present outlook on New Deal legislation. He thought that if all PWA projects should be suspended as the result of an adverse decision by the Supreme Court, it would be all to the good. . . . There doesn't seem to me to be any doubt that he is entirely willing to have the Supreme Court knock out every New Deal law. It is clear that he is willing to go to the country on this issue but he wants the issue to be as strong and clear as possible, which means that he hopes the

[92] *Id.* at 530.

[93] *Id.* at 531–32. Ickes added: "It happens that I am fully in accord with the President's view on this matter. I believe that this issue will have to be fought out sooner or later and no more important issue has arisen since the Civil War. Naturally, I would like to be in this fight and be a member of the Administration that is carrying it on."

> Supreme Court will declare unconstitutional every New Deal case that comes before it.

Yet, while blithely accepting this prospect of a constitutional Armageddon, the President continued to say nothing publicly. Early in February, George Fort Milton confided:[94]

> I thought a month ago that the Court and the Constitution were very definitely going to be in this year's presidential debate. But everything in Washington is of the hush, hush attitude. . . . What I am feeling is that maybe he is depending too much on his resourcefulness and that he could do some thinking on what would be the usefulness of being re-elected if he was going to have to go into a second term denied the essential powers of nationality. Wouldn't he be all dressed up and have nowhere to go?

Roosevelt's silence, which some interpreted as acquiescence in the Court's decisions, left the initiative for public action to Congress. In the 1936 session, congressmen introduced more than a hundred proposals to restrict the federal courts. Some measures, such as the "Human Rights Amendment," aimed to expand the powers of Congress to enact social legislation. Others, like the Cross bill, sought to strip the courts of the prerogative of judicial review. Still others resorted to enlarging the bench. In January, 1936, Representative Ernest Lundeen of Minnesota filed a bill to increase the Supreme Court by two Justices so that the Court could handle more work and because "new blood will mean a more liberal outlook on constitutional questions." Lundeen pointed out that when his bill had been adopted, and when Justice Willis Van Devanter carried out his purported plan to retire, the President would be able to name three new Justices and thus assure a liberal majority. A week earlier, Representative James L. Quinn had gone even further; he had introduced a measure to expand the Court to fifteen Justices.[95]

On February 12, 1936, George Norris delivered a major address on the floor of the Senate. He denounced the Supreme Court as a "continuous constitutional convention." To the contention that the processing tax was invalid because agricultural production was not mentioned in the Constitution, Norris retorted: "Nowhere in

---

[94] Milton to George Foster Peabody, Feb. 10, 1936, Milton MSS, Box 19.

[95] Thomas R. Amlie to W. Jett Lauck, Mar. 6, 1937, Amlie MSS, State Historical Society of Wisconsin, Madison, Wisc., Box 6; O. H. Cross to Stanley Reed, Jan. 17, 1936, NA Dept. of Justice 235868.

that great document is there a syllable, a word, or a sentence giving to any court the right to declare an act of Congress unconstitutional." Norris expostulated: "The members of the Supreme Court are not elected by anybody. They are responsible to nobody. Yet they hold dominion over everybody."[96] Rejecting the amendment procedure he had once favored as "impracticable," Norris asked Congress to have the "courage" to enact legislation requiring a unanimous decision to invalidate an act of Congress.

The columnist Robert S. Allen wrote Norris:[97]

> I have been wondering for weeks what the hell this session was for. Your matchless speech on the Supreme Court this afternoon cleared up the mystery. The session was solely so you could deliver this superb exposition—so it could go into the Record for all history to read—so you could say what everybody was thinking, but no other leader had the guts to say out loud.
>
> It was a grand and unequaled job, Senator. And what was no less significant was the tremendous response it is being accorded. It is really amazing the extraordinary press coverage it has received. Even the filthy Hearst jackals carried almost a column of your remarks. It was also amazing to me how deeply moved the press gallery was. Reactionary old bastards who haven't had an intelligent idea in decades spoke respectfully of your views.

Norris' concern over the Court question was long-standing, but it was heightened during these weeks by anxiety over the fate of the Tennessee Valley Authority, of which he was acknowledged to be the "father." In January, Norris had written: "Up to the time this decision was rendered in the AAA case, I had no doubt whatsoever that the Supreme Court would sustain the TVA Act. . . . Since the AAA decision, however, I would not be surprised if the Court would hold the TVA Act unconstitutional."[98] On February 17, the Court, by a surprising 8-to-1 vote, diminished these

---

[96] "Legislation by the Judiciary," Copy in the George Norris MSS. See, too, Norris to Francis Heney, Apr. 25, 1936, Heney MSS, Bancroft Library, University of California, Berkeley, Calif. The Norris idea was a familiar one. In January, a Tacoma assessor had written the President: "The extreme penalty is not exacted from the vilest culprit, save on a unanimous verdict. Why should the will of the people be crucified for less?" Fred A. Smith to FDR, Jan. 9, 1936, NA Dept. of Justice 235773.

[97] Allen to George W. Norris, Feb. 12, 1936, Norris MSS, Tray 27, Box 4.

[98] George W. Norris to Irving Brant, Jan. 11, 1936, Norris MSS, Tray 27, Box 5.

anxieties by upholding the power of the TVA to dispose of power generated at Wilson Dam.[99]

Although some critics pointed out that the Court still had not rendered a decisive judgment on the constitutionality of the TVA, friends of public power were delighted by the opinion. "I had completely resigned myself to a bad decision, only holding out hope that we would have some crumb of comfort in that unlike AAA and NRA we would not be swept completely out to sea, bag and baggage," wrote David Lilienthal.[100] "The decision, clearing away so many of the clouds hanging over us, makes me feel very humble. We are given an almost incredible grant of power."[101] The opinion served, for the moment, to quiet demands for reform of the judiciary.[102] By showing the fairness of the Court, the decision, observed the Washington *Post*, "should do more than anything else to end the campaign for limitation of the Court's authority."[103] From Chattanooga, George Fort Milton wrote gleefully:[104]

> Well, after TVA, I think we ought to start talking about "one old man and the eight young men." . . .
> I suspect that some of the members of the Court set themselves forward deliberately to show that they could render other than a Tory decision. Would you call this modernizing Mr. Dooley, so that the Supreme Court precedes the election returns?

The respite provided by the TVA decision proved short-lived. Six weeks later, the Court rebuked the Securities and Exchange Commission,[105] and on May 18, 1936, it went out of its way in the *Carter* case[106] to strike down the Guffey Coal Act in an opinion that appeared to doom not only the Wagner Labor Relations Act

---

99 Ashwander v. T.V.A., 297 U.S. 288 (1936).

100 1 Journals of David E. Lilienthal 59 (1964).

101 Lilienthal to Felix Frankfurter, Feb. 17, 1936, Lilienthal MSS, Princeton University Library.

102 Knoxville News-Sentinel, Feb. 18–20, 1936, clippings, David Lilienthal Scrapbooks, Lilienthal MSS, Princeton University Library.

103 Knoxville News-Sentinel, Feb. 18, 1936.

104 George Fort Milton to Francis Coker, Feb. 18, 1936, Milton MSS, Box 19. *Cf.* Newton Baker to James M. Beck, Mar. 19, 1936, Beck MSS.

105 Jones v. S.E.C., 298 U.S. 1 (1936).

106 Carter v. Carter Coal Co., 298 U.S. 238 (1936).

but any attempt by act of Congress to control wages and hours. The *Carter* decision started a new wave of condemnations of the Court and demands for restrictions. Once more, the age of the Justices and the possibilities offered by "packing" were pointed out. "We permit old men 90, probably as childish as boys of 9, to sit on the Supreme Court bench and in case of a 5 to 4 vote one old man controls the affairs of the nation," one critic wrote the President. "In reviewing the Constitution of the United States," noted a Pennsylvania man, "it comes to my attention the fact that there is no limit to the Personell of the Supreme Court." A Los Angeles man urged the President to name four more Justices. He added helpfully: "For these four positions I nominate Senator Hiram Johnson of California and Senator Geo. W. Norris of Nebraska. Now you name two." Yet Roosevelt not only would not heed such advice but when newsmen pressed him for a statement on the *Carter* decision he brusquely closed off that line of questioning.[107]

The *Carter* decision turned out to be only the first in a series of rapid-fire blows the Court delivered at the New Deal. On successive Mondays in the spring of 1936, the Court handed down the *Carter* opinion, overturned the Municipal Bankruptcy Act,[108] and, in the most momentous ruling of all, invalidated the New York state minimum-wage law in the *Tipaldo* case.[109] Each decision came from a divided court.

For critics of the Court, the *Tipaldo* opinion was the last straw. Before that decision, even some New Dealers hoped to avoid a direct confrontation with the Court. After it, Tugwell has written, liberals agreed that "something must be done."[110] Not since the *Dred Scott* disaster had the Court inflicted on itself so deep a wound. As Alpheus T. Mason has observed: "At any time up to June 1, 1936, the Court might have retreated and thus avoided a showdown. The New York Minimum Wage opinion, handed down

---

107 Wendell Berge to E. L. Woodcos, May 20, 1936, Berge MSS, LC, Box 10; L. C. Weiss to FDR, May 20, 1936; H. C. Holland to FDR, May 23, 1936; Jan Byrd to FDR, May 20, 1936, NA Dept. of Justice 235773; Washington Post, May 20, 1936; John D. Miller to the New York Times, May 19, 1936, Miller MSS, Cornell University Collection of Regional History.

108 St. Joseph Stockyards Co. v. United States, 298 U.S. 38 (1936).

109 Morehead v. New York *ex rel.* Tipaldo, 298 U.S. 587 (1936).

110 Tugwell, *op. cit. supra* note 55, at 391.

that day, convinced even the most reverent that five stubborn old men had planted themselves squarely in the path of progress.[111]

The *Tipaldo* decision produced a national outcry against the Court. Ickes noted angrily: "The sacred right of liberty of contract again—the right of an immature child or a helpless woman to drive a bargain with a great corporation. If this decision does not outrage the moral sense of the country, then nothing will."[112] But it was not only New Dealers who objected to the opinion. The Court had embarrassed Administration critics who had argued that protection of the rights of labor should be left to state action. "Hereafter," wrote Franklyn Waltman in the Washington *Post*, "whenever New Dealers are taunted with trying to break down the rights of the States to manage their own affairs, the taunters will have this decision tossed in their faces."[113] The *Post* labeled the opinion "An Unfortunate Decision," and Herbert Hoover called for an amendment to restore to the states "the power they thought they already had."[114]

Once more, Roosevelt was pressed to act. From California, the head of the Stockton Democratic Club wrote the President: "By another 4 to 5 decision on the part of JUDOCRACY, *one man* has been able . . . to nullify the progress of half a century along humanitarian lines, exposing the Motherhood of America to further exploitation on the part of unscrupulous employers. If this be Democracy—may God save the mark!" A telegram from Brooklyn urged: "Increase number of justices in Supreme Court with men in their fifties." The head of a New York printing firm warned the President that it would be "useless" for him to pursue his program unless he pushed through an amendment. "You can't side-step the issue," he scolded. "The people who will re-elect you will expect you to have something to say about this matter."[115]

At a press conference on June 2, 1936, Roosevelt broke his silence. For the first time since the "horse-and-buggy" meeting,

---

111 MASON, *op. cit. supra* note 89, at 438.

112 1 ICKES 614.

113 Washington Post, June 2, 1936.

114 N.Y. Times, June 7, 1936.

115 James A. Metcalf to FDR, June 3, 1936, NA Dept. of Justice 224196; E. Larkin to FDR, June 4, 1936, FDRL OF 41-A, Box 116; Earl Salley to FDR, June 5, 1936, FDRL OF 274, Box 3.

he commented on a decision of the Court. Of the *Tipaldo* opinion, he said:[116]

> It seems to be fairly clear, as a result of this decision and former decisions, using this question of minimum wage as an example, that the "no-man's-land" where no Government—State or Federal—can function is being more clearly defined. A State cannot do it, and the Federal Government cannot do it.

But when a reporter asked, "How can you meet that situation?" the President replied, "I think that is about all there is to say on it."

Roosevelt was no less circumspect about drafting the 1936 Democratic platform. Both the President and Senator Robert Wagner of New York, chairman of the Resolutions Committee, were urged to incorporate in the platform commitments to specific proposals, such as requiring a 7-to-2 majority to invalidate a law, or amending the Constitution to empower Congress and the states to enact minimum-wage laws.[117] But the Administration was determined to keep the platform ambiguous, not only because it wanted to remove the Court issue from the campaign, but because it had not yet decided on any particular plan.

In drafting their platform, the Democrats had to cope with the fact that the Republicans had already committed themselves to an amendment to overcome the *Tipaldo* decision. As Cummings warned the President, if the Democrats sought to outbid the Republicans they ran the risk of going so far as to shift the whole emphasis of the campaign to the constitutional question. Cummings hoped to avoid any specific plank, but if one were necessary he favored one so vaguely worded that it should leave the door open "to the thought that perhaps, after all, an amendment may not be necessary." Four days earlier, Donald Richberg, who had been a prominent labor attorney and chairman of the National Industrial Recovery Board, had also submitted a draft which was adroitly phrased to escape any definite commitment.[118]

On the Sunday before the 1936 Democratic convention, Roosevelt, Wagner, and several others met after dinner in the White

---

[116] 5 PUBLIC PAPERS 191–92.

[117] Louis Boehm to Robert Wagner, June 6, 1936; Clarence V. Tiers to Stephen Early, June 24, 1936, FDRL OF 1871-A.

[118] Detroit News, June 25, 1936, clipping, Blair Moody Scrapbooks, Moody MSS, Michigan Historical Collections of the University of Michigan, Ann Arbor, Mich.; Cummings to FDR, June 20, 1936, FDRL PSF Justice; Richberg to FDR, June 16, 1936, FDRL PSF Supreme Court.

House to draft the platform. When they encountered difficulties, it was decided to ask two of the participants, Samuel I. Rosenman, another member of the original Brain Trust, and Stanley High, a skillful phrase-maker, to try their hands after the meeting broke up. They worked all night at a typewriter, and by morning the President had their draft on his breakfast tray. Certain parts, including a Supreme Court plank, were still missing. After breakfast, Rosenman and High went into the President's bedroom, where they found Donald Richberg.

Recognizing that more aid might be required, the President had summoned Richberg to the White House. Richberg, who guessed why he had been called, turned up shortly after breakfast with a carbon of his proposed plank in his pocket. When Roosevelt told him that Wagner needed help, Richberg handed him the draft to read. After going over it, the President whistled softly and said, "I think this is it." The others gathered in the President's bedroom agreed, and, with minor changes, Richberg's plank was incorporated in the platform. Purposely vague, it proposed an attempt to achieve a "clarifying amendment" only "if these problems cannot be effectively solved by legislation."[119]

In the 1936 campaign, Roosevelt maintained a studied silence on the Court question despite counsel from different sides that he urge action to alter the Court or that he assure the country that he would not pack the Court. The President wanted the campaign to center not on the Constitution but on the concrete achievements of the New Deal and the past iniquities of Herbert Hoover. Within the Roosevelt circle, Felix Frankfurter and Frances Perkins opposed making an issue of the Court's rulings, and even Ickes conceded that the groundwork for it had not been laid.[120] One correspondent urged the President to leave the Court matter "till after the campaign, so as not to supply ammunition to the 'constitution cryers.' When the campaign is over, Congress could proceed in a calm mood and adopt certain changes. . . . Congress could suggest to the President to add to the present Tribunal two, four or six justices to make the number 11, 13, or 15."[121]

Nonetheless, the constitutional issue surfaced in different parts

---

119 Richberg, My Hero 204–05 (1954); Rosenman, Working with Roosevelt 100–03 (1953); Moley 346–47.

120 1 Ickes 524, 531, 602.

121 Jacob Hayman to FDR, Feb. 24, 1936, FDRL OF 41-A, Box 116.

of the country where conservatives warned that a Roosevelt victory would menace the Court. They were unpersuaded by New Deal avowals of reverence for the Constitution. Rexford Tugwell's theology was acceptable, noted one writer, but his actions were unorthodox, "like a Renaissance cardinal with children." Conceivably, a few votes may have been swung by the Court question. One man wrote: "In my opinion any man who sneered at the United States Supreme Court like he did in May 1935, when they ruled against N.R.A., is not worthy of my vote though I have been voting the Democratic Ticket since 1884." Yet Roosevelt's studied silence made it possible for Stephen Duggan, director of the Institute of International Education, to write a long letter, which the *New York Times* published, urging support of the President, who "has given no evidence that he wants to 'pack' the court," and for a conservative senator like Josiah Bailey of North Carolina to defend Roosevelt on the Court question. Enlarging the Supreme Court, wrote Frederick Lewis Allen shortly before the election, "need hardly be regarded as a serious possibility in the immediate future: it would be too obviously a cowardly move."[122]

V. Election Landslide

In November, 1936, Franklin Roosevelt rolled up the greatest landslide victory in the history of two-party competition by capturing the electoral votes of all but two of the forty-eight states. His political opponents routed, his policies vindicated, he could now give full attention to the challenge posed by the Supreme Court. Time was short. In just two more months the Court would reconvene; awaiting it were tests of the validity of the Social Security Act, the Wagner Labor Relations Act, the Railway Labor

[122] Sternsher, Rexford Tugwell and the New Deal 349 (1964); Raymond Clapper MS Diary, Aug. 24, 1937; S. H. Boddinghouse to Daniel Roper, Nov. 6, 1936, FDRL OF 41-A, Box 116; Henry Teigan to C. Schoening, Feb. 16, 1937, Teigan MSS, Minnesota Historical Society, Box 14; Chicago Tribune, July 24, 1936, clipping, Frank Murphy Collection, University of Michigan Law School; Frank Gannett to Alexander Falck, Mar. 7, 1936, Gannett MSS, Cornell University Collection of Regional History, Box 16; James H. Winston to FDR, Aug. 1, 1936, FDRL PPF 1786; J. A. Mulhern to Newton Baker, Oct. 22, 1936, Baker MSS, Box 52; Stephen Duggan to FDR, Nov. 13, 1936, FDRL OF 274; John Robert Moore, "Josiah William Bailey: A Political Biography," unpublished Ph.D. dissertation, Duke University, 1965; James Hamilton Lewis to Arthur Vandenberg, Sept. 18, 1936, Lewis MSS, LC; Allen, *Behind the Campaign*, 173 Harper's 476 (Oct., 1936).

Act, the Commodity Exchange Act, state minimum-wage and unemployment compensation laws, and of the powers of the PWA, the SEC, and the Federal Communications Commission. Even the gold clause resolution faced another contest.

In view of this prospect, what was Roosevelt to do? He might just wait for vacancies to develop. The laws of nature were on his side, for never in our history had a Court been composed of so elderly a group. Moreover, Justices Van Devanter and Sutherland had talked of retiring. Yet Roosevelt had seen nearly four years go by without one opportunity to make an appointment, an experience that had occurred in no other full presidential term save for the special instance of Andrew Johnson's tenure. Anyone familiar with the conversation of Justices knew enough to place a high discount on talk of retiring, and these particular Justices seemed determined to stay on the bench so long as Roosevelt was in the White House. At the first cabinet meeting after the election, the President, in a spirit of gallows humor, said that Justice McReynolds would still be on the tribunal when he was 105.[123]

Still, Roosevelt might wait to see whether the Court would follow the election returns. The switch of even one Justice could be decisive. It might be anticipated that the emphatic outcome of the election would surprise some Justices who had believed that they were speaking for a nation outraged by the New Deal. (It is clear from Van Devanter's correspondence that he thought the election would be close.)[124] Nor, it has been argued, was Justice Roberts as set against the New Deal as he appeared to be.

Yet there were risks in waiting. The Court had behaved so arrogantly in the spring of 1936 that the prospects for a change of views seemed slim. Not only did the Court's line of reasoning in its last Term leave little reason to suppose that the Court would

---

[123] John H. Clarke to Newton Baker, Apr. 6, 1934, Jan. 3, 1936, Baker MSS, Box 60; Detroit News, June 2, 1937; Willis Van Devanter to Mrs. John Lacey, Jan. 11, 1933, Van Devanter MSS, Vol. 46; 1 ICKES 705.

It is not clear why the Administration did not move more forcefully to expedite the Sumners bill to make retirement more attractive. On the early history of this bill, see James M. Landis to Donald R. Richberg, Richberg MSS, LC, Box 1; Alexander Holtzoff to the Attorney General, Mar. 5, 1935, NA Dept. of Justice 235241. For post-election response, see Cummings to FDR, Dec. 29, 1936, FDRL PSF Supreme Court.

[124] Van Devanter to Dennis Flynn, Oct. 19, 1936; Van Devanter to Mrs. John W. Lacey, Nov. 2, 1936, Van Devanter MSS, Vol. 52.

not strike down such landmarks as the Wagner Act and the Social Security law, but it barred the way to new legislation. Returned to office with a tremendous grant of power, Roosevelt might be denied by the Court the opportunity to use that power. If he waited to see what the Court did, he might find himself with his past achievements obliterated and the momentum for future change lost.

Roosevelt had a strong sense of his own place in history. He would not countenance being written off in the history books as a man who had been frustrated in his attempts to lead the country out of the depression and to create a more humane social order. "When I retire to private life on January 20, 1941," he remarked, "I do not want to leave the country in the condition Buchanan left it to Lincoln."[125] Nor did he wish to be known as a President who had permitted judicial usurpers to impair the office of the Executive. Finally, it should be noted, the Court, by such decisions as that in the *Humphrey* case, had wounded his self-esteem, and, by other acts, had convinced Roosevelt that it was personally hostile to him.[126] He now sought a way not merely to liberalize the Court but to chastise the Justices for their past behavior.

Six days after the election, Roosevelt returned to Washington from Hyde Park; on his very first night in the capital, he summoned Cummings to the White House to report to him on what progress had been made at the Justice Department. Cummings told him that, over the summer, work had intensified as men like Edward S. Corwin, professor of jurisprudence at Princeton University, and William Draper Lewis of the American Law Institute had been asked for advice. Within the department, under the direction of Cummings and Solicitor General Stanley Reed, arguments were being assembled for and against specific proposals.

Both Roosevelt and Cummings had a tacit understanding that at some point action would have to be taken, and they now agreed that the Court was unlikely to be changed in its ways by the election returns. Yet the President still did not indicate that the time to act had come. He treated the meeting as yet another occasion on which the Attorney General had been asked for a progress

125 29 TIME 13 (Mar. 8, 1937).

126 For Roosevelt's belief that he had been snubbed by the Justices in 1936, see the penciled memorandum, "Court story," Harry Hopkins MSS, FDRL, Box 325. The account in SHERWOOD, ROOSEVELT AND HOPKINS 94 (1948) is slightly inaccurate.

report, and told him to come back as soon as he had something new to recommend. Meanwhile he was to maintain the closest secrecy on his research.[127]

Cummings, who may have sensed that Roosevelt was more disposed to act than he indicated, sped back to the Justice Department to order his research aides to devote full time, and overtime, to preparing reports and digests of reports for the President. Speed was important, because Roosevelt was to leave on a South American cruise on November 18. For the next nine days, messengers carried memorandums from the Justice Department to the White House and the President's comments back in the other direction. Almost every day, the Attorney General, arriving secretly through a private entrance, conferred at the White House with the President.[128]

Day after day they went over the great variety of recommendations that had come to them in the past two years. The uninvited counsel the President had received in the aftermath of the election indicated that opinion was still unsettled and that no one solution had emerged as the inevitable answer. Some urged pressing for an amendment. A Philadelphia attorney wrote, "We hope . . . you will recommend an amendment clearly adequate in scope, not only for today but for tomorrow also, when even broader needs will arise but may be met by stronger reactionary barriers." Similarly, a group of five Utah labor organizations wanted their legislature to memorialize Congress for an amendment to give Congress the power to regulate the hours of labor.[129] But other letters recommended packing the Court and emphasized the old-age theme. A Baltimore lawyer wanted "a law to be enacted at once that the personnel of the Supreme Court be increased to not less than two more judges," and a Memphis man wrote: "I think you the grandest President we have ever had, and I think God will give you a hand. . . . Mr. President, the labor people want you and Congress

---

127 ALSOP & CATLEDGE, THE 168 DAYS 20, 23–24 (1938) (hereinafter ALSOP); N.Y. Times, Feb. 12, 1937; Raymond Clapper MS Diary, Feb. 8, 1937.

128 ALSOP 27.

129 L. Stauffer Oliver to FDR, Nov. 12, 1936; George C. Christiansen *et al.* to C. W. Spence, Dec. 12, 1936, FDRL OF 274, Box 4. See, too, Virgil V. Johnson to FDR, Nov. 13, 1936, FDRL PPF 200, Reelect Cong–J.

to curb the Supreme Court. You all know just 9 old men should not rule this grand country."[130]

Roosevelt dismissed the amendment route as unacceptable for a number of reasons. In the first place, he thought an amendment would be difficult to frame. Two years of study in the Justice Department had not yet yielded a satisfactory draft, and liberals outside the government were far from a consensus. When the National Consumers' League, which had spearheaded the drive for minimum-wage legislation, polled national legal experts after the *Tipaldo* decision on whether a campaign for an amendment should be launched, the results were discouraging. Half of those polled—including Felix Frankfurter—opposed agitation for an amendment, and the other half were so far apart on what kind of an amendment should be sought that the League decided against any action at all.[131]

Even if an amendment could be framed, and approved by two-thirds of each house of Congress, it would have to run the gantlet of ratification by three-fourths of the states. If ratification was by state legislatures, as seemed most likely, it would require an adverse vote by only one house in thirteen legislatures to defeat an amendment, and the state legislatures were known to overrepresent conservative interests. Nor did Roosevelt have much faith in the probity of these assemblies. As he wrote a prominent New York lawyer three months later: "If you were not as scrupulous and ethical as you happen to be, you could make five million dollars as easy as rolling off a log by undertaking a campaign to prevent the ratification by one house of the Legislature, or even the summoning of a constitutional convention in thirteen states for the next four years. Easy money."[132] In a conversation with Ickes, Tom Corcoran had no trouble in ticking off the thirteen states "that would naturally be against a broadening amendment or in which money could be used to defeat it."[133]

---

[130] John B. McGraw to Stephen Early, Dec. 8, 1936, FDRL OF 274, Box 4; L. L. Wilson to FDR, Dec. 3, 1936, NA Dept. of Justice 235773. See, too, B. F. Welty to FDR, Dec. 29, 1936, FDRL OF 41, Box 114.

[131] Report of the Committee of Inquiry to the Board, Nov. 5, 1936, Mary Dewson MSS, FDRL, Box 6. The Dewson Papers also contain the original replies.

[132] FDR to Charles C. Burlingham, Feb. 23, 1937, 1 Letters 662.

[133] 2 Ickes 33–34.

At best, ratification would take a long time, and time was invaluable. Conscious of the brief span allotted to reform movements, Roosevelt wanted to exploit his landslide victory to drive through legislation such as a wages and hours bill while Congress still felt the full force of his popular indorsement. To be sure, the Norris lame-duck amendment had been adopted quickly, but that, he thought, was because it had not been opposed by any strongly entrenched interest. A constitutional amendment affecting the courts would not only be rejected by business interests but would encounter state legislatures largely composed of lawyers, who would be likely to be more disapproving of tinkering with the courts than would other groups.[134]

Roosevelt was especially influenced by the long, unsuccessful experience with attempting to win ratification for the child-labor amendment, a struggle then in its thirteenth year. As LaRue Brown, formerly Assistant Attorney General under Wilson, told the National Consumers' League:[135]

> My personal experience with the Child Labor Amendment leads me to view with great dubiety the prospect of ratification of an amendment increasing federal power. Our side is at so tremendous a disadvantage as to resources and so many truly liberal folk are so questioning as to the ultimate intendments of increasing the federal authority that I fear we should simply wear our hearts out in another hopeless fight.

Subsequently, Stephen Early, Roosevelt's press secretary, summed up the objections for Raymond Clapper. Clapper set down in his diary:[136]

> Steve said that the president had given him sidelight this morning on court proposal that he thought he would pass on to me to use or not as I saw fit. It was this—that people who talked about an amendment either didn't realize difficulties in that method or else did realize them and for that reason advocated this course. Steve said that to seek an amendment meant

134 Mallon, *Purely Confidential*, Detroit News, Feb. 13, 1937; N.Y. Times, Feb. 12, 1937.

135 Brown to Lucy R. Mason, Sept. 9, 1936, Mary Dewson MSS, Box 6. See, too, Donald Richberg to Raymond Clapper, Feb. 26, 1937, Richberg MSS, Box 2. Advocates of amendments pointed out that the child-labor amendment had been improperly drafted, and that the ratification process could involve conventions rather than legislatures.

136 Raymond Clapper MS Diary, Feb. 8, 1937.

> getting two-thirds of both houses and then submitting it to states where ¾ needed. He said suppose 13 governors refused to submit amendment. It dead then. He said all of us who ever been around legislatures know how easy be for moneyed interests to buy up enough legislatures to prevent action. Said this not like prohibition—here are vast and powerful groups determined to prevent action. Said another reason would be that to follow amendment course would make this an issue in 1938 campaign and might lose a number of "our congressmen." Might cost them their seats.

Even if all these objections were overcome and an amendment went through, any legislation enacted under authorization of such an amendment would still be subject to review in the courts, unless such an amendment was purely procedural. "In view of what Mr. Justice Roberts did to a clause as broad and sweeping as 'the general welfare,'" wrote Charles A. Beard, "I can see other justices of his mental outlook macerating almost any clarifying amendment less generous in its terms. If there is any phrase wider than providing for the general welfare, I am unable to conjure it up in my mind."[137] Besides, if the President should sponsor an amendment enlarging federal powers, it might seem tantamount to conceding that he had been wrong and the Supreme Court right in their dispute over the constitutionality of New Deal measures, and this Roosevelt, especially after his bracing election triumph, was less willing than ever to do.[138]

After eliminating amendment proposals, Roosevelt and Cummings next looked into various suggestions that would require only an act of Congress. First, they considered a bill stipulating more than a majority of Justices to invalidate a law; they dismissed this, because they feared that the Court would void such a statute. As Richberg later explained: "A mere statute to this effect would either be disregarded by the court, or have the result that Justices anxious to preserve the prestige of the court would join unwillingly with the majority so as to make a decision of the court effective." Moreover, such a law would limit the Court's role as a protector of civil liberties. They then examined a bill to withdraw appellate

[137] Beard, *Rendezvous with the Supreme Court*, 88 New Republic 93 (Sept. 2, 1936); Beard to Nicholas Kelley, Aug. 8, 1936, Mary Dewson MSS, Box 6.

[138] Washington Herald, Mar. 14, 1937, clipping, Frank Murphy Collection, University of Michigan Law School.

jurisdiction, but they were troubled by the recognition that the Court would still have original jurisdiction, especially in cases involving conflicts among states, and that the lower courts would retain their powers. By the end of the nine days, both men were leaning toward court-packing as the only feasible solution, but they were not yet committed to it, nor had they decided on the form it should take.[139]

Just before departing for South America, Roosevelt met once more with Cummings in the President's office. This time the President told an elated Cummings that he had made his decision; he would present a Court bill to Congress as soon as one was ready. Cummings gave him two stout volumes of proposed amendments and bills to take aboard ship to study, and they agreed that if any new ideas were developed they would be dispatched to the President at his ports of call. Roosevelt also took with him two lengthy memorandums from Donald Richberg, which stated that he "should not simply *defend* reasonable exercises of legislative power, but should aggressively *attack* the unconstitutional exercise of judicial power." On November 18, the President set sail for southern waters, after charging Cummings to have a plan ready for him on his return.[140]

VI. McReynolds' Petard

During the four weeks the President was touring South America, Cummings and his aides worked prodigiously at canvassing the possibilities for judicial reform. But when Roosevelt returned on December 15, they still had not found a solution. The main result of their labors was an exhaustive 65-page report which W. W. Gardner submitted to Reed, and the Solicitor General forwarded to Cummings. ("This matter has been handled confidentially," Reed assured him, "and I have my copy of the memorandum under lock.") Scholarly, shrewd, carefully written, the report was more valuable for warning of the pitfalls in various proposals than in pointing out what should be done.[141]

---

139 Alsop 28–30; N.Y. Times, Feb. 12, 1937; Washington Post, Feb. 13, 1937; Richberg to Clapper, Feb. 26, 1937, Richberg MSS, Box 2.

140 Alsop 30–31; Richberg to FDR, Nov. 16, 1936, FDRL PPF 2418.

141 Raymond Clapper MS Diary, Feb. 8, 1937; Reed, Memorandum for the Attorney General from the Solicitor General, Dec. 19, 1936, NA Dept. of Justice 235773.

Meanwhile, a much more fruitful exchange was being carried on between Cummings and Professor Corwin. The author of numerous articles and books excoriating the infringement by the Court on the prerogatives of other branches of government, Corwin had developed a close relationship with the Justice Department. Like other constitutional authorities, he had oscillated between different answers to the conflict between the President and the Court—from believing the Court should correct its own errors to favoring amendments, especially one to require more than a simple majority to invalidate laws.[142] His thinking may have been turned in a new direction by a letter he received early in September from Charles E. Clark, dean of the Yale Law School: "I do think that the possibility of increasing the size of the Court ought to be more considered in Congress than apparently it has."[143]

After the election, Corwin wrote a series of newspaper articles on the Court question. On December 3, Cummings wrote the President, who was still in South America:[144]

> Professor Corwin, of Princeton, has prepared a series of articles dealing with some of our Constitutional difficulties. These articles will shortly be published in the Philadelphia Record. They are especially pertinent to the last discussion I had with you on this subject. I have just received from Doctor Corwin the proof sheets of the articles, which I enclose herewith. I am very sure that you will find them well worth reading.

Corwin's series was a curious performance. With corrosive wit, he derided the record of the Court during the New Deal. In exposing the inadequacies of the panaceas that had been offered, he wrote brilliantly. But his own remedies were murky and even contradictory. After showing with devastating clarity why the Administration should not resort to amendments, he stated that some amendments might be needed. He called for the Court to reform itself, yet conceded that this particular Court could not be expected to do so. But one sentence in the final article emerged boldly: "No reform could be better adopted than the requirement, to be laid

---

142 Corwin had helped prepare the Government's brief in the *Carter* case. CORWIN, THE COMMERCE POWER VS. STATES RIGHTS 263–67 (1936); Corwin to Lucy R. Mason, Sept. 24, 1936, Mary Dewson MSS, Box 6; John Dickinson to Corwin, June 15, 1936.

143 Clark to Corwin, Sept. 3, 1936, Corwin MSS, Princeton University Library.

144 Cummings to FDR, Dec. 3, 1936, FDRL OF 41-A, Box 116; Cummings to Corwin, Dec. 3, 1936, Corwin MSS.

down by an act of Congress, or, if necessary, by constitutional amendment, that no Judge may hold office under the United States beyond his seventieth birthday."[145]

In the series, Corwin appeared to be trimming some of his beliefs in order to avoid exciting unnecessary quarrels. In particular, his deference to the amendment approach seemed less than heartfelt. On December 16, he wrote Cummings:[146]

> It is probably utopian to hope that the Court will supply the needed remedy for a situation which it has itself created. Hence we must turn either to constitutional amendment or Congressional action.
>
> As to the latter, I did not care to go on record as favoring a *tour de force;* yet it is essential to face the fact that Congressional action may be necessary.

Nor, he added, had his articles exhausted the possibilities of action. Corwin continued:

> A friend of mine has made this ingenious suggestion: that the President be authorized, whenever a majority of the Justices, or half of the Justices, are seventy or more years old, to nominate enough new Justices of less than that age to make a majority. This, too, would require only an act of Congress, and something of a legislative precedent for such a measure is furnished by § 375 of title 28, of the U.S. Code.
>
> Mr. Reed appears to think that I put too much emphasis on my age-limit proposal, but I'm not so sure. A 70-year age-limit would secure more rapid replacement of justices. Furthermore, it might serve to draw the attention of the appointing power more frequently to the faculties of our great Law-schools where superior talent emerges at an earlier age than in practice at the Bar.

---

[145] The proofs are in FDRL OF 41-A, Box 116. Clark argued that Corwin had underestimated the possibilities of the amendment process. Clark to Corwin, Dec. 11, 1936, and Corwin's reply, Dec. 16, 1936. See, too, Clark to Corwin, Aug. 18, 1936, Corwin MSS.

[146] The penciled draft of this letter in the Corwin Papers is undated. The letter could have been sent at any time between December 4 and 16, but December 16 seems highly probable. That same day, Corwin wrote Reed: "I was glad to get your comments on those articles—I believe that my age limit proposal, if adopted, may have considerable effect. It might not get more liberal judges, but it would assure a more rapid replacement of the Bench. Today Jefferson's complaint is well justified: 'Few die and none resign.'—indeed the statement might be made stronger. . . . I believe it could be validly accomplished by an act of Congress." Corwin to Reed, Dec. 16, 1936, NA Dept. of Justice 235868. Reed appears to have been unenthusiastic about the plan both at this point and when it finally emerged.

Since Corwin had pointed out in his series the folly of enlarging the Court, this suggestion marked an important new departure. For the first time, compulsory retirement at 70 was linked to the appointment of new Justices. On the very next day, Cummings replied to Corwin:[147]

> Of course, I realize that there is a good deal of prejudice against "packing the Court." I have been wondering to what extent we have been frightened by the phrase.
>
> Quite apart from immediate consideration, and as a mere matter of general policy, I have often thought that much was to be said for a constitutional amendment requiring retirements when the age of 70 is reached. I am wondering if there would be much opposition to such an amendment if it were so framed as not to affect the present judiciary by making it apply to future appointments only.

Corwin's contribution reached Cummings at a propitious moment. Both the Attorney General and the President had been attracted to "court-packing" for some weeks, but they recognized that the proposition violated taboos and that some principle would have to be found to justify it. Corwin offered such a formula by relating new appointments to the ages of Justices. If Corwin's suggestion (or that of Corwin's "friend") was adopted, Cummings could exploit growing popular resentment at the age of the bench.

By now, it had become commonplace to refer to the Justices as the "nine old men." A. A. Berle had used the term in passing in 1933,[148] and a column in a Kentucky newspaper reflected a popular notion when it referred to the Court as "nine old back-number owls (appointed by by-gone Presidents) who sit on the leafless, fruitless limb of an old dead tree." But it was the publication on October 26, 1936 of *The Nine Old Men* by Drew Pearson and Robert S. Allen which made the phrase a household word. The book quickly climbed onto the best-seller lists, and it was serialized in newspapers across the country. Even critics of the Justices were disturbed by the book's tone and by its inaccuracies, but this exposé helped concentrate popular attention on both the age and the viewpoint of the Court as a more sober account might not have done. Representative Thomas Amlie of Wisconsin, while regretting the book's innuendos, thought "that Pearson and Allen have done a particu-

---

[147] Cummings to Corwin, Dec. 17, 1936, Corwin MSS.

[148] Berle, *Law and the Social Revolution*, 22 SURVEY GRAPHIC 594 (Dec., 1933).

larly good job on the Constitutional law angle," and Senator Joseph Guffey of Pennsylvania called for a Senate investigation of the allegations made in the book. Guffey called the volume "the most disturbing—I would say shocking book on public officials I have ever read. Its purported disclosures are sensational."[149]

After receiving Corwin's letter, Cummings was close to the end of the trail. Yet Corwin still had not shown him the precise route the Attorney General was seeking, and Cummings' reply suggests that he was still thinking that an amendment might be required, and that the present Justices might be exempted. However, once Corwin had blazed the path this far, it did not take Cummings long to discover the rest of the way.

At some point in the next five days, Cummings found his answer. While carrying on his other duties, the Attorney General had also been writing a history of his department, in collaboration with his aide, Carl McFarland. One passage in *Federal Justice*, which was about to be published, now stood out from the pages as it had not before, a recommendation that Justice McReynolds, when serving as Wilson's Attorney General, had made in 1913.

McReynolds' recommendation stated:[150]

> Judges of the United States Courts, at the age of 70, after having served 10 years, may retire upon full pay. In the past, many judges have availed themselves of this privilege. Some, however, have remained upon the bench long beyond the time that they are able to adequately discharge their duties, and in consequence the administration of justice has suffered. ... I suggest an act providing that when any judge of a Federal court below the Supreme Court fails to avail himself of the privilege of retiring now granted by law, that the President be required, with the advice and consent of the Senate, to appoint another judge, who would preside over the affairs of the court and have precedence over the older one. This will insure at all times the presence of a judge sufficiently active to discharge promptly and adequately the duties of the court.

149 Charles N. Crewdson to Louis Howe, Jan. 7, 1936, FDRL OF 41-A, Box 116; Thomas Reed Powell to William O. Douglas, n.d., Douglas MSS, LC, Box 20; Herbert Hoover to Charles Evans Hughes, Feb. 19, 1937, Hughes MSS, Box 6; James A. Stone to William T. Evjue, Mar. 17, 1937, Stone MSS, Minnesota Historical Society, Box 28; Thomas R. Amlie to Donald A. Butchart, Mar. 6, 1937, Amlie MSS, Box 36; N.Y. Times, Jan. 27, 1937.

150 Report of the Attorney General for the Fiscal Year Ending June 30, 1913 5, Cummings & McFarland, Federal Justice (1937).

Cummings now reasoned that McReynolds' prescription, which had been limited to the lower courts, might also be applied to the Supreme Court. Once the principle of retirement was adopted, any age might be stipulated, but 70 seemed especially compelling. It had been the age that, on different occasions, McReynolds, Cummings, and Corwin had all hit upon, and it had the not inconsiderable advantage of having biblical sanction. That summer, an Oklahoma newspaper had proposed to retire Supreme Court Justices at seventy, "as set out in Holy Writ as the reasonable span of human life."[151] With the retirement age fixed at 70, Roosevelt would be able to name six new Justices, thus practically assuring a bench that would approve New Deal legislation.

Before presenting the plan to Roosevelt, Cummings directed his assistants in the Justice Department to prepare a series of reports. He deliberately parceled out work so that the scheme would be kept a secret even from his own aides. Except for Cummings and Reed, no one in the department save for Holtzoff and McFarland appears to have known the full scope of the proposal until it was announced. When his assistants reported back to Cummings, each gave a favorable reply. One report approved the plan's constitutionality. Another turned up historical precedent in an 1869 bill that had passed the House of Representatives. A third pulled together statistics to show that the formula would also supply enough new judges for the lower courts.[152]

Cummings' search had ended. On December 22, he sent a penciled note to the President: "I am 'bursting' with ideas anent our constitutional problems; and have a plan (of substance & approach) I would like to talk over with you when you have the time."[153] By this point, Roosevelt was already determined to "pack" the Court, but he did not yet know how, and he still thought of the idea as a birch rod to be taken out of the closet only if the Court did not mend its ways in the new Term.

He now summoned George Creel to the White House once more to prepare an article, this one to be called "Roosevelt's Plans and Purposes." During the afternoon and evening they worked to-

151 *The Federal Constitution,* Shawnee (Okla.) County Democrat, Aug. 7, 1936, clipping, FDRL OF 274, Box 4.

152 Alsop 34; Raymond Clapper MS Diary, June 12, 1938.

153 Cummings to FDR, Dec. 22, 1936, FDRL PSF Supreme Court.

gether, Creel was struck by the fact that the President, understandably, viewed the election as a purely personal victory. He told Creel that the social objectives he cherished would all have to run the gantlet of the Supreme Court. But his face brightened as he said: "I've thought of a better way than a constitutional amendment stripping the Court of its power to nullify acts of Congress. The time element makes that method useless. Granted that Congress could agree on such an amendment for submission to the several states, it would be two, three, or four years before the legislatures could or would act. What do you think of this?"[154] From a drawer in his desk, he extracted a heavily marked copy of the Constitution and riffled the pages as he read off passages and commented on the powers of Congress to act for the general welfare.

After reading Article III, § 1, he asked: "Where is there anything in that which gives the Supreme Court the right to override the legislative branch?" As the President talked, Creel wrote afterward, "I was amazed by his reading on the subject and by the grip of his mind on what he conceived to be essential facts. For example, he quoted at length from Madison's *Journal* and Elliot's *Debates*, citing them as his authority for the statement that the framers of the Constitution had voted on four separate occasions against giving judges the power to pass upon the constitutionality of acts of Congress."[155]

If Congress was to reclaim the powers that had been usurped from it, Roosevelt reasoned, it should add a rider to each bill at the next session charging the Supreme Court to remember that the Constitution vested all legislative power in Congress and authorized it to provide for the general welfare. Suppose this proved ineffective? Creel related: " 'Then,' said the President, his face like a fist, 'Congress can *enlarge* the Supreme Court, increasing the number of justices so as to permit the appointment of men in tune with the spirit of the age.' " When *Collier's* published this article on December 26, with three columns discussing the Supreme Court, Creel expected an explosion in Congress and the press. Yet, once again, the President's explicit words were ignored.[156]

On the same day that Creel's article appeared, Cummings went

154 CREEL, *op. cit. supra* note 65, at 292–94; Richberg to FDR, Nov. 16, 1936, FDRL PPF 2418.

155 CREEL, *op. cit. supra* note 65, at 293–94.

156 *Ibid.*

to the White House to report to Roosevelt. According to one account, not altogether probable, the Attorney General handed the President a packet of plans with the new scheme on the bottom. He then watched agitatedly while Roosevelt turned over each in turn until he came to Cummings' favorite; to the Attorney General's immense pleasure, Roosevelt was delighted. However it happened, it is clear that the President gave his approval that day. He was gratified that the proposal was unquestionably constitutional, and he took a mischievous pleasure in the fact that it could be attributed to McReynolds.[157]

Buoyed by the President's approval, Cummings now turned his hand to sketching the remaining details of the plan. He wanted not only to liberalize the Court but to reform the entire judiciary. By presenting "court-packing" in the guise of judicial reform, he would make the plan more palatable. Yet Cummings' interest in reform was not just expedient. He had long cherished the aim of overhauling the structure of the courts, and Roosevelt shared some of his ardor. Once they launched what they knew would be a historic fight, they wanted it to be remembered for improving the judicial system as well as for overcoming the intransigence of the Supreme Court.

For two years, William Denman, Judge of the Ninth Circuit Court of Appeals, had been bombarding Roosevelt with pleas for more lower-court judges in order to relieve congestion in the courts and prevent miscarriages of justice. Denman also argued that the lower-court system was illogically organized, and, he proposed, among other suggestions, the appointment of a proctor of the Supreme Court to supervise lower courts and the creation of "roving judges" to clear up congestion. The Judicial Conference had also, more than once, pointed out the need for additional district judges. Cummings now decided to tie all these ideas together into a single package, but to relate the call for more lower-court judges to the principle of age.[158]

---

[157] ALSOP 34–35; Raymond Clapper MS Diary, June 12, 1938. Rexford Tugwell has written: "Of all the ways open to him Franklin does seem to have chosen the one most upsetting to judicial dignity." TUGWELL, *op. cit. supra* note 55, at 392.

[158] Raymond Clapper MS Diary, Feb. 8, 1937; Denman to Cummings, Mar. 19, 1936; Denman to FDR, Mar. 20, 1936, FDRL OF 209-I; Memorandum for the Attorney General, Apr. 29, 1936; Denman to M. H. McIntyre, Mar. 17, 1936, FDRL PPF 336; Denman to FDR, Sept. 5, 1936, FDRL OF 41, Box 114; Charles Evans Hughes

By the end of the year, the Justice Department had prepared the first draft of the bill. In all, it went through twelve full drafts and numerous minor revisions. The measure embraced four proposals: (1) that when a judge of a federal court who had served ten years did not resign or retire within six months after his seventieth birthday, the President might name another judge as coadjutor; (2) that the Supreme Court should not have more than six added Justices, nor any lower-court bench more than two, nor the total federal judiciary more than fifty; (3) that lower-court judges might be assigned to exceptionally busy courts; and (4) that the lower courts should be supervised by the Supreme Court through a proctor.[159]

Roosevelt and Cummings decided it would be helpful to accompany the bill with both a message from the President and a letter from the Attorney General. Instead of concentrating on the desirability of a more liberal court, both documents would stress the incapacity of aged judges and the need for additional appointments to get the Court abreast of its work. By emphasizing the theme of greater efficiency, they hoped the whole plan would be accepted as a project for judicial reform rather than a stratagem to pack the Court. Once again, Cummings parceled out assignments within the department so that men were called on to supply statistics on denial of certiorari or the ages of judges without ever being told why this information was wanted or being given enough to do to be able to piece together what was happening.

When all three documents were taken to the White House, the President offered little comment on the bill, but he gave the letter, to which Holtzoff had made important contributions, a thorough going-over, and Cummings had to revise it before Roosevelt would give his approval. Even more care was lavished on the President's message, which Roosevelt recognized would be an important state paper. In the third week in January, Donald Richberg was called in to polish the draft, and on the night of January 30, when Judge Rosenman arrived at the White House for the President's birthday party, he was asked to contribute his talents. It was the first he had

---

to FDR, May 30, 1934, FDRL OF 41-A; Mallon, *Purely Confidential*, Detroit News, Apr. 2, 1937; ALSOP 31–35.

[159] By January 5, the bill had reached a fifth draft. "Draft No. 5, January 5, 1937," FDRL PSF Supreme Court.

heard of the plan, even though he had helped write both the State-of-the-Union message and the Inaugural Address that month. When Rosenman told Corcoran, who had also been kept in the dark, what was happening, the President agreed that Corcoran, too, should be asked to go over the final draft of the message. But he instructed Rosenman not to let Cummings know that Corcoran was involved.[160]

The President's insistence on secrecy combined fear of premature disclosure that might promote bickering with his love of the dramatic. Save for Cummings, no one in the cabinet, not even the ubiquitous Ickes, knew of the plan. Indeed, Roosevelt, at one cabinet meeting in January, deliberately misrepresented what was going on. Nor was any member of Congress told. Some of the men who would soon bear the burden of defending it were busy drafting quite different proposals, and Henry Fountain Ashurst, who would shortly be called on to move the President's proposal through the Senate Judiciary Committee, was publicly denouncing court-packing as "the prelude to tyranny."[161]

Through all of this, the President gave almost no indication of the surprise he was about to spring. As Moley later wrote: "Roosevelt's pronouncements in the course of his good-will trip to South America would not have frightened the birds of St. Francis."[162] Despite some shafts aimed at the Supreme Court, Roosevelt's State-of-the-Union message was praised for its good-tempered restraint, and he made no mention at all of the Court in his Inaugural Address. Informed observers predicted that the President would wait to see

---

[160] ALSOP 43–47; RICHBERG, *op. cit. supra* note 119, at 221–22; Raymond Clapper MS Diary, Jan. 14, 1938; ROSENMAN, *op. cit. supra* note 119, at 145–50. Two drafts of the message have been retained in the Samuel I. Rosenman MSS, FDRL, "Message to Congress on the Judiciary" folder.

[161] Washington Post, Feb. 13, 1937; 2 ICKES 31; Henry Morgenthau, Jr., MS Diary, FDRL, Feb. 6, 1937; Raymond Clapper MS Diary, Feb. 5, 1937; Edward Rees to William Allen White, n.d., White MSS, Box 186; CONG. REC., 75th Cong., 1st Sess., 562. After the plan was announced, Clapper reported on an interview with the President's press secretary, Stephen Early: "Steve says that only five people were told of plan by President. He said president wouldn't want him to reveal names but he thought I knew them. Said none was in Congress. . . . Steve said reason Rvt didn't talk it over with more people was that he was afraid of a leak which would tip off opposition and enable them to start hostile build up before he got his plan out." Clapper MS Diary, Feb. 8, 1937.

[162] MOLEY 356.

how the Court disposed of the Wagner cases before taking any action. On January 24, Dean Dinwoodey, editor of *United States Law Week,* wrote that "last week it was made plain that he does not at the present time have in mind any legislation directed at the Court."[163]

VII. Roosevelt Entertains the Court

By the beginning of February, the bill, the letter, and the message had all been drafted, except for a few final details. All that remained was to decide when to launch the plan. It is conceivable that Roosevelt might have waited until the Wagner cases had been decided, although this seems unlikely, but if he had any such intention, he felt compelled to abandon it. The situation in Congress, where more and more members were committing themselves publicly to divergent proposals, was getting out of hand. Outside the government, progressives had called a national conference to reach agreement on an amendment. Most important, word of Roosevelt's own plan had begun to leak out, and speculation about what the President intended was getting closer and closer to the mark.[164]

Not everyone had thought that Roosevelt's State-of-the-Union address signaled inaction. Breckinridge Long noted in his diary:[165]

> After I heard the speech I went home and read the printed speech twice. It is rather mysterious in that it is enshrouded somewhat in mystery in that he makes no intimation of his specific plan, but it is very plain that he has something definitely in mind. I say it is very plain, but I mean that it is very plain to those who read with a discriminating eye the words of his message and use as a background his whole history in connection with the Supreme Court.

The conservative Republican congressman from Minnesota, Harold Knutson, also found the address unsettling. He wrote: "I rather

---

[163] 29 Time 13–14 (Jan. 18, 1937); N.Y. Times, Jan. 5, 7, 10, 24, 1937.

[164] Mallon, *Purely Confidential,* Detroit News, Feb. 13, 1937; Mary Dewson to Stanley Reed, Dec. 10, 1936; Dewson to Mrs. Armstrong, n.d.; Elmer F. Andrews to Members of the New York State Minimum Wage Conference, Jan. 26, 1937; Mrs. J. C. Pryer to Mary Dewson, Jan. 11, 1937, Dewson MSS; Alfred M. Bingham to Thomas R. Amlie, Jan. 5, 1937, Amlie MSS, Box 35. Subsequently, Clapper summed up what Cummings had told him: "Didn't know until last minute whether Rvt would go through with it or not." Clapper MS Diary, Feb. 8, 1937.

[165] Breckinridge Long MS Diary, Jan. 6, 1937.

thought the President's message contained one or two disquieting features and the question that is bothering me is, will he attempt to 'pack' the Supreme Court. There is no limit on the number of judges that may be appointed to the Supreme Court and by adding two or three he could easily secure control of the judiciary. Will he go that far?"[166]

In divining the President's intentions, Long had an advantage. On the same day that Roosevelt gave his address, Long had lunched with Cummings. Afterward, he set down in his diary:[167]

> Homer has devised a means and has a specific draft to carry out the provisions intimated. It contemplates a large treatment for the whole judicial system and is not confined to the Supreme Court alone. He thinks the President has the matter definitely in mind. Procedure along that line would permit the drafting of a bill to disqualify members of the judiciary over the age of 70 years, if they have not retired voluntarily within six months after they have passed that age, and the appointment of a successor. More than that, it makes various changes in the structure of the judiciary and mobilizes the framework of the system. Whether anything will come of it is to be determined only in the future, but in the light of the President's Annual Message to the Congress it seems to my mind clearly that he has some definite proposal in mind, and after my conversation today I am of the opinion that it is this proposal.

Roosevelt's speech-writers were no more discreet than his Attorney General. Over cocktails on January 20, Donald Richberg let slip what was going on. Ray Clapper noted in his diary:[168]

> Richberg says Rvt has a number of bombshells ready to shoot which will astound country—says Rvt is in audacious mood and is even thinking of proposing to pack Supreme Court by enlarging it. R seems favor instead compulsory retirement. He says Rvt is determined to curb the court and put it in its place, and will go ahead even if many people think it unwise.

Before the month was out, the Senate began to sense what was happening. On January 24, Irving Brant, who as editor of the editorial page of the St. Louis *Star-Times* had often written on constitutional subjects, wrote the President: "Several senators have

[166] Knutson to Elmer E. Adams, Jan. 11, 1937, Adams MSS, Minnesota Historical Society, Box 42. See, too, Ray Lyman Wilbur to Dr. Arthur H. Daniels, Jan. 8, 1937, Wilbur MSS, Stanford University Library.

[167] Breckinridge Long MS Diary, Jan. 6, 1937.

[168] Raymond Clapper MS Diary, Jan. 20, 1937.

told me that you expect to make a statement about the Supreme Court within a few days."[169] On February 2, in a speech that seemed to imply more than it said, Senator William Borah of Idaho deprecated the "purloining" of state powers by the federal government and lauded the Supreme Court as the shield of individual liberties.[170] Alert Washington columnists knew that something was in the wind, but they had not yet discovered what it was. "Strange things are being said in Congress," Paul Mallon noted in his column of February 4. First there had been a speech by Ashurst, then one by Congressman Samuel Pettengill, now Borah. But what were they aiming at? Borah, he pointed out, "left the definite impression he was attacking something Mr. Roosevelt was going to propose, but he did not say what."[171]

Roosevelt could wait no longer. Since the Court was scheduled to begin hearings on the constitutionality of the Wagner Act on Monday, February 8, he wanted to submit the message before then so that it would not be interpreted as a threat to the Court. On February 2, he was scheduled to entertain the judiciary at dinner at the White House; so he could not very well present the plan before then.[172] Richberg later recalled that the President had said impishly that "his choice should be whether to take only one cocktail before dinner and have it a very amiable affair, or to have a mimeographed copy of the program laid beside the plate of each justice and then take three cocktails to fortify himself against their reactions."[173] The President was thus limited to the interval between February 3 and February 6. On February 3, the Senate recessed until February 5; so Friday, February 5, became the day the President chose to act.

The real ending of the odyssey of the search for the Court plan came not on February 5 but three days earlier when the guests assembled in the East Room of the White House for the judiciary dinner. It was a gala evening. Among the ninety guests were most of the Supreme Court Justices, Mrs. Woodrow Wilson, Senator Borah, and the Gene Tunneys. In the room sat men like Reed, whom the Justices did not suspect might soon be their colleague,

169 Brant to FDR, Jan. 24, 1937, FDRL PPF 2293; Washington Post, Feb. 13, 1937.

170 N.Y. Times, Feb. 2, 1937; Detroit News, Feb. 2, 1937.

171 Mallon, *Purely Confidential*, Detroit News, Feb. 4, 1937.

172 Washington Post, Feb. 13, 1937; Raymond Clapper MS Diary, Feb. 8, 1937.

173 RICHBERG, *op. cit. supra* note 119, at 222.

and Cummings, who was told by Rosenman that he had the lean and hungry look proper to a conspirator.[174] Two of those present, Senator Ashurst and Representative Hatton Sumners, chairmen of the Senate and House Judiciary Committees, would in three more days be handed a bill to curb the power of the honored guests of the evening. As the guests filed out of the dining room, Roosevelt, in high spirits, remained seated talking to Justices Hughes and Van Devanter. Borah, seeing them together, remarked: "That reminds me of the Roman Emperor who looked around his dinner table and began to laugh when he thought how many of those heads would be rolling on the morrow."[175]

VIII. The Reality and the Myth

To put together the complete puzzle of the origins of the Court plan, one still needs a few pieces. The opening of the Homer Cummings papers, now privately held, and of the Stanley Reed memoir in the Columbia Oral History Collection, now closed, should be instructive. But most of the pieces are now available. It is clear that many of the men alleged to have been authors of the plan either knew nothing of it or played quite minor roles. The main operation, from beginning to end, involved a very few men, all of them concentrated in the Justice Department. Of those who exerted influence from outside the department, Corwin, a department consultant, was more important than such putative architects as Corcoran.

Of the plan itself, few have found much good to say. Much of this criticism is surely justified. Yet the presentation of the plan was not a capricious act but the result of a long period of gestation. During this time, other alternatives were carefully examined, favored for a while, and then discarded on not unreasonable grounds. Throughout this same period, Roosevelt was called on repeatedly to take action, and it appeared, in particular, that he would have a sizable following for a recommendation which would justify the appointment of additional Justices by stressing the infirmity of the Hughes Court. That Roosevelt misjudged the state of opinion seems probable in retrospect, but, at the time, the plan seemed to have an inherent logic and even inevitability.

---

[174] Rosenman, *op. cit. supra* note 119, at 153–54.

[175] Richberg, *op. cit. supra* note 119, at 222; 29 Time 15 (Feb. 15, 1937); *id.* at 13 (Mar. 1, 1937).

Court-Curbing Periods in American History

Stuart S. Nagel[*]

Seven periods of intense Court-curbing have occurred in American history. Due to the Court's unavoidable involvement in the political process, conflict between the legislative and judicial branches will occur again when certain judicial provocations and catalytic factors are present. Professor Nagel examines the factors which have an affirmative correlation with the occurrence of Court-curbing bills, and the factors which have an affirmative correlation with the success of Court-curbing bills.

Due to its unavoidable involvement in the political process, the Supreme Court has often been an object of congressional attack. Excellent descriptive studies have been made of certain periods of conflict between Congress and the Court,[1] but there is a lack of writing which systematically analyzes relations between Congress and the Court throughout American history. It is the purpose of this paper to analyze in a partially quantitative manner some of the factors which seem to account for the occurrence or nonoccurrence and for the success or failure of congressional attempts to curb the Court.

I. Research Design

One hundred and sixty-five instances of bills designed to curb the Supreme Court were compiled along with information concerning their content, sponsor, and fate from a perusal of *The Congressional Record* and its forerunners and also from the previous literature in the field.[2] In order to keep the data within manageable limits, resolutions and constitutional amendments were not included although they are introduced frequently and often contain proposals which would

* Assistant Professor of Political Science, University of Illinois; member of the Illinois Bar. The author is very grateful to Nancy J. Fahrnkopf, a former graduate student at the University of Illinois, for the extensive research work she did for an early draft of this article.

1. Walter F. Murphy concentrates on the problems of the Warren Court in his book, CONGRESS AND THE COURT (1962) as does PRITCHETT, CONGRESS VERSUS THE COURT (1960). Robert Jackson concentrates on the 1937 Court-packing plan in THE STRUGGLE FOR JUDICIAL SUPREMACY: A STUDY OF A CRISIS IN AMERICAN POWER POLITICS (1941). Walter Murphy's book was especially suggestive in writing some parts of this paper.

2. *Ibid.* See also Culp, *A Survey of Proposals to Limit or Destroy the Power of Judicial Review by the Supreme Court of the United States*, 4 IND. L.J. 386, 474 (1929); Warren, *The Early History of the Supreme Court of the United States in Connection with Modern Attacks on the Judiciary*, 8 MASS. L.Q. 1 (1922).

substantially reduce the powers of the Court.[3] Relatively narrow bills designed to reverse a single decision were also excluded. Relying on the distribution of bills as well as the consensus of historians, seven time periods as shown in Table I were labeled high-frequency Court-curbing periods. This identification is both quantitative and qualitative. For example, the first period covering the years from 1802 to 1804, had only two instances of overt congressional attempts to curb the Court, one of which was the unsuccessful impeachment of Justice Chase. While it may well be a quantitatively marginal period, most writers agree that this was a time of high friction between the Federalists on the bench and the Jeffersonians in Congress and the Administration.

TABLE 1. HIGH AND LOW FREQUENCY PERIODS OF COURT-CURBING IN AMERICAN HISTORY

High-Frequency			Low-Frequency		
Years	# of Bills	% of 165	Years	# of Bills	% of 165
1. 1802-1804	2	1%	1. 1789-1801	0	0%
2. 1823-1831	12	7	2. 1805-1822	0	0
3. 1858-1869	22	13	3. 1832-1857	1	1
4. 1893-1897	9	5	4. 1870-1892	8	5
5. 1922-1924	11	7	5. 1898-1921	6	4
6. 1935-1937	37	22	6. 1925-1934	2	1
7. 1955-1957	53	32	7. 1939-1954	2	1
Total	146	87%		19	12%

A criterion by which to judge the relative success or failure of any one Court-curbing period is more difficult to establish. A total of only nine out of the 165 bills regulating the Court have passed Congress. This group of "absolutely successful" bills, representing approximately five per cent of the total instances, is too small to work with for the purposes of this study. Three criteria of "relative success" will therefore be used. First, *how many* anti-Court bills during each period were reported from committee, the lowest stage of the legislative process aside from introduction? Second, *what per cent* of the bills introduced were reported out of committee? The third criterion of success, as shown in Table 2, is that of determining whether a congressional at-

3. Twenty-five joint resolutions were proposed in 1937 while thirty-three constitutional amendments were introduced during the two year period from 1935 to 1937. Several attempts have been made, for example in 1867 and 1871, to establish via Constitutional amendment a new court representing all the states which would have jurisdiction over constitutional questions. A joint resolution in 1861 demanded the abolition of the federal judicial system.

tack has had the effect of changing within the immediate future the pattern of voting behavior of the Court on the issues which originally provoked the attack. In four of the seven attacks, the Court did retreat from its previous controversial policy by executing a tactical abstention from further similar provocation (as was the case in the years following the 1804 conflict) or by effecting a reversal of policy (as was the case in 1937). At the climax of the seventh period, the Court drew back from its stand on one of the issues which antagonized Congress—namely a broad interpretation of free speech—but remained firm on its policies toward segregation and criminal procedure which were also under congressional fire.

TABLE 2. Relative Success of Seven High-Frequency Court-Curbing Periods

Years	Number of Bills Out of Committee	Per cent of Bills Out of Committee	Judicial Retreat	Composite Success	Rank Order of Composite Success
1. 1802-04	1	50%	Yes	Yes	3
2. 1823-31	3	25	Yes	Yes	4
3. 1858-69	11	50	Yes	Yes	1
4. 1893-97	1	11	No	No	7
5. 1922-24	2	18	No	No	6
6. 1935-37	6	16	Yes	Yes	2
7. 1955-59	2	4	Partial	No	5
	Avg. = 3.7 (N = 26)	Avg. 25% per period	Usually Yes	Usually Yes	

The fourth column in Table 2 provides a composite index of overall success. Thus, a high-frequency period can be considered successful if it is above average on the number of bills that were reported out of committee (*i.e.*, four or more); if it is above average on the per cent of successful bills (*i.e.*, 25% or above); and if it was climaxed by retreat of the Court on the majority of the issues involved. A period will be termed relatively successful if it is above average on at least two of these three criteria. Using this composite standard, four of the seven high-frequency periods have been classified as relative overall successes, and each period has been given a rough success ranking as shown in the last column of Table 2.

The variables influencing the occurrence and success of the seven court-curbing periods seem to fit into a model like the psychological model of stimulus-organism-response. In the political phenomenon of Court-curbing, the stimulus is represented by judicial provocation.

The organism is represented by the political system which may contain certain catalytic or conditioning factors which shape the perception of the provocation and the response. The response manifests itself in certain types of Court-curbing bills and Presidential action. This response may feed back on the judiciary and thereby stimulate judicial counter-action. Having this overall model in mind helps one to see better the interrelations between the more specific variables discussed in this paper.

II. JUDICIAL PROVOCATION

A. *Quantity of Judicial Review*

To what extent does a high quantity of judicial review of legislative acts provoke Court-curbing regardless of the type of interests involved? Table 3 shows that almost 50 of the total 86 instances of judicial nullification of federal statutes in American history have occurred during or within three years prior to the seven Court-curbing periods. Thus, over half of the instances of judicial nullification have occurred during a time span equaling less than one-third of the history of the Supreme Court. The use of judicial review for the first time in *Marbury v. Madison,*[4] was certainly an irritant in the Federalist-Jeffersonian dispute over relative amounts of judicial and executive power in the early 1800's. The nullification of state bankruptcy and debtor laws as well as the invalidation of a Maryland act taxing the Bank of the United States provoked the wrath of congressmen in the 1820's.[5] The 1858 Dred Scott case[6] nullified a federal statute, and congressional anticipation of judicial review of Reconstruction legislation led to the court-packing and restrictions on habeas corpus in the 1860's. The 1890's attack was precipitated in part by the invalidation of a federal income tax law, and nullification of federal and state economic legislation led to another Progressive attack on the Court in the 1920's. The judicial review of fifteen New Deal statutes was a prime causative factor in the 1930's conflict. In the 1950's, portions of federal and state laws were held unconstitutional, and proposed legislation such as the Jenner bill was clearly aimed at several decisions. In short, all the periods of intense Court-curbing have been provoked to some degree by the judicial review of legislative acts. Nullification of federal statutes, however, seems to provide a greater provocation than nullification of state statutes since judicial review of state statutes seemed to be a prime factor only in the 1820's Court-curbing period and

4. 5 U.S. (1 Cranch) 137 (1803).
5. 17 U.S. (4 Wheat.) 316 (1819).
6. 60 U.S. (19 How.) 393 (1857).

partially in the 1950's. Congress is apparently more protective of its own lawmaking than it is of the various state legislative bodies.

TABLE 3. Occurrence of Judicial Review During and 3 Years Prior to the High-Frequency Court-Curbing Periods

Years	Instances of judicial review of federal acts during or 3 years prior
1802-04	1
1823-31	0*
1858-69	5
1893-97	3
1922-24	13
1935-37	15
1955-59	5
Total:	42

*Judicial review of state acts present

If the seven periods are divided into the periods of relatively high judicial review of federal legislation and relatively low, then as Table 4 shows, a slightly greater proportion of the relatively high review periods involved relatively successful Court-curbing bills than did the relatively low review periods. Thus, the intensity of judicial review may be a partial determinant of the success of controversial Court-curbing bills as well as a determinant of the introduction of Court-curbing bills. There are, however, more important determinants of Court-curbing success as will be shown later.

TABLE 4. The Relation Between Intensity of Judicial Review and Court-Curbing Success

	Judicial Review of Federal Acts: Relatively Low	Judicial Review of Federal Acts: Relatively High
Relatively Successful	1800's 1820's	1930's 1860's
Relatively Unsuccessful	1890's 1950's	1920's

B. *Subject of the Provoking Cases*

The specific issues over which conflict has occurred whether from judicial review cases or other cases can be divided into four categories —economic regulation, civil liberties, federal-state relations, and general separation of powers. Table 5 indicates that first, economic regulation has been involved to some extent in four of the seven high-frequency periods. Civil liberties and federal-state relations have each been at issue in two periods, while general separation of powers at the national level has been the main controversy in only the earliest period.

TABLE 5. INTERESTS INVOLVED IN COURT-CURBING DURING AMERICAN HISTORY

Issues	Period	Overall Success
1. Economic Interests		
a. Business Regulation	1930's	Yes
	1890's	No
	1820's	Yes
b. Labor Relations	1890's	No
	1920's	No
c. Taxes	1890's	No
2. Civil Liberties		
a. Segregation	1950's	No
b. First Amendment	1950's	Partial
	1860's	Yes
c. Criminal Procedure	1950's	No
	1860's	Yes
3. Federal-State Relations		
	1800's	Yes
	1820's	Yes
4. Separation of Powers in the National Government	1800's	Yes

Trends in the frequency or occurrence of certain issues are apparent. For example, the attacks during the first half of the nineteenth-century were largely concerned with federal-state relations and separation of powers, a fact which can be explained in part by the youth of the country. At this time, the power distribution between the parts of the newly established federal system was not at all clear, this question being a dividing point between the two political parties as well as a major public issue. From the latter half of the nineteenth century through 1937, the basic issue in Congress-Court relations was that of economic regulation. Conflict over civil liberties has occurred intermittently but particularly in recent years.

From the data in Table 5 one might also be able to say that

court-curbing bills are more likely to succeed where federal-state relations or separation of powers represent the prime subject matters involved. On the other hand, where intensely held economic interests or civil libertarian interests are involved, the likelihood of court-curbing success is decreased.

C. *Unanimity of Provoking Cases*

Does the degree of conflict within the Supreme Court influence the occurrence of congressional Court-curbing? The degree of conflict within the Court can be measured by the degree of unanimity in key decisions at a given time. Using the statements of various writers and congressmen as to what cases provoked the anti-Court bills, the voting split on these controversial decisions was determined. The average degree of unanimity for all the periods was 76% which means that there was an average of two to three dissents in the cases provoking the attacks. This number contracts with the higher degree of unanimity normally found in the totality of Supreme Court cases. The results of Table 6 support the hypothesis that during periods in which there is a relatively high (*i.e.*, above average) degree of disagreement between members of the Court (and thus high controversy), congressional attack is more likely to occur.

TABLE 6. DEGREE OF UNANIMITY IN THE SUPREME COURT AND THE EFFECT ON OCCURRENCE AND SUCCESS OF COURT-CURBING

Periods	Degree of Unanimity	Relative Success
1800's	100% relatively high	Yes
1820's	89 rel. high	Yes
1860's	59 rel. low	Yes
1890's	72 rel. low	No
1920's	69 rel. low	No
1930's	69 rel. low	Yes
1950's	76 rel. high	No
	Avg. = 76%	

Contrary to what one might expect Table 6 shows that a slightly greater proportion of the high unanimity (rather than the low unanimity) periods involved relatively successful Court-curbing bills. However, the high unanimity in the 1800's and the 1820's does not necessarily indicate complete unity on the part of the Court. It may merely indicate that dissenting had not yet become an established practice.

III. Catalytic Factors

A. *Parties and Factions in Congress*

To what extent does party composition and the presence of factions in Congress during high-frequency time periods act as a catalytic or enabling factor influencing the occurrence and outcome of the attack? In five of the seven high-frequency periods, the Democratic party or its forerunners have dominated the Congress. A tabulation of the party affiliation of the individual sponsors of the bills also reveals that Democrats have sponsored over twice as much anti-court legislation than have Republicans. This relationship, however, does not mean that having a Democratic Congress is sufficient to provoke Court-curbing bills, for many Democratic Congresses have enjoyed smooth relations with the Court. It does suggest that, when other factors have been present, the existence of a Democratic Congress may have stimulated the occurrence of Court-curbing. Thus, the pattern has been such that when the Court has been defending property rights as in the 1930's and 1820's, the Democrats were more likely to attack it, and the Republicans were more likely to defend it. On the other hand, although to a lesser extent, when the Court has been defending civil liberties as in the 1950's and 1860's, the Republicans were more likely to be attacking it, and the Democrats (at least the Northern Democrats) were more likely to be defending it. This phenomenon can be explained by the socio-economic bases of the two parties, and the frequent attacks of the Democrats point up the fact that the Supreme Court has more often defended property rights than civil liberties.

Perhaps a more adequate description of the groups attacking the Court would replace the party labels with conservative or liberal designations. Table 7 shows that liberal groups have attacked the Court in six of the seven periods, and conservative groups (representing a coalition between wings of the Republican and Democratic parties) attacked the Court for the first time in the 1950's. Future attacks on the Supreme Court will also probably come from conservative forces given the increased power of liberal urbanism in the United States, a power which since 1932 has been increasingly making itself felt in the electoral college system that chooses the President, and thus indirectly in the President's choices for Supreme Court Justices.

TABLE 7. The Relation Between Party in Congress and the Occurrence of Court-Curbing Bills

High-Frequency Period	Party or Faction Sponsoring Bills
1800's	Jeffersonians

1820's	Democrats
1860's	Radical Republicans
1890's	Democrats and Populists
1920's	Liberal Republicans
1930's	Democrats
1950's	Conservative Republicans & Conservative Democrats

The above discussion focused on the relation between party (or faction) and the occurrence of a Court-curbing period. There is also a relationship between the party sponsoring Court-curbing legislation and the success of the attacks. Thus, when the percentage of Democrats in Congress is high (over 65 per cent), Democratic bills are more likely to succeed, and less likely to succeed when the percentage of Democrats in Congress is low.[7] Similarly, Republican bills are more likely to succeed when the percentage of Republicans in Congress is high as is shown in Table 8. These relations, however, are much weaker than one would expect to find in a more disciplined two-party system. A group's leadership in Congress may be as important as its numerical strength and may strongly influence the cohesiveness of the group. For example, the skillful leadership of Senators O'Mahoney and Wheeler in 1937, and Lyndon Johnson in 1958, is credited by some writers as being an important factor in the defeat of anti-court legislation.[8]

TABLE 8. Relations Between Sponsoring Party and Relative Success of Court-Curbing Bills
(Where Sponsor and Party are Known)

	Democratic Bills		Republican Bills	
	65% or less Dems. in Cong.	More than 65% Dems. in Cong.	65% or less Reps. in Cong.	More than 65% Reps. in Cong.
Relative Success	6 (9%)	7 (20%)	5 (20%)	7 (44%)
Relative Failure	60 (91%)	28 (80%)	20 (80%)	9 (56%)
	66 (100%)	35 (100%)	25 (100%)	16 (100%)

7. "Per cent Democrats in Congress" equals

$$\frac{1}{2}\left(\frac{\text{House Dems}}{\text{House Dems} + \text{Reps}} + \frac{\text{Senate Dems}}{\text{Senate Dems} + \text{Reps}}\right)$$ and likewise with "per cent Republicans in Congress."

8. Murphy, *op. cit. supra* note 1, at 249.

B. *Party and Factional Differences Between Congress and the Court*

Is there a relationship between (1) party or factional differences between Congress and the Court, and (2) the occurrence of Court-curbing bills? As Table 9 shows, a slightly greater proportion of Congresses having a dominant (*i.e.*, majority) party different from the Court's dominant party were Congresses from the Court-curbing periods. It is also relevant to note that of 142 Court-curbing bills for which the Democratic or Republican affiliation of the sponsor was known, 39 were introduced by Congressmen of the party opposite to the party that dominated the Court when the bill was introduced. Congresses where the same party did not dominate both houses of Congress were eliminated from Table 9, as were Congresses where the Court had an equal number of Democrats and Republicans.

TABLE 9. PARTY DIFFERENCES BETWEEN CONGRESS AND THE COURT DURING THE HIGH AND LOW COURT-CURBING PERIODS

	Congresses Dominated by a Party Also Dominating the Court	Congresses Dominated by a Party Not Dominating the Court
Court-Curbing Periods	12 (21%)	9 (39%)
Non-Court-Curbing Periods	44 (79%)	14 (61%)
	56 (100%)	23 (100%)

The above analysis tends to show a weak causal relation between Congress-Court party splits and an upsurge of Court-curbing bills. If, however, one hypothesizes that a party split between Congress and the Court is an important *condition* or *catalyst* rather than a cause, then Table 10 below is more relevant. It shows that all seven high frequency periods involved party or factional differences between Congress and the Court.

TABLE 10. THE RELATION BETWEEN CONGRESS-COURT PARTY OR FACTIONAL SPLITS AND THE OCCURRENCE OF COURT-CURBING BILLS

High Occurrence Period	Party Sponsoring Majority of Bills	Party Dominating the Court
1800's	Jeffersonians	Federalists
1820's	States-Rights Dems.	Nationalists
1860's	Republicans	Democrats
1890's	Democrats	Republicans
1920's	Liberal Reps.	Conservative Reps.
1930's	Democrats	Republicans
1950's	Conservative Reps. and Dems.	Liberal Dems.

The degree of composite success of a congressional attack also correlates with the degree of party split between Congress and the Court. All three periods during which there was a sharp party split can be considered successful, whereas three out of the four periods during which there was not so sharp a split can be considered relatively unsuccessful as is shown in Table 11. This table like Table 9 but unlike Table 10 only considers party splits and not factional splits. The relationship between relative success and party differences can be accounted for in part by the fact that when Congress represents a different party than the Court, then legislation introduced by members of that party and particularly legislation directed against policies of the opposite party will be more apt to get out of committee than legislation introduced by the minority party. In addition, when there is a party split between Congress and the Court, public opinion is more apt to be on the side of Congress since that body, by virtue of its short terms, is more responsive to changes in the public sentiment. It follows that when the public consensus is at odds with the policies of the Supreme Court, anti-Court legislation will not only increase in volume but will have a better chance of being seriously considered.

TABLE 11. Relation Between Congress-Court Party Differences and the Relative Success of Court-Curbing Bills

	Not so sharp a split	Sharp split
Relatively Successful	1820's	1800's 1860's 1930's
Relatively Unsuccessful	1890's 1920's 1950's	

C. *Crises*

A third catalytic or enabling factor which may accelerate or decelerate congressional reaction to judicial provocation is the presence or absence of a crisis. Although the outbreak of war or depression may not directly cause attacks on the Court, one might hypothesize that when judicial provocation has first occurred, the presence or absence of a crisis may affect the speed and manner with which Congress reacts. Crisis may be defined as a period of depression, economic panic, war (including cold war), or post war readjustment. In light of these definitions, during almost all of the Court-curbing periods some degree of crisis has been present as is shown in Table 12. The two classic examples of this relationship are the periods of the 1860's and 1930's. These attacks, which are perhaps the most famous and serious attempts to curb the Court, occurred during or just after two of the most serious crises which this country has had to suffer, the Civil War and the Great Depression.

TABLE 12. RELATION BETWEEN CRISIS AND THE OCCURRENCE OF COURT-CURBING BILLS

High Occurrence Period	Type of Crisis
1800's	None, other than establishing a federal government
1820's	None
1860's	Civil War
1890's	Economic Panic
1920's	Post-War Readjustment
1930's	Depression
1950's	Cold War

The relationship between crisis and the success of Court-curbing is more difficult to determine, but a positive correlation is suggested by the outcome of at least two of the high frequency periods. The attacks of the 1860's and 1930's which followed or accompanied great crises in American history were both highly successful in relation to the other periods. The two most unsuccessful attacks, the 1890's and 1920's, occurred during periods of low degrees of crisis. The other three Court-curbing periods, however, fail to follow this pattern.

TABLE 13. RELATION BETWEEN CRISIS AND THE SUCCESS OF COURT-CURBING BILLS

	Not so severe Crisis	Severe Crisis
Relatively Successful	1800's 1820's	1860's 1930's
Relatively Unsuccessful	1890's 1920's	1950's

D. *Public Opinion and Pressure Groups*

The element of public opinion should also be included in the discussion of catalytic or enabling factors which, through their presence or absence, accelerate or temper congressional attacks upon the Supreme Court. The lack of extensive public opinion polls prior to recent years hinders scientific research and measurement of the impact of this factor on Court-curbing activity. An estimation of public support or disapproval for legislative policies toward the Court could be made through the rather crude method of analyzing the results of elections occurring immediately prior to or during periods of congressional attacks on the Court. An analysis of this sort would point, for example, to the landslide of 1936 which Roosevelt interpreted as a mandate for the New Deal and possibly for some kind of Court-curbing scheme. Public opinion polls taken at various stages of the fight over Roosevelt's Court-packing bill in the Senate indicate, however, that public opinion turned against his scheme after the election.[9] Another technique would involve the detailed analysis of newspaper comment, comments from the *Congressional Record,* and other contemporary publications which tend to record the issues and sentiment of the time. This type of analysis would, however, primarily reflect the sentiments of the upper, more literate classes just as election analysis would reflect the sentiment in respect to broad policy rather than the specific Court-curbing issue.

Pressure groups, representing certain segments of public opinion, have been active during legislative attacks upon the Court. Again, their influence cannot be measured, but general comments about their probable roles can be made. In the 1930's the American Bar Association, the National Association of Manufacturers, and the American Liberty League were the principle defenders of the Court, while the AFL-CIO was a principle attacker. In the 1950's the NAACP and ACLU defended, and the White Citizens Councils and American Legion did some of the attacking. In both of these instances, the liberal pressure groups only partly won the battle since the actual outcome was dependent on the operation of a number of variables. One can readily hypothesize, however, that when strong, prestigious groups are on the side of Congress, the attack is strengthened, and when such groups defend the Supreme Court, the attack is weakened.

E. *Regionalism*

Regionalism is a catalytic factor like political party. When a judicial policy particularly affects one region of the country, the concerted efforts of that region's congressional representatives can strengthen the negative response of Congress. For example, ten of the twelve anti-Court bills introduced during the 1820's were sponsored by

9. Murphy gives the results of Gallup polls taken during the Court fight in 1937, *op. cit. supra* note 1, at 61. Not only did the public increasingly disapprove of the Court-packing plan, but the President's personal popularity also fell during this period.

Southerners in general and Kentuckians in particular who had been provoked by the Court's invalidation of land and debtor laws. Does one region of the country generally tend to be involved in Court-curbing more than others? Table 14 indicates that of the three main regions of the country—south, west, and north—the west and north have been slightly more involved in Court-curbing than the south. This pattern is explained in part by considering the relationship between regionalism and issues. Economic issues such as those at stake in the 1890's, 1920's, and 1930's evoke a northern and western response, while the states rights issues of the 1800's, 1820's, and 1950's evoke a southern response. This relationship is explained by the socio-economic makeup of the various regions with the north and west being industrial and populist-wheat centers, while the south has been the locus of plantation agriculture and the negro problem.

TABLE 14. Relationship of Regionalism to the Occurrence and Success of Court-Curbing

Period	Regional Sponsors	Success
1800's	Southern and Western	Yes
1820's	Southern and Western	Yes
1860's	Northern	Yes
1890's	Northern and Western	No
1920's	Northern and Western	No
1930's	Northern and Western	Yes
1950's	Southerners and Northern Conservatives	No

In terms of success, the south has enjoyed success in two-thirds of its attempts to curb the Court, while the north and west have been successful in approximately half of their attempts. If the Court-curbing periods are ranked as in Table 2, however, two of the most successful periods, the 1860's and 1930's, were predominantly northern sponsored attacks. An explanation for this is the fact that the northern states are more heavily represented in Congress, and the north enjoyed an additional advantage in the 1860's conflict since the south and the Democratic Party were largely incapacitated. An analysis of regionalism points up the fact that congressional attacks upon the Supreme Court are often regional attacks, and that the Court has never really been faced with a united, national enemy which, along with public opinion and other factors, may account in part for the generally low degree of success Court-curbing bills have had.

F. *House and Senate Procedure*

The House of Representatives has been almost twice as active in Court-curbing as the Senate, sponsoring 98 bills to the Senate's 57. What accounts for the greater volume of bills originating in the House? First, the difference may not be as great as it seems. Since the membership of the House is over four times as large as that of the Senate, one would expect the House to sponsor a greater amount of bills than the Senate on any issue. Second, House members, subject to biennial elections, might be more sensitive to short-run changes of sentiment than are Senate members. In addition the smaller, more homogeneous constituencies of House members are possibly more conducive to sponsoring Court-curbing bills and other extreme legislation which would be too divisive in a larger constituency. A third factor is that Senate members may sponsor bills jointly, whereas House bills can carry the name of only one sponsor, a practice tending to produce duplicate bills. Procedure then is a catalyst tending to affect the relative volume of bills generated in each house of Congress.

The Senate, in spite of its lower number of bills, has had a greater degree of success in getting its Court-curbing legislation out of committee. Almost one-fourth of the Senate bills got out of committee while only 13% of the House bills ever did. For reasons mentioned above, the House possibly tends to introduce harsher measures which therefore have a smaller chance of success. In addition, the practice of introducing duplicate bills in the House lowers its average of success for individual bills.

IV. Congressional and Presidential Response

A. *Congressional Response*

Several courses of action are available to the congressmen seeking to attack the policies of the Supreme Court. At the local level, he can participate in nullification movements to register disapproval of a particular decision. In Congress, he can attempt retaliation via the fiscal powers, introduce restrictive constitutional amendments, sponsor legislation to overturn a statutory interpretation, initiate joint resolutions or investigations, or, if a Senator, he can attempt to block a Presidential nominee for the bench. Although these methods account for a good share of the activity during congressional attacks on the Court, this paper and the following table is concerned only with specific bills designed directly or indirectly to change some general policy of the Court.

TABLE 15. TYPES OF BILLS PROPOSED TO CURB THE SUPREME COURT

	Frequency		Relative Success	
	Number	% of 165	Number	% of Type
1. Judicial Review				
a. Special concurrence needed	41	25%	5	12%
b. Miscellaneous regulate	5	3	0	0
c. Abolish	3	2	0	0
Total:	49	30%	5	10% Avg.
2. Personnel				
a. Qualifications	24	15	0	0
b. Size of Court	13	8	5	38
c. Retirement	7	4	3	43
d. Appointing.	4	2	1	25
e. Give states equal representation	1	½	0	0
Total:	49	29½%	9	18% Avg.
3. Jurisdiction				
a. Regulate and define general appellate jurisdiction	23	14	3	13
b. Repeal Supreme Court jurisdiction over state	3	2	1	33
c. Limit jurisdiction in special cases:				
1) Habeas corpus appeals	3	2	2	67
2) Reconstruction	1	½	0	0
3) Public schools	7	4	0	0
4) Other specific areas	8	5	1	12
Total:	45	27½%	7	16% Avg.
4. Procedure				
a. General reorganization	6	4	3	50
b. Amend judicial code	4	2	2	50
c. Amend rules of practice and procedure	1	½	0	0
d. Facilitate decisions on constitutional questions	1	½	0	0
Total:	12	7%	5	42% Avg.
5. Curtail Contempt or Injunction Powers	4	2	3	75
6. Miscellaneous				
a. Let lower court ignore non-legalistic Sup. Ct. decisions	2	1	0	0
b. Change doctrine of pre-emptive federalism	1	½	1	100

c. Postpone meeting of Court	1	½	1	100
d. Impeachment	1	½	1	100
e. Give some body direct review over Sup. Ct. decisions	1	½	0	0
Overall Total:	165	100%	32	19% Avg.

After the congressman has decided to attack the power of the judges and to do it through legislative means, he still has a range of alternatives from which to choose. Table 15 indicates that about 30% of the Court-curbing bills dealt with regulating or abolishing judicial review which particularly includes bills requiring special concurrences to declare statutes unconstitutional. Another 29% dealt with matters of Court personnel, particularly qualifications (like lengthy prior judicial experience) for holding a Supreme Court judgeship. Within this 29% are also included thirteen bills designed to increase or decrease the size of the Court so as to allow a new President to make new appointments or to keep him from making new appointments. About 28% of the bills attempted to restrict the court's appellate jurisdiction, and the relatively few remaining bills dealt with various procedural and miscellaneous matters.

Some measures have been peculiar to one time period. Bills curtailing the contempt and injunction powers were predominant, for example, during the period of the Progressives' attack on the Court, particularly before the enactment of the Clayton Act.[10] Bills pertaining to the appellate jurisdiction of the Court in respect to public schools, and bills abolishing the doctrine of pre-emptive federalism were characteristic of the 1955-1959 conflict. The broad historic trend has been away from bills which would remove or circumscribe a broad area of the Court's power and toward those bills which would limit a small, more specific part of the Court's functions. For example, the only serious attempt at impeachment occurred in 1804. Bills advocating the repeal of the 25th section of the Judiciary Act of 1789 which would be tantamount to removing the Court's appellate jurisdiction over state courts were concentrated in the first half of the nineteenth century. Unsuccessful bills providing for equal representation of the states on the Court were proposed prior to 1870, and thus those groups favoring such a change have recently resorted to a constitutional amendment via a constitutional convention. In contrast, many bills proposed during the intense conflict in 1937 were designed to effect changes in the quorum, retirement of Justices, and size of the Court. In the attack on the Warren Court, many bills prescribed limitation of jurisdiction in special cases dealing with subversion,

10. 64 Stat. 1125 (1950), 15 U.S.C. § 12 (1958).

public schools, and (after 1961) reapportionment. More extreme bills in the earlier years may be attributable to the fact that in the early nineteenth century, the role of the judicial branch of the government was not yet established, and the obvious partisanship of some justices during the very early years was a hindrance to the growth of the judicial myth. In addition, history has shown that bills removing comparatively smaller amounts of the Court's power have the greatest prospect of success. Astute congressmen may well have taken note of this fact. One, however, should note that although the severity of bills during the Warren and Roosevelt courts was lower than in prior periods, the quantity of bills was higher. This possibly indicated a more widespread discontent toward specific decisions and a lack of cohesive leadership by the anti-Court forces which kept these forces from centering on one or a few bills.

With regard to the matter of success, ten of the twenty-three categories of bills had a higher percentage of relative success (*i.e.*, got out of committee) than the average of 19%. These ten types of bills included repealing jurisdiction over state supreme courts, limiting jurisdiction in regard to habeas corpus appeals, changing the rules concerning retirement and the size of the Court, restricting the Court's procedure, and limiting the Court's contempt and injunction powers. Most of the ten types could be considered as limited means of curbing the Court. The substantially higher rate of success for the relatively milder bills can be explained by the fact that during all the time periods, there has been a sizable opposition in Congress to any attempts to curb the Supreme Court—a factor which necessitates compromise.

B. *Presidential Response*

To what extent have Presidents become involved in Court-curbing and what effect has their participation had on the outcome of congressional court conflicts? Four Presidents have been openly critical of the Court during the high-frequency periods, *i.e.*, Jefferson, Jackson, Lincoln, and Roosevelt, but not Eisenhower or the Presidents of the 1920's or 1890's. Presidents have been hesitant to openly initiate Court-curbing legislation. FDR's Court packing plan of 1937 was an exception, but it was only one of numerous anti-Court bills introduced in the 1930's. This presidential reluctance is possibly due to a fear of alienating the Court's numerous defenders in Congress and the public (as well as a respect for the independence of the judiciary), and in some instances to a favorable presidential attitude toward the Court's policies.

With regard to the success of individual bills, Roosevelt's Court-packing bill was reported out of committee unfavorably. This is attributable to inadequate cultivation of support in Congress and among the public and to reversals by the Court itself. In view of the Court's retreat, however, the Roosevelt period can be considered a relative success. Presidents also have administrative weapons to either thwart or aid orders of the Supreme Court, and ultimately via his appointive power the President can change the Court's policies. Nevertheless, with the astute use of his tools of leadership, the President can be a powerful figure both in the initiation and successful outcome of Court-curbing bills. With his active support Court-curbing legislation is probably more likely to pass, and without it, such legislation is more likely to fail.

V. Judicial Counteraction

The behavior pattern of the Court-curbing process does not end with the action taken by Congress and the President. The Supreme Court can affect the outcome of legislative attacks by its reaction. First, the members of the Court can individually refute the charges made by congressmen. Prior to 1937, however, the judicial myth of aloofness from political disputes was generally followed by the Court. The only exceptions to this pattern was Marshall's criticism of Jefferson in *Marbury v. Madison,* Chase's partisan opinions, and Taney's criticism of Lincoln. The 1937 conflict involved the direct participation of members of the Court and included Brandeis' testimony before the Judiciary Committee, Hughes' letter to the sympathetic leaders in Congress defending the Court, and the timeliness of Van Deventer's retirement.

Second, the Court as a whole can counteract legislative attack by retreating from the policy stand which originally provoked the attack. In terms of frequency, this has happened in four of the seven high frequency periods. The four periods involve the early 1800's conflict, the 1820's, the 1860's, and the 1930's. In 1959, the Court retreated in one of the three fields (free speech, segregation, and criminal procedure) which originally provoked the attack. In the 1890's and 1920's on the other hand, a conservative Court protected by a Republican Congress easily withstood the disorganized attacks of the Democrats, Populists, and Progressives without having to resort to a retreat. Since the composite index of success includes retreat as a major criterion, all four of the above mentioned Court-curbing periods, by definition, can be called successful. In short, when the Court removes the provocation for the conflict, the attack dissipates but can be considered a success.

VI. CONCLUSIONS

Periods of intense Court-curbing bills have occurred only seven times during the 170 year history of the United States. Nevertheless, this mode of conflict between the legislative and judicial branches will no doubt recur when certain judicial provocations and catalytic factors are present.

The factors which have an affirmative correlation with the occurrence of Court-curbing bills are (in the order presented) as follows: (1) judicial review of federal and state statutes, (2) economic issues rather than other issues, (3) low degree of unanimity within the Supreme Court, (4) Democratic or liberal Congress when the Court is conservative, (5) Republican or conservative Congress when the Court is liberal, (6) crisis present, (7) public opinion and powerful pressure groups favor the attack, (8) the process for introducing bills in the House, and (9) the lack of cohesive Congressional leadership.

The factors which have an affirmative correlation with the success of Court-curbing bills (in the order presented) are as follows: (1) sponsored by the majority party in Congress, (2) party split between the Court and Congress, (3) crisis present and allegedly made more severe by the Court's decisions, (4) public and pressure group support, (5) northern sponsored attack, (6) introduced in Senate, (7) limited in purpose, and (8) has presidential support and cohesive congressional leadership.

Although an accurate measurement of the relative importance of these factors to Court-curbing cannot be made, a behavior pattern which invariably occurs in such conflicts can be described. The sequence of events involves judicial provocation, the existence of circumstances which act as catalysts or as retarders, a set of congressional and presidential responses, and judicial counteraction. This model which is based on the psychological model of stimulus, organism, response, and feedback can perhaps also be profitably applied to analyzing other legal and political phenomena.

The President and the Court: Reinterpreting the Court-packing Episode of 1937

MICHAEL NELSON

On 5 February 1937, Franklin D. Roosevelt, reacting to a long string of Supreme Court decisions that were hostile to the New Deal, asked Congress to empower him to "pack" the Court with as many as six new justices, one for every sitting justice 70 years or older who, having served at least ten years, declined to retire. The proposal was highly controversial from the start, and whatever chance for passage it may have had was lost that spring when the Court abandoned its anti-New Deal posture in a series of cases that was instantly dubbed "the switch in time that saved nine." A watered-down version of the Court-packing plan was tabled into oblivion on 22 July 1937 by a Senate vote of 70 to 20.

In 1939, reflecting on two years experience with a now compliant Court, Roosevelt proclaimed that although he had lost the Court-packing battle, he had won the war. Seventeen years later, James MacGregor Burns concluded that in view of the breakdown of the "Grand Coalition" in the Democratic party that the Court-packing episode had triggered, "it could be better said that he had lost the battle, won the campaign, but lost the war."[1]

[1] James MacGregor Burns, *Roosevelt: The Lion and the Fox* (New York: Harcourt, Brace, and World, 1956), 315.

MICHAEL NELSON is associate professor of political science at Vanderbilt University. He has written numerous articles about American politics and books about the presidency.

Political Science Quarterly Volume 103 Number 2 1988

Students of the New Deal era have divided along these lines since 1937, with most arguing that the Court fight was not worth the costs for Roosevelt.[2] But regardless of their position on the controversy, scholars generally have accepted the premises of the Roosevelt-Burns "debate." First, they have examined the Court-packing case on an ad hoc basis, either as an incident in and of itself, or as one to be understood in the context of the Roosevelt presidency. Second, most have analyzed the success or failure of the Court-packing effort in hindsight, that is, in terms of its consequences.

Can the Court-packing episode be understood better if it is studied not solely as a unique historical event or as part of one administration's tenure, but also as a case study of attempted presidential leadership in the cause of dramatic, nonincremental political change? Can Roosevelt's strategy, granted his goal of Supreme Court approval or at least acquiescence in the New Deal, be assessed in terms of the challenges, obstacles, and resources he faced at the time? Can alternative courses of action be assessed from this same vantage point?

THE COURT AND THE PRESIDENT

Franklin Roosevelt's problems with the Supreme Court are an oft-told tale. Four of the nine justices who served on the Court during his first term were ardent conservatives who appeared to regard the New Deal brand of governmental intervention in the economy as constitutionally unacceptable almost by definition. Dubbed the Four Horsemen, they were: Willis Van Devanter, James C. McReynolds, George Sutherland, and Pierce Butler. Another group of three justices seemed more disposed to allow the elected branches of government wide latitude in framing public policies: Louis D. Brandeis, Harlan Fiske Stone, and Benjamin N. Cardozo. The remaining two justices, Chief Justice Charles Evans Hughes and Owen J. Roberts, were swing votes, not consistently aligned with either bloc. By the end of Roosevelt's first term, six of these justices, including all four conservatives, were in their seventies, the oldest collection of justices ever to sit on the Court.[3] Roosevelt had appointed none of them; he was the first president since James Monroe to serve a full term with no opportunities to nominate one or more justices.

Sensing the Court's hostility almost from the start, the Roosevelt administration delayed cases that challenged the constitutionality of New Deal measures

[2] The standard accounts are Joseph Alsop and Turner Catledge, *The 168 Days* (Garden City, N.Y.: Doubleday, Doran, 1938); Leonard Baker, *Back to Back: The Duel Between FDR and the Supreme Court* (New York: Macmillan, 1967); and three articles by William E. Leuchtenburg: "The Origins of Franklin D. Roosevelt's 'Court-packing' Plan," *Supreme Court Review* (1966): 347–400; "Franklin D. Roosevelt's Supreme Court 'Packing' Plan" in Harold M. Hollingsworth and William F. Holmes, eds., *Essays on the New Deal* (Austin: University of Texas Press, 1969), 69–115; and "FDR's Court-Packing Plan: A Second Life, A Second Death," *Duke Law Journal* (June–September 1985): 673–689.

[3] Laurence H. Tribe, *God Save This Honorable Court* (New York: Random House, 1985), xv. The average age for justices was 72.

from coming before the Court for as long as possible, but the judicial hammer blows began falling in 1935. In May the justices invalidated the Railway Pension Act, the National Industrial Recovery Act, the Frazier-Lemke Act, and a presidential decision to fire a member of the Federal Trade Commission.[4] (The last three decisions were handed down on 27 May, thenceforth known as Black Monday to New Dealers). In January 1936 the Court voided the tax provision of the Agricultural Adjustment Act, then in May (after approving the Tennessee Valley Authority Act in February) struck down the Guffey Coal Act and the Municipal Bankruptcy Act.[5] Finally, in *Morehead v. Tipaldo*, its most controversial decision of all, the Court ruled in June that New York's minimum-wage law for women was unconstitutional, thus nearly precluding even a state government role in depression-fighting.[6] In all these cases the Four Horsemen voted against the New Deal; sometimes they were joined by Roberts, sometimes by Roberts and Hughes, sometimes (as in the three Black Monday decisions) by all the other justices.

What, from the vantage point of mid-1936, was Roosevelt to do? Simply to wait for the justices to change their minds or leave the Court was to him intolerable. The logic of the majority opinions in the Court's recent decisions seemed to leave no room for other New Deal measures whose constitutionality had not yet been tested, such as the Social Security Act and the Wagner Labor Relations Act, much less for legislation concerning wages and hours and other subjects that Roosevelt was planning to introduce. And he was convinced that no vacancies on the Court would occur for him to fill: McReynolds would still be on the bench when he was 105, the President groused.[7] Conflict with the Court seemed inevitable.

Yet Roosevelt knew from experience that to attack the Court would create serious problems of its own. In the aftermath of Black Monday, he had chastised the justices for "relegat[ing] us to the horse-and-buggy definition of interstate commerce." The outraged public reaction to this offhand remark, not just from conservatives, was evidence enough that any effort to change the situation by law or constitutional amendment would require Roosevelt to do nothing less than summon all the elements of political power that he had been able to bring together in the first term.[8] What constellation of political forces did Roosevelt need to reassemble in order to prevail? The main ingredients of his dramatic first-term legislative successes—and of the dramatic legislative successes of other twentieth

[4] *Railroad Retirement Board v. Alton Railroad Co.*, 295 U.S. 330 (1935); *Schechter v. United States*, 295 U.S. 495 (1935); *Louisville Joint Stock Land Bank v. Radford*, 295 U.S. 555 (1935); *Humphrey's Executor v. United States*, 295 U.S. 602 (1935).

[5] *United States v. Butler*, 297 U.S. 1 (1936); *Ashwander v. Tennessee Valley Authority*, 297 U.S. 288 (1936); *Carter v. Carter Coal Co.*, 298 U.S. 238 (1936); *Ashton v. Cameron County Water District*, 298 U.S. 513 (1936).

[6] *Morehead v. New York ex rel. Tipaldo*, 298 U.S. 587 (1936).

[7] Leuchtenburg, "Origins of Court-packing Plan," 381.

[8] Alsop and Catledge, *The 168 Days*, 7; Leuchtenberg, "Origins of Court-packing," 357–359.

century presidents who have attempted and achieved them—were three: an empowering election, suitable ideas, and requisite political skills.[9]

Election. A president is empowered for legislative achievement if, in the election that brings or returns him to power, he campaigns with promises, however general, of significant reform; is elected by a landslide majority; and sees large gains for his party in the accompanying congressional elections.

The requirement for a personal landslide is obvious, the others perhaps less so. Clearly, though, unless the president has campaigned on a reformist theme, he cannot interpret his victory (or expect others to) as any sort of mandate for massive policy change. It also is hard to persuade Congress to accept such an interpretation unless his victory is joined to gains for his party's legislative candidates. Indeed, the size of the gains, even more than the size of his party's contingent in Congress, is what matters, because the gains invariably are attributed, accurately or not, to the president-elect's coattails or to a mandate that he and Congress share. Either way, the election creates a heightened disposition among legislators of both congressional parties to support the president's legislative initiatives—fellow partisans because they want to ride his bandwagon, members of the opposition to avoid being flattened by it.[10] A president whose election is not accompanied by large gains is more likely to be seen by representatives and senators as politically tangential to their own political fortunes. For similar reasons, a president could be empowered for legislative achievement if in the midterm elections his party made gains in Congress, violating the historical pattern.

Roosevelt's election in 1932 had met all the requirements of an empowering victory. Entering the race as the clear progressive candidate, based on his active efforts as governor to ease the ill effects of the depression in New York and his determination to make the economy the main issue in 1932 (rather than prohibition, which conservative Democrats wanted), Roosevelt spoke at various times during

[9] No value judgments are implied by the term "dramatic legislative success." "Dramatic" means that the effect of the new legislation was to alter significantly the role of the national government in American society. "Success" means simply that the President was able to persuade Congress to pass his proposals. Woodrow Wilson, Lyndon Johnson, and Ronald Reagan are the other modern presidents who have achieved dramatic legislative success. For a full exposition of the theory of presidential power that underlies this analysis, see Erwin C. Hargrove and Michael Nelson, *Presidents, Politics, and Policy* (Baltimore: The Johns Hopkins University Press and New York: Knopf, 1984), esp. chaps. 3, 4, 6, 7, and 8; and Hargrove and Nelson, "The Presidency: Reagan and the Cycle of Politics and Policy" in Nelson, ed., *The Election of 1984* (Washington, D.C.: Congressional Quarterly Press, 1985), 189–213.

[10] Members of Congress will make this calculation if they intend to seek reelection. Available data for the post-World War II era indicates they do: from 1946 to 1982 an average 83.7 percent of senators sought reelection in each term-ending election. To see if this generalization applied to the Roosevelt period, the author examined Senate elections in the period 1928–1936 and found the average reelection-seeking rate to be 83.8 percent. Author's calculations from Norman J. Orstein, et al., *Vital Statistics on Congress* (Washington, D.C.: American Enterprise Institute, 1982), 46–68; and *Guide to U.S. Elections* (Washington, D.C.: Congressional Quarterly, 1975), parts IV and VI.

the campaign in support of farm relief, unemployment insurance, national planning, public power, public works, reforestation, tariff reduction, and securities legislation.[11] But far more significant than any list of promises extracted from Roosevelt's speeches was the sense of commitment he conveyed that as president he would do whatever he could to remedy the awful plight of "the forgotten man at the bottom of the economic pyramid." Again and again, he harked back to the theme he had stated in April in a speech at Oglethorpe University: "We need to correct, by drastic means if necessary, the faults in our economic system from which we now suffer. . . . The country needs and, unless I mistake its temper, the country demands bold, persistent experimentation. . . . Above all, try something."[12]

The results of Roosevelt's reformist campaign completed the task of empowering him for legislative success. His own landslide victory over President Herbert Hoover was the most overwhelming in history against an incumbent president. Equally important, Roosevelt's party gained ninety seats in the House of Representatives and thirteen in the Senate. The House gains were the largest ever for a president's party; the Senate results turned a one-seat deficit for the Democrats into a twenty-five seat majority. A veritable explosion of New Deal legislation occurred shortly after the new President's inauguration.

In singular fashion, the midterm elections of 1934 provided the impetus for continued presidential leadership. During the campaign, Roosevelt pledged to introduce a far-reaching program of social insurance, housing, and resource development in the next Congress.[13] The results of the elections were unprecedented in their endorsement of the President. Historically, the president's party loses seats at midterm; the average loss since 1906 had been forty-two seats in the House and five in the Senate. As election day neared, Vice President John Nance Garner judged that to lose only thirty-seven House seats would be a victory and most doubted that the party would do that well. Instead, Democrats gained nine seats in the House and added ten senators. Arthur Krock described the 1934 election in *The New York Times* as "the most overwhelming victory in the history of American politics."[14] Thus, it is not surprising that just as the 1932 elections set the stage for the First Hundred Days, so did the 1934 results lay the groundwork for the second New Deal of 1935: social security, the Wagner Act, a progressive income tax, and so on.

Skill. In order to make their imprint on policy, presidents are called upon to

[11] Arthur M. Schlesinger, Jr., *The Crisis of the Old Order, 1919–1933* (Boston: Houghton Mifflin, 1957, Sentry ed.), 277, 289–291, 313; William E. Leuchtenberg, *Franklin D. Roosevelt and the New Deal, 1932–1940* (New York: Harper and Row, 1963, Torchbook ed.), 11–12. Roosevelt's oft-noted promise to balance the budget was made contingent on the absence of "dire need" in the country.

[12] Schlesinger, *Crisis of Old Order*, 289, 290.

[13] Leuchtenburg, *Roosevelt and New Deal*, 93.

[14] Average seat loss is author's calculation from data in Ornstein, *Vital Statistics*, 41. Arthur M. Schlesinger, Jr., *The Coming of the New Deal* (Boston: Houghton Mifflin Co., 1959), 506–507.

demonstrate a challenging array of leadership skills. They require above all a strategic sense of the grain of history—an ability to sense, define, and articulate the public mood and to shape and fulfill the historical possibilities of the time.[15] Such presidents also must be able to present themselves and their policies to the general public through effective rhetoric and symbolic action and to deal in a tactically skillful way with other Washington politicians through negotiation, persuasion, and various forms of gamesmanship. Finally, they must be adroit in managing the talents of administration lieutenants in the quest for workable and appealing policy proposals. A requirement for the exercise of any of these skills is a continuing effort by the president to ground himself in political reality.

The first-term Roosevelt had been a marvel of leadership skill. He had understood that the public desire was less for a particular agenda of action to cure the depression than for action itself, a commitment on the President's part to keep trying cures until he found one that seemed to work. Roosevelt coupled action with an exuberant sense of optimism, competence, and confidence, jauntily displayed in newsreels, photographs, personal appearances, and, of course, on radio. He was an adroit manager of lieutenants in the task of developing administration policies. The heart of Roosevelt's success in this regard, Arthur Schlesinger pointed out, was his realization that "the first task of an executive . . . was to guarantee himself an effective flow of information and ideas." As for tactical skills, Roosevelt was Richard Neustadt's exemplar of mastery and success.[16]

Ideas. The rhetoric of dramatic change may be enough to get a president elected if that is what the public wants to hear, but once in office it must be translated into specific ideas for legislation. Successful ideas are characterized not just by their grounding in expert knowledge but also by their fit with American political values and the public expectations of the day. Roosevelt had a brains trust to advise him during the first term, but he also had a legacy of ideas from the 1920s and earlier to draw upon. As James MacGregor Burns notes, Roosevelt "had grasped the standard of Wilsonian reform in his measures for federal supervision of securities, friendliness to labor, business regulation. He had trod Cousin Theodore's old path in conservation and in the elements of planning in the AAA [Agricultural Adjustment Administration]. He had filched a plank from American socialism in the public ownership features of TVA [Tennessee Valley Authority]," and later, in the social security and tax bills.[17]

[15] This is similar to the skill Woodrow Wilson described as "interpretation." See Jeffrey Tulis, "The Two Constitutional Presidencies" in Michael Nelson, ed., *The Presidency and the Political System* (Washington, D.C.: Congressional Quarterly Press, 1984), 59–86.

[16] Schlesinger, *Coming of New Deal*, 522–24; Richard E. Neustadt, *Presidential Power* (New York: John Wiley, 1960). Leuchtenburg, "Origins of Court-packing" is the definitive work on the development of the President's proposal and, except where noted, is the source for this section. Alsop and Catledge also provide a good account in *The 168 Days*, chap. 1.

[17] Burns, *Roosevelt*. 179.

The Court-packing Episode

As in the first term, so in the second: in order to accomplish a dramatic legislative victory of the kind he felt he needed over the Supreme Court, Roosevelt would require intellectually and politically suitable policy ideas, an empowering election, and a fully deployed repertoire of political skills.

Ideas. Roosevelt had no shortage of ideas to draw from about how to resolve his problems with the Supreme Court. The populist and progressive movements of the late nineteenth and early twentieth centuries had made courts a target of reform. As William Leuchtenburg notes, "Roosevelt began his political career at the time that his distant cousin Theodore was assaulting the sanctity of the courts and the air was loud with cries for the recall of judges and judicial decisions."[18] In the 1920s, such proposals increasingly were aimed at the Supreme Court, which seemed under Chief Justice William Howard Taft to have gone to the extreme in its conservatism. More recently, the first round of anti-New Deal Court decisions in early 1935 (including the anticipation, false as it turned out, that the Court would rule against Roosevelt and Congress in the gold clause cases)[19] had lent unprecedented urgency to some liberals' desire to rein in the Court. The years 1935–1937 saw more "Court-curbing" bills introduced in Congress than in any other three-year (or thirty-five year) period in history.[20] A few of these, including some endorsed by Vice President Garner and Senators James M. Byrnes and Robert M. LaFollette, Jr., proposed to amend the Constitution to define Congress's legislative powers more expansively.[21] Most, however, were aimed at the Court itself, some in the form of constitutional amendments, others as simple legislation.

Proposals to create new vacancies on the Supreme Court were the preferred method of Court-curbing for some members of Congress, whether by increasing the size of the Court to eleven or fifteen, mandating retirement at age 65 (or 70), or establishing a ten-year term for judges.[22] Other bills addressed the issue of judicial review, including some that would have forbidden it altogether. Senator George Norris proposed an amendment that would require the agreement of seven justices in order to declare a federal law unconstitutional, then endorsed a bill mandating unanimity. LaFollette wanted to empower the president to demand advisory opinions from the Court regarding the constitutionality of proposed federal statutes.[23] At one time or another, Roosevelt was attracted by almost all of these ideas, including composite measures in one bill to allow the president and Congress to

[18] Ibid., 346.

[19] *Norman v. Baltimore and Ohio Railroad Co.*, 294 U.S. 240 (1935). The vote was 5–4.

[20] Author's calculation from Table 1 in Stuart S. Nagel, "Court-Curbing Periods in American History," *Vanderbilt Law Review* 18 (March 1965): 926.

[21] Raymond Moley, *After Seven Years* (New York: Harper and Brothers, 1939), 307; Arthur M. Schlesinger, Jr., *The Politics of Upheaval* (Boston: Houghton Mifflin Co., 1960), 491.

[22] Leuchtenburg, "Origins of Court-packing Plan," 373, 366; Schlesinger, *Politics of Upheaval*, 491.

[23] Leuchtenburg, "Origins of Court-packing Plan," 359; Schlesinger, *Politics of Upheaval*, 491.

demand, receive, and reject advisory opinion from the Court, or in another to repass an overturned law after an intervening congressional election.[24] Ultimately, he decided to adopt the essential elements of still another composite that Edward S. Corwin suggested in correspondence with Attorney-General Homer Cummings. It stipulated that whenever the Court included half or more justices who were 70 years or older, a new justice could be appointed for each justice in his seventies who declined to retire.[25]

Not every suggestion to break the impasses between the justices and the New Deal involved an assault on the Court. Representative Hatton Sumners of Texas, the chairman of the House Committee on the Judiciary, proposed legislation to guarantee retirement pay for justices over 70. One effect of the Economy Act of 1933 had been to cut former Justice Oliver Wendell Holmes's benefits in half, and Sumners believed that at least two of the Four Horsemen, Van Devanter and Sutherland, were delaying their own retirements for fear of a similar fate.[26] Another suggestion came from Arthur N. Holcombe of Harvard, who, in the spirit of Mr. Dooley's observation that "the Supreme Court follows th'illiction returns," urged that Roosevelt simply wait: "If these elections [of 1936] turn out satisfactorily, I cherish a strong hope that there will be a better prospect for liberal interpretation of the Constitution from the Supreme Court."[27]

Elections. In contrast to the elections of 1932 and 1934, the political implications of the 1936 results were ambiguous. Indisputably, the presidential landslide met one criterion for an empowering election – Roosevelt's margin of victory over Governor Alfred M. Landon was the largest in history. To interpret the congressional results was more difficult. Democrats gained only nine seats in the House, considerably less than the historical average.[28] Their seven-seat gain in the Senate was smaller than in either 1932 or 1934, but it was impressive nonetheless. Certainly, few Democrats could deny that the main explanation for their party's rapid rise to majority status lay with Roosevelt. Some doubtless began to wonder, however, whether their personal political fortunes still were joined to the President, especially since the general assumption was that he was beginning his last term.

The aspect of the 1936 elections that was least empowering for the second term was the campaign Roosevelt waged. Early in the year, he made very few requests to Congress for new legislation. Then, after a fighting acceptance speech to the Democratic convention, he carefully struck a president-above-the-fray pose in public appearances during the late summer and early fall. And even when he sharpened

[24] Leuchtenburg, "Origins of Court-packing Plan," 363–365, 371.

[25] Ibid., 388–391.

[26] Alsop and Catledge, *The 168 Days*, 40–41. Justice Stone shared this view. Alpheus Thomas Mason, *Harlen Fiske Stone: Pillar of the Law* (New York: Viking Press, 1956), 454.

[27] Schlesinger, *Politics of Upheaval*, 493.

[28] From 1900 to 1932, the average gain in House seats for the president's party in presidential election years was 34. Author's calculation from data in James Q. Wilson, *American Government*, 2nd ed. (Lexington, Mass.: D.C. Heath, 1983), 644–645.

his rhetoric in October, records Burns, "Roosevelt talked very little about the future . . . . He was making the New Deal record, not the New Deal promises, the issue."[29]

Roosevelt's inattention to the Court controversy during the 1936 campaign warrants special mention. At the Republican convention, former President Hoover and the Republican platform had pledged to defend the judiciary and dared Roosevelt to state his own position. Landon and other party leaders made much of the issue.[30] But Roosevelt was convinced that any intimation of his intention to confront the Court would create confusion and controversy among voters.[31] Delegates to the Democratic convention, responding to Roosevelt's explicit instructions, fuzzed the Court issue: to the extent that the platform suggested that any action might be needed, it spoke of "clarifying amendments" that would allow government intervention in the economy.[32]

Privately, Roosevelt had ambitious plans for the second term. "Wait until next year, Henry," he told Secretary of the Treasury Henry Morgenthau in May 1936, "I am really going to be radical."[33] Certainly he had decided that a drastic remedy for the Court impasse was required, although he did not know specifically what it would be. But publicly the campaign urged voters to treat the election as a referendum on the first term. The Court issue continued to be ducked; Roosevelt never spoke of it during the fall campaign. Harold Ickes, who had urged Roosevelt to raise the issue as far back as January, later remarked ruefully that "the groundwork had not been laid," recognizing at least that some groundwork was required in the election campaign before taking the issue to Congress.[34]

Skill. Of the three main elements that make possible dramatic presidential leadership of Congress—suitable policy ideas, an empowering election, and the adroit exercise of presidential leadership skill—the last took on particular importance in the Court fight. The abundance of available ideas about how to break the impasse between the Court and the administration was both an advantage and a disadvantage to Roosevelt; he had no shortage of approaches to choose from, but there was little consensus about which was best. The verdict of the 1936 election, overwhelming in its endorsement of the legislative achievements of Roosevelt's first term, was ambiguous in its implications for the second. In this uncertain situ-

[29] Schlesinger, *Politics of Upheaval*, 504; Burns, *Roosevelt*, chap. 14.

[30] Baker, *Back to Back*, 45–46.

[31] Kenneth S. Davis, *FDR: The New Deal Years, 1932–1937* (New York: Random House, 1986), 632–633.

[32] Schlesinger, *Politics of Upheaval*, 581–582.

[33] Ibid., 513.

[34] *The Secret Diary of Harold Ickes*, vol. 1 (New York: Simon and Schuster, 1953), 602, 524, 530, 531. In 1937, Ickes argued rather disingenuously to a Republican editor that since the Republicans had sounded their opposition to Court-curbing in 1936 and lost, Roosevelt could claim a mandate. Leuchtenburg, "Roosevelt's Plan," 84. Of course, Republicans had declaimed against totalitarian rule as well.

ation, unusually skillful presidential leadership clearly was needed if there were to be any hope of success.

For this challenge Roosevelt seemed particularly well-suited. His strategic sense, capacity to manage administration lieutenants for the development and promotion of policy ideas, presentational abilities in persuading and mobilizing the general public, and shrewd use of tactics within the Washington community are unrivaled among modern presidents.[35] Yet with few exceptions, these skills were notably absent in the Court fight of 1937.

Strategic Sense. In democratic polities, a leader's effort to discern the historical possibilities of the time requires above all an ability to interpret the public mood. On matters involving the judiciary, Roosevelt was ill-equipped to do so by experience or temperament and made few efforts to remedy these shortcomings.

Americans generally have regarded the judicial process as somehow outside and above politics. This underlying regard was challenged in the 1930s by the Supreme Court's rebuke of the New Deal, but other aspects of that decade seem to have made the public's appreciation of the Court all the more profound. Ironically, the depression was one: "The greater the insecurity of the times," Leuchtenburg notes, "the more people cling to the few institutions which seem changeless."[36] The number of justices had been fixed at nine since 1869, long enough for many people to regard it as set by the Framers.[37] The rise of Hitler and Mussolini in Europe also made some feel especially protective of the independence that the American judiciary enjoys. "Even many people who believe in President Roosevelt . . . ," said Senator Henry Ashurst, "were haunted by the terrible fear that some future President might, by suddenly enlarging the Supreme Court, suppress free speech, free assembly, and invade other Constitutional guarantees of citizens."[38] Apprehension about tampering with the ability of the Court (which had a strong record on civil liberties) to protect minorities was greatest among ideological liberals and certain religious, racial, and regional groups, including for different reasons many blacks and white southerners. Interestingly, almost every Catholic senator opposed the Court-packing plan.[39]

Roosevelt lacked an intuitive appreciation of the public's regard for the judiciary. He had come of age in politics during a period of court-bashing and, as a lawyer, was particularly receptive to the emerging realist school of legal intellectual thought, which considered judges to be policy makers motivated in large part by their own opinions and prejudices. Once, delivering a 1932 campaign speech,

[35] Hargrove and Nelson, *Presidents, Politics, and Policy*, chap 4.

[36] Leuchtenburg, *Roosevelt and New Deal*, 235–236.

[37] Robert Scigliano, *The Supreme Court and the Presidency* (New York: Free Press, 1971), 52. One woman protested: "If nine judges were enough for George Washington, they should be enough for President Roosevelt." Leuchtenburg, "Roosevelt's Plan," 86–87.

[38] Baker, *Back to Back*, 47–48. Felix Frankfurter shared this fear. Alsop and Catledge, *The 168 Days*, 76.

[39] Ibid., 80–82; Leuchtenburg, "Roosevelt's Plan," 87–88, 85.

Roosevelt spoke from a prepared text that read: "After March 4, 1929, the Republican party was in complete control of all branches of the government – the Legislature, with the Senate and Congress, and the executive departments." Then he improvised: "and, I may add, for full measure, to make it complete, the United States Supreme Court as well." Soon after his inauguration in 1933 Roosevelt judged Chief Justice Hughes one who "wouldn't cooperate" when the chief justice declined to give informal advisory opinions on proposed legislation.[40]

Compounding Roosevelt's difficulty in intuitively grasping public sensitivities on issues involving judicial independence was his more general tendency to over-interpret his mandate from the 1936 election. Although he had made his first term the issue, Roosevelt evidently felt that in giving him a forty-six-state majority, the voters had written a blank check to take the government in any direction he chose, by any means. He was encouraged in this view by aides such as Thomas Corcoran, Benjamin Cohen, and Harry Hopkins.[41] Campaigns can educate candidates as well as voters; by gauging audiences' responses to particular appeals in campaign speeches, for example, the candidate can gain a sense of which issues are working and which are not. But even though Roosevelt never mentioned the Court in 1936, he spoke to a Democratic victory dinner on 4 March 1937 as if he had: "We gave warning last November that we had only just begun to fight. Did some people really believe we did not mean it? Well, I mean it and you meant it."[42]

After the election, Roosevelt closed himself off from sources of information that would have informed his reading of public opinion, and neglected or downplayed available evidence that seemed to contradict that reading. Although Roosevelt regarded the labor, farm, and liberal lobbies' support for Court reform as vital, he did not consult with their leaders before launching his attack. Had he done so, he probably would have learned that for various reasons (the narrowness of organized labor's concern, extending mainly to the Wagner Act; the farmers' general conservatism, except when the issue was their own government benefits; liberals' apprehensions about civil liberties) such support would be limited, especially if the object of reform was the Court itself.[43] As for the general public, evidence was available that should have given the President pause before claiming a mandate for reformist legislation in general and Court-curbing in particular. A Gallup poll taken in November 1936 found that 50 percent of a sample of voters hoped the second term would be more conservative than the first; 15 percent hoped

[40] Baker, *Back to Back*, 108–110; Leuchtenburg, "Origins of Court-packing," 346; Alsop and Catledge, *The 168 Days*, 16.

[41] Alsop and Catledge, *The 168 Days*, 21; Burns, *Roosevelt*, 305.

[42] Burns, *Roosevelt*, 299. James Farley made a similar claim in late May: "Why compromise? The Democratic senators were elected on the basis of supporting the president's program. It is up to them to back it now." Leuchtenburg, "Roosevelt's Plan," 99.

[43] Baker, *Back to Back*, 86–89, 202–205; Alsop and Catledge, *The 168 Days*, 47–48, 53–54. Organized labor also was divided at this time between a feuding American Federation of Labor and Committee for Industrial Organization.

it would be more liberal.[44] Occasional Gallup polls in late 1935 and 1936 showed public resistance to proposals to restrict the Court's power to invalidate laws.[45] Yet even the harsh and massive influx of congressional mail after the Court plan was introduced in early 1937 and subsequent Gallup polls that consistently demonstrated the absence of public enthusiasm for Court-packing did not intrude into Roosevelt's oft-repeated belief that: "The people are with me. I know it."[46] Instead he clung to straws such as Lyndon Johnson's April 1937 victory in a special congressional election in Texas, even though Johnson was the only candidate in an eight-man field who favored the Roosevelt plan, and he won with only 28 percent of the vote.

Lack of empathy with the public regard for the Supreme Court, inattentiveness to opinion leaders, neglect of disagreeable evidence, an overly expansive interpretation of the meaning of the 1936 election—of all these explanations of the President's dulled strategic sense in the Court-packing episode, the election seems to have been the most important. Roosevelt had maintained a shrewd and studied silence in 1935 and 1936 while the Court was overturning his New Deal legislation; from 31 May 1935, when he made his "horse-and-buggy" remark, until 2 June 1936, when the *Tipaldo* decision provoked him to complain that the justices had created a constitutional "no-man's-land," Roosevelt made no public comment about the Court, biding his time and letting anti-Court sentiment grow on its own.[47] But when Ickes, Norris, and others encouraged Roosevelt to reap the harvest of his patient waiting by taking the Court issue to the voters, he declined. He wanted the election to be fought on the least controversial basis possible, even though such a strategy meant that little about the second term would be taught or learned in the campaign. To the extent that Roosevelt's purpose was to create the largest possible landslide on election day, he succeeded. But then, having chosen to seek no mandate for future action from the voters, he claimed one anyway.

Management of Lieutenants. As with the skill of strategic sense, Roosevelt did better managing lieutenants in the Court fight prior to the 1936 campaign than afterward. Beginning no later than an 11 January 1935 cabinet meeting, which took place on the eve of the Supreme Court's decision in the gold clause cases, Roosevelt began the process of discussing and considering various Court-curbing proposals with a variety of aides and advisers, including the cabinet as a body, Secretaries Ickes and Cummings individually, Senator Norris, journalist George

[44] George H. Gallup, *The Gallup Poll: Public Opinion, 1935–1971*, vol. 1 (New York: Random House, 1972), 41.

[45] Walter F. Murphy, *Congress and the Court* (Chicago: The University of Chicago Press, 1962), 61.

[46] Burns, *Roosevelt*, 298; Alsop and Catledge, *The 168 Days*, 72, 74, 78, 79, 184, 210; Frank V. Cantwell, "Public Opinion and the Legislative Process," *American Political Science Review* 40 (October 1946): 924–935.

[47] Leuchtenburg, "Origins of Court-Packing," 377–378; and Gregory A. Caldeira, "Public Opinion and the U.S. Supreme Court: FDR's Court-Packing Plan," *American Political Science Review* 81 (December 1987): 1139–1153.

Creel, Breckinridge Long (the American ambassador to Italy), and many others. He not only ranged widely in his search for solutions, but winnowed them on prudential, if not indisputable, grounds. Constitutional amendments as a class ended up being discarded, mainly because of the difficulties (or at the very least, the time) involved in gaining ratification from three-fourths of the states. Certain ideas for bills were rejected in the expectation that the Court would void them.

But having considered proposed solutions to the Court problem from a variety of sources in 1935 and in early and mid-1936, Roosevelt abruptly narrowed his range of advisers to one, Attorney-General Cummings. After the election, Cummings and Roosevelt met nearly every day in secret to discuss their progress in designing a proposal. Security was complete. White House advisers Corcoran and Cohen actually were working up a Court-curbing bill on their own, ignorant of the activities of the President and attorney-general;[48] even Justice Department aides who conducted research for Cummings (including Solicitor General Stanley Reed) did so in ignorance of its purpose.

Not until December, and then only in response to an initially unsolicited suggestion from Professor Corwin, did Roosevelt and Cummings settle on a plan: to seek legislation that would empower the President to appoint one additional justice (up to a maximum of six) for every sitting member of the Court with at least ten years service who declined to retire when he reached his seventies. Hughes, Brandeis, and the Four Horsemen fit this definition on the current Court. Both Cummings and Roosevelt had spoken approvingly of creating new justiceships as far back as January 1935; Roosevelt often invoked, although in garbled form, a British incident in which the prime minister had threatened to create new peerships to pack the House of Lords. Late in December 1935, however, he called simple Court-packing "a distasteful idea."[49] The lure of the Corwin plan was that with it the administration could define the mental and physical capacities of the elderly justices, not their conservative opinions, as the issue. What made the idea all the more delicious was Cummings's discovery that in 1913, then-Attorney-General McReynolds had made a similar recommendation with regard to lower court judges.

Delighted with the plan and its rationale ("the answer to a maiden's prayer," he exclaimed), Roosevelt approved the main elements of the Court proposal on 26 December. Responding to Cummings's longstanding desire for general federal court reform and seeing an opportunity to thicken still further the smokescreen around his Court-packing motive, Roosevelt allowed the attorney-general to add other provisions: additional lower court judges (also based on the age of the incumbent judiciary), reassignment of judges to busy courts by the chief justice, and a Court-appointed proctor to help supervise the flow of federal litigation.[50] Finally, Roosevelt approved Cummings's draft of the accompanying presidential

[48] Alsop and Catledge, *The 168 Days*, 36–37.
[49] *Secret Diary of Ickes*, 495.
[50] Alsop and Catledge, *The 168 Days*, 36.

message to Congress, a message that in stressing the age issue never mentioned the real basis of the President's desire to alter the Court. So complete had Roosevelt's veil of secrecy been that a brief meeting before the sending of the message on 5 February 1937 was the first word that any member of Congress got about the President's proposal.

The extent of the political problems that were created by Roosevelt's decision to formulate his approach to the Court issue in secret consultation with just one adviser would become apparent only when he tried to sell the Court plan to the public through rhetoric and to the Washington community with tactical skills. That there would be such problems, however, was inherent in the post-election policy development process that Roosevelt used for the Court issue. By locking out all lieutenants but Cummings after mid-1936, Roosevelt denied himself the benefits of the very advisory system that had worked so well during the first term. To some degree, a fluid and pluralistic process was needed to overcome Roosevelt's own excesses—his love of clever indirection, his impatience with procedural barriers, and his belief that he was in a real sense an anointed agent of Providence.[51] To some degree, too, such a process was needed to remedy the limitations of any single adviser—in Cummings's case, his ambition to sit on the Court.[52] Whether Corcoran, Cohen, or others would have discouraged Roosevelt from trying to pack the Court is uncertain, but they certainly would have recognized (and did, as soon as they heard—too late— about it) how politically damaging the plan's deceptive presentation would be.[53] The delight in a smart trick that made the age rationale irresistible to Roosevelt and Cummings as they conspired in secret would have been punctured by advisers more detached from the plan's cuteness.

Two consequences for subsequent relations between Roosevelt and his lieutenants flowed from the Court-packing policy development process: one predictable, one curious, both harmful to the President. The predictable consequence was that Roosevelt's customary advisers, puzzled by their leader's behavior, became wary of passing on disturbing news that they heard during the battle for congressional passage, thus allowing the President to become further detached from political reality.[54] The curious consequence was that Roosevelt, having excluded White House aides from the advisory role they performed so well, charged them, rather than the congressional leaders he had relied on in the first term, to direct the battle in Congress. This was a task for which they were ill-suited; Corcoran, in particular, was contemptuous of legislative politics, which he regarded as messy and ego-ridden. The aides' lack of good sources in the Senate made it hard to know

[51] Burns, *Roosevelt*, 297; James David Barber, *The Presidential Character: Predicting Performance in the White House* (Englewood Cliffs, N.J.: Prentice-Hall, 1972), 211-212; Kenneth B. Davis, "FDR As a Biographer's Problem," *The American Scholar* 53 (Winter 1983-1984): 107.

[52] Ted Morgan, *FDR: A Biography* (New York: Simon and Schuster, 1985), 469; Alsop and Catledge, *The 168 Days*, chap. 1 and p. 4.

[53] Alsop and Catledge, *The 168 Days*, 49.

[54] Baker, *Back to Back*, 47.

what the situation was, much less to influence it; even in late May, when the battle was all but lost, they rejected opportunities for a compromise in the illusion that they still could win.[55]

Why did Roosevelt abandon the system he had used so well in the first term to manage lieutenants for policy formation? The answer offered by Joseph Alsop and Turner Catledge, contemporary chroniclers of the Court-packing episode, is still the most plausible one:

> Nothing could illustrate better how the election had altered the Washington scene. A year earlier, in planning so momentous a step as an attack on the Supreme Court, the President would have followed a well-established program of general consultation. First his brilliant intellectual advisers . . . would have been called in to prepare the measure. And then, when the measure was ready, his congressional leaders . . . would have been summoned to advise on its presentation to Congress. . . .
>
> Now, however, the President felt no compulsion to make his consultation general. . . . He and Cummings could work out a solution together, and even though Cummings was a politician and not a constitutional expert, the solution would certainly be acceptable to a postelection Congress.[56]

Public Presentation. Roosevelt's decision not to address the Court issue in the 1936 election made the task of convincing and rallying the public both more difficult and more essential when he introduced the Court-packing plan in early 1937. Yet despite occasional glimpses of the customary Rooseveltian flair for skillfully presenting himself and his policies to the citizenry, the President's persuasive efforts were notably unsuccessful. He never was able to undo the ill effects of the deceptive design that he and Cummings had given to the plan.

Part of Roosevelt's problem was his apparent but curious belief that people either would take the plan's age-and-efficiency rationale at face value or, if they saw through to its real Court-packing purpose, would share his delight at its clever indirection. Either assumption was dubious; together they were poison. Yet at the press conference in which he first told the public about his intention to reform the Court, Roosevelt mixed careful reading and explication of the bill with winks and smiles. "He seemed to be asking the assembled newspapermen to applaud the perfections of his scheme, to note its nicely calculated indirections and praise its effectiveness," wrote two journalists.[57]

The effects of Roosevelt's deceptive presentation were disastrous. As he conceded four years later, "I made one major mistake when I first presented the plan. I did not place enough emphasis on the real mischief—the kind of decisions which,

[55] Alsop and Catledge, *The 168 Days*, 82–83, 186–187, 214. Aides also bungled by asking for only two weeks to present the administration's case in the Senate judiciary committee hearings, in the hope that the opposition would follow suit. Instead, opponents kept up an incessant drumbeat of hostile testimony for well over a month.

[56] Ibid., 24–25.

[57] Alsop and Catledge, *The 168 Days*, 167.

as a studied and continued policy, had been coming down from the Supreme Court."[58] The trumpet call he had issued to rally the faithful sounded false and uncertain. Deceptiveness disgusted some potential allies, notably Norris. It left the Court plan open to simple refutation of the facts that were its purported rationale. "The Supreme Court is fully abreast of its work . . . ," wrote Chief Justice Hughes in a public letter that was addressed to Senator Burton K. Wheeler, signed by Brandeis and Van Devanter, and supported, Hughes implied, by all the justices. Having thus disposed, with accompanying statistics, of Roosevelt's public diagnosis of the Court's maladies, Hughes went on to challenge the efficacy of his prescription: "An increase in the number of justices of the Supreme Court . . . would not promote the efficiency of the Court. There would be more judges to hear, more judges to confer, more judges to be convinced and to decide."[59] The age issue—raised by passages in the President's message like: "A lower mental or physical vigor leads men to avoid an examination of complicated and changed conditions"—offended many old people, including a goodly number of septuagenarian members of Congress and legions of liberal admirers of the 80-year-old Brandeis.[60] And not the least of the problems with the administration's public presentation of its case was that it was all but impossible to maintain. Even Cummings succumbed to candor when asked at a Senate hearing whether "after the six additional members of the Supreme Court are appointed, the Court should divide seven to eight, this entire plan would fail." He replied, "It would depend upon which side the seven were on and upon which side the eight were."[61]

Perhaps the worst thing about Roosevelt's presentation of the Court plan was that it made him seem ashamed of his best and truest argument for reform. In January 1935, he had been prepared to make a ringing radio speech if the Court ruled against the New Deal in the gold clause cases. Neither he nor Congress would "stand idly by," the President planned to say, "and . . . permit the decision of the Supreme Court to be carried through to . . . imperil the economic and political security of the nation."[62] Yet in the 1936 election he eschewed open confrontation with the Court, which by then had overturned a dozen laws enacted by the elected branches in their effort to meet the national crisis. In 1937 he launched his assault with circumspection so complete that one could barely find evidence in Roosevelt's public statements that he found the Court's conservative defiance objectionable.

An about-face by the President in March helped his case somewhat. Realizing

[58] Mason, *Harlan Fiske Stone*, 444.

[59] Baker, *Back to Back*, 158–159. As Hughes pointed out in his letter, in 1925 Congress had empowered the Court to decide which appeals it thought were important enough to hear. Some justices, including Stone, did not see the letter and were privately unhappy that Hughes implied their support.

[60] Leuchtenburg, "Roosevelt's Plan," 75, 85–86.

[61] U.S. Congress, "Reorganization of the Federal Judiciary," Hearings before the Committee on the Judiciary, U.S. Senate, 75th Congress, first sess. (Washington, D.C.: U.S. Government Printing Office, 1937), 15.

[62] Leuchtenburg, "Origins of Court-packing," 353–354.

the ineffectiveness of his efforts to date, Roosevelt took dead aim at the Court's obstructiveness in a fighting speech to a Democratic victory dinner on 4 March and a quieter but no less pointed fireside chat on 9 March. He displayed his gifts for dramaturgy later that spring, stopping in Texas in April, for example, to draw attention to the public endorsement of Court-packing that Johnson's election seemed to indicate.[63]

But coming as late in the game as they did, these gestures were of little consequence and the speeches, although probably the source of the Court-packing proposal's only advance in the Gallup poll, prompted no outpouring of mail to wavering legislators, which had been the speeches' main purpose.[64] Strangely, Roosevelt's frank admission of the real rationale behind Court-packing in early March did not lead him to make a logical accompanying change in tactics—to abandon the bill that he and Cummings had drafted and settle for a readily obtainable compromise that would create two or three new justiceships and thus allow him to tip the balance on the Court in favor of the New Deal.[65]

Tactics. In addition to his deficient exercise of strategic, managerial, and presentational skills, Roosevelt was tactically maladroit in his dealings with other Washington politicians during the Court-packing episode. Roosevelt's first misstep was to keep his intentions secret, even in their broadest outlines, from those whose support he would need. His announcement of the plan to a called meeting of the cabinet and congressional leaders on the morning of 5 February, a half-hour before he had scheduled a session with the press, was the first word of his purposes that any of them other than Cummings heard; Roosevelt actually had dissembled to the cabinet in January.[66] Most students of the Court-packing episode have rightly noted the damaging effects of Roosevelt's arrogance in all this. Even when he did summon leaders from the cabinet and Congress, he did nothing more than brief them and send them on their way.[67] The post-briefing reactions of certain participants have entered the realm of folklore: Sumners's "Boys, here's where I cash in my chips"; Garner holding his nose with one hand and pointing thumbs-down with the other; Sam Rayburn's conclusion that Roosevelt was becoming a tin god.[68]

But there were further, equally damaging effects of Roosevelt's policy of secrecy.

[63] Baker, *Back to Back*, 198–202; Leuchtenburg, "A Second Life, A Second Death," 677–679.

[64] Alsop and Catledge, *The 168 Days*, 113. The Gallup poll showed that public opinion, which was 48 to 41 percent against the Court plan on 1 March, climbed to 45 to 41 percent in favor by 29 March, before sliding down to 44 to 31 percent against on 17 May and 50 to 35 percent against on 7 June. Cantwell, "Public Opinion"; Caldeira, "Public Opinion," 1147.

[65] Such a compromise was proposed to the administration by Senate leaders frequently and as late as the end of May. Alsop and Catledge, *The 168 Days*, 78, 108, 152–153, 210, 214.

[66] Leuchtenburg, "Origins of Court-packing," 396.

[67] Baker, *Back to Back*, chap. 1.

[68] Alsop and Catledge, *The 168 Days*, 67; Leuchtenburg, "Roosevelt's Plan," 101; Morgan, *FDR*, 471. Rayburn also was furious that Roosevelt had physically attached his message to the proposed bill, as if to suggest that no alterations by Congress would be tolerated.

For one, it left him tactically unprepared for unexpected resistance. The consensus was that the House would be the best place to begin the battle for passage, but that possibility was effectively foreclosed when Speaker William Bankhead, Majority Leader Rayburn, and Sumners (chairman of the judiciary committee) surprised Roosevelt by indicating their opposition to Court-packing.[69] Sumners quickly rallied a majority of his committee (the rules committee also was opposed), and Bankhead and Rayburn decided to forestall any effort to bring the bill to the floor by a discharge petition.[70]

Roosevelt's decision to keep congressional leaders in the dark hurt his cause in other ways. Throughout 1936 and at the start of the 75th Congress in 1937, many Washington politicians made commitments on the Court issue that later were difficult to reverse. Senator Ashurst, for example, denied during the 1936 campaign (as did Senator Joseph Bailey) that the President had any intention of packing the Court and denounced the idea as "the prelude to tyranny."[71] Bankhead, Norris, Sumners, and others introduced reform measures when Congress opened in 1937, usually explaining why their ideas were better than Court-packing or other alternatives would be. By bringing these legislators in on the policy development process (even at a late stage), Roosevelt could have taken advantage of their desire to do something about the Court. By locking them out, he all but guaranteed that they would go their own ways. Ashurst endorsed Roosevelt's plan, but did not give it the kind of enthusiastic support the President needed from the chairman of the Senate Judiciary Committee. Secrecy from congressional allies also hurt Roosevelt when Senator Hugo Black left the judiciary committee for reasons of his own at the start of the January session, thus denying Roosevelt his one staunch and effective supporter on the committee. Had Black known anything of Roosevelt's plans, he almost certainly would have stayed where he would have been of greatest service.

Secrecy was not Roosevelt's only tactical error in the Court-packing fight. He also seriously underestimated his opposition. In at least one case, this was unavoidable: who could have foreseen that Senate Republicans would maintain a conspiracy of silence after the plan was introduced, leaving Democrats to lead the opposition to Court-packing and denying Roosevelt the opportunity to portray its critics as bitter-end partisans?[72] But for the most part, Roosevelt's errors in judging his opponents were careless. To discount, as Roosevelt did, the political wiles of former New York governor, former secretary of state, former Republican presidential nominee Charles Evans Hughes was to leave his plan wide open to

[69] Leuchtenburg, "Roosevelt's Plan," 77–78. In February, a poll of the House by Representative Fred Vinson showed a 100-vote margin for the Court plan. Alsop and Catledge, *The 168 Days*, 92.

[70] Alsop and Catledge, *The 168 Days*, 88; Burns, *Roosevelt*, 314.

[71] Burns, *Roosevelt*, 294; Leuchtenburg, "Origins of Court-Packing," 396.

[72] Karl A. Lamb, "The Opposition Party as Secret Agent: Republicans and the Court Fight, 1937," *Papers of the Michigan Academy of Sciences, Arts, and Letters* (1961), 539–550; Baker, *Back to Back*, 89–99.

the sort of subtle attack Hughes later launched with his letter to Wheeler. Similarly, for Roosevelt to think that corporate America was politically impotent just because he had overcome its opposition in 1936 was reckless. In truth, led by publisher Frank Gannett, the business-funded National Committee to Uphold Constitutional Government fought Court-packing both ardently (sending out ten million mailings that urged recipients to write Congress) and skillfully (Gannett even advanced civil libertarian arguments against the plan to Jews and blacks).[73]

How does one account for Roosevelt's deftless approach to both his allies and his foes prior to announcing the Court-packing plan? Fear of leaks that would provoke a preemptive attack by administration opponents and divide the ranks of its supporters was the stated reason for Roosevelt's policy of secrecy.[74] Even putting aside both the obvious costs of excluding needed and demonstratedly loyal allies and the clear value of airing the issue among voters in the campaign, this explanation would be easier to credit if Roosevelt himself had not leaked his intention to pack the Court to George Creel, who promptly published the news in the 26 December issue of *Collier's*.[75] Burns, an admiring biographer, probably has a truer understanding of Roosevelt's motives:

> The explanation lies deeper—deep in Roosevelt's personality. He had won what he considered to be a personal election victory over the Old Guard. Now the Old Guard remained entrenched in the ramparts of the judiciary. The stage was set for a Rooseveltian onslaught against the citadel [that] . . . combined in a curious fashion two Rooseveltian traits—his instinct for the dramatic and his instinct for the adroit and circuitous stratagem rather than the frontal assault.[76]

Less attractive personality traits, notably the impulse to punish as well as to overcome administration opponents, may explain Roosevelt's blindness to the political skills of big business and the Court itself. Business, of course, had provoked his astonishing 1936 election-eve statement: "I welcome their hatred . . . . I should like to have it said that in the second term these forces met their master."[77] Roosevelt's opposition to the Court also was bitter; curiously, of all the justices' anti-New Deal decisions, the one that infuriated him most was *Humphrey's Executor*, which overturned the President's firing of a by then dead regulatory commissioner. Roosevelt took this as a personal insult by the justices, so much so that aides Rexford Tugwell and Robert H. Jackson later traced the origins of Court-packing to his reaction to this decision.[78] He also was angry that Hughes, after refusing to

[73] Baker, *Back to Back*, 74–77, 80–81.

[74] Leuchtenburg, "Origins of Court-packing," 396; Burns, *Roosevelt*, 297.

[75] George Creel, "Roosevelt's Plan and Purposes," *Collier's*, 26 December 1936, 7–9ff; Creel, *Rebel at Large* (New York: G. P. Putnam's, 1947), 292–294.

[76] Burns, *Roosevelt*, 297.

[77] Ibid., 283.

[78] William E. Leuchtenburg, "The Case of the Contentious Commissioner: Humphrey's Executor v. U.S." in Harold M. Hyman and Leonard W. Levy, eds., *Freedom and Reform* (New York: Harper

give advance warning in the form of informal advisory opinions on the constitutionality of proposed legislation, had joined the Four Horsemen and ruled against the New Deal. Finally, Roosevelt believed that to amend the Constitution to broaden Congress's powers would be an intolerable concession that the Court had been correct in its interpretation of the existing Constitution.[79]

As Burns suggests, Roosevelt's 1936 election landslide figures prominently in any explanation of why he behaved so uncharacteristically in launching the Court fight. During the first term, his temperamental inclinations notwithstanding, political uncertainty and shrewd tactical sense kept Roosevelt cautious. He consulted with congressional, cabinet, and interest group leaders; allowed them at least the illusion of influence over the administration's policies and strategies; and gauged the opposition carefully. Now, after the election, convinced that "the people are with me," Roosevelt shrugged off these self-imposed restraints and gave full vent to his desire for mastery.

Even after he introduced the Court-packing plan, election-born overconfidence continued to blur Roosevelt's tactical decision making. Virtually from the week of the plan's introduction in February 1936 until the last week in May, offers and pleas to compromise by settling for a simple two or three-seat expansion of the Court came into the White House from the Senate. Roosevelt correctly saw no need to strike a deal quickly, although his loud laughter in the faces of Garner and some congressional leaders when they proposed a three-seat increase in February was unhelpful.[80] Pressures to settle for two additional justices increased by mid-April. Hughes had written his letter (March 22); Roberts's switch-in-time had effectively reversed the Court's nine-month-old *Tipaldo* ruling (March 29) and upheld the Wagner Act (April 12);[81] and public support for the Court plan had severely waned. Senator Charles O. Andrews even provided a face-saving rationale: growth in the number of federal judicial circuits, which historically had been the main basis for increasing the Court's size, could be said to imply ten associate justiceships, one for each circuit, and a chief justice serving at-large.[82]

Roosevelt was implacable. A reasoned worst-case scenario provides part of the explanation. If Roberts reverted to conservatism and Senate Majority Leader Joseph Robinson, to whom Roosevelt had promised the first vacancy on the Court, voted with the Four Horsemen, the New Deal still would be at a 5–6 deficit. Reason also dictated, however, that with chances for any sort of victory fading, the President would do well to take what he could get, not only to settle the Court issue

---

and Row, 1967), 310–311; Rexford G. Tugwell, *The Democratic Roosevelt* (Garden City, N.Y.: Doubleday, 1957), 392.

[79] Leuchtenburg, "Origins of Court-packing," 396.

[80] Alsop and Catledge, *The 168 Days*, 78.

[81] *West Coast Hotel Co. v. Parrish*, 300 U.S. 379 (1937); *NLRB v. Jones and Laughlin Steel Corporation*, 301 U.S. 1 (1937).

[82] Alsop and Catledge, *The 168 Days*, 152–153, 160, 196–197; Scigliano, *Supreme Court and the Presidency*, 52.

but also to end the bitter fight that was splitting his party and tying up the rest of his legislative agenda. Yet even in late May, by which time Justice Van Devanter had announced his retirement (May 18) and the Court had upheld the Social Security Act (May 24), Roosevelt stood his ground.[83] He still wanted to teach a lesson about the dangers of defying the President to congressional Democrats, whom he regarded as his political debtors, and to the Court, which he was certain had changed course just to deny him victory for his plan.[84]

On 3 June, Roosevelt finally accepted Senator Robinson's plea to authorize him to work out the best compromise he could. Robinson latched on to a proposal by Senator Carl Hatch that would empower the President to nominate a new justice for every 75-year-old member of the Court, at a rate of one such appointment per year. This guaranteed Roosevelt at least two appointments in 1937 and one each in 1938, 1939, and 1940. Robinson, who had labored without ceasing for the original Court-packing plan, redoubled his efforts. Roosevelt helped matters by playing genial host to Democratic legislators at the Jefferson Island Club on the Chesapeake Bay.[85]

The President's turnabout came too late. Robinson thought he had engineered a narrow majority for a time, but opposition leaders had both the will and, with more than forty senators in their ranks, the way to conduct and sustain a filibuster.[86] Then there was the House to overcome, its leaders still implacable and well-positioned to resist.[87] In any event, defections by freshmen Democrats probably lost Robinson his majority even in the Senate by 13 July.[88] Ashurst told a Roosevelt aide, "If anyone's telling the president he can pass this Court bill he's doing him a great disservice."[89] On 14 July Robinson died. Shortly after his funeral, the Senate voted to table the bill, and the Court-packing episode of 1937 was over.

Alternatives to Court-packing

William Leuchtenburg has defined the challenge sensibly for students of the Court-packing episode. "Before they are allowed to dismiss [Roosevelt's] proposal out of hand," he argues, "they should be required to examine the difficult situation he faced and to indicate what alternative he might have adopted that was truly feasible." Stated differently, the challenge is this: given the knowledge that was available to the President and accepting his view that to win Supreme Court ac-

[83] *Steward Machine Co. v. Davis*, 301 U.S. 548 (1937); *Helvering v. Davis*, 301 U.S. 619 (1937).

[84] Alsop and Catledge, *The 168 Days*, 153–154.

[85] Ibid., 219–223; Leuchtenburg, "Roosevelt's Plan," 101; Leuchtenburg, "A Second Life, A Second Death," 677–679.

[86] Leuchtenburg, "A Second Life, A Second Death," 680–682; Alsop and Catledge, *The 168 Days*, 248–250; Baker, *Back to Back*, 233.

[87] Baker, *Back to Back*, 218; Burns, *Roosevelt*, 314. Sumners by now was furious in his opposition. Alsop and Catledge, *The 168 Days*, 264–265.

[88] Alsop and Catledge, *The 168 Days*, 265.

[89] Ibid., 264.

quiescence in the New Deal was an important second-term goal, "What then was Roosevelt to do?"[90]

The analysis of presidential leadership that is presented in this article suggests an answer to Leuchtenburg's challenge. During the 1936 election campaign, Roosevelt's best strategy was to attack the Court frontally in order to lay the groundwork for post-inauguration reform; after the election, considering that he had not done so, his best remaining alternative was simply to wait.

Before the Election: Attack Frontally. The reasoning of the majority opinions in the anti-New Deal Court decisions had convinced Roosevelt, quite understandably, that social security, the Wagner act, and other achievements of the first term would be declared unconstitutional when the Court ruled on them, as would the sorts of proposals he had in mind for the second term, such as wages and hours legislation.[91] Roosevelt had heard and discussed the many and varied ideas that members of Congress, White House advisers, and others had suggested to end the Court's resistance; as much as anything, this experience had shown him that there was growing support in Washington to do something. He had determined in the aftermath of his much-criticized horse-and-buggy attack on the Court that time and presidential self-restraint were needed for public opinion to come around. He even suggested to the cabinet in January 1936 that he hoped the justices would void enough bills so that, in Ickes's account, "a real issue will be joined on which we can campaign to the country."[92] The justices had more than cooperated, and Ickes, Norris, and others had urged the President to reap the harvest sown with his public patience by raising the Court issue in his speeches. Finally, Roosevelt had concluded that he was going to win reelection—in January, June, August, and October, his tallies of electoral votes, always cautious, showed that he saw himself well in the lead.[93]

The sensible decision for Roosevelt—given the obstacles and opportunities he confronted, as he saw them—was to make his intention to end the Court's obstruction of the New Deal clear during the campaign, then claim a mandate for action after he won. His own hindsight, not future scholars', should have led him to this strategy. Certainly the lesson of 1932 had been that a presidential candidate did not need to be specific in his proposals. Simply to raise high an issue and pledge to remedy it in office was sufficient if he won a large victory. The experience of the first term also gave clear guidance about what the President should do after the election—consult with trusted and experienced advisers to develop a plan, bring in his ever-reliable congressional allies to advise him on how to promote the plan, then let them take the lead in Congress while he took his case to the voters.

After the Election: Wait. Roosevelt, of course, did not attack the Court fron-

[90] William E. Leuchtenburg, "The Court Packing Crisis of 1937," *News For Teachers of Political Science* 45 (Spring 1985): 13.

[91] In truth, the reasoning of *Carter v. Carter Coal Co.* and *Railroad Retirement Board v. Alton Railroad Co.* seemed to doom the Wagner act and social security act, respectively.

[92] *Secret Diary of Ickes*, 524.

[93] Schlesinger, *Politics of Upheaval*, 571, 608, 640.

tally before the 1936 election. The desire for the largest reelection majority possible that kept him from raising controversial issues in the campaign, the fear of leaks that prevented him from consulting even with allies and advisers, the fondness for indirection that made coy approaches so appealing – considerations such as these governed Roosevelt's behavior and left him in a much-changed situation after the election. A direct assault on the Court still would be better than a deceptive one, consultation better than secrecy. But if a frontal attack remained a better post-election alternative than the Court plan, it no longer was a good one: the President had sought no mandate and could claim none. Nor did his best remaining strategy seem all that appealing: simply to wait in the hope that the justices would come to appreciate the improved craftsmanship that had gone into the more recent New Deal laws that now were coming before them; that vacancies would occur on the Court; or that the Court would fulfill Mr. Dooley and yield to the voters' endorsement of the New Deal.

Improved Legal Craftsmanship. The legislation of the first New Deal was not well drawn; it too often tied sweeping assertions of federal power to slap-dash justifications like the doctrine of emergency powers from the World War. By 1934, a new group of draftsmen had joined the administration. Trained by Felix Frankfurter at Harvard Law School and by Brandeis or Holmes in Supreme Court clerkships, Corcoran, Cohen, James Landis, and their colleagues were far more attentive to the need when writing legislation to skirt the legal landmines that were sprinkled through the Court's decisions and to offer the justices a plausible constitutional rationale for voting to uphold.[94] Few, if any, expected that craftsmanship alone would move the Supreme Court, but in the event that one or more justices were open to persuasion for other reasons, intelligent administration rationales based on the commerce clause or the taxing power could only make the task easier.

Vacancies. "It will fall to your lot to nominate more justices of the Supreme Court than any other president since General Washington," Senator Ashurst told Roosevelt in 1936. "Father time, with his scythe, is on your side. Anno Domini is your invincible ally."[95] American history writ large provided a basis for Ashurst's prophecy: presidents prior to Roosevelt had appointed an average of one justice every twenty-three months, and previous "old" Courts usually had broken up quickly.[96] But American history writ small was of greater interest to Roosevelt: his first four years had produced no vacancies and the hostile decisions of 1935 and 1936 had convinced him that all of the conservative justices would postpone retirement as long as he was president and that none of them would die. (Metropolitan Life's actuarial tables gave even the oldest justice another five years).[97] In the meantime, the New Deal remained in constant jeopardy.

[94] Paul L. Murphy, *The Constitution in Crisis Times 1918–1969* (New York: Harper and Row, Torchbook, 1972), 140–148.
[95] Baker, *Back to Back*, 8.
[96] Author's calculation. Tribe, *God Save This Court*, xviii.
[97] Schlesinger, *Politics of Upheaval*, 493.

Others thought they had reason to be less pessimistic than the President about the prospect of judicial retirements. Frances Perkins, the secretary of labor, had been told by McReynolds that some of his colleagues would retire if their full pensions were guaranteed against the kind of action that had reduced Holmes's by half.[98] Stone said the same thing to Irving Brant, the editorialist of the *St. Louis Star-Times* and a sure conduit to the White House. Stone also hinted to Representative Emmanuel Celler that passage of Sumners's retirement bill, which was designed to protect the justices' benefits, would prompt two members of the Court to depart in six months to a year.[99] Sumners himself was certain that Van Devanter and Sutherland, two of the Four Horsemen, would step down soon after his bill was passed.[100] Three days after Roosevelt introduced the Court-packing proposal, Ashurst tried to interest him in the Sumners bill as an alternative. Rather than respond favorably (he regarded retirement legislation as a useless diversion), Roosevelt took Ashurst's suggestion as cause to doubt the senator's loyalty.[101]

Congressional leaders rushed the Sumners bill to passage on 1 March, even though they feared that Roosevelt's assault on the Court would discourage justices from retiring quickly for fear of seeming weak. But Van Devanter, coaxed by Senator William Borah, who thought that a quick retirement would help the anti-Court-packing cause, stepped down just three months later, and Sutherland followed in January.[102] Brandeis's retirement and Butler's death in 1939 gave Roosevelt his third and fourth appointments of the second term; by the time he left office, he had appointed nine justices.

Election Aftershocks. Incredible though it may seem in view of the results, until the 1936 election was over, conservatives on the Court had some reason to think that the public agreed with them about the New Deal and that Roosevelt might be defeated. The *Schechter* decision overturning the National Industrial Recovery Act had been widely applauded, and a poll printed in the *Washington Post* on the eve of *U.S. v. Butler* showed the public opposed to the Agriculture Adjustment Act.[103] On 19 October, Van Devanter wrote to a friend that he thought the election would be close.[104] Roosevelt could not have known how Van Devanter and perhaps some of his colleagues felt, but he was aware of information in the public record that might be leading the justices to that conclusion. The fledgling Gallup poll indicated that the Republicans had nominated by far their most popular candidate and placed Landon within four or five percentage points of Roosevelt all summer.[105] The prestigious *Literary Digest* poll, which had come within three points

[98] Morgan, *FDR*, 469.
[99] Mason, *Harlan Fiske Stone*, 454–455.
[100] Alsop and Catledge, *The 168 Days*, 41.
[101] Baker, *Back to Back*, 67–68.
[102] Ibid., 229.
[103] Alsop and Catledge, *The 168 Days*, 7; Leuchtenburg, "Origins of Court-packing," 368.
[104] Leuchtenburg, "Origins of Court-packing," 381.
[105] *Gallup Opinion Index* (December 1980), 28, 40.

of the final tally in 1932, predicted a Landon victory with 57 percent of the popular vote and 370 electoral votes.[106]

After the election, Cummings and Roosevelt discussed the possibility that the President's landslide would convince the Court that it was isolated and should yield, however grudgingly, to political reality.[107] Although they decided that McReynolds and the other three conservative justices were too stubborn to change, there was some reason to think that the election results really had made a difference. Government lawyers noticed, for example, that the Four Horsemen now treated them with respect rather than contempt when they argued before the Court.[108] And Hughes was on record, in a just-published book, as arguing that when the Court departed from "its fortress in public opinion," it "suffered severely from self-inflicted wounds." Did this not give reason to think the chief justice might change course now that he knew which way the political wind was blowing?[109] Stone thought so; he also thought that Roberts might desert the Four Horsemen after election day.[110]

Roberts, in fact, did desert: it was his vote in *West Coast Hotel v. Parrish* and the Wagner act and social security cases that constituted the switch in time. That Roberts abandoned the conservatives in the aftermath of the election but before the President's Court plan was introduced is clear. He told Hughes in December that he would vote to affirm the Washington state minimum wage law.[111] Curiously, however, one could argue just as plausibly that the election postponed Roberts's alliance with the moderates as that it hastened the switch. Roberts had shown an early willingness to sustain New Deal-style programs. In 1934, for example, he wrote the majority opinion in *Nebbia v. New York*, strongly asserting the primacy of the public interest when in conflict with property rights, much to the fury of the Four Horsemen.[112] But in 1935 Roberts's name began to be mentioned as a possible presidential nominee for the Republicans in 1936, in the spirit

[106] Gallup, *Gallup Poll*, 39. James L. Sundquist, *Dynamics of the Party System*, rev. ed. (Washington, D.C.: Brookings Institution, 1983), 218.

[107] Alsop and Catledge, *The 168 Days*, 24.

[108] Ibid., 138–139.

[109] Charles Evans Hughes, *The Supreme Court of the United States* (Garden City, N.Y.: Garden City Publishing Co., 1936), 24, 51–53.

[110] Mason, *Harlan Fiske Stone*, 454.

[111] Merlo J. Pusey, *Charles Evans Hughes* (New York: Macmillan Co., 1952), 757, 766–772. Roberts always maintained that his votes in *Tipaldo* and *Parrish* were consistent, because in *Tipaldo* the controlling issue of *Parrish*, that is, whether to override *Adkins v. Children's Hospital* (261 U.S. 525 [1923]), was not properly brought before the Court by the plaintiffs. This explanation, unlikely though it seems, might be plausible if his vote in *Parrish* had not been followed so quickly by other switches in the Wagner act and social security cases. See Felix Frankfurter, "Mr. Justice Roberts," *University of Pennsylvania Law Review* 104 (December 1955): 311–317; and John W. Chambers, "The Big Switch: Justice Roberts and the Minimum-Wage Cases," *Labor History* 10 (Winter 1969): 44–73.

[112] *Nebbia v. New York*, 291 U.S. 502 (1934). Roberts also sided with the moderates in the gold clause cases.

of the draft of then-Justice Hughes in 1916.[113] In view of the party's conservative center of gravity at the time, a shift to the right to draw the contrast between himself and the New Deal would have been sensible.[114] In summer 1936, however, Roberts saw not just his own chances dashed but the nomination of a centrist candidate and the adoption of an anti-*Tipaldo* platform by the Republican convention. The results in November only underscored how far the country had moved from conservatism.

In 1954, a then-retired Roberts appeared before a Senate committee to warn of Supreme Court justices who

> have had in the back of their minds a possibility that they might get the nomination for president. Now, that is not a healthy situation because, however strong a man's mentality and character, if he has this ambition in his mind it may tinge or color what he does . . . . I happen to have a personal knowledge of what that pressure is like, for twice ill-advised but enthusiastic friends of mine urged me to let my name go up as a candidate for president while I was on the Court.

Roberts added: "Of course I turned a hard face in that thing. I never had the notion in my mind."[115]

For Roosevelt to attack the Supreme Court in the 1936 campaign would have been risky. What if the issue backfired and made his reelection so narrow that he could not persuasively claim a mandate for Court reform afterward?[116] After the election, to wait, even if waiting included an endorsement of Sumners's retirement bill and offered the hope that one or more of the hoped-for changes in the Court would come about naturally, meant gambling that the justices would not continue on the course they had followed since 1935. But presidential power is never a sure thing. In this case, as in all cases, the most that one can conclude is that in view of the situation Roosevelt faced at the time, to fight or to wait were more likely to achieve his goals than any of the alternatives, including the Court-packing plan.

Conclusion

The Court-packing episode of 1937 may be understood well as a case study in presidential leadership, not just a unique historical event or an aspect of a partic-

[113] Baker, *Back to Back*, 123–124.

[114] There are alternative explanations for Roberts's growing affinity with the conservatives: fondness for McReynolds, sympathy with big business, constitutional philosophy, etc. Alsop and Catledge, *The 168 Days*, 6–7.

[115] U.S. Congress, "Composition and Jurisdiction of the Supreme Court," Hearings before a Subcommittee of the Committee on the Judiciary, U.S. Senate, 83rd Congress, second sess. (Washington, D.C.: U.S. Government Printing Office, 1954), 8–9.

[116] Yet if anyone should have been immune to this fear, it was Roosevelt. As noted earlier, he had little appreciation for the public's veneration of the Court; what is more, he had decided in January 1935, on the eve of the gold clause cases, that to attack and even defy the Court was a course he was willing to take.

ular presidency, and from the perspective of Roosevelt's political situation at the time, rather than in hindsight. But is there a larger issue as well? Roosevelt's dramatic first-term legislative accomplishments already have been analyzed as manifestations of a pattern of presidential leadership success that includes an empowering election, suitable ideas, and the adroit exercise of political leadership skills. His second-term failure on Court-packing may illustrate another, more destructive pattern of the modern presidency.

It seems more than coincidental that the four twentieth-century presidents who have won the largest reelection victories (thus demonstrating their sensitivity to public opinion) instantly breached the bounds of permissible political action in a way that brought down the public's wrath. Roosevelt's Court-packing proposal in 1937, Johnson's unilateral escalation of the Vietnam war in 1965, the cover-up of the Watergate scandal by Richard M. Nixon in late 1972 and 1973, and Reagan's Iran-contra affair in 1985 and 1986. Compounding their problems, each then circled up the wagons, all of them manned by deferential aides and cronies, to seal out unpleasant but necessary political knowledge when things went badly. From the heights of political unity and consensus in the reelection, each president and the nation descended into varying depths of stalemate and suspicion during the second term.

The common feature of each of these self-inflicted wounds seems to have been the reelected president's errant conclusion that the voters had handed him blanket authorization to rule during the second term as he saw fit, rather than, as was more likely, that they had endorsed his conduct during the first term, expressed a lack of confidence in his opponent, and shown some faith that he would continue to lead as the skillful head of one branch of a three-branch government. There is nothing inevitable about such a reaction from presidents who are landslide reelection winners, but the temptation to a "*L'etat, c'est moi*" way of thinking in such an instance—and the need to resist it—are obvious.*

* I would like to thank Erwin Hargrove, Paul Conkin, Kenneth Finegold, and Sam MacSeveney of the History and Politics Group of the Institute for Public Policy Studies at Vanderbilt University for their helpful comments on an earlier draft of this article.

Reflections on the Separation of Powers and Judicial Review at the End of the Reagan Era

Peter E. Quint*

I. *Introduction*

As a review of the past eight years clearly shows, the Reagan period was marked by severe clashes of power between the President and Congress. These disputes extended across a number of areas in foreign and domestic policy.

The administration's military policy—certainly the most adventuristic since the end of the Vietnam War—raised issues of presidential authority in the stationing of Marines in Lebanon, the invasion of Grenada, the bombing of Libya, the reflagging of Kuwaiti ships in the Persian Gulf, and the military support of the *Contra* rebels in Nicaragua and of government forces in El Salvador. In part to support its Nicaraguan venture, the administration apparently created a secret operational foreign policy apparatus in the National Security Council.

In domestic affairs, the administration sought to extend policy controls over administrative agencies by requiring cost-benefit analyses supervised by the Office of Management and Budget. The President also issued directives requiring more than two million government employees to sign secrecy agreements, a program undertaken in the absence of any explicit statutory authority. Finally,

* Professor of Law, University of Maryland. For helpful comments on an earlier draft of this essay, I am grateful to my colleagues, William Reynolds, Palma Strand, Edward Tomlinson, Robin West, and Gordon Young.

January 1989 Vol. 57 No. 3

the administration bitterly opposed congressional measures that it believed infringed upon executive prerogatives—such as the legislative veto, the Gramm-Rudman-Hollings budget control legislation, and provisions for the appointment of independent counsel to investigate alleged crimes of high executive officers.

Contests with Congress also marked the administrations of Mr. Reagan's recent predecessors, Nixon, Ford and Carter, but tension between Congress and the President is not a new phenomenon of recent decades. Indeed, the Framers of the Constitution recognized that a rather extreme system of divided powers—with the executive elected independently, rather than chosen by the legislature as in the British system—would naturally raise questions about the precise boundaries of governmental authority. The authors of *The Federalist Papers* foresaw that there would be struggles for power between the branches, and believed that these struggles would restrain each branch and protect the people against overbearing governmental power.[1]

An early interbranch conflict arose in 1793 when President Washington proclaimed American neutrality in the war between England and France, without the participation of Congress. In this episode, two authors of *The Federalist Papers* divided on the propriety of Washington's action.[2] Hamilton defended the proclamation and argued that extensive foreign-policy authority was included in the "executive power" confided to the President by Article II.[3] Madison, in contrast, asserted the importance of congressional participation in foreign affairs and emphasized the "danger of the [presidential] prerogative contended for [by Hamilton.]"[4]

The tension between the policymaking assertions of the President and Congress continued throughout the nineteenth and into the twentieth century. Sometimes, as in the early days of the Civil War, presidential power prevailed almost absolutely. In the late nineteenth century, in contrast, the weakness of the President yielded to a form of "congressional government."[5] Sometimes, as in disputes over Reconstruction and the impeachment of Andrew Johnson, these struggles took a particularly dramatic form. Yet, as the authors of *The Federalist* contemplated, these disputes between the President and Congress over the allocation of governmental authority are an inextricable part of the American constitutional system.

To this extent, then, these disputes of the Reagan administration and its recent predecessors represent nothing new in American political life. Yet, in another very important sense, the separation of powers disputes of the past twenty years do indeed reflect a new development of profound dimension, and the full implications of

1. THE FEDERALIST No. 51 (J. Madison).

2. *See* A. HAMILTON & J. MADISON, THE LETTERS OF PACIFICUS AND HELVIDIUS (1845) WITH THE LETTERS OF AMERICANUS (R. Loss ed. 1976).

3. *Id.* at 9-15.

4. *Id.* at 102.

5. *See* W. WILSON, CONGRESSIONAL GOVERNMENT (1885).

this development are not yet entirely clear. Before the early 1970s, *judicial* intervention in separation of powers disputes between the President and Congress was relatively rare. Although the underlying disputes were common, courts rarely intervened to decide these matters. The scarcity of great separation of powers decisions in the Supreme Court in the nineteenth and early twentieth centuries provides a striking contrast to the abundance of federalism cases—raising questions of the allocation of power between the federal government and the states—decided during the same period. Thus, the great separation of powers decision of the early post-war period—the *Steel Seizure Case*[6]—was a relatively isolated phenomenon when it was decided, and its novelty was underscored by Justice Jackson, who remarked that comparatively little in the way of authoritative guidance was available to the Court in deciding such momentous but generally unresolved issues.[7]

All this changed in the early 1970s under the pressure of the Vietnam War and the events of the Nixon administration.[8] In that period the Supreme Court, and other courts, began to decide questions of the allocation of power between the President and Congress with a frequency that has continued, and even increased, into the present. The reasons for this development are complex. Certainly the general success of judicial action in the civil rights revolution of the 1950s and 1960s accustomed courts and litigants to more dramatic judicial action, and afforded the courts increased confidence in their ability to confront other branches of government in politically sensitive matters. Perhaps the executive claims of the Nixon administration also made clear to some judges that judicial action was necessary to avoid a profound distortion of the constitutional system; cases such as *United States v. Nixon*[9] and *United States v. United States District Court*[10] suggest this possibility. Finally, and for our purposes perhaps most important, it was in the 1970s—in light of the Vietnam War and the excesses of the Nixon administration—that Congress began to enact legislation on a broad scale for the express purpose of limiting or restraining the burgeoning power of the presidency. In the ordinary course of enforcing several of these statutes, courts were confronted with constitutional questions that the judges could not easily avoid.

Judicial intervention in separation of powers disputes raises its own problems. Earlier, when few separation of powers cases came

6. Youngstown Sheet & Tube Co. v. Sawyer, 343 U.S. 579 (1952).
7. *Id.* at 634-35.
8. I have previously explored this point in an article written for readers in the Federal Republic of Germany. *See* Quint, *Gewaltenteilung und Verfassungsauslegung in den USA*, 1987 DIE ÖFFENTLICHE VERWALTUNG 568, 569.
9. 418 U.S. 683 (1974).
10. 407 U.S. 297 (1972).

to the courts, constitutional arguments over the allocation of power were naturally employed in political debate. The actual resolution of these issues, however, reflected the political strength of the respective branches and often involved compromises that were not necessarily susceptible of any clear theoretical explanation. When the judiciary decides a separation of powers issue, in contrast, it is ordinarily obliged to explain its result on the basis of some coherent rationale. The text of the Constitution, however, says very little about the power of the President in general, and it is particularly delphic about the distribution of powers between the President and Congress. In some separation of powers decisions, therefore, the courts may seek to construct a more or less far-reaching principle in order to support a particular decision. Such a theory may be based on the justices' (perhaps tendentious) reading of constitutional history, their more or less abstract views of what a proper constitutional system should look like, their concrete judgments about the practical impact of the decision on the operations of government, or a mixture of all of these. To some unclear extent, governmental practice—the manner in which the political organs of government have ordinarily allocated power—may also play a role. On the other hand, to the extent that the court is willing to defer to congressional power under the Necessary and Proper Clause, the necessity of constructing innovative judicial theories may be avoided.

In deciding how to approach separation of powers cases, the courts must often make their way without much guidance from a developed body of experience: as noted above, the long history of judicial trial and error in nineteenth century case law, which marks the courts' consideration of constitutional relations between the federal government and the states, is generally lacking with respect to separation of powers disputes. Nonetheless, it may be possible to discern certain evolving patterns in the methods employed by the courts in handling these cases. Moreover, a review of these patterns suggests that some judicial tendencies, especially those emerging in the last few years, raise substantial cause for concern.

II. Judicial Review of Executive Action

The possible techniques available to the judiciary in separation of powers cases may vary, depending on the type of problem presented. One important question is whether it is the action of the executive or the action of Congress that is being challenged. As indicated below, a somewhat broader range of techniques is ordinarily available to the courts when questions are raised about the constitutionality of the executive's action.

The executive's action, in turn, can take various forms. In some cases, for example, the President may seek to promulgate formal legal rules—through executive order or international agreement—in a manner that is claimed to exceed his authority. Thus, President Carter entered into an executive agreement with Iran—relating to assets and reciprocal claims—when American hostages were released at the end of his administration. The Reagan administration issued a regulation restricting most American travel to Cuba by prohibiting normal expenditures incident to that travel. Reagan also issued a directive requiring a broad range of executive officials to sign agreements limiting their ability to disclose certain types of information.

In other cases—often cases involving the military—the President can just act, and the actions that he orders may be challenged as exceeding his authority. This kind of action is seen, for example, in the invasion of Grenada, the bombing of Libya, and other notable military undertakings of the Reagan period.

When presidential measures are challenged, it is possible for the President to argue that his action falls within an area of his direct constitutional authority. Arguments of this sort are often made in war-powers disputes; President Reagan asserted, for example, that the invasion of Grenada and the bombing of Libya fell within his constitutional power over foreign affairs or his power as Commander-in-Chief of the armed forces.[11] An argument of direct presidential power to settle international claims was also made by the Reagan and Carter administrations with respect to President Carter's action in entering into the United States-Iran Executive Agreement.[12] In a few scattered cases involving foreign affairs, arguments based on direct presidential power have prevailed in the Supreme Court,[13] but in *Youngstown Sheet & Tube Co. v. Sawyer*[14]—a case that probably still remains the central decision in the area—broad claims of direct presidential authority in domestic affairs were decisively rejected where Congress had apparently indicated a contrary intent.

A second form of argument in litigation considering the lawfulness of presidential action is the assertion that some form of *congressional* authority exists to support the action. This form of argument has generally been more successful than assertions of direct presidential power in the Supreme Court. In disputed cases of this kind, however, statutory authority is rarely explicit; rather, authority is often claimed on the basis of general and sometimes quite obscure

---

11. *See* Letter to the Speaker of the House and the President Pro Tempore of the Senate on the Deployment of United States Forces in Grenada, 2 PUB. PAPERS 1512, 1513 (Oct. 25, 1983); Letter to the Speaker of the House and the President Pro Tempore of the Senate on the United States Air Strike Against Libya, 22 WEEKLY COMP. PRES. DOC. 499, 500 (Apr. 16, 1986). Assertions of direct presidential authority thus formed the background of contentious disputes over the conformity of these executive actions with the requirements of the War Powers Resolution.

12. *See* Dames & Moore v. Regan, 453 U.S. 654 (1981).

13. See, for example, United States v. Pink, 315 U.S. 203 (1942) and United States v. Belmont, 301 U.S. 324 (1937), upholding presidential authority to enter into an executive agreement in connection with recognition of a foreign government.

14. 343 U.S. 579 (1952).

statutory language.[15] A common supporting argument, often urged by the executive in cases of this sort, is that the court should give substantial weight to the President's constitutional position in its process of statutory interpretation.[16] According to this view, the courts should consider the President's independent role when they interpret an unclear or inconclusive statutory structure, and accordingly reach out to find a measure of congressional authority for the President's actions. Courts have sometimes been willing to grant very sweeping executive power under the rubric of statutory interpretation, because this technique does not force the courts to make a clear decision between Congress and the executive and appears to leave Congress the opportunity (illusory as it may often be) to withdraw the authority by subsequent statute.

Techniques of this sort were used by the Court in deciding *Dames & Moore v. Regan*[17] and *Haig v. Agee*,[18] important cases of the late Carter and early Reagan periods. Similar questions of statutory interpretation were also raised when the Reagan administration sought to limit most travel to Cuba by issuing a treasury regulation prohibiting expenditures, such as payments for hotels and meals, ordinarily incident to that travel.[19] Here there was no claim that the executive possessed any form of independent power to issue such a regulation. Rather, when the regulation was challenged in the federal courts, the administration argued that relevant statutes of Congress could be interpreted to grant the executive the necessary authority.

As is often true in such disputes, this case presented a difficult statutory tangle. The administration asserted that 1977 legislation seeking to limit the President's peace-time emergency powers had preserved his authority to prohibit financial transactions incident to normal travel to Cuba without undertaking the special procedural steps required in the 1977 act. However, the conclusion that the statute did indeed preserve the executive's authority in this context was far from clear. Furthermore, other legislation of the late 1970s seemed to indicate that Congress was unwilling to allow the executive to impose restrictions on travel to specified localities in the absence of special health or safety considerations.[20] Accordingly, in its opinion below, the First Circuit rejected the government's claim.[21]

In *Regan v. Wald*,[22] a bare majority of the Supreme Court accepted

---

15. *See* Quint, *The Separation of Powers Under Carter*, 62 TEX. L. REV. 785, 791-94, 848-52 (1984) [hereinafter *Separation of Powers Under Carter*]; Quint, *The Separation of Powers under Nixon: Reflections on Constitutional Liberties and the Rule of Law*, 1981 DUKE L.J. 1, 27 [hereinafter *Separation of Powers Under Nixon*].

16. *See generally* Koh, *Why the President (Almost) Always Wins in Foreign Affairs: Lessons of the Iran-Contra Affair*, 97 Yale L.J. 1255, 1309-13 (1988).

17. 453 U.S. 654 (1981).

18. 453 U.S. 280 (1981); *see Separation of Powers Under Carter*, *suprà* note 15, at 816-21, 848-52; Koh, *supra* note 16, at 1309-10.

19. 31 C.F.R. § 515.560 (1983).

20. *See, e.g.*, Farber, *National Security, the Right to Travel, and the Court*, 1981 SUP. CT. REV. 263, 282.

21. Wald v. Regan, 708 F.2d 794 (1st Cir. 1983), *rev'd*, 468 U.S. 222 (1984).

22. 468 U.S. 222 (1984).

the government's position. Although the Court's opinion focused particularly on inferences to be drawn from the complicated legislative history, the Court seems to have taken the President's independent foreign-policy role into account in its process of statutory interpretation. *Regan* was also notable because the Court refused to extend a line of Warren Court doctrine that required clear legislative authorization for executive action that might threaten the right to travel or certain other important constitutional rights. The court below had relied upon this doctrine to fortify its view that the executive's order lacked adequate congressional authorization.[23]

In interpreting statutory language in cases like *Regan*, the courts may find that inferences from presidential power are sometimes pitted against inferences that may be drawn from constitutional rights: the inferences from presidential power may operate to extend congressional authorization of doubtful executive action, but the inferences from individual constitutional rights can operate to limit that authority in the absence of clear congressional approval.[24] Although the Court's opinion focused mainly on more technical questions of statutory interpretation, *Regan v. Wald* may be viewed as the most recent in a line of Carter and Reagan era cases—including *Snepp v. United States*[25] and *Haig v. Agee*—in which inferences from executive power have prevailed over countervailing inferences from constitutional rights, with the result that congressional authorization of executive action has been found on the basis of unclear or fragmentary legislative materials. As we will see below, the influence of presidential power on statutory interpretation continues to play an important role in the opinions of the Supreme Court.

In other cases involving disputed presidential action—especially those in which the President has employed military force—the government may argue (and the courts may well agree) that the issues present a nonjusticiable "political question" or are otherwise inappropriate for judicial resolution. In Reagan-era litigation, for example, lower courts have taken such a position in dismissing actions alleging that assistance to the Nicaraguan *Contras* or to the government of El Salvador violates the Constitution, the War Powers Act, or other federal law.[26] Like a decision finding statutory authority, this technique also seems to play an intermediate role because it does not require a clear position on the ultimate scope of executive

23. 708 F.2d at 800, 803. *See* Koh, *supra* note 16, at 1312.
24. *See Separation of Powers Under Carter, supra* note 15, at 849, 855.
25. 444 U.S. 507 (1980).
26. *See* Sanchez-Espinoza v. Reagan, 770 F.2d 202, 210 (D.C. Cir. 1985); Crockett v. Reagan, 558 F. Supp. 893, 898-99 (D.D.C. 1982), *aff'd*, 720 F.2d 1355 (D.C. Cir. 1983), *cert. denied*, 467 U.S. 1251 (1984). *See generally Separation of Powers Under Nixon, supra* note 15, at 4; Koh, *supra* note 16, at 1313-17.

authority. In reality, however, such decisions almost certainly indicate that the executive's power in the relevant area will not be restricted by the judiciary.[27]

On the other hand, certain executive activities that ordinarily would not be susceptible to judicial examination may sometimes be subjected to a form of review through the criminal process. For example, if a foreign-policy unit exceeds the authority granted to it by Congress, its activities might come under judicial scrutiny if those activities violate criminal statutes. Although the use of National Security Council officers for "operational" purposes might well not be subject to declaratory judgment or injunction by a court, some sort of review of those activities can be exercised in the trials of Oliver North and others under the general provisions of the criminal law. In the same way, creation of an extra-statutory "plumbers" unit in the Nixon White House—designed to investigate opponents of Nixon's foreign policy in Vietnam and find the source of disclosures to the press—fell under judicial scrutiny because its members undertook actions that violated federal criminal statutes.[28]

III. *Judicial Review of Congressional Action*

Another type of separation of powers dispute, however, is not generally susceptible of a form of intermediate determination through statutory interpretation, or through the "convenient apologetics" of the political-question doctrine. In the 1970s—in reaction to the extraordinary executive claims of the Nixon administration and the tragedies of executive policy during the period of the Vietnam War—Congress attempted to reassert its policymaking authority in a number of areas, and sought to impose explicit statutory limits on the power of the presidency. Among other actions, Congress sought to limit the asserted war powers of the President, regulate executive budgetary authority, impose limitations on the exercise of emergency power, rationalize the use of information from presidential papers, and provide for independent investigation of high executive officers suspected of committing criminal offenses. Moreover, in several disparate areas, Congress sought to limit executive policymaking powers through the widespread use of one or another of the devices known as the legislative veto.

In several instances, the Reagan administration took the position that certain statutory restrictions could not be validly applied against the President or executive officers in general. In some of these cases—for example, in the dispute over the legislative veto—the administration pursued arguments that had also been invoked by its predecessor.[29] In other important instances—in the dispute over the independent counsel legislation, for example—it claimed more extensive (and more exclusive) executive power than had been

27. *See Separation of Powers Under Nixon, supra* note 15, at 7-8.
28. *See, e.g.*, United States v. Ehrlichman, 546 F.2d 910 (D.C. Cir. 1976), *cert. denied*, 429 U.S. 1120 (1977).
29. *See* INS v. Chadha, 462 U.S. 919 (1983).

asserted under President Carter.[30]

In many of these cases, some sort of intermediate argument based on statutory construction was ordinarily not available to the administration. Perhaps it was occasionally possible to argue that a statutory scheme should be interpreted so that it does not apply to the executive in specific cases, or even that it might actually *grant* power to the President under certain circumstances.[31] In many important instances, however, the language and purpose of these statutory schemes of the mid-1970s were so clearly directed toward specific limitation of the executive, that such arguments were not plausible. Rather, in these cases the administration was required to argue that the statutes themselves were unconstitutional.

One implication of the assertion of executive power in this context, therefore, was that the administration was required to argue that a number of far-reaching and complex statutory schemes must be dismantled or significantly impaired. In the case of arguments for the unconstitutionality of the legislative veto, for example, almost two hundred statutory programs—many of very great importance—would in some way be affected. In seeking to nullify the Comptroller General's role in budget control, the administration was also endeavoring to undo a complex statutory compromise that—at least to some—represented "one of the most novel and far-reaching legislative responses to a national crisis since the New Deal"[32] and "unquestionably ranks among the most important federal enactments of the past several decades."[33] Finally, in the independent-counsel litigation, the executive again argued for the invalidation of an important statutory program reflecting a deeply held political consensus.

Perhaps even more interesting than its assertion that broad statutory plans should be invalidated is the form of argument that the administration was required to employ in such cases. As noted above, the allocation of powers between the President and Congress is generally not the subject of clear and unambiguous regulation in the constitutional text. If the executive seeks to invalidate congressional statutes on separation of powers grounds, the necessary argument must generally be constructed from supposed theoretical principles underlying the distribution of power.[34]

30. *See* Morrison v. Olson, 108 S. Ct. 2597 (1988).

31. The War Powers Resolution is perhaps an example of these possibilities. *See Separation of Powers Under Nixon, supra* note 15, at 8.

32. Bowsher v. Synar, 478 U.S. 714, 759 (1986) (White, J., dissenting).

33. *Id.* at 777-78 (Blackmun, J., dissenting).

34. In rare cases, a convincing argument may be based on explicit language in the constitutional text. Perhaps Buckley v. Valeo, 424 U.S. 1, 109-43 (1976) is such a case. Some say that *Chadha* is also, but I disagree. *See Separation of Powers Under Carter, supra* note 15, at 826-37.

In *Bowsher v. Synar,*[35] for example, the administration attacked a central provision of the Gramm-Rudman-Hollings Deficit Control Act on the ground that it required the President to make budget reductions that had been determined (pursuant to statutory guidelines) by the Comptroller General, an officer removable by Congress for cause by joint resolution. The administration maintained that such determinations could not constitutionally be made by an officer who was independent of presidential removal and control. The Constitution, however, contains little express guidance on the removal of an officer such as the Comptroller General; indeed, the Constitution says nothing at all about the removal of officers except by impeachment. Consequently, the government was required to construct a complex conceptual argument: the powers sought to be exercised by the Comptroller General under the statute are "executive" powers;[36] such powers must accordingly be exercised by an "executive" officer; the Comptroller General is not an executive officer because he is removable by congressional joint resolution,[37] or perhaps because in the totality of the circumstances he is under the control of Congress;[38] in any case, the Comptroller's statutory duties "are so central to the administration of the Executive Branch" that they can be performed only by the President or an officer who is removable by the President at the President's will.[39]

Ultimately, a majority of the Supreme Court adopted variations of these arguments: the Court held that the "executive" powers accorded to the Comptroller General under the statute cannot be exercised by an officer removable by Congress;[40] a concurring opinion found the statutory scheme unconstitutional because, in the totality of the circumstances, the Comptroller General is an agent of Congress, and Congress cannot "set policy that binds the Nation" through acts of its agents, but rather must embody that policy in a statute enacted pursuant to the procedure contained in Article I.[41] These views evoked a vigorous dissenting opinion by Justice White, who argued that the Court's view of the separation of powers was "distressingly formalistic"[42] and a "rigid dogma."[43] White argued that in reality Congress's "control" of the Comptroller General is minimal, and that Congress has the power under the Necessary and Proper Clause to further statutory goals by creating certain officers that are insulated from distracting political pressures.[44]

35. 478 U.S. 714 (1986).

36. Brief for the United States at 27-29, Bowsher v. Synar, 478 U.S. 714 (1986) (No. 85-1377), *reprinted in* 160 LANDMARK BRIEFS & ARGUMENTS OF THE SUPREME COURT OF THE UNITED STATES: CONSTITUTIONAL LAW 348-50 (P. Kurland & G. Casper eds. 1987) [hereinafter LANDMARK BRIEFS].

37. *Id.* at 31-35, *reprinted in* LANDMARK BRIEFS, *supra* note 36, at 352-56.

38. *Id.* at 36-44, *reprinted in* LANDMARK BRIEFS, *supra* note36, at 357-65.

39. *Id.* at 44-51, *reprinted in* LANDMARK BRIEFS, *supra* note 36, at 365-72.

40. Bowsher v. Synar, 478 U.S. 714, 732-34 (1986).

41. *Id.* at 756-59 (Stevens, J., concurring).

42. *Id.* at 759.

43. *Id.* at 776.

44. *Id.* at 760-62, 773-76.

A particularly striking example of the construction of elaborate formalist theories in an attempt to invalidate congressional legislation is presented by the government's argument in *Morrison v. Olson,*[45] the "independent counsel" case. In this case, as in *Bowsher,* the administration objected to congressional creation of an office that was significantly insulated from executive control: the office of "independent counsel" established to investigate high executive officers accused of serious criminal offenses. The basic argument of the administration in *Morrison* was that, because of its "executive" functions, the "independent counsel" must be appointed by the President and must also be subject to unrestricted removal by the President; the independent counsel, in other words, must be unambiguously a member of the executive branch for all purposes whatsoever. Under the Ethics in Government Act[46] the independent counsel did not satisfy these criteria, because she was appointed by a special panel of federal judges and could be removed by the Attorney General only for "good cause" or other similar grounds. According to the administration, therefore, the statutory scheme providing for independent counsel was unconstitutional.

In making this argument, the administration was not only required to contend with the general lack of textual guidance that is ordinarily found in separation of powers cases. The administration was also confronted by a specific constitutional provision in Article II granting Congress the power to lodge the appointment of "such inferior Officers, as they think proper, in the President alone, in the Courts of Law, or in the Heads of Departments."[47] This language explicitly allows Congress to empower the courts to appoint at least some "inferior" officers.

In light of the general lack of favorable textual guidance—and the actual presence of an unfavorable constitutional provision—the administration (as amicus curiae) was forced to construct an elaborate argument from structural inferences in order to maintain that the statute should be found unconstitutional. First, the government argued that because of the importance of maintaining the separation of powers, the relevant language of Article II should be read to allow courts of law to appoint inferior "judicial" officers but not inferior "executive" officers;[48] moreover, according to the government, the functions of the independent counsel are "inescapably executive."[49] The government also argued that the independent counsel

45. 108 S. Ct. 2597 (1988).

46. Pub. L. No. 95-521, § 601(a), 92 Stat. 1867 (1978) (current version at 28 U.S.C. §§ 49, 591-599 (1982 & Supp. IV 1986)).

47. U.S. CONST. art. II, § 2, cl. 2.

48. Brief for the United States as Amicus Curiae Supporting Appellees at 17-24, Morrison v. Olson, 108 S. Ct. 2597 (1988) (No. 87-1279).

49. *Id.* at 9.

is not an "inferior" officer within the language of Article II because she exercises her powers independently and is not under the direct supervision of any other officer; therefore, she cannot be appointed by the courts, but rather must be appointed by the President with confirmation by the Senate.[50] Finally, the government argued that because the powers of the independent counsel are purely "executive" in nature, she must be removable by the President at his sole discretion[51]—an argument also made with respect to the Comptroller General in *Bowsher,* but not adopted by the Court in that case.

Exactly how these arguments should be evaluated—the extent to which they are convincing based on any given theory of constitutional interpretation—is not the only question raised here. Rather, the most striking point is that in seeking to assert executive power and invalidate the statute, the executive was forced to devise complex constitutional formulations supported by very little in the way of textual or historical materials. Moreover, these arguments were "formalist" in that they established rigid theoretical categories—derived from a conceptual view of the nature of certain governmental functions—and sought to apply those categories in an uncompromising manner, without any significant recognition of the impact of contemporary governmental realities on the appropriate treatment of the underlying problems.[52] The administration was seeking to put forward a rigid conceptual view in disregard of more pragmatic judgments made by congressional majorities.

Thus, in seeking to invalidate the statute, the administration was urging the Court to exercise broad-ranging judicial power. Indeed, the administration was advocating an exercise of judicial power that was in important ways clearly "activist" in nature. As we have seen, the judicial activism urged by the administration is reflected in two interlocking aspects of its position. First, in these cases, the administration sought to invalidate statutory programs of great importance, reflecting carefully determined congressional judgments of policy and frequently resting on broad political consensus. Second, the arguments to which the administration was forced to resort to invalidate the legislation involved the creation of elaborate formalist structures based on fragile premises.

It is important to understand, however, that this form of activism is not adventitious; it is an inevitable product of a policy of asserting strong executive power in the courts in the contemporary historical context. When Congress has sought to place some limitations on executive power, as it did in the 1970s, an administration's policy of strong assertions of executive power in the courts has the inevitable consequence of urging an activist judicial role, as the executive

50. *Id.* at 24-29.

51. *Id.* at 29-33. In making this argument, the government sought to rely on Myers v. United States, 272 U.S. 52 (1926). *Id.* at 29-31.

52. For discussions of "formalism" and "functionalism" in separation of powers adjudication, see, e.g., Strauss, *Formal and Functional Approaches to Separation-of-Powers Questions—A Foolish Inconsistency?* 72 CORNELL L. REV. 488 (1987); Sunstein, *Constitutionalism After the New Deal,* 101 HARV. L. REV. 421, 493-500 (1987).

pushes to become free of what it sees as irksome legislative restraints. This activist role is then further heightened by the lack of textual and historical guidance on separation of powers questions, requiring judicial elaboration of extensive conceptual principles.

Thus, when the executive seeks to assert broad presidential power in the face of congressional attempts to restrain that power, executive advocacy of judicial activism is the essential result. But these assertions of executive power, with their concomitant approval of an activist judicial role, seemed to place this particular administration in a somewhat paradoxical position. As has been occasionally noted, the administration's arguments for a form of judicial activism in separation of powers cases like *Morrison* contrast dramatically with its general calls for judicial restraint in other areas, such as school prayer and abortion.[53]

Moreover, from a somewhat broader perspective, the administration's call for judicial activism evokes some disturbing historical echoes.[54] Although there are also significant differences, these formalist arguments recall techniques employed by an activist Supreme Court in other structural decisions of the past: the federalism cases of the late nineteenth and early twentieth centuries in which the Court struck down a number of federal statutes on the ground that they exceeded congressional power under the Commerce Clause, thereby invading the power of the states. In these cases, also, the Court invalidated important statutory programs reflecting broad political consensus on the basis of its own general views of proper constitutional structures, in decisions that failed to defer to congressional discretion under the Necessary and Proper Clause. These cases also required the creation of elaborate doctrine more or less out of whole cloth, relying on rigid conceptual categories. For example, in these cases the Court took the position that "manufacture" is not "commerce," and that activity affecting commerce "indirectly" rather than "directly" cannot be regulated by Congress under the Commerce Clause.[55] The Court also held that "prohibition" of commerce is not "regulation" except when Congress prohibits the interstate shipment of goods that are "evil" in

53. *See, e.g.*, Remarks and a Question-and-Answer Session with Women Leaders of Christian Religious Organizations, 2 PUB. PAPERS 1451 (Oct. 13, 1983); Statement on Senate Confirmation of Sandra Day O'Connor as an Associate Justice of the Supreme Court of the United States, 1 PUB. PAPERS 819 (Sept. 21, 1981); Remarks in Denver, Colorado, at the Biennial Convention of the National Federation of Republican Women, 1 PUB. PAPERS 811 (Sept. 18, 1981) (statements by President Reagan advocating judicial restraint).

54. For an earlier version of the following argument, *see* Quint, *supra* note 8, at 578; for a contrary view, *see* Strauss, *supra* note 52, at 513-15.

55. Carter v. Carter Coal Co., 298 U.S. 238 (1936); United States v. E.C. Knight Co., 156 U.S. 1 (1895).

themselves.[56]

Although these earlier Commerce Clause cases have long been overruled, similar techniques reappeared recently in *National League of Cities v. Usery*,[57] when the Court struck down the application of federal minimum-wage laws to the states as violating the Tenth Amendment. The Court found that even though the regulation might otherwise be justifiable under the Commerce Clause, Congress had no power "to directly displace the States' freedom to structure integral operations in areas of traditional governmental functions."[58]

In time, with the experience of continued litigation (and, in some cases, political change), the Court came to adopt the view that the formalist intellectual structures erected to justify limits on the power of Congress under the Commerce Clause could not be sustained. Most recently, the Court overruled *Usery* in an opinion that emphasized the states' practical political power. In *Garcia v. San Antonio Metropolitan Transit Authority*,[59] the Court found that the states exercise significant influence on the composition of Congress and the nature and extent of congressional action. The result was that the states retain adequate political power to represent their own interests in the political arena. Accordingly, the Court has decided that federalism limitations on Congress should ordinarily be effected through political action of the states, and not through formalist judicial doctrine elaborated from general structural notions of the justices.

In the same way, the time may come when the rigid view reflected in decisions such as *Chadha* and *Bowsher* will give way to the judgment that the formalist doctrines established in those cases are not tenable. Moreover, it may come to be appreciated by the Court that, just as the states retain considerable political influence on Congress, the President also retains practical political power of a similar nature. Indeed, that power is certainly as great as—and probably substantially greater than—the political power of the states. Certainly under contemporary circumstances the President's effective influence on the actions of Congress goes far beyond the significant power formally conferred upon the President through the veto authority. In the same way that the Court decided in *Garcia* that the judiciary should leave broad areas of relations between Congress and the states to a process of political accommodation, the Court may ultimately determine that the constitutionality of statutes touching on executive authority should also generally be left to the

56. Hammer v. Dagenhart, 247 U.S. 251 (1918). On the other hand, these earlier Commerce Clause cases had the effect of protecting property interests in a way that generally has not occurred in the separation of powers decisions. Undue protection of property might become an issue, however, if the independent regulatory agencies were to be significantly impaired by separation of powers decisions, or if the invalidation of the legislative veto were to make it difficult to enact and enforce regulatory programs involving broad delegations of authority.

57. 426 U.S. 833 (1976).

58. *Id.* at 852.

59. 469 U.S. 528 (1985).

process of political accommodation between the majoritarian power represented by Congress and the majoritarian power represented by the President—powers representing, in effect, the same majorities.[60] Indeed, it appears that a position of this nature lies behind the impressive (and rather lonely) dissents of Justice White in *Chadha* and *Bowsher*, emphasizing that deference should be accorded to the views of Congress when it legislates in the area of separation of powers.[61]

IV. Morrison v. Olson

In this context the recent decision in *Morrison v. Olson*[62] may appear portentous. Against the immediate background of *Chadha* and *Bowsher*—cases in which the Court used formalist techniques to strike down important statutes of Congress—the *Morrison* decision upheld congressional power against far-reaching executive assertions. *Morrison* therefore poses the intriguing question of whether the decision signals at least a partial retreat from the activist techniques of *Chadha* and *Bowsher*, and a general tendency toward greater deference to congressional judgment in separation of powers cases.

Perhaps some clues to the answer can be gleaned from examining the background of the case, and from a review of the opinion itself.

The true background of *Morrison v. Olson* must be sought in the last years of the Nixon administration, when allegations of serious criminal actions were leveled against high executive officers, including the President. When these allegations were made, many doubted that an adequate investigation of the charges could be assured, in light of the President's control of the Attorney General, and thus of the Justice Department. Under considerable congressional and popular pressure, therefore, a special prosecutor was appointed by the Attorney General for the purpose of investigating the

---

60. Justice Rehnquist suggests a similar comparison in his opinion for the Court in *Usery*, 426 U.S. at 841 n.12, but he uses it as an argument against deferring to Congress in federalism cases rather than as an argument for the abandonment of formalist techniques in separation of powers decisions. *See also Garcia*, 469 U.S. at 567 n.12 (Powell, J., dissenting) (supporting Rehnquist's argument in *Usery*). On the similarity between techniques of adjudication in federalism and separation of powers cases, see J. CHOPER, JUDICIAL REVIEW AND THE NATIONAL POLITICAL PROCESS (1980) (arguing that separation of powers questions, as well as most federalism issues, should be decided through the political process rather than by courts). *But see* Strauss, *supra* note 52, at 513-15 (arguing that the "political process" principles of *Garcia* probably cannot be transferred from federalism to the separation of powers context).

61. *See, e.g.*, Bowsher v. Synar, 478 U.S. 714, 776 (1986) (White, J., dissenting); *cf.* Northern Pipeline Constr. Co. v. Marathon Pipe Line Co., 458 U.S. 50, 92-118 (1982) (White, J., dissenting) (urging deference to Congress's judgment in allocating judicial powers to non-Article III courts).

62. 108 S. Ct. 2597 (1988) (upholding a statutory plan for "independent counsel" to investigate alleged crimes of high executive officers).

charges. The role of the special prosecutor and the stability of his office remained central political issues until the fall of the Nixon administration. The administration's dismissal of the first special prosecutor, Archibald Cox, evoked a popular outcry that marked an important turning point in the history of the period, and the tenure of his successor, Leon Jaworski, was assured only by the highly charged political atmosphere of that extraordinary era. Nonetheless, the subpoena of tapes that ultimately resulted in the case of *United States v. Nixon*[63] was directed by Mr. Jaworski, and the decision in that case perhaps can be viewed as assuming the constitutionality of a special prosecutor's office insulated from unrestrained executive dismissal.

The somewhat fragile structure of the ad hoc special prosecutor, however, was unsatisfactory as a permanent plan. In 1978, therefore, Congress enacted the Ethics in Government Act, which authorizes the appointment of special prosecutors (now called "independent counsel") by a special panel of federal judges, subject to removal by the Attorney General only for "good cause" or other specified grounds. The independent counsel's office was therefore insulated from political pressure as a practical matter. This statute reflected a broad political consensus, including substantial majorities of both houses of Congress and enthusiastic approval by President Carter.

As was the case in the Nixon administration, the last years of the Reagan administration were marked by charges of possible criminal violations by high executive officers. Some were allegations of more or less individual personal wrongdoing, but others involved the serious misuse of executive agencies to further certain goals of administration policy in an allegedly unlawful manner—in some ways a reprise (indeed on a more serious level) of charges directed against Nixon administration officials. In the misuse of the National Security Council in the Iran-Contra affair—as in certain actions of Nixon's White House "plumbers" unit—the desire for greater efficiency in pursuing foreign policy goals had animated the allegedly illegal actions of executive officers. As was also the case under Nixon, the investigations of a special prosecutor (in this case, actually, the activity of several "independent counsel") marked the final months of the Reagan administration. The general background of *Morrison* therefore shares some important points of similarity with the background of *United States v. Nixon.* I will return to some possible conclusions to be drawn from that similarity after a brief review of the opinion in *Morrison* itself.

For our purposes, the most important aspect of the *Morrison* opinion is that its language contains very little to suggest a general trend toward greater deference to congressional discretion. Indeed, the opinion in *Morrison* is compact, matter-of-fact, and quite circumspect. The Court upheld the statutory plan but generally avoided

63. 418 U.S. 683 (1974).

taking positions that would significantly constrain its decisions in future cases. At a number of points, moreover, it seemed to take particular pains to preserve a significant role for executive power, even though it held against the executive in the particular case. In interpreting the Appointments Clause, for example, the Court rejected the government's sweeping view that "inter-branch" appointments—such as the appointment of "executive" officers by a court of law—are prohibited in all cases; on the other hand, the Court indicated that under some circumstances (not spelled out in the opinion) a provision for judicial appointment of executive officers might be unconstitutional if it has "the potential to impair the constitutional functions assigned to one of the branches" or if there is an "incongruity" between the appointment and the courts' ordinary functions.[64] Moreover, the Court emphasized the importance of executive participation, by noting that under the statute the judiciary may appoint independent counsel only when the Attorney General, an executive officer, has recommended that it do so.[65] Similarly, the Court found that the assignment of certain miscellaneous or incidental powers to the appointing "special court" did not exceed the boundaries of Article III; nonetheless, it cautioned special courts against an attempted expansion of powers that might risk such a constitutional violation, and noted examples of judicial action that could exceed proper limits.[66]

Probably the most adventurous part of the *Morrison* opinion was the Court's abandonment of its apparent prior view that the constitutionality of congressional limits on the removal of an official depends on whether the official exercises "quasi-legislative" and/or "quasi-judicial" power. Instead, the Court adopted a less categorical position, permitting congressional restrictions on the removal of officers if those restrictions are not "of such a nature that they impede the President's ability to perform his constitutional duty."[67] Through such an open formula, the Court upheld the specific provisions for the independent counsel's removal without relinquishing control over more general questions of congressional limitations on the removal of government officials. Moreover, even here, the Court seemed to caution that ultimate presidential removal power remained important; the Court emphasized that the statute preserved the Attorney General's power to remove the independent counsel for "good cause."[68] Some sort of ultimate executive control (although restricted in scope) appears to remain requisite.

64. *Morrison*, 108 S. Ct. at 2609-11.
65. *Id.* at 2621.
66. *Id.* at 2611-15.
67. *Id.* at 2619.
68. *Id.* at 2616-20.

There is very little in this fundamentally cautious and laconic opinion that suggests a general tendency toward greater deference to Congress. In this connection, the opinion in *Morrison* is notable for the absence of two forms of argument which, had they been present, might have indicated the possibility of such a change.

First, as Justice Scalia pointed out in dissent, the Supreme Court majority nowhere expressly stated that in reviewing the Ethics in Government Act, the Court owed any general deference to the judgment of Congress. Rather, in Scalia's view, as apparently in the Court's, "[t]he playing field . . . is a level one. . . . Congress, no more than the President, is entitled to the benefit of the doubt."[69] Although Scalia argued that the Court did not "faithfully" observe this doctrine in *Morrison*,[70] he was absolutely correct in noting that there is little express indication in the majority opinion of any general deference to congressional judgment. Indeed, in the one instance in which the Court expressly conceded congressional discretion, it did so because specific language in the constitutional text seems to grant that discretion: Article II confers on Congress the power to "vest the Appointment of such inferior Officers, *as they think proper* . . . in the Courts of Law . . . ."[71] Even here, the Court suggested that Congress's textually based discretion can be limited by the judicially constructed concept of "incongruity" (and perhaps other limitations), noted above.

The second form of argument that could have been recognized by the Court is closely related. It is a view that sees the separation of powers as a "fluid, functional" doctrine whose purpose is to preserve a reasonable balance among the departments in light of the present realities of government. It acknowledges the lessons of contemporary history and recognizes that if the strength of one branch has become clearly overpowering in reality, innovative countermeasures might be permissible to redress the balance. Thus, if contemporary history indicates that Presidents have engaged in certain abuses, congressional measures of redress must be examined in light of this general idea of balance. Such a view was suggested by Justice White in his dissenting opinion in *Chadha*,[72] and the acknowledgment of such a position by the Court in *Morrison* could have been significant. Interestingly, this form of argument is found in the dissenting opinion of Judge Ruth Bader Ginsburg in the court below—an opinion whose result, but not whose reasoning, was adopted by the Supreme Court. Judge Ginsburg remarked:

> [The Ethics in Government Act] strives to maintain the structural design that is the genius of our Constitution—the system of mutual checks and balances; the Act's sole purpose is to curb or avert abuses of executive branch power. . . .
>
> . . .

69. *Id.* at 2626.
70. *Id.* at 2625.
71. U.S. CONST. art. II, § 2, cl. 2 (emphasis added).
72. 462 U.S. 919, 1002 (1983).

> The Ethics Act is designed to function as a control against abuse of executive branch power. It implements the checking aspect of the separated powers. The independent counsel provisions of the Act were developed in response to the Watergate era abuses of executive branch powers, *abuses which themselves threatened the balance among the three branches of government.* . . . The Act thus operates as a means of maintaining the executive's proper—and properly circumscribed—constitutional role.[73]

There is little indication of this more "fluid, functional" approach—an approach that would tend to defer to Congress in the face of executive excesses of power—in the Supreme Court's cautious and reserved opinion in *Morrison.*[74]

The absence of such arguments in the majority's opinion, and the absence of other expressed concessions to the discretion of Congress, should caution against the view that *Morrison* signals the beginning of a trend toward an increased general deference toward congressional decisions in conflicts between legislative and executive authority. This seems especially true when the opinion is read against the background of such immediately preceding cases as *Chadha* and *Bowsher,* cases in which congressional judgments in broad separation of powers areas were quite resoundingly rejected by the Court.

In light of these factors, it may well be that *Morrison* is essentially sui generis. The case may represent an exception to current trends favoring the executive, because of its historical setting, its specific subject, and the distinctive echoes that it evokes. Indeed, as suggested above, it may be that this case is most accurately viewed as a sequel to *United States v. Nixon.* Both are cases in which the executive sought to assert broad claims of presidential authority in a context in which, had those claims prevailed, the President or high executive officers might well have been insulated from criminal liability. Both are cases that arise against the general historical background of a

73. *In re* Sealed Case, 838 F.2d 476, 518, 527 (D.C. Cir. 1988) (emphasis added), *rev'd sub nom.* Morrison v. Olson, 108 S. Ct. 2597 (1988).

74. The *Morrison* opinion should also be compared with the recent decision in Mistretta v. United States, 109 S. Ct. 647 (1989), in which the Court upheld the constitutionality of the United States Sentencing Commission. The *Mistretta* opinion refers to "flexibility" in the separation of powers and contains language suggesting deference to congressional judgment—language quoted, ironically, from a concurring opinion in *Bowsher. See id.* at 661. Although *Mistretta* may be viewed as indicating an increased measure of deference to Congress in separation of powers decisions generally, it seems more likely to be a continuation of a narrower trend toward deference to Congress in its allocation of *judicial* power between Article III courts and other judicial or quasi-judicial agencies. *Compare* Northern Pipeline Constr. Co. v. Marathon Pipe Line Co., 458 U.S. 50 (1982) *with* Commodity Futures Trading Comm'n v. Schor, 478 U.S. 833 (1986). *See also* Thomas v. Union Carbide Agricultural Prods. Co., 473 U.S. 568 (1985); Strauss, *supra* note 52, at 515-16.

dramatic scandal in which executive actions spilled over into massive patterns of illegal or allegedly illegal activity, in a manner that called into question public confidence in government. *Nixon* may be viewed as finding that executive claims of power will not succeed in protecting members of the executive branch itself against serious charges of criminality, because such use of those claims would be viewed as cynical and self-serving and could impair confidence in the governmental system.[75] For all the complexities of its analysis, *Morrison* may be viewed in the same light. Even though the independent counsel in *Morrison* was not investigating matters involving the Iran-Contra affair, the implications of the decision for that and other closely watched investigations was perfectly clear. Perhaps the Court just could not envision upholding arguments by which the executive would be able to insulate its own officers from criminal prosecution, thereby striking down a popular and measured congressional scheme designed to achieve a degree of independence in the criminal prosecution of high executive officials. As in *Nixon,* the Court may have seen its role as that of protecting the perceived equality and fairness of the criminal justice system in the prosecution of government officers, an area in which perceptions of partiality might gravely impair public confidence in the judicial system and in government in general.

The nature of the administration's arguments in *Morrison* suggests one other point of similarity with *Nixon.* It may have been the case in *Morrison* that some implications of the government's positions were just too revolutionary for the justices to accept. Beyond the arguments over removal lay the government's asserted position that the entire apparatus of independent regulatory agencies is unconstitutional, because the members of the relevant boards and commissions exercise "executive" authority without being subject to an unfettered power of removal by the President. Adoption of the government's position in *Morrison,* at least in some of its forms, might cast doubt on a significant portion of the judicial legacy of the New Deal, and perhaps for the justices those implications seemed just too far-reaching to countenance. It is one thing to strike down a newly enacted budget plan and a device of legislative control which, while originating decades ago, achieved its position of real significance only in recent years; it is another thing entirely to cast serious doubt on the independent agencies, one of the central features of the New Deal legacy. In *Nixon,* too, the President's broad claim of power to enforce executive confidentiality without judicial review, viewed together with other extraordinary claims of executive power advanced by the same administration, seemed to suggest an almost revolutionary reworking of the governmental system. In both of these cases, therefore, the Court could perceive itself as the voice of good sense rejecting extraordinary positions that raised threats of fundamental structural change.

---

75. *See* J. CHOPER, *supra* note 60, at 337-38.

Thus, *Morrison* is certainly a crucial decision in its specific area—limitations on the appointment and removal of officers—and certainly the independent agencies appear less vulnerable after the decision. But it is not necessarily a decision that portends a more accommodating general view of congressional power under the Necessary and Proper Clause over the broad range of separation of powers cases. Extensive claims of presidential power in a number of areas—for example, in defense and "national security," an area not directly at issue in *Morrison*—may well remain basically untouched by the decision. We are likely to see continuing efforts by the executive to persuade the courts to strike down congressional limits on executive power in this and other areas, and the decisions in those cases may not be much affected by the decision in *Morrison.*

V. Prospects for the Immediate Future: Secrecy and "National Security"

One of the great themes of the Reagan administration's eight years in office was a sustained assertion of broad executive power in foreign affairs and national security matters. Among other things, this position involved a concerted drive toward greater secrecy in government, including a renewal of covert activities in foreign affairs and a great expansion of secrecy requirements applicable to government employees. Issues of this kind generally tend to raise problems for judicial review because of the courts' uncertainty over judgments of policy in "national security" and foreign affairs (and the factual predicates underlying those judgments), as well as the general proximity of these problems to other factors underlying the political-question doctrine.

Two important "national security" controversies of the Reagan period have been litigated in the lower federal courts and raise serious problems for the future. In my opinion, these two cases consider extremely important issues of executive authority and also raise serious questions about the general techniques that the courts have employed in reviewing separation of powers cases. In these cases the executive's "national security" claims collide with assertions of individual constitutional rights, and so these cases implicate the problems of individual-rights decisions such as *Haig v. Agee, Snepp,* and *Regan v. Wald,* as well as the more purely structural issues of *Chadha, Bowsher,* and *Morrison v. Olson.*

The first of these cases is *United States v. Morison,*[76] in which the executive argued that two seldom-used sections of the Espionage

76. 844 F.2d 1057 (4th Cir.), *cert. denied,* 109 S. Ct. 259 (1988).

Act,[77] and a statute prohibiting the theft of government property,[78] should be construed to criminalize the transmission by a government employee of classified photographs for the purpose of their publication in a widely distributed journal. Although the broad language of the espionage statutes could cover this action, the legislative history seems to indicate that Congress did not intend to criminalize the transmission of information to the press.[79] Moreover, Congress has reinforced its understanding of the limited coverage of the Espionage Act by "repeatedly" and "consciously" refusing to enact statutes that would expressly criminalize this activity.[80] In *Morison,* however, the Fourth Circuit accepted the administration's arguments to the contrary and upheld the employee's conviction. In October 1988, the Supreme Court denied certiorari.[81] In *Morison,* therefore, the executive prevailed upon the courts to construe espionage and theft statutes, many years after their enactment, to punish certain "leaks" of classified information to the press.

The only previous use of these statutes to prosecute similar leaks of information was the conspiracy indictment of Daniel Ellsberg and others for actions related to the delivery of photocopies of the Pentagon Papers to the *New York Times.* Ellsberg's prosecution was dismissed for governmental misconduct, but it vividly illustrates the possibilities opened up by the decision of the Fourth Circuit in *Morison.*[82] The result may approach the judicial establishment of a British-style official secrets act, applicable to leaks of information from sources in the government.[83]

Although this may not be a typical separation of powers case, the dangers that it evokes—the risk of circumventing Congress's role in passing upon legislation that may have a limiting effect on individual rights—raises central separation of powers concerns.[84] The result of this statutory construction might seem to be a *judicial* encroachment on the powers of Congress but, in reality, it represents an enlargement of *executive* power. The executive made the decision to

77. 18 U.S.C. § 793(d), (e) (1982).

78. 18 U.S.C. § 641 (1982).

79. *See* Edgar & Schmidt, *Curtiss-Wright Comes Home: Executive Power and National Security Secrecy,* 21 HARV. C.R.-C.L. L. REV. 349, 395-96 (1986).

80. *See* United States v. Truong Dinh Hung, 629 F.2d 908, 927-28 (4th Cir. 1980) (opinion of Winter, J.), *cert. denied,* 454 U.S. 1144 (1982); Edgar & Schmidt, *supra* note 79, at 401.

81. *See* 109 S. Ct. 259 (1988).

82. On the theft count, the government's case against Morison presented an issue not raised by Ellsberg's activities, because while Morison transferred actual government photographs to the press, Ellsberg apparently furnished photocopies that he had made himself. Thus, Morison transferred tangible government property (plus information) whereas Ellsberg furnished government information alone, because the tangible paper belonged to him. In light of the First Amendment interests equally implicated in both cases, however, it may be questioned whether this distinction of property law should be determinative under the circumstances. *But see* United States v. Morison, 844 F.2d 1057, 1077 (4th Cir.), *cert. denied,* 109 S. Ct. 259 (1988) (emphasizing that in *Morison,* "[w]e are dealing with specific, identifiable tangible property," not just information).

83. *See* Edgar & Schmidt, *supra* note 79, at 356, 399.

84. *See Separation of Powers Under Carter, supra* note 15, at 862.

commence the prosecution, and it was the executive's theory and arguments that ultimately formed the framework of the court's decision: of course, the result could not have been achieved without the court's cooperation, but the animating force came from the executive. Furthermore, it is future *executive* power—to enforce its views of secrecy through the criminal process—that is greatly expanded as a result of this decision.

Perhaps lawmaking by the executive and judiciary, without the majoritarian participation of Congress, may be inevitable in some areas. Perhaps in some areas, too, judges need not be particularly assiduous in searching out statutory ambiguity in response to doubts raised by legislative history. Where First Amendment rights are involved, however, the central importance of those rights should counsel that Congress must have clearly considered the relevant issues before speech and press interests may be constitutionally burdened—if indeed, under the circumstances, they may be burdened at all.[85] In *Morison,* in contrast, the court discounted legislative history and clear congressional understanding in order to apply espionage statutes—for the first time since their enactment—in a manner that severely burdened First Amendment interests.

Certainly none of the opinions in *Morison* adequately acknowledged the impact of First Amendment rights on the relevant questions of statutory construction. Indeed, the principal opinion in the Fourth Circuit seemed to argue that the First Amendment was not relevant in the case at all,[86] although the opinion did discuss (and reject) defendants' claims of First Amendment vagueness and overbreadth. Two separate opinions more clearly acknowledged that the First Amendment issues were "real and substantial," but concluded that any problem is cured if the jury finds that the leaked information is "potentially" injurious to the country or "*might* be useful to an enemy."[87] Certainly, however, a formula of such breadth could cover almost all classified information; the Pentagon Papers, for example, could have been so described. In any case, it should be up to Congress in the first instance, and not up to the joint action of the executive and the courts, to determine the extent to which the benefits of public discussion are outweighed by the risks of possibly remote "potential" injury.

In construing the relevant statutes in *Morison,* the court in effect elevated inferences drawn from the claims of executive power over the countervailing First Amendment implications. In so doing, the Fourth Circuit followed a general path marked out by the Supreme

85. *See id.* at 837-38; *Separation of Powers Under Nixon, supra* note 15, at 63-65.
86. 844 F.2d at 1068, 1070.
87. *Id.* at 1085-86 (Phillips, J., concurring) (emphasis added); *id.* at 1084 (Wilkinson, J., concurring).

Court in *Snepp, Haig v. Agee,* and *Regan v. Wald,* cases of the last few years in which a similar technique was employed.[88] Apparently the Reagan administration indicated that it would not be likely to use the *Morison* precedent to launch conspiracy or other prosecutions against the press itself.[89] Yet, whatever vague assurances may be given at any particular moment, this decision clearly raises the ominous possibility of further espionage prosecutions of government employees, and perhaps of journalists also, arising from "leaks" of classified information to the press.

This prospect, serious enough in itself, leaves the saving possibility (however remote in fact) that Congress may intervene to make clear that the Espionage Act was intended to cover only the secret transmission of information to a foreign country, and that the concept of "theft" does not include the transmission of government information to the press for purposes of publication and open debate. Congress has on occasion protected First Amendment interests even when the executive and the courts, in construing statutory material, have failed to do so.

The second of these Reagan-era cases, however, does not appear to admit of the saving possibility of congressional intervention, and in this respect I believe it is one of the most chilling decisions in the area of separation of powers ever handed down by an American court. In certain ways this case reflects the furthest judicial extension of executive power against the actions of Congress, going well beyond the decisions in *Chadha* and *Bowsher* in its theoretical implications. In some ways a companion-piece to *United States v. Morison,* this decision also concerns the subject of governmental secrecy and the extent to which the executive can require that information be withheld from the public and Congress.

In 1983, following general ideas suggested by the Supreme Court's *per curiam* opinion in *Snepp,* President Reagan issued "National Security Decision Directive 84," which called for a broad new governmental secrecy program. Acting under this "Directive," the administration required that over two million executive-branch employees with possible access to classified information sign secrecy agreements prohibiting the unauthorized disclosure of classified or "classifiable" government information. In the case of certain employees, a separate agreement required prepublication review of material that contains or relates to "sensitive compartmented information," a particularly secret category of classified material. Both forms of agreement contemplated civil sanctions for violations. There was no express statutory authority for this program—indeed, the classification system in general has proceeded without comprehensive statutory authorization—and the plan was seen by many as

88. *See supra* text accompanying notes 23-25.

89. Denniston, *Court Affirms Conviction for Leaking U.S. Secrets,* Baltimore Sun, Oct. 18, 1988, at 1, col. 5.

posing a threat to criticism of the government that relied on material originating within the government itself. Certainly such a program could greatly impair disclosures of corruption, illegality, and other forms of "whistleblowing" in the Department of Defense and other agencies in which classified or classifiable information is widespread. Indeed, the agreements could significantly limit the information available for public discussion of defense and other important public issues, and thus raise serious First Amendment concerns. For example, such a regime, if enforceable, could have penalized (and perhaps prevented) public disclosure of the classified Pentagon Papers. Federal employees and their unions filed an action challenging the program on various statutory and constitutional grounds, including asserted First Amendment violations.

After this action was filed, Congress enacted a statute that prohibited the expenditure of funds to "implement or enforce" secrecy agreements limiting disclosure of "classifiable" (but not classified) information or restricting the confidential transmission of information to Congress.[90] This statute placed significant limits on the use of the secrecy agreements, and the government accordingly took steps to discontinue or modify parts of the program. The administration continued to assert, however, that the statute imposed an unconstitutional limitation on the executive's national security power.

In *National Federation of Federal Employees v. United States,*[91] a federal district judge accepted the administration's arguments and *invalidated* the congressional statute limiting the executive's use of secrecy agreements. In an extraordinary endorsement of executive power, the court not only found in effect that no statutory basis was necessary for a broad requirement of executive department secrecy agreements, but also went on to hold that a significant congressional attempt to limit or qualify such a program was unconstitutional. The district court's opinion in this case goes well beyond decisions like *Haig v. Agee* and *Snepp,* in which the Supreme Court strained to find legislative authorization for executive action but did not question the principle of ultimate control by congressional lawmaking. Here, the district court simply rejected the constitutional possibility of congressional control of the executive in this area of national security. Coming in the final months of the Reagan period, this opinion seems to be the most thorough judicial endorsement of the

90. Continuing Appropriations, Fiscal Year 1988, Pub. L. No. 100-202, § 630, 1987 U.S. CODE CONG. & ADMIN. NEWS (101 Stat.) 1329, 1329-432. For fiscal year 1989 this statute has been replaced by an identical provision, Treasury, Postal Service and General Government Appropriations Act, 1989, Pub. L. No. 100-440, § 619, 1988 U.S. CODE CONG. & ADMIN. NEWS (102 Stat.) 1721, 1756.

91. 688 F. Supp. 671 (D.D.C.) (Gasch, J.), *vacated and remanded sub nom.* American Foreign Serv. Ass'n v. Garfinkel, 57 U.S.L.W. 4441 (U.S. No. 87-2127, April 18, 1989).

Reagan administration's vision of the separation of powers in national security affairs.

In a *per curiam* decision issued in April of this year, the Supreme Court vacated the district court's opinion on procedural grounds, and remanded the case for further proceedings.[92] The Court's remand, however, does not express an opinion on the underlying merits, and the district court could well adhere to its original view after procedural and statutory questions are resolved.[93] Such a decision could therefore ultimately return the constitutional issue to the Supreme Court in a future term. Moreover, this case is likely to be only the first in a series of disputes in which the executive claims that congressional regulation—in the area of secrecy agreements as well as a range of other matters—infringes on a broad "plenary" power of the President in national security or foreign affairs.[94] Thus the *Federal Employees* case heralds a form of argument that could become increasingly familiar in the future. In light of this possibility—and in light of the revolutionary potential of this case—it will be useful to analyze the district court's constitutional theory and consider the reception that views of this sort might ultimately receive in the Supreme Court.

The sweeping opinion of the district judge in *Federal Employees* was an extraordinary *coup de main.* The portion of the opinion striking down the statute is conclusory and short, relying on "the constitutional and traditional role of the Executive in assuring the nation's security and gathering and protecting the information essential to that security."[95] The district court's reliance on tradition and history illustrates some of the perils of employing "custom" in separation of powers disputes. The "tradition" of executive classification is of relatively recent origin, and the system has only existed in anything resembling its present form since the period following World War II. Indeed, the entire classification system could be subject to question because of its lack of comprehensive legislative authority, although individual statutes have enforced its provisions in specific circumstances. With time, however, a practice that at first may have presented a borderline question of executive authority seems to

92. American Foreign Serv. Ass'n v. Garfinkel, 57 U.S.L.W. 4441 (U.S. No. 87-2127, April 18, 1989). The Court noted that amended secrecy agreement forms now comply with the statute, at least in part. Accordingly, certain questions of mootness, in addition to other issues of statutory construction and ripeness, should be resolved by the district court before it considers the constitutional question. According to the Court, a constitutional issue of such magnitude should not be decided without a clear resolution of these preliminary points. *Id.* at 4442.

93. *Id.* The Court did caution, however, that the district court should not decide the underlying constitutional issue, unless it "finds it imperative to do so." *Id.*

94. Indeed, the statute considered in *Federal Employees* was intended only as a temporary "moratorium," pending a more thorough congressional review directed toward permanent legislation regulating secrecy agreements in the future. Thus the congressional regulation of executive secrecy agreements may present continuing constitutional issues. *See generally* HOUSE COMM. ON GOVERNMENT OPERATIONS, LEGISLATION NEEDED TO CURB SECRECY CONTRACTS, H.R. REP. No. 991, 100th Cong., 2d Sess. at 6-7 [hereinafter cited as HOUSE REPORT]. *See also infra* note 111.

95. 688 F. Supp. at 685.

have become an institution that is not only clearly permitted, but is also viewed as so central that congressional limitations in the area may actually be excluded.

In general, moreover, the district court in *Federal Employees* seemed to ignore the basic proposition that all aspects of the vast executive apparatus—including the CIA, Defense Department, and all other departments whose employees are now covered by secrecy agreements—are created by Congress under the Necessary and Proper Clause. Under that clause, Congress has broad authority to determine the functions and attributes of the offices that it creates in the executive branch. Congress created the CIA in 1947, and it is generally assumed that Congress could abolish the entire intelligence apparatus tomorrow if it wished. Does the theory of the district court imply that Congress has a constitutional *duty* to establish and maintain intelligence agencies for the collection of secret information if the President so requires?

It is important to note that there was no question in this case of confidential relationships between the President and his close advisors—relationships that might implicate the privilege of confidentiality established in *United States v. Nixon.* Yet the district court's doctrine in *Federal Employees* may be viewed as a lineal descendant of Chief Justice Burger's footnote 16 in *Nixon,*[96]—indicating that the President possesses certain "implied powers," analogous to those recognized as belonging to Congress in *McCulloch v. Maryland*—and the further suggestion, implicit in *Nixon,* that those executive powers may prevail in some circumstances even though they did not prevail in *Nixon* itself.[97]

The President no doubt does possess certain exclusive powers explicitly set forth in the constitutional text, and he may also have a constitutional relationship with certain high officers (such as the Secretary of State) that Congress generally would have to respect.[98] The extent of exclusive executive power asserted by the district court, however, reaches far beyond any reasonable conception of that irreducible core.[99] Most important, the secrecy agreements imposed on more than two million employees heavily burden First

---

96. 418 U.S. 683, 705 n.16 (1974).

97. *See also id.* at 706, 710-11, 712 n.19 (indicating that, in contrast with the result in *Nixon,* a court's need for information might be subordinated in the case of "military, diplomatic, or sensitive national security secrets").

98. *Cf.* Marbury v. Madison, 5 U.S. (1 Cranch) 137, 169 (1803) (noting the "intimate political relation subsisting between the President of the United States and the heads of departments").

99. This case of course falls within the third category set forth by Justice Jackson in his famous opinion in the *Steel Seizure Case,* the category in which presidential measures are "incompatible with the expressed or implied will of Congress." Youngstown Sheet & Tube Co. v. Sawyer, 343 U.S. 579, 637 (1952) (Jackson, J., concurring). In this category the President's power "is at its lowest ebb," and such executive claims "must be

Amendment interests, and the statute at issue in *Federal Employees* was a legislative attempt—in the best traditions of Congress—to strike the appropriate balance between the First Amendment interests and the government's interest in secrecy.[100] Indeed, a requirement of explicit statutory authorization for measures that may threaten constitutional rights is a doctrine that is essential for preserving those rights;[101] consequently, a holding that deprives Congress of *any* role in protecting certain powerful First Amendment interests seems to stand the constitutional system on its head. Significantly, however, in deciding the question of executive power, the district court in *Federal Employees* ignored the very weighty First Amendment interests at issue in the case. Indeed, those interests received absolutely no mention in the passages holding the statute unconstitutional.[102]

In at least one other significant respect, the district court's decision in *Federal Employees* went beyond *Chadha* and *Bowsher,* the recent Supreme Court decisions invalidating congressional action on separation of powers grounds. *Chadha* and *Bowsher* were, at bottom, procedural cases. They did not find that congressional lawmaking must be subordinate to executive decisions in a specific area of governmental activity; rather, they found that if Congress wished to act in a particular area, it was required to act in one manner rather than in another. If the Supreme Court were ultimately to sustain the district court's position in *Federal Employees,* it would be the Court's first holding that executive power totally excludes Congress in an important area of general policymaking.[103]

Although the district court's opinion in *Federal Employees* seems extreme, remarks in recent Supreme Court opinions suggest that, at least in the minds of some justices, its underlying principles might be worthy of serious consideration. Last term, in *Department of Navy v. Egan,*[104] the Court proclaimed an independent presidential power over "national security" information and, in particular, over classification of secret material. In an opinion that gave a very narrow interpretation to a statute allowing administrative review in certain security-clearance cases, the Court declared that the authority to

scrutinized with caution, for what is at stake is the equilibrium established by our constitutional system." *Id.* at 637-38. *See* House Report, *supra* note 94, at 16-17.

100. *See generally Separation of Powers Under Nixon, supra* note 15, at 54-62.

101. *See id.* at 63-65.

102. The district judge did indicate, however, that he would review First Amendment issues in a later opinion considering the constitutionality of the secrecy agreements themselves. In that opinion, the court found that the agreements' requirement of secrecy for "classifiable" information was unconstitutionally vague; the vagueness would be cured, however, if the government's limiting definition of "classifiable" information appearing in the Federal Register was distributed to all employees signing the agreements. In all other respects, the plaintiffs' First Amendment claims were rejected. National Fed'n of Fed. Employees v. United States, 695 F. Supp. 1196 (D.D.C. 1988).

103. *See, e.g.,* Brief of the Speaker and Leadership Group at 17-18, American Foreign Serv. Ass'n v. Garfinkel, 57 U.S.L.W. 4441 (April 18, 1989) (U.S. No. 87-2127); *cf.* House Report, *supra* note 94, at 15 (views of Professor Michael Glennon).

104. 108 S. Ct. 818 (1988).

classify national security information "flows primarily from [a] constitutional investment of power in the President and exists quite apart from any explicit congressional grant. . . . The authority to protect such information falls on the President as head of the Executive Branch and as Commander in Chief."[105] Apparently, the Court's acceptance of extensive executive power over national security information was the prime determinant of its narrow interpretation of the congressional grant of administrative review in security-clearance cases.

This language in *Egan* was invoked by the district court as a basis for its opinion in *Federal Employees.* In a recent dissenting opinion, moreover, Justice Scalia has taken *Egan* one step closer to *Federal Employees,* by raising the possibility that certain statutes in the area of "national security" might unconstitutionally invade the executive's power. Specifically, Scalia cast doubt on whether Congress could constitutionally authorize judicial review of a CIA director's decision to discharge an intelligence agent. Dissenting in *Webster v. Doe,*[106] Scalia remarked that a "serious constitutional question" is presented by the issue of "whether Congress could constitutionally *permit* the courts to review all [personnel decisions of the Director of Central Intelligence] if it wanted to."[107] In suggesting that an area of CIA personnel policy remained constitutionally free from some forms of congressional or judicial control, Scalia relied on the *Curtiss-Wright* case[108] and *Snepp,* and also quoted relevant language from *Department of Navy v. Egan.*[109]

Scalia's opinion, of course, was a dissent, and the Court's opinion on administrative review in *Egan* considered an issue that was rather different from the limitations on secrecy agreements presented in *Federal Employees. Egan* also contained somewhat ambiguous language that could be interpreted as acknowledging ultimate congressional control over national security affairs.[110] Moreover, in contrast with *Egan,* the Court in *Webster v. Doe* recently construed a statute of Congress to allow judicial consideration of asserted *constitutional* violations in CIA firing decisions. Thus, here is one recent case in which the implications drawn from constitutional rights may have prevailed, at least in a preliminary procedural skirmish, against the radiations of executive power in the process of statutory interpretation.

Nonetheless, the recent statements of the Court in *Egan* asserting

105. *Id.* at 824.
106. 108 S. Ct. 2047, 2055-63 (1988).
107. *Id.* at 2059.
108. United States v. Curtiss-Wright Export Corp., 299 U.S. 304 (1936).
109. *See Webster,* 108 S. Ct. at 2060 (Scalia, J., dissenting).
110. 108 S. Ct. 818, 825 (1988).

an independent national security power of the President—combined with Scalia's fairly clear suggestion that this power may under some circumstances prevail against explicit congressional limitation—seem to indicate that the ideas put forth by the district court in *Federal Employees* might well receive a serious hearing in the Supreme Court. The possibility of a broad constitutional imperative of executive secrecy that would not only be enforced on the basis of some sort of ambiguous *statutory* authority, but would also be imposed by courts even against the express will of Congress, is a stark and frightening prospect. It is a possibility, however, that could conceivably flow from the line of recent decisions favoring executive power in a number of areas. Whether this sort of argument indeed represents the wave of the future may be indicated if the Supreme Court passes on this case in a later term. Even if the *Federal Employees* decision does not re-appear in the Supreme Court, however, the district court's opinion will almost certainly be a harbinger of further arguments seeking to restrict Congress's ability to regulate the asserted national security power of the President.[111] In general, the fate of views of this sort may depend on the prospect of likely changes in the Court over the next few years. Acceptance of these arguments, however, would clearly represent a significant change in the constitutional structure.

VI. Conclusion

If one looks over the history of separation of powers decisions in the last twenty years, certain rough outlines of development seem to emerge.[112] The Court's increased intervention in separation of powers disputes began in the early 1970s, and its cases since that period seem to fall, with a certain amount of overlap, into three basic stages. The early and mid-1970s was a period of serious public concern about extraordinary assertions of executive power under President Nixon, and important decisions of the period imposed limits on executive power or upheld congressional limits on that power. Thus, in *United States v. Nixon*,[113] the Court required the President to deliver tape recordings of confidential communications to the courts, even though the opinion recognized the existence of a general presidential privilege of confidentiality. Thereafter, the Court upheld a congressional statute placing Nixon's presidential papers (and tapes) in the custody of the government.[114] During the

111. *See, e.g.*, Koh, *supra* note 16, at 1303 n.218 (The Reagan administration argued that the Boland Amendments, limiting expenditure of funds to support Nicaraguan Contras, unconstitutionally infringed the President's foreign affairs power.) *See also supra* text accompanying note 94.

112. This historical summary draws in part on Quint, *The Separation of Powers in American Constitutional Law: Perspectives and Recent Trends*, 1984 ANNALS OF THE FACULTY OF LAW IN BELGRADE 86 (copy on file at the *George Washington Law Review*).

113. 418 U.S. 683 (1974).

114. Nixon v. Administrator of Gen. Servs., 433 U.S. 425 (1977).

same period the Court also denied the Nixon administration's request for an injunction against the publication of the Pentagon Papers; a number of justices concurring in the Court's *per curiam* decision emphasized lack of statutory authority as well as First Amendment grounds.[115]

The cases of the late 1970s and early 1980s, however, seem to reflect a rather different atmosphere in the Supreme Court. In the context of severe international crises—particularly those arising from the change of government in Iran—the Court upheld far-reaching exercises of executive power as falling within the radiations of congressional authorization.[116] Indeed, two cases of this period involved significant executive inroads on constitutional rights.[117] But even in these cases the Court appeared to reserve the ultimate allocation of authority to Congress, if Congress desired to act.

Finally, in two notable decisions of the mid-1980s, the Court began to show an increased willingness to intervene *against* Congress by striking down important statutory programs on separation of powers grounds.[118] The *Chadha* and *Bowsher* decisions—invalidating various forms of congressional limitations on the executive—required the erection of complex structures of formalist judicial doctrine. These cases are also notable for their refusal to defer to congressional power under the Necessary and Proper Clause.

Against the background of *Chadha* and *Bowsher,* however, the Court last term in *Morrison v. Olson*[119] upheld the independent-counsel legislation, a particular target of the Reagan administration. It is conceivable that this case heralds a tendency toward greater judicial deference to Congress in separation of powers cases. Yet, an examination of the background and opinion in this case suggests that the case may not portend a general swing toward greater deference to

115. New York Times Co. v. United States, 403 U.S. 713 (1971) (per curiam).

116. *See, e.g.*, Dames & Moore v. Regan, 453 U.S. 654 (1981) (upholding executive agreement with Iran); *cf.* Goldwater v. Carter, 444 U.S. 996 (1979) (finding that the President's unilateral termination of Taiwan Mutual Defense Treaty was non-justiciable).

117. Haig v. Agee, 453 U.S. 280 (1981) (upholding withdrawal of passport); Snepp v. United States, 444 U.S. 507 (1980) (enforcing CIA secrecy agreement). For a later example, see Regan v. Wald, 468 U.S. 222 (1984), discussed *supra* at text accompanying notes 19-25.

118. Bowsher v. Synar, 478 U.S. 714 (1986); INS v. Chadha, 462 U.S. 919 (1983). For a forerunner, see Buckley v. Valeo, 424 U.S. 1 (1976) (statute vesting power to appoint Federal Election Commissioners in certain members of Congress held unconstitutional). In addition, in the early 1980s the Court rejected possible implications from the first two *Nixon* cases and found that an absolute immunity protects the President from civil liability for violations of citizens' constitutional rights. The Court, however, did not decide whether Congress could limit the scope or nature of that immunity. Nixon v. Fitzgerald, 457 U.S. 731 (1982).

119. 108 S. Ct. 2597 (1988); *see supra* Part IV.

Congress in separation of powers disputes, but rather that the decision represents a special case—analogous to *United States v. Nixon*—in which the Court perceived itself as furthering confidence and governmental stability by refusing to insulate high executive officers from criminal liability. Indeed, certain recent pronouncements of the Court in the "national security" area suggest, with increased clarity, the acceptance of independent executive power in that area—power that might possibly be found impervious to limitation or regulation by Congress, to an extent defined by the courts.

* * *

There was a time not too long ago when a strong legislature and a limited presidency formed a cornerstone of the conservative political position; it was the Progressives and New Deal liberals who sought stronger executive power. With the growth of the national security state and the crucial historical episode of the Vietnam War, however, these positions have substantially reversed themselves, and it is the conservatives who seek stronger and more absolute executive authority. Accordingly, it is one of the youngest and most recently appointed justices, Antonin Scalia, whose positions favoring executive power seem to be the most forthright, plainly expressed, and uncompromising. The results of the recent presidential election strongly suggest, at least, a continuation of this position among prospective new justices of the Supreme Court.

In past years, political forces favoring congressional power could always console themselves with the thought that imbalances of presidential power could ultimately be redressed through the political process. In recent years, however, the courts have been intervening with increased frequency in separation of powers disputes. In light of recent decisions canvassed here—and what may be continuing trends, especially in national security affairs—such a political approach to separation of powers problems may become significantly more limited in its possibilities. If these trends continue to develop, important aspects of executive power could be fortified by constitutional decisions of the judiciary, which might be insulated in almost all practical respects from political change.

UNFULFILLED ASPIRATIONS: THE COURT-PACKING EFFORTS OF PRESIDENTS REAGAN AND BUSH

Christopher E. Smith and Thomas R. Hensley***

I. INTRODUCTION

During 1993, the American public was reminded yet again of the perceived link between the Supreme Court's composition and its decisions affecting law and public policy. Before selecting Judge Ruth Bader Ginsburg[1] to replace Justice Byron White,[2] President Clinton considered the probable impact of various potential nominees on future Supreme Court decisions concerning abortion and other controversial issues.[3] There was nothing unusual about the attention paid by Clinton, as well as by senators[4] and interest groups,[5] to Ginsburg's probable impact on the Rehnquist Court's decision mak-

* Associate Professor of Political Science, University of Akron. A.B., 1980, Harvard University; M.Sc., 1981, University of Bristol (England); J.D., 1984, University of Tennessee; Ph.D., 1988, University of Connecticut.

** Professor of Political Science, Kent State University. B.A., 1965, Simpson College; M.A., 1967; Ph.D., 1970, University of Iowa.

The authors gratefully acknowledge the contributions to this Article made by data drawn from the United States Supreme Court Judicial Database, Harold J. Spaeth, principal investigator and available through the Interuniversity Consortium for Political and Social Research (ICPSR Study Number 9422). A version of this work was presented at the 1993 annual meeting of the American Political Science Association.

1 Richard L. Berke, *Clinton Names Ruth Ginsburg, Advocate for Women, to Court*, N.Y. TIMES, June 15, 1993, at A1.

2 Linda Greenhouse, *White Announces He'll Step Down From High Court*, N.Y. TIMES, Mar. 20, 1993, at A1.

3 In announcing his selection of Ginsburg, Clinton did not state any specific expectations about how she would decide abortion or other particular issues. However, his remarks made clear that he had expectations about how she would decide cases affecting women:

> It is important to me that Judge Ginsburg came to her views and attitudes by doing, not merely by reading and studying. . . . Having experienced discrimination, she devoted the next 20 years of her career to fighting it and making this country a better place for our wives, our mothers, our sisters and our daughters.

Transcript of President's Announcement and Judge Ginsburg's Remarks, N.Y. TIMES, June 15, 1993, at A24.

4 During the confirmation hearings, senators sought to learn Ginsburg's views on abortion, capital punishment, and other issues. Ginsburg was the first nominee to strongly endorse the right of choice for abortion. Neil A. Lewis, *Ginsburg Affirms Right of a Woman to Have Abortion*, N.Y. TIMES, July 22, 1993, at A1. However, she declined to discuss her views on capital punishment and other issues. *See* Neil A. Lewis, *Ginsburg Deflects Pressure to Talk on Death Penalty*, N.Y. TIMES, July 23, 1993, at A1.

ing. Studies on the appointment process of Supreme Court Justices demonstrate the acceptance by previous Presidents and other political actors of the view that membership changes can affect the Court's decisions in fundamental ways.[6] As one scholar has noted: "[B]ecause the Court's major role in policy making [is] well understood . . . Presidents recognize that the capacity of their appointees to help shape the Court's policies is among their major legacies."[7] Thus Presidents have attempted to pack the Supreme Court with nominees whom they believe will move the Court's decisions in a direction favoring the Presidents' values and policy preferences. President Franklin Roosevelt, for example, attempted to pack the Court with nominees who would end the judicial obstruction of his New Deal policies.[8]

Like their predecessors, Presidents Reagan and Bush sought to use their power to appoint Supreme Court Justices and other federal judges as a means to shape constitutional law and public policy in directions consistent with their policy preferences. President Reagan applied "the most systematic ideological or judicial philosophical screening of judicial candidates since the first Roosevelt administration"[9] in selecting judicial officers for all levels of the federal courts. Similarly, the Bush administration "moved deliberately in its screening process and had to be reasonably satisfied that the nominee was not only professionally qualified but also shared the president's judicial philosophy."[10] The Reagan-Bush era presented a significant opportunity for two like-minded Presidents to make a concerted effort to reshape the Supreme Court because five Justices, constituting a majority on the high court, retired between 1981 and

[5] *See, e.g.*, Margaret Carlson, *The Law According to Ruth*, TIME, June 28, 1993, at 38, 40 ("Women's groups are also worried over criticism the pro-choice Ginsburg leveled at the *Roe v. Wade* decision in a speech last March.").

[6] *See* HENRY J. ABRAHAM, JUSTICES AND PRESIDENTS: A POLITICAL HISTORY OF APPOINTMENTS TO THE SUPREME COURT (3d ed. 1992).

[7] LAWRENCE BAUM, THE SUPREME COURT 41 (4th ed. 1992).

[8] *See* ABRAHAM, *supra* note 6, at 212. Abraham noted:

> No mystery attends Roosevelt's motivations in selecting his Supreme Court nominees. There were three major criteria: (1) absolute loyalty to the principles of the New Deal, particularly to governmental regulatory authority; (2) firm adherence to a libertarian and egalitarian philosophy of government under law—at least as it was viewed contemporarily; and (3) (once it had become clear that war clouds would cover the New World as well as the Old) full support of FDR's war aims, which necessitated a generous interpretation of the extent of executive power.

Id.

[9] Sheldon Goldman, *Reagan's Second Term Judicial Appointments: The Battle at Midway*, 70 JUDICATURE 324, 326 (1987).

[10] Sheldon Goldman, *Bush's Judicial Legacy: The Final Imprint*, 76 JUDICATURE 282, 286 (1993).

1992.[11] Although the fortuitous timing of five Justices' departures enabled conservative Republican Presidents to pack the Court with carefully selected appointees, Reagan and Bush ultimately failed to achieve complete fulfillment of their objectives. As this Article will discuss, the opportunity for and appearance of "Court packing" do not necessarily produce the intended results for Presidents who seek to move the high court in specific directions.

II. The Creation of the Rehnquist Court

A. *The Warren and Burger Court Eras*

In seeking to pack the Supreme Court with political conservatives, Presidents Reagan and Bush were reacting to the legacy of the Warren- and Burger-era Supreme Courts. A widespread consensus exists among scholars[12] that the Warren Court engaged in "what can only be described as a constitutional revolution, generated by a group of justices who were perhaps the most liberal in American history."[13] The Warren Court era was characterized by decisions "striking down state restrictions on individual rights"[14] and enabling "minorities . . . to win victories they had not been able to obtain from reluctant legislatures and executives."[15] Although the Court's liberal composition during that era clearly facilitated its decision making in favor of individual rights and liberties, scholars disagree about whether the appointment of Arthur Goldberg or other specific Justices during the 1960s caused the Supreme Court to make particular liberal decisions.[16]

---

11 Potter Stewart retired in 1981 and was replaced by Sandra Day O'Connor. When Warren Burger retired in 1986, William Rehnquist was elevated to Chief Justice and Antonin Scalia was appointed to the Court. In 1987, Lewis Powell retired and was replaced by Anthony Kennedy in 1988. David Souter replaced William Brennan in 1990, and Clarence Thomas replaced Thurgood Marshall in 1991. Baum, *supra* note 7, at 266.

12 *See, e.g.*, Robert H. Bork, The Tempting of America: The Political Seduction of Law 61 (1990) ("[T]he [Warren] Court's change of direction and its assumption of a power to be used for new ends meant a revolution in our society as well."); Robert A. Carp & Ronald Stidham, The Federal Courts 8 (2d ed. 1991) ("Without doubt, [the Supreme Court] gave its strongest and most active support for civil liberties and civil rights during the 1953-1969 period, when Earl Warren served as chief justice.").

13 Thomas G. Walker & Lee Epstein, The Supreme Court of the United States: An Introduction 19 (1993).

14 Stephen L. Wasby, The Supreme Court in the Federal Judicial System 11 (4th ed. 1993).

15 *Id.*

16 The prevailing view is that "[o]nly when Justice Felix Frankfurter retired in 1962 and was replaced by Justice Arthur Goldberg did the Court have a fifth reliable civil liberties vote, reinforced by Thurgood Marshall, the Court's first black member. Their presence and that of Abe Fortas, who replaced Goldberg, explains the later Warren Court's high level of support for

During the Warren Court era, the Supreme Court made many notable—and controversial—decisions. The underlying principles from some of their decisions, such as the proclamation in *Brown v. Board of Education*[17] that government-sponsored racial discrimination violates constitutional principles of equal protection, have become well-accepted by liberals and conservatives alike.[18] Many of the Court's other decisions, however, have generated persistent criticism and political conflict. For example, the Warren Court's decisions that strengthened the rights of criminal defendants by expanding the application of the exclusionary rule for evidence obtained through improper searches,[19] and the requirement that police officers inform arrestees of their rights,[20] became targets for political conservatives. As one scholar observed, "The *Miranda* decision unleashed a storm of criticism of the Court for its alleged coddling of criminals, and some scholars shared the . . . view that *Miranda* represented a radical break in which the Court had made a 'new law and new public policy.'"[21] Similarly, Warren Court decisions that barred organized prayer in public schools[22] and recognized a constitutional right of privacy[23] generated sustained opposition from, respectively, conservative politicians[24] and conservative scholars.[25]

civil liberties." WASBY, *supra* note 14, at 13. An alternative view, based on a systematic study of the Warren Court's decisions, asserts that "the [liberal] shift occurred before Goldberg joined the Court, and probably would have occurred even if he had never been nominated and confirmed." Jeffrey A. Segal & Harold J. Spaeth, *Decisional Trends on the Warren and Burger Courts: Results From the Supreme Court Data Base Project*, 73 JUDICATURE 103, 104 (1989).

17 Brown v. Board of Educ., 347 U.S. 483 (1954).

18 For example, Edwin Meese, the conservative Attorney General during the Reagan administration, lavished praise on the Supreme Court's decision in the *Brown* case while he simultaneously attacked the Court's doctrines and decisions in many other areas. *See* Christopher E. Smith, *Jurisprudential Politics and the Manipulation of History*, 13 W. J. BLACK STUD. 156, 158-60 (1990). As one commentator observed about Meese's diplomatic treatment of the Court's school desegregation decisions, Meese portrayed himself as a supporter of *Brown* because "[a]nybody who opposed [*Brown*] today would be assailed as a segregationist crank." Stuart Taylor, Jr., *Meese v. Brennan: Who's Right About the Constitution?*, NEW REPUBLIC, Jan. 6, 1986, at 17, 21.

19 Mapp v. Ohio, 367 U.S. 643 (1961).

20 Miranda v. Arizona, 384 U.S. 436 (1966).

21 MELVIN I. UROFSKY, A MARCH OF LIBERTY: A CONSTITUTIONAL HISTORY OF THE UNITED STATES 819 (1988).

22 Engel v. Vitale, 370 U.S. 421 (1962).

23 Griswold v. Connecticut, 381 U.S. 479 (1965).

24 *See* John A. Murley, *School Prayer: Free Exercise of Religion or Establishment of Religion?*, *in* SOCIAL REGULATORY POLICY: MORAL CONTROVERSIES IN AMERICAN POLITICS 5 (Raymond Tatalovich & Byron Daynes eds., 1988).

25 For example, Robert Bork has described the Warren Court's recognition of a constitutional right to privacy as a "constitutional time bomb." BORK, *supra* note 12, at 95.

President Richard Nixon seized his opportunity to pack the Court when the quirks of timing of Justices' retirements gave him four vacancies to fill.[26] Because "Nixon was among the first to recognize that expanded rights for the criminally accused touched the nerves of a majority of Americans,"[27] he criticized the Warren Court's decisions and used his appointment power to nominate new Justices who would limit the Warren Court's expansion of rights for criminal defendants.[28] According to Nixon, "Some of our judges have gone too far . . . in assuming unto themselves a mandate which is not there, and that is, to put their social and economic ideas into their decisions."[29]

Under Chief Justice Warren Burger, a Nixon appointee, the Supreme Court moved in a markedly conservative direction on criminal justice issues,[30] and limited judicial policy making in some other areas.[31] However, it never reversed the Warren Court's fundamental and controversial precedents on the exclusionary rule and *Miranda* warnings. Moreover, the Burger Court actually expanded constitutional rights in other areas through important liberal decisions concerning abortion,[32] gender equality,[33] and affirmative action.[34] Although the Justices on the Burger Court provided less support than their Warren Court predecessors for individual civil

---

26 Although only two Justices, Hugo Black and John Harlan, would have naturally retired due to age and ill health during Nixon's administration, Nixon was also able to replace Earl Warren and Abe Fortas because of political miscues by President Lyndon Johnson in unsuccessfully seeking to have Fortas elevated to Chief Justice in place of Warren. As a result of ensuing political controversies, Fortas resigned after Nixon took office so Nixon was able to appoint replacements for both Warren and Fortas. *See* Christopher E. Smith, *"What If. . . .": Critical Junctures on the Road to (In)Equality*, 15 THURGOOD MARSHALL L. REV. 1 (1989-90).

27 LEE EPSTEIN & THOMAS G. WALKER, CONSTITUTIONAL LAW FOR A CHANGING AMERICA: RIGHTS, LIBERTIES, AND JUSTICE 334 (1992).

28 *Id.* at 334-36.

29 MELVIN I. UROFSKY, THE CONTINUITY OF CHANGE: THE SUPREME COURT AND INDIVIDUAL LIBERTIES 1953-1986, at 18 (1991).

30 *See* Yale Kamisar, *The "Police Practice" Phases of the Criminal Process and the Three Phases of the Burger Court*, *in* THE BURGER YEARS: RIGHTS AND WRONGS IN THE SUPREME COURT, 1969-1986, at 143 (Herman Schwartz ed., 1987).

31 For example, the Burger Court limited district judges' ability to redress school segregation by limiting remedies to single school districts in the absence of proof that other specific school districts were at fault. Milliken v. Bradley, 418 U.S. 717 (1974). This decision effectively assured that schools in many of the largest cities would remain essentially composed of poor, minority students who have access to fewer educational resources than their counterparts in nearby suburbs. *See* Thomas F. Pettigrew, *A Sociological View of the Post-*Bradley *Era*, 21 WAYNE L. REV. 813 (1975).

32 *E.g.*, Roe v. Wade, 410 U.S. 113 (1973).

33 *E.g.*, Fronteiro v. Richardson, 411 U.S. 677 (1973).

34 *E.g.*, United Steelworkers v. Weber, 443 U.S. 193 (1979).

rights and liberties claims,[35] the Court did not engage in wholesale reversals of liberal precedents. In fact, despite Nixon's success in appointing Justices who would limit rights for criminal defendants, his appointees ultimately disappointed conservatives because they moved the Court in liberal directions on so many other important issues, most notably in abortion and affirmative action.[36]

Because President Carter had no opportunities to appoint new Justices to the Supreme Court during his four-year term in the White House, President Reagan's administration inherited a Court composed of holdover Justices from the Warren and Burger Court eras. Only Justice John Paul Stevens, a Republican appointee of Gerald Ford who replaced Warren Court liberal William O. Douglas, had altered the Court's composition since Nixon's four appointments in the early 1970s. Reagan and his political supporters wanted to reverse the liberal judicial policy patterns established by the Warren and Burger Courts with respect to abortion, affirmative action, school prayer, criminal defendants' rights, and other issues.[37] Reagan and his allies recognized, however, that they could not easily achieve their policy goals through legislative action because Democrats remained powerful in Congress. Thus they opted to use the presidential appointment power to remake the federal judiciary, including the Supreme Court, through the appointment of conservative judicial officers who would reverse the liberal trends established by the Warren and Burger Courts.[38] As one scholar observed, "It

[35] During the Warren Court era, the Court's support level for individuals' civil liberties claims exceeded 70% during seven of its terms, while the Burger Court's support exceeded 50% during only three terms and otherwise ranged only from 33% to 48%. Segal & Spaeth, *supra* note 16, at 104.

[36] *See, e.g.*, ABRAHAM, *supra* note 6, at 349 ("The Burger Court, far from reversing or otherwise undoing its predecessor Warren Court, was marked by a generally surprising penchant for judicial activism, even in such unexpected areas as civil rights and civil liberties.").

[37] *See* LEE EPSTEIN & JOSEPH F. KOBYLKA, THE SUPREME COURT AND LEGAL CHANGE 18 (1992) (Reagan "had no trepidation about criticizing the Burger Court's 'activist' stances on abortion, affirmative action, and other issues. Neither did he make any bones about his strategy of judicial appointment: he would nominate jurists who shared his values."); *see also* LINCOLN CAPLAN, THE TENTH JUSTICE: THE SOLICITOR GENERAL AND THE RULE OF LAW 268-77 (1987) (describing Reagan administration efforts to use the Office of the Solicitor General to urge the Supreme Court to reverse liberal precedents on abortion, affirmative action, and other issues); Kristen Norman-Major, *The Solicitor General: Executive Policy Agendas and the Courts*, 57 ALB. L. REV. 1081 (1994) (discussing the politicization of the role of the Solicitor General).

[38] *See* HERMAN SCHWARTZ, PACKING THE COURTS: THE CONSERVATIVE CAMPAIGN TO REWRITE THE CONSTITUTION 175-76 (1988) ("In order to govern, however, a Republican president, even one as 'right-minded' as Reagan, must disappoint the true-believing conservatives . . . because he cannot deliver what they want, such as constitutional amendments or legislation on abortion, school prayer, affirmative action, and busing. . . . The one thing a president can do

was undoubtedly with [the Warren and Burger Courts'] history in mind that President Reagan resolved to endeavor to fill . . . two [Supreme Court] vacancies with replacements of whose conservative, strict constitutional constructionist, jurisprudence he could be relatively comfortably secure."[39] Reagan's Vice-President, George Bush, later continued this approach when he subsequently served a single term as president.[40] Thus two like-minded, consecutively serving Presidents had the opportunity to pack the Supreme Court with a new majority of five appointees who were chosen, in large part, with the intention of moving constitutional law and judicial policy away from the liberal precedents established during the Warren and Burger Court eras.

B. The Reagan and Bush Appointees to the Supreme Court

In important ways, the five Justices appointed to the Supreme Court by Presidents Reagan and Bush were all more conservative than the Warren and Burger Court era Justices whom they replaced. The evident conservatism in the judicial philosophies of the five appointees reflected the conscious efforts of the Reagan and Bush administrations to pack the Supreme Court with Justices who would undo the objectionable liberal decisions of the preceding three decades.

President Reagan's first opportunity to appoint a new Justice came with the retirement of Eisenhower appointee Justice Potter Stewart, a moderate Republican. During the 1980 presidential campaign, Reagan had pledged to appoint the first woman to the Supreme Court,[41] and he fulfilled that promise by nominating Sandra Day O'Connor, an experienced state appellate judge and former state senator from Arizona.[42] As a Justice, she has been more conservative than Stewart in many respects. While Stewart was a member of the seven-member majority in *Roe v. Wade* that sought to remove government interference from women's decisions about terminating early stage pregnancies,[43] O'Connor has explicitly criti-

for these supporters—and this will ultimately be just as effective on social issues—is to give them the judges they want.").

[39] ABRAHAM, *supra* note 6, at 349-50.

[40] *See* Goldman, *supra* note 10, at 282-86.

[41] DAVID G. SAVAGE, TURNING RIGHT: THE MAKING OF THE REHNQUIST SUPREME COURT 113 (1992).

[42] *Id.* at 112-13.

[43] *See* Roe v. Wade, 410 U.S. 113, 115 (1973).

cized the reasoning in *Roe*[44] and has endorsed government restrictions on abortion.[45] While Stewart was the author of an important opinion permitting Congress to prohibit racial discrimination by private individuals under its Thirteenth Amendment power,[46] O'Connor sought reconsideration of Congressional power to regulate private discriminatory conduct[47] and voted to narrow the scope of existing statutory protections.[48] In addition, although the cases are arguably distinguishable, Stewart joined the five-member majority to overturn a conviction in the Supreme Court's original flag burning case,[49] while O'Connor joined the Justices who in later cases refused to recognize flag burning as a protected form of political expression.[50]

Reagan's second appointee was Antonin Scalia, who filled William Rehnquist's spot on the Court when Rehnquist was elevated to Chief Justice upon Warren Burger's retirement in 1986. Scalia was a former law professor and a judge on the U.S. Court of Appeals for the District of Columbia Circuit.[51] His outspokenness as a law professor had made him a favorite of political conservatives, and he was "billed as the intellectual lodestar who would pull the Court to the right by the force of his brilliance."[52] Scalia sailed through an easy confirmation process because he was viewed as simply one conservative replacing another conservative and, therefore, not threatening to the ideological balance of power on the Court. In addition, he benefitted from being the first Italian-American nominee to the Supreme Court. Moreover, liberal senators and interest groups were

---

44 *See* City of Akron v. Akron Ctr. for Reprod. Health, 462 U.S. 416, 453-59 (1983) (O'Connor, J., dissenting), *overruled by* Planned Parenthood v. Casey, 112 S. Ct. 2791, 2816-17 (1992).

45 For example, over the objections of the remaining members of the original *Roe* majority (Justices Blackmun, Brennan, and Marshall), O'Connor endorsed a Missouri statute which declared that life begins at conception, required fetal testing before mid-term abortions, and limited patients' access to public hospitals as a source of abortions. Webster v. Reproductive Health Servs., 492 U.S. 490, 522-31 (1989) (O'Connor, J., concurring).

46 Jones v. Alfred H. Mayer Co., 392 U.S. 409 (1968).

47 Stuart Taylor Jr., *Court, 5-4, Votes to Restudy Rights in Minority Suits*, N.Y. TIMES, Apr. 26, 1988, at A1, A24.

48 *See* Patterson v. McLean Credit Union, 491 U.S. 164 (1989); Wards Cove Packing Co. v. Atonio, 490 U.S. 642 (1989).

49 Street v. New York, 394 U.S. 576 (1969).

50 United States v. Eichman, 496 U.S. 310, 319 (1990); Texas v. Johnson, 491 U.S. 397, 421 (1989).

51 *See* Christopher E. Smith, *Justice Antonin Scalia and the Institutions of American Government*, 25 WAKE FOREST L. REV. 783, 786-87 (1990).

52 Tony Mauro, *High Court Adjourns for Summer Intact*, LEGAL TIMES, July 9, 1990, at 10.

distracted by their efforts to block the elevation of Justice Rehnquist to Chief Justice in a simultaneous confirmation process.[53]

Contrary to perceptions that Scalia would be, in effect, simply replacing a fellow conservative when Chief Justice Burger retired, Scalia proved to be more conservative than Burger on several issues. For example, Chief Justice Burger wrote the opinion that endorsed a congressional affirmative action statute requiring a percentage of federal contract funds to be directed to businesses owned by members of specified minority groups.[54] By contrast, as a law professor Scalia condemned affirmative action[55] and he continued his strident opposition to such policies as a Justice by voting consistently against affirmative action programs,[56] including a federal affirmative action program for awarding broadcast licenses.[57] While Chief Justice Burger authored the employment discrimination decision which declared that Congress sought to eradicate "the *consequences* of [discriminatory] employment practices, not simply the motivation,"[58] Scalia was a member of a five-member majority that altered Burger's precedent by emphasizing discriminatory motivations over discriminatory consequences.[59]

When Lewis Powell retired in 1987, Reagan was unsuccessful in his effort to appoint his ideal choice, Judge Robert Bork, but Powell's ultimate replacement,[60] Judge Anthony Kennedy from the U.S. Court of Appeals for the Ninth Circuit, proved to be more conservative than his predecessor. The defeat of Bork's nomination in the U.S. Senate was attributable, in part, to the belief that a strident conservative would be replacing the Court's perceived moderate.[61] Although Kennedy was a less controversial choice, "the Court's swing seat no longer functioned as a vote that balanced the liberal and conservative blocs by siding with one or the other from case to case. Instead, Kennedy's vote most often served as a tie-breaker that could tip the balance in favor of the conservatives."[62]

---

53 ABRAHAM, *supra* note 6, at 353-54.

54 Fullilove v. Klutznick, 448 U.S. 448 (1980).

55 *See* Antonin Scalia, *The Disease as Cure*, 1979 WASH. U. L.Q. 147.

56 *See* City of Richmond v. J. A. Croson Co., 488 U.S. 469 (1989); Johnson v. Transp. Agency, 480 U.S. 616 (1987).

57 Metro Broadcasting Inc. v. FCC, 497 U.S. 547 (1990).

58 Griggs v. Duke Power Co., 401 U.S. 424, 432 (1971).

59 Wards Cove Packing Co. v. Atonio, 490 U.S. 642 (1989).

60 Reagan's second nominee, Judge Douglas Ginsburg of the U.S. Court of Appeals for the District of Columbia Circuit, had his nomination withdrawn after revelations about his marijuana use as a law professor. ABRAHAM, *supra* note 6, at 359.

61 *Id.* at 357-59.

62 *Id.* at 361.

For example, although Powell was a member of the majority in *Roe v. Wade* and subsequently issued a plea for preservation of the abortion precedent,[63] Kennedy joined the Justices who subsequently endorsed governmental regulations affecting abortion choices.[64] While Powell crafted the compromise opinion endorsing affirmative action programs,[65] Kennedy actively opposed affirmative action programs in his decisions.[66]

When William Brennan retired in 1990, the Court's remaining liberal wing lost its "center of gravity" because of Brennan's "intellectual force [and] magnetic personality."[67] President Bush nominated David Souter to replace Brennan because "[i]t was abundantly clear . . . based on his five years of service on the New Hampshire Superior Court and seven on its Supreme Court, that here was a jurist firmly committed to Bush's desire for a strict constructionist, a judicial restraintist, dedicated to legal and constitutional precedent and history."[68]

During his very first Term on the Supreme Court, Souter quickly demonstrated that he was much more conservative than his predecessor, one of the leading Justices on the liberal Warren Court. Souter cast the decisive fifth vote in eleven five-to-four cases that produced conservative outcomes, cases which would have turned out the other way if Brennan had remained on the Court. For example, while Brennan was a member of the original *Roe v. Wade* majority and a consistent defender of a right of choice in abortion, Souter cast the deciding vote to endorse the Bush administration's so-called gag rule that prevented doctors at federally funded clinics from advising patients about abortion options.[69] While Brennan was openly skeptical of governmental efforts to regulate pornography and other sexually explicit forms of expression,[70] Souter cast the deciding vote to

---

63 City of Akron v. Akron Ctr. for Reprod. Health, 462 U.S. 416, 420 n.1 (1983), *overruled by* Planned Parenthood v. Casey, 112 S. Ct. 2791, 2816-17 (1992).

64 Webster v. Reproductive Health Servs., 492 U.S. 490 (1989).

65 Regents of the Univ. of Cal. v. Bakke, 438 U.S. 265 (1978).

66 City of Richmond v. J. A. Croson Co., 488 U.S. 469 (1989); Metro Broadcasting Inc. v. FCC, 497 U.S. 547 (1990).

67 Linda Greenhouse, *An Activist's Legacy*, N.Y. TIMES, July 22, 1990, at 1, 22.

68 ABRAHAM, *supra* note 6, at 367.

69 Rust v. Sullivan, 500 U.S. 173 (1991).

70 After spending many years as the Court's resident expert who attempted to develop a definition for "obscenity," *see* Roth v. United States, 354 U.S. 476 (1957), Brennan eventually decided that is was virtually impossible to develop a workable definition and therefore the government should be limited in its ability to proscribe or punish such expression. Paris Adult Theatre I v. Slaton, 413 U.S. 49 (1973). Even when Brennan was working with definitions of obscenity, he produced definitions that effectively prevented the government from seeking many opportunities to limit sexually explicit expression.

endorse an Indiana statute barring nude dancing at bars, despite the fact that the Court majority acknowledged such dancing to be a form of artistic expression rather than obscenity.[71] Souter also cast the decisive vote against claims of individuals in seven criminal justice cases in which the claimants would have prevailed if Brennan had remained on the Court.[72]

The retirement in 1991 of the last remaining liberal from the Warren Court, Thurgood Marshall, presented Bush with the opportunity to reinforce significantly the Court's strong conservative wing. Bush nominated Judge Clarence Thomas of the U.S. Court of Appeals for the District of Columbia Circuit, the controversial former Chairman of the Equal Employment Opportunity Commission during the Reagan administration. By saying at the nomination press conference that "the main consideration, in addition to excellence in qualification, is this concept of interpreting the Constitution and not legislating from the Federal bench,"[73] Bush used the familiar conservative code words for advocating a judicial counterattack against the Warren- and Burger-era legacy of liberal judicial activism.

After stormy confirmation hearings that included allegations of sexual harassment by Thomas against subordinates,[74] Thomas was confirmed by the narrowest of margins (fifty-two to forty-eight),[75] and he immediately set to work establishing himself as a virtual conservative antithesis of his predecessor, Thurgood Marshall. During his first Term on the Court, Thomas agreed with the consistently conservative Scalia in 79% of nonunanimous cases, the highest interagreement rate of any two Justices on the Court.[76] His lowest agreement rates (below 30%) were with Marshall's former allies, Blackmun and Stevens.[77] While Marshall had been a member of the original *Roe* majority,[78] Thomas, despite confirmation hearing claims that he had no views on the issue and had never discussed it

---

[71] Barnes v. Glen Theatre, Inc., 111 S. Ct. 2456 (1991).

[72] *See* Christopher E. Smith & Scott P. Johnson, *Newcomer on the High Court: Justice Souter and the Supreme Court's 1990 Term*, 37 S.D. L. Rev. 21, 39-41.

[73] *Excerpts From News Conference Announcing Court Nominee*, N.Y. Times, July 2, 1991, at A14.

[74] *See* Christopher E. Smith, *Politics and Plausibility: Searching for the Truth About Anita Hill and Clarence Thomas*, 19 Ohio N.U. L. Rev. 697 (1993).

[75] *Id.* at 703.

[76] Christopher E. Smith & Scott P. Johnson, *The First-Term Performance of Justice Clarence Thomas*, 76 Judicature 172, 175 (1993).

[77] *Id.*

[78] Roe v. Wade, 410 U.S. 113, 115 (1973).

with anyone,[79] immediately joined the Justices who advocated reversal of *Roe*.[80] Marshall had been a leading defender of criminal defendants' and prisoners' rights,[81] but Thomas established himself as among the most conservative of all Justices in such cases.[82]

All of the Reagan and Bush appointees were more conservative than their predecessors on important civil rights and liberties issues, and several of them had replaced the only remaining liberals from the Warren Court era. Thus it appeared that Reagan and Bush had successfully packed the Rehnquist Court in a manner that would produce new conservative trends in constitutional law and judicial policy making.

III. The Rehnquist Court: Image and Reality

A. *Perceptions About the Rehnquist Court*

The addition of the Reagan and Bush appointees produced notable decisions indicating that the Presidents' efforts to move the Court in a conservative direction had succeeded. The Supreme Court approved governmental regulations affecting women's choices about abortion that would never have been approved by the Justices comprising the majority in *Roe v. Wade*.[83] The Court's new conservative majority produced a series of decisions in 1989 that limited the scope of established employment discrimination doctrines and thereby made it more difficult for people to succeed in bringing employment discrimination claims into court.[84] These decisions spurred Congress

---

[79] *Excerpts From Senate's Hearings on the Thomas Nomination*, N.Y. Times, Sept. 11, 1991, at A22.

[80] Planned Parenthood v. Casey, 112 S. Ct. 2791, 2855 (1992) (Rehnquist, C.J., dissenting).

[81] Between 1986 and 1991, Marshall supported the claims of individuals in 94% of nonunanimous criminal justice cases, the highest percentage of any justice on the Supreme Court. Christopher E. Smith, *Justice Antonin Scalia and Criminal Justice Cases*, 81 Ky. L.J. 187, 193 (1992-93).

[82] For example, in Hudson v. McMillian, 112 S. Ct. 995, 1004 (1992), Thomas and Scalia were the only Justices to argue that no Eighth Amendment issues were raised when correctional officers beat a prisoner. In Dawson v. Delaware, 112 S. Ct. 1093, 1103 (1992), Thomas was the only Justice to argue that no constitutional rights were violated when a prisoners' affiliation with a racist organization was considered by a death penalty jury in a case in which there was no racial motivation in the killing of one white person by another white person.

[83] *See* Webster v. Reproductive Health Servs., 492 U.S. 490 (1989).

[84] *See* Patterson v. McLean Credit Union, 491 U.S. 164 (1989) (limiting applicability of certain employment discrimination actions to the formation but not the execution of employment contracts); Wards Cove Packing Co. v. Atonio, 490 U.S. 642 (1989) (limiting the ability of discrimination claimants to use statistical proof to create inference of discriminatory hiring and promotion practices); Martin v. Wilks, 490 U.S. 755 (1989) (creating increased opportunities for challenges to consent decrees designed to redress discrimination).

to react by overruling the statutory interpretation decisions and expanding the legal remedies available to victims of discrimination.[85] In 1991, the Court reversed precedents that had been established in 1987[86] and 1989[87] by permitting victim impact testimony in death penalty sentencing hearings.[88] Such actions enhanced the perception that the conservative Justices would aggressively attack precedents with which they disagree rather than manifest the qualities of judicial restraint.[89]

Numerous commentators concluded that Presidents Reagan and Bush had succeeded in packing the Court effectively because, in the words of one scholar, the Reagan and Bush appointees produced a Supreme Court in which "the conservative bloc has become the most cohesive that it has been in half a century."[90] The results of conservative effort to pack the Court were summarized by one scholar in stark terms: "[T]he Supreme Court has turned a cold shoulder to most of those who asked for judicial redress in the fields of civil rights and liberties. Discarding earlier rulings that reflected a national consensus on protecting hard-won rights, the Court has taken a narrow, restrictive approach to constitutional claims."[91] Based on the Supreme Court's notable decisions affecting various civil liberties issues, scholarly analysis has concluded that the Rehnquist Court is much more conservative than the Burger Court. For example, one analyst noted that

> [t]he appointment of an astute, forceful, and ideological chief justice [i.e., Rehnquist] who has regularly opposed the civil-liberties orientation of the Court, the emergence of an ostensibly cohesive conservative bloc on the Court, and some initial

---

85 *See* Bob Cohn, *A Turnabout on Civil Rights*, NEWSWEEK, Nov. 4, 1991, at 32.

86 Booth v. Maryland, 482 U.S. 496 (1987).

87 South Carolina v. Gathers, 490 U.S. 805 (1989).

88 Payne v. Tennessee, 111 S. Ct. 2597 (1991).

89 The Reagan administration criticized Warren Court Justices for being too active in remaking constitutional law in a liberal fashion. *See* CAPLAN, *supra* note 37, at 66-67. President Bush indicated that he shared the Reagan administration's preference for jurists who practice judicial restraint by declaring that he wanted Supreme Court Justices who would "avoid the tendency to legislate from the bench." *Excerpts From News Conference Announcing Court Nominee*, N.Y. TIMES, July 2, 1991, at A14. However, one characteristic of a restrained jurist is "interpretive stability," namely adherence to precedential court decisions, doctrines, and interpretations. *See* Bradley C. Canon, *Defining the Dimensions of Judicial Activism*, 66 JUDICATURE 236, 239 (1983). Thus the active reversal of precedents gave the appearance that the appointees to the Rehnquist Court were activist conservatives rather than judicial restraintists. *See* Christopher E. Smith, *The Supreme Court's Emerging Majority: Restraining the High Court or Transforming Its Role*, 24 AKRON L. REV. 393, 420-21 (1990).

90 SHELDON GOLDMAN, CONSTITUTIONAL LAW 151 (2d ed. 1991).

91 PETER IRONS, THE COURAGE OF THEIR CONVICTIONS 413 (rev. ed. 1990).

[case decisions] from the Court itself all point in [the] direction [of a new, consistent conservatism].[92]

The *Los Angeles Times* reporter who covered the Supreme Court summed up the Court's conservative transformation with a dramatic flair when Justice Thurgood Marshall retired in 1991: "[H]is resignation added an exclamation point to the term's end. The last of the Warren Court liberals was gone. Rehnquist and the conservatives had control, and now even the voice of liberalism had vanished."[93]

B. Performance of the Rehnquist Court

Although individual decisions and doctrinal changes produced by the Rehnquist Court moved constitutional law and judicial policy making in the conservative direction sought by Reagan and Bush, systematic analysis of the Court's decisions indicates that the Court did not shift as far right as the Presidents had hoped and intended. As indicated in table 1,[94] an overall assessment of the liberalism-conservatism[95] of the Rehnquist Court's civil rights and liberties decisions indicates that in numerical terms the Rehnquist Court is not more conservative than the Burger Court.[96]The percentage of liberal civil liberties decisions produced during the Rehnquist Court era when Reagan and Bush packed the Court with appointees is, despite the contemporary Court's reputation for unique conservatism, virtually identical to that of the Burger Court, with its recognized liberalism in many issue areas.[97]

Presidents seek to pack the Supreme Court because they, like scholars,[98] believe that "major policy change on the Court results

92 Charles M. Lamb & Stephen C. Halpern, *The Burger Court and Beyond*, *in* THE BURGER COURT: POLITICAL AND JUDICIAL PROFILES 433, 455 (Charles Lamb & Stephen Halpern eds., 1991).

93 SAVAGE, *supra* note 41, at 420.

94 Christopher E. Smith & Thomas R. Hensley, *Assessing the Conservatism of the Rehnquist Court*, 77 JUDICATURE 83, 85 (1993).

95 The data employ standard definitions for liberal and conservative case decisions used by scholars who apply empirical methods to the study of judicial decision making:

> Civil liberties issues include cases involving criminal procedure, civil rights, the First Amendment, due process and privacy .... Liberal decisions in the area of civil liberties are pro-person accused or convicted of a crime, pro-civil liberties or civil rights claimant, pro-indigent, pro-[Native American] and anti-government in due process and privacy.

Segal & Spaeth, *supra* note 16, at 103.

96 The data contained in this Article are drawn from the United States Supreme Court Judicial Database, an ongoing research project funded by the National Science Foundation and available through the Interuniversity Consortium for Political and Social Research.

97 *See supra* note 36 and accompanying text.

98 *See, e.g.*, DAVID M. O'BRIEN, SUPREME COURT WATCH—1992, at xiii (1992) ("Changes in the composition of the Supreme Court often bring changes in constitutional law as well.").

TABLE 1
SUPREME COURT SUPPORT FOR CIVIL LIBERTIES DURING THE WARREN, BURGER, AND REHNQUIST COURT ERAS, 1953-1992

Direction of Decision	Warren era (1953-69)		Burger era (1969-86)		Rehnquist era (1986-1993)	
	%	(n)	%	(n)	%	(n)
LIBERAL	71.4	(728)	43.8	(698)	42.8	(195)
CONSERVATIVE	28.6	(291)	56.2	(896)	57.2	(261)
TOTAL	100.0	(1,019)	100.0	(1,594)	100.0	(456)

from presidential appointments."[99] Thus it is useful to look more closely at the Rehnquist era to assess the impact of individual Reagan and Bush appointees. Table 2 shows the Supreme Court's support for civil liberties during each "natural court" period during the Rehnquist era. Each natural court reflects the time period during which the Supreme Court's composition remained unchanged.[100] The addition of a new member starts the Court into a new natural court period that lasts until the next new member begins to participate in the Court's decision making.

TABLE 2
PROPORTIONS OF CASE OUTCOMES FAVORABLE TO CIVIL RIGHTS AND LIBERTIES CLAIMANTS, NATURAL COURT PERIODS, 1986-1992

Natural Courts	% Favorable	Change From Previous Natural Court	N
Rehnquist I (1986-1987)	44.8	+6.7	105
Rehnquist II (1987-1990)	40.3	-4.5	221
Rehnquist III (1990-1991)	44.3	+4.0	61
Rehnquist IV (1991-1992)	45.9	+1.6	61

During the first natural Rehnquist Court period, after Scalia was appointed and Burger retired, the Court's support for civil rights and liberties increased 6.7% over the last natural court period of the

[99] BAUM, *supra* note 7, at 3.
[100] *See* Christopher Banks, *The Supreme Court and Precedent: An Analysis of Natural Courts and Reversal Trends*, 75 JUDICATURE 262 (1992).

Burger Court, rising from 38.1% to 44.8%. Given Scalia's reputation as a strongly conservative Justice,[101] one would not have expected the Court's support for civil rights and liberties to have increased, especially by such a substantial amount. The Rehnquist Court's support score dropped during the next natural court period from 1987 to 1990 when Kennedy replaced Powell, falling from 44.8 percent to 40.3 percent. This result is perhaps also surprising, because the scholarly literature suggests that a much more dramatic decrease occurred in support for civil rights and liberties when Kennedy took Powell's seat. For example, a prominent professor wrote in *Harvard Law Review* that: "For liberals, it is a time of despair. The 1988-1989 Term was devastating for civil rights and civil liberties."[102] The data presented here do not support this strong of an assessment of the Rehnquist Court's conservative movement.

The results presented in table 2 are especially surprising for the last two natural court periods covering the 1990 and 1991 Terms. Souter replaced Brennan in the 1990 Term, and Thomas replaced Marshall in the 1991 Term. Brennan and Marshall had been the Court's two leading liberals, and commentators generally believed that their departures had made the Supreme Court significantly more conservative.[103] The data show, however, that this did not happen with respect to decisional patterns in civil liberties cases. Quite remarkably, in the 1990 Term when Souter replaced Brennan, the Court's support for civil rights and liberties increased 4% from 40.3 to 44.3. Furthermore, in the 1991 Term when Thomas replaced Marshall, the Court's support score increased again, reaching 45.9%, the highest support score for the four natural court periods of the Rehnquist Court era.

C. *Explaining the Gap Between Image and Reality*

There are several possible explanations for the surprising developments which seem to indicate that Reagan and Bush failed to achieve their policy objectives from packing the Court with conservatives. The membership change in the Court, stemming from the infusion of Reagan and Bush appointees, did not produce the expected conservative results. However, membership change is not the only influence over changes (or the lack thereof) in the Supreme Court's

---

101 *See* Richard A. Brisbin, Jr., *The Conservatism of Antonin Scalia*, 105 POL. SCI Q. 1 (1990).

102 Erwin Chemerinsky, *Foreword: The Vanishing Constitution*, 103 HARV. L. REV. 43, 45 (1989).

103 *See, e.g.*, *supra* note 91 and accompanying text.

decisions affecting constitutional law and judicial policymaking.[104] Trends in the Court's decisions can also be shaped by individual position change when specific Justices change the way that they make decisions. The most notable example of individual position change is Harry Blackmun, who transformed himself from a conservative "Minnesota Twin" of life-long friend Warren Burger to a leading liberal on the Rehnquist Court.[105] The other possible cause of the trends in the Court's decisions is issue change, which involves the Court being confronted with different types of legal questions within a particular area of law. For example, in school desegregation cases, the Court was initially confronted with the relatively simple issue of rigid, government-sponsored separation of school children by race. As these cases evolved, however, the Court was faced with difficult implementation issues such as metropolitan busing[106] and judicially-ordered taxes to support integration.[107] Thus the Court's decisions may move in unexpected or new directions simply because the Justices are responding to new and different kinds of issues.

It is very difficult to measure precisely the extent to which issue change occurs and affects the Supreme Court's decisions.[108] It is clear, however, issue change cannot be the lone source of the unexpected liberalism of the Rehnquist Court. Even when all of the Reagan and Bush appointees were in place, the Court endorsed Warren and Burger Court policies targeted by Reagan and Bush, includ-

---

104 *See* Lawrence Baum, *Membership Change and Collective Voting Change in the United States Supreme Court*, 54 J. POL. 3, 5-6 (1990).

105 After enduring scathing attacks from conservatives because of his majority opinion in *Roe v. Wade*, "Blackmun's jurisprudence appeared to begin actively to change. With the possible exception of the criminal-justice sector, where he would still more often than not be found at Burger's side—although even there he left the proverbial reservation on occasion—Justice Blackmun began to move toward the Court's liberal wing." ABRAHAM, *supra* note 6, at 308-09 (citation omitted). Although Blackmun was a consistent conservative in his initial terms on the Court, "as he realized that the system he had assumed would function benignly was not doing so, he came to side more with the individual against the government, demanding that his colleagues pay heed to problems of the 'real world' that he himself had not closely examined in his early opinions, and calling for great judicial protection of those individuals." Stephen L. Wasby, *Justice Harry A. Blackmun: Transformation from "Minnesota Twin" to Independent Voice*, *in* THE BURGER COURT: POLITICAL AND JUDICIAL PROFILES 96 (Charles M. Lamb & Stephen C. Halpern eds., 1991).

106 Milliken v. Bradley, 418 U.S. 717 (1974).

107 Missouri v. Jenkins, 495 U.S. 33 (1990).

108 BAUM, *supra* note 7, at 6 ("Empirically, it is relatively easy to distinguish between the impact of membership change and the impact of the other two sources of voting change. It is far more difficult to distinguish between change in individual policy positions and change in the issues that come before a body, because both are manifested in voting change by 'continuing' members . . . . [I]t is probably impossible to develop an adequate direct measure of issue change in a field as broad as civil liberties.").

ing the ban on government-sponsored prayers in public schools[109] and the right of choice for abortion.[110] Moreover, the Court also expanded some rights by, for example, recognizing that a nonsmoker prison inmate could possess a constitutional protection against physical harm from the second-hand smoke of a cellmate.[111]

It appears that the Court disappointed Reagan and Bush on specific issues because of changes in the decisions of Justice Kennedy,[112] and perhaps those of O'Connor and Souter, too. For example, in the surprising 1992 decision in which the Court upheld the underlying principle of *Roe v. Wade*,[113] Kennedy, O'Connor, and Souter wrote a co-authored opinion that placed great emphasis on the need to preserve stare decisis.[114] The trio of Justices asserted that "[a] decision to overrule *Roe*'s essential holding under the existing circumstances would address error, if error there was, at the cost of both profound and unnecessary damage to the Court's legitimacy, and to the Nation's commitment to the rule of law."[115] Thus these Justices emphasized their concerns about stare decisis and the preservation of the Court's legitimacy[116] over, from O'Connor's[117] and Kennedy's[118] perspective, previously expressed criticisms of *Roe v. Wade*. Similarly, Kennedy switched from being a consistent accommodationist with respect to the Establishment Clause[119] to being the author of a majority opinion barring prayers at public school graduations.[120]

---

109 Lee v. Weisman, 112 S. Ct. 2649 (1992).

110 Planned Parenthood v. Casey, 112 S. Ct. 2791 (1992).

111 Helling v. McKinney, 113 S. Ct. 2475 (1993).

112 *See* Christopher E. Smith, *Supreme Court Surprise: Justice Anthony Kennedy's Move Toward Moderation*, 45 OKLA. L. REV. 459 (1992).

113 410 U.S. 113 (1973).

114 *Casey*, 112 S. Ct. at 2804 ("After considering the fundamental constitutional questions resolved by *Roe*, principles of institutional integrity, and the rule of *stare decisis*, we are led to conclude this: the essential holding of *Roe v. Wade* should be retained and once again reaffirmed.").

115 *Id.* at 2816.

116 *Id.* at 2814 ("The Court must take care to speak and act in ways that allow people to accept its decisions on the terms the Court claims for them, as grounded truly in principle, not as compromises with social and political pressures having, as such, no bearing on the principled choices that the Court is obliged to make. Thus, the Court's legitimacy depends on making legally principled decisions under circumstances in which their principled character is sufficiently plausible to be accepted by the Nation.").

117 *See supra* notes 44-45 and accompanying text.

118 *See supra* note 64 and accompanying text.

119 *See* Christopher E. Smith & Linda Fry, *Vigilance or Accommodation: The Changing Supreme Court and Religious Freedom*, 42 SYRACUSE L. REV. 893, 939 (1991).

120 Lee v. Weisman, 112 S. Ct. 2649 (1992).

The movement of such Justices as Kennedy, O'Connor, and Souter away from their usual conservative allies on key issues may also reflect an effort to disassociate themselves from the judicial style and behavior of Justices Scalia and Thomas. Justice Scalia consistently employs sarcasm, strident condemnations, and other undiplomatic language in castigating both liberal and conservative colleagues when they disagree with him.[121] Such irritating attacks on colleagues may have driven Kennedy and O'Connor, in particular, away from Scalia in key cases.[122] Thomas has emulated Scalia's abrasive style[123] and, moreover, reportedly offended other Justices with his responses and reactions during and immediately after his controversial confirmation hearings.[124]

Reagan's and Bush's efforts to achieve specific judicial policy goals by packing the Supreme Court may also have been undermined by their inaccurate predictions about how their appointees would decide specific issues. For example, Bush appointed David Souter because Souter's record as a state judge and his endorsements from politicians indicated that he would be a consistent conservative.[125] Bush's appointment of Souter also stemmed from a "desire to finger a conservative judge with no controversial written opinions (especially on the emotional abortion issue) that would trigger sustained ideological conflict on the eve of the 1990 midterm elections."[126]

---

[121] Smith, *supra* note 51, at 804-08.

[122] *See* CHRISTOPHER E. SMITH, JUSTICE ANTONIN SCALIA AND THE SUPREME COURT'S CONSERVATIVE MOMENT 91-112 (1993).

[123] Smith & Johnson, *supra* note 76, at 177.

[124] According to journalists, Thomas "infuriated some, if not all, of the Justices" by staging a large celebration and insisting that he be sworn in as a justice on the day after the funeral for Chief Justice Rehnquist's wife. TIMOTHY M. PHELPS & HELEN WINTERNITZ, CAPITOL GAMES xv (1992). In addition, Thomas appeared with his wife on the cover of *People* magazine with an accompanying article in which Virginia Thomas described the confirmation hearings as "spiritual warfare. Good versus evil." Virginia Lamp Thomas, *Breaking Silence*, PEOPLE, Nov. 11, 1991, at 108, 111. The article, which included a "candid" photograph of the couple reading *The Bible* together, was an unusually blatant attempt to rehabilitate Justice Thomas's public image after the bruising confirmation battle and controversy surrounding allegations of sexual harassment raised by his former assistant, Anita Hill. This apparently calculated effort to pander to segments of the American public did not fit with his colleagues' expectations of how a Supreme Court Justice should remain aloof from public controversy: "The *People* magazine piece, according to Court insiders, was greeted with abject horror in the chambers of many of the justices and it brought the Court down to a different level as did the charges against Thomas." Karen O'Connor, *The Effects of the Thomas Appointment to the Supreme Court*, 25 P.S.: POL. SCI. & POL. 492, 495 (1992). Moreover, according to a national news magazine, "two conservative justices who watched the [confirmation] hearings told their clerks that they thought [Justice] Thomas lied to the Judiciary Committee." David A. Kaplan, *An Uncomfortable Seat*, NEWSWEEK, Oct. 28, 1991, at 31.

[125] ABRAHAM, *supra* note 6, at 366-67.

[126] *Id.* at 366.

Thus Bush lacked a solid basis to predict how Souter would decide the particular judicial policy controversies lingering from the Warren and Burger Court eras that Reagan and Bush hoped their new appointees would reverse. Souter joined the conservative Justices consistently during his first term,[127] but he established himself as an independent thinker in the middle of the Court's ideological spectrum as he gained experience during subsequent terms.[128]

IV. CONCLUSION

Presidents Reagan and Bush made concerted efforts to pack the Supreme Court with appointees who would reverse the liberal constitutional law and judicial policy decisions of the Warren and Burger Courts. Despite enjoying the opportunity to appoint a majority of the Court's members, these like-minded conservative Presidents ultimately fell short in pursuit of their underlying policy objectives. Although the Reagan and Bush appointees helped to produce conservative outcomes on a variety of issues, many of the liberal precedents most despised by political conservatives, including Reagan and Bush, remained fundamentally intact, including *Roe v. Wade*,[129] *Engel v. Vitale*,[130] *Mapp v. Ohio*,[131] and *Miranda v. Arizona*.[132] Moreover, the Rehnquist Court's pattern of support for individuals in civil rights and liberties cases was no more conservative than that of the Burger Court.

The unfulfilled aspirations of Reagan and Bush serve as a lesson to Presidents about the difficulties involved in seeking to the pack the Supreme Court in order to achieve specific policy objectives. As the performances of the Reagan and Bush appointees on the Rehnquist Court indicate, Presidents can predict neither how their appointees will decide the complete range of issues presented to the Court nor how individual Justices will interact with and react to each other in the Court's collegial decision-making processes. The long, protected tenures in office enjoyed by the Supreme Court Justices permit these human beings in black robes to alter their approaches to decision making in response to changing conditions in

[127] Scott P. Johnson & Christopher E. Smith, *David Souter's First Term on the Supreme Court: The Impact of a New Justice*, 75 JUDICATURE 238, 239-40 (1992).

[128] *See* Paul M. Barrett, *Independent Justice: David Souter Emerges as Reflective Moderate on the Supreme Court*, WALL ST. J., Feb. 2, 1993, at A1, A6; Jeffrey Rosen, *Poetic Justice*, NEW REPUBLIC, Mar. 8, 1993, at 26.

[129] 410 U.S. 113 (1973) (abortion).

[130] 370 U.S. 421 (1962) (school prayer).

[131] 367 U.S. 643 (1961) (exclusionary rule).

[132] 384 U.S. 466 (1966) (arrestees' rights).

society, changes in the kinds of issues presented to the Court, or personal changes in their own values and philosophies. Because Presidents cannot control their appointees to the Supreme Court, Justices may move several feet or many miles away from the objectives that originally motivated Presidents to select them as nominees for the high court.

Acknowledgments

Bean, Ralph J., Jr. "The Supreme Court and the Political Question: Affirmation or Abdication?" *West Virginia Law Review* 71 (1969): 97–134. Reprinted with the permission of the *West Virginia Law Review.*

Beck, Leland E. "Constitution, Congress, and Court: On the Theory, Law, and Politics of Appellate Jurisdiction of the United States Supreme Court," *Hastings Constitutional Law Quarterly* 9 (1982): 773–850. Reprinted by permission. Copyright by University of California, Hastings College of Law.

Comiskey, Michael. "Can a President Pack — or Draft — the Supreme Court? FDR and the Court in the Great Depression and World War II," *Albany Law Review* 57 (1990): 1043–1059. Reprinted with the permission of the *Albany Law School.*

Eskridge, William N., Jr. "Reneging on History? Playing the Court/Congress/President Civil Rights Game," *California Law Review* 79 (1991): 613–84. Reprinted with permission. Copyright 1991 by the California Law Review, Inc.

Feinberg, Wilfred. "Constraining 'The Least Dangerous Branch': The Tradition of Attacks on Judicial Power," *New York University Law Review* 59 (1984): 252–76. Reprinted with the permission of the *New York University Law Review.*

Frankfurter, Felix, and James M. Landis. "The Supreme Court Under the Judiciary Act of 1925," *Harvard Law Review* 42 (1928): 1–29. Copyright 1928 by the Harvard Law Review Association.

Leuchtenburg, William E. "The Origins of Franklin D. Roosevelt's 'Court- Packing' Plan," *Supreme Court Review* (1966): 347–400. Reprinted with the permission of the University of Chicago Press, publisher. Copyright 1966 by the University of Chicago Press.

Nagel, Stuart S. "Court-Curbing Periods in American History," *Vanderbilt Law Review* 18 (1965): 925–44. Reprinted with the permission of Vanderbilt University.

Nelson, Michael. "The President and the Court: Reinterpreting the Court- Packing Episode of 1937," *Political Science Quarterly* 103 (1988): 267–93. Reprinted with the permission of the author and The Academy of Political Science.

Quint, Peter E. "Reflections on the Separation of Powers and Judicial Review at the End of the Reagan Era," *George Washington Law Review* 57 (1989): 427–58. Reprinted with the permission of *George Washington Law Review.* Copyright 1988.

Smith, Christopher E., and Thomas R. Hensley. "Unfulfilled Aspirations: The Court-Packing Efforts of Presidents Reagan and Bush," *Albany Law Review* 57 (1994): 1111–1131. Reprinted with the permission of the Albany Law School.

For Product Safety Concerns and Information please contact our EU representative GPSR@taylorandfrancis.com
Taylor & Francis Verlag GmbH, Kaufingerstraße 24, 80331 München, Germany

www.ingramcontent.com/pod-product-compliance
Ingram Content Group UK Ltd.
Pitfield, Milton Keynes, MK11 3LW, UK
UKHW022207190926
475702UK00003B/250